Sport Finance

Gil Fried, JD
Steven J. Shapiro, PhD
University of New Haven
Timothy D. DeSchriver, EdD
University of Massachusetts

Human Kinetics

Library of Congress Cataloging-in-Publication Data

Fried, Gil, 1965-
  Sport finance / Gil Fried, Steven J. Shapiro, Timothy D. DeSchriver.
      p. cm.
  Includes bibliographical references and index.
  ISBN 0-7360-0183-2
  1. Sports--Finance. 2. Sports administration. I. Shapiro, Steven J.,
1955- II. DeSchriver, Timothy D., 1968- III. Title.
  GV716 .F75 2003
  796'.06'9--dc21

                            2002007423

ISBN: 0-7360-0183-2

The Web addresses cited in this text were current as of November 4, 2002, unless otherwise noted.

Acquisitions Editor: Amy N. Clocksin; **Developmental Editor:** Melissa Feld; **Assistant Editor:** Susan C. Hagan; **Copyeditor:** Joyce Sexton; **Proofreader:** Erin Cler; **Indexer:** Susan Danzi Hernandez; **Permission Manager:** Dalene Reeder; **Graphic Designer:** Nancy Rasmus; **Graphic Artist:** Dawn Sills; **Photo Manager:** Leslie A. Woodrum; **Cover Designer:** Keith Blomberg; **Photographer (cover):** Tom Roberts; **Photos (interior):** © 1999 Terry L. Brandt (pp. 247 and 261), Frank DiBrango (pp. 91, 151, and 297), Gittings & Lorfing (p. 375, top), © ImageState (p. 279), © ImageState/Ken Levinson (p. 57), © ImageState/Michael Paras (p. 35), Richard B. Levine (p. 223), Steve Long (p. 376), © Joe Robbins 2002 (p. 7), W. Lynn Seldon, Jr. (pp. 127 and 189), Stuart Shapiro (p. 375, bottom), © Sportschrome East/West (p. 213), © Sport the Library/Al Messerschmidt (p. 21), © Sport the Library/SI (p. 297), © Sport the Library/SPUK (p. 103), © Brian Spurlock/SportsChrome USA (p. 67), © Robert Tringali, Jr./Sportschrome East/West (p. 171); **Art Manager:** Kelly Hendren; **Illustrator:** Brian McElwain; **Printer:** Transcontinental

Printed in Canada   10 9 8 7 6 5 4 3 2

Human Kinetics
Web site: www.HumanKinetics.com

United States: Human Kinetics
P.O. Box 5076
Champaign, IL 61825-5076
800-747-4457
e-mail: humank@hkusa.com

Canada: Human Kinetics
475 Devonshire Road, Unit 100
Windsor, ON N8Y 2L5
800-465-7301 (in Canada only)
e-mail: orders@hkcanada.com

Europe: Human Kinetics
107 Bradford Road
Stanningley
Leeds LS28 6AT, United Kingdom
+44 (0)113 255 5665
e-mail: hk@hkeurope.com

Australia: Human Kinetics
57A Price Avenue
Lower Mitcham, South Australia 5062
08 8277 1555
e-mail: liaw@hkaustralia.com

New Zealand: Human Kinetics
Division of Sports Distributors NZ Ltd.
P.O. Box 300 226 Albany
North Shore City, Auckland
0064 9 448 1207
e-mail: blairc@hknewz.com

To my parents, Louis and Haya Fried,
who inspired in me the pursuit of excellence;
and to the proud men and women of the Israeli Defense Forces.
Gil Fried

To my parents of blessed memory, Philip and Charlotte Shapiro,
who taught me that success comes to those
who are not afraid to ask the right questions.
Steven Shapiro

To my parents, Richard and Jean, who have
inspired me to be an educator.
Tim DeSchriver

Contents

Part V Profits

Part VI Financial Troubleshooting

Preface

If you saw the movie *Jerry Maguire*, you might have thought about studying sport law or becoming a players' agent. Similarly, if you tracked Michael Jordan's phenomenal success in endorsing various products from Nike®, shoes to Gatorade®, you might want to study sport marketing. If you enjoy watching Super Bowl advertisements more than the games themselves, you might want to enter the exciting field of sport advertising. Sport finance can be more exciting than all these disciplines. Marketing, sponsorship, facility construction, sport law, and all the other sport management disciplines cannot be undertaken without knowledge of the financial position of the team, business, or organization. Thus, sport finance is the linchpin for all decisions and actions in sport business. Students who feel that sport accounting and finance are not as exciting as sport law, marketing, or advertising are wrong. Some of the most interesting jobs in sport focus on finance-related issues. For example, National Football League and National Basketball Association teams normally have "capoligists" who are directly responsible for ensuring that the team does not violate the salary cap for its players. Financial numbers can tell us many important facts about a business. So, even though sport finance has never been considered an exciting component within any sport and fitness administration curriculum, it might be one of the most important topics that you study.

No business, organization, or government entity can survive without money. The saying "Money makes the world go 'round" accurately reflects the sport industry, with some professional teams now worth over a half-billion dollars and with television networks spending billions to air premiere events. Sport finance analyzes where the money comes from, where the money goes, and how to effectively utilize any remaining money to help foster future growth. Thus, sport finance is the key for any sport business decision-making process, and a thorough knowledge of sport finance is the key to making it into high-level managerial positions where the decisions are made.

The stock market skyrocketed several hundred percent in the 1980s and 1990s. If you had invested $18.50 in 1986 in one partnership unit in the Boston Celtics, would that unit be worth $180 today? Why have Boston Celtics shares remained a stock market outcast, dropping to $11 per share in 2002? Does such a decline indicate that the Celtics are in poor financial shape? What factors helped drive the stock price down? Does such a decline represent market conditions alone, or can the Celtics' board of directors develop policies that can reduce the stock's value? Was it worthwhile for the Celtics to hire Rick Pitino as a coach at $5 million per year? Would any resulting turnaround in the team's performance significantly enhance the team's value? What can the Celtics do to increase their stock value? Would a high stock value indicate financial strength for the Celtics? If the team traded its most expensive players and reduced overall salaries by $20 million per year, would the stock value increase as a result of the increased savings? A thorough financial analysis can help answer these questions. This book is designed to help you understand the numerous financial issues faced by any sport or fitness business or entity.

The need for a strict sport finance text has come to the fore over the past several years with the push to build new sport facilities and the financial projections made by the facilities' opponents and proponents. Similarly, fitness facilities have fueled significant career opportunities, and managers in this industry encounter numerous unique financial issues. Sport entrepreneurs have to deal with financial issues such as how to develop a business plan with a pro forma budget, what finance vehicle is most effective for raising start-up capital, and how to control inventory. With professional football teams selling for $700 million, a team owner or general manager will not trust anyone to make financial decisions who does not have a strong background in finance. Last, with Title IX affecting many high school and college athletic programs, schools need to know how to work with the dollars they have in order to comply with the law. These represent just some of the issues you might face in your future career, and an aim of this text is to give you a framework to help you deal with these issues.

Although professional sport presents some very useful examples, this text focuses on the following four case studies that are discussed throughout. As concepts come up in the text, we highlight how the concepts would apply to one of the following case studies. Icons will alert you to the application of the case study. Read the Introduction to the Case Studies (pp. 1–4) for background on each example.

1. **The Smiths** just graduated from Minnesota State and want to open their own fitness center with a little gift shop and juice bar. You will proceed step-by-step with Bob and Cheryl as they explore how they might raise the necessary capital, where they should locate the fitness center, how to decide whether to buy or rent the needed space, how many employees to hire, and how best to purchase necessary supplies and handle related concerns.

2. **Sport Manufacturing Company (SMC)** manufactures golf clubs and tennis rackets. The company acquires raw materials and processes these materials into high-end equipment. It has been in business for over 20 years and is publicly traded on the NASDAQ exchange. The company's seasonal business requires careful financial planning so that the company can maximize revenue during the peak months and borrow as little cash as possible during the winter.

3. **The University of Houston** is a large urban university serving over 30,000 students. The athletic department has a rich tradition, having produced such stars as Hakeem Olajuwon, Clyde Drexler, Andre Ware, Elvin Hayes, Carl Lewis, and a host of others. Unfortunately, in the mid-1990s the athletic department fell on hard times and was losing about $5 million a year. You have been retained as an outside consultant to help determine what fiscal steps need to be taken to help develop new women's sports (to comply with Title IX), reduce expenditures, and increase revenue.

4. **The Boston Celtics** have given you the dream job you wanted with a professional team. You are now the chief financial officer for the Boston Celtics. You have been hired to examine the team's financial

statements and to reinterpret the numbers and explain them in "plain English" for the shareholders. You will analyze such issues as the financial impact the new arena will have on team income and whether the team's win-loss record will affect the team's profitability.

Whenever possible, the case studies are analyzed with use of financial data obtained from real businesses or government entities.

Our goal in writing this text was to create an intermediate finance text that would be ideal for business school-based sport and fitness administration programs, sport finance classes, and graduate programs in various other disciplines. The point of the designation is to emphasize that the book is comprehensive, but we felt it was also important to develop the text for people who had never read a finance or accounting text. With this book you will be able to grasp fundamental finance and accounting concepts regardless of your knowledge level. If you have some finance or accounting skills, this text will help expand your knowledge and provide some real-world application of that knowledge. The real-world situations in the case studies provide a strong framework within which you will be able to apply financial principles in your future career. If you are already an industry professional, you could rely upon the text to help you understand financial markets, develop money-saving strategies, learn how to properly invest for future growth, and develop business finance strategies.

To date, no single text has covered critical sport finance topics such as balance sheets, income statements, industry ratios, banking policy, venture capital, stock markets, inventory systems, accounting strategies to maximize financial returns, and related topics deemed critical for a sound knowledge in sport finance. This text aligns itself with the requirements set forth by the National Association for Sport and Physical Education and the North American Society for Sport Management for a sport finance course:

Required Content (All Topics Must Be Addressed)

Basic accounting principles—types of accounting

Financial statements

Sources of revenue for financing—public sector versus private sector, governments, membership, fees, PSLs, taxes, bonds, etc.

Principles of budgeting—types (capital, master, departmental, line item, zero-based, PPBES)

Budget as a method of control, organization, and reallocation

Budget development

Spreadsheet utilization (Lotus®, Excel®, or Quicken® Quickbooks)—basic laboratory experiences

Financial aspects of facilities management

Recommended Content (A Minimum of 50% Must Be Addressed)

Present financial status of the sport industry—collegiate, professional, private, manufacturers

Concessions and merchandising—trademark licensing, inventory, cost control, cash management

For-profit and not-for-profit budgeting

Development and fund-raising principles and methodology (campaigns, alumni, auctions)

Financing facilities ("Sport Management," 2000, pp. 7–8).

Sport Finance is designed to walk you through the finance process. It provides you with the basic skills needed to help raise, manage, and spend money in sport settings. It covers a number of key financial concepts:

- What a business needs to succeed
- What makes businesses operate
- Where businesses obtain necessary start-up capital
- How to determine how much money is available
- How to read newspaper business pages for meaning
- What typical expenses sport organizations incur
- Why sport businesses succeed
- Why sport businesses fail
- How sport organizations can grow

Part I deals with the importance of finance in the sport industry, including a thorough analysis of the various issues that compose sport finance. Since financial planning is impossible without an understanding of accounting basics, part I gives special attention to fundamental finance and accounting issues. Part I also stresses the various environments that affect finance, ranging from business structures and financial markets to government entities that control taxes and interest rates.

Part II addresses the information needed in order to answer questions or solve problems posed by the case studies. Through analyzing data contained in the income statement and balance sheets, students will learn how to analyze a business' strengths and weaknesses. Industry ratios, financial statements, the time value of money, and the financial planning process are highlighted in this section of the book.

Part III examines where the money is located. These chapters look at the ways in which businesses find the capital they need to operate. Discussions focus on funding options for various types of entities, ranging from a government entity that needs to raise more taxes to a business that is searching for venture capital, pursuing a public offering, or selling corporate bonds.

Part IV discusses where the money goes. What are the typical expenses, and how do businesses budget for them? This part of the book also highlights short-term planning and how to document monetary needs. These discussions are especially appropriate for those interested in developing business plans and the accompanying pro forma budgets. An additional focus is on ways to manage the money you obtain or owe as a sport manager. Lastly, this part of the book provides a comprehensive overview of the inventory management and production control processes, which are critical for concession and sporting goods businesses.

Part V centers on the profit distribution process, including retained earnings, dividends, and company growth through acquisition of additional businesses. This part of the book also analyzes several financial issues, including taxation and fiscal risk management.

Part VI covers the tracking of money and details accounting techniques that you can implement to make sure that financial auditing is successful. A final topic in part VI is how to close a business through bankruptcy or other techniques.

Each chapter ends with suggested assignments, research projects, and class discussion topics. These suggestions are designed to help channel dialogue among students and to give instructors ideas for helping students engage with the material over and above just reading the text. Bolded words in the text are found in the glossary at the back of the book. Key points are highlighted throughout each chapter. In addition, an instructor guide is available that provides more discussion topics and material.

Acknowledgments

I could not have asked for two better coauthors. They diligently wrote their chapters and assisted with the instructor guide, making this one of the best texts I have had the pleasure to work on. Tim was helpful throughout the entire process, and his patience and understanding during some of our unexpected delays were greatly appreciated. Steven was a significant boost to the project as an economics and finance department chair helping write a finance book. His participation provided significant credibility and knowledge unmatched by any other author we could have used. My two coauthors went beyond the call for this text, and I thank them for their effort.

I would like to extend a special thanks to Dr. Allen Sack, Dr. Ron Dick, Dr. Abbas Nadim, Dean Zeljian Schuster, and the entire School of Business faculty and staff at the University of New Haven for all their assistance. I would also like to thank my research assistants Brian Rec and R. Dylan O'Connor for their help.

A special thanks also goes out to my wife and children (Gavriella, Arieh, and Rebecca) for all their patience during the writing and revising of this text. It was a multiyear process with several major snafus that created delays. However, the final text shows that the wait was worth every second and the final combination of authors was outstanding. Each coauthor brought significant value to the text and helped shape it into one of the strongest texts in the sport management area.

Gil Fried

It has been a pleasure to be involved in this project with my talented coauthors. Their patience and support were appreciated while I "got up to speed" after replacing one of the original authors on the project. The extensive sport management backgrounds of both Gil and Tim were especially helpful as they suggested industry-specific pedagogical examples. The anonymous reviewers of the text provided critical insight that makes this a better book. I am sure that my coauthors would agree with the standard statement that although the reviewers were important in finding pedagogical and other errors and making this a more readable book for the sport finance community, we take the blame for any shortcomings that remain.

I want to extend special thanks to Dean Zeljian Schuster of the School of Business at the University of New Haven for providing support that helped make it possible for me to work on this book. The encouragement and feedback of colleagues at the University of New Haven made it easier to complete the project. I am also appreciative of the research assistance provided by Secil Taras.

Finally, I especially want to acknowledge my wife, Phyliss, and my children, Stuart and Lauren, for their understanding while I worked on this time-consuming project. Over the years, they have been continuously supportive while competing with teaching, research, writing, and consulting activities for my time.

Steven Shapiro

I would like to extend a special thanks to my two coauthors. Gil Fried has been the driving force behind this project since its inception. His guidance and persistence were critical to ensuring the successful completion of this book. Steve Shapiro did a marvelous job of stepping into a project that was already in progress. The addition has been invaluable, and his background in financial management was very helpful. I would also like to thank Amy Clocksin, Melissa Feld, and the staff at Human Kinetics. Their patience and willingness to see the project through to completion have been greatly appreciated.

I would also like to thank my colleagues on the sport management faculty at the University of Massachusetts. Their encouragement and kind words have not gone unnoticed. There is no finer group of sport management academicians in the world. It is truly an honor to work with them on a daily basis.

Last, I would like to thank my parents, Richard and Jean DeSchriver, for loving and supporting me for all these years. I may be getting older, but they are still the two most important people in my life. They instilled within me a passion for education and teaching that will last forever.

Tim DeSchriver

The authors would like to acknowledge the following individuals for their hard work and dedication in helping make this text a reality. A special thanks goes out to the diligent and hard work of Amy Clocksin, Melissa Feld, Susan C. Hagan, and the rest of the Human Kinetics staff who worked so hard on this project.

Introduction to the Case Studies

As mentioned in the preface, the following case studies are discussed throughout the book. In this section, we provide the background information that you'll need to understand the case studies when they are applied in the main text. The icons shown here next to the case studies are also used to identify the case studies in the chapters to follow. You will also want to refer to this section to answer discussion questions and do assignments.

The Smiths

Bob and Cheryl Smith are recent graduates of the sport and fitness administration program at Minnesota State. Both have loved being certified fitness instructors and thought that after they earned their degrees they would have all the skills necessary to open their own fitness center in the Minneapolis-St. Paul area. Neither had ever owned a business before, but they felt that their combined five years' experience with the YMCA qualified them to understand and operate their own business.

Bob and Cheryl start planning for their future facility. They want to include the following options:

- A 5,000-square-foot wood-floored aerobics area, with mirrors on the wall, that can be used for aerobics and various dance classes
- A 5,000-square-foot free-weight and exercise machine room for those interested in weight training and cardiovascular workouts
- Two 1,000-square-foot locker rooms for male and female patrons
- A 1,000-square-foot office and reception area
- A gift shop and juice bar where fitness apparel and food and beverages can be sold

Although the Smiths have big ambitions, they are also realistic. They know they are not going to get rich. However, they want to control their own destiny and make it or break it by themselves.

They do not come from wealthy families, but they feel they can work hard and put in as many hours as necessary to make their dream come true. They have $5,000 saved to help pay their start-up expenses. They have 50 friends who are willing to sign five-year contracts at $600 per year for using the fitness center. Each friend would pay the first year's dues up front when the plans are finalized. The $30,000 will help pay for equipment or help secure a bank loan. There are 20 other clubs in the metro area, but there's only one other club in a 2-square-mile area with 30,000 residents.

Sport Manufacturing Company

Sport Manufacturing Company (SMC) is a seasonal business that requires constant financial analysis to optimize its profits. The business has several owners and is publicly traded. SMC was formed to manufacture golf clubs; however, over the years it has added tennis rackets to its product inventory. SMC manufactures all the clubs and rackets around the same schedule so that the manufacturing side of the business can stop production in December and January, reducing operating costs. However, if the company did not maintain its trained employees on a payroll it would lose valuable employees and would have to pay that much more to train new employees. Thus, even when the machines are down, the company is incurring expenses. Similarly, sales expenses increase during the springtime as commission-sales staff members start turning in their sales orders. Thus, the other side of the business (besides manufacturing) is the sales department, which works all year long to secure orders from various retailers. The secret for the company is to balance its financial obligations through obtaining funds from the bank for its financial needs during the winter and to properly invest its income in the spring and summer to maximize revenue. This cyclical pattern has been successful for 20 years. The company's production and sales volumes in 1999 are shown in table 1.

Table 1 SMC's Production and Sales Volumes

Month	Manufacture (units)	Sales (units)
January	0	10,000
February	400,000	30,000
March	400,000	60,000
April	400,000	300,000
May	400,000	600,000
June	400,000	700,000
July	400,000	600,000
August	400,000	500,000
September	400,000	400,000
October	400,000	500,000
November	400,000	50,000
December	0	250,000
Total	**4,000,000**	**4,000,000**

Sport Manufacturing Company incurs $15 million in fixed costs each year. Variable costs, such as the raw materials used for making the equipment, are $7 per piece. The company also incurs $1.25 per piece in administrative and selling expenses. The total cost per piece, excluding fixed costs, is $8.25. If SMC manufactures 4 million units, then the total production costs are as follows:

$15,000,000 fixed costs

+ $33,000,000 per piece cost ($8.25 × 4,000,000)

$48,000,000 total production costs

Dividing the $48 million by 4 million pieces yields a per piece total cost of $12.

University of Houston Athletic Department

The University of Houston (UH) has a proud history of athletic success. However, the financial picture has not been marvelous over the past several years. Dwindling attendance, not playing football games on campus, low student interest, low season-ticket base, and a host of other concerns led to threats from the university's president that the entire athletic program could be canceled by the year 2000 (Barron, 1996).

The revenue and expenditures from 1991 through 1995 for the University of Houston athletic department are highlighted in table 2.

Table 2 University of Houston Athletic Department's Revenues and Expenditures—Overview

Year	Revenues	Expenditures
1991	$3,321,496	$6,889,332
1992	5,965,735	7,763,595
1993	5,478,830	8,678,124
1994	3,749,819	9,119,937
1995	3,368,915	10,741,181

Reprinted, by permission, from University of Houston Athletic Department, 1995, *Schedule of Revenues and Expenses.*

Although the deficit numbers seem large, they are not unusual in the world of "big-time" athletics. In fact, in a 1995 audit of Texas state-supported universities, each university posted a deficit in its athletic programs (Barron, 1996). The combined losses, based on over $95 million in expenses and only $56 million in revenue, totaled just over $39 million. With the addition of almost $23 million in student service fees, the combined losses were reduced to just over $16 million, with the University of Houston being responsible for $5 million of those losses (Barron, 1996). In 1996, the University of Houston offered seven men's and seven women's sports with 226 athletes on full or partial scholarships and a total of 295 student athletes. The 1996-2000 projected revenues and expenses are shown in tables 3 and 4. These projections were based on a number of assumptions, including moving home football games back to the main campus, adding women's soccer, moving concession operations to a new company, strengthening the caliber of opposing teams, and building luxury boxes at the football stadium and basketball arena.

Boston Celtics

The Boston Celtics were owned by a publicly traded limited partnership, with Celtics, Inc. being the corporate general partner (Much & Friedman, 1996). The team went public in 1986 after it was bought by three individuals for $19 million. About $48 million was raised after 40% of the team was sold through the public stock offering (Much & Friedman, 1996).

The Celtics have gone through several major changes over the years that included the purchase and sale of radio and television stations. In 1998 the stocks went through additional changes forced by legislative requirements. The consolidated balance sheets from 1997 and 1998, prior to the change, are available

Table 3 University of Houston's Projected Revenue

Income category	Actual 1996	Projected 1997	Projected 1998	Projected 1999	Projected 2000
Ticket sales	1,085,600	1,559,017	1,664,215	1,550,430	1,650,351
Premium seating	67,900	–	–	–	–
Concessions	70,000	100,000	90,000	95,000	100,000
Parking fees	6,000	6,600	6,500	6,700	7,000
Advertising	17,000	20,000	25,000	50,000	75,000
Sponsorship	76,000	100,000	125,000	150,000	200,000
Novelty/program sales	15,000	18,000	20,000	22,000	24,000
Guarantees received	1,125,000	860,000	885,000	1,215,000	1,300,000
Guarantees paid	(725,000)	(845,000)	(810,000)	(885,000)	(800,000)
Miscellaneous revenues	31,254	30,000	30,000	32,000	35,000
Conference distribution	1,864,000	500,000	550,000	600,000	650,000
Subtotal	**3,632,754**	**2,348,617**	**2,585,715**	**2,836,130**	**3,241,351**
Student service fees	2,329,256	2,329,256	2,329,256	2,350,000	2,350,000
Endowment revenue	2,435,150	2,440,000	2,445,000	2,450,000	2,455,000
Gifts	524,850	–	–	–	–
Houston Athletics Foundation:					
Premium seating	80,000	100,000	140,000	140,000	
Annual fund	600,000	700,000	800,000	900,000	
Net nonathletic special events revenue	25,000	100,000	125,000	150,000	175,000
Total athletic revenue	**8,947,010**	**7,897,873**	**8,284,971**	**8,726,130**	**9,261,351**
Plus university support	4,099,700	5,930,371	6,231,677	6,520,787	6,361,277
Total revenue	**13,046,710**	**13,828,244**	**14,516,648**	**15,246,917**	**15,622,628**

Reprinted, by permission, from University of Houston Athletic Department, 1995, *Schedule of Revenues and Expenses.*

Table 4 University of Houston's Projected Expenditures

Expenditure category	Actual 1996	Projected 1997	Projected 1998	Projected 1999	Projected 2000
Salaries, wages, and benefits	4,340,240	4,584,215	4,584,215	4,584,215	4,584,215
Printing	139,050	146,000	153,300	160,900	169,000
Utilities	600,000	590,000	607,700	625,900	644,700
Postage and telephone	239,375	241,700	244,100	246,600	249,000
Advertising and fund-raising	10,000	100,000	125,000	127,000	129,000
Rentals, leases, and maintenance	357,810	360,000	362,000	365,000	368,000
Insurance	285,000	290,700	296,500	302,400	308,400
Uniforms and equipment	202,400	206,000	210,000	214,000	218,000
Administrative fees	631,059	662,629	700,733	738,027	755,039
Game expenses	387,150	390,000	409,500	429,975	451,474
Scholarships	1,917,766	2,000,000	2,100,000	2,200,000	2,300,000
Travel	1,163,200	1,395,800	1,465,600	1,538,900	1,615,800
Other marketing and operations	875,660	963,200	1,060,000	1,166,000	1,282,000
Addition of women's sports (Title IX)	0	0	300,000	650,000	650,000
Total athletics expenditures	**11,148,710**	**11,930,244**	**12,618,649**	**13,348,917**	**13,724,628**
Debt service	1,998,000	1,898,000	1,898,000	1,898,000	1,898,000
Total expenditures	**13,046,710**	**13,828,244**	**14,516,648**	**15,246,917**	**15,622,628**

Reprinted, by permission, from University of Houston Athletic Department, 1995, *Schedule of Revenues and Expenses.*

at **www.sec.gov/edgar.shtml**. In 1987 Congress passed the Revenue Act of 1987, which required taxing limited partnerships at the standard partnership rate. The Celtics were reorganized to take advantage of this new requirement. On the basis of a grandfather clause, the Celtics limited partnership was going to be taxed at the corporate rate beginning July 1, 1998. In June 1998, the Boston Celtics Limited Partnership reorganized into two separate entities:

1. The Boston Celtics Limited Partnership II (BCLP), which was formed to remain on the New York Stock Exchange and to be taxed as a corporation
2. Castle Creek Partners, LP, which was formed as a nonpublic entity with "pass-through" tax treatment (Much & Phillips, 1999)

BCLP is the publicly traded partnership that owns 48% of the NBA's Boston Celtics. The partnership originally owned all of the team, but that changed after the split. Now, the family of BCLP chairman and CEO Paul Gaston controls Castle Creek Partners, a private partnership that owns the remaining 52%. There are 2,703,364 publicly traded units of a master limited partnership that can be traded on the New York Stock Exchange. Unlike common stock, which could entitle the owner to an equity position (ownership) in the team, the units are only claims against the company's cash flow. In September, 2002, the Celtics were bought for $360 million and once again became a privately owned team (Frost, 2002). Figure 1 shows the stock's performance over the past 5 years.

The Boston Celtics currently offer 104 luxury suites at the new FleetCenter as compared with only 36 in the old Boston Garden. Luxury suites are currently being rented for between $168,000 and $258,000 per year (Greenberg & Gray, 1996). FleetCenter also has 2,350 club seats that average between $10,650 and $12,250 (Much & Friedman, 1996). In addition to these payments, luxury box holders have to pay $40 per ticket per game for boxes that hold between 12 and 18 seats (Much & Friedman, 1996). Tickets for "clubhouse" seats were $43 per game in 1996, over and above the yearly cost for the club seats (Much & Friedman, 1996). By the 2001-2002 season, these tickets were selling for $85 each. The FleetCenter's name was acquired by Fleet Bank for $30 million over 15 years, and the company can also use the facility for company and promotional functions (Greenberg & Gray, 1996).

When playing at the Garden, the Celtics regularly had all 38 home games sold out and averaged 565,820 fans a year for six years through 1994-1995 (Much & Friedman, 1996). The team's attendance at the FleetCenter was 660,936 in the 2001-2002 season, which was an average of 16,120 fans per game. The team had $83 million in revenue in 2001 with $35.8 million coming from ticket sales.

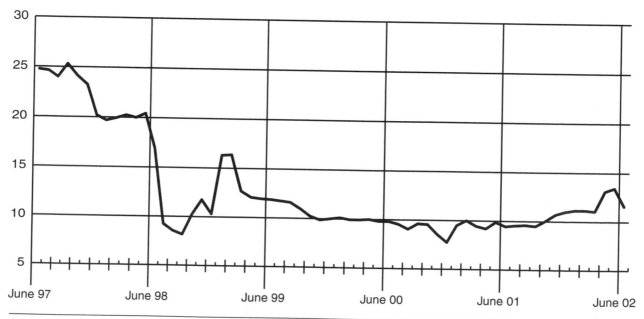

Figure 1 Although the Boston Celtics have not had the greatest success on the court over the past several years, the stock has performed steadily.

PART I

The Basics of Sport Finance

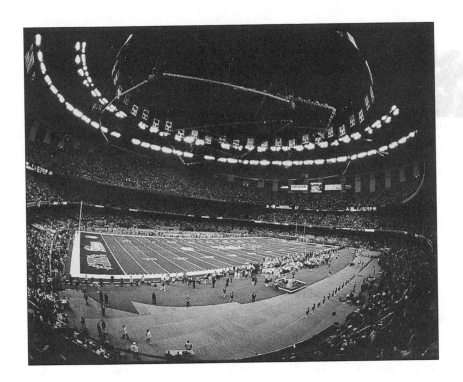

Financial Issues in Sport

CHAPTER OBJECTIVES

After studying this chapter, you should be able to do the following:

- Understand how money affects every facet of the sport industry.
- Understand how industry trends and economic conditions affect every aspect of sport.
- Analyze why the sport apparel industry faces financial hardships.
- Appreciate that some sport businesses are owned by individuals and some by the public.
- Understand major developments in stadium construction trends.
- Describe some of the concerns associated with economic impact analysis for planned stadiums and arenas.

Imagine a world without money. How would we obtain the items we need? How could businesses grow? How could we save for the future? These are typical questions that could arise if our society did not utilize money. More practically, what would happen to us if our checking account did not balance? What would happen to us if our car broke down and we needed to buy a new car? Would we have a favorable credit history for obtaining a loan? Would we need someone to **cosign** a loan, agreeing to pay the balance if we defaulted on the loan? How would we balance our financial obligations with another obligation added to the mix? Would the new car increase our insurance costs to the point that we might not be able to afford the monthly payments? These are questions that typically arise when we make personal financial decisions.

Similar questions are raised by businesses concerning every decision made. Should a new franchise join a league? Should an athlete be signed at $5 million or $6 million a year? How much should ticket prices rise in any given year? If someone wants to start her own sport business, where can she obtain the funds? These questions are asked and answered every day by means of financial analysis. Monetary issues come up throughout the business day, and each business needs individuals who are trained to analyze where the money is or where to obtain additional funds if necessary.

Although **money** is important for everyday decisions, money is not an end in itself for most people. We strive for personal financial independence, but we also normally realize that money only helps us enjoy our life to the fullest. What good is a million dollars if we cannot enjoy spending the money? Individuals traditionally work hard to earn money to enjoy the finer things in life, for example, traveling, retiring, or spoiling family members. However, businesses traditionally do not have the same vision concerning the role money plays in their existence. Businesses exist solely to make money for their owners and stockholders. If a company has other goals besides earning profits, it still has to focus on the bottom line in order to pay **bills** and meet its payroll. For example, even if a company has as its primary goal to make ecologically friendly products to save the rain forest, the company will not be in business if it is unable to sell these products at a price sufficient to cover the costs of running the business. Nonprofit organizations also exist to make money in order to further their primary goals. The Special Olympics needs to engage in selling products, sponsorship, and advertising to raise the funds necessary to offer programs for its athletes.

Besides paying the bills, making and managing money provide the framework for future growth. Finding, managing, tracking, and spending money refer to specific finance-related functions within a company or business. Failure to properly manage funds will cause a business to fail. Successful financial management results in business growth. The best product in the world would not survive if sound financial planning did not support the sales effort. Economic forecasts help determine potential sales patterns or the times when raw goods need to be purchased. If sales are expected to be phenomenal, then it might be necessary to borrow money from a lending institution or the public to finance new manufacturing facilities. Sound financial planning is especially critical when the development process for a product is expected to be long. For example, new nutritional supplements typically require several years of development and testing on humans before they are approved by the Food and Drug Administration (FDA) for consumer distribution. Sport nutrition products such as Gatorade are a good example. Gatorade had to go through the entire FDA review process (which is cumbersome and involves multiple hurdles that can take years to overcome) before it could be sold, and then it had to meet government guidelines concerning the health information on the label. Most pharmaceuticals do not make it through the review process and do not get FDA approval to be sold. During the years the FDA review process takes, a company might not have any income but still needs to pay bills, wages, and operating expenses. Through wise money management and working with potential investors such as venture capitalists, the company could generate the needed finances without jeopardizing product development. The key to financial success, as highlighted by this simple example, is financial planning.

All managerial decisions require a comprehensive review of internal and external constraints. Environmental factors such as the cost of borrowing money involve both internal and external constraints. Internal constraints can include a company's past credit history, sales volume, product lines, accounts receivable, inventory balances, and management structure. External constraints can include inflationary conditions, significant competition, high interest rates, weak **economic indicators,** shrinking of the money supply by the government, and the political environment. Although it takes money to make money, you cannot make money unless you understand all the internal and external variables that affect your ability to properly manage your finances. Thus, a team owner cannot start budgeting for future growth based on a new stadium if the voters have not yet approved public funding for the stadium. Internal constraints, such as ticket prices, are moot issues until the external constraints, the votes, are finalized.

Basic financial principles apply to every business, nonprofit organization, and government entity. People are concerned about the financial health of the Social Security system and whether it might go bankrupt in the future. Some nonprofit organizations have suffered from scandals involving key executives who abused financial control to live a lavish lifestyle. Countless businesses have filed for bankruptcy protection because they failed to make required payments in a timely manner. All these scenarios are examples of poor financial planning. The sport world is not immune to such problems. From the building of a public stadium that sits almost dormant for years to the folding of a new league due to a stronger rival league's aggressive marketing efforts, problems in the sport world often result from the lack of critical financial planning. And the main common denominator in most professional sport strikes involves financial planning. For example, some owners have raised the salary bar for other owners, and once the bar has been raised it becomes almost impossible, without violating antitrust laws, to lower the salaries. That has led to an environment of haves and have-nots. Some teams are able to survive and generate enough revenue to constantly put forth a strong product while other teams flounder with low salaries. Other teams use strategic financial planning to help their bottom line.

As an example, the San Diego Padres spent a significant amount on top-level talent during the 1998 season to help win the National League championship. They also won a vote to utilize public funds to help build a new ballpark. The team spent $53 million in 1998 compared with only $32.8 million in 1997 (Truex, 1999). Thereafter, the team was dismantled and some of the top talent either was traded, was not signed, or signed with other clubs as free agents, thus significantly reducing the payroll (Truex, 1999). Analysts conjectured that the owners spent lavishly to produce a great product and a winning team. Voters would have a harder time voting against a new stadium for a winning team. In contrast, voters would probably not feel bad turning down a stadium bond vote for a team that had never won. Once the team had received the positive vote, the need for a winning and expensive team ended; and the Padres could return to a lower payroll level. Team payrolls do not occur by chance. Financial planning sets the stage for team success.

A Typical Job Description for an Entry-Level Sport Finance Position

Company: Sports Inc.
Department: Business Office
Official Title: Accounts Payable Coordinator

General Statement of Duties

Administrative responsibilities include coordination of accounts payable, cash reconciliation, and other related duties. The position reports to the Assistant Controller and requires the supervision of clerical staff.

Core Duties

Coordinate and perform accounts payable functions
Handle vendor inquiries and resolve problems
Reconcile bank accounts, general ledger accounts
Provide assistance to the payroll function
Prepare journal entries

Secondary Duties

Perform budget analysis
Update and maintain inventory records
Prepare bank deposits
Perform all related duties as assigned

(continued)

(continued)

Required Qualifications

Experience in accounts payable functions utilizing computerized systems
A bachelor's degree in business administration
Strong organizational and interpersonal skills
Experience with Excel or other spreadsheet software
Ability to work under pressure of heavy workload during peak times

A Typical Job Description for a High-Level Sport Finance Position

XYZ is a sport management company seeking a highly motivated Chief Financial Officer. This person will serve as a strategic partner and internal consultant through providing guidance to all individuals associated with our various financial systems. Responsibilities will include, but are not limited to: company-wide budgeting, financial forecasting, statistical reporting, audits, new business development, payroll preparation, state and federal tax compliance, and information systems. Qualified candidates should hold a certificate such as a CPA, CMA, or possess an MBA in conjunction with an accounting bachelor's degree. Five to eight years of senior level financial experience is necessary in order to gain a full understanding of projections, techniques, systems, and methodology. The ideal candidate will also possess strong leadership and managerial skills to help lead a group of 20 employees in various areas such as ticket processing, accounts receivable/payable, and outside contracts administration.

Numerous Sport-Related Organizations Need Individuals With Finance-Oriented Skills

The following two advertisements appeared in the same 1999 Sunday paper in Houston.

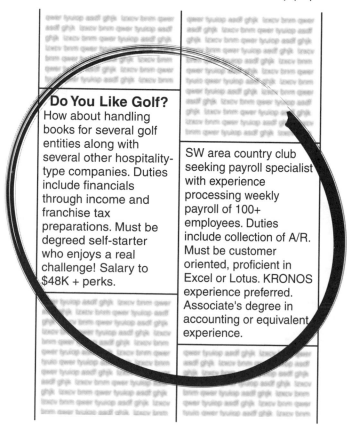

Do You Like Golf? How about handling books for several golf entities along with several other hospitality-type companies. Duties include financials through income and franchise tax preparations. Must be degreed self-starter who enjoys a real challenge! Salary to $48K + perks.

SW area country club seeking payroll specialist with experience processing weekly payroll of 100+ employees. Duties include collection of A/R. Must be customer oriented, proficient in Excel or Lotus. KRONOS experience preferred. Associate's degree in accounting or equivalent experience.

Sport finance entails numerous unique issues, but these nevertheless mirror the finance issues faced by all other businesses. This chapter highlights those similarities. The chapter focuses on current sport finance issues, beginning with the valuation of sport teams and the borrowing of money or issuance of stock by pro sport teams. We then consider mergers of larger sport businesses, changes in the sport apparel area, some of the changes that are affecting sport sponsorship, and the financing of new stadiums and arenas. The background material in this chapter should give you a strong foundation in some of the basic concepts you must understand in order to appreciate the complexities of sport finance.

Every sport business needs to engage in financial planning, just as other businesses, nonprofit organizations, and government entities engage in financial planning.

Newspapers throughout the world are replete with sport finance articles. Whether such articles are on the front pages or in the business or sport sections, many people meticulously follow sport finance stories because of their fan interest or the thrill associated with seeing multimillion-dollar deals. It would be impossible to highlight a year's worth of such headlines in a single text. However, the following represent some key sport finance-related issues raised over the past several years that indicate the breadth of the field. Because of numerous internal and external constraints posed by teams, athletes, facilities, communities, and other variables, no two stories or issues are the same.

Billion-Dollar Teams

The 21st century might witness the first professional team in the United States selling for over $1 billion, now that the Washington Redskins and their stadium have been sold for $805 million, surpassing the previous record of $530 million paid for the Cleveland Browns just several months earlier (Hiestand, 1999). The Redskins appeared to be a strong investment vehicle, as the new stadium, with over 200 luxury suites, was capable of generating over $20 million a year from just those suites and an estimated $5 million a year in stadium naming rights. These figures, added to shared ticket, broadcasting, and licensing revenue, made even $800 million seem like a wise investment (Hiestand, 1999).

Even with such large sums offered for a team, team values can be affected by numerous variables, such as what is included in the deal, whether a new or existing franchise is being sold, or the league's financial strength. In fact, the $800 million offer from New York Islanders' owner Howard Milstein was rejected by the other National Football League (NFL) owners ("Owners Unlikely to OK," 1999). While the Redskins deal included both the team and a stadium, several months after that sale a new NFL franchise was awarded. The NFL sold a franchise to Houston for $700 million (Zimbalist, 1999). National Football League teams have shown more **appreciation** than baseball teams because of the hard salary cap limiting the amounts teams can pay their players, a loyal fan base interested in attending the limited number of games played, and huge television broadcast contracts. However, every sport business has to face the ups and downs of economic conditions, and team values can fluctuate as well. Thus even though a **recession** was occurring as the 21st century began, the sport industry was not anticipating significant layoffs. Major League Baseball (MLB) and Major League Soccer (MLS) were discussing eliminating troubled teams due to financial hardships. Financially strapped MLS had lost $250 million from 1996 through 2001; and one owner, billionaire Phil Anschutz, in essence controlled the destiny of the league by owning 5 of the league's 10 teams (Wahl, 2001). Nonetheless, a financially strong team can still attract buyers, as evidenced by the $755 million sale of the Boston Red Sox along with storied Fenway Park and the New England Sports Network (Farhi, 2001).

The Most Valuable Teams in the World

According to a book titled *Keeping Score: The Economics of Big Time Sports,* in 1996 the Dallas Cowboys were the most valuable sport team in the world, valued at $428 million. Three college teams—Michigan, Florida, and Notre Dame—were also listed among the 25 most valuable sport franchises, even though the college teams could not be sold (Sheehan, 1996). Only three years later, $428 million would appear to be a steal compared to the selling prices for the Houston Texans and the Redskins. However, the downturn in the economy that started the 21st century could lower team values and make the $428 million figure more realistic.

Talk About Appreciation!

With NFL franchises valued at around a half-billion dollars, it is hard to believe the teams' values when the original franchises were issued. Curly Lambeau paid $50 in 1922 for the Green Bay franchise. In 1925, Tim Mara paid $500 for the New York franchise. Art Rooney acquired the Pittsburgh franchise in 1933 through an unconventional method—he won the rights in a card game ("From $50 in 1922," 1999).

In 1995, the NFL sold two franchises for $140 million each. In 1998, the Cleveland Browns franchise sold for $530 million, and the Washington Redskins sold for $805 million (including $160 million for assuming the Redskins' stadium debt). In 1999, Houston won an NFL franchise for $700 million. As of this book's publication, the Houston Texans had yet to play a game, but the franchise's purchase price still appeared to be a steal. Although making a **profit** might appear impossible after paying so much for a franchise, the newest franchise should still make money. The team would receive income of $90 to $100 million the first year from stadium-related revenue (gate receipts, luxury suites, concessions, parking, sponsorships, etc.) and $75 million from NFL central funds. The team costs would include an $80 to $90 million payroll and administrative costs of $40 to $45 million. After all the math is done, the team still should generate $30 to $50 million a year for a **net** return of 4% to 6%. In addition, up to 50% of the team's purchase price is attributable to player contracts. This means that the contracts can be amortized over five years, allowing the team to deduct $70 million annually before calculating the tax liability. Player salaries can also be written off as a business expense (Zimbalist, 1999).

> If player salaries can be reduced and alternate revenue streams such as international sponsorship increased, it is conceivable that some teams, such as NFL teams, could be worth over $1 billion.

North American sport teams are not alone in their high valuations. At one point in 1999 it appeared that England's most famous soccer club, Manchester United, might be the first team to be worth $1 billion. Thereafter, the stock dropped to less than half that value and now trades on the London stock exchange for 740 million euros (Kapner, 2001). Why would a team's **value** fluctuate so much in such a short time period? The simple answer could be the team's profit margin or total **assets** as discussed later in this text. Another reason could be an arbitrary value based on fan and investor speculation rather than true financial value. Some wealthy individuals are interested in owning an expensive toy and could throw all logic out the window if they are in a bidding war with a rival and want more than anything to own a professional team. As Dallas Mavericks' owner Marc Cuban said, "It's every little kid's dream . . . to own their favorite team. I think it's a tremendous opportunity" ("Web Billionaire," 2000).

Can Anyone Loan Me Several Billion?

For a period of time in 1998, the NFL was considering the sale of asset-backed securities to raise $600 million. An asset-backed security is a type of promissory **note** such as a car loan in which the car serves as **collateral.** If the loan is not repaid, the car (asset) is forfeited to the lender. Similarly, the NFL wanted to have available for teams the opportunity to borrow funds using assets such as anticipated television revenue to guarantee loan repayment. The trust financing instruments were to be 12-year certificates that each team could borrow against. The **securities** were to be secured by revenue generated from an 8-year broadcasting contract worth approximately $18 billion and revenue from NFL Properties, which licenses team logos ("Offering for Investors," 1998). The offering was withdrawn when investor interest turned out not to be strong enough (Kaplan, 1998, August-September).

In contrast, the New York Yankees have successfully issued bonds to fund future growth. That growth included a merger with the New Jersey Nets into a company called YankeeNets. The merger was undertaken to **leverage** the cable TV market, but each team still runs its own affairs separately. The cash raised from the bond issue was used in part to try to buy the New Jersey Devils. The team was slated to be sold to Puck Holdings, which is an affiliate of YankeeNets ("YankeeNets Affiliate," 2000). The YankeeNets were working in 2001 on obtaining state support to build a new sport arena for the Nets in Newark and another facility in Hoboken for the Devils ("Hoboken Arena," 2002).

Stocks for Sale

Individuals now have greater opportunities than in the past to invest in their favorite teams. People can invest in public stock offerings for teams such as the Boston Celtics, Green Bay Packers, and Orlando Predators. Individuals can also purchase stock in sport-related businesses such as International Speedway Corp. (which owns 12 NASCAR racetracks),

internationally recognized companies such as Nike or Disney, and even sport-specific stock funds. Some sport-specific investment funds have attempted to focus on such areas as auto racing, golf, sport sponsors, and sporting goods manufacturing companies ("Investing's Fast Track?" 1999). An investment fund called the Sportsfund was launched in 1996 but never succeeded. The company's brochure included the following warning:

Since the fund focuses its investment on a set of industries related to a single theme, it may be more volatile than a fund that does not focus its investments in this manner. Because sport activities are not a necessity, companies focused on sports may be more affected by economic downturns than other companies. (Sportsfund, 1996)

Specialty Sport Stock Indexes and Funds

Specialty sport stock indexes became popular in the late 1990s, but few showed significant success. Among approximately 7,300 specialty **mutual funds,** several specialized in the sport industry. The StockCar Stock Index, with assets of about $5 million, was down while the rest of the market was up for part of 1999. The Value Trends Links Fund had trouble finding golf-oriented stocks, so it started acquiring stocks in companies that sponsor golf events. By October 1999, the fund's value had increased 8.8% (O'Brian & Tam, 1999).

> *Unlike any other time in the past, fans can buy shares in their favorite sport team as easily as they can cheer for the team.*

Merger Mania

The sporting goods industry sustained significant growth in the 1990s through the success of shoe brands such as Air Jordans®. However, the industry experienced a major downturn in the late 1990s, with several manufacturers losing significant earnings. These losses led to a consolidation within the retail sales side of the industry. For example, in 1998 Woolworth Corp. (now Venator) agreed to buy Sports Authority for stock valued at $579.6 million and the **assumption** of $179 million worth of Sports Authority debt ("Woolworth Corp.," 1998). Sports Authority was expected to report losses of $0.12 a share before the acquisition was announced. The acquisition allowed its shareholders to receive 0.8 shares in Woolworth stock for each Sports Authority share.

Woolworth already owned over 3,000 athletic shoe stores, including Foot Locker®, Lady Foot Locker®, and Champs Sports stores, and would add the 202 Sports Authority stores to its family of sporting goods sales units that generated over $5.5 billion in annual worldwide sales ("Woolworth Corp.," 1998).

Investors did not view the merger positively when it was first announced. In May 1998, the Venator Group and Sports Authority, Inc. announced the planned merger when both companies' shares were trading at approximately $20 per share. Six months later, shares of both companies' shares were valued at around $10 with Sports Authority, Inc.'s stock dropping to as little as $4.06—signaling lack of investor interest in the merger (Bernstein, 1998). However, Venator was able to successfully complete the merger and start producing strong returns. For the quarter ending January 2000, Venator's net income rose to $73 million on sales of $1.33 billion. For the year, Venator's 4,529 stores produced a $48 million profit, or $0.35 per share. The prior year (1998), the company had had losses of $136 million, or a $1 loss per share. On the basis of the reported goods news, Venator's stock rose $0.25 to $7 per share ("Venator Net Surges," 2000). This example shows that even when significant planning goes into a financial decision such as a merger, numerous problems can arise. One major problem can be investor response. In this case the investors were proven wrong and the merger was a success.

Major industry consolidations also occurred in the sport agency arena; for example, SFX Entertainment purchased Falk Associates Management Enterprises for $100 million. Super agent David Falk is most famous as Michael Jordan's agent. That acquisition occurred less than one year after Interpublic Group, an ad agency, purchased Advantage International, Inc., which represents over 200 athletes (Fatsis, 1998, May 8). However, not long after SFX started its acquisition spree (see chapter 15), it was acquired by another company. Clear Channel, which owns 867 radio stations, 19 TV stations, and over 500,000 outdoor billboards, offered to acquire SFX for $2.99 billion. Ironically, SFX obtained a significant amount of its cash needed to purchase other companies by selling its radio stations. SFX's class A shareholders were to receive about $40.125 for each share. However, class B shareholders were given one share of Clear Channel (valued at over $66.00) for each class B share. This deal structure caused some concern, since the only holders of class B shares were SFX's chairman and CEO (Tejada, 2000). Individuals could be concerned with this purchase structure since the class B shareholder would be compensated at a higher level than other stockholders. While class A and class B stocks are technically different, if they paid the same amount for their interest and had the same risks, investors would be concerned if they did not receive similar compensation, and in this case the difference was over $25 per share. The potential exists for class A stockholders to believe that their compensation for selling their interest in SFX was inadequate given the higher amount paid to class B stockholders for their shares.

Additional consolidation occurred in the broadcasting industry. Disney's acquisition of ABC and ESPN appeared to be a natural fit for the entertainment giants, which positioned themselves to bid for large packages such as the National Basketball Association (NBA) broadcast contract in 2001 (Fendrich, 2001). Another major merger that occurred in 2000 involved America Online (AOL), which merged with Time Warner to form the media, entertainment, and sport giant AOL Time Warner. Mergers such as these are covered in greater detail in chapter 15.

> During the late 1990s, a number of companies in the sporting goods manufacturing industry and the entertainment industry were acquired by larger companies.

Sport Apparel Blues

Product repositioning represents one of the major transitions facing the sport, or athletic, shoe industry. In the 1980s, almost every player in the NBA had a shoe deal. However, by 1998, only about half of the 400 players in the league had shoe contracts, and that number was dwindling rapidly (Fatsis, 1998, May 14). Reebok alone dropped over 110 NBA players who had been under contract previously. Reebok also slashed its baseball sponsorship lineup from 280 to 140 athletes and its football players from 550 to around 100 (Fatsis, 1998, May 14). Major stars such as Shaquille O'Neal had their contracts terminated or bought out. Larry Johnson had earned around $800,000 a year from Converse in the early 1990s, but in 1998 he received only $7,500 in free merchandise (Fatsis, 1998, May 14). The sponsorship downturn was the result of a significant downturn in the $8 billion U.S. athletic shoe market. Reebok sales in the United States slumped 12% in early 1998. Converse sales plummeted 50%, and Nike sales fell 18%, resulting in Nike's laying off 7% of its workforce (1,600 employees) (Fatsis, 1998, May 14). Analysts thought the primary reason Nike was experiencing slower gains than expected was the numerous shoe stores that had closed or filed for bankruptcy. For example, Just For Feet, Inc. filed for bankruptcy in 1999, depriving Nike of numerous outlets for selling its products (Gomes, 2000). Nike sales have rebounded and fluctuated since 1998, with third-quarter sales ending in February 2000 hitting $2.16 billion and the company beating analyst projections with earnings per share of $0.52 ("Nike Net Rose," 2000). By the second quarter ending November 30, 2001, Nike sales had hit $2.3 billion, but the earnings per share had declined to $0.48 (Pritchard, 2001). These figures indicate that volatility exists with any business from year to year or even month to month. Sales can be flat in the winter except for a spike in Christmas-related purchases and then often heat up when spring arrives and people are once again participating in sports.

Season can also affect the sport apparel area, in which sales are often best right before schools are back in session. However, sales had declined to such an extent in the sport apparel industry in the late

1990s that one of the nation's premiere sport clothing manufacturers, Starter Corp., filed for chapter 11 bankruptcy in 1999 and was liquidated shortly thereafter ("Starter Seeks Chapter 11," 1999). Creditors pushed the company into bankruptcy even though Starter had a significant number of orders to fill for the pre-school buying cycle (Sack & Nadim, 2002). A similar fate befell Pro Player, which went bankrupt in 1999 (although there is still a stadium in Miami named after the now defunct brand) (Sack & Nadim, 2002). Furthermore, licensed sport apparel company Logo Athletic, Inc. filed for chapter 11 bankruptcy protection in 2000 ("Logo Athletic," 2000).

Financial hardships in the sport shoe and apparel industries were not the result of decreased sales alone. Converse suffered from decreased sales, but its bankruptcy was not entirely related to falling sales. According to Converse's spokesperson Mark Shuster, "[I]t's not a lack of business, but our debt structure that made it difficult for the company to thrive" (Byrt, 2001).

> *Manufacturers of athletic shoes and other sport-related apparel are affected by ups and downs in the larger economy as well as by internal finance-related issues.*

Sport Sponsorship

The sport shoe and apparel industries were not alone in experiencing financial turmoil in the late 1990s. Sport sponsorship in general was facing some hard times late in the decade and into the 21st century. Sponsors sometimes have difficulty placing a value on a sponsorship property, so any reinvestment decision is subject to significant fiscal scrutiny. Coca-Cola had a 12-year relationship with the NFL through 1998. However, the latest deal, crafted in 1998, pays the NFL only $6 million a year as compared with $15 million in prior years ("Coke Signs," 1998). The reduced sponsorship package allows teams for the first time in many years to negotiate their own local sponsorship deals. The reduced value associated with the new contract was possibly the result of Dallas Cowboys owner Jerry Jones striking his own deals with competing sponsors. Jones sold sponsorship rights to Pepsi for Pepsi's sponsorship of Texas Stadium. Since it was the stadium that was sponsored by the competing soft drink manufacturer, not the team, Jones was technically not violating the old NFL and Coca-Cola contract. However, because the Cowboys were the only team that played in Texas Stadium, the sponsorship agreement implied indirect sponsorship of the Cowboys by Pepsi. The resulting confusion reduced the sponsorship value for Coca-Cola, leading to the subsequently smaller sponsorship agreement.

Sponsorship can come in various forms. For example, a professional league can sponsor a farm team. The NBA in fact had a partnership arrangement with the Continental Basketball Association (CBA) through 2001. The NBA then decided to move away from the CBA and start its own developmental league. The loss of the NBA as a sponsor doomed the CBA, which filed for bankruptcy in 2001 ("CBA Ceases Operations," 2001). Losing sponsors also hurts smaller events, community events such as run-a-thons, and even larger events such as collegiate football bowl games.

> *Sport sponsorship faced some hard times in the late 1990s and the opening years of this century.*

Financing New Stadiums and Arenas

The most dynamic sport finance topic in the 1990s was stadium construction deals. Currently there are 111 major professional sport franchises in America, and 91.9% (102) moved into new or significantly renovated stadiums in the 1990s (Smith, 2001). Bond issues, economic factors, taxing issues, financial guarantees, legal wrangling, and political shenanigans can all be examined when one is looking at stadium construction deals. Venerable Yankee Stadium was built in 1923 for $2 million. In 1973, New York City refurbished the stadium for $100 million. In 1996, New York City proposed a new stadium on the west side of Manhattan with an estimated cost of $1.06 billion (Sportsfund, 1996). In 2001, New York recommended two new $800 million stadiums for both MLB teams, which would require the teams and cities to split $50 million a year in **debt service** (to repay the money borrowed to build the stadiums) ("Double Play for New York," 2001). The total taxpayers' cost for stadiums or arenas built from 1995 through 2000 has been estimated at over $9 billion (Kraker, 1998). Another estimate capped the building boom at $7 billion from 1998 through 2006, and the number keeps increasing when new stadiums and arenas are approved by voters (Noll & Zimbalist, 1998). Although numerous facilities are being built to keep or attract professional sport teams, such investments might not always make economic sense or stand on sound financial analysis.

The Rockies' Stadium Deal

The Colorado Rockies built their stadium with a 1%, six-county-area sales tax, with the team contributing $53 million and Coors Brewing making **scheduled payments** of $1.5 million a year for naming rights. Under the 17-year lease, the city received 20% of parking revenue on game days and 3% of the revenue from a brew pub. The team receives 100% of net concession revenue (Rogus, 1997).

In a 1990 study, the Heartland Institute examined 14 stadiums from 1954 through 1986; these facilities had a net accumulated value of negative $139.3 million ("Sports Stadiums," 1990). The city that had lost the least was Buffalo, New York: the War Memorial Stadium had lost taxpayers only $836,021. In contrast, the New Orleans Superdome lost Louisiana taxpayers $70,356,950 ("Sports Stadiums," 1990). After the construction boom in the 1990s, additional research showed that the stadiums and arenas were not a wise financial investment if examined strictly from an economic perspective (Smith, 2001).

Municipalities interested in luring a new team or keeping an existing team argue that tax dollars should help finance facility construction because entertainment dollars are brought from outside the community, thus infusing "new" moneys into the local economy (Howard & Crompton, 1995). While the municipalities are urging voters to approve allocating funds to build the facilities, the teams are also supporting these efforts. However, the average level of team contribution to a new NFL stadium is only 29%, or $82 million, of the typical construction cost for a football stadium ("NFL Stadium," 2001). Even without any team contributions, some municipalities are willing to foot the entire price of a facility to become a "big-league" city. Besides increased economic activity and increased sales, income, and employment tax revenues from those attending games and working at the facilities, proponents argue that the facilities help promote community image (Baim, 1994).

Although significant benefits can be derived from new sport facilities, numerous projections highlighting potential increased tax revenue or other benefits are often significantly inflated to help support the case for building a new facility (Howard & Crompton, 1995). In fact, the combined revenue of the five major professional sport teams in Chicago accounts for only 0.08% of the personal income throughout the city of Chicago (Kraker, 1998). One recent study concluded that the departure of an NBA team from a city results in no measurable impact on a region's per capita income and thus that building a new arena does not make sense as a

cornerstone for economic development ("Football Strike?" 2001). One of the reasons that projected economic impacts may conflict has to do with the individuals who determine potential economic impact. Consultants who prepare economic impact reports can utilize incorrect multipliers, or assume that everyone who attends the facility would not have spent money elsewhere in the city, or build in a host of other incorrect assumptions (Baim, 1994). Thus, as is the case for all issues associated with financial analysis, the numbers are only as good as their source and need to be verified, more or less the same way financial statements should be **audited** by a neutral third party.

Although numerous consulting reports show potential profits attributable to a facility, many studies have shown that very few facilities are able to cover their costs (Baim, 1994; Noll & Zimbalist, 1998; Smith, 2001). One major study concluded that older arenas with little debt and numerous scheduled events (NBA, NHL, Ice Capades, family shows, circuses, etc.) tended to make the highest profit while new stadiums for outdoor sports were least profitable (Baim, 1994). The disparity among economic impact studies is highlighted by two studies conducted in 1992 when the San Francisco Giants were considering a move to San Jose, California. A study conducted in San Francisco estimated economic losses of $3.1 million per year if the team moved. A study conducted for San Jose produced different results. The San Jose study concluded that if the team moved the approximately 45 miles from San Francisco to San Jose, the yearly economic impact to San Jose would be between $50 and $150 million annually (Howard & Crompton, 1995).

The potential hypocrisy associated with stating the financial need to build a stadium or arena was highlighted in a suit by former Tampa Mayor William Poe, who tried to stop a referendum to build a new stadium for the Tampa Bay Buccaneers. The Buccaneers were claiming significant financial hardship and the need for a new stadium in order to be economically competitive with other NFL teams. Poe was able to show that at no time did any city official ever ask to see the Buccaneers' financial

A Good Deal for the Ravens?

The Baltimore Ravens have a financially lucrative stadium deal, with the team receiving revenue from seat licenses and 100% of the revenue from concessions, suites, club seats, and naming rights—and the team pays no rent. Ticket, novelty, parking, sponsorship, and advertising revenues are split between the team and government (Rogus, 1997). Unfortunately, several years later, PSINET (the company that held the naming rights) went bankrupt. Similarly, the Houston Astros bought their way out of their naming-right contract with Enron to disassociate themselves from that company.

The United Center in Chicago

The Chicago Bulls play in the United Center, built in 1994 at a cost of $175 million; 80% of the financing was with funds from private bank loans and 20% was with funds from the building owners. The entire project was privately funded by the United Center Joint Venture, which is headed by William Wirtz (owner of the Chicago Blackhawks), and Jerry Reinsdorf (majority owner and team chairman of the Chicago Bulls) ("Building Information," 2001). United Airlines pays $1.8 million a year for naming rights (Rogus, 1997). The original Chicago Stadium, which housed the Bulls and Blackhawks for years, was built for $7 million in 1926. The new center is almost four times the size of the first stadium, and its average electric bill is around $155,000 each month ("Building Information," 2001).

statements to ensure that the team owner was telling the truth (Henderson, 1996). The following examples point to the **economics** and financing backdrop behind several stadium or arena deals.

Louisiana Superdome

In *The Sports Stadium As a Municipal Investment* (1994), Dean Baim highlighted several unique stadium deals, including the Louisiana Superdome deal. In 1966, Louisiana voters approved the state constitutional amendment that formed the Louisiana Superdome Authority and allowed the state to borrow $35 million for the project. The facility was completed at a cost of $125 million. The original bond issue was to be backed by a 4% hotel and motel occupancy tax. The full faith and credit of the state of Louisiana was to be *excluded* from backing the bond offering. Since the costs far exceeded the initial $35 million price tag, the state agreed to lease the stadium at an annual rent equal to the shortfall experienced by the authority for servicing the facility's debt obligation. Thus, the state's credit was not utilized to secure the debt obligation (Baim, 1994).

Chase Manhattan Bank led a syndicate prepared to underwrite the Superdome's bonds, but the syndicate collapsed when a gubernatorial candidate threatened to derail the project if he was elected.

This led to collaboration between a local banker and an Arkansas bank to sell the $113 million in bonds needed to start construction (Baim, 1994).

To become economically successful (self-sufficient), the Superdome needed to earn between $26,000 and $35,000 in daily rental income (Baim, 1994). This number was projected even before any tenants were being considered for the facility. Thus, Louisiana was hoping for a dream to come true—"If you build it, they will come." Louisiana is not alone. Stadium and arena projects are routinely passed even if no host tenants exist or the facility cannot cover its own debt obligations once it has been completed (Andelman, 1993). Opponents of a San Diego facility referendum explicitly projected that the stadium could not pay for itself, yet the measure passed with 72% of the votes (Baim, 1994). Such possibly foolish investments in a losing venture are made not for strictly financial reasons, but for the prospect of economic growth, urban revitalization, or possibly improvement in the quality of life in the area.

Arrowhead Pond of Anaheim

Located in the heart of Southern California, Arrowhead Pond is a 650,000-square-foot arena that serves as home to the NHL Mighty Ducks, owned by Disney. Arrowhead Pond of Anaheim was constructed through a comprehensive financing package involving several parties. The city of Anaheim issued $103 million in a certificate of participation bond. This bond was guaranteed by a **letter of credit** from Ogden Facility Management. As the city of Anaheim was *not* forced to underwrite the bond with its own security, it repaid Odgen by giving Ogden an exclusive right to manage the arena for 30 years. Ogden also receives a management fee and can earn between 75% and 85% of all yearly profits from the facility (Greenberg & Gray, 1996).

Rose Garden

The Rose Garden in Portland is a 785,000-square-foot facility that hosts a range of events from NBA and Women's National Basketball Association games to college basketball; professional hockey; and other events such as concerts, rodeos, ice shows, and monster truck rallies. In a complex blend of private and public funding, the Rose Garden was built with Portland Trailblazers owner Paul Allen contributing $46 million in cash. Three major banks loaned a total of $16 million to the pot. Last, nine insurance companies purchased $155 million in privately placed bonds paying 8.99% interest over 27 years (Greenberg & Gray, 1996). The city of Portland paid $34.5 million for street, parking, and related improvements. These city-funded projects will be paid for by a ticket tax of 6.5%, which will pay off the city's contribution in six years and thereafter provide the city with a perpetual return on its investment (Greenberg & Gray, 1996).

Stadiums and Job Creation

Although stadium proponents claim that building a stadium creates jobs, the cost of creating a stadium-related job is over $100,000 per job versus a job at a retail shop or supermarket, which often costs under $10,000 (Rogus, 1997).

Texas Motor Speedway

Stadiums and arenas for professional sport teams are not the only facilities currently being built. Several companies with nationally traded stock are developing and building racetracks throughout the United States. The largest such track to date is the Texas Motor Speedway. The Speedway was paid for by Speedway Motorsports, Inc. but received significant government assistance; for example, the city of Fort Worth spent $7 million on road improvements and $4 million for water and sewer improvements, with the county throwing in $5 million for road improvements. The Speedway can hold over 250,000 spectators for a race. Before the Speedway was built, economists pegged the potential economic impact at between $11 and $200 million annually for only several events each year (Moffeit, 1999). The potential economic impact was greatly reduced by a "sweetheart deal" in which the owners would not have to pay any city or county property taxes for 30 years—a benefit valued at over $100 million. Each year the city captures approximately $700,000 in Speedway-related tax revenue. The figures are fairly new, as the Speedway opened only in 1997. However, the initial numbers indicate that the $700,000 in added tax revenue represented 10% of the city's sales tax revenue in 1998. Furthermore, the Speedway helped increase motel and hotel tax revenue by 20% in 1997. A unique aspect of the Speedway is that condominium and Speedway Club towers have been built on the property, and all the condominiums are already sold. The facilities and track contribute 400 full-time jobs to the local economy year-round and 5,000 part-time jobs during race week (Moffeit, 1999).

Stadiums and Income Growth

While stadium proponents claim significant benefit to building a new stadium, one researcher studied per capita income growth in 48 metropolitan areas. In the 30 cities that had facility changes in the preceding 10 years, 27 showed no significant relationship between income growth and building a facility, and three areas experienced reduced income (Baade, 1994).

Funding Facilities

Projects such as the Louisiana Superdome, Arrowhead Pond, the Rose Garden, and Texas Motor Speedway rely on various funding techniques ranging from private contributions to **municipal bonds.** Municipal notes and bonds are publicly traded securities that have the benefit of not having to comply with some of the same registration requirements that other publicly traded securities do (Greenberg & Gray, 1996). Chapter 10 covers several different types of municipal bonds including general obligation, special tax, revenue, and lease-backed financing bonds, as well as certificates of participation. Municipal bonds utilize public funds to help build new facilities. For example, by negotiating a strong agreement requiring the municipality to pay the bulk of the costs, the team interested in playing in the facility can preserve its capital and increase its revenue stream. In addition to considering municipal bonds, facilities and various government entities can examine other critical financing issues such as the tax status of the bond interest income (taxable or tax-exempt), the credit strength of the bond-issuing entity, the collateral or security that would be utilized to secure the bonds, and related concerns. All these concerns come into play when the final financing package for the facility is being negotiated. Negotiations represent the opportunity to creatively design a comprehensive financing package containing any necessary bells and whistles to encourage all parties to commit to the project.

> Among sport finance-related topics in the news during the 1990s, the stadium construction boom was the hottest.

CONCLUSION

The financial examples presented in this chapter help demonstrate the breadth of financial issues that can affect a sport administrator. Other issues not yet touched upon include Title IX compliance for high school and college athletic programs, fund-raising for youth sport, ways in which a sporting goods company might issue stock to gain critical expansion funds, and countless others. These topics suggest the wide range of issues that intertwine sport and finance. As these examples indicate, financial concerns permeate every decision made in the sport industry. Even a decision that might seem innocuous from a financial standpoint, such as whether to play a given athlete, presents critical financial consider-

ations. Any time a player participates, he may draw additional fans, may foul a significant number of pitches and so give rise to more commercial break opportunities, or may get a hit that qualifies him for a financial benefit. If the player is injured, the team can lose revenue, face higher workers' compensation premiums, and incur higher rehabilitation-related costs.

ASSIGNMENTS

1. Using an Internet search engine, look up Nike, Boston Celtics, Churchill Downs, Disney, or Comcast. See if you can find any financial data about the company. Where did you find the information? What information did you find?

2. Go onto the Internet and try to find information on a stadium or arena built in the past five years. Investigate whether the new facility increased the primary tenant's (home team's) attendance, and track the attendance numbers since the facility was opened to see whether the new facility can continue to attract more fans. Does the team's record affect attendance totals for a new facility?

RESEARCH PROJECT

Research one of the professional sport facilities (either stadium or arena) built in the past five years. After you decide on a facility to look into, conduct extensive research through Internet and other sources to find the following information:

1. Who built the facility?
2. Who was the architect that designed the facility?
3. Who paid for the facility, and how was it financed?
4. What events are held at the facility?
5. What have been the attendance numbers since the facility was built?

Besides finding the information, make sure you cite where you obtained your information to receive full credit.

CLASS DISCUSSION TOPICS

1. How many pairs of sport or athletic shoes do you own? What are the brands? Did you buy the shoes? How much did you pay? What is your most expensive model?

2. Who went to a professional sport event within the last year? Where did you go? Did you buy the tickets? How much did you pay? Did you buy any concession items? What items did you buy? How much did you pay? Is price a factor in your purchase decisions as they relate to sport?

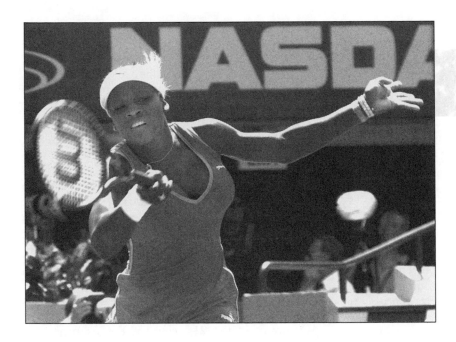

Basic Financial Concepts

CHAPTER OBJECTIVES

After studying this chapter, you should be able to do the following:

- Analyze the problems or failures that might result from inaccurate financial and economic analysis.
- Understand the basics of how a business uses a budget.
- Distinguish between revenue and expenses.
- Understand basic financial goals and how to maximize shareholders' wealth.
- Describe the difference between finance and accounting.
- Understand the objectives of an accounting system.
- Understand the basics of "T-accounts" and general data entry techniques.
- Understand the difference between cash and accrual accounting systems.
- Explain the need for accuracy in accounting and financial data.
- Explain the importance of audited financial statements.

This chapter deals with basic financial terms and principles. The chapter begins with an analysis of revenue and expenses. We then examine the principles of budgeting and the importance of proper documentation. Next we discuss the issues that managers must consider when determining financial objectives and, in a final section of the chapter, present an overview of accounting concepts.

Revenues and Expenses

We all have bills to pay. We also normally have a source of funds whether from a job, loans, or family. This section highlights how we get and spend money in the sport business. **Revenues** represent money coming into a sport business. Revenue can come from ticket sales, broadcast contracts, concession sales, sponsorship agreements, and a host of other opportunities. The opposite of revenues are expenses. **Expenses** represent costs that are incurred. Typical expenses for a professional team include player salaries, equipment, travel, executive salaries, and other expenses ranging from rent to insurance premiums. Each business has different revenues and expenses and they are constantly changing. A health club might have revenues of $1 million one year, but if 100 members do not renew their membership the revenues can plunge. Similarly, if you have ever spent more than you could afford on a credit card, your expenses might be out of control and create debt. **Debt** is the owing of money to others. If you pay all your expenses as they arise, you can avoid debt.

The following example presents the revenues and expenses that a typical public high school athletic program might have:

Revenues	Expenses
Local and city school taxes	Facility repair and maintenance costs
Federal tax subsidies for education	Uniform and equipment costs
State taxes	Travel and lodging costs
Participation fees	Insurance costs
Donations	Umpire costs
Booster clubs	Utility costs
Concession revenue	Salaries and benefits
Attendance revenue	Advertising costs
Broadcasting revenue	Promotional costs
Advertising revenue	Office supplies
Fund-raising efforts	

Licensing revenue

Sponsorship revenue

For a multitude of reasons, many revenue-generating techniques do not work in a given community. Parents may not want to support a program. Possibly no local advertisers are willing to spend their advertising dollars with the school. City regulations may prohibit utilizing certain fund-raising techniques. Although the revenue-generating options may be limited, the expenses normally do not share the same fate. Expenses were outpacing revenues by such a large amount in the early 1990s that some schools started charging students for each sport they played; canceling busing to road games; and eliminating sports such as golf, water polo, and junior varsity sports (Chi, 1992). While financial concerns affecting high school sports surfaced in the 1990s, they became paramount in the 21st century. For example, the towns of Simsbury and Ledyard in Connecticut are charging parents $100 for the privilege of having their children play football during the 2002-2003 academic year. Budget cuts were also felt by colleges. Given various concerns such as compliance with Title IX and the Americans with Disabilities Act, numerous collegiate athletic programs are facing difficult financial times. The problems are compounded by the fact that most Division I athletic programs operate at a deficit. At one point in the 1990s, the Illinois state legislature was even considering eliminating all state funds for intercollegiate athletics (Hiestand, 1992). But the revenue and expense problems in intercollegiate and interscholastic sports are not unique, as the same concerns can affect any business.

Revenues and expenses are often very similar for almost all industries. For example, all businesses, nonprofit organizations, and government entities need to pay rent in some manner or have salary expenses. In professional or collegiate sport, revenues are primarily derived from ticket sales, broadcasting rights, or both, while the primary expenses are salaries and benefits (Howard & Crompton, 1995). Regardless of the team or league, every sport organization has the same basic revenue streams from the sale of goods or services and the same basic expenses of salaries, rent or mortgage, maintenance, advertising, raw goods, and various supplies. Any of these numbers can be large and may appear impressive. However, after critically examining such numbers, anyone trained in financial analysis can see that many businesses with substantial revenue streams are not profitable. Many professional sport teams earn significant revenue from attendance and broadcast rights, but fail to cover their fixed operating costs (Howard & Crompton, 1995). No business can survive a constant monetary wound that keeps bleeding. That is why so many Canadian teams have packed their bags or are considering packing their bags to move to greener pastures in the United States (Harper, 1999). By the 2001 National Hockey League (NHL) season, only four teams remained in Canada after teams left Winnipeg and Quebec City for the United States (Kowall, 2001). Teams were leaving Canada because of such economic hardships as high taxes (expenses), payment of players in American dollars (expenses), and the lower value of the Canadian dollars (revenues) (Harper, 1999).

A Costly Rain Delay

An example of a team's revenue and expenses gives an idea of the potential monetary gains and losses that may be present in professional sport.

Professional Baseball Team X Income Statement

Revenue:	
Baseball attendance revenue	$650,000
Revenue from facility rental	60,000
Revenue from concessions	35,000
Total revenue	**$745,000**
Expenses:	
Players' salaries (35 players)	$235,000
Price for new players	90,000
Transportation bills	15,000
Hotel bills	15,000
Rental expenses and salaries	85,000
Maintenance costs	20,000
Spring training costs	25,000
Players' supplies	11,000
Insurance costs	12,000
Scouts' salaries/expenses (3 scouts)	20,000
Expenses for 12 newspapermen	38,400
Sundries	11,600
Total expenses	**$578,000**
Profit before taxes	**$167,000**

Adapted from J. Lewis, 1936, "Basehits, incorporated," *Liberty:* 48–49.

Although it does not appear that the team's economic condition is all that bad, the revenue, expenses, and pretax profits can swing sharply in any given moment. In fact, the numbers shown are not hypothetical; rather they are the actual revenue and expense numbers for a professional team in 1935. The numbers appeared in an article by a professional team owner who was highlighting the potential perils associated with a team's bottom line. The writer also recounted how in 1934 another team, the New York Giants, had been within a game of first place and had been scheduled to play a doubleheader against the Philadelphia Phillies. A capacity crowd of 50,000 was expected for the games. But a drizzle began to fall, resulting in postponement. When the games were later replayed, the Giants were already out of the pennant picture, and a crowd of only 2,000 attended the doubleheader. Because of the rain delay the Giants lost over $55,000 (Lewis, 1936).

Professional sport has changed drastically since the 1930s. Contractually obligated revenues such as broadcasting contract and luxury box revenue have made the prospects for significant one-day losses highly unlikely. However, sport has a way of producing strange results, and rain delays, freak injuries, and unexpected economic conditions can all affect a team's bottom line. The following paragraph appeared in the same 1936 article:

Last year the New York Yankees sent Ruth to the Boston Braves. It was soon apparent that they had made a big mistake, for their attendance fell off even though the team was leading the league. Ruth, despite the fact that he had slowed to a walk, was still a terrific drawing card in New York. When the Braves made their first 1935 appearance in Tammany Town, 42,000 fans turned out to cheer him. Ruth, with the Braves for less than half the season, made enough money for them in that short space of time to allow them to break even on the season despite the fact that they finished in last place. (Lewis, 1936)

The Babe Ruth example is not an isolated case of a financial blunder involving trading or releasing an athlete. In any given year, a player might be a low-level player for one team but blossom for another. Conversely, a player can be a star one day and "washed up" the next. Thus, the business of managing sport teams, organizations, or facilities is fraught with potential profit centers or with traps that can lead to financial ruin. The convergence of numerous variables that can increase or decrease revenue in a moment makes sport management traditionally more complex than financing in other, traditional business sectors. However, by analyzing a company's financial objectives, sport finance students can often determine that a short-term loss might be beneficial for generating larger profits in the long run. Financial objectives are often found in financial **disclosure** documents required by federal regulators. For example, the Boston Celtics' financial objectives are included in their **Form 10-K** annual report. The team's annual 10-K and quarterly **Form 10-Q** reports are filed with the Securities and Exchange Commission (SEC) as required by law. The reports can be accessed from numerous financial Web sites, including the SEC's own Web site at **www.sec.gov**.

From seeing how revenues and expenses change over time, students can learn much about an industry. For example, in the 1930s, professional sport was not as popular as it is today, and the teams had to promote themselves constantly. That is why the team referred to earlier spent $38,400 to pay the travel expenses of 12 newspaper reporters. Since the team was paying the way for the reporters, they were less likely to write negative stories. The resulting positive publicity was designed to help sell more tickets. Teams no longer have to pay reporters to travel to cover them. However, teams still need to include a line item in their budget to pay for food that is given to reporters in the pressroom.

Revenues (money coming in) and expenses (money going out) are fundamental to sport organizations and sport businesses as with any other type of business.

Budgets

Revenues and expenses are included in various types of **financial statements,** such as budgets, income statements, and balance sheets. A **budget** is a road map that shows where the sport business intends to spend its money. All members of the business can use the budget to help make decisions. If the budget allocates a certain amount of money for marketing and the marketing department reaches that limit halfway through the year, then it may be difficult for the department to receive additional funds for the rest of the year. The only way this is likely to happen is if sales are exceeding the sales forecast or if another area in the budget, such as customer service, is reduced to free money for the marketing department. Budgets, as will be discussed in chapter 7, are often developed through use of prior income statements and balance sheets. An income statement highlights a company's **income** and expenses over the past year. A balance sheet shows the worth of a company at a specific time. These are just two of the types of financial statements discussed in greater detail in chapter 5. Investors, stakeholders, analysts, and government officials are the primary readers of most financial statements. The following two examples illustrate the stories that can unfold when one critically analyzes income statements, as well as showing how budgets influence sport businesses. By examining past income statements, a business can help plan for its future budget and also determine whether or not its prior budget was accurate.

Two Budgets

The Texas Special Olympics reported $7.1 million in income and expenses in its 1995 annual report. The following table shows how the numbers broke down in amounts and percentage of total funds for various categories.

1995 Texas Special Olympics Income Statement

Income:	
Fund-raising/Annual campaign (45.4%)	$3,220,266
Direct mail/Telemarketing (27.2%)	1,936,589
Investment income (11.8%)	838,773
Program services (5.6%)	395,540
Game sponsors (5.2%)	366,930
Foundations/Grants (3.0%)	215,007
Souvenir sales (1.8%)	126,895
Total income	**$7,100,000**
Expenses:	
Program services (52.8%)	$3,742,385
Revenue development (17.6%)	1,252,106
Net asset increase (14.1%)	1,001,196
Direct mail/Telemarketing (8.9%)	634,965
Management/General (6.6%)	469,348
Total expenses	**$7,100,000**

Data from "Texas Special Olympics," 1996.

Among the stories these numbers tell are the following:

- Over 50% of all moneys raised helped pay for program services.
- Investment income will increase on an annual basis if the Texas Special Olympics continues increasing its net assets, because the primary assets are investment securities that will generate future income.
- Only 6.6% of expenses were dedicated to managerial tasks while 26.5% of expenses helped raise operating funds.
- Although direct mail and telemarketing costs were $634,965, this investment was very successful in helping to raise almost $2 million.
- The greatest revenue source comprised fund-raising efforts and donations by individuals to the annual campaign.

The income statement of the 1996 Olympic Games in Atlanta (see p. 26) tells a completely different story. The sheer magnitude of million-dollar budgets presents a sharp contrast to relatively small budgets like the Texas Special Olympics budget. Most sport-related budgets are for midsized companies and range from $2 million to $8 million.

These numbers indicate that revenue is derived primarily from broadcasting rights, ticket sales, and national sponsorship programs. Construction and venue operating expenses dominate the Atlanta Olympic Organizing Committee's (AOOC) expenses. However, the human resource expenses are fairly large and compose a significantly higher percentage than the human resource expenses generated by the Texas Special Olympics. The budget also highlights that while the AOOC earns interest income from excess

(continued)

(continued)

1996 Atlanta Olympic Organizing Committee's Income Statement

Revenue and support:	(millions)
Broadcast rights	$568.3
Ticket sales	427.2
Joint marketing—USOC	426.7
Top III sponsorship	81.1
Rate card rentals	63.2
Merchandising margin	34.6
Interest	19.4
Local sponsors	14.8
Housing	14.2
Ticket fees	12.6
Contributions	10.2
License plate sales	9.5
Parking and transportation	9.3
Disposal of assets	8.0
Other	30.0
Total revenue	**$1,729.4**
Less royalties	6.4
Net revenue	**$1,723.0**
Expenses:	
Salaries and wages	$315.7
Benefits	21.1
Professional services	209.7
Construction and venues	541.2
Contracted services	94.5
Rent and occupancy	147.2
Equipment	197.1
Materials and supplies	68.5
Insurance	25.2
Conference, travel, hospitality	55.0
Interest and other financing	19.0
Other	10.3
Reserve—liabilities	21.3
Reserve—operations	17.8
Total expenses	**$1,723.0**

Data from Glier, 1997.

cash reserves invested in various interest-earning **accounts,** it also has to pay interest on various loans. The interest earned ($19.4 million) and the interest paid ($19 million) are almost equal, but the strategy did generate an additional $400,000 in revenue. Any budget utilizing such large numbers would be impossible to follow without proper documentation to track all the funds.

A budget is a road map that shows where a business plans to spend its money. The budget forms the basis for decisions about allocating resources.

Proper documentation of revenues and expenses is crucial to a sport business' ability to analyze and evaluate its performance.

Proper Documentation

Finance affects all business decisions, from acquiring funds to allocating various resources and tracking performance (Spiro, 1996). The documentation of these funds and their **expenditures** and returns forms the basis for stockholders' decisions concerning the company. However, while record-keeping is stressed throughout this text as an integral component of financial success, record-keeping should not be seen as an end in itself. Record-keeping is a tool. If just developing the right documents is overemphasized, managers will not be able to see the forest for the trees and may make decisions that look great on paper but become major disasters. Nevertheless, the documentation process is critical and is highlighted throughout this text. At the same time, documentation is only one of the many functions required by law or contract for obtaining necessary funds. That is why analyzing revenues and expenses is so critical. Finance necessitates analyzing the financial feasibility of various projects based on the projected revenues to be gained, the expenses that will be incurred, and the availability of moneys to fund the project through to completion. When potential income from a project is properly documented, a potential investor is more inclined to back that project.

The ability to make appropriate financial decisions is predicated on proper documentation. The AOOC had to pay an accounting firm to develop an audited financial statement that could be shown to the government and other stakeholders. When a sport business finds itself in a financial plight, the only way it can analyze the situation accurately is through proper documentation. Did someone fudge the sales numbers? Is someone embezzling money? Is the company carrying too much inventory? Are the costs of employee benefits out of control? Is extra cash just lying around in unknown accounts? Proper documentation enables you to find the answers to these types of questions. Thus, when examining a balance sheet or income statement, people need to ask themselves if they can trust the numbers. If the financial statements are not audited or otherwise certified by an independent party as accurate, the reader should be cautious.

Determining Financial Objectives

For many managers, making the highest profit possible is a financial objective. However, profit is not the only criterion for financial success. Most managers of corporations are interested in one primary overall objective—keeping stockholders happy. If a manager is interested in keeping stockholders happy, then she should focus more on earnings per share than on total corporate profits (Brigham & Gapenski, 1994). A company that earned $10 million and had over 100 million outstanding shares would generate earnings of $0.10 per share. In contrast, a company that earned only $1 million with only 100,000 outstanding shares would generate earnings of $10 per share. The shareholders of the second company would have higher earnings per share and would probably feel they had a better investment. This assumes that the criterion for analysis used by the shareholders was earnings per share rather than stock price appreciation or total earnings.

Earnings can also be reflected in increased stock value. Especially for stocks that do not pay dividends, the increase in share value will be the hallmark for determining financial success. Thus, if two companies (Company A and Company B) have earnings of $50 million each, the hallmark of yearly success could be the companies' stock values. If Company A's stock rose $2 per share from $28 to $30 and Company B's shares rose $1 from $4 to $5 per share, most analysts would consider Company B more successful. Since the earnings were identical, the focus turned to increased stock value, and Company A's 7.125% increase in stock value paled in comparison's to Company B's 25% rise.

Earnings per share is just one of the factors that help influence the health of a corporation. A corporation is a business entity that is incorporated under state law and is entitled to issue ownership interests in the form of stock certificates (see chapter 4 for a thorough analysis of business structures). Individuals interested in investing in stocks, also called **shares** in a corporation, are interested in determining if their investment will generate a return such as **dividend** payments or an increased stock price. Besides whether or not the stock will pay a dividend, a potential investor might want to know the following:

- How often the dividends are paid
- How risky future earnings might be
- How much debt the company carries
- What the corporate policies are (e.g., whether they are going to try and purchase a competitor or what dividend rate they pay)

All these questions become critical for financial analysis because corporate policies concerning stocks and bonds help dictate stockholder and analyst interest in the stock.

If the Celtics need to build a new practice facility, they could possibly lower their dividend rate to current stockholders and retain the extra funds to help finance the new building. However, if the Celtics did not want to upset the investors, they might attempt to borrow the funds instead. But increasing the Celtics' total debt could also have negative ramifications, such as lowering their creditworthiness. Because both positive benefits and negative repercussions are associated with each decision, the Celtics would have to thoroughly analyze each potential financing option before deciding which one to pursue. Furthermore, stock analysts critically examine any decision a major corporation makes. If the Celtics made a decision that the analysts thought was wrong, the analysts could send the stock into a nosedive by publishing a negative opinion.

The Celtics example demonstrates the numerous concerns an entity faces when financing any business decision. Furthermore, it demonstrates that any business decision needs to be made in light of the fact that numerous external individuals and entities will critically analyze those decisions. The organization needs to examine all these variables when determining the financial objectives. Are the Celtics going to build the practice facility to increase revenue? Will any increased revenue benefit the individual stockholders? Is the facility being built to appease creditors or analysts?

Chapter 7 looks at the planning process in greater detail. However, it is worth mentioning here that whether one is examining a stadium construction project or a team's revenue stream, any analysis is futile if it does not address where the team was financially last year, what it projects this year, what its financial goals are, and how success or failure will be measured. Critically analyzing financial objectives can hold the key to business success or failure. But it is also impossible to analyze any financial decision without understanding the underlying objectives. Just as a corporate executive might sponsor a golf tournament because of love of the game rather than business sense, financial decisions can be made on grounds other than business sense. Unless one knows the true underlying objective for any financial decision, it becomes a matter of guesswork to determine what a team or business is trying to accomplish. Chapter 7 covers long-term planning and the tools needed to help develop more informed financial objectives.

> Businesses can define their financial objectives in a number of ways. Making the highest possible profit, returning the highest possible earnings per share to shareholders, and increasing the value of stock are some example objectives.

An Overview of Accounting Concepts

Finance and financial management cannot be understood without knowing basic accounting concepts. Accounting is the art of processing the revenue and expense numbers to develop appropriate reporting procedures upon which financial decisions are made. Accounting issues that we touch on in this chapter are basic T-accounts, understanding how cash is received and processed within a business, and methods by which businesses make sure that the numbers managers rely on are correct. It is impossible to understand a balance sheet or income statement without knowing how the numbers were obtained. This section presents some of the basic accounting concepts that you will need to know once you start analyzing comprehensive financial records.

Accounting requires the identification, measurement, recording, and communication of financial information associated with various critical events. A high school might be required to engage in statistical accounting to track students or supplies and might have to engage in financial accounting to track revenues and expenses (Horine, 1999). This text overviews financial accounting and the methods that a sport business manager might use to track revenues coming into the business and expenses flowing out of the business. Although keeping track of the number of towels used at a health club might seem a simple task, financial accounting can be very difficult and complex. See the following case study example.

 Suppose the Smiths' fitness center has 2,000 members who pay at different times during the month, or possibly not at all. Some members may have the funds electronically removed from their bank account. Others may pay with their credit card, in which case the health club has to process all the credit card transactions and then track them and pay the credit card company a small percentage of the amount charged. Other members may pay with cash, or pay late and have to pay a late fee, or demand a refund.

On top of all the issues in the preceding case study example, accountants must track all the money that is owed to countless vendors, employees, or even the government. All in all, financial accounting is a complex art and science that tracks revenues and expenses from numerous areas to provide an accurate record of a business' financial position.

The objective of accounting for any organization is to provide information for the following purposes:

1. Making decisions concerning the use of limited resources, including the identification of crucial decision areas and determination of objectives and goals

2. Effectively directing and controlling an organization's human and material resources

3. Maintaining and reporting on the custodianship of resources

4. Contributing to the overall effectiveness of the organization (Freeman, Shoulders, & Lynn, 1988, p. 6).

Finance emphasizes recording, monitoring, and controlling the financial consequences of various activities and analyzing the need for additional funds to meet current and future demands (Spiro, 1996). These tasks cannot be completed without economic analysis and the data system that has been developed through accounting. Accounting is often performed by a controller who is responsible for documenting what happened, not what should have happened. Thus, the focus is on accuracy as dictated by industry-defined rules. Managerial accounting is the process utilized to develop financial forecasts and monitor various budgets and costing models (Spiro, 1996). The output produced by the controller provides the opportunity for a company to open the lines of communication among different divisions or echelons to help achieve the company's goals and objectives. Through managerial accounting the controller can produce data designed to facilitate internal success, but the same data can be utilized for external needs, such as shareholder relations.

In contrast to the responsibilities of a controller and the managerial accounting process, a treasurer has distinct responsibilities that focus mostly on external factors. Thus, while the controller manages internal financial and accounting-based concerns, the treasurer deals with banks, stockholders, institutional investors, bondholders, and other stakeholders or potential stakeholders. The information developed by the accounting process assists the treasurer in obtaining additional funds to help achieve business goals and objectives.

The accounting objectives just identified are highlighted in detail by Larry Horine of Appalachian State University in his book *Administration of Physical Education and Sport Programs.* Horine (1999) highlights 12 important objectives for a sport organization's accounting system:

1. The data should be collected to help plan for the program's future.

2. The financial records must be kept in an orderly manner.

3. An orderly and professional accounting method must be implemented to track authorized expenditures.

4. Appropriate forms must be prepared to help standardize and create a definite paper trail for receipts and expenditures.

5. A system or process needs to be developed and implemented to coordinate the receipt of goods and services and to ensure that all such goods and services meet required standards before any final payments on the goods or services are made.

6. Transactions need to be documented in such a way that an independent auditor can examine the transaction and determine to whom money was paid and for what purpose.

7. Revenue must be tracked to determine if fiscal obligations can be paid. Tracking should determine what funds were obtained, from whom, and for what purpose.

8. Special funds need to be accounted for in a separate accounting manner to track such

items as planned giving and major gifts, which are nontraditional revenue sources.

9. All information documented through the accounting process needs to be prepared in such a way that an external reviewer can adequately audit all accounts.

10. Any accounting system must be adequate to meet the organization's needs with special consideration for size and complexity.

11. Any accounting system must meet all state, federal, regional, and association standards and guidelines.

12. Any accounting system must provide the opportunity to critically analyze management decisions and produce appropriate reports to evaluate past managerial decisions and pave the way for future decisions (Horine, 1999).

When we are analyzing accounting issues, it is imperative to understand the difference between the concepts of stock and flow. Stock refers to wealth, in a variety of forms such as cash, assets, real estate, and **accounts receivable,** that is available at any specific point in time. In contrast, flow refers to expenditures or receipts between two specific points in time. These two concepts are associated with two of the most important types of documents produced through the accounting process. Stock is shown on a balance sheet that documents the value of a company at a specific time. The income statement, on the other hand, portrays the flow that has been occurring in a company throughout a specified business year. Every company needs to utilize both the stock and flow concepts to analyze its financial position.

In order to track revenues and expenses between balance sheet dates, accountants utilize their own unique systems. Accountants have developed the T-system to document monetary transactions. This text includes a brief discussion of T-accounts; students who take a course in accounting can spend several weeks on T-accounts. The discussion of T-accounts here is intended to overview the process through which the final total numbers used in financial statements are determined. For additional information on T-accounts, please refer to a basic accounting textbook.

Accountants refer to entries made on the right side of the "T" as **credits** and to entries on the left side of the "T" as **debits** (see figure 2.1a). Whereas people who are not accountants might interpret the terms *debit* and *credit* to mean specific activities, such as paying a bill or buying on credit, for the purpose

of accounting these terms just refer to sides of the "T" where various transactions are recorded (Spiro, 1996). A company's balance sheet may provide the best example of the application of the "T" system (see figure 2.1b). Corporate assets are listed on the left side (debits), and liabilities and **owners' equity** are represented on the right side (credits). In conventional usage of the terms, something that is owned by the business would be thought of as a credit to the bottom line, not a debit or reduction in the company's value. But in the T-system, when assets are added to the company's bottom line, the process is referred to as debiting that asset. Similarly, if liabilities are increased, then the specific liability account is credited. The confusion associated with accounting terms can be easily set aside if the terms are not the focal point of analysis; rather, the reader should just know that certain entries are placed on the right and others on the left side of the "T."

Although the terminology might be confusing, the process is important and is universally utilized to properly document financial transactions.

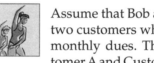 Assume that Bob and Cheryl Smith have two customers who owe money on their monthly dues. The T-accounts for Customer A and Customer B would show the monthly $100 fee added to accounts receivable for the business (see figure 2.2).

If these customers are the only two individuals who owe money to the Smiths, then the Smiths would have $200 debited to their accounts receivable account. Assume that the Smiths also have $10,000 in their cash account. Figure 2.3 shows how these two accounts would look.

If Customer B pays $50 toward his overdue **balance,** the following changes would need to be made to the T-accounts (see figure 2.4). Customer B's prior obligation of $100 has been reduced by the $50; the Smiths are now owed only $150 through accounts receivable and have gained $50 for their cash account.

Because multiple accounts are being changed, the process is often referred to as double-entry bookkeeping. Use of this technique, along with other accounting practices, must comply with generally accepted accounting practices in order to be accepted by the greatest number of potential readers, such as government officials, shareholders, and financial analysts. If troublesome questions arise that have to do with documenting more complex transactions, an accountant might refer to guidelines called generally accepted accounting prin-

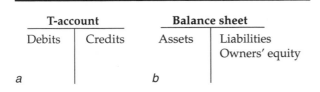

Figure 2.1 A T-account *(a)* and the T-system applied to a company's balance sheet *(b)*.

Customer A		Customer B	
$100		$100	

Figure 2.2 T-accounts for two of the Smiths' customers who owe money on their monthly dues.

Accounts receivable		Cash	
$200		$10,000	

Figure 2.3 T-accounts showing the Smiths' accounts receivable and cash accounts.

Customer B		Accounts receivable		Cash	
$100	$50	$200	$50	$10,000	
				50	

When these entries are synthesized, they will appear as follows:

Customer B		Accounts receivable		Cash	
	$50	$150		$10,050	

Figure 2.4 T-accounts reflecting Customer B's $50 payment.

ciples (GAAP), as interpreted by the Financial Accounting Standards Board (FASB) and the American Institute of Certified Public Accountants. FASB is mostly relevant to public companies.

The T-system is a system that accountants have developed to document monetary transactions.

Cash Versus Accrual Basis

It is beyond the scope of this text to analyze many accounting-related issues, but a key topic that requires discussion here is the method for reporting income. Although most business owners charged with keeping their own business records would record a cash receipt the day it is received and would record a payment the day the bill has been paid, this technique might not be correct. According to GAAP, revenues and expenses can be recorded either on a cash basis or on an **accrual** basis. The accrual basis is the preferred technique, but the cash method is allowed by GAAP under specific limited circumstances, such as when a business conducts all transactions with cash. With use of the cash basis method, transactions are recorded when cash is actually received or paid. **Cash basis budgeting** recognizes income and expenses when cash is actually received or paid and therefore does not recognize sales made on credit or bills that are owed until they are actually paid. This process is also referred to as the **cash system of accounting.** The accrual method recognizes revenues when they are earned and recognizes expenses when they are incurred. In other words, accrual-based reporting does not consider when money is received or paid, only when the act occurred that resulted in the revenue or expense. Normally GAAP requires the use of accrual accounting regardless of the size of the business. Only in rare circumstances when all transactions are in cash will the GAAP allow a company to use the cash system of accounting. Thus, the Smiths would have to record income when lessons are given or memberships are due regardless of whether or not the customer has paid.

Art of Accounting

Many refer to accounting as an art rather than a science (Griffin, 1991). Although financial analysis cannot exist unless accounting systems have developed the appropriate numbers for analyzing past performance, there is never any guarantee that the numbers relied upon are actually correct. Accounting produces financial statements consisting of numbers. However, the numbers refer only to those components of a business that are quantifiable.

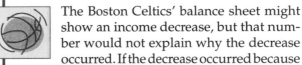 The Boston Celtics' balance sheet might show an income decrease, but that number would not explain why the decrease occurred. If the decrease occurred because another team was having a banner season, then nothing internal to the Celtics resulted in the

decreased revenue. The financial statements would not indicate the objective reason for the decline, but only present the quantifiable results. That is why one needs to analyze the financial objectives for the business in order to learn the entire story that the numbers might not disclose.

Accounting systems also utilize professional judgments and estimates when absolute objective evidence does not exist (Griffin, 1991). Although such judgments are typically very accurate, anyone reading financial statements has to assume that there is some risk that the information includes inaccuracies. There is never a sure bet in finance, and the best you can hope for from financial statements is a very accurate portrait of a business based on data analyzed by an accountant—a human being who can also make errors.

Audited Financial Statements

Accountants can make errors; an auditor is often the last individual who can possibly discover any discrepancies. Most companies attempt to obtain an independent audit of the work performed by their accountants. Such an audit is often undertaken even if an external accounting firm was used to prepare the initial financial statements. An auditor utilizes the Statements of Auditing Standards issued by the Auditing Standards Board of the American Institute of Certified Public Accountants. These standards were developed to help ensure that audits are conducted in a systematic manner. After thoroughly analyzing all the financial statements, the auditor prepares a report including the statement that

1. the auditor is independent from the company's management,
2. the financial statements were audited, and
3. the financial statements are management's responsibility and that the auditor's role is to express an opinion on the financial statements (Griffin, 1991).

Once the audit is completed, the auditor prepares an opinion that addresses the fairness of the financial statements, the degree to which the financial statements comply with GAAP guidelines, and any noticeable changes in accounting principles from industry norms (Griffin, 1991). The final opinion reached by the auditor can be

- an unqualified opinion that the statements are accurate,
- a qualified opinion,
- an adverse opinion indicating that the statements do not conform with required principles, or
- a **disclaimer** indicating that the auditor was unable to complete the report because the company failed to provide certain data.

A typical unqualified opinion might include a statement such as the following: "In our opinion, the financial statements above present fairly, in all material respects, the financial position of the Boston Celtics as of June 31, 2000, and the results of its operations and its cash flows for the year then ended in conformity with generally accepted accounting principles." Auditing is covered in greater detail in chapter 16.

The accounting system objectives discussed in this section relate to what has already happened. Accounting statements are reviewed to determine what occurred during the designated time period. However, accounting does not indicate what should occur in the future. Budgeting is the process that can indicate what steps should be taken in the future. The budget sets the company's road map for the future and is based on the company's goals and objectives. Budgeting, which is covered in chapter 7, is the first step in the financial process after the accountants analyze past performance.

CONCLUSION

This chapter provides an initial glimpse into sport accounting and finance. Sport finance is a numbers game. Numerous revenues and expenses constitute the game pieces. Profits and losses are highlighted in the game's final outcome. Through adherence to basic accounting protocol, the finance game is played with a host of additional rules such as tax considerations and stock regulations that affect a sport entity's movements in the game. By understanding all the necessary moves and the various strategies available to the contestants, a sport organization can win the game. While this game metaphor may appear contrived, it represents a reality in sport finance. Sport finance is as much a game as the games played on athletic fields or courts are. Sport finance professionals need to play a heads-up game to take advantage of various laws, economic conditions, or other variables to maximize their value. Through intelligent financial manipulations, a skilled player can turn a loss into a profit. As Paul Beeston, former president of the Toronto Blue Jays, said, "[U]nder generally accepted accounting principles, I can turn a $4 million profit into a $2 million loss, and I can get every national accounting firm to agree with me" (Howard & Crompton, 1995, p. 12). This text does not analyze the ethical issues associated with such conduct, but raises the red flag for readers to understand that financial data can be manipulated. Thus, care should be exercised in reviewing all financial statements and whenever a question arises you have the ultimate responsibility to ask questions and not just assume that others have done the analysis work for you.

The free enterprise system centers on finance. Any business dealings need to entail significant financial analysis. Finance involves three primary areas of analysis: money and the **capital markets,** investments, and financial management (Brigham & Gapenski, 1994). These three skills are critical for anyone interested in working in the sport industry and, more specifically, for anyone responsible for fiscal oversight in a sport-related program. An individual charged with financial-related duties will have to assume the following responsibilities:

- Forecasting and planning to help lay the foundation for future success

- Investing in major assets such as plants and equipment

- Coordinating other employees and managers to ensure that individuals are working in the most effective manner

- Managing the business' interaction with financial markets, for example determining how much money to raise and in what manner (Brigham & Gapenski, 1994)

This text provides a general overview, but it cannot fully prepare any student to assume complete responsibilities in managing a finance department or performing a similar job. Financial managers need to obtain more specific knowledge in areas such as which assets a firm should purchase and why, how to finance those assets, how to forecast future revenue streams, and how to effectively manage existing resources. Although the skills discussed in this chapter are important, financial managers are judged primarily on whether or not they have been successful in maximizing the corporation's stock value. Accomplishing increased stock valuation is an immense task that requires every unit within the business to operate together (Brigham & Gapenski, 1994).

ASSIGNMENTS

1. Develop appropriate T-accounts for the following scenario.

The Smiths have five customers (A, B, C, D, and E) whose $100 membership fee is coming due. Customer A pays on the 1st of each month, B pays on the 5th, C pays on the 15th, and both D and E pay on the 30th. The Smiths currently have $500 in cash and nothing in accounts receivable. Assuming that each customer at the start of the month owes no money, prepare T-accounts for the 1st, 15th, and 30th of the month for each customer account, accounts receivable, and cash.

2. When is the best time to repay accounts payable?

3. Should you pay accounts payable early, or should you wait until you are sent an overdue notice?

4. Which technique is best if discounts for early payments are offered or interest is charged for late payments?

5. From your general life experience, list five techniques that you think can help uncover financial fraud.

6. Why are earnings important?

RESEARCH PROJECT

Take any of the recently completed stadium or arena projects and critically analyze the construction costs, the political issues associated with this construction, the benefit to the local residents, and the net worth of the investment in terms of costs versus benefits.

CLASS DISCUSSION TOPICS

1. What is the difference between accounting and finance?

2. Why is accounting important for financial analysis?

3. What is the value of budgeting?

4. Analyze the revenue and expense projections for the University of Houston (see p. 3), and try to determine some of the potential financial objectives for the athletic department.

5. Compare the team expenses for a baseball team in the 1930s versus today and identify the greatest differences.

6. What are the key items that need to be documented in order for a business to accurately analyze its financial performance?

7. Develop a list of revenue and expense streams for a professional baseball team.

Financial Systems and How They Operate

CHAPTER OBJECTIVES

After studying this chapter, you should be able to do the following:

- Describe what a financial market is.
- Compare the different types of financial markets and how they affect sport.
- Understand the differences among marketable securities such as stocks and bonds.
- Explain how a sport business can acquire needed capital through institutions such as banks and savings and loans.
- Comprehend government's role in influencing financial systems and sport industries.
- Understand the forces that propel the stock market and the various publicly traded sport-related stocks.

This chapter deals with the key elements in various financial systems and institutions and how they interact to help sport businesses. The primary focus is on what constitutes value and how value can be exchanged to help facilitate business transactions. Financial systems are affected by financial markets, financial institutions, government influences, and environmental factors. Financial **markets,** such as stock markets, are the arenas in which value is transferred. Financial institutions, such as banks, are entities that help transfer value. **Interest rates** are controlled by a combination of economic factors and government regulations. Two final sections of this chapter address government's greater role in regulating businesses through such strategies as taxes, and the effect of environmental conditions on a sport investment.

Financial systems represent mechanisms that allow anything of value to be exchanged between different parties. Financial systems are involved when individuals receive their paycheck from their employer. The employer draws the check from the employer's bank, credit union, savings and loan, or other type of financial holding entity. The money that is drawn might have been received from the employer's customers or from other sources such as borrowed funds or extra cash in the employer's accounts. If the bank does not have enough cash to cover the check, the bank may have to borrow money from the Federal Reserve System. The paycheck will have some taxes withdrawn, reflecting participation by various government units in the financial exchange. Various financial institutions are also utilized when the employee deposits the check and starts paying bills such as credit card bills and the mortgage on a home loan.

This is an oversimplified example of some financial systems and institutions at work. The financial systems work in a cyclical manner, with the same types of transactions occurring on a regular basis. Businesses face the same cyclical patterns in their financial dealings. Each month new orders are received, meaning new funds. However, some debts are paid immediately, while others might not be paid for several months. Money will be trickling in from accounts receivable while the business attempts to pay its own **obligations,** which are **accounts payable.** If there is not enough money to pay outstanding debts, the business may have to turn to financial institutions such as banks, the bond market, the **stock market (stock exchange),** or possibly venture capitalists to obtain money.

Financial Markets

Businesses and individuals needing funds are brought together in financial markets. There are numerous financial markets where funds can be obtained; every business will have several markets from which to obtain funds. The following are the primary types of markets:

1. Tangible or physical markets involve items of value such as products or property. Examples of items in these markets are golf clubs, tennis rackets, golf courses, race cars, and manufacturing machinery.

2. **Financial asset** markets involve evidence of value or ownership such as stocks, bonds, loans, and mortgages.

3. Spot markets are markets involving assets that are bought and sold and will be delivered within several days. Precious metals are an example of such assets.

4. Futures markets are markets involving assets that are bought and sold and will be delivered at a later date, which could be 6 months or several years later. A sport drink company might buy ingredients for its drinks on the futures market if it anticipates that certain ingredients might increase in price and wants to lock in a lower price.

5. Money markets are markets for **debt securities,** such as loans with a very low risk of default, that mature in a shorter time period—usually less than one year.

6. Capital markets are markets in which long-term debt such as bonds or ownership rights such as stocks are traded.

7. The **mortgage** market is a market in which residential loans or business loans backed by real estate are traded.

8. International markets are available for individuals in one country to tap financial resources in another country. As an example, Canadian professional teams that have to pay players in U.S. dollars may wish to exchange currency on the international market to obtain good exchange rates.

9. **Primary markets** are markets in which businesses raise new capital by offering securities for sale. A primary market exists for a particular security only the first time the security is issued and sold.

10. Secondary markets exist after a security has been sold in the primary market. Thus, the first time the Boston Celtics issued their stock, the stock was offered in the primary market. After the initial issues were sold, someone who wanted to buy shares from other owners could acquire the shares only in the secondary market (Brigham & Gapenski, 1994).

This listing indicates the numerous arenas in which businesses can obtain or sell assets. Businesses are not required to use only one market exclusively. Businesses can use several markets, and most businesses utilize several markets concurrently. Furthermore, most businesses utilize several different markets when raising capital. A sport business could raise money on the capital market, or possibly from foreign markets. The markets listed above are primarily markets based in the United States; however, a business can also raise money from foreign markets in any place in the world that offers a market, such as the London stock exchange or the European currency market. A financial manager's job could include constantly tracking these markets to minimize borrowing expenses or to raise additional funds. No matter what market is utilized, the key to funding business growth and facilitating movement within all financial markets is money.

Money

Money is the means by which commerce can occur. A dollar bill has no value in and of itself, without agreement on the part of the government and people that it has value. We are accustomed to taking a dollar out of our wallet and buying a candy bar. We probably do not think twice about such a transaction. But the situation is different if we are buying something for $1 million. No one would expect us to bring in one million dollar bills. Over time, the growth of commerce necessitated the creation of instruments that functioned similarly to money but were easier to use for conducting business. Checks are an everyday example. Although money is the backbone of most financial transactions, numerous individuals and businesses are starting to use alternative payment options, such as automatic withdrawals and bill payments through electronic fund transfers (EFTs).

Money, credit, and checks are not the only instruments of commerce. Wealth can be transferred and documented through other instruments as well. A

History of Financial Institutions

Date	Activity
600 B.C.	Lydia, a Greek state in Asia Minor, uses coins for the first time.
600 to 200 B.C.	The Athenian drachma and Roman denarius are first used.
54 A.D.	Roman Emperor Nero is the first official to start reducing the amount of gold and silver in coins.
1409	The first stock exchange is established in Brussels.
1587	One of the first public banks is established in Venice, Italy.
1661	The first paper money is printed by the Swedish National Bank.
1816	England introduces gold as an official currency.
1918	The international gold standard ends.
1925	England returns to the gold standard.
1929	All major international currencies are once again linked to gold, and that link continues until the Great Depression ends gold's influence.
1945	After World War II, the world's monetary systems start operating on a standard linked to the U.S. dollar.
1978	The European monetary system is introduced.
1999	Euro coinage is phased in for all nations in the European Economic Union.

Data from "From coins to credit cards," 1999.

deed to a piece of land demonstrates that you own the land and have certain rights that might include the right to transfer the land. Similar rights are conferred by marketable securities, which represent documentation of ownership or indebtedness that can be transferred under the right circumstances to others. Stocks and bonds are typical examples of marketable securities and are discussed in the sections to follow.

> *Financial markets are arenas in which businesses and individuals can obtain needed funds and in which value or ownership is transferred from one party to another.*

Marketable Securities

Marketable securities are instruments so widely accepted and purchased by others that they are very similar to cash (Brigham & Gapenski, 1994). For example, common stock in a publicly traded company can be sold through a broker and the resulting cash deposited into the seller's account within a day. In contrast, hard assets are assets that a company might not be able to convert to cash as quickly but that still can have significant value. A factory building that has significant value, but might take a year to sell, is an example of a hard asset. Accounts receivable (A/R) and inventories are between these two extremes. An A/R is an owed obligation. If you have a yearly club membership requiring payment of $50 a month, one payment that you miss becomes a receivable owed to the club. The club may develop a group of similar obligations that are past due; these obligations are categorized as accounts receivable. Although significant value exists in A/R and inventories, it may take a business several months to collect these funds, and some funds will be lost because they are uncollectible or lost due to spoilage. However, factoring (discussed in chapter 8) makes it possible to sell A/R and inventories within several days and to use the proceeds to pay other expenses. Thus, through factoring, some assets are more **liquid** than they were in the past and might be classified as marketable securities.

Marketable securities are the most liquid assets available for investment because of their shorter **maturity** periods (T-bills), ability to sell on a daily basis (stocks), and/or because they are relatively risk free (certain bonds and government securities). Relatively risk free means that the chances of the borrower's not paying are negligible. The U.S. government is considered one of the most risk-free

investments because of the very low risk that the government will collapse. Examples of marketable securities include the following:

- Treasury bills: **Treasury bills,** or **T-bills,** are direct obligations of the U.S. government that mature in 3 to 12 months. Direct obligation means that the U.S. government must repay the debt itself when the loan comes due, which is called the maturity date. The U.S. government regularly borrows and repays money—which is often how a national deficit is created.

- Treasury notes: Similar to T-bills, **Treasury notes** are obligations of the U.S. government, but they mature in 1 to 5 years.

- Government agency securities: The maturity on these obligations can be up to 30 years. These securities differ from Treasury notes, however, in that although individual government agencies can issue them, the taxing authority of the U.S. government does not directly back them.

- Certificates of deposit: **Certificates of deposit,** or **CDs** as they are commonly called, represent cash deposited in commercial banks, savings and loans, and credit unions. CDs normally mature in 1 month to 5 years. **Jumbo CDs** are for deposits of over $100,000. These investments have very low risk, especially if they are maintained in a federally insured savings institution.

- Commercial paper: **Commercial paper** (CP) is a **short-term debt** obligation issued by a large corporation for an amount over $25,000. These debt obligations can have maturity dates ranging from one day to a year. Most of these promissory notes mature in 90 days and carry an interest rate around the prime interest rate based on the company's credit rating. A promissory note is a simple contract in which the borrower agrees to repay the **lender** for money borrowed. The **prime interest rate** is the interest rate charged by banks on loans to their best customers (those with minimal credit risk).

Table 3.1 lists both liquid securities and investments or securities that are not as liquid. Riskiness represents the potential of a borrower's defaulting on an obligation. A default-free investment is basically guaranteed, so the lender is certain to be repaid. A low default risk is the next best protection;

Table 3.1 Securities From Risk Free to High Risk

Security	Typical maturity	Riskiness
Liquid investments for near-cash reserves		
U.S. Treasury bills—sold by the U.S. Treasury	91 days to one year	Default free
Banker's acceptance—promise to pay backed by a bank	Up to 180 days	Low risk if backed by a strong bank
Commercial paper—issued by large firms	Up to 270 days	Low default risk
Negotiable certificates of deposits (CDs)	Up to one year	Low default risk
Money market mutual funds—investment in T-bills, CDs, commercial paper, and so on.	No specific maturity	Low degree of risk
Euro market time deposits	Up to one year	Based on issuing bank
Consumer credit loans—banks, credit unions, finance companies	Variable	Based on issuing bank
Floating rate and market auction preferred stocks	Variable	Based on issuer
Liquid investments not suitable for near-cash reserves		
U.S. Treasury notes—price can change based on interest rate changes	3 to 10 years	Default free
U.S. Treasury bonds	Up to 10 years	Default free
Corporate bonds (rated AAA)	Up to 40 years	Based on issuer
State and local government bonds (rated AAA)	Up to 30 years	Based on issuer
Preferred stocks (rated AAA)	30 years to perpetual	Based on company
Common stocks in corporations	Unlimited	Variable

with this level of risk there exists the potential for the borrower to default. When a risk is identified as based on the insurer, the meaning is that the risk of default is contingent on the entity that borrowed the money. Some companies are so strong that the risk of default is minimal, while other companies have a high default risk. See chapter 8 for a discussion of the role of credit ratings in assessing credit risk.

Most CP is very liquid, as only the top corporations with strong credit histories can effectively issue this type of security. Commercial paper is an effective funding source in that it can be issued very inexpensively compared to bonds and stocks, which take considerable time and money to issue. Commercial paper also entails less governmental regulation, can help raise significant cash, and does not require the issuer to maintain any compensating balances with a bank. (A **compensating balance** is a required amount of cash kept with the lending institution that serves as a type of security. Since the corporation itself issues the CP, there is no need for any compensating balance to protect the lender.) A final benefit associated with CP is the prestige a company can generate from being financially strong enough to issue this type of instrument (Griffin, 1991). Thus, as with government-issued securities that can be treated much like **cash,** a corporation's CP can inspire a high level of investor confidence.

The previous section has covered the most liquid types of investment vehicles, which are almost like cash. However, other assets are also considered liquid assets but are not as liquid as cash or cash equivalent assets. Thus, ownership of a business can also be considered a liquid asset if the ownership is evidenced through publicly traded stock. However, in contrast to the situation with cash, T-bills, or CDs, which all have a definite value, if you have ever owned stock and sold it, you might have obtained less than the stated value of the stock. Stock redemption refers to the process of selling stocks back to the open market or to the original issuing company. A stock may be hard to sell if investors are not interested in it. Furthermore, market volatility can affect the value of the investment. When times are good and a **bull market** keeps driving up the value of stocks, more companies put excess cash into acquiring shares in various other companies. If a balance sheet indicates $1 million in investment assets such as stocks, that value will drop $100,000 in one day if the stock price declines 10%. When investors redeem their shares of stock, they might receive less than they originally paid for the shares. Thus, the **liquidity** of stocks is lower than cash or cash equivalents because of the volatility of the stock market.

Sport Examples of Valuation

At the start of 2002, World Wrestling Entertainment, Inc. (WWE) had a market capitalization of $949 million; shares were selling at $13 each, and the 52-week range for the stock price was $10 to $22. As of October 26, 2001 (a couple of months earlier), the company had had total current assets of over $332 million. The company also had over $90 million invested in property, plant, and equipment. WWE's net tangible assets combined with the total shareholders' equity totaled over $361 million and included $68 million in retained earnings and $296 million in capital surplus (Yahoo! Finance—WWF, 2002).

On the same day, the Boston Celtics had a market capitalization of $29.2 million. Shares were trading at $10.80, and the 52-week range was $8.80 to $12.11. The team had $32 million in current assets with $2 million in cash and $30 million in short-term investments. The team had over $87 million of total liabilities as of their last reported quarter at that time (September 30, 2001). With liability so much higher than total assets, the team had a negative stockholders' equity of over $53 million (Yahoo! Finance—BOS, 2002).

These examples highlight the fact that two stocks can be trading at very similar price ranges but represent completely different pictures, with WWE having significant assets and shareholders' equity and the Celtics having significant debt.

Stocks

Obviously, value can be demonstrated in other vehicles besides money. Currently one of the strongest value indicators is stocks. A stock certificate is a document demonstrating ownership **interest** in a company. This ownership interest is often referred to as equity value. The equity value in companies has increased over the past 10 years. The **Dow Jones Industrial Average** (Dow), one of the major **market indexes (market averages),** was flirting with 11,000 in 1999 and by 2000 had reached 12,000 before declining to around 10,000 in 2002 (Lamiell, 1999). The average rose over 1,000 points ($1,000) in only a 24-day period in 1999. The previous record for the length of time it took the Dow to rise 1,000 points (from 6,000 to 7,000 points) had been 89 trading days in 1996 through 1997. Similar to what happened with the Dow, the NASDAQ® index also showed significant strength in 1999. The index was so strong due to Internet stocks that it increased more than 84% for the 1999 year and closed at over 4,000 for the year ("Up, Up and Away," 1999). However, just two years later the NASDAQ was down over 50%, at around 1,990 ("Dow Jones Continues," 2002).

Charles Dow established the Dow in 1896 as an index to be used in *The Wall Street Journal.* The Dow closed its first day at 40.94, and it was almost 10 years before the index passed 100. The stock market went through some tumultuous times in the early 1900s; there were large drops in 1901 and 1907, and the famous "Black Thursday" occurred on October 24, 1929. The Dow started to rise in the World War II period and soared through the 1950s, reaching 500 in 1956. In 1970, the Dow ended the year at 838.92 (Dunphy, 1998). In 1972, the Dow surpassed 1000 points. In 1979, the index ended at 838.74; and in 1987, it passed the 2,000-point mark, having entered the bull market leading to the 1999 level. By mid-1999, the Dow had surpassed 10,000. However, even during the "good" times of the bull market when prices advance at an aggressive pace, a **bear market,** or even a day of large losses, can significantly alter such a run. In 1987, "Black Monday" occurred on October 19 when the index collapsed 508.32 points, which represented a 22.6% drop in one day. This drop was approximately twice as large, in percentage terms, as the drop in 1929. However, the prospect of war pushed the Dow up again in 1991, with the Persian Gulf War fueling a rise past 3,000 (Yip, 1999). These highlights suggest the volatility of the Dow in relation to financial, political, and global concerns. For example, right after the attacks in New York and Washington, D.C., on September 11, 2001, the Dow dropped to 8,235, but it rose 20% again within four months ("Dow Jones Continues," 2002).

The Dow does not value stocks. It is just one tool to measure investor confidence in the stock market. During strong economic times, individuals are willing to invest in companies by acquiring stocks. Investors hope that the company will do well enough that the stock will increase in value and any profits will be split with the stockholders through dividend payments or increased share values. The value of the Dow increases as the values of the businesses that compose the Dow increase. Conversely, if the stocks of companies on the Dow decline, so will the Dow. This very visible volatility helps dictate whether analysts consider the market to be a bull or bear market. A bear market is a stock market in which investors are scared and prices drop approximately 20%. A bull market, on the other hand, occurs when investors are optimistic and the stock market increases more than 20%. Instead of analyzing all stocks, analysts can look to the Dow and other market indexes to develop a quick barometer of market conditions.

Changes to the Dow Jones Industrial Average

Recently, the Dow has undertaken a major renovation to more effectively reflect the change in the economy from smokestacks to high tech. Several major corporations were removed from the Dow in 1999, including such household giants as Chevron, Goodyear, Sears Roebuck, and Union Carbide. These businesses were replaced by Intel, Microsoft, Home Depot, and SBC Communications to complete the 30-stock list. The change also represented the first time that the Dow has included two stocks (Intel and Microsoft) from the NASDAQ rather than just New York Stock Exchange-listed shares ("High-Tech Injection," 1999).

Bonds

Bonds represent another measure of value. Unlike stocks, which denote ownership interest in a company, bonds represent an obligation owed by a company or institution. The entity issuing the bond is the **debtor,** and the purchaser of the bond is the **creditor.** Creditors are interested in investing their money in bonds that provide a reasonable **yield (rate of return)** with the lowest possible risk level. Similar to the situation with CP, the greater a company's financial strength, the easier it is for that company to issue bonds. A company that has a poor financial picture has to pay investors a premium to interest them in buying their bonds. Bonds issued by established companies normally pay lower interest but present a significantly lower default risk.

Bonds are not as frequently seen in the sport industry as in the consumer goods or manufacturing industries. However, the recent strong increase in professional team values may create more opportunities for issuing bonds. For example, the New York Yankees and the New Jersey Nets merged and undertook a bond offering through YankeeNets LLC that raised $250 million. Proceeds were used to help purchase the New Jersey Devils. Analysts thought that the YankeeNets offering was unusual and that most bond offerings would still come from stadium and arena construction projects because facilities have a more predictable revenue stream than teams, whose revenues can be volatile based on their win-loss record ("Corporate Debt," 2000).

Marketable securities, stocks, bonds and other methods utilized to finance a business are discussed in greater detail in chapters 8, 9, 10, and 11. They are relevant in this chapter as vehicles that help facilitate financial transactions. An issuing company can use these instruments to raise money, or companies can purchase these instruments in an effort to acquire another business or as an investment vehicle to earn a return. The only limits concerning which corporations can issue stocks and bonds are internal or external variables such as a corporation's articles of incorporation or its credit rating. If a corporation's bylaws only allow the corporation to issue one million shares, then after that number is reached no more shares can be issued without amending the bylaws. No matter who issues or acquires value, institutions need to help facilitate the flow of value through these documents.

Marketable securities, such as stocks and bonds, are so widely accepted that they function much like cash.

Financial Institutions

Several major types of financial institutions help facilitate the transfer of capital. These institutions are involved in the process in order either to obtain an interest in the transaction or to be paid a fee for their services. For example, seats on the New York Stock Exchange (NYSE) are sold to companies wishing to engage in buying and selling listed stocks. A seat gives the seat owner the right to trade stocks on the NYSE. A seat is similar to a personal seat license (PSL) for a sports team. Once you buy a PSL you can use it, sell a game-day ticket to someone else or leave it empty. Similarly, a seat on the NYSE allows the owner to personally buy and sell shares or to allow others to do the buying and selling on his behalf. Thus, a seat is the right to be able to do business. Other institutions such as banks charge various fees for services and also obtain revenue by acquiring money at a low interest rate and then turning around and loaning the same money to others at a higher rate.

Banks

The Babylonians are often credited with developing the first true banks sometime around 2000 B.C. These banks were run by the Babylonian temples and were involved both in lending and in safekeeping of valuables. The temples charged as much as one-sixth of the deposits for the safekeeping of gold, silver, and other valuables entrusted to them. A temple then charged people who borrowed deposits around 20% interest, compounded monthly (Rodgers, 1966). Fifteen hundred years later, the Greeks also turned their temples into safes for the wealthy. Athens developed a specific body of law covering banking transactions, as well as a court system, which required repayment of debts within 30 days (Rodgers, 1966).

The Roman *argentarii* (silver dealers) began offering additional services such as lending money, selling mortgages, and providing letters of credit. However, they often made loans to individuals such as politicians who were unable to pay them back. These high-risk loans caused significant losses that forced the Roman bankers to seek higher interest payments from other borrowers. Through stringent control, the Roman Empire was able eventually to rein in interest rates to 2.5% per year (Rodgers, 1966). However, by that time the damage had been done and the bankers had developed a poor image. Banking was not as commonly utilized in the Dark Ages because of edicts of the Christian Church, which did not distinguish between interest and **usury** and thus forbade any payments for using money. This edict did not affect other religions, whose adherents were still able to loan money and collect interest (Rodgers, 1966).

The first publicly owned bank was the Bank of Venice, founded in 1171 A.D. The success of the Bank of Venice in its limited lending role spawned future banks such as the Bank of Barcelona in the 14th century, the Bank of Amsterdam in 1602, and the Bank of England in 1694 (Rodgers, 1966).

Banking in the American colonies experienced numerous failures in the early years. In 1791 Alexander Hamilton convinced Congress to charter a national bank called the Bank of the United States, which failed shortly thereafter (FDIC, 2002).

Banking history has had numerous success stories, such as the Bank of England, which started as a 1,200,000-pound loan to the English government in 1694 and is still around today. However, many disasters befell the French banking system, which collapsed numerous times from unbridled spending and abuses. Banks as we know them today have learned many lessons from the past, but greed has crept into the system at various times and led to problems such as the Great Depression and the savings and loan scandal of the 1980s.

Even with all the faults one can see in the commercial banking system, the system is essential for economic and financial survival. For example, if bankers start reducing the credit offered to businesses, then economic growth is slowed and the standard of living for all citizens decreases. Conversely, if too much credit is extended to the business community, the rate of growth and the standard of living will rise significantly, but also will reach a pace that is not economically sustainable. It may happen, for example, that the demand for money is great but that there is not enough money to meet the demand; this can cause significant competition for funds and higher interest rates. These two examples of banks influencing the economy in the direction of success or failure are commonly referred to as "boom and bust" (Rodgers, 1966).

Clearly, our everyday bankers wield significant power and help run the monetary system for the entire economy by helping to establish, either directly or indirectly, prices, interest rates, economic growth, and capital creation (Rodgers, 1966). The power of bankers can be diminished to some extent in markets where there is competition from nonbank lenders or when the government significantly manipulates the banking system by changing interest rates. In order to obtain funds to help foster economic development, banks need to acquire money from other sources. The primary sources include invested capital, borrowing, primary deposits, and borrowing from the Federal Reserve Bank.

Capital

A bank's capital can come from money initially used to start the bank. Several major investors might each contribute $20 million to create a bank. Publicly traded banks might issue stock to raise more capital. Capital can also take the form of retained earnings accumulated from income generated by the bank. A bank may choose not to pay dividends and instead use the accumulated earnings as capital. Banks need extra capital to pay daily bills and to extend credit to a broad base of individuals and businesses that need to utilize that capital. The amount of capital required by any bank for its own reserves is set by law. Capital reserves are also analyzed by the **Federal Deposit Insurance Corporation** (FDIC) when a bank makes a request to reduce its capital stock, establish a new branch, merge or consolidate, or move its main office (Rodgers, 1966). The amount of capital available for issuing loans is also affected by the risks associated with other loans, the liquidity of other assets, whether deposits are increasing, and whether enough profit is being made to sustain shareholder confidence. If a bank loaned a significant amount of money to a real estate company and the real estate market collapsed, the bank would lose significant money if it was unable to recover its investment. This loss would deplete the bank's available capital since money would be spent covering losses and paying for attorneys to help recover as much of the investment as possible. Thus, banks need to critically analyze every loan decision to make sure that the investment will not jeopardize their loan portfolios or their available credit reserves.

One of the primary reasons banks are required by law to maintain adequate capital reserves is to prevent a run on the bank. If depositors felt that their deposits were at risk, they could pull out their deposits, and the bank has to have enough capital to repay all such demands. Before depositing funds, people need to feel comfortable that the bank's management will take care of their money. Although there is no guarantee that any bank or savings and loan will not face financial hardships, investors have federal protections that have been designed to help safeguard their deposits. This protection includes reserve requirements, which are funds that cannot be loaned out, and can include account insurance offered by the federal government, which is discussed later in the chapter.

Borrowing

Just the way everyday citizens do, banks sometimes run out of money and have to borrow money in order to continue their operations. Banks can turn to other banks for short-term loans or, if they are a member, can approach the Federal Reserve Bank for additional funds. To obtain these funds, a bank might conduct a temporary sale of assets or a temporary deposit of primary funds (short-term funds deposited by other banks; see below), or might just borrow money and pay the prevailing market rate for loans to banks.

Borrowing by a bank most often occurs when a bank has to fund a special deal or when a client needs a large sum for several days. At other times a bank might borrow to build new offices or to fund other ventures without creating any reserve-related concerns. If the bank uses its own funds, it may not have the amount of money in reserve that is required by federal banking regulations. But if the bank borrows money from the Federal Reserve, it does not dip into funds of its own that are fulfilling the reserve requirements.

Federal Reserve System

The **Federal Reserve System** (Fed), established by Congress after 1913, comprises 12 Federal Reserve district banks, 25 branches, and over 5,800 national and state banks (see figure 3.1) (Klise, 1972). The Fed, as it is commonly called, was established to provide central banking facilities for the entire United States. The system operates to manage the nation's money supply by raising or lowering the reserve amount banks need to keep on hand, changing the discount rate (which is the rate charged to commercial banks for borrowing money), and purchasing and selling government securities (Siegel, Shim, & Hartman, 1992). The Fed has jurisdiction over the following activities:

- Commercial bank regulatory function
- Reserve requirements and bank discounts
- Selective credit control
- Open market operations
- International operations (Spiro, 1996)

The Fed is responsible for conducting field audits of member banks but typically conducts such audits only for state-chartered banks. Nationally chartered banks are under the statutory domain of the Comptroller of the Currency and can be examined by that

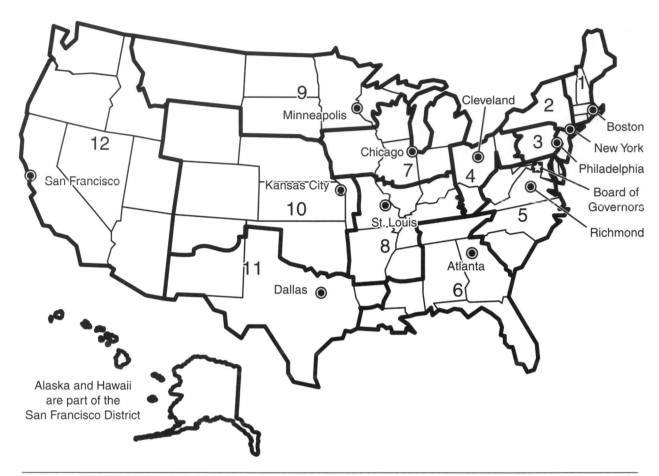

Figure 3.1 The 12 Federal Reserve districts.

office rather than the Fed. The Comptroller of the Currency also audits banks under its charge and works with the Fed in controlling the practices and procedures of nationally chartered banks. The Fed is responsible for administering the Bank Holding Act of 1956, which was enacted to prevent bank monopolies while permitting banks to expand into some nonbank endeavors such as the credit card business or investment management (Spiro, 1996). Another federal law that the Fed is responsible for promulgating and enforcing compliance with is the **Truth in Lending Act** of 1968 (also called the **Consumer Credit Protection Act**), which requires lenders to provide user-friendly information about the true terms and interest rates on loans.

The Fed is responsible for some regulations concerning credit-related borrowing and lending. For example, the Fed can specify which securities can be purchased on credit and the amount or percentage of credit that lenders are able to extend to purchase the securities. Although the Fed engages in significant policy making, its decisions and actions do not

require any governmental approval from either the executive or the legislative branch. The Fed is run by a board of governors who are appointed by the president of the United States with the Senate's consent. After being appointed, the governors and the Fed chairperson work autonomously but report on a yearly basis to Congress. The current Fed chairman is Alan Greenspan, who was nominated for the position in 1986 and has served several terms. On the basis of his strong performance in the 1990s, Greenspan was renominated by President Clinton in 1999 for another term. The six other members of the Board of Governors serve staggered terms, and no member can be reappointed.

The Fed operates similarly to a bank in that member banks can deposit funds with and borrow funds from the Fed. Member banks are required to keep a specific fraction of their deposits as a cash reserve. The money can be kept by the banks in their vaults or can be deposited with the Fed. The Fed determines what percentage needs to be kept on reserve and varies this amount to help stimulate the economy. The Fed can also influence the economy through its discount window. A discount window is the range of interest rates at which a bank can borrow money from the Federal Reserve. The discount window allows banks to borrow against their loan portfolio to raise additional money for offering more loans. By changing the discount rate that it charges commercial banks, the Fed can either encourage more loans (by offering a lower rate) or discourage more loans (by increasing the rate banks have to pay to borrow the funds) (Spiro, 1996).

Primary Deposits   Primary deposits are deposits in a bank that come from other banks. Banks that have excess cash, but not enough borrowers, may deposit the extra cash in another bank in order to obtain some interest. If the funds just sit in a bank, that bank is forced to pay interest to the depositors but the funds do not generate any revenue. Depositing the funds in another bank makes it possible to obtain some interest, but the funds can also be quickly withdrawn if other borrowers need the money.

These funds can be utilized to increase reserves with the Fed, which frees more capital for investing. The Fed can also affect bank reserves. The Fed is responsible for maintaining the nation's money supply, and one technique entails purchasing securities. When the Fed buys securities, the funds used to pay for the securities end up as increased deposits in the banking system, which ultimately translates into higher reserves. Thus Fed member banks can increase their reserves without having to deposit any more cash into their reserves. During World War II, the Fed purchased over $22 billion in securities to help create reserves to finance the war. The banks throughout the nation had more capital that they could loan but did not have to do anything to acquire the extra capital.

Bank Deregulation   After the 1930s, banks were heavily regulated so that they were prevented from engaging in other business enterprises such as selling insurance or providing investment advice. However, new laws passed in the late 1990s resulted in bank deregulation. Commercial banks are now allowed to establish or acquire investment banking and merchant banking subsidiaries that can engage in purchasing ownership interests, extending loans, or underwriting bond offerings. Banks can now invest in as much as 5% of a company outright or purchase up to 49% of a company through bank-owned subsidiaries. This opportunity to own other businesses has fueled significant investment by banks in high-tech start-

ups. Banks can derive significant profit from venture capital investment, which is one of the first stages of investing in a new business. Chase Manhattan Corp.'s venture capital arm had $2.5 billion in revenue in 1999 and generated $1.4 billion of Chase's profits (Mclean, 2000).

Deregulation created an environment with significant banking investments in potentially riskier businesses, which resulted in the threat that banks could lose a large amount of their deposits. The Fed was called in to analyze this concern and developed policies in 2000 to address the situation. Banks are now required to set aside more capital to cover riskier equity investments. An **equity investment** is not a loan, but a purchase of an ownership interest in a business. The new policies could significantly reduce the amount of venture capital available, as up to one-third of the $48 billion that poured into venture capital in 1999 could have been affected by the new rules (Sapsford, 2000). Analysts feel that the ruling will not affect large banks with diverse portfolios, but will hurt smaller banks.

Bank Lending Rules

The various rules and regulations enforced by the Fed can also interact with a bank's own written or unwritten rules. All banks utilize a loan-to-deposit ratio according to which they will not loan money as freely once their loans reach more than a certain percentage—often 70% to 75%—of all deposits. The remaining percentage is kept in reserves or invested in short-term or other liquid investments such as **Treasury bonds.** If the loan-to-deposit ratio is reaching the tip of a bank's comfort zone, a borrower could be caught in a credit squeeze. A credit squeeze occurs when a business borrows too much money and a bank or other lending institution tells the business they will not loan them any more money unless they repay previously incurred obligations. This is similar to when a bartender sees a person has had too much to drink and refuses to serve that person any more alcohol. A bank will put a credit squeeze on a company if it feels the company is overextended or cannot repay debts as they become due. A credit squeeze could be caused by a bank, lender, borrower, the economy, or any other external conditions. To avoid such a problem, most financially astute managers develop multiple banking relationships so they can approach several different banks for the same loan.

Banks may also establish specific rules concerning the types of loans they might entertain. Banks typically do not want to issue capital loans, because the repayment for loans to help start a business takes much longer to collect than repayment for typical commercial loans. Thus, it would be much more difficult for the Smiths to obtain initial financing from a bank than it would for Sport Manufacturing Company to get a loan. Banks can demand a security pledge from someone who wants to obtain a loan. These **secured loans** can utilize anything of value as a pledge from which repayment can be extracted if a borrower defaults. Sport loans are often secured by the item purchased. If a golf course borrows money to purchase a golf cart, the cart can become the collateral securing the loan repayment. Each bank has specific rules concerning each facet of a loan, from the application process through repayment requirements. These rules are not designed to waste valuable paper, but rather to help reduce the risks associated with collecting the loan.

Bank Services

Besides providing loans and facilitating economic growth by making money available to borrowers, banks perform various additional services. These services include

- allowing individuals to deposit their money in a bank account for safekeeping,
- allowing checking account holders to write checks demanding that the bank pay another party a specific amount,
- providing clients with cashier's checks or certified checks when necessary,
- providing numerous specialty savings accounts for customers, and
- acting as general depositaries for U.S. Treasury funds.

These services are provided at different costs, depending on the bank and the special programs offered by each bank. Many banks charge a fee for every check written; other banks provide interest payments to customers who write fewer checks. The costs or interest rates available are based on supply and demand factors as well as competition from other banks. When rates are fairly equal among banks, the banks often engage in sales promotion strategies to encourage business and may offer potential customers various prizes, from stuffed animals and piggy banks to toasters or other kitchen appliances. All sport businesses utilize checking accounts; and if a business has enough money in an account, that business can negotiate how much it will pay for the services it receives.

Protecting Deposits

While banks can use numerous gimmicks to win clients, the primary concern depositors might have is whether their money will be safe. Through the 1930s, the history of banking made depositors skeptical concerning their ability to remove funds. There were several early attempts to protect deposits, but they all failed. In fact, the depression was further flamed by the failure of approximately 15,000 banks in the 1920s through the 1930s. The federal government was asked to step in to help protect depositors' money. The government, though, was skeptical about taking on this role, as guaranteed accounts would provide a disincentive for bankers to be vigilant with depositors' money. In 1933 the first form of federal **deposit insurance** was developed as an attempt to facilitate better banking (Rodgers, 1966). The Banking Act of 1933 helped establish the FDIC as a government unit charged with insuring bank deposits. In 1950, the law was superseded by the Federal Deposit Insurance Act. The FDIC is now privately owned by the banks rather than the government. Similar to the Fed, the FDIC is run by a board of directors that includes the comptroller of the currency and two other individuals appointed by the president with the Senate's consent. The FDIC reviews reports from insured banks, including insured banks that are not members of the Fed. The FDIC has a strong weapon to help ensure compliance with safe banking practices. If a bank engages in and is found guilty of unsafe, unsound, or illegal banking activities, the FDIC can terminate that bank's insurance. Part of the insurance termination process involves contacting all depositors to let them know that the insurance coverage will be terminated.

If a bank cannot cover withdrawals, the FDIC can pay all claims and liquidate the bank's assets. This is an extreme measure and one that produces negative publicity. If at all possible, the FDIC tries to find another bank willing to assume the defaulting bank's deposit liabilities. Furthermore, under the 1950 act, the FDIC can purchase assets from, extend a loan to, and make deposits in any insured bank facing financial hardships.

The insurance covers funds not on the basis of the depositor but on the basis of the account, covering the first $100,000 in any account. Thus, if a depositor has $400,000 in an account, only the first $100,000 is insured. In contrast, if a depositor has four different accounts each of which contains $100,000, each is fully insured.

Account protection through insurance is critical to ensure the availability of funds. For example, suppose that a sport team kept all moneys from ticket and broadcasting sales in one bank account and that the bank faced financial problems and closed. Even if the team had $40 million in the account, only $100,000 would be insured. Thus the team could face significant financial trouble and be unable to cover bills because of the bank's closing. To avoid this problem, the team would probably keep only smaller amounts in each bank (a maximum of $100,000 per account), possibly only bank with the largest and strongest banks, or possibly keep a smaller amount in their bank and invest more of the money in marketable securities. Such exercises in distributing money—constantly juggling money to provide the greatest return and protection—are among the key duties of financial managers.

Quasi Bankers

The discussion so far has focused on commercial banks. However, a host of other banking-related businesses also provide needed capital for corporations and individuals. These entities can range from savings and loans, which are very similar to banks, to mortgage companies, which are discussed further on. Investment bankers specialize in raising long-term funds for both corporate expansions and capital needs. Insurance companies, on the basis of their large cash reserves, can also provide significant capital for corporations seeking additional funds. **Pension funds** and retirement accounts are often utilized as borrowing sources. The largest teacher pension/retirement fund in the world, TIAA/CREF, has provided significant financial support to several major stadium construction projects ("Top Holders," 1997). Credit unions also can provide substantial capital based on their large membership numbers. Since credit unions receive money from members and loan money only to members, they are often the cheapest source for borrowing funds. However, it is sometimes impossible to join a credit union without being affiliated with a specified employer or social group. For example, if the Smiths currently work for a company that is affiliated with a credit union, it might be easier for them to secure a loan and obtain more favorable terms.

Other sources of funds include **consumer finance companies,** sales finance companies, pawnbrokers, and even unlicensed lenders such as loan sharks. An example of consumer financing is a car purchase agreement in which the car serves as the collateral for the amount financed by the purchaser. If the purchase price of the car was $20,000 and $5,000 went for the down payment, then $15,000

would be the financed amount. The $15,000 note could be sold to large finance companies that purchase millions in loans to consumers for numerous products. A sales finance company sells items such as photocopiers, or even zambonis, and instead of accepting cash also can finance the item through loans secured by the equipment.

Mortgage companies loan money to individuals willing to pledge their homes as collateral. Mortgage companies rarely receive deposits except for initial capital infusions by investors. Since mortgage companies are very specialized, they can offer additional services and can often provide comprehensive benefits.

If the Smiths are willing to mortgage their house to start their business, they might approach both a bank and a mortgage company to determine which would offer the best value. The mortgage company might have a lower initial interest rate, but also might charge a special handling fee (often called **points**) for writing the loan. The mortgage company might also allow repayment without any penalties. The bank might impose an early-payment penalty if the Smiths paid early. The Smiths would need to analyze each option carefully to determine which would give them the greatest value.

Stock Exchanges

There are very specific requirements for admission to established stock exchanges, as well as regulations concerning who can **trade** the shares. Only firms that are members of a particular exchange can trade stocks on that exchange. This policy was established when the **security exchanges** were chartered. Since the exchanges are owned and operated by their members, they can establish rules for future members. One rule is that any company wishing to buy a seat (place) on a particular exchange must purchase the seat from a departing member and must pay the prevailing market rate for the seat, which can exceed $2 million on the New York Stock Exchange. Having a seat makes the company a member of the exchange. Someone who wants to purchase shares of a stock listed on an exchange contacts a member to purchase the shares. Nonmembers cannot purchase the shares.

Three major stock exchanges exist in the United States. The most prestigious is the **New York Stock Exchange** (NYSE), which was founded in 1792 and still exists as a private entity. Approximately 3,000 companies meet the stringent requirements for size and profitability that a company must fulfill in order to be listed on the NYSE (Dunphy, 1998). To be listed, a company typically must have at least 2,000 shareholders, must have a market value of at least $100 million, and must have been profitable for the last three years with earnings of at least $6.5 million per year during those years ("U.S. Standards," 2002). Normally, only the most prestigious companies can be listed on the NYSE.

The **National Association of Securities Dealers Automated Quotations** (NASDAQ) system is a computerized national trading system for more than 4,000 publicly traded companies. The NASDAQ began operating on February 8, 1971, with several larger companies such as American Express and Anheuser-Busch (Ip, 2000, March 10). Both companies are now listed on the NYSE. Some companies listed on the NASDAQ, such as MCI, Microsoft,

Major International Exchanges

Market/ exchange	Year founded	Avg. daily no. shares traded	Avg. daily trading volume	Market capitalization	Largest stocks
NYSE	1792	1.08 billion	$35 billion	$12 trillion	GE, Exxon, Wal-Mart
NASDAQ	1971	1.76 billion	$41.5 billion	$5.02 trillion	Intel, Cisco, Microsoft
Deutsche	1585	N/A	$4.5 billion	$1.5 trillion	Siemens, Allianz
London	1801	2.1 million	$13.5 billion	$2.8 trillion	British Telecom, BP Amoco
Tokyo	1878	0.6 billion	$6.8 billion	$4.1 trillion	Toyota, Nippon Tel. & Tel.
Australian	1837	1.02 billion	$0.78 billion	$370 billion	News Corp., Aust. Bank
Toronto	1878	197.5 million	$2.85 billion	$1.7 trillion	Nortel, Seagram, BCE

Data from Calian & Latour, 2000.

Intel, Compaq, Starbucks, Apple Computer, Coors Brewing, and Ben and Jerry's, have become big and profitable enough to be listed on the NYSE but for various reasons have not moved their stock from the NASDAQ. One reason may be that many start-up and high-tech companies are launched on the NASDAQ and there is an image that NASDAQ companies are more cutting edge than some of their more established counterparts trading on the NYSE. The NASDAQ is also the primary U.S. market for trading securities in overseas companies such as Toyota, Volvo, Canon, Fuji Photo, and Cadbury Schweppes.

Besides listing major national and international companies, NASDAQ also has several ancillary services that help people trade securities in smaller companies. The OTC (over-the-counter) Bulletin Board is an electronic market for securities not listed on NASDAQ or any other U.S. exchange. Bid and ask quotations are captured and displayed in real time so that trades can be accomplished almost instantaneously. The **ask,** or **offer, price** is the price that a seller would like to receive for the item they wish to sell. The **bid price** is what amount a poten-

tial buyer might want to spend to acquire the item. Somewhere between these two amounts a compromise might be reached. However, numerous deals are based on firm asking prices or bid prices where the party making the firm offer refuses to budge. Similar to what occurs with bidding on eBay or other Internet auctions, the highest price offered at the designated time wins and the item is automatically shipped or transferred once the payment is verified.

The **National Association of Security Dealers** (NASD) regulates the NASDAQ and other **over-the-counter exchanges.** Regulation is accomplished through education programs, on-site examination of member firms, automated market surveillance, registration and testing of security professionals, review of members' sales and advertising practices, an arbitration program to resolve disputes, and review of underwriting arrangements associated with new offerings (*An Introduction,* 1992). Automated market surveillance and reviewing of underwriting arrangements are undertaken through close examination of the launching and selling of stocks to ensure that no improprieties are occurring. For example, the system can track whether weird spikes in stock prices are due to manipulation or insider trading. These powers are derived through federal legislation such as the 1938 Maloney Act amendments to the Securities Exchange Act of 1934, which established NASD. The NASD was organized through the joint effort of Congress and the Securities and Exchange Commission. Although NASD was given significant power by federal legislation, it is a privately financed and managed company, with its members and listed companies contributing to its approximately $200 million annual budget ("NASD," 1992). The NASD is responsible for regulating more than 5,200 brokers/dealers and 430,000 registered sales representatives ("NASD," 1994).

Another exchange is the American Stock Exchange (AMEX), which has 700 small to midsized businesses, with a large number of these companies servicing the oil industry. Smaller regional exchanges exist throughout the United States, such as the Boston, Cincinnati, Chicago, Pacific, and Philadelphia stock exchanges and specialty exchanges such as the Chicago Board Options Exchange and the Chicago Mercantile Exchange. There are also international exchanges; the most prominent are those based in Tokyo, London, Madrid, Paris, Tel Aviv, and Hong Kong.

These exchanges have their shares prices listed on a daily basis in major financial papers such as *The Wall Street Journal*. Typical daily newspaper business sections list only the most active shares from the biggest exchanges. Typical stock listings show the bid and ask prices, the difference from the prior day if any, the 52-week high and low prices for the shares, and possibly the price-to-earnings ratio (PE ratios are covered in chapter 5).

The major stock exchanges operate quite differently from one another. The NYSE and the AMEX utilize an auction style, with investors sending orders through their brokers to the stock exchange floor. The floor is the trading area where buyers and sellers have a chance to swap stocks or other commodities. Brokers on the floor gather together in groups to buy and sell a particular company's stock. The brokers utilize the time-honored negotiation tool of supply and demand to develop a fair market price for the stock. If someone asks too much for her shares, they will go unsold. If someone offers to sell a stock at a low price, numerous brokers may try to buy. Through negotiations the parties reach a mutually acceptable price. If a block of shares is offered for sale or purchase and no one steps forward to make a deal, an exchange specialist can sell or purchase from his company's own account (Dunphy,

1998). An exchange specialist typically sells shares from a range of stocks sold on a specific exchange. If someone wishes to purchase the shares, a deal is concluded and the shares exchange hands. Actual stock certificates are not exchanged on the floor; instead, slips of paper evidencing the deal are exchanged, and ownership changes are recorded at a different time.

The NASDAQ and OTC markets operate differently than the NYSE in that there is no trading floor. Brokers do not gather in any specific location, but negotiate with others through computers. Thus, NASDAQ is a computer-driven dealing system in which orders are bought and sold based on prices posted by various buyers and sellers (Dunphy, 1998). An OTC brokerage operates as a normal securities retailer and wholesaler and also trades in select securities from its own accounts (Spiro, 1996). Security retailers and wholesalers buy and sell whatever stocks are being demanded in either small or large lots. Brokers are often called market makers, as they advise other brokers and the investment community at large of the price at which they are willing to buy or sell shares. With the speed of today's top computers, buying and selling stocks can occur in just seconds.

Electronic trading is the current rage among investors, who can now utilize Internet-based trading companies to purchase and sell stocks at the touch of a button. Commissions on these trades are often lower than traditional commissions, which run approximately $50 and up depending on the volume traded; electronic commissions are often less than $20 per trade. For example, if you purchase 100 shares of Nike for $50 a share, you are buying an entire lot, or **even lot** (100 shares). For the $5,000 paid for the stock you might have to pay an extra $20 to possibly $200 dollars to compensate the broker who purchased the stock for you. You would also have to pay a commission when you sell the stock. If you were to purchase an **odd lot,** which is anything but an even lot (1-99 shares), you might have to pay a higher commission since it might be harder for a broker to find a buyer for the shares. Commissions can be negotiated with the brokerage house based on the number of stocks traded, the number of trades each month, or the dollar value of your account.

On the basis of the changing dynamics presented by online trading and the potential for new online stock exchanges, in 2000 the NYSE was considering a merger with NASDAQ. The announcement came after both exchanges had announced plans to convert to for-profit companies to compete with newer computerized trading systems ("Markets Consider Merger," 2000). New exchanges have already been created; the first major new exchange, Archipelago, created a trading alliance through the Pacific Stock Exchange in 2000 (Ip, 2000, March 15). In the Pacific Stock Exchange, founded in 1882, the 552 member seat owners traded 23 million shares on a daily basis. Archipelago was started in December 1996, its ownership including Merrill Lynch, Goldman Sachs, ETrade Group, J.P. Morgan, CNBC TV, and Instinet. The young screen-based trading service had a daily volume of 50 million shares and generated enough revenue to buy the Pacific Stock Exchange to launch its effort to deal in NYSE-listed shares (Ip, 2000, March 15).

Various techniques are used to assess market conditions and track stock movement. As discussed earlier in this chapter, the most famous barometer of the stock market is the Dow, which includes 30 large U.S. companies. The representative mix of companies ranges from computer giant IBM to Disney. The primary benefit of the Dow is that it has an established track record. The primary disadvantage is that the average represents only a small spectrum of all available stocks.

Another indicator is the Standard & Poor 500 Stock Index, which tracks the 500 largest companies based on market capitalization. Since the Standard & Poor Index has more stocks than the Dow, it is considered a more reliable indicator of market movement. The only indexes that provide more in-depth coverage are the Russell Indexes, which cover either 1,000; 2,000; or 3,000 different stocks. The NASDAQ also has a composite to track its shares. The NASDAQ Composite Index first closed over 1,000 on July 17, 1995. Due to skyrocketing Internet offerings, the index had shot up to over 5,000 by the year 2000 (Ip, 2000, March 10). The opening months of the 21st century saw a rapid decrease in the technology-heavy NASDAQ. The collapse of the "dot-com" economy from overspeculation caused the NASDAQ to lose over 3,000 points ("Dow Jones Continues," 2002). This downturn represents one of the major concerns associated with exchanges that specialize in a given industry segment. If that industry segment experiences a downturn, the exchange will also suffer significantly.

Examples of sport-related stocks available on the NYSE include the Boston Celtics, Disney, Tribune, and many companies in the golf, shoe, fitness, and auto and horse racing industries. The NASDAQ system also includes similar prestigious companies. Table 3.2 highlights some of the major publicly traded sport-related companies that are traded on various exchanges.

Table 3.2 Major Publicly Traded Sport-Related Companies

Company symbol	Company name	Primary sport product	Exchange
AASP	All-American Sportpark	Sport parks	OTC
ACTN	Action Performance	Motor sport	NASDAQ
ADGO	Adams Golf	Golf club manufacturer	NASDAQ
AK	Ackerley Group	Seattle Supersonics and media	NYSE
ALDA	Aldila, Inc.	Golf clubs	NASDAQ
ASHW	Ashworth	Golf	NASDAQ
BFT	Bally Total Fitness Holding	Fitness centers	NYSE
BIKE	Cannondale Corp.	Bicycles	NASDAQ
BOLL	Bollinger Industries, Inc.	Fitness equipment	OTC
BOOT	LaCrosse Footwear, Inc.	Sport shoes	NASDAQ
CHDN	Churchill Downs	Thoroughbred racing	NASDAQ
CLEAR	Clear Channel	Event management/Agents	NYSE
CMCSK	Comcast	Media and team	NASDAQ
CVC	Cablevision	Knicks/Rangers and media	NYSE
DIS	Walt Disney	Anaheim teams, ESPN, ABC	NYSE
DVD	Dover Downs Entertainment	Motor sport	NYSE
ELET	Ellett Brothers, Inc.	Outdoor recreation products	OTC
ELY	Callaway Golf	Golf	NYSE

Company symbol	Company name	Primary sport product	Exchange
ERTS	Electronic Arts	Video games	NASDAQ
FGLF	Renaissance Golf Products	Golf accessories	OTC
FINL	Finish Line	Apparel	NASDAQ
FLH	Fila	Shoes	NYSE
FTS	Footstar	Shoes	NYSE
FUSA	Football USA Inc.	Licensed goods	NASDAQ
GET	Gaylord Entertainment Co.	Media and resorts	NYSE
GSPT	Global Sports Interactive	Internet	NASDAQ
GTA	Golf Trust of America, Inc.	Golf course owner	AMEX
SSPY	Sports Supply Group, Inc.	Sporting goods	OTC
HIBB	Hibbett	Apparel retail	NASDAQ
HUF	Huffy	Bicycle manufacturer	NYSE
ISCA	International Speedway	Motor sport	NASDAQ
KSWS	K-Swiss, Inc.	Athletic footwear	NASDAQ
KTO	K2	Skis	NYSE
MIEC	Magna Entertainment	Horse racing tracks	NASDAQ
MPH	Championship Auto Racing Teams	Motor sport	NYSE
MTN	Vail Resorts Inc.	Skiing	NYSE
NIKE	Nike	Shoes	NYSE
NWS	News Corp.	Dodgers and media	NYSE
OO	Oakley	Sunglasses	NYSE
OSH	Oshman's Sporting Goods	Sport retail	AMEX
PAR	CoastCast	Golf	NYSE
PRED	Orlando Predators	Arena football team	NASDAQ
PTII.OB	PTI Holding, Inc.	Bicycle accessories	OTC
PVII	Princeton Video Image, Inc.	Broadcasting	NASDAQ
RACN	Racing Championship Corp.	Licensed goods	NASDAQ
RAWL	Rawlings Sporting Goods	Sporting goods	NASDAQ
RBK	Reebok	Shoes	NYSE
RDL	Riddell Sports Inc.	Sporting goods	AMEX
RIFL	Royal Precision, Inc.	Golf clubs	NASDAQ
ROLL	Rollerball International	In-line equipment	OTC
RST	Boca Resorts	Resorts	NYSE
SCY	The Sports Club Co.	Fitness centers	AMEX
SGDE	The Sportsman's Guide, Inc.	Catalog retailer	NASDAQ
SPCH	Sport Chalet, Inc.	Sporting goods retail	NASDAQ
SPLN	SportsLine USA	Internet	NASDAQ
SPOR	Sport-Haley, Inc.	Golf apparel	NASDAQ
SRR	Stride Rite Corp.	Shoes	NYSE
TDRP	TearDrop Golf Co.	Putter manufacturer	NASDAQ
TEE	National Golf Properties, Inc.	Golf course owner	NYSE
TRB	Tribune	Cubs and media	NYSE
TRK	Speedway Motorsports	Motor sport	NYSE
WWE	World Wrestling Entertainment	Wrestling	NYSE
Z	Venator Group	Foot Locker Stores	NYSE

AMEX = American Exchange; NASDAQ = regular NASDAQ; NYSE = New York Stock Exchange; OTC = NASDAQ's over-the-counter Bulletin Board.

The securities industry is regulated by its own rules, but also needs to comply with federal regulations. In the following section we consider how the government also affects financial systems.

> Two of the most important financial institutions through which capital is transferred are the banking system and the various stock exchanges, such as the NYSE and NASDAQ.

Government's Influence on Financial Markets

In addition to the Fed, discussed earlier in connection with banking, numerous federal and state government units can exert considerable influence over financial systems. Various regulatory bodies at the state or federal level make laws in many areas, from how to incorporate to what taxes are to be paid. One such federal regulatory agency is the Securities and Exchange Commission (SEC), which was formed after the 1929 stock market crash and started operating in 1934. The SEC's primary emphasis initially was on ensuring accuracy in the underwriting of stock offerings and proper disclosure (Spiro, 1996). The goal was to ensure equal access among investors to information from companies. Activities of the SEC have evolved into analyzing practices at the private exchanges and monitoring the accounting practices used by companies in their initial security offerings and subsequent annual reports.

The SEC's current primary focus is on proper disclosure. The scandals affecting publicly traded companies such as Enron, Worldcom, and Global Crossing highlight the importance of following the SEC's disclosure rules. Proper disclosure often centers on **annual reports;** proxy statements; audited financial statements, including management's analysis of operating and financial conditions (Form 10-K); and quarterly reports, including unaudited financial statements (Form 10-Q) prepared by the corporation but not verified by an independent auditor (*Securities Regulation,* 1994). Certain decisions made by a corporation's board of directors, such as election of new board members or a change in the bylaws, are subject to shareholder voting. At a corporation's annual meeting, stockholders who cannot attend are allowed to vote by proxy. A **proxy** enables someone else to vote in the shareholder's place. The proper disclosure of proxy-related issues is designed to ensure that all stockholders have the opportunity to air their ideas or concerns. A proxy statement needs to disclose the date, time, and location of the meeting; which types of stockholders (those holding class A or class B stock) are allowed to vote on certain issues; information about directors, including their compensation; and any significant decisions to be made such as changing the charter, issuing new securities, or decisions about mergers and acquisitions (*Securities Regulation,* 1994). While most annual meetings are not contentious, companies going through tough times or internal strife may have critical issues to be discussed at the annual meeting. The government steps in to ensure that the competing groups provide appropriate and accurate information to all shareholders.

Insider Trading

One key concern addressed by the SEC is insider trading. Pursuant to Section 1b of the Securities Exchange Act of 1934, insider trading is illegal. The definition of an insider has expanded over the years. Initially only the top corporate officials had confidential information that could help guide their buying or selling practices associated with the company's securities. Over the years, the definition of an **insider** has come to cover other investors, even those not associated with the company, who acquire confidential information and utilize that information for their own or another's financial gain.

A good example of an insider trading case was publicized in 2000. A former temporary employee with several securities trading firms used his position to find information in garbage cans, desks, and on computer printers (McMorris, Smith, & Schroeder, 2000). The case was the first case of an insider trading ring on the Internet, in which information on 23 corporate deals was discussed with friends who met in chat rooms. In all, 19 people were charged with insider trading for their activities, which generated $8.4 million in profits. Some of those charged were fairly distant from the initial illegal tip. The case showed that the government was serious about all individuals involved in insider trading. The government was willing to go so far as to prosecute individuals who had heard the news from others who had heard the news from another source who could be traced to the original insider. Thus, the government does not care where people might have heard the inside information; the fact that they used inside information makes them liable (McMorris et al., 2000).

Power of the Securities and Exchange Commission

Congress tracks the securities industry through the Committee on Banking, Housing, and Urban Affairs in the Senate and the Committee on Energy and Commerce in the House of Representatives. The Securities Exchange Act of 1934, mentioned earlier, concerns the sale and trading of existing securities and created the **Securities and Exchange Commission** (SEC). In contrast, the Securities Act of 1933 primarily concerns the issuing of new securities. The 1934 act provides the primary underpinning for rules governing brokers/dealers, financial responsibility requirements, regulations restricting borrowing to purchase securities, and rules concerning manipulation of security prices. The numerous regulatory requirements are beyond the SEC's scope. Thus, the SEC has delegated significant regulatory authority to several self-regulatory organizations that oversee their respective markets. The NYSE, NASDAQ, and AMEX are examples of self-regulatory organizations. However, as already mentioned, the NYSE and NASDAQ are both considering a change to for-profit status, which could possibly change the manner in which the government might try to regulate them.

> *Among government agencies that regulate many aspects of financial systems and individual companies to protect the interests of citizens, one of the most important is the Securities and Exchange Commission.*

State Regulations

In addition to federal regulations, state regulations apply to any company issuing securities. A company issuing securities needs to ensure first that it follows all corporate laws in the state in which it is issuing stocks. Next, the certificate of incorporation needs to comply with all applicable state laws. The certificate of incorporation is the formal application and approval form from the state authorizing the corporation's formation and ability to operate. Last, the corporation's bylaws must not conflict with either state laws or the certificate of incorporation (*Securities Regulation,* 1994). State laws can cover such diverse areas as classes of stocks that can be issued, limitations on dividend policies, restrictions on transferring stocks, the rights and obligations of officers and directors, amending corporate charters

to change capital structure, mergers and consolidations, selling corporate assets, and final corporate dissolution. Some laws are similar in the federal and state systems but provide for different legal conclusions. For example, state laws can cover mergers or consolidations, but many mergers require federal approval to avoid antitrust violations. Similarly, while state laws cover corporate dissolution, most dissolutions revolve around bankruptcy proceedings, which are covered by federal laws.

Government regulations affecting financial systems abound. Chapters 14 and 17 of this text cover additional issues such as laws affecting business structures, tax considerations, and bankruptcy protection. Government units can also work to shore up failing financial systems. After the stock market crash in 1929, states as well as the federal government tried to protect the banking industry. In late 1932 and early 1933, several governors called banking holidays, which prohibited depositors from removing their funds. Congress followed the lead and passed the Emergency Banking Act (Klise, 1972). The strategy could not save all banks, but it saved a large number of banks that were able to use the holiday closure to reorganize and strengthen. Although the government is supposed to protect the public, the following sport finance examples might point to the scenario of the wolf guarding the sheep.

In God We Trust

Government entities are elected to represent the interests of citizens within their jurisdiction. However, government interaction with sport can produce mixed results that affect the bottom line. A good example of such a connection is in the Olympic bribery scandal that unfolded in 1998-1999. Officials within the Salt Lake Olympic Committee were accused of misappropriating funds to bribe International Olympic Committee members involved in the host city bidding process ("Briefly," 2000). Some officials might consider such payments justified to help secure an event that could bring tremendous growth and income to Utah. Others would consider such actions an affront to the notion of amateurism and fair play. Moreover, such conduct can also be illegal as a violation of federal or state laws, or both, against corruption and bribery.

Financial wrongdoing was also alleged in a case involving the Tampa Bay Lightning. Former city and Lightning officials were cleared of criminal charges after the team officials allegedly altered their balance sheets before city officials reviewed them (Gilpin, 1998). Charges were dropped by the prosecutor, possibly because of perceived difficulty in prosecuting the case. City officials backed a $160 million arena deal and agreed to guarantee $1 million a year in the package. Former Lightning executive David LeFevre allegedly ordered the removal of $1.1 million in short-term liabilities from the balance sheet and transferred the funds to another building project that did not become active until nine months later (Gilpin, 1998). Thus, the balance sheet did not accurately reflect all of the team's debt. The criminal probe failed because there was no proof that the city had relied upon the altered documents to make the decision (Gilpin, 1998).

In a lawsuit against the city of San Francisco, plaintiffs alleged that city officials failed to comply with voting secrecy requirements and allowed early voting at four public housing projects during the elections that would decide on the proposed San Francisco 49ers' new stadium (Chiang & Wilson, 1998). The two propositions authorized $100 million in lease revenue bonds for the proposed stadium and changed some land zoning restrictions. A state court of appeals dismissed the suit (Chiang & Wilson, 1998).

But not all government interaction with sport entities results in litigation or fiascoes. The relations between government entities and sport organizations are often very amicable and frequently produce positive results for both sides. A good example is in the action the Canadian government was considering in order to protect Canada's professional teams. Canadian teams have fared poorly over the years because of a weak Canadian dollar (compared with the stronger U.S. dollar) and heavy tax burdens. The Vancouver Canucks, for example, had $54.8 million in 1998 revenue but anticipated losing between $20 and $25 million. A portion of these losses was attributed to the Canuck players' salaries, which increased over 30% in one year to $55.4 million (Canadian) (Schreiner & Damsell, 1998).

The Canucks are not alone. Combined, the Ottawa Senators and Montreal Canadiens pay more property tax than all 21 U.S.-based NHL teams combined (Harper, 1999). Some of the taxing shortfalls that affect the Senators are the following:

- $17 million in provincial and federal income taxes for employees, including players
- $4.5 million in property taxes for the Corel Centre
- $5.6 million in amusement taxes on ticket sales

- $5 million in general sales taxes
- $2.1 million surcharge for a highway overpass built for the arena
- $1.1 million in corporate and capital taxes
- $450,000 in withholding taxes for nonresident employees on the team

In total, the Senators and the Corel Centre paid $36.6 million in taxes—not including the arts tax on broadcast rights, which forces the Senators to pay 5% of their television revenue to help fund the making of Canadian films (Harper, 1999). Interestingly enough, the Ontario government levies the amusement tax because under provincial law an NHL game is not considered "Canadian entertainment" (Harper, 1999). The taxes listed are often avoided by U.S. teams, which might pay only sales, income, and a ticket tax to help repay facility construction costs. United States teams can also negotiate away some of these tax obligations when they move to a new facility and obtain significant incentives to relocate.

On the basis of such losses, the Canadian legislature was examining an annual government subsidy of $5 million Canadian ($3.3 million U.S. dollars) to each of the nine professional teams in Canada (only NBA, NHL, and MLB teams). The government was also examining a 150% tax **deduction** for corporate sport sponsorship, including the purchase of luxury boxes ("Canada Eyes," 1998). However, after a significant public outcry, the Canadian government backed out of the pledged aid for professional teams (Beltrame, 2000). As of 2001, only seven professional teams remained in Canada.

Environmental Conditions

The fact that the Canadian economy does not help professional teams in Canada represents a critical environmental condition. Professional teams might seem like a very solid investment if one considers how some franchises increased in value in the 1990s. However, there is no such thing as a guaranteed financial winner. Numerous environmental concerns can affect any sport investment. The following quote from a Baltimore Orioles annual report highlights the various threats that can affect a sport investment.

Escalating player salaries have become our most serious problem; baseball is experiencing a rapidly changing environment. We have entered a period of financial extravagance and, while it lasts, salaries will continue to escalate wildly and the stability of our game will be put to a severe test. (Much, 1997, December 1, p.1)

The rapidly escalating salaries for professional athletes have fostered the tremendous boom in new arena and stadium construction as new revenue streams are needed to fund salary increases. The quote might have appeared in a press release from MLB concerning the aftermath of the 1994-1995 player strike and the continuing increase in player salaries through the beginning of the 21st century. However, the quote appeared in the 1977 Baltimore baseball club's annual report. Baseball salaries in 1977 averaged $76,066 (Ruxin, 1989). By 1998, the average baseball salary was $1.4 million, with 750 players expecting to earn over $1 million (Singer, 1998). By 2001, the average salary in baseball was $2.138 million, with four teams (New York Yankees, Los Angeles Dodgers, Boston Red Sox, and Cleveland Indians) averaging over $3 million per player on their roster ("Salary Scoreboard," 2001). The team with the lowest average payroll in 2001 was the Montreal Expos, which averaged $926,333 per player and was being considered for elimination through contraction ("Salary Scoreboard," 2001). Player salaries represent just one internal constraint that affects a professional team's financial bottom line.

Internal constraints are factors within a business that can be controlled. Player personnel issues can involve both internal and external constraints. A baseball team may have a farm system to help train young players. The team may also have gifted scouts who can help sign top talent. The team can also carefully plan the payroll to optimize bonuses and planned player retirement or free agency. These internal variables must be contrasted with external variables such as whether baseball is losing popularity, whether fewer high school teams are being formed, whether other sports are drawing greater fan support, whether other teams are paying their players more, and whether a municipality taxes the team or athlete in an unreasonable manner.

Conditions in the environment, such as social forces and the economy, can have a strong impact on a sport business.

CONCLUSION

Every business has to balance the internal and external constraints in its financial environment. The Smiths need to deal with their own banks, their customers' banks, and possibly the financial institutions of their suppliers or landlord. The Smiths can face a multitude of other financial systems and concerns, from having to manage their accounts to

ensure that they are protected from a bank default to understanding the SEC's authority if they wish to sell shares in their business. Although the number of entities involved is limited, the interactions can be highly complex. The interactions are that much more complex for the Celtics. Imagine the millions of interactions each season that relate to attendance alone, with fans buying their tickets with bank **drafts** or credit cards, and remember that each transaction requires the involvement of at least two financial institutions. In addition, when the Celtics need funds, they will need to go beyond the banks if they wish to issue additional stocks or bonds.

Every successful business at one point or another handles money, stocks, bonds, and other assets, ranging from liquid to hard assets. Similarly, every business needs to be concerned with the inner workings of all the financial institutions. It is impossible to know where you might have to obtain your next round of capital infusion. One year a business might obtain necessary funds from a bank or a **public offering.** The next year the business might have to borrow from an insurance company or pension fund. The options are only limited by the various internal and external constraints. These constraints can include such elements as the corporation's own bylaws or articles of incorporation (discussed in chapter 4) or its credit rating (discussed in chapter 8). Government regulations can dramatically affect the options if interest rates rise or if borrowing regulations are tightened. No matter what capital criteria might arise, businesses need to be proactive in their capital funding operations to help reduce borrowing or capital acquisition expenses and to increase their ability to raise any necessary funds.

ASSIGNMENTS

1. List five internal and external constraints that can affect each scenario featured in this text.

2. Develop capital campaigns for each scenario with an emphasis on raising $1 million. You can use any potential capital acquisition approach. However, the analysis should be based on current data, such as the prevailing prime rate during the week you do this exercise.

RESEARCH PROJECTS

1. Examine the banking policy in any other country, and try to compare the manner in which that government interacts with banks and controls inflation with how the Fed controls banking and interest rates in the United States.

2. Take any one of the sport companies or corporations traded on any of the exchanges and critically analyze the company by examining its stock trading history, annual reports, earnings projections, price-to-earnings ratio, and any additional information that could help you reach a decision whether or not to buy shares in that company. Some of this information can be obtained by looking at business papers, but a majority of the information will be found on the Internet. Appendix C provides some Web sites to help locate additional information.

CLASS DISCUSSION TOPICS

1. What is the difference between the NYSE and the NASDAQ?
2. What determines value?
3. Why would the price of a stock increase or decrease?
4. What is the difference between stocks and bonds?
5. Should governments control banks?
6. Should governments control monetary policies?
7. Why would a bank want or need to borrow money?
8. Should banks be allowed to sell insurance, securities, and related products or services?
9. Discuss some of your positive and negative banking experiences, such as bouncing a check.
10. What is the difference between a bank and a savings and loan?
11. What are the differences between the various stock exchanges?

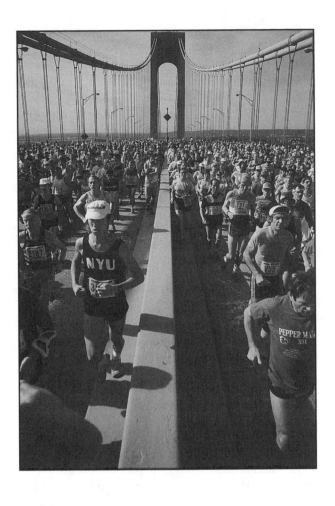

Business Structure

CHAPTER OBJECTIVES

After studying this chapter, you should be able to do the following:

- Understand why a business structure can affect a company financially.
- Understand when each type of business structure should be used.
- Define the requirements for each type of business structure utilized in sport.
- Compare the advantages and disadvantages of sole proprietorships, partnerships, corporations, and limited liability corporations or limited liability partnerships.

The previous chapter highlighted the financial systems that come into play when we examine financial issues, but the structure of a sport business can also generate particular financial benefits or hardships. Thus, it is just as important to understand business structures as it is to understand financial systems. The Smiths could form their business as a sole proprietorship, a partnership, an S corporation, a C corporation, or a limited liability corporation; and each business type would have different tax and legal concerns or benefits. A company such as Nike needs funds to expand and grow, and corporations have the ability to issue stocks and bonds as a vehicle for acquiring additional funds.

The various options for raising funds highlighted in chapters 8 through 10 are often contingent on the type of business structure that is seeking funds. This chapter covers the various types of business structures that exist and considers the advantages and disadvantages associated with each structure type.

Most businesses start as small single-owner companies and expand from that point if they are successful. The owner of a sporting goods store could invest his life savings in a business and own the entire business with no obligations to any lenders. However, if the business is not structured properly, it could be lost through litigation. Assume that Mr. Jones owns a business himself and never incorporated. He operates the business himself, within the most popular type of business structure in the United States, the sole proprietorship. As discussed in more detail later, a sole proprietor is completely liable for any business debts. Thus, if Mr. Jones sold a defective product and was sued, he could lose his life savings and possibly any other money or property he might have. However, if Mr. Jones had utilized a different business structure, his financial picture could have been significantly brighter.

The various types of business entities that exist include governments, nonprofits, sole proprietorships, partnerships, limited partnerships, limited liability corporations (LLCs) or limited liability partnerships (LLPs), **subchapter S corporations,** and C corporations. This text does not focus on government and nonprofit structures, even though they can be found in sport, but they are highlighted here. Government entities can run numerous sport entities, from high school athletic departments to collegiate athletic programs. Since such programs are government entities, their liability and financial status are significantly different from those of traditional private businesses. For example, a business that exceeds its budget may have to borrow funds to survive but will still owe the funds even if it goes out of business. In contrast, an institution such as the University of Houston can exceed its budget by millions and traditionally the state will assume the obligation and pay the bills, even if the expenses were not authorized, since the state government is ultimately responsible for the debts of its own agencies.

Similarly, nonprofits can own and operate sport businesses. It is easy to find examples of nonprofit organizations that operate sporting events; some examples are the New York City Marathon, Special Olympics, Pop Warner Little Scholars, Little League Baseball, and health clubs associated with YMCAs and hospitals. Nonprofits can also own professional sport teams. For example, the Massachusetts attorney general was investigating the sale of the Boston Red Sox in 2002 to ensure that charities received the largest amount possible under the proposed sale. The Yawkey Trust, which was the majority owner of the team, benefits numerous charities; and the state was examining the sale to ensure that the highest price was received so that the **trust** would be able to give the greatest amount back to the various charities ("Attorney General," 2001). Nonprofits face different financial concerns primarily in relation to raising funds. Although some nonprofits can use traditional bank lending, the primary fund-raising options for nonprofits are donations and the selling of various items, from memberships and registration fees to participate in special events to television and sponsorship rights. Chapter 14 includes additional discussion of the tax consequences of raising funds for nonprofits.

Sole Proprietorships

A sole proprietorship is a business entity owned by a single person. If the Smiths decided not to form a partnership, but to have one person as the sole owner, then the business would be classified as a sole proprietorship. The primary benefits of this business structure are that no formal paperwork is needed to start the business, the cost of organizing the business is not significant, and profits and organizational control do not need to be shared with anyone else (Siegel, Shim, & Hartman, 1992). The primary disadvantages are that a single individual has limited ability to raise significant capital, the owner can face unlimited personal liability, and the business ends when the owner dies (Siegel et al., 1992). Another disadvantage is that a sole proprietorship is normally a single-person operation without access to support from partners. This lack of support can render decision making more difficult.

Table 4.1 lists other advantages and disadvantages associated with a sole proprietorship.

Most businesses in the world are sole proprietorships (Cheeseman, 1998). In the sport world, many entities are classified as sole proprietorships. In thinking about sole proprietorships in sport, you may envision small mom-and-pop businesses such as a specialized sporting goods store, a bowling alley, or a martial arts studio; but this leaves out another whole classification of sole proprietorships. Independent contractors are often sole proprietors and are prevalent in many sports—for example, professional bowlers, skiers, skaters, or race car drivers. These individuals have a minimum of expenses apart from travel and entry expenses and are often living on meager purses won at events. Once they become more successful and have larger income streams and expenses, they can become incorporated (incorporation is discussed later in this chapter).

Table 4.1	Advantages and Disadvantages of a Sole Proprietorship	
Advantages	**Disadvantages**
Total control over decision making	Limited managerial experience
Revenues taxed only once	Unlimited personal liability
Great flexibility	Lasts only as long as owner lives
Easy to form	Limited access to capital funds
All profits retained by owner	
Less concern about confidentiality	
Easy to sell	
Fewer government restrictions	

The majority of businesses in the world are owned by one person; likewise many sport businesses are owned by one person.

General and Limited Partnerships

If the Smiths decide to run the business equally and if each owns 50% (or any other division of ownership) of the business, they are considered partners. A partnership's primary benefits are minimal formation costs and few government regulations. The primary disadvantages are difficulty in raising capital, unlimited personal and business liability for all partners, and immediate termination of the partnership once one partner dies or withdraws from the partnership (Siegel et al., 1992). Table 4.2 highlights the advantages and disadvantages associated with a partnership.

There are two primary types of partnerships. In a general partnership, individuals or groups combine their resources to share in operating, managing, and controlling a business and also share in all profits and liabilities. This type of partnership has several advantages. General partnerships have greater access to capital than sole proprietorships do; profits are taxed only once when distributed to the partners; and the combination of at least two parties helps enhance managerial decision making.

The primary disadvantages are that this type of partnership has a limited longevity based on the partners' lives/existence (i.e., a human partner's death or if a partner is a corporation or other business structure, when that business structure terminates from dissolution or by court order); partners are jointly and severally liable for partnership debt or liability; capital acquisition is limited compared with that of corporations; and the managerial talent pool is often limited to only those individuals who are partners versus corporations that possibly have many more voices from which to harness expertise.

A general partnership can be created in one of two ways. An express partnership can be developed through a written contract. An implied partnership can be created through the actions of the parties.

 If the Smiths did not formalize any agreement, but their conduct of the business was similar to that of a partnership, their business would be considered a partnership. If the Smiths shared profits, managed the facility together, and were each able to sign the company's checks, the business would be an implied partnership.

In contrast to a general partnership, a limited partnership involves a general partner who is responsible for managing the company and one or more "limited" partners who provide only financial input (Cheeseman, 1998). A **limited partner** is entitled to share profits but is not engaged in day-to-day management. Because the limited partner's stake in the company is purely financial, her liability is limited to her financial contribution. Limited liability provides a strong incentive for people to invest in a partnership. Other benefits associated with a limited partnership include the ability to generate more capital than sole proprietorships, maintenance of a pass-through benefit for the profits paid to a limited partner (i.e., limited partners are paid their profits without the partnership being taxed first), and the fact that limited partners can invest in several different businesses without exposing themselves to significant liability. The two biggest disadvantages of a limited partnership are the lack of managerial involvement by the limited partner and the fact that the general partner is still subject to unlimited liability.

Both general and limited partnerships can be ended through express language in the partnership agreement or through addition or subtraction of a partner. By law, a partnership ends when a partner dies, a partner goes bankrupt, or the partnership engages in any illegal activity. A partnership can also end if a partner is adjudicated insane by the courts, if a partner can no longer perform his duties, if a partner engages in improper conduct, or if the partnership can never make money (Cheeseman, 1998). Some businesses, no matter how hard they try, might not make any money. If a partnership has entered this trap and cannot make any money, a partner can ask the court to dissolve the partnership. This is a last alternative if the other partners refuse to close the business and one partner does not want to invest any more money due to the business' inability to make a profit. The partner that wants to exit the partnership will have to prove that there is no likelihood that the partnership will ever make money.

A partnership—a business owned jointly by two or more people—is inexpensive to form and subject to few government regulations, but compared to some other business structures may have difficulty in raising capital.

Subchapter S Corporations

Subchapter S corporations (often called S corporations) represented 45% of all businesses at one point in the 1990s (Marullo, 1997, February). S corporations can have up to 35 shareholders and can own subsidiaries, and S corporations that are tax-exempt organizations such as charities can own shares. The primary advantage of S corporations is that their income flows through the corporation to the shareholders, who pay taxes as personal income. This avoids the double-

Table 4.2 Advantages and Disadvantages of a Partnership

Advantages	Disadvantages
Some control over decision making	Limited managerial experience
Revenues taxed only once	Joint personal liability
Great flexibility	Limited access to capital funds
Easy to form	Lasts only as long as partnership survives
All profits retained by owners	
Easy to sell	
Fewer government restrictions	

taxation situation inherent in C corporations, in which the corporation is taxed and dividend income to the shareholders is also taxed. The option of owning subsidiaries allows S corporations to insulate themselves further from liability (Marullo, 1997, February).

Assume that the Smiths incorporate their fitness center as an S corporation and become very successful. They decide to branch out into manufacturing exercise equipment. They can start a separate subsidiary company under the S corporation to manufacture the equipment. Someone who was injured on the equipment could sue the manufacturer, but because the manufacturer is a subsidiary, the fitness center could not be touched, nor could any other subsidiary of the Smiths' S corporation.

A major disadvantage for an S corporation is that the corporation can issue only one form of stock. A traditional corporation can issue various types of shares that entitle shareholders to different **voting rights,** or can issue preferred stock that entitles stockholders to better dividends. An S corporation must be based in the United States, and no more than 20% of its income can be derived from passive investments (providing financial resources without any other assistance). Furthermore, corporations, partnerships, and international investors cannot invest in an S corporation. Lastly, an S corporation cannot own 80% or more of another corporation's stock (Cheeseman, 1998).

The S corporation fell somewhat out of favor through advancements in LLCs in the 1990s. Limited liability corporations, as discussed later on, are simpler to form and manage than S corporations. Thus S corporations are not as popular, and numerous S corporations are being converted to LLCs. At the same time, numerous S corporations still exist in the sport industry and in all other industry segments.

There are a number of subchapter S corporations in the sport industry. Subchapter S corporations have the advantage that their income flows directly to shareholders and is not subject to double taxation.

C Corporations

Corporations are entities whose formation complies with specific state laws. Thus, corporations are "fictitious" legal entities that exist only through the rights given to them by specific statutory law. Corporations are often referred to as C corporations to distinguish them from S corporations. Corporations need to de-

velop bylaws and articles of incorporation that specify how they will conduct business. The articles of incorporation typically contain the corporate name, the number of shares the corporation will issue, the corporation's initial address, and the name and address of each of the initial incorporators (Cheeseman, 1998).

A corporation can be formed in any state as long as it complies with specific rules. Rules may relate to activities such as conducting annual meetings, keeping minutes from each meeting, and electing boards of directors. Delaware is the "friendliest" corporation state, with laws that assist a company in fending off a takeover attempt. The Delaware business laws are very favorable to corporations and contain numerous advantages compared to laws in other states, as highlighted in the sidebar.

Advantages of Forming a Corporation in Delaware

The following advantages are available for corporations domiciled in Delaware:

- Delaware has a court of chancery, which is a business court that hears only business cases, without a jury and with appointed judges.
- Fees are low; corporate formation charges can be as little as $74, and franchise taxes can be as low as $50 a year.
- Shares of stock are not subject to Delaware taxes if the owner lives outside the state.
- Delaware-based corporations do not have to pay taxes on income earned outside the state as long as no income is earned in the state (Delaware InterCorp, 2000).

Favorable laws have helped develop Delaware as the premiere state for incorporating businesses; more than half of publicly incorporated companies in the United States were formed there (Lipin, 2000). These favorable laws include a dedicated judge that only handles business-related cases; such cases are not heard by a jury. Due in part to these legal advantages afforded to a business incorporated in Delaware, a research study indicated that Delaware-based businesses from 1991 to 1996 were worth 5% more than corporations formed in other states (Lipin, 2000).

Corporations have several major advantages and disadvantages. The primary advantage sought by those seeking to incorporate is the liability protection available to the owners (shareholders). The primary disadvantages of incorporating are double taxation and the complexities associated with complying with all pertinent government regulations. The various advantages and disadvantages associated with incorporating are highlighted in table 4.3.

The primary disadvantages for corporations are the cost involved in forming the corporation and the prospect of double taxation. The paperwork associated with incorporating can be voluminous, including initial filings, annual reports, Securities and Exchange Commis-

sion filings (for public corporations only), and so on. The expenses associated with documentation represent only one cost and do not include the costs associated with state filing fees (which can be thousands of dollars), hiring entities to represent the corporation in each state where the corporation conducts business (called an agent for service of process), preparing audited financial statements, and a host of additional fees. The other major financial drain for any corporation is the prospect of double taxation.

 If the Smiths earned a $100,000 profit as a sole proprietorship or partnership, they might pay $30,000 in taxes and take home

Table 4.3 Advantages and Disadvantages of a Corporation

Advantages	Disadvantages
Unlimited life of the corporation	Complex formation process
Liability of the corporation limited to the extent of corporate assets	Need to answer to shareholders who might have ulterior motives
Creditors not permitted to come after individual investors for payment over and beyond their equity investment	Sometimes onerous government regulations
Ownership interest easily transferable in the form of shares	Double taxation
Ability to hire a broad base of talented managers	
Tax benefit—dividends paid to corporation are 70% tax free	
Greater bargaining position with vendors who are more willing to provide credit to a corporation versus a single owner	
Ability to issue publicly traded debt and equity	

or reinvest $70,000 (this assumes that the tax rate is 30%). However, if the Smiths formed a corporation that returned the same profit, they would take home much less. Assume that the corporation and the Smiths' personal tax rate were 30%. After the corporation paid $30,000 in taxes, the corporation could distribute up to $70,000 to its shareholders in dividends. If the Smiths received the entire $70,000 as a dividend, they would owe 30% of that amount in taxes. Thus, the after-tax amount that the incorporated Smiths would take home would be only $49,000. But, while the Smiths would lose $21,000 in take-home pay by incorporating, they might gain much more valuable benefits in that they would not face liability on personal assets and their odds of obtaining external funding would increase dramatically.

Another concern is the potential for shareholders to rebel and demand a managerial change. If the shareholders are dissatisfied with the corporate strategy or management team, they can vote to change the corporate direction or management. Most major companies have departments that work exclusively with shareholders to address their concerns and to help produce **shareholders' reports.**

> C corporations are formed in accordance with specific state laws and are subject to considerable government regulation.

Limited Liability Corporations and Partnerships

Forming a traditional corporation can be complex, expensive, and time-consuming. Adding the burden of going public to the already considerable burden can encourage entities to form an LLC in place of a traditional corporation. Limited liability corporations and LLPs are quickly gaining favor in the United States because of their simplicity. The primary benefit for LLCs and LLPs is their classification as a partnership for federal income tax purposes (Revenue Ruling 88-76, 1988). Besides the tax benefit, LLCs and LLPs obtain the liability protection afforded to corporations. In contrast to the S corporation, which cannot be owned by either a corporation or a partnership, an LLC or LLP can be owned by another corporation or partnership. Thus, Sport Manufacturing Company can purchase another business that is an LLC, and keep that unit separately as an LLC. The major disadvantage of LLCs is their newness. There is no national standard, and each state has unique rules and regulations that will take several years to work their way through the legal systems. However, once all the legalities are settled, LLCs and LLPs will become a primary business structure for new businesses (Cheeseman, 1998).

An LLC or LLP is created through the filing of articles of partnership in the state where the business will be organized. Although the SEC typically does not regulate LLCs and LLPs, it can regulate some of the LLCs' and LLPs' activities, such as issuing publicly traded debt. The Boston Celtics are an example of a partnership that has to file reports with the SEC because of having publicly traded securities. The lack of SEC oversight can save a significant amount of money, especially if the LLC or LLP does not have to pay for audited financial statements and other related expenses.

Limited liability corporations and limited liability partnerships are gaining in popularity because the process of formation is simple and inexpensive.

CONCLUSION

This chapter covers the various business forms that exist and some of the positive and negative aspects of each. Although the form of a business is typically a legal issue, it also involves important financial considerations. A sole proprietorship can never issue stock, so its capital acquisition options are very limited. In contrast, a corporation can go public; but such an action raises numerous financial reporting requirements. Thus, it is imperative to consider the business structure before you examine what financing options are available or what industry ratios might serve as appropriate frames of reference for comparing one business to another. As highlighted throughout the rest of this book, industry benchmarking standards might exist, but they are irrelevant if you are comparing two different types of business structures.

ASSIGNMENT

Go to a small sport business and ask about the ownership structure.

1. Is the business a sole proprietorship?
2. Is it a partnership?
3. Does the company issue stock, and if so, who can purchase the stock?
4. What type of financing does the company use?
5. What are the company's strengths and weaknesses? Consider both internal and external environmental conditions facing the company in your answer.

RESEARCH PROJECTS

1. Obtain a copy of any report required by the SEC of any publicly traded sport corporation and examine the report to determine if you think the reporting requirements are onerous.
2. Obtain an annual report from a publicly traded company and summarize the key legal issues in the report.

CLASS DISCUSSION TOPICS

1. If you were the Smiths, what type of business structure would you try to establish?
2. The NFL currently does not allow any team other than the Green Bay Packers to have any shareholders. Should the NFL change this rule? Give pros and cons for public ownership of a sport franchise.

PART II
Principles of Financial Analysis

Financial Statements, Forecasts, and Planning

CHAPTER OBJECTIVES

After studying this chapter, you should be able to do the following:

- Identify the elements of the balance sheet.
- Identify the elements of the income statement.
- Discuss the cash flow statement and relate it to the income statement and the balance sheet.
- Define common financial ratios that can be used to assess an organization's liquidity, activity, financial leverage, profitability, and inventory, as well as the firm's collection cycle.

- Understand the information that needs to be gathered before beginning forecasting.
- Forecast sales, as well as profit and loss.
- Understand what drives the need for capital.
- Forecast the balance sheet.
- Relate the projected profit and loss and balance sheet to industry norms as a reasonableness check.
- Discuss how to use break-even analysis as a planning tool.

To achieve success in their ventures, it is essential for sport administrators and managers to know how to analyze financial statements and to develop skills in financial forecasting and planning. In this chapter, we discuss the "nuts and bolts" of financial statements as well as show how cash flow is derived from the basic financial statements. We also introduce you to the steps involved in doing financial forecasting and planning. In addition, we describe the basic accounting statements that are used for reporting purposes by businesses. The techniques we discuss are critical for starting new businesses, investing in new equipment, and making appropriate operating decisions. The following are key concepts underlying financial analysis that the chapter addresses:

- Types of financial statements
- Interpreting financial statements
- Preparing financial forecasts and budgets
- Break-even analysis

Types of Financial Statements

Financial statements are compiled from a firm's accounting records. These financial statements include the balance sheet, the income statement, and the statement of cash flows. Financial statements are intended to provide information to individuals about a business in a consistent manner, as a result of efforts by accountants to follow generally accepted accounting principles (GAAP). Two private organizations, the American Institute of Certified Public Accountants and the Financial Accounting Standards Board, as well as the Securities and Exchange Commission, an agency of the federal government, are the authoritative bodies that determine GAAP. For example, GAAP set forth policies concerning how to categorize depreciation or properly record losses. However, although GAAP are considered appropriate standards, they have come under attack because of loopholes that allowed the accounting scandals highlighted in the Enron collapse in 2001.

The **balance sheet** displays the financial condition of a business at a single point in time. The balance sheet gives information concerning assets, liability and owners' equity. The **income statement** describes how much profit or loss was earned by a business over a given length of time, such as a month, quarter, or year. The income statement provides information about a business' operating performance over that period of time. The **statement of cash flows** provides information about how the cash position of a business has changed over a given period of time. For example, the firm may see its cash position depleted through the purchasing of machinery or supplies. By contrast, the firm's cash position can be diminished through the paying down of debt or the paying of dividends to stockholders. It is possible for the income statement to show that a business had a profitable year, but for the business to have a cash shortage. The statement of cash flows can be used to determine what happened to the cash.

Throughout this chapter, we refer to the Celtics' and Nike's financial statements. Due to copyright restrictions, we cannot include those statements here. Follow the instructions in each section to locate and print out the financial statements.

Balance Sheet

The balance sheet is used by accountants to give a picture of the business at a single point in time, as if the business were standing still. To print out the balance sheet for Nike, Inc. as of May 31, 1999; May 31, 2000; and May 31, 2001, go to **www.sec.gov/edgar.shtml** and search for company filings. You'll want to find form 10-K (listed by year). Access the same Web site to print out the balance sheet of Celtics Basketball Holdings, L.P., which owned and operated the Boston Celtics of the NBA, as of June 30, 1999; June 30, 2000; and June 30, 2001. Again search for company filings and then locate the Celtics' 10-K forms by year. The balance sheet is divided into two sides with assets on the left and liabilities and capital provided by investors (or stockholders'

equity) on the right. The basic definition that all balance sheets follow is

(5.1) assets = liabilities + capital provided by owners

This basic definition must always hold. Therefore, capital provided by investors is related to the assets and liabilities of the firm as follows:

(5.2) capital provided by owners = assets − liabilities

In a balance sheet, the assets of the firm are listed according to the length of time it takes to convert them to cash. The asset side normally is determined by the nature of the business, the industry it operates in, and financing and operational decisions made by management. In many businesses, management has to make decisions concerning whether sales are cash sales or whether credit will be extended, whether equipment should be purchased or leased, and whether cash balances should remain as cash or should be invested in short-term securities that can earn a return.

Liquidity refers to the ease and quickness with which assets can be converted to cash. The entries shown under **current assets** are the most **liquid** since they are expected to be converted to cash in one year or less. Examples of current assets that appear on balance sheets are cash and short-term financial assets. In addition, current assets include accounts receivable, which consist of the dollar amounts not yet collected from customers for goods and services sold to them (after adjustments for bad debts). Inventory consists of raw materials that are used in manufacturing, in work in process, or in finishing goods. Current assets are discussed in more detail in chapter 12. **Fixed assets** are the assets on the balance sheet with the least liquidity. These assets include real estate, plant, and equipment. Unlike current assets, fixed assets normally are not converted to cash for such day-to-day activities as meeting payroll or paying vendors.

As found in Nike's consolidated balance sheet from their form 10-K filing, Nike's current assets include cash, cash equivalents (e.g., liquid bank accounts, such as checking accounts), accounts receivable, and inventory. Nike's current assets also include deferred income taxes and prepaid expenses. The deferred income taxes include tax benefits associated with the purchase of a business asset that are classified as a current asset because they accrue to Nike within one year. Prepaid expenses are for items of value that have future usefulness in business operations, such as payment in advance of an insurance premium that makes the unexpired portion of the insurance premium into a current asset.

For Celtics Basketball Holdings (Celtics), most of the current assets consist of cash and cash equivalents (see the Celtics' 10-K form on the SEC Web site). An additional major category of current assets is accounts receivable. The Celtics also report prepaid expenses, which are combined with other current assets. A major difference between Nike and the Celtics is that since the Celtics are primarily not a manufacturer or distributor of merchandise, the Celtics' balance sheet does not include inventory as a current asset.

Both Nike and the Celtics report equipment and property as fixed assets. Other fixed assets for the Celtics include the value of the Celtics franchise itself as a fixed asset and the value of its share of NBA Media Ventures, which provides income to the team as a result of its share in NBA media licensing and broadcast contracts. Nike includes deferred income taxes, which are the tax benefits that accrue to the firm after one year, and the value of intangible assets and goodwill. The value of intangible assets and **goodwill** includes the value of Nike's trademarks and brand names, which are valuable in that they provide Nike with a major recognizable presence in the marketplace. Goodwill represents an expectation of a greater-than-normal level of earnings for a business in relation to its particular industry.

On the other side of the balance sheet, liabilities are listed in the order of when they must be paid. For example, current liabilities consist of obligations that must be paid down in one year or less, while long-term liabilities consist of items that will not be paid down completely for more than one year. The liabilities and stockholders' equity (capital provided by investors) portions of the balance sheet typically reflect decisions made concerning the sources of financing for the business. For example, decisions concerning the mix of financing provided by debt versus stockholders' equity, and short-term versus long-term debt financing, are reflected in the entries shown on the liabilities and stockholders' equity side of the balance sheet.

The Celtics' primary current liability is accounts payable, which comprises bills to vendors that have not yet been paid. In addition, the Celtics, like other professional sport teams, are locked into long-term compensation arrangements with many of their players. Player salaries can be broken down into two categories: long-term liabilities and current liabilities. When a player signs a 10-year contract, only a portion will be immediately due, so the entire contract should not be considered a current liability to the business even though the entire debt will be owed at a later date. The compensation that is known to be due to players, coaches, and management within a year or less is included in the current portion of deferred compensation. This makes sense for financial and practical reasons because the future liability can be very speculative. If a player or coach is injured, retires, or is traded, then the Celtics would no longer owe that obligation.

Accounts payable are also an important current liability for Nike. In addition, Nike's current liabilities include the notes payable and the current portion of its long-term debt, that is, interest and principal on short-term and long-term debt that are payable within one year. Nike reports accrued liabilities—that is, records expenses when they are incurred, but before they are paid—as a current liability as well.

 The Celtics list the noncurrent portion of deferred compensation under long-term liabilities because this includes compensation to players, coaches, and management under employment contracts that will be payable beyond one year into the future. More than 80% of the Celtics' long-term liabilities are in the form of bank financing.

The bulk of Nike's long-term liabilities is long-term debt, which is in the form of various bonds held by investors. Nike also reports deferred income taxes and other liabilities as a long-term liability. The deferred income taxes represent future anticipated income taxes that will be owed as a result of current business activity.

Because Nike is a publicly traded corporation, the owners who have invested in Nike are the stockholders. Shareholders' equity represents the value of the stockholders' investment in Nike.

 For the Celtics, the investment in the business by its owners is denoted by the term *partners' capital* instead of stockholder equity. The reason is that rather than the Celtics' having issued shares of common stock as a means of obtaining investment capital, the team is structured as a partnership. All partners in the team provided capital to the Celtics when they purchased partnership shares.

The net working capital, or working capital, of any business is current assets less current liabilities. When net working capital is positive, this means that the firm expects the cash paid out over the next year to be less than the cash that will become available over the next year. Nike's net working capital equaled $1,818 million ($3,264.9 million – $1,446.9 million) on May 31, 1999; $1,456.4 million ($3,596.4 million – $2,140.0 million) on May 31, 2000; and $1,838.6 million ($3,625.3 million – $1,786.7 million) on May 31, 2001. This indicates that Nike's current assets have substantially exceeded its current liabilities.

 By contrast, the Celtics have had negative net working capital, which means that the team's short-term obligations have exceeded the team's short-term assets. As reported by the Celtics, the net working capital equaled –$20,664,393 ($5,240,634 – $25,905,027) on June 30, 1999; –$13,583,239 ($21,378,081 – $34,961,320) on June 30, 2000; and –$14,807,986 ($16,423,720 – $31,231,706) on June 30, 2001.

The term *investment in working capital* refers to an increase in net working capital between points in time on the balance sheet. See the following case study example.

 Between June 30, 1999, and June 30, 2000, Celtics Basketball Holdings' negative net working capital actually decreased from –$20,664,393 to –$13,583,239, which represented an increase of $7,081,154 in net working capital. Although this was an improvement in the short-term cash position of the Celtics, their expected cash outflows were still exceeding expected cash inflows, as of June 30, 2000.

Income Statement

The income statement measures a business' profitability over a specific period of time, such as a year or a quarter. Income is defined as follows:

(5.3)   income = revenue – expenses

Whereas the balance sheet provides us a snapshot at a single point in time, the income statement can be viewed as a film that portrays how the organization performed between the single snapshots depicted on the balance sheet. To view the income statements for Nike and the Celtics, access their 10-K forms on the SEC Web site.

The income statement typically consists of three sections. The first section includes the revenues and expenses from the company's operations. Second, a non-operating section of the income statement includes financing costs and any income earned by financial investments. Typically the non-operating section of the income statement includes all taxes that are paid by the enterprise. The third section of the income statement is the net income of the business.

 In contrast to Nike, the Celtics do not report taxes paid because the profits and losses flow directly to the tax returns of the Celtics Basketball Holdings partners themselves. As a result, there are no taxes paid directly by the Celtics operations.

Under GAAP, revenue is generated when an exchange of goods or services has occurred. In addition, revenues and expenses are reported when they occur, even though cash inflows or outflows may or may not have occurred. For example, when goods and services are sold for credit, associated sales and profits are reported even if payment has not yet been received. This is also known as accrual basis accounting as opposed to cash basis accounting (discussed in chapter 2), in which revenues and expenses are not recognized until there are actual cash inflows and outflows.

The value of a firm's assets is linked to the future incremental cash flows that they will generate, but cash flows do not show up on the income statement. As a result, there are expenses that appear on the income statement but are not actual cash outlays. One such expense is depreciation. **Depreciation** represents an estimate by the firm's accountants of the cost of equipment and property that are used up by the organization in the process of producing and distributing goods and services. Unlike the Celtics, Nike does not separately report depreciation but instead includes it with selling and administrative expenses.

 The Celtics also have a noncash expense related to the amortization of the NBA franchise and other intangible assets. Intangible assets represent nonphysical fixed assets of the business that provide value to the business, such as goodwill, patents, licenses, trademarks, and copyrights. Owning an NBA franchise represents an intangible asset because there is value in being the only organization that

is allowed to function as an NBA franchise in the Greater Boston area and to collect all available broadcast royalties and other NBA-related revenues. Unless one is ready to assume that an intangible asset has unlimited life for accounting purposes, it is necessary to claim amortization over a reporting period, as a result of either obsolescence or the "wearing out" of the intangible asset. As with depreciation, this amortization of intangible assets does not result in a cash outflow for the Celtics.

Numerous companies report as cost of goods sold those expenses that are directly related to the production and distribution of goods and services. Nike uses the term *cost of sales* to report cost of goods sold on its annual income statements. Such costs include raw materials, direct labor, and manufacturing overhead costs. Other costs are allocated by the accountants preparing the financial statements to the time period covered by the income statement. Such costs are reported separately as selling and general and administrative costs, although Nike combines these categories under "selling and administrative costs."

 The Celtics separately report general and administrative and selling and promotional costs, but report no cost of goods sold. The Celtics do not report cost of goods sold because the Celtics are engaged in the business of entertaining their fans with 41 home games and then appearing on the road for 41 more games. As a result, the Celtics report costs and expenses associated with playing over the regular season, which can be viewed as a team sport franchise's productive activity.

It is also interesting to note that the Celtics reported a net income of $9,010,550 for the year ending June 30, 2000, but a loss of $424,255 for the year ending June 30, 1999. This difference in profitability is attributable to the labor dispute between the NBA Players Association and the NBA owners during the 1998-1999 season. As a consequence of the dispute, the owners locked out players. When the labor dispute was settled, the end result was an abbreviated playing season. Although the Celtics' expenses were substantially less because of the abbreviated season, revenues from gate receipts and television and radio broadcasting dropped more steeply than expenses.

Statement of Cash Flows

From the perspective of financial analysis, the importance of financial statements is in their ability to provide information about an organization's cash flows. Firms have value when they generate cash flows for investors. By cash flows, we are referring directly to cash flowing into the business, as well as cash flowing out of the business. To see this distinction between cash flows and accounting measures of income, recall from earlier that income statements include noncash expenses such as depreciation. The amount of depreciation that is reported on the business' income statement has no impact whatsoever on the cash generated by the business. The reason is that when the business reports depreciation, the dollar amount reported as depreciation is not directly paid to any vendors or employees, as would be the case with other operating expense categories. The statement of cash flows is a financial statement that reports changes in a company's cash holdings over a particular period.

To view Nike's statements of cash flows for the years ending May 31, 1999; May 31, 2000; and May 31, 2001, go to **www.sec.gov/edgar/shtml** and search for Nike's 10-K form. Statements of cash flows for Celtics Basketball Holdings for the years ending June 30, 1999; June 30, 2000; and June 30, 2001 can also be found at **www.sec.gov/edgar/shtml**. (Search for the Celtics under company filings and then find form 10-K.) In the statements of cash flows for Nike and the Celtics, there are three primary sources of cash flows as a result of business activities. These include cash flows from (used in) operating activities, cash flows from (used in) investing activities, and cash flows from (used in) financing activities.

Cash flow refers to the difference between what a company brings in and what they pay out. Thus, cash flow from (used in) operating activities refers to both positive and negative cash flows that result from the firm's basic operating activities. These cash flows are equal to operating revenues less all operating expenses other than noncash operating expenses, such as depreciation. When a firm earns revenue, there are positive cash flows, whereas cash expenses are associated with **negative cash flows.**

As reported in Nike's 10-K form on the SEC Web site, Nike's operating activities generated positive cash flows between $650 million and $950 million for the years ending May 31, 1999; May 31, 2000; and May 31, 2001. As reported in the Celtics' 10-K form on the SEC Web site, the Celtics reported negative cash flows from operating activities for the year ending June 30, 1999, because cash outflows exceeded cash inflows as a result of the labor dispute during the 1998-1999 season, while for the years ending June 30, 2000, and June 30, 2001, there were positive cash flows from operating activities.

 Note that the Celtics' $14.3 million in cash flows from operating activities (see the Celtics' statement of cash flows from form 10-K) is higher than the $11,859,004 in earnings before interest for the year ending June 30, 2000 (see the Celtics' income statement from form 10-K). The earnings before interest, which are reported on the income statement, measure the profits from the operating activities of the Celtics and include noncash expenses, such as depreciation and the amortization of the NBA franchise and other intangible assets. The cash flows from operating activities are higher, as depreciation and amortization represent costs that are not associated with actual negative cash flows. We should note also that no firm can operate for long periods of time with negative operating cash flows, since this implies that the firm does not generate enough cash internally to meet its actual operating costs.

The cash flows from investing activities are cash flows associated with the business' making additions to current or fixed assets. Purchases of current and fixed assets lead to negative cash flow resulting from the use of cash to purchase these assets. When current and fixed assets are reduced, that is, sold or disposed of, during the year, this can be viewed as a positive cash flow because of the cash generated by the sale of the asset. In addition, when current liabilities are increased, there is a positive cash flow from investing activities because of the postponement of the use of cash.

As shown in the statement of cash flows from Nike's form 10-K, Nike reported negative cash flow from investing activities equal to $342.3 million for the year ending May 31, 2001. Nike's $419.9 million in negative cash flow associated with purchases of property, plant, and equipment, and $51.3 million in negative cash flow associated with the purchase of other assets, were only partially offset by positive cash flows associated with the purchase of other assets and disposal of property, plant, and equipment during the year ended May 31, 2001.

 As shown in the statement of cash flows from the Celtics' form 10-K, the Celtics reported negative cash flow of $144,541 resulting from capital expenditures (purchases of fixed assets) for the year ending June 30, 2000. The reason was that between June 30, 1999, and June 30, 2000, the Celtics purchased fixed assets (plant, property, or equipment) that cost them $144,541, which in effect was a negative outflow for the Celtics' investors. According to the cash flow statement, the Celtics also accrued $309,664 in cash inflows as a result of selling other assets. Overall, the Celtics' investment activities generated $165,123 in cash flow for the year ending June 30, 2000.

The cash flows associated with financing activities are cash flows to and from creditors and owners. Such cash flows include changes in the firm's debt and equity. When the firm increases its borrowings, the cash that is created is a positive cash flow. By comparison, paying off a loan results in negative cash flow. When dividends are paid out to stockholders, there is negative cash flow, whereas proceeds from stock issues (i.e., new owners purchasing stock) result in positive cash flow.

As shown in the statement of cash flows from form 10-K, for the three years ending in May, 2001 (May 31, 1999; May 31, 2000; and May 31, 2001), Nike reported negative cash flows from financing that ranged between $252 million and $444 million. For example, for the year ending May 31, 2001, substantial negative cash flows resulted from the payment of dividends to stockholders, the repurchase of stock (buying back stock from existing stockholders), and reductions in debt (reductions in long-term debt and decreases in notes payable).

 On the statement of cash flows from form 10-K, the Celtics also reported the cash flows associated with their financing activities. Specifically, they reported $7 million in positive cash flows as a result of increased bank borrowing (reported as proceeds from bank borrowings), but there was an exactly offsetting negative cash flow of $7 million because the Celtics also reported paying off a $7 million loan (reported as payment of bank borrowings) during the year ending June 30, 2000. The Celtics Basketball Holdings partners received $8 million in cash distributions during the year ending June 30, 2001, which generated an $8 million negative cash flow from financing activities. However, since the partners received the $8 million, individually they had a positive cash flow.

> *Financial statements, including a company's balance sheets, income statements, and statements of cash flows, are intended to provide information about the business in a systematic, consistent manner.*

Types of Financial Ratios

Information from financial statements can be used to compute financial ratios that provide insight into a business' condition. Specifically, we define commonly used financial ratios that focus on the following areas:

- Liquidity
- Activity
- Financial leverage
- Profitability
- The value of the firm

Liquidity

The liquidity ratios measure the ability of a business to meet short-term financial obligations. Liquidity ratios are associated with the firm's net working capital. A common liquidity ratio is the **current ratio.** The current ratio is computed by dividing current assets by current liabilities.

(5.4)   current ratio = total current assets /
                              total current liabilities

For Nike, the current ratio, as of May 31, 2001, is

current ratio = $3,625.3 million / $1,786.7 million
              = 2.03

This means that Nike can sell its current assets and cover its liabilities two times over.

 The current ratio for the Celtics as of June 30, 2001, is

current ratio = $16,423,720 / $31,231,706
              = 0.53

Unlike the ratio for Nike, the Celtics' current ratio is below 1, which indicates that current assets cannot cover current liabilities. Under such circumstances, the Celtics may be unable to pay their bills on time without further borrowing or more cash provided by owners.

A second measure of liquidity is the **acid test**

ratio, or **quick ratio,** which is obtained by subtracting inventories from current assets and dividing the resulting difference by current liabilities. Since inventories are the least liquid of any current assets, the quick ratio allows one to examine whether a firm can pay its current liabilities without relying on the sale of inventories.

(5.5)   acid test ratio, or quick ratio =
(total current assets – inventories) /
current liabilities

For Nike, the quick ratio, as of May 31, 2001, is

quick ratio = ($3,625.3 million – $1,424.1 million) /
$1,786.7 million
= 1.23

Even with inventories removed from current assets, Nike still has sufficient current assets to pay off short-term liabilities.

The quick ratio was not computed for the Celtics for the year ending June 30, 2001, because there were no inventories to deduct from current liabilities. As a result, the quick ratio for Celtics Basketball Holdings is identical to its current ratio.

Two other liquidity measures are the solvency ratio and working capital. The **solvency ratio** determines how strong the business is in terms of being able to cover its liabilities. The solvency ratio is calculated by dividing net worth by total assets.

(5.6)   solvency ratio = net worth / total assets

Net working capital is not a ratio, but it helps highlight the amount of current assets that is available after all the current liabilities are paid. Net working capital shows how much cash or other liquid assets might be available if the business had to repay all the liabilities that are due in the next several months. Net working capital is calculated as follows:

(5.7)   net working capital = current assets –
current liabilities

Activity

Activity ratios measure how effectively a firm manages its assets. The **total asset turnover ratio** is computed by dividing total revenues for a particular accounting period by the average total assets for that period.

(5.8)   total asset turnover ratio =
revenues / total assets (average)

For the year ending May 31, 2001, Nike's total asset turnover ratio is

total asset turnover ratio = $9,488.8 / $5,838.3 million
= 1.63

For the year ending June 30, 2001, the total asset turnover ratio for the Celtics is

total asset turnover ratio = $83,142,436 /
$28,635,812
= 2.90

The asset turnover ratio gives an indication of how effectively a firm uses its assets to generate sales. If the asset turnover ratio is relatively high, the firm is efficiently using its assets to generate sales. If the ratio is relatively low, the firm is not using its assets as effectively and may wish to consider selling off assets if sales are not increased.

The **inventory turnover ratio** is equal to the cost of goods sold over a particular period divided by the average inventory level during that same period.

(5.9) inventory turnover ratio = cost of goods sold /
inventory (average)

For Nike, the inventory turnover ratio for the year ending May 31, 2001, is

inventory turnover ratio = $5,784.9 million /
$1,435.1 million
= 4.03

The inventory turnover ratio tells us how many times during the year the inventory is purchased and sold. A relatively high turnover ratio is usually preferable, although the appropriate ratio is industry specific. For a company like Nike, the inventory turnover ratio can be easily affected by the technologies used to produce the goods that it sells, as well as by distribution techniques. Inventory management is covered in more detail in chapter 13.

To calculate the **receivables turnover ratio,** we divide revenues by average receivables during the collection period. The ratio of receivables can then be used to derive the **average collection period,** which equals the number of days in the period divided by the receivables turnover ratio. The values of these ratios are highly dependent on a firm's credit sales policies. A firm with generous credit terms will have a higher amount of receivables.

(5.10) receivables turnover ratio = total revenues / average receivables

(5.11) average collection period = number of days in the period / receivables turnover ratio

For Nike, the receivables turnover ratio and the average collection period are computed for the year ending May 31, 2001 (note that as a result, the number of days in the period is set equal to 365):

receivables turnover ratio = $9,488.8 million / $1,595.4 million
= 5.95

average collection period = 365 days / 5.95
= 61.3 days

 The Celtics' receivables turnover and average collection period for the year ending June 30, 2001, are

receivables turnover ratio = $83,142,436 / $4,525,055
= 18.37

average collection period = 365 days / 18.37
= 19.9 days

Comparing the Celtics' ratios with those of Nike, the Celtics do not rely as heavily on credit sales, which is reflected in a higher receivables ratio for the Celtics. The average collection period for the Celtics is also low, relative to that for Nike, because most Celtics sales (primarily from ticket sales and broadcast rights) do not involve the granting of credit through extended payment terms. A rule of thumb is that the collection period should not exceed the time allowed for payment in a company's credit terms by more than 10 days (see Ross, Westerfield, & Jaffe, 1996, p. 34).

Financial Leverage

Financial leverage ratios provide information concerning the extent to which a business relies on debt (loans), rather than equity (stocks), for financing. Firms with high financial leverage ratios relative to other firms in their industry have a greater likelihood of financial distress and bankruptcy. One measure of financial leverage is the debt ratio, which equals total liabilities divided by total assets.

(5.12) debt ratio = total liabilities / total assets

The May 31, 2001, debt ratio for Nike is

debt ratio = $2,325.1 million / $5,819.6 million
= 0.3995

 By contrast, the June 30, 2001, debt ratio for the Celtics is

debt ratio = $86,414,527 / $26,161,019
= 3.30

The Celtics are much more leveraged than Nike. The term "leveraged" refers to the extent to which a company relies on borrowing to finance its operations. The Celtics are highly leveraged; thus they are paying higher interest costs relative to the value of their assets. Most businesses cannot survive with a high debt ratio. However, because of the inherent value of an NBA team, the Celtics can have significant debt, with their players as their only significant asset. Thus, a high debt ratio does not mean they are in financial trouble. The team can still earn significant returns on their minimal assets as reflected in their high profit margin, highlighted in the next section.

Similar to the debt ratio is the **debt-equity ratio,** which also analyzes a business' leverage but from the standpoint of the owners equity rather than all the assets. The debt-equity ratio is calculated as follows:

(5.13) debt-equity ratio = total debt / total shareholders' equity

This ratio helps highlight how much of the debt is financed by shareholders. The higher the ratio, the greater the reliance on shareholder support. A low ratio might indicate that the debt is being purchased through retained earnings or internal sources rather than through shareholders.

An additional financial leverage measurement is the **interest coverage** ratio. To calculate the ratio of interest coverage, we divide **earnings before interest and taxes** (EBIT) by interest. This ratio provides insight into whether a firm has sufficient earnings to cover its interest expense.

(5.14) interest coverage ratio = earnings before interest and taxes / interest

For the year ending May 31, 2001, Nike's interest coverage ratio is

interest coverage ratio = $980.1 million / $58.7 million
= 16.70

The Celtics' interest coverage ratio for the year ending June 30, 2001, is

$$\text{interest coverage ratio} = \$11{,}548{,}004 / \$3{,}299{,}931 = 3.50$$

The higher ratio of interest coverage for Nike is further confirmation that Nike is substantially less leveraged than Celtics Basketball Holdings. In other words, Nike does not rely as much on borrowing funds to keep operating.

Profitability

One of the most critical figures to examine a company's success is **corporate earnings.** The bottom line for companies is their ability to generate sufficient earnings to continue growth and reward shareholders. Earnings are calculated by subtracting total costs from total sales or revenue. In form 10-K, Nike's corporate earnings are $980.1 million. This figure does not include any reduction for interest expenses or taxes due. The earnings or the corporate losses if costs exceed sales are the key point of analysis for future progress, dividend payments, bankruptcy, and any other potential corporate decision.

There are numerous commonly used measures of profitability. These include profit margin (gross and net profit margin), return on assets, return on equity, and return on investment. Profit margins are calculated by dividing profits by revenues. **Net profit margin** is computed using net income (profits after interest and taxes) as a proxy for profits; **gross profit margin** uses earnings before interest and taxes to represent profits.

(5.15)   net profit margin = net income / revenues

(5.16)   gross profit margin = earnings before interest and taxes / revenues

For the year ending May 31, 2001, Nike's profit margins are computed as

net profit margin = $589.7 million / $9,488.8 million = 6.21%

gross profit margin = $980.1 million / $9,488.8 million = 9.71%

The Celtics' profit margins for the year ending June 30, 2001, are

net profit margin = $8,674,854 / $83,142,436 = 10.43%

gross profit margin = $11,548,004 / $83,142,436 = 13.89%

When a firm's net profit margin is high relative to that of other firms in its industry, this is an indication that the firm is able to provide its products at either a low cost or a high price.

For example, if the Celtics have a 10.43% net profit margin and another team has only a 4.5% profit margin, there could be very specific reasons for the difference. The differences could be attributable to better local television rights contracts, a better arena revenue-sharing deal, differences in payroll, or just the fact that some markets can command higher ticket prices for any number of reasons.

Stockholders are primarily concerned with the return on their investment, thus the dividend per share is an important calculation for their return on investment. If the stock price increases, stockholders can realize this gain only if they sell the stock. In contrast, if the corporate board of directors decides to issue a dividend, then stockholders can earn an immediate return on their investment without having to sell.

According to form 10-K Nike paid $129.7 million in dividends in 2001. Assume, for ease in calculation, that there are 100 million outstanding shares of Nike stock currently on the market. Then we can calculate the dividend per share.

(5.17)   dividend per share = dividends / outstanding shares
= $129.7 million / 100 million
= $1.29

Thus, if you owned 10 shares of Nike you would have earned $1.29 per share, or a total of $12.90, as the return on your investment. In actuality, Nike has 273.3 million shares outstanding, which means that the dividend per share was: $129.7 million / 273.3 million = $0.47 a share.

Other measures of profit do a better job than profit margins in reflecting the investment in capital by the firm or its shareholders. One such measure of profitability is **return on assets** (ROA), which is defined as profits divided by average assets for the reporting period in question. The average assets can be found on the balance sheet.

(5.18)   return on assets = net income / average total assets

For the year ending May 31, 2001, Nike's return on assets is

return on assets = \$589.7 million / \$5,838.3 million
= 10.10%

For the year ending June 30, 2001, the return on assets for the Boston Celtics is

return on assets = \$8,674,854 / \$28,635,812
= 30.29%

Return on assets (often referred to as ROA) is also known as return on investment because it reflects the amount of profits earned on the investment in all assets of the firm. Any new asset purchased by the firm should be able to generate increased returns over and beyond what could have been earned if the funds had been placed in an equally risky financial investment.

A profitability measure that is related to ROA is the **return on equity** (ROE), which is net income divided by average stockholders' equity. Return on equity measures profitability in terms of profits earned on investment in the firm's assets by stockholders only—as opposed to ROA, which measures profitability earned on investments in a firm by all providers of funds, such as lenders, creditors, and stockholders.

(5.19)   return on equity = net income / average
stockholders' equity

For the year ending May 31, 2001, Nike's ROE is

return on equity = \$589.7 million / \$3,315.3 million
= 17.79%

The ROA or ROE can be used to compare one business to others in the same industry or as a stand-alone measure to help determine success. If Nike's goal was to obtain a 15% ROE for its investors, then it exceeded its own goals by 2.79%. However, if Nike wanted to exceed the competition by 5% and all the other sport shoe manufacturers had an ROE averaging around 20%, then Nike did not meet its goal.

The ROE is not computed for the Celtics because stockholders' equity (partners' capital) is negative as a result of the fact that liabilities substantially exceed assets. Consequently, ROE is not a meaningful measure for the Celtics.

The last return on investment calculation is **return on investment capital** (ROIV). The ROIV attempts to analyze the company's performance by all the long-term investments that help fund growth, such as long-term bank loans, bonds, and stocks.

(5.20)   return on investment capital = net income /
long-term debt + owners' equity

For the year ending May 31, 2001, Nike's ROIV is

return on investment capital = \$589.7 million / (\$435.9
million + \$3,315.3
million)
= 15.7%

A 15.7% return is a fairly strong rate of return if similar businesses are only generating a 12% rate of return.

Determining the Value of the Firm

As we have seen so far, financial statements give information about the basic condition of the firm, but they do not tell us anything about the firm's market value. The market value of the firm is based on what stock buyers and sellers establish when they buy and sell shares in the business. For a publicly traded company, the **market value** is simply the price per share of common stock, based on reported prices of shares traded on stock exchanges, multiplied by the number of shares of common stock outstanding.

(5.21)   market value = price per share of common
stock × average number of outstanding shares

On May 31, 2001, Nike's common stock shares traded at a price of \$41.10. Since there were 273.3 million outstanding shares of Nike common stock during the year ending May 31, 2001 (this financial information comes from Nike's 10-K filing with the Securities and Exchange Commission), Nike's market value, as of May 31, 2001, can be expressed as

market value = \$41.10 × 273.3 million outstanding
shares
= \$11,233 million

Whereas market value tells an investor what the investing public thinks a company is worth, a company's book value presents a different version of the company's worth. **Book value** is based on historic cost of assets minus accumulated depreciation. Although book value represents the value of assets on paper, it does not necessarily represent the true value because an asset might have a replacement cost that is higher than its book value. Thus, an asset might cost \$1 million to replace, but the book value could be only \$500,000 (\$2 million purchase price – $1.5 million in accumulated depreciation). Book value is calculated by subtracting total liabilities from total assets.

(5.22)   book value = total assets – total liabilities

For Nike, book value as of May 31, 2001 would be:

book value = $5,819.6 – $2,325.1
= $3,494.5 million

The book value for a company is also called the owners' equity because that represents the value the owners have in the business. Owners' equity is also calculated by adding retained earnings and the value of common stocks. Since this is a company's true value, it is also called the **net worth.**

The **book value per share** is another measure of a company's value based on owners' equity. If one stockholder wanted to see how much value she had, she could look at book value per share.

(5.23)   book value per share = owners' equity /
total outstanding shares

The calculation is as follows for Nike as of May 31, 2001:

book value per share = $3,494.5 / 273.3 million
= $12.79

Thus, if we assume that Nike shares were selling for $62 per share in 2001, then $12.79 of that amount was value over and beyond any value such as goodwill or expected potential future growth.

Techniques to Determine an Investment's Value

Besides all the calculations a corporation can make concerning its value, earnings, liquidity, and so on, investors can use several different techniques to determine the value of their investment. The book value calculation above is one such technique that can help an investor make appropriate investment decisions. Other techniques include annual return, holding period return, simple rate of return, and dividend payout ratio.

The annual return per share and the annual rate of return for an investment analyze whether there was any increase or decrease in a stock's value and whether any dividends were given. Assume that an investor purchased a stock on January 1, 2002, and sold it on December 31, 2002. The stock was purchased at $8 per share and sold for $10 per share. During the year the company paid dividends of $0.04 per share. The annual return per share and annual rate of return would be calculated as follows:

(5.24)   annual return per share = increase or decrease in value + dividends
= ($10 – $8) + $0.04
= $2.04

(5.25)   annual rate of return = annual return / initial investment
= $2.04 / $8.00
= 25.5%

The 25.5% return helps highlight how good of an investment the stock purchase was that year. However, this analysis is effective only for a quick snapshot in time and if the stock was actually sold. If the stock went down the next day, then the annual return would still be an accurate reflection of the value the prior year, but not the investment's true value. This is often referred to as **paper profit.** That is, the stock might have produced a great annual return, but if the stock is not sold the profit could vanish in an instant if the stock price declines.

In contrast to annual return, the holding period return takes into consideration the fact that the stock was possibly not sold. The **holding period return** indicates for the stock being analyzed, what happened to the investment, independent of what might happen in the future. Since the return on the investment during the one-year holding period was 25.5%, then that is the holding period return rate.

A less complex calculation is the **simple rate of return** (SRR), which analyzes what the stock was initially purchased for and what returns were earned by the stock. Thus, if the stock did not pay any dividends there would be no return under this formula even if the stock increased in value $10 per share. The simple rate of return is calculated as follows:

(5.26)   simple rate of return = investment's annual income / initial investment
$$= \$0.04 / \$8.00$$
$$= 0.005, \text{ or } 1/2 \text{ of } 1\%$$

Thus, through SRR, we can see that without the increase in stock price, this stock purchase was a bad decision if the investor was looking for a strong annual return from this investment.

Another method to examine the success of an investment is to examine the dividend payout ratio. The **dividend payout ratio** examines the dividends per share in contrast to how much the company earned per share. The formula is as follows:

(5.27)   dividend payout ratio = dividends per share / earnings per share

Using the Nike numbers as of May 31, 2001, we would obtain:

$$21.76\% = \$0.47 / \$2.16 \text{ (see below)}$$

This means that 21.76% of Nike earnings were repaid to the stockowners as dividends.

To get a sense of how the stock market is valuing a company, one can compute the **price-earnings ratio** (PE ratio). The PE ratio is equal to the price per share of common stock divided by the earnings per share of common stock. **Earnings per share** is calculated as follows:

(5.28)   earnings per share = net income / average
                number of shares outstanding

If two competing firms in the same industry reported earnings per share equal to $5, but Company 1's shares sell for $15 and Company 2's shares sell for $20 each, then the PE ratio for Company 1 is

(5.29)   price-earnings ratio = price per share /
                      earnings per share
                   = $15 / $5
                   = 3

By contrast, the PE ratio for Company 2 is

price-earnings ratio = $20 / $5
                   = 4

Note that the stock market is valuing Company 2's shares at a higher multiple of earnings than it is valuing Company 1's shares. This disparity in PE ratios is usually related to differences in how the financial markets view the quality of earnings, past profitability, or expected future earnings growth, or a combination of two or more of these factors. Typically, established firms have a PE ratio around 20, whereas the "dot-com" companies in the late 1990s, with almost no income and huge stock prices, had PE ratios in the thousands.

This concept is discussed in greater detail in chapter 9.

In order to compute Nike's PE ratio, it is first necessary to compute Nike's earnings per share using equation (5.28). For the year ending May 31, 2001, Nike's earnings per share is calculated as follows:

earnings per share = $589.7 million /
                273.3 million shares
             = $2.16

Using equation (5.29), Nike's PE ratio, as of May 31, 2001, is then calculated as follows:

price-earnings ratio = $41.10 / $2.16
                   = 19.03

Financial statements provide important information about the condition of a firm. By using numbers in financial statements we can get key information that allows us to summarize an organization's liquidity, activity, financial leverage, and profitability. These ratios also allow a firm to critically examine its operations and ratios in comparison with publicly traded firms in the same industry. However, when appropriate information is available, market values of the firm should be used as a supplement to these accounting-based ratios. Market value is the true street value for a business—that is, what someone would pay for a business today. However, such a value can be affected by deception. Thus, Enron had a high market value based on financial shenanigans, and the company was not really worth the exaggerated street value.

Many different ratios are used to compute various aspects of a business' financial condition, including the business' ability to meet short-term obligations, the effectiveness with which it manages its assets, the extent to which it relies on debt versus equity, and its profitability.

Preparing Financial Forecasts and Budgets

Now that we have introduced the basics of financial scorekeeping as it relates to income statements, balance sheets, statements of cash flow, and financial ratios, in this section we apply the tools of basic financial measurement to track financial results and prepare financial forecasts. The basic financial statements are probably the most important source of numbers for managing any organization. It is extremely critical for any organization, regardless of size and complexity, to make sure that a solid accounting and financial information system has been developed and that up-to-date information is compiled. An accounting and financial information system generates detailed financial reports, including income statements, balance sheets, and statements of cash flow. It is also crucial that an accountant be available to help interpret the data provided by the accounting and financial information systems.

Although it may sound like a daunting task for small organizations to develop an accounting and financial information systems, in part because of the elaborate record-keeping and report-generating activities required, there are quite a few widely distributed bookkeeping and accounting packages for business that can be operated on inexpensive personal computers. Thus even sole proprietors can generate monthly income statements and current balance sheets with a minimum of effort. These systems also offer a convenient way to archive past records. Having a historical record of income statements and balance sheets is important in order for a business to prepare budgets and projections of future financial results.

As we continue through the remainder of this chapter, we introduce financial forecasting and budget preparation as a tool for planning purposes. We also demonstrate the relationship between sales growth and a business' capital requirements.

In order to prepare financial forecasts and budgets, a business needs to follow a sequential process.

The sequence of steps consists of the following:

1. Gathering information
2. Forecasting sales
3. Projecting profits and losses
4. Comparing to industry norms
5. Determining capital needs

All forecasts are based upon assumptions, educated guesses, and hunches. The assumptions and hunches included in a forecast should not come out of the blue, however, but rather from experience in combination with the gathering of extensive information. Since forecasts involve an unknown future, it is impossible to be 100% correct. For a business owner, attaining 80% accuracy is very good. Thus, even though a forecast is not absolute, it is better for an organization to use a forecast with an 80% level of accuracy than none at all. Proceeding blindly without any forecasts or budgets for the future increases the odds of poor future financial results and ultimately insolvency.

In the sequence just outlined, sales forecasts are prepared before any profit and loss or cash flow forecasts are made. As discussed next, it is reasonable to assume that at least some expenses will have some relationship to sales. Thus, it is fruitless to forecast expenses (and resulting profit and loss or cash flow) without using sales forecasts as a foundation.

Gathering Information

In order to prepare financial forecasts, it is first necessary to have information on hand concerning the basic factors that contribute to the success or failure of the business. See the following case study example.

 Manufacturers such as Sport Manufacturing Company (SMC) follow trends involving bookings of business, billings, and backlog that signal whether the business will be profitable. If SMC does not book new business, then its customer billings will be down and manufacturing backlog will be reduced. This can spell trouble for SMC in the form of less profitable production. Since SMC produces an item that for many consumers is a discretionary purchase, SMC needs to be aware of the first signs of a slowing economy because in this type of environment, consumers at the retail level will presumably reduce their purchases of products made by SMC and other sporting goods manufacturers.

Similar to the case study example, as witnessed in the early 2000s, a down economy reduced ticket sales, which reduced the revenue for most professional teams and was the first major economic downturn since the major facility construction boom of the 1990s. Teams that saw the downturn coming renegotiated luxury box holders' contracts and locked in the holders to long-term contracts before the downturn took place. Those that did not gather and analyze appropriate economic data were in trouble when businesses stopped signing contracts because of reduced funds.

As part of the information-gathering process, it is imperative to define the business' target markets. Key questions that must be answered include the following:

- How big are the target markets?
- What is the business' penetration of these markets?
- What is the potential that is remaining for the business to exploit in these markets?
- Who are the competitors, what are their market shares, and what is their pricing strategy?

Answers to these questions are important in order to generate more accurate revenue forecasts.

As the business projects its revenues, it is important to include a "reality check." In particular, is the future projected sales growth truly sustainable? High growth will consume substantial sums of cash and capital, as well as any capital provided by lenders and investors. It is critical to determine whether the firm has sufficient resources to sustain the level of growth built into revenue forecasts. In addition, for technology companies that invest heavily in research and development and capital equipment, high sales growth is necessary to cover costs and earn profits ("Tough Equations," 2001).

Information also needs to be obtained concerning the extent to which expenses vary directly with revenues. If most of the expenses are variable, this means that they are tied to the volume of sales. If the expenses of the firm are primarily variable, it may be possible to look at ways of reducing the costs per unit produced in order to improve profitability. When expenses are fixed, this means that they are not tied to the volume of sales. See the following case study examples.

 Examples of variable costs for SMC include costs of labor and material. If SMC finds that it is selling fewer golf clubs, it will reduce production. As production is reduced, SMC can reduce the number of people employed in production, as well as reducing the purchase of materials used in the manufacture of the golf clubs.

As an example concerning fixed expenses, it would be reasonable to assume that SMC has extensive machinery and equipment in its manufacturing facilities. The machinery and equipment, along with the manufacturing premises, are long-term capital assets whose costs are considered fixed over any particular time period. If the machinery and equipment are used in a facility that fabricates golf clubs, the annual expense is incurred even if no golf clubs are produced and sold to customers. When expenses are mostly fixed, higher profitability will be associated with higher sales because the cost per unit sold will automatically fall as sales increase. If we assume that the majority of SMC's expenses are the fixed costs associated with its machinery and equipment, SMC needs to maximize golf club sales in order to boost profitability through lowering the cost per golf club sold when sales increase. In the short run, a major constraint in SMC's attempts to maximize profitability through increased golf club sales is the maximum production capacity of the manufacturing facility. A production constraint is also a sales constraint. If SMC can produce only 800,000 golf clubs in a given year, SMC will be unable to sell more than 800,000 golf clubs annually. Even if there is demand for 1 million golf clubs per year, SMC will still be unable to sell that many golf clubs unless it can find some way to increase production.

To obtain key information that is needed in order to prepare financial forecasts and budgets, executives can look to publications issued by trade and professional organizations. Trade and professional organizations have also begun to provide information on the Internet. Small Business Institutes at colleges and universities, which are funded and sponsored by the federal government's Small Business Administration, are excellent sources of information for small business owners. SCORE, an organization that consists of retired business executives who volunteer their time, provides free consulting and information to start-ups. In addition, attending trade shows can be a way to gain insight through networking and attending seminars. Consultants, vendors, customers, and the company's own sales force can also be useful information sources. More detail on obtaining information of this type is provided in appendix C.

It is also important to obtain benchmark data, either for other firms in the industry or for the industry as a whole. Benchmark data include information on revenues, expenses, profits, net worth, and assets for other firms, making it possible to get a financial profile of the average, or typical, firm in the industry. These data can be used to construct benchmark ratios, such as profitability ratios for the average firm, that serve as a reasonableness check (comparing the results of a forecast for a particular business with the financials of the typical firm) on forecasts of sales and profits (Pratt, Reilly, & Schweihs, 2000).

 For example, SMC could conceivably find it useful to collect financial information about other manufacturing firms. In addition, as the Smiths begin their efforts to operate a fitness center, they should obtain financial information for other representative firms or for the industry as a whole in such sectors as

- health clubs,
- retail establishments, and
- service establishments.

Without such benchmarking information, the Smiths and SMC would have no idea if the breakdown of expenses versus revenues and profitability ratios as implied by their financial forecasts is realistic.

 The Smiths could rely on fitness industry data from the health club area. From this data the Smiths might learn, for example, that the average fitness-only club earns about $778 per member each year, which translates to $65 per square foot of facility space (based on 14 square feet per member). They could learn that the attrition rate is approximately 39% and that marketing costs constitute approximately 3.4% of a facility's total budget (*Profiles of Success*, 2001). On the basis of such data, the Smiths could calculate that if they have a 4,000-square-foot facility and their dues are similar to those of other clubs in the industry they should be able to generate $260,000 ($65 per square foot × 4,000 square feet) in annual revenue.

Detailed composite financial information is available from *RMA Annual Statement Studies*, available on CD-ROM and in printed format. These studies give detailed information on revenues, expenses, and profitability as reported by businesses on commercial loan applications. The *RMA Annual Statement Studies* data are broken down by detailed industry category and size of business (as measured by total assets), and include historical information that allows one to analyze historic growth in sales. Additional detailed composite financial information is available from the Internal Revenue Service. The Internal Revenue Service's company financial statistics are published by disaggregated industry categories in the following annual publications: *Corporation Source Book, Partnership Source Book,* and *Sole Proprietorship Source Book.*

Generalized industry data are also available from *U.S. Industry & Trade Outlook,* which is produced annually by the U.S. Department of Commerce and published by McGraw-Hill. *Standard & Poor's Industry Surveys* provides information on 52 basic industry groups and includes discussions of the industry's market structure, trends in the industry, the future outlook of the industry, and financials for publicly traded firms in the industry. Specifically, *Standard & Poor's Industry Surveys* provides coverage of the entertainment industry, which can serve as a reasonable proxy for many types of sport businesses.

Additional relevant information can be obtained via a thorough online search. Given the rapidly changing nature of the Internet, it is impossible to give a comprehensive guide to online sources in a textbook, but such sources can be located through the use of appropriate keywords in Internet search engines such as Yahoo!®. An example of an online site that provides useful information is Hoover's Online (**www.hoovers.com**). Hoover's Online is an Internet-based subscription service that provides financial information, major news, and background for major industry groupings, as well as for specific companies within an industry grouping. Industry groupings on Hoover's Online include "Professional Sports Teams & Organizations," "Sporting Goods Retailing," manufacturing of "Sporting Goods," and "Professional Sports Gear & Apparel."

Knowledge of an industry's SIC code—the Standard Industrial Classification code—can also enhance research. The SIC system is a government classification system for industries. There are several sport-related SICs in the 7,000 category range, including 7,199, which represents health clubs. Knowing this code could help the Smiths gain additional information from various government and nongovernment sources. As always, though, people need to remember that the data they obtain are only as good as the source.

Forecasting Sales

To generate sales forecasts for an established business, the starting point is to use the most recent full year's sales. It is useful to list sales separately by product line, by sales distribution method (e.g., direct sales, retail sales, online sales), or by geographic market.

As an example, SMC sold 4 million units in 1999. Assuming that SMC charged $15 per unit sold, its 1999 total revenues equaled $60 million. In table 5.1, SMC's 1999 revenues of $60 million are broken down by sales distribution channel, that is, by the method for distributing SMC's products to its final customers. As table 5.1 shows, SMC relies heavily on sales to retail chains, with 60% of sales through that distribution channel. There are also significant sales to independent stores and abroad. Sport Manufacturing Company has also invested in distribution on the Internet, although online sales in 1999 were still only 6% of total sales.

Once potential sales have been analyzed from various projections by sales force and marketing executives, historic sales are examined in order to project future sales. At a minimum, three to five years of the most recent historic sales should be reviewed. This allows one to examine recent trends that are useful in forecasting future sales growth.

The research process, specifically an examination of historic sales data, has shown that over the last 20 years SMC has maintained its position as a sporting goods manufacturer with seasonal sales patterns and that those sales have grown an average of 8% per year. In individual years, sales have been dependent on the strength of the U.S. economy. The forecasts for Year 2000 sales will be based on the historical information, supplemented by the experience and research of SMC's analysts.

In table 5.2, three scenarios are presented for forecasting purposes. These include a best-case scenario and a worst-case scenario, as well as a most likely scenario. The most likely scenario is based upon pulling together the best and worst cases. The two extreme cases give the analyst a way to better understand opportunities, as well as potential barriers to success (Copeland, Koller, & Murrin, 2000).

The worst-case scenario assumes that most of SMC's sales are stable and that as a result, 90% of 1999 sales is a reasonable assumption for the worst-case scenario. The 90% range is designed as a cushion in case sales are lower in a subsequent year. If SMC's historic sales had fluctuated substantially from year to year, a worst-case scenario could involve sales of even less than 90% of

Table 5.1 SMC Corp.'s 1999 Sales

	1999 Sales	Percent of total
Chain stores	$ 36,000,000	60%
Independent stores	12,525,000	21%
Individual (direct)	375,000	1%
Internet	3,750,000	6%
Foreign	6,000,000	10%
Other	1,350,000	2%
Total	**$60,000,000**	**100%**

Table 5.2 SMC Corp.'s Sales Forecast for 2000

Distribution channel	1999 Sales	Worst case	Most likely	Best case	Increase/ Decrease
Chain stores	$ 36,000,000	$ 32,400,000	$ 38,880,000	$ 43,200,000	8%
Independent stores	12,525,000	11,272,500	13,527,000	15,030,000	8%
Individual (direct)	375,000	375,000	375,000	375,000	0%
Internet	3,750,000	2,250,000	6,525,000	9,375,000	74%
Foreign	6,000,000	5,400,000	6,480,000	7,200,000	8%
Other	1,350,000	1,350,000	1,350,000	1,350,000	0%
Total	**$60,000,000**	**$53,047,500**	**$67,137,000**	**$76,530,000**	**12%**

1999 sales. In the case of sales over the Internet, that distribution channel is still in its infancy and is subject to greater risk, particularly if other manufacturers decide to use the Internet as a distribution medium. Thus in a worst-case scenario, sales over the Internet are shown as a 40% decline. Sales to individuals are expected to remain the same, even in a worst-case scenario, because SMC does not place any marketing effort into individual sales, and annual sales to individuals have stayed relatively constant over the last decade.

Note that historic sales were used to determine the worst-case scenario. In the event of a new trend that is not reflected in the historic sales information, it is very easy to underestimate the potential sales decline under the worst-case scenario. For example, if a new movement toward consolidation took place in the retail sporting goods sector and certain retail chains that had been SMC customers went out of business, SMC's sales might be subject to unforeseen declines. Furthermore, if SMC made nothing but snow skis and the winter snowfall was poor, or if SMC missed the snowboarding trend, then sales could plummet.

The best-case scenario assumes that with properly focused marketing efforts, the chain store, independent store, and foreign sales can increase by 20% under extremely favorable conditions. By contrast, since Internet sales are in their infancy, a best-case scenario includes Internet sales growing by a multiple of 2.5 in the event that SMC's efforts to enter this market segment begin to bear immediate fruit. The 2.5 times increase is just an estimate based on either an educated hunch or market expectations.

The most likely scenario represents a composite of the worst-case and best-case scenarios. The best- and worst-case scenarios do not have to be weighted evenly. Instead the weight applied to each should represent subjective judgment concerning the relative likelihood that each of these scenarios will occur. In terms of a reasonableness check, note that SMC's sales in its traditional chain store, independent store, and foreign distribution channels are expected to grow at rates that match recent historic growth rates for the business as a whole. Since the Internet is an entirely new distribution channel with a lot of upside potential for growth, Internet sales are projected to grow 74% in 2000 under a most likely scenario. The Internet sales growth causes overall projected sales growth to be 10% for the year 2000, which will surpass the 8% historic norm.

So far, we have developed a sales forecast based on a "bottom-up" approach. In effect, we have separately forecast each component of sales and then summed up the total sales across components (or distribution channels in our example) to determine total sales.

Generating a Longer-Term Forecast

Now that we have prepared a one-year sales forecast, based upon a most likely scenario, it is necessary to generate a longer-term forecast. Typically, lenders and investors require at least a three-year projection, shown in table 5.3.

In the case of SMC, we assume that in the chain store, independent store, and foreign distribution channels, sales will continue to grow at their historic 8% average annual growth rate. In the case of the Internet, we assume that growth will decline from 74% in 2000 to 40% in 2001 and 20% in 2002. This is perfectly consistent with the notion that a new business line will demonstrate extremely high sales growth that declines over time (Ross et al., 1996). We also continue to assume that sales to individuals and other sales will remain constant over time.

Table 5.3 SMC Corp.'s Three-Year Sales Forecast

Distribution channel	1999 Actual sales	2000 Most likely sales	2001 Sales	2002 Sales
Chain stores	$ 36,000,000	$ 38,880,000	$ 41,990,400	$ 45,349,632
Independent stores	12,525,000	13,527,000	14,609,160	15,777,893
Individual (direct)	375,000	375,000	375,000	375,000
Internet	3,750,000	6,525,000	9,135,000	10,962,000
Foreign	6,000,000	6,480,000	6,998,400	7,558,272
Other	1,350,000	1,350,000	1,350,000	1,350,000
Total	**$60,000,000**	**$67,137,000**	**$74,457,960**	**$81,372,797**

Special Situations

There are special situations that we have not considered in our discussion of preparing sales forecasts. These situations include

- start-ups,
- ownership changes, and
- fast growth.

Start-Ups Sales forecasts for start-ups are particularly difficult because there is no established track record for the business. In addition, trade group and industry data comprise sales figures for ongoing and successful businesses, which are not necessarily relevant for a new business. New businesses tend to have sales that are lower than the sales of an established business with the same level of expenses. In addition, new businesses tend to be strapped for the capital that is necessary to generate sales sufficient to translate into profitable financial results. As a result, pro forma balance sheets and income statements for new businesses are very speculative. This is discussed in greater detail in chapter 7.

A way of performing a reasonableness check on any sales forecast is to find data on the ratio of sales to net worth for other businesses in the same industry. These ratios are available from the previously mentioned *RMA Annual Statement Studies.* The amount of capital invested in the business or borrowed can be multiplied by a ratio of sales to net worth to derive an attainable sales level. If other manufacturers comparable to SMC, an established sporting goods manufacturer with stable earnings, have sales to net worth ratios equal to 8%, then the $67,137,000 in forecast sales for 2000 would imply net worth equal to $839,212,500 ($67,137,000 / 0.08). If SMC follows industry norms as represented by the benchmark sales to net worth ratio, and its forecast net worth is substantially less than $839,212,500, it is questionable whether SMC has sufficient investment capital to generate the projected sales.

The use of benchmarking ratios to examine a start-up is more difficult than for an established firm. For example, assume that the top 25% of firms in the industry have a net sales to net worth ratio of 15, that the bottom 25% have a net sales to net worth ratio of 8, and that the start-up has borrowed $40,000, in initial capital. This implies that if the start-up matched the performance of the top 25% of firms in the industry, its sales would equal 15 × $40,000, or $600,000. If its sales matched the bottom 25% of the industry, then projected sales would be 8 × $40,000, or $320,000. This provides a range to work with in forecasting sales.

Ownership changes If there is an ownership change, the operating history of the business may not be a useful guide to developing future sales forecasts. If the ownership change resulted from poor business performance, new ownership is probably going to institute changes in management. This means that the business must halt its negative momentum and engineer a turnaround before sales growth can occur. In addition, ownership changes can result in the loss of customers or key employees, especially in smaller, closely held businesses in which the business' success is tied to the efforts of a key person. Under these circumstances, businesses tend to have to reexamine their product lines and markets.

 For example, the Smiths might be able to sell a successful fitness facility, but memberships could plummet immediately after the sale. Perhaps members are no longer joining because the Smiths are no longer associated with the fitness facility, or perhaps the Smiths have chosen to open another facility several miles away.

This example indicates why buyers of existing small businesses often insist that the sales agreement include a noncompete clause. Noncompete clauses prevent the sellers from competing in the same line of business from a location within the same geographic region for a specified number of years. Another way around this problem is for the buyer of the business to retain the seller of the business as a consultant for a specified length of time after the sale is completed.

Fast Growth In the case of businesses that are characterized by fast-growing sales, it is a mistake to assume that this fast growth will continue forever into the future. For example, if corporate sales in the economy have been growing annually at a rate of 6% per year over the past five years and a particular business has been growing at a rate of 20% per year, it is unreasonable to assume that this divergence will continue. Typically, successful start-ups have extremely high growth rates that slow down as the business matures. Businesses that seize new market niches or enter new and growing markets are typically the ones associated with abnormally high growth, and these are the types of businesses that are at risk as other entrants, having witnessed the explosion in growth, try to steal market share (Pratt et al., 2000).

Projecting Profits and Losses

Thus far, we have generated sales forecasts. Although sales forecasts are useful for planning purposes, we are really interested in profit-and-loss projections and cash flow projections. As we discuss further on, sales can be viewed as a key driver of the expenses shown on an income statement and ultimately drive the statement of cash flow.

On the basis of the figures shown for SMC in the Introduction to the Case Studies (p. 2), as well as the sales figures in table 5.3 (p. 84), we have produced an income statement for SMC for 1999 that is shown in figure 5.1. In order to generate figure 5.1, we have assumed that the $15 million in fixed costs for SMC, as reported in the Introduction to the Case Studies, is split between depreciation ($10 million) and interest expense ($5 million). Depreciation is an accounting-based expense that represents an allowance for wear and tear on plant and equipment. Depreciation is a fixed cost to the business because it does not change with the volume of sales. Interest expense, which represents interest on money borrowed by the business, is also a fixed cost because the firm would have to repay interest expense even if it shut down production facilities. In order to calculate net income, which is income after corporate taxes are paid, in figure 5.1 we have assumed that the combined federal and state corporate tax rate is 40%.

In figure 5.1, the gross margin was calculated by subtracting cost of goods sold from sales. Cost of goods sold includes the variable costs of production. Cost of goods sold in figure 5.1 was obtained by multiplying the $7 per unit produced by the 4 million units sold. The $32 million gross margin shown in figure 5.1 indicates that SMC is earning $32 million in profits after deducting direct costs of production from sales, but not factoring in other costs of doing business. It is

important to examine gross margins because if a business has trouble covering its direct costs of production, even a restructuring and substantial reduction of administrative and overhead costs will not restore the business to profitability.

Normally, operating expenses include all other expenses, other than cost of goods sold, which represents the cost of doing business. In our example, to keep things simple we have included only administrative and selling costs and depreciation as operating expenses. The administrative and selling costs are obtained by multiplying the $1.25 cost per unit sold by the 4 million units sold. The $10 million annual depreciation expense shown in figure 5.1 represents an estimate by SMC's accountants of the cost of equipment and property that are used up by the organization in the process of producing and distributing goods and services. As noted in the discussion of financial statements earlier in this chapter, depreciation expense is not an actual cash outlay.

As shown in figure 5.1, SMC's EBIT equal $17 million. The EBIT are equal to sales less cost of goods sold less operating expenses. The EBIT measure the level of profits that are available to all investors and to pay the firm's corporate income tax liabilities.

As reported in figure 5.1, SMC also incurs $5 million in annual interest expense. **Pretax earnings,** or earnings before taxes (EBT), are equal to EBIT less interest expense. In figure 5.1, SMC's EBT equal $12 million, which means that after payment of interest to lenders, SMC has $12 million available for distribution to stockholders (owners) and to pay tax liabilities. Net income is equal to EBT minus corporate taxes. In the case of SMC, net income is $7.2 million, which equals the $12 million EBT minus $4.8 million in corporate income taxes. The company's net income represents the profits available to stockholders after accounting for cost of goods sold, operating expenses, interest expense, and corporate income taxes.

Table 5.4 consists of projections of profits over the period from 2000 through 2002, with our sales forecasts from table 5.3 (p. 84) serving as the driver of expenses and ultimately the profits shown in figure 5.1 (Copeland et al., 2000). In table 5.4, we have assumed that interest expense and depreciation expense are unchanged, since they are fixed costs.

Since cost of goods sold and selling and administrative expenses are variable costs, these expense items must grow as sales grow over the forecast period. To forecast the variable expenses, we use as an illustration the **percent of sales method.** The

	($000)
Net sales	60,000
Cost of goods sold	28,000
Gross margin	**32,000**
Selling and administrative expenses	5,000
Depreciation	10,000
Earnings before interest and taxes	**17,000**
Interest expense	5,000
Earnings before taxes	**12,000**
Taxes at 40%	4,800
Net income	**7,200**

Figure 5.1 Income statement of SMC for the year ending December 31, 1999.

Table 5.4 SMC Corp.'s Profit Forecasts for 2000-2002

	2000	**2001**	**2002**
Net sales	$ 67,137,000	$ 74,457,960	$ 81,372,797
Cost of goods sold	31,554,390	34,995,241	38,245,214
Gross margin	**35,582,610**	**39,462,719**	**43,127,583**
Selling and administrative expenses	5,370,960	5,956,637	6,509,824
Depreciation	10,000,000	10,000,000	10,000,000
Earnings before interest and taxes	**20,211,650**	**23,506,082**	**26,617,759**
Interest expense	5,000,000	5,000,000	5,000,000
Earnings before taxes	**15,211,650**	**18,506,082**	**21,617,759**
Taxes at 40%	6,084,660	7,402,433	8,647,104
Net income	**$9,126,990**	**$11,103,649**	**$12,970,655**

percent of sales method directly ties variable costs to sales, based upon assumptions concerning each variable expense as a percentage of sales. In 1999, cost of goods sold was 47% of sales while selling and administrative expense was 8% of sales. In our example, we assume that these percentages correspond to historic averages, and we assume that cost of goods sold and selling and administrative expense as a percentage of sales will remain at their 1999 percentages over the forecasting period.

Forecasts of profit and loss are shown in table 5.4 as seen in the net sales row. You should note that the percent of sales approach used to develop the three-year forecast is accurate only if financial statement ratios remain constant over time. There are times when these ratios may not be constant, for example when there are economies of scale. When economies of scale exist, the average cost per unit of sales declines as sales increase, which implies changing ratios of expense items to sales over time. Economies of scale are particularly prevalent when a firm has fixed costs that represent a substantial portion of total costs.

As an example, if a firm has $10 million in fixed costs associated with operating factories, the fixed cost per unit sold is $20 if the firm sells 500,000 units, but $10 if the firm sells 1 million units. The fixed cost per unit sold is calculated by dividing the total fixed cost by the total number of units sold (i.e., $10,000,000 / 500,000). If the variable cost per unit sold is $2, then total cost per unit sold (variable cost per unit sold plus fixed cost per unit sold) equals $22 per unit sold when the firm's annual sales equal 500,000 units, and $12 per unit sold when sales equal 1 million units. Clearly, cost per unit sold declines as sales increase. When expenses are not expected to

be a constant percentage of sales, it may be necessary to employ sophisticated statistical techniques, such as regression analysis, that are beyond the scope of this text, to forecast the variable expense items. Such economies of scale may actually exist for a manufacturer like SMC.

Comparing to Industry Norms

Once profit-and-loss projections have been computed, it is worth referring to industry norms as a reasonableness check. Using the information sources discussed earlier, it is possible to obtain various income entries as percentages of sales for the average firm in an industry. In the case of *RMA Annual Statement Studies*, such data are also available for firms that are the top 25% and bottom 25% performers. These figures provide reasonableness checks for the expense forecasts derived from sales forecasts. Data on industry norms for ratios such as net income to net worth (return on equity) are available as well for assessing the reasonableness of financial projections.

 Assume that SMC's net worth is projected to equal $76 million in 2000. On the basis of SMC's projected $9,126,990 net income for 2000 (see table 5.4), SMC's return on equity is equal to $9,126,990 / $76,000,000, or 12%. If the average ROE for firms comparable to SMC is 13%, then the profit projections certainly are reasonable. If, on the other hand, comparable firms are earning 8% rates of ROE, then it might be advisable to revisit SMC's profit-and-loss projections, unless there is something unique about SMC that differentiates it from other firms in the same market or industry.

Determining Capital Needs

Once sales and profit forecasts are complete, it is necessary to see whether the forecast sales and profits can be accomplished with the firm's current assets. If the forecast sales and profits grow at too high a rate in the future, it may be necessary for a company to obtain additional capital or assets in the form of inventory and fixed assets. These assets can be acquired only with money obtained through either increased borrowing or the issuance of stock. If the company cannot raise the money to obtain the capital, it can face a crisis caused by inability to finance the high growth.

To determine capital needs, sustainable growth rate analysis is used. If the annual sales growth rate exceeds the sustainable annual growth rate, then external capital is needed to finance the necessary growth. The sustainable growth rate is calculated as follows:

(5.30) $g^* = [P(1 - D)(1 + L)] / [T - P(1 - D)(1 + L)]$

g^* = sustainable growth

P = net income / sales

D = target level of dividends paid out to stock holders / net income

L = total liabilities / net worth

T = total assets / net worth

 From our example in figure 5.1 (p. 86), net sales in 1999 for SMC equaled $60 million, and net income equaled $7.2 million. Thus P = 12%. Assume that SMC's board sets D at 50% and that the calculations for L and T are 50% and 80%, respectively. Note that L and T are hypothetical numbers to make the example read better.

$$g^* = [0.12(1 - 0.50)(1 + 0.50)] /$$
$$[0.80 - 0.12(1 - 0.50)(1 + 0.50)]$$
$$= 0.09 / 0.51$$
$$= .12676, \text{ or } 12.676\%$$

Based upon the formula above, the sustainable growth rate is 12.7%. Note that this is just above the 12% projected growth rate used to project future annual profits for SMC in table 5.2 (p. 83). Consequently, no external capital requirements are needed to fund SMC's projected sales growth.

On the basis of SMC's projected 12% sales growth rate, SMC will barely miss needing a capital infusion to fund growth. Assume that SMC's actual annual growth in sales ended up averaging 14% per year over the next several years, instead of the forecast 12% per year. The company's growth would exceed the 12.7% sustainable growth rate, and SMC would require additional capital to fund its growth. The company's options for obtaining new capital would be to issue new common stock, reduce dividend payouts to current stockholders, or increase borrowing (see chapters 8 through 10). The sustainable growth rate formula also implies that SMC can reduce its assets-to-sales ratio by renting and leasing, as opposed to owning fixed assets, since this will reduce the need for capital. In addition, if SMC is a closely held business, reducing compensation to owners is an option.

Note that our discussion of capital and cash needs did not focus on variations of capital needs during the course of a year when businesses face seasonal sales patterns. For example, SMC is characterized by lower sales in December and January relative to the rest of the year. Even though it might appear that SMC does not have to finance sales growth through a capital infusion, SMC still needs to have cash available to meet operating expenses in December and January when cash inflows are relatively lower. One way in which businesses handle such seasonal patterns in demand is through bank lines of credit, which are drawn down during slow periods of demand and then repaid when sales improve.

Sustainable growth rate analysis suggests that when planning for high rates of sales growth, businesses have to factor in the likelihood of further capital infusions. High sales growth uses up cash and capital.

> *In order to plan for the future, businesses prepare financial forecasts and budgets through a series of steps that begin with gathering information and end with determining future capital needs.*

Break-Even Analysis

So far this chapter has covered various financial calculations to determine strengths and weaknesses and examined forecasting and planning. A key concept that embodies all three elements is break-even analysis. Because of its relevance to inventory and production management in addition to its usefulness for guidance in financial forecasting and planning, break-even analysis is also covered in chapter 13.

Break-even analysis is used to determine the level of unit sales that is required for the business to just cover its expenses. In other words, break-even analysis provides the base sales level that is needed to ensure profitability. **Break-even** occurs when EBIT equal zero, that is, when pretax operating profits, independent of financing considerations, are zero. Break-even can be expressed as

(5.31)   EBIT = revenues − variable costs − fixed costs of production = 0

The preceding equation can also be expressed as

(5.31) $EBIT = PQ − VQ − F = 0$

EBIT = earnings before interest and taxes

P = the selling price per unit sold

V = the variable cost per unit sold

F = the fixed costs of production

Q = unit sales

Equation (5.32) can be solved in order to determine the break-even level of unit sales (Q_{BE}) as follows:

(5.32) $Q_{BE} = F / (P − V)$

Q_{BE} = break-even level of unit sales

F = the fixed costs of production

P = the selling price per unit

V= the variable cost per unit sold

The break-even formula in equation (5.32) states that the break-even level of unit sales will be higher if fixed costs are higher. The difference between unit price and unit variable cost (P − V) can be viewed as the gross profit per unit sold. The higher the level of gross profit per unit sold, the lower will be the number of units that need to be sold to break even.

The break-even formula can be demonstrated using the assumptions concerning SMC's 1999 financials from earlier in the chapter. The company's per unit price (P) is $15. The per unit variable cost (V) is $8.25, which is the sum of the $7 per unit in direct manufacturing costs and the $1.25 per unit in selling and administrative costs. The fixed cost of production is $15 million, which is the sum of the $10 million depreciation expense and the $5 million interest expenses. Plugging these values into the break-even formula, we get

Q_{BE} = $15,000,000 / ($15 − $8.25) = 2,222,222 units

As our analysis shows, the 4 million units that are driving the 1999 financial results for SMC are substantially above the number of units required to just break even. On the basis of the break-even formula, SMC's annual fixed costs would have to increase to $27 million per year in order for SMC to just be breaking even at 4 million units.

Note also that SMC's per unit gross profit margin on each sale is equal to $15 − $8.25, or $6.75 per unit sold. If fixed costs remain at $15 million per year, the per unit gross profit margin would have to be reduced to $3.75 in order for SMC to be breaking even at 4 million units. This indicates that SMC is in good shape because any reductions in per unit profits could only come about through severe price reductions, significantly reduced sales, or substantial increases in variable costs.

Break-even analysis helps a business determine the point at which revenues will be sufficient to cover the business' expenses.

CONCLUSION

In this chapter we discuss the rudiments of financial statement analysis, as well as financial forecasting and planning. Specifically, we provide an introduction to financial statements. We discuss the elements of the balance sheet, which summarizes the firm's financial condition at a particular point in time, and the contents of the income statement, which is used to measure a business' profitability over a period of time. The balance sheet and the income statement provide a lead-in to explain changes in the cash position of a firm over some period of time. Specifically, we describe changes in cash flows that result from operations, investing activity, and financing. The elements of the balance sheet and income statement are used to compute financial ratios that summarize the firm's liquidity, activity, financial leverage, profitability, and market value.

We also review methods of forecasting future sales and using the sales forecasts to project future profits. Finally, we discuss how sales and profit forecasts are used in the planning process to determine capital needs and break-even sales.

ASSIGNMENTS

1. Prepare an income statement for the Tallahassee Flyers minor league baseball team using the

following information. Assume that the Flyers pay corporate income tax equal to 35% of the difference between EBIT and interest expense.

Operating revenues from ticket sales and advertising	$500,000
Team and game expenses	200,000
Administrative expenses	100,000
Interest expense	50,000

2. Use the following data for the Acme Racquet Company to construct the company's balance sheet.

Cash	$ 4,000
Patents	82,000
Accounts payable	6,000
Accounts receivable	8,000
Taxes payable	2,000
Machinery	34,000
Bonds payable	7,000
Accumulated retained earnings	6,000
Capital surplus	19,000

3. What are the differences between accounting-based measures of profits and cash flow?

4. Explain why the leverage of a sporting goods manufacturer might be different from that of a professional sport team.

5. Discuss how companies can reduce the break-even level of sales.

6. How would reducing the break-even level of sales affect a company's financial results during a general downturn in the economy?

7. Discuss the implications of high growth for a company.

8. Discuss the problems inherent in projecting sales and profit and loss for a start-up company.

RESEARCH PROJECTS

1. Examine the financials of a publicly traded sport company or corporation. Assess that company's financial condition in terms of its liquidity, financial leverage, profitability, activity, and PE ratio.

2. Examine the financials of a publicly traded sport company or corporation. Prepare a three-year forecast of sales and profit and loss.

3. On the basis of current-year financials for a publicly traded sport company or corporation, calculate the sustainable growth rate.

CLASS DISCUSSION TOPICS

1. Discuss the pros and cons of using the various measures of profitability to examine a company's performance.

2. Discuss the pros and cons of using the measures of leverage to assess whether a company faces financial distress.

3. How would you finance the high growth of a business like Nike if you were not willing to borrow or raise additional capital?

4. How do you reconcile unique characteristics about your business with the information gained through use of industry averages to forecast sales and profit and loss?

Time Value of Money

CHAPTER OBJECTIVES

After studying this chapter, you should be able to do the following:

- Understand the concept of future value, including its calculation for a single amount of cash received today.
- Understand the concept of present value, including calculation of the present value of a single payment at a particular time in the future.
- Calculate the present value of multiple payments received in the future, including perpetuities and annuities.
- Describe basic concepts of risk and return and their relationship to computing the present value of future payments.
- Use risk statistics to define risk, including relating the performance of financial assets to risk.

The book to this point has highlighted the importance of finance in making business decisions and the issues associated with determining value based on various ratios or industry benchmarking standards. However, any analysis cannot be complete without examining the time value of money. It is impossible to examine a $1 investment today versus one from 50 years ago without realizing that $1 from 50 years ago might be worth $50 in today's dollars. This chapter highlights why money is sensitive to time and how to calculate changes in value based on time constraints.

How Much Is Money Worth?

In chapter 5 we discussed how to analyze sales and costs, evaluate cash flows, measure profitability, and prepare financial forecasts. A key issue in valuing these flows is their timing. A dollar received today is worth more than a dollar received in the future. **Time value of money** represents the concept that money decreases in value over time. With this concept in mind, any investor or business needs to examine the time in which investment decisions will be made and to critically examine how that time frame will ultimately affect the invested amount and projected payout.

Whenever an investment takes time to collect, there is a greater likelihood of a larger return as well as a greater likelihood of loss. That is, if an investment takes long to mature it might generate a significant return if the money is not lost due to the investment going bad. That is why some investors prefer to have a safe investment, such as government bonds, and forgo a potentially larger future return, which could have possibly been received if the money was invested in a **junk bond** that would have paid a higher interest rate but would have been a riskier investment. As long as the government bond pays more than the current rate of inflation, the government bond would be a secure investment with a return that exceeds the time value of money. However, if inflation rises significantly, then the bond's value would be lost due to the time value of money making the earnings worth less than if the bond paid a return greater than the current inflation rate. A simple example will illustrate this.

 Assume that Sport Manufacturing Company (SMC) has a parcel of real estate that it wishes to sell. Assume that SMC has lined up two prospective buyers. One buyer, Speedy Enterprises, is willing to enter into a contract to pay $100,000 immediately for the parcel of land. A second buyer, Acme Limited, has offered to pay $102,500 for the land, but with actual payment to be made in one year's time. At first glance, it may appear that SMC should take the Acme Limited offer, since Acme is willing to pay more for the land, but looks can be deceiving!

The way to evaluate which offer SMC should accept is to note that if SMC accepted the offer from Speedy Enterprises, it could hypothetically deposit the funds in a one-year certificate of deposit (CD) that earns 5% interest per year. Sport Manufacturing Company would start out with $100,000 in the bank (principal) and would earn interest equal to $0.05 \times \$100,000$. As a result, SMC would have the following on deposit in one year:

$$\$100,000 + 0.05 \times \$100,000 = \$105,000$$
$$\text{or}$$
$$\$100,000 \times 1.05 = \$105,000$$

In other words, SMC would have on deposit its initial $100,000 principal plus $5,000 in interest, which equals $105,000. Factoring in the interest earned during the year, the initial principal is multiplied by (1.05), that is, 1 plus the interest rate, to obtain the $105,000 on deposit at the end of the year.

By contrast, if SMC accepted the Acme offer, it would have only $102,500 available in one year, compared to the $105,000 it would have on hand in one year if it accepted the Speedy offer. By taking the offer from Acme, SMC would have $2,500 less than if it had invested the initial $100,000 in the one-year CD. Clearly, SMC is better off taking the offer from Speedy Enterprises.

In working through this example we made use of the concept of future value. **Future value** (FV) is the value of an initial lump sum of money after it is invested over one or more periods of time. The future value in one year's time of the $100,000 received from Speedy Enterprises is $105,000. Note that the future value of any given sum reflects the interest earned on that investment.

Another way of looking at this example is to examine how much money SMC must deposit in a one-year CD that earns 5% in order to have $102,500 in one year. The amount of money that would yield $102,500 if invested today at a 5% interest rate is the **present value** (PV) of $102,500 received in one year. We can solve for this PV as follows:

(6.1) $$PV \times 1.05 = \$102,500$$

Solving for PV gives us:

(6.2) $$PV = \$102,500 / 1.05 = \$97,619$$

In general, the formula for the present value can be written as shown in equation (6.3).

(6.3) $$PV = C_1 / (1 + r)$$

C_1 = cash flow received at the end of one year

r = appropriate interest rate

The variable r, the interest rate or percentage return that can be earned on an initial amount of money, is also known as the **discount rate.** In our example, the 5% annual return that SMC earns on its financial investment, that is, a one-year CD, is used as the discount rate in order to value the $102,500 received in one year.

Our analysis of present value indicates that a payment of $102,500 received in one year from Acme has a present value of $97,619 today. In other words, at a 5% interest rate, SMC would find receiving $97,619 today from Acme or $102,500 in one year equally acceptable alternatives. Given $97,619 today, the company can deposit the funds in a one-year CD that will allow it to receive $102,500 in one year.

Since the offer by Speedy Enterprises was for $100,000 to be received today, the Speedy Enterprises offer has a present value of $100,000. Thus our present value analysis suggests that SMC should take the Speedy Enterprises offer.

Future Value More Than One Period Into the Future

So far, we have looked at the concept of present value and future value in the context of cash flows over a single period of time. We will now show how this can be generalized over more than one period. This process is critical because most business deals do not start and end in one year, but rather last several years.

Assume that Adrian Jones owns shares of SMC common stock and that the return on SMC stock is 8%. To keep things simple, let us also assume that Jones paid $1 per share for SMC's common stock. At the end of one year, she will have $1 plus the return on that dollar at r% for each share. Since r% equals 8%, she will have at the end of one year:

$$\$1 + \$1r = \$1 \times (1 + r)$$
$$= \$1 \times 1.08$$
$$= \$1.08$$

r = expected rate of return

At the end of the year, Jones has two choices. She can cash out her stock and take the $1.08 per share or hold the stock for a second year. This process of holding the stock and accruing a further return over the second year is what is referred to as **compounding.**

If Jones decides to hold the stock for another year, then at the end of two years she will have

$$\$1 \times (1 + r) \times (1 + r) = \$1 \times (1 + r)^2$$
$$= \$1 \times (1.08) \times (1.08)$$
$$= \$1 \times (1.08)^2$$
$$= \$1.1664$$

At the end of two years, she will have transformed $1.00 into $1.1664. Notice that at the end of two years, she will generate $0.1664 in **compound interest** or return. That is, each payment of interest or return that is reinvested earns a return also.

This process can be generalized over many periods of time **(t)** by the following formula for the future value (FV) of an investment:

(6.4) $$FV = C_0 \times (1 + r)^t$$

C_0 = the initial amount of cash that is invested today

r = the interest rate or rate of return

t = the number of years over which the cash is invested.

We can do this calculation for the example by hand or with the help of a table. Table A.1 in appendix A (pp. 310–311) presents future values of $1 at the end of t periods, which means a variable number of time periods into the future over which the $1 is earning interest. Traditionally, t periods on a future value chart range from 1 year to 20 or 30 years. To use the table, locate the appropriate interest rate or return on the horizontal axis and the appropriate number of periods on the vertical axis. For example, you could find that the future value of $1 that is received two years into the future is $1.1664. This figure is reached if you assume an 8% rate of return. If you started out with $500 and earned an 8% annual return over two years, then the future value at the end of two years would be:

(6.5) $FV = 500 \times 1.1664$
  $= \$583.20$

As another example, suppose an investor buys a \$1,000 bond issued by SMC. The bond pays 10% interest and is redeemable in 20 years. Going to table A.1 (pp. 310–311), you can look at 20 years as the t period and then go across to 10% interest. The number on the chart is 6.1159. Thus, FV = \$1,000 × 6.1159, which yields a future value for the \$1,000 investment after 20 years of \$6,116. Through compounding interest, the bond increases more than sixfold if kept for the entire 20 years. This example highlights how the federal government can sell U.S. bonds for \$50 now and guarantee payment of \$100 in 10 years: through compounding, the \$50 investment can produce a 4 to 5 times greater return in 10 years while still allowing the government to pay the investor double his money.

Present Value Over More Than One Period Into the Future

Assume that James Slugger has signed a contract including \$2 million in deferred compensation that will be paid at the end of two years. Assume that if he were to receive compensation today, he could invest that money in a financial vehicle (such as a CD) that earns a 4% annual return. We would like to know how much money received today would be worth \$2 million in two years after earning a 4% annual return for two years. This can be written as

(6.6) $PV \times (1 + r)^t = FA$

PV = present value

r = annual rate of return

t = number of years

FA = future value

  $PV \times (1.04)^2 = \$2,000,000$

In (6.6), PV stands for present value, the amount of money that would have to be invested today in order to grow to \$2 million in two years.
Solving for PV in (6.6), we get

(6.7) $PV = \$2,000,000 / (1.04)^2$
  $= \$2,000,000 / 1.0816$
  $= \$1,849,112$

Equation (6.7) indicates that if Slugger received \$1,849,112 today, invested it, and earned a 4% an-

nual return, he would have \$2 million at the end of two years. This process of obtaining a present value is known as **discounting.** Based on equation 6.7, the \$2 million is discounted by a **discount factor,** or **present value factor,** which equals 0.9246 [1 / (1.04)²] in this example. Using this discount factor we can calculate the present value as 2,000,000 × 0.9246, or \$1,849,200 when rounded up.

An alternative way to calculate the results obtained in (6.7) is to use table A.2 in appendix A (pp. 312–313) in order to obtain a present value factor. This table shows the present value of \$1 to be received after t periods. To use the table, locate the appropriate number of periods on the vertical axis and the interest rate on the horizontal axis. In our example, the number of periods is 2 and the interest rate is 4%. Thus the present value factor is 0.9246. If we multiply \$2 million by the present value factor 0.9246, we find that the present value of \$2 million received in two years is \$1,849,200.

In general, the present value of a sum of money received t periods in the future can be written as

(6.8) $PV = C_t / (1 + r)t = C_t \times PVF_{r,t}$

C_t = the cash flow received at the end of t periods

$PVF_{r,t}$ = the appropriate present value factor for \$1 received t periods into the future

r = annual return of interest

We can extend this example to finding the present value of multiple payments. Assume that Carrie Smith, a player in the Women's National Basketball Association, has signed a contract that will pay her \$100,000 immediately, \$110,000 at the end of one year, and \$115,000 at the end of two years. Assume that she can earn a 4% annual return investing the money. The present value of the cash flows is shown in table 6.1.

Table 6.1 Present Value of Carrie Smith's Cash Flows Over Several Years

Year	Cash flow (\$)	Present value factor	Present value (\$)
0	100,000	1.0000	100,000
1	110,000	0.9615	105,769
2	115,000	0.9246	106,324
Total			**\$312,093**

The present value of the cash flows under this contract equals $312,093. In other words, the payment structure under this contract is equivalent to paying Smith $312,093 in one lump sum today.

> *Future value refers to the value of an initial sum of money after it is invested over one or more periods of time. Present value is the current value of a future amount of money.*

Perpetuities and Annuities

For certain types of finance problems, there are shortcuts for calculating present values. In particular, we discuss shortcut methods for two types of cash flow streams:

1. Perpetuities
2. Annuities

Perpetuities

A **perpetuity** consists of a single cash flow per year forever into the future. Although perpetuities may not seem to have any real-world relevance, there are certain financial instruments that are in effect perpetuities. These instruments are called consols, which are bonds issued by the British government. The holder of a consol receives yearly interest from the British government forever into the future. As a hypothetical sport example, imagine a solid company such as Nike agreeing to give the founder and his family, for an unlimited number of generations, a $1 million per year payment for eternity. Although consols are not common, people do use them. The present value of a perpetuity is equal to

(6.9) $PV = C / (1 + r) + C / (1 + r)^2 + C(1 + r)^3 + \ldots$

C = a constant annual cash flow

r = the interest rate or rate of return

The dots at the end of the formula indicate that there are an infinite number of terms that complete the formula. Equation (6.9) is an example of what math texts call an infinite series. Based on mathematical formulas used to solve infinite series, (6.9) can be simplified to

(6.10) $PV = C / r$

In other words, the present value of a perpetuity is simply the annual cash flow divided by its discount rate (Ross, Westerfield, & Jaffe, 1996). Assume that the perpetuity pays $100 per year at an interest rate of 8%; then the present value of the perpetuity is

(6.11) $PV = \$100 / 0.08$
                         $= \$1,250$

If interest rates fell to 6%, the present value of the perpetuity would be

(6.12) $PV = \$100 / 0.06$
                         $= \$1,666.67$

Note that formulas (6.11) and (6.12) indicate that the value of the perpetuity rises as the interest rate declines and falls as the interest rate increases. This is an illustration of a general principle, which is that the present value of any stream of cash flows (whether or not they are in the form of a perpetuity) is inversely related to the discount rate. At higher interest rates, the present value of any future cash flows declines because one can start out with a smaller initial lump sum; as this sum earns a return, it will grow to equal the future cash flow.

Annuities

An **annuity** is a constant stream of payments that is received for a fixed number of periods. Annuities are common in the real world. Home mortgages, leases, and pensions paid at retirement are all examples of annuities. When evaluating annuities, we utilize the following formula:

(6.13) $PV = C / (1 + r) + C / (1 + r)^2 + C / (1 + r)^3 + \ldots + C / (1 + r)^t$

PV = present value

C = constant cash flow per period

r = annual rate of return

t = number of periods during which the cash flow will be received

Equation (6.13) is cumbersome, but fortunately, it can be simplified to yield the following formula for an annuity that is paid over T periods (Ross, Westerfield & Jaffe, 1996):

(6.14) $PV = C\{1 - [1 / (1 + r)^n]\} / r$

PV = present value

C = constant cash flow per period

r = annual rate of return

t = number of periods during which the cash flow will be received

Calculating Rick Pitino's Compensation Package

An example of an annuity is the compensation package that was received by Rick Pitino, the former president and director of basketball operations and head coach of the Boston Celtics. On May 6, 1997, Pitino signed a contract that would pay $6,750,000 in salary through May 6, 2003.[1] For our purposes, this is treated as a six-year annuity, effective May 6, 1997. If the appropriate discount rate is 7%, then plugging these values into equation (6.14), we obtain

$$(6.15) \qquad PV = \$6,750,000 \times \{1 - [1 / (1.07)^6]\} / 0.07$$
$$= periodic\ payment \times annuity\ factor$$
$$= \$6,750,000 \times 4.7665$$
$$= \$32,173,875$$

The present value of Pitino's contract, as of May 6, 1997, when he signed it (and assuming a 7% discount rate), equaled $32,173,875. The numbers in braces in equation (6.15) are the present value factor for an annuity. In this example involving the value of Pitino's salary, the present value factor for the annuity equals 4.7665. Table A.3 in appendix A (pp. 314–315) is titled "Present Value of $1 per Period for t Periods." Again, interest rates are shown on the horizontal axis, and number of periods is shown on the vertical axis. Consulting the table, you will see that for an interest rate of 7% and an annuity that is received for six periods, the present value factor is 4.7665, which we obtained in the calculation in (6.15).

In doing these calculations of the value of Rick Pitino's contract at the time it was signed, we have not factored in any potential uncertainty concerning the receipt of salary in the future. This uncertainty can be viewed as risk, which is our next topic.

Perpetuities, which consist of a single cash flow forever into the future, are not common in the United States. In contrast, annuities, which consist of single payments received for a fixed number of periods, are very common.

Risk

When we calculated the present value of future cash flows, we did not discuss how to choose a discount rate. As we explain here, the choice of discount rates is tied to the risk of the future cash flows. By risk, we are referring to uncertainty concerning the future cash flows.

Whenever we compute the present value of a stream of future cash flows, we do not know with 100% certainty that those cash flows will be received. In the previous sidebar, we calculated the present value of a portion of Pitino's compensation package, as of May 6, 1997, when he was named president and director of basketball operations and head coach of the Boston Celtics. In that example, we calculated the cash flows without making any allowances for future uncertainty about whether Pitino would actually re-

ceive all of that compensation. As it happened, Pitino resigned from the Boston Celtics in January 2001 and as a result would not receive all of the compensation that was included in his initial employment contract ("Pitino Resigns as Celtics Coach, President," 2001).

A common way to adjust for uncertainty is to use a discount rate that reflects the riskiness of the cash flows. As we will show, the higher the level of risk of a financial instrument, the higher its rate of return. This implies that we need to use higher discount rates when there is greater riskiness associated with the cash flows being valued.

Returns

In order to measure risk, we need to examine the behavior of returns on different types of financial assets. Thus, before we go any further, it is necessary to focus on what we mean by the term "return." As a first step, we wish to distinguish between dollar returns and rates of return.

 Assume that you bought 100 shares of stock in SMC at $10 per share. Your initial investment would be equal to

---

[1]This information was obtained from Form 10-K for the fiscal year ending June 30, 2000, filed with the Securities and Exchange Commission by Boston Celtics Partnership II on September 15, 2000. These figures do not include an additional $2 million per year in salary paid from May 6, 2003, through May 6, 2007, and bonuses that were also part of Pitino's compensation package.

$$100 \text{ shares} \times \$10 = \$1,000$$

Suppose that SMC paid an annual dividend to all shareholders equal to $0.50 per share. During the year, you would receive dividend income equal to

$$100 \text{ shares} \times \$0.50 = \$50$$

In addition, assume that the price of SMC's stock increased over the year to $11 per share. Since the stock increased in price, you would have a capital gain equal to the change in the stock price over the year multiplied by the number of shares held or

$$
\begin{aligned}
\text{capital gain} &= (\text{current price} - \text{initial price}) \times \\
&\quad \text{number of shares} \\
&= (\$11 - \$10) \times 100 \text{ shares} \\
&= \$100
\end{aligned}
$$

The capital gain is equal to the dollar increase in the value of the SMC stock.

Conversely, if the stock declined in price to $9 per share, there would be a capital loss (the negative change in price over the year) equal to

$$
\begin{aligned}
\text{capital loss} &= (\$9 - \$10) \times 100 \text{ shares} \\
&= -\$100
\end{aligned}
$$

Since the stock declined in value over the year, the capital loss is equal to the dollar decline in the value of the stock.

In general, capital gain is defined as the dollar amount by which a financial instrument, for example, shares of stock, changes over some time period. The term *capital loss* is used when the value of the financial instrument declines.

The **capital gain or loss,** like the dividend income, is part of the total return earned by stockholders. In general, the total dollar return on a security is

$$
\begin{aligned}
\text{total dollar return} = \text{capital gain or loss} + \\
\text{dividend income}
\end{aligned}
$$

In our first example with the increase in the price of the stock, the total dollar return is equal to

$$
\begin{aligned}
\text{total dollar return} &= \$100 + \$50 \\
&= \$150
\end{aligned}
$$

In our second example with a decreased stock price, the total dollar return is equal to

$$
\begin{aligned}
\text{total dollar return} &= -\$100 + 50 \\
&= -\$50
\end{aligned}
$$

Rates of return allow us to measure gains and losses in percentage terms. In particular, they pro-

vide us with a means to standardize measuring the performance of a financial asset, regardless of the dollar amount invested, which is useful for comparing the performance of different financial assets. Going back to our earlier example, assume that the initial price of the stock (P_0) is $10, that at the end of one year the price of the stock (P_1) is $11, and that the dividend paid per share (D_{t+1}) is $0.50. The return on dividend, called the dividend yield, is equal to the dividend divided by the initial price of the stock, or

$$D_{t+1} / P_0$$

D_{t+1} = dividend paid per share in a given year

P_0 = price when the stock was initially purchased

$$\text{or } \$0.50 / \$10 = 0.05 = 5\%$$

The rate of return resulting from the capital gain is equal to the change in the price of the stock over the year divided by the initial price.

$$\text{rate of return} = (P_1 - P_0) / P_0$$

P_0 = price when the stock was initially purchased

P_1 = stock price at the end of year 1

If the stock price increases to $11 per share, then the rate of return resulting from the capital gain is equal to

$$
\begin{aligned}
\text{rate of return} &= (\$11 - \$10) / \$10 \\
&= \$1 / \$10 \\
&= 0.10, \text{ or } 10\%
\end{aligned}
$$

We now combine our results to obtain the total return, from both the dividend payout and the capital gain, which is equal to

$$
\begin{aligned}
\text{total return} &= \text{dividend return} + \\
&\quad \text{return resulting from the} \\
&\quad \text{capital gain} \\
&= 5\% + 10\% \\
&= 15\%
\end{aligned}
$$

Risk Statistics

Now that we have discussed how to measure returns, we need to define what we mean by risk. In a nutshell, one can measure the risk of any financial asset by examining the extent to which the returns on that asset fluctuate over time. In particular, we want to measure the performance of the asset with reference to the extent to which the returns fluctuate relative to their average value. This requires us to develop some statistical measures of performance and risk.

The stock returns shown in table 6.2 are for the portfolio of stocks that make up the Standard & Poor (S&P) 500 Composite Index. Given data such

Table 6.2 S&P 500 Composite Index Returns From 1960 Through 2001

Year	Annual percent return	Year	Annual percent return
1960	–2.67%	1981	7.80%
1961	18.66%	1982	–6.51%
1962	–5.87%	1983	34.00%
1963	12.01%	1984	0.03%
1964	16.46%	1985	16.44%
1965	8.36%	1986	26.49%
1966	–3.30%	1987	21.36%
1967	7.82%	1988	–7.34%
1968	7.36%	1989	21.46%
1969	–0.87%	1990	3.64%
1970	–14.94%	1991	12.43%
1971	18.11%	1992	10.52%
1972	11.10%	1993	8.58%
1973	–1.62%	1994	2.00%
1974	–22.88%	1995	17.66%
1975	4.00%	1996	23.77%
1976	18.40%	1997	30.27%
1977	–3.73%	1998	24.28%
1978	–2.22%	1999	22.28%
1979	7.28%	2000	7.53%
1980	15.31%	2001	–16.33%

Average	**8.26%**
Standard deviation	**12.84%**

as those shown in table 6.2, we can calculate the average or mean. To compute the mean, we add up all of the annual returns and divide by 42 because we have 42 years of data. If R_t is the rate of return in year t, then the formula for the average rate of return $\bar{R}$ over t years is

$$\bar{R} = (R_1 + R_2 + \ldots + R_t) / t$$

$\bar{R}$ = average rate of return

t = number of years

The mean of the returns from 1960 to 2001, shown in table 6.2, is 8.26%. The mean tells us what the average of the annual returns is for a particular time period. In other words, in our example, annual returns on average tended to be 8.26%. But an examination of table 6.2 reveals that in any given year, the return can be either above or below the average. For example, even though the average return tended to be 8.26% over the 42-year period from 1960 to 2001, in 12 of those years the return was actually negative.

Since returns in any year of a historic period can differ from the average, we want to measure the extent to which this occurs for a sample of returns. The most common measures of dispersion or variability are the **variance** and its square root, the standard deviation. The variance (s^2) of a sample of annual returns over t years is equal to

$$s^2 = [1 / (t-1)] [(R_1 - \bar{R})^2 + (R_2 - \bar{R})^2 + (R_3 - \bar{R})^2 + \ldots + (R_t - \bar{R})^2]$$

This formula instructs us that in order to calculate the variance, it is necessary to take each of the individual annual returns, subtract the average return $\bar{R}$, square the result, and add all the years together. We then divide the result by the number of years minus one. The standard deviation (s) is the square root of the variance as follows:

$$s = \sqrt{s^2}$$

 To see the calculation of these statistics as used to analyze the performance of financial securities, assume that SMC issues common stock and that its returns from 1997 through 2000 equaled 0.1170, 0.1236, 0.3896, and –0.0965, respectively. The average return for SMC from 1997 through 2000 is calculated as:

$$\bar{R} = (R_1 + R_2 + R_3 + R_4) / 4$$
$$= [0.1170 + 0.1236 + 0.3896 + (-0.0965)] / 4$$
$$= 0.5337 / 4$$
$$= 0.1334$$

The variance in SMC's returns over this four-year period is calculated as follows[2]:

$$s^2 = 0.0396$$

The standard deviation, which is the square root of the variance, is

$$s = \sqrt{0.0396} = 0.1990$$

---

[2]The formal calculation of the variance using our formula is:

$s^2 = [1 / (4 - 1)] [(R_1 - \bar{R})^2 + (R_2 - \bar{R})^2 + (R_3 - \bar{R})^2 + (R_4 - \bar{R})^2]$
$= [1 / 3][(0.1170 - 0.1334)^2 + (0.1236 - 0.1334)^2 + (0.3896 - 0.1334)^2 + (-0.0965 - 0.1334)^2]$
$= (1 / 3) (0.1189) = 0.0396$

The standard deviation is a measure of the spread, or dispersion, of a sample. The significance of the standard deviation is that unlike the variance, it is measured in the same units as the returns in our sample. Statistical theory suggests that there is a probability of approximately 2/3 that the observations in a sample are in a range between the mean less the standard deviation and the mean plus the standard deviation.[3] Going back to our example, there is a probability of approximately 2/3 that the returns lie between (0.1334 – 0.1990) and (0.1334 + 0.1990), that is, between –0.0656 and 0.3324.

As shown in table 6.2, the standard deviation of the annual returns in the S&P 500 Composite Index equals 12.84% from 1960 through 2001. This means that for the years 1960 through 2001, there is approximately a 2/3 probability that the annual returns for the S&P 500 Composite Index lie between (8.26% – 12.84%) and (8.26% + 12.84%), or between –4.58% and 21.10%.

Average Returns and Risk

Table 6.3 consists of summary statistics concerning annual returns for the portfolio of stocks that make up the S&P 500 Composite Index. In addition, the table includes summary statistics for three-month U.S. Treasury bills. What stands out in table 6.3 is that the standard deviation of the returns on three-month U.S. Treasury bills is very small relative to that for common stocks. Treasury bills are sold once per week by the federal government at an auction. Treasury bills typically mature in less than a year. Since the federal government can use its taxing power to pay its debt obligations, this debt has very little likelihood of default. As a result, we can think of the return on Treasury bills as **risk-free return.**

The lower standard deviation is a reflection of the virtual nonexistence of risk for Treasury bills. Since the annual returns on Treasury bills have a very low standard deviation, they do not fluctuate substantially from their average value. This means that there is relatively more certainty that an individual investor will receive the return on an investment in Treasury bills.

By contrast, the standard deviation of the annual returns on common stock equals 12.84%, which is substantially higher than the 2.53% standard deviation in the annual returns on Treasury bills. This results from the greater year-to-year fluctuation in the annual returns of common stock, which means that the annual returns on common stocks can deviate substantially from the long-term average in any given year. Although the average return on common stock was 12.41% from 1960 to 2001, there is a greater potential in any given year of a large negative return compared to that for Treasury bills. The larger standard deviation or variance in annual returns is an indicator of greater risk.

Table 6.3 indicates that Treasury bills have less risk than common stock but that common stocks on average outperformed Treasury bills, as shown by a comparison of the average annual returns of the S&P 500 Composite Index with the average yields on three-month Treasury bills. Over the period from 1960 to 1999, an investor on average could have earned 8.26% by holding common stock but would have earned only 5.95% holding Treasury bills. In other words, an investor in the portfolio of stocks included in the S&P 500 Composite Index earned an excess return of 2.31%, based on the difference between the average returns on stock and the yields on Treasury bills. This excess return can be viewed as a **risk premium,** that is, the additional annual return that the holders of common stock earned relative to that for a risk-free asset, Treasury bills.

Table 6.3	Means and Standard Deviations for U.S. Treasury Bills and Common Stocks	
	Yield on newly issued 3-month treasury bills	Return on the S&P 500 Composite Index
Mean	5.95%	8.26%
Standard deviation	2.53%	12.84%

[3]We have assumed that the population (theoretical distribution) of returns for SMC, that is, all possible outcomes over all possible years, follows the normal distribution, which is the bell-shaped curve that many students may be familiar with. Since we are working with a sample that is drawn from a population, there is no guarantee that the annual returns will cleanly fit on the bell-shaped normal distribution. Statistical theory does suggest that as one analyzes larger samples of annual returns (i.e., covering more years), the actual historic data will begin to resemble the theoretical distribution. If we look at SMC's stock returns over a long period of time, we know that there may be some sampling error in our individual sample of returns; but this error is small relative to that for a sample consisting of four years of data. Students interested in going beyond the thumbnail sketch in this footnote should consult a business statistics text, such as Siegal, 2000.

The data in table 6.3 show that investors in the stock market are rewarded with much higher returns than investors in the relatively risk-free Treasury bills. This is not to suggest that an individual should not invest in Treasury bills. Instead, the information in table 6.3 suggests that investors in riskier assets are rewarded with higher average returns. By contrast, investors in Treasury bills receive lower returns because the investment is virtually without risk.

A way to understand the choice of the risk undertaken by an individual investor is from the standpoint of the length of time that the money is to be invested. If the investor plans to use the proceeds of the investment to buy a house in one year, it would be prudent to purchase Treasury bills, since a riskier investment has a higher likelihood of resulting in a capital loss over the year. By contrast, for an investor who is saving for retirement but who will not retire for another 30 years, the greater risk of investing in a stock portfolio may be acceptable because of the potential for higher expected returns over a longer time horizon.

Risk and the Choice of a Discount Rate

Up to this point, we have discussed the concept of risk and the ways in which investors are compensated for taking on more risk in the financial markets. This brings us full circle, to the issue of putting a value on cash flows that will be received in the future when the cash flows have an element of uncertainty, or risk. As we discuss next, risk is dealt with through the choice of a discount rate that factors in risk. We consider this issue under two assumptions:

1. Risk is the same as for the overall stock market.
2. Risk is different from that for the overall market.

Risk Is Identical to That for the Overall Stock Market

For argument's sake, assume that at the time Pitino signed his long-term contract to serve as the head coach and president of the Celtics, he viewed the riskiness of the cash flows as equivalent to that of the overall stock market. In that case, Pitino would have used the current expected return on an index of stock market performance such as the S&P 500 Composite Index. We can anticipate that the S&P 500 Composite Index return can be earned on a financial investment of equivalent risk to the cash flows associated with Pitino's contract at the time of the signing. The expected return on the market index (S&P 500 Composite Index) can be expressed as:

expected return on the market index = risk-free rate + expected risk premium

We can look at the return on the S&P 500 Composite Index as the sum of the risk-free rate of return plus a premium for taking on the risk of investing in a stock portfolio. The risk premium is what investors must receive in the financial markets in order to be induced to take on the additional risk associated with holding a diversified stock portfolio such as the S&P 500 Composite Index.

The estimation of the expected return on the market portfolio is straightforward. Assume that the current three-month Treasury bill rate is 6.50%. We can then use 6.50% as our estimate of the risk-free rate. Table 6.3 shows that from 1960 through 2001, the average Treasury bill rate was 5.95%, while the average annual return on the S&P 500 Composite Index was 8.26%. Thus the historic risk premium from 1960 to 2001 is 2.31% (8.26% − 5.95%). The historic risk premium is a common estimate of the expected risk premium in the future (Ross et al., 1996, p. 238). Adding the historic risk premium of 2.31% to the estimated 6.50% riskless rate, we end up with an estimated expected return on the S&P 500 Composite Index equal to 8.81%. The estimated 8.81% return on a portfolio of stocks contained in the S&P 500 Composite Index can then be used as the discount rate for these cash flows.

Risk Is Different From That for the Overall Market

So far we have assumed that the risk of the future cash flows being valued is equal to the overall risk of the stock market, as represented by returns on the S&P 500 Composite Index. If the risk of the cash flows differs from that for the overall stock market, then we cannot use the expected return on the S&P 500 Composite Index as the discount rate. In order to decide which discount rate to use, we look at the risk that matters to individual investors.

The S&P 500 Composite Index is a highly diversified stock portfolio that contains 500 common stocks. The standard deviations of the returns of individual stocks tend to be considerably higher than the standard deviation of the returns of the

S&P 500 Composite Index.[4] The reason for the difference is **diversification**. With diversification, individual stocks can be combined into portfolios. As long as the stocks in the portfolio do not completely move together over time, stocks in the portfolio that earn poor returns are offset by other stocks that earn higher returns. As a result, returns on the portfolio fluctuate less than the returns on individual stocks. Since people have the ability to diversify their portfolios, we can argue that when analyzing the risk of an individual security, we are really concerned with the impact of an individual security on the overall risk of a well-diversified portfolio such as the S&P 500 Composite Index. Specifically, when we measure the risk of an individual security, we are interested in how the risk of a well-diversified portfolio is affected by adding that security to the portfolio.

Under the assumption that investors hold well-diversified portfolios, the **capital asset pricing model** (CAPM) shows that the risk of an individual security can be represented by its beta coefficient.[5] Beta tells us the extent to which the return on the individual security moves with the overall market (the S&P 500 Composite Index). The S&P 500 Composite Index itself has a beta of 1. The beta of a stock that is less risky than the overall market is less than 1. A stock that is more risky than the overall market has a beta exceeding 1.

Under CAPM, the expected return on an individual security is as follows:

expected return on an individual security = current risk-free return + (beta of the individual security × historic market risk premium)

Assume that SMC has a beta equal to 1.20, that the current risk-free rate is 6.50%, and that the historic market risk premium is 2.31%. Based on CAPM,

SMC's expected return = 6.50% + (1.20 × 2.31%)
= 9.27%

If SMC is valuing the cash flows of an individual project funded entirely by common stock, then 9.27% is an appropriate discount rate. CAPM and the choice of an appropriate discount rate when firms obtain funding via issuance of bonds, loans, and internally generated cash is discussed further in chapter 11.

> *To measure risk, we examine the behavior of returns on different types of assets and also examine the degree to which the returns on a given asset vary over time.*

CONCLUSION

In this chapter, we cover principles of financial analysis that we will use throughout the rest of this textbook. In particular, we discuss

- the time value of money, with particular emphasis on computing future values of monies received today, as well as discounting future expected cash flows to present values;
- the concept of risk as analyzed when choosing between risk-free and risky investment choices; and
- the concept of risk, with particular emphasis on the problems inherent in factoring in risk in the valuation of cash flows.

ASSIGNMENTS

1. What effect does an increase or decrease in (a) the interest rate and (b) the time period of an investment have on its future value?

2. Art Passer, a star quarterback in the NFL, has been asked by the owner of his team to have $100,000 of his current salary deferred for one year in order to reduce payroll expenses. By how much would the present value of Passer's salary contract change if he agreed to the salary deferral?

3. A famous pitcher just signed a $50 million contract that provides $10 million per year for five years, while an outfielder signed a $45 million contract that pays $15 million now and $6 million per year for five years. If the interest rate is 10%, which player's contract is worth more?

---

[4]This is confirmed by estimates of standard deviations in the individual returns of Apple, Chrysler, Cray Research, General Motors, Homestake Mining, IBM, and Mattel for 1990 through 1994, which were all higher than the standard deviation for the returns on the S&P 500 Composite Index, as reported by Ross et al. (1996).

[5]In formal statistical terms, beta is equal to the covariance of the return of an individual security with the overall market portfolio divided by the variance on the market portfolio. See Ross et al., 1996, for a more detailed discussion of the assumptions and derivation of the capital asset pricing model.

4. SMC has a beta of 1.2 and Acme Sports Stores has a beta of 0.7.

   a. Which stock is the least risky?

   b. Which stock would perform better when the stock market declines?

   c. Which stock would perform better when the stock market is rallying?

RESEARCH PROJECTS

1. Research current sport contracts for five players in the same professional sport league, as reported in the news media. Compare the present values of all the contracts.

2. Pick a 10-year period, and obtain Nike's closing stock price at the end of each year. For the same 10-year period, also obtain the end-of-year value of the S&P 500 Composite Index. Nike's closing price and values of the S&P Composite Index can be obtained from **http://chart.yahoo.com/d** on the Internet.

Use this information to compute annual returns for Nike and the S&P 500 Composite Index. Based on a review of mean returns for the 10-year period, does Nike's stock outperform the overall market? Based on a review of the standard deviations of Nike's and the S&P 500 Composite Index's returns, is Nike's stock more risky than the overall stock market?

CLASS DISCUSSION TOPICS

1. Evaluate the following statement: "Since a well-diversified portfolio of stocks tends to outperform U.S. Treasury bills, there is no reason to invest in Treasury bills."

2. There has been increased criticism of corporate executives for being too short-term oriented and not focused enough on the long-run performance of their companies. Should there be an emphasis by companies on maximizing long-term profits?

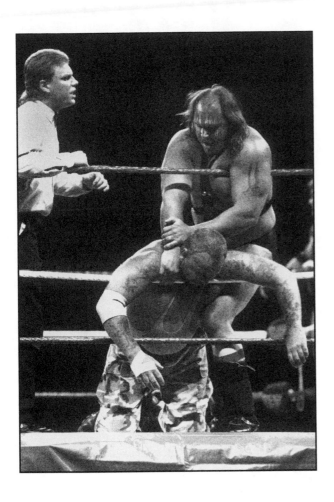

Approaches to Financial Planning

CHAPTER OBJECTIVES

After studying this chapter, you should be able to do the following:

- Define financial planning.
- Describe how to acquire financial data from internal and external sources.
- Understand how to utilize financial data to help make business decisions.
- Distinguish between long-term and short-term financial planning and understand how to minimize risk.
- Understand how to use pro forma budgets and business plans.

Financial planning entails examining future income and expenses to help steer a company in a given direction. Chapter 6 emphasizes how critical foresight is for financial planning. Pro forma projections provide guidance for making decisions and represent a basic instrument in the financial planning process. Every business decision requires planning. Strategic planning has gained popularity as a way of critically analyzing given business scenarios to generate appropriate solutions. This same strategic planning perspective applies to financial planning. Every monetary issue needs to be examined for fiscal soundness. Every dollar needs to be planned for in order to maximize that dollar's impact. Planning for most typical contingencies can help a business operate smoothly and save money.

This chapter highlights the various components necessary to plan effectively for the future. The first step is to obtain the necessary internal and external data on which to base decisions. The next step is to make use of the data for both short-term and long-term planning. The last section of this chapter deals with the final step: how to develop a pro forma budget as a key to writing an effective business plan.

 As an example, the Celtics might examine their energy costs for the FleetCenter. By computing the energy costs associated with any given luxury box, the Celtics could determine how much of a luxury box's budget should be allocated to energy. This amount could be billed to the luxury box owner as a pass-through expense. A pass-through expense is any item that can be calculated separately and added to a client's bill. On the other hand, if the Celtics saw the potential for monetary savings in relation to energy use, they might develop an energy management policy in order to achieve the savings. A box that remains vacant during an event does not require the same amount of energy as when it is filled. The Celtics could decide to give a refund to any luxury box renter who informed the Celtics 24 hours before an event that the box would remain vacant for that event. If the Celtics were charging $50 a night as a pass-through energy expense, they might offer the renter a $25 refund in return for providing the appropriate notice. While the Celtics would lose $25, they also would reduce energy costs in an amount closer to $50. Thus, the Celtics would in fact come out ahead due to appropriate financial planning. Such an analytical approach to developing policies and procedures is an example of how financial planning can help squeeze every penny possible in a tight budget or help develop larger profits.

Another example of financial planning comes from the Texas Rangers. After signing Alex Rodriguez for approximately $250 million, the team needed to generate sufficient funds to cover this expense. One technique the team used was to raise ticket prices, by an estimated 10.4%, from an average of $20 to $22.08 ("Sports in Brief," 2001). Both this and the preceding example highlight the importance of planning and the potential impact if only several hundred dollars or as much as several million dollars are either saved through facility-related policies or raised through adapting marketing strategies.

Financial planning can help to provide appropriate solutions for the types of problems businesses face every day, such as the need to

- develop new products,
- spend more money on research and development,
- retire a given product line,
- borrow funds for future expansion,
- issue commercial paper,
- issue more stock,
- issue more bonds,
- sell existing assets,
- purchase new assets,
- move the business to another location,
- acquire a competing company, or
- file for bankruptcy protection.

As the list suggests, every future action a business might undertake entails financial planning. For example, every company that undertakes an advertising campaign needs to develop an advertising budget incorporating forecasts of future advertising expenditures. Table 7.1 in the following case study is an example of an advertising budget worksheet that could help a company establish priorities for future advertising campaigns. These are critical for financial planning because a sales forecast will be based on the anticipated advertising campaign and the anticipated resulting sales. If a new product is launched and only a small marketing budget has been provided, the anticipated sales could be severely compromised. At the same time, a large marketing budget that is misspent on the wrong advertising means can be counterproductive.

If Sport Manufacturing Company decides to switch from advertising primarily in magazines to using athletes as endorsers, this planning decision will be shown on a completed form that will let management know how the strategy will be implemented (see table 7.1).

The marketing budget reflects the new emphasis on endorsing athletes, along with a dramatic cut in the magazine advertisement budget. Note that some high-priority areas may have a lower budget than certain lower-priority items. For example, posters have one of the lowest allocations in the budget, but are a high priority. Since the new campaign emphasizes the endorsing athletes, giving away posters of the athletes may be a major initiative; but it still does not represent a major expenditure. Other items might have higher budgeted amounts but have a lower priority. For example, the company might purchase certain ads even though they are not a major part of the marketing effort because of a long-standing relationship with the advertising medium or in order to avoid an image backlash. The major declines in the marketing budget are in radio (–34.6%), magazine (–31.25%), and television advertisements (–20%).

Table 7.1   2000 Advertising Budget Categories

Category	Priority	# Insertions	1999 Budget ($)	2000 Budget ($)	% Difference
Magazine	2	200	8,000,000	5,500,000	–31.25
Newspaper advertisements	7	40	1,000,000	1,000,000	0.00
Newspaper supplements	5	26	2,000,000	2,300,000	15.00
Radio	11	900	1,300,000	850,000	–34.60
Television	8	150	2,500,000	2,000,000	–20.00
Endorsements	1	10	1,000,000	8,500,000	750.00
Posters	4	50,000	60,000	140,000	133.00
Special media	3	100	800,000	1,000,000	25.00
Agency fees	16	N/A	1,200,000	1,000,000	–16.66
Trade media	6	60	700,000	750,000	7.14
Consumer incentives	9	100,000	500,000	500,000	0.00
Sales conferences	10	12	230,000	250,000	8.69
Merchandising material	12	400	130,000	150,000	15.38
Trade allowances	13	N/A	100,000	100,000	0.00
Trade free goods	14	2,000	1,000,000	1,050,000	5.00
Sundries	15	N/A	120,000	130,000	8.33
Totals	**N/A**	**153,898**	**$20,640,000**	**$25,220,000**	**22.19%**

Advertising variables may not be as clear to upper management if different segments of the business submit different marketing budgets. A large business may have several different segments that have their own budgets; if these budgets are not consolidated into a final marketing budget, upper management will not have a correct picture of the marketing goals and associated costs. For example, the Celtics might have different marketing budgets for ticket sales and the team's Web page or souvenir store. If the various budgets are not consolidated into a simple-to-read document, management will make decisions without all the relevant facts. The planning process cannot be accomplished without this information, and the information paves the way for the overall corporate budget. While it might appear that examining individual budgets might be easier for some executives, the inability to completely compare and contrast each budget in a synthesized manner can reduce the effectiveness of various techniques such as zero-based budgeting (see p. 106). Thus, some executives like to examine individual unit budgets but insist on examining a consolidated budget to see what impact any changes in one budget will have on other units.

The chart shown (table 7.1) is one that upper management can examine to determine where the marketing emphasis will be in the coming year and what areas represent the greatest spending growth and decline. This information can be correlated with sales forecasts to help management understand why a certain advertising strategy is being suggested. For example, if sales stemming from magazine advertisements increased 20% in the past year, it would make sense for the advertising campaign to show an increase in magazine ads to help spur additional sales from that outlet. However, if the sales force informed management that utilizing athletes as endorsers was expected to produce the greatest surge in exposure, management could understand why magazine advertising was actually declining even though one could expect additional magazine advertisements to increase sales. Thus, the marketing budget chart serves as a tool that management can use to make a logical plan for the future.

As with any business, a sport team like the Boston Celtics or the Texas Rangers must plan effectively for the future by collecting good data on which to base both short- and long-term decisions.

Data Gathering

Companies and organizations cannot plan without appropriate data. They should compare planning data with internal projections and with external projections such as industry standards.

The information from which spending and revenue sources can be identified includes internal data and external data. Internal data are often referred to as primary data since these are data generated by the business itself. External data, or data obtained from other sources, have already been developed and published and so are often referred to as secondary data.

Internal Data

As the preceding sidebar example highlights, forecasting cannot be accomplished without reliable internal data. The economic impact study could have significant value, but if it is not accurate, then any reliance on the data would be erroneous. It is critical to have reliable internal as well as external data in order to make decisions. Internal data can include past balance sheets and income statements, audited financial records, annual reports, research and development reports, and countless other documents generated by employees or consultants. Paper trails should not be used to the exclusion of

other data. For example, e-mails may contain valuable data that researchers may miss if they examine printed material only.

Internal data can come from various other sources. Information can be derived from personal observation or through conversation around the water cooler. Numerous additional sources may include surveys conducted by the business to analyze customer concerns. Many sport teams conduct fan surveys to determine why people attend games and how to provide more valuable services. Information on how much and what types of soda or beer are sold can be useful. By analyzing the numbers for sales in the grandstands and at concession stands, a team can plan its strategy for increasing beverage sales. Similarly, by breaking its operation down into its basic elements, the team can develop a more appropriate budget. This process is often seen in zero-based budgeting.

Many companies utilize zero-based budgeting as a technique to justify future expenditures. In **zero-based budgeting** (ZBB), every expenditure is justified in comparison with other potential projects. If a team will have $1 million for its marketing budget, every department that wishes to receive some of that money needs to indicate how much money it is requesting and provide justification for the request. If a department has been successful in a particular campaign, those numbers can be used as a justification for receiving a given amount of the funds. Each unit, division, or department might be required to produce formal documentation to justify requested expenditures. Objective documentation is the key. If the existence of a department could be under review, there may be a temptation to manipulate data to ensure continued employment. For example, if the National Aeronautics and Space Administration (NASA) operated under ZBB principles, its entire Mars program might be under review after several major disasters costing millions of dollars. Individuals in an affected program might try to paint a picture that is better than what really occurred. However, objective data can help eliminate potential bias or distortion. An excellent way to uncover objective information is to go to external sources.

Financial Numbers From a Minor League Baseball Team

The following are excerpts from an interview with Chris Canetti, the former general manager of a minor league baseball team at the time of the interview in 2000. The information reflects the importance of internal data and how the internal data can generate strategies for future growth.

I receive a lot of resumes where someone says in the cover letter that they love sports and that's great. You have to love baseball to work in baseball and you have to love sports to work in sports, but the bottom line is that it is a business. When I have to hire someone I can care less if they played Little League baseball, I want to know what positives they can bring to my business and me and how they can benefit the bottom line. This might encourage or discourage you, but when I went to college I was a communications major. I never took an accounting, marketing or finance course. For a bachelor's degree in my school the only thing I needed was Economics 101. I wish differently now that I had taken those courses, but a few years ago before I became general manager, the former GM came to me one day and said I want you to do the budget. A minor league baseball team makes millions a year in revenue and I have to make a budget. You can't tell your boss no, so you have to figure it out. I wish I had a course like this [sport finance], it would have made my life a lot easier.

A budget is a model that is set by the team to try and forecast the goals they want to meet for the coming year. . . . If you look at some budgets, they might show a cash-positive year. However, if the team has debt service that is amortized out over the course of time, it will show up as an expense, even though it is not a hard cash expense. With the debt service expense included in the budget, the budget could show a loss. I use a piece by-piece approach to developing the numbers in this budget. The primary source for these numbers is from historical data. History describes what occurred last year and serves as the base for predicting what might happen in the coming year. For example, if we look at fictitious numbers for last year [pp. 108–109], we see that the team had $1.4 million in [game day] concession sales. Assume 200,000 fans attended games last season. By dividing the $1.4 million by the 200,000 fans, we can calculate that an average fan spends $7 each game on concessions. If we anticipate a 10% increase in attendance, then our budget should also reflect that 10% increase. Our ticket sales would increase 10% and our concession sales would also increase. If fans once again spend on average $7 each, then we can multiply $7 by 220,000 fans (200,000 fans plus the 10% increase in fans), resulting in a budgeted $1.54 million for concession revenue for next season.

A team's stadium lease will always be a major factor in determining an organization's financial picture. The lease is a key consideration when going through the budgeting process. The lease outlines how the parties involved will split the responsibility and control of major expense and revenue categories. These elements often include things such as concession revenue, suite revenue, parking revenue, ticket taxes, stadium maintenance, and utilities. The factors within a lease are unique in almost every team's case. In some instances, a team's lease is written so that a percentage of annual revenues are used to pay debts incurred from stadium construction or renovation. Such cases will affect the team's annual financial statement.

When asked about profit centers, Canetti responded:

[C]oncessions represent one of the greatest profit centers for a team. While a minor league team makes a significant amount on ticket revenue and does not pay players'/coaches' salaries, which are paid by the parent club, concessions is still the best profit center. A team can generate between 50% and 60% profit on concession sales. A team could possibly outsource concession to another company, but then would only receive 35%. This significant potential decline in concession revenue has encouraged us to keep taking care of concessions ourselves to maximize the revenue and flexibility.

(continued)

(continued)

Hypothetical Minor League Baseball Team Budget for the 2000 Season

Category	($000)
Revenue	6,140
Direct costs	1,806
Gross profit	**4,334**
Park and game expenses (schedule 1)	992
Team expenses (schedule 2)	196
General/Admin. expenses (schedule 3)	2,422
Debt service (schedule 4)	840
Total expenses	**4,450**
Operating income	**–116**
Sources of revenue:	
Ticket revenue	2,000
Direct ticket costs:	
Facility fee	200
Payment to MLB	60
Ticket production	14
Total costs	**274**
Gross profit	**1,726**
Advertising revenue	1,400
Direct costs:	
Paint/Material	–
Printing	–
Radio	10
Promotional spots	200
Total costs	**210**
Gross profit	**1,190**
Game day concessions	1,400
Group concessions	600
Total concession revenue	**2,000**
Direct costs:	
Food	380
Soft drinks	70
Beer	80
Supplies/Uniforms	60
Equipment leasing	8
Payroll	240
Payroll taxes	30
Total costs	**868**
Gross profit	**1,132**
Merchandise revenue	340
Direct costs:	
Beginning inventory	70
Purchases	130
Payroll	14
Total costs	**214**
Ending inventory	48
Final costs	**166**
Gross profit	**174**
Other revenue:	
Parking	40
Programs	40
Other	320
Total other revenue	**400**

Category	($000)
Direct costs:	
Program	80
Other	160
Total costs	**240**
Gross profit	**160**
Total gross profit	4,382
Departmental gross profit margin:	
Ticket department	1,726
Advertising department	1,190
Concessions department	1,132
Merchandise department	174
Other departments	160
Total gross profit	**4,382**
Gross profit margin	**71.37%**
Schedule 1—Park and Game Expenses:	
Stadium rent	150
Real estate taxes (waived)	0
Utilities	130
Maintenance—grounds	280
Security	110
Umpires	70
Game day payroll	190
Game day payroll taxes	18
Equipment rental	16
Miscellaneous	28
Total park and game expenses	**992**
Schedule 2—Team Expenses:	
Transportation	80
Lodging	96
Laundry/Clubhouse	10
Uniforms	10
Total team expenses	**196**
Schedule 3—General and Administrative:	
Salaries	800
Payroll taxes	74
Office operations	4
Dues and fees	60
Promotion and advertising	550
Other (schedule 5)	984
Total general and admin.	**2,422**
Schedule 4—Debt Service Plus Other Expenses:	
Interest	180
Depreciation	260
Amortization of contracts	400
Total debt service plus other expenses	**840**
Schedule 5—Other Expenses:	
Amortization	370
Auto expenses	18
Bad debt expenses	10
Bank service charge	40
Contributions	2
Entertainment	10
Insurance	160

Category	($000)	Category	($000)
Professional fees	60	Supplies	32
Miscellaneous	2	Taxes—others	60
Outside services	16	Telephone	80
Postage	40	Travel	16
Rent	2	**Total other expenses**	**934**
Repairs	16	**Total expenses**	**4,450**

External Data

The preceding sidebar highlights the importance of internal data for decision making. By knowing how successful internal operations are, a business can more appropriately plan for the future. External data can serve the same purpose. External data and documentation are critical for successful planning. External data can be used to help shape various decisions to properly reflect the true business environment. For example, the Ravens' data show the extent to which marketing efforts were succeeding. If the team was facing financial trouble, it could examine prior expenditures to see what efforts were and were not successful. The team could examine the $275,000 spent on promotion and advertising and determine whether a different campaign was needed based on customer response to the prior campaign. In addition, if the stadium landlords were having trouble with the local officials, as evidenced by news stories and city hearings, the team could attempt to renegotiate the lease to both save money and project a positive public image for the landlord. These are only two examples of the use of external data to help shape sport business decisions.

There are many other ways in which external data can help to shape decisions. The following are examples of gathering external data:

- Monitoring international terrorist activities to determine if an event needs to be canceled
- Analyzing industry trends to develop appropriate pricing for concession items
- Tracking culinary advances to determine the most effective means of packaging and selling food items
- Reading current articles in trade publications to stay abreast of industry changes
- Attending conferences and hearing what other executives are saying about the industry
- Reviewing government census reports to understand demographic changes in the pos-

sible fan base

Publications such as *Barron's, Forbes, Business Week,* and *The Wall Street Journal* provide significant general information. More specific information can be obtained from such sources as *Dun & Bradstreet's Key Business Ratios,* which analyzes 14 key ratios for various industries. Both state and federal governments produce significant useful data such as statistical abstracts. Industry trade groups can also produce valuable data to assist with financial planning. Appendix C is a resource section with information on these publications and how to access them.

Among the best information sources for the sport industry are industry publications such as *Athletic Business, Athletic Management, Fitness Management, The NCAA News,* and a host of other specialized publications. Each one has unique special features, reports, and surveys that can provide invaluable assistance. One of the premiere publications in the industry is *Street & Smith's Sports Business Journal.* This weekly publication has special sections devoted to attendance numbers, a stock market index for sport-related companies, and information on sponsorship deals, among other features.

Industry-related data come from a variety of sources and appear in a variety of formats. The Small Business Administration publishes free business plan formats online to help businesses understand what data they will need and what to do with the data. More specific data are often needed from specific industry groups or associations.

 If the Smiths wanted to build a softball complex they could turn to the Sportsplex Operators and Developers Association (SODA), which publishes industry-specific data. To determine how much it would cost to build a park, they could possibly obtain the information shown in table 7.2, which is derived from a facility cost comparison published by SODA in 1993.

Table 7.2 Comparison of Two Sizes of Complexes

Description	Six-field complex in Arizona		Three-field complex in Florida	
	Actual cost ($)	Avg. per field cost ($)	Actual cost ($)	Avg. per field cost ($)
Engineering/Arch. plans	40,000	6,666.67	350,000	116,666.67
Site mobilization	140	23.33	122,938	40,979.33
Site grading and prep	65,480	10,913.33	166,367	55,455.67
Storm drains	0	0	71,632	23,877.33
Sewers	19,036	3,172.67	14,860	4,953.33
Water system	45,000	17,000.00	14,894	4,964.67
Underground cable	6,000	1,000.00	10,000	3,333.33
Well costs	100,000	16,667.67	5,000	1,667.67
Topsoil	6,000	1,000.00	24,000	8,000.00
Sod and soil	69,000	11,500.00	139,445	46,481.67
Shrubs/Trees	23,230	3,871.67	298,000	99,333.33
Paths/Walls	66,100	11,016.67	72,000	24,000.00
Warning tracks	5,015	835.83	12,000	4,000.00
Area lighting	21,201	3,533.50	131,000	43,666.67
Sports lighting	185,000	30,833.33	220,000	73,333.33
Parking paving	101,450	16,908.33	100,000	33,333.33
Fencing	57,900	9,650.00	65,000	21,666.67
Scoreboards	15,000	2,500.00	22,000	7,333.33
Batting cages	48,890	8,148.33	63,775	21,268.33
Tot lot	27,785	4,630.83	62,542	20,847.33
Volleyball court	20,403	3,400.50	27,551	9,183.67
Basketball courts	0	0	88,223	29,407.67
Picnic area	11,772	1,962.00	5,000	1,666.67
Entryway	4,000	666.67	10,000	3,333.33
Snack bars	290,150	48,358.33	446,150	148,716.67
Trash enclosures	4,700	783.33	4,000	1,333.33
Maintenance shed	14,215	2,369.17	66,500	22,166.67
Admin. building	300,000	50,000.00	13,750	4,583.33
BBQ area	25,000	4,166.67	3,000	1,000.00
Fees and permits	103	17.17	8,900	2,966.67
General conditions	10,950	1,825.00	109,000	36,333.33
Maintenance equipment	35,000	5,833.33	22,500	7,500.00
Concessions equipment	65,000	10,833.33	40,000	13,333.33
Park furnishing	3,000	500.00	8,000	2,666.67
Computers	0	0	10,000	3,333.33
Video security/PA	17,000	2,833.33	6,000	2,000.00
Bleachers	10,600	1,766.67	20,000	6,666.67
Signage	2,900	483.33	6,000	2,000.00
Inventory and supplies	22,000	3,666.67	8,000	2,666.67
Preopening expenses	16,000	2,666.67	20,000	6,666.67
Legal/Accounting	8,500	1,416.67	30,000	10,000.00
Feasibility study	3,800	633.33	25,000	8,333.33
Development fees	144,600	24,100.00	225,000	75,000.00
Total	**$1,641,920**	**$273,653.33**	**$3,168,027**	**$1,056,009.00**

Data from SODA, 1993.

Fitness Facility Benchmarking

Various organizations regularly research specific industry benchmarks that can help establish criteria for success or failure. The numbers in the following table represent averages for the fitness club industry as researched by the International Health, Racquet and Sportsclub Association (IHRSA); this information helps provide guidance for fitness facilities establishing their budgets.

Fitness Club Industry Benchmarks

Category	Industry average
Total revenue from non-dues sources	27%
Payroll as a percentage of revenue	42%
Total operating expenses as a percentage of revenue	66%
Total fixed expenses as a percentage of revenue	10.7%
EBITDA	23.2%
Spending to maintain the facility and all equipment	6.2%
Revenue per square foot	$45
Revenue per member	$871

Data from Winters, 2000.

Regardless of the type of external data, the reader of such reports needs to compare apples with apples. Some publications calculate return on equity as **net income** divided by average common equity, while others divide net income by the year-end common equity. Comparing data that have been obtained using different equations will lead to inaccuracies. Referring back to NASA's trouble with its Mars program, one expensive blunder occurred, in part, because of human error in which measurements were not converted correctly from the metric to the traditional English system. Such a "simple" mistake led to the crashing of a spaceflight. Similarly, incorrectly analyzing an internal rate of return or price-earnings ratio can destroy an investment decision. Thus, all financial statements should be carefully scrutinized to determine what equations and measurement techniques were used and when the data were collected to insure proper comparisons.

Sport businesses analyze their own internal data in order to make financial decisions and also gather data from many external sources ranging from local news to industry publications.

The Financial Planning Process

Financial planning requires two major activities: forecasting potential revenues and budgeting for future expenses, commonly called budgeting. Once the appropriate data are collected, it is incumbent on management to act on the data. Management cannot hide behind the numbers and not make a decision. Stockholders and voters demand that a business or government entity make decisions that will maximize their investment. The most common managerial decisions have to do with maximizing revenue sources and minimizing expenses.

Financial planning is often based on behavior learned from previous bad habits or mistakes. Failing to turn over inventory quickly enough or not collecting overdue bills in a timely manner leads to reduced income and higher expenses. Both inventory levels and uncollected accounts can significantly increase or decrease profitability if they are high. If excess inventory and uncollected accounts receivable appear on the balance sheet, then a significant amount of money may be tied up and unusable. Both of these problems also can be easily corrected through the implementation of efficiency control mechanisms such as posting systems (based

Revenue and Expenses in NCAA Division I-A Programs

The following examples highlight how an organization's data can be compared with industry data to determine if revenue and expenses match figures for other similar entities. While the dollar amounts might differ, a percentage analysis can be very useful and appropriate. The data in the following table show where the typical National Collegiate Athletic Association (NCAA) Division I-A monies come from.

NCAA Division I-A Revenues

Category	Percent of income
Home gate receipts	30.9
Cash gifts	13.7
Radio/Television	12.6
Postseason compensation	7.1
Auxiliary income	7.0
Institutional support	7.0
Student fees	6.6
Away game guarantees	5.8
Other income	5.7
Investment income	2.0
State aid	1.5

Data from "Fiscally Friendly Football," 1996.

Expenses for typical NCAA Division I-A programs are expressed as percentages in the table that follows.

NCAA Division I-A Expenses

Category	Percent of income
Salaries and benefits	28.9
Grants-in-aid	16.5
Other expenses	9.2
Operations and maintenance	6.5
Team travel	6.4
Opponents' payments	6.1
Equipment and supplies	5.5
Contract services	3.9
Debt service	3.9
Capital expenses	3.2
Recruiting	2.3
Publicity	2.2
Fund-raising	1.8
Insurance	1.1
Nonathletic	1.0
Taxes	0.9
Administrative travel	0.6

Data from "Fiscally Friendly Football," 1996.

When people talk about revenue sports, they are talking about men's football and basketball. The greatest percentage of revenue is derived from the categories in the following table.

Revenue Percentages for NCAA Division I-A Programs

Category	Percentage
Football	63.3%
Men's basketball	20.2%
Student fees, state and institutional aid	15.2%
Other men's sports	0.8%
Women's sports	0.5%

Data from "Fiscally Friendly Football," 1996.

Expenses (as a percentage of total expenses) for NCAA Division I-A members of the College Football Association in 1995-1996 are shown in the next table.

Expense Percentages for NCAA Division I-A Programs

Category	Percentage
Football	23.9%
Support staff	12.9%
Women's sports	11.8%
Other expenses	9.2%
Other men's sports	8.8%
Operations/Maintenance	6.5%
Men's basketball	6.3%
Contract services	4.0%
Debt service	3.8%
Other	12.8%

Data from "Fiscally Friendly Football," 1996.

College sports have been turning a profit in recent years. The average Division I-A program earned $660,000 in 1993; this figure increased to $1.2 million in 1995. However, the black ink was made possible by institutional support. Without institutional support, the average Division I-A program operated at a $237,000 deficit, and only 46% of programs were profitable. In 1993, 51% of programs generated a profit (Naughton, 1996). By the time of the next report three years later in 1998, the average Division I-A program's profit had decreased to $437,000 (in 1997). Excluding the institutional support, the average Division I program lost $823,000, resulting in an average of over a half-million-dollar increase in losses for each institution ("NCAA Study," 1998).

The following table shows which sports produce the highest concession sales average per attendee at professional sport facilities, regional arenas, and NCAA stadiums.

(continued)

(continued)

Ranking of Sports and Events With Highest Expenditure per Attendee

Sport	Average expenditure per attendee ($)
NFL	6.10
NHL	6.10
NBA	5.40
MLB	5.30
Motor sport	3.50
Concerts	3.40
Minor league hockey	2.90
Family shows	2.50
NCAA men's basketball	2.30
NCAA football	1.60

Data from *1997 Stadium & Arena Managers' Annual Report*, 1997.

on the due dates of outstanding accounts receivable) or the establishment of guidelines for inspecting the inventory. Many steps that one might categorize as financial planning are just plain commonsense tactics. For example, the following are simple tactics promoted by American Express Small Business Services to help manage cash flow:

1. Organize billing schedules so overdue bills can be flagged for quicker follow-up.

2. Stretch out repayment of suppliers to the maximum time allowed by contract.

3. Try to pay bills earlier if suppliers offer incentive for early repayment.

4. If suppliers do not offer an incentive program for early payment, ask for such a program.

5. Do not hesitate to raise prices, as clients are accustomed to small, but regular, increases.

6. Eliminate any unnecessary inventory, which just wastes money.

7. Consider leasing rather than buying to free your credit line and to take advantage of tax write-offs.

8. Buy from various suppliers to prevent harm if a supplier faces a problem and to take advantage of special offers that other suppliers might make ("Steps for Improving," 1998).

These simple strategies are in fact decisions that can be reached through the planning process. A business can decide to pay bills within 10 days if a discount is offered and to reinvest any savings into interest-bearing Treasury bonds. Such a planning process appears simple, but numerous managers live "by the seat of their pants" when making decisions and do not consider the long-term ramifications. Planning helps determine potential long-term ramifications.

One of the most important planning issues is determining the capital structure for a business. Chapter 11 explains the importance of determining the capital mix or target capital structure. The planning process can help determine the most appropriate structure for a given year based on economic variables and countless additional pieces of information acquired in the data collection process. If Nike is overburdened by bond obligations, it might not be able to generate enough return to interest potential stockholders. However, if Nike's equity is overdiluted, it may be difficult for the company to ever buy back its shares. Nike could be in trouble if it has issued too many shares and its equity is primarily composed of shareholders' equity rather than retained earnings. This could be a problem if Nike ever wanted to buy back its stock to go private or buy back some of its shares to reduce the number of shareholders and increase the share value for the remaining shareholders.

Economic conditions are an excellent example of the concerns raised in the planning process. **Inflation** and prosperity typically cause a sharp need for corporate capital so that the company can continue to produce more. However, if bonds and preferred stock are issued too quickly, a company can go bankrupt if the economy changes and the company owes too much in interest, **principal,** and required dividend payments. Furthermore, during periods in which interest rates are low, bank borrowing may be more economical than issuing bonds. If a bank loan is obtainable at a relatively low interest rate, the main savings will be the costs associated with issuing bonds (vs. the minimal costs associated with obtaining a bank loan). If the long-term bond interest rate is lower than the obtainable bank interest rate, then it may be worthwhile to issue the bond, as the issuing cost can be recouped over the long term. The opposite result is seen when interest rates are high, which means a business would have more difficulty issuing long-term bonds. The business would have trouble selling long-term bonds to investors if their interest rate is lower than what an investor might be able to obtain in the short-run from other investments. Planning helps prevent making the wrong decision and issuing securities that might not be attractive to investors.

Short-Term Planning

Short-term planning dictates how a business should proceed within a short time frame, usually less than two years. Short-term planning cannot be undertaken without examining the potential implication of current decisions on the long-term profitability or success of any business. Long-term planning is more oriented toward the future and allows executives to be more creative since there are so many options and uncertainties that play into such decision making. Short-term planning is based on specific research and requires individuals to meet specific goals. Regardless of the time frame used for planning, accuracy and the ability to properly interpret internal and external data are the keys to success. For example, if the short-term analysis fails to adequately examine internal debt-related issues and the external borrowing environment, a business may not last more than several months before creditors file for involuntary bankruptcy.

The short-term planning process requires close scrutiny of internal variables such as cash flow and debt-related issues. Key aspects of short-term planning include how to effectively understand and make decisions based on working capital, net working capital, current ratio, acid test ratio, and the cash budget. These ratios are discussed in chapter 5.

Deciding whether or not to hire a new basketball coach is normally a long-term planning process. Most coaches are not hired for the short term, but are hired to build a program around their skills and strengths. This does not mean that short-term plan-

ning will not influence the decision, as ticket sales and player recruiting still need to be undertaken during the hiring process to ensure continued success or prevent falling further behind competing programs. Thus, the hiring process, similar to almost all planning decisions, entails a blend of short- and long-term planning. Actions taken by the University of Houston surrounding a hiring decision may serve as an example of poor short-term planning and inadequate capital management.

 The University of Houston hired a former star basketball player at the university and one of the top 50 players in the NBA's history, Clyde Drexler, as the head basketball coach. Almost immediately thereafter, the university spent a considerable sum to remove several rows of seats and install luxury boxes. Although the initial demand for the boxes was high based on the prospect that the new coach would bring a winning team, those hopes quickly faded. The team performed unremarkably during Drexler's two-year term, and after two years he resigned.

Effective planning would have included a cost-benefit analysis of installing the luxury boxes based on the potential failure of the coach, rather than only on the expectation that a miracle would occur and that the hiring would erase years of debt. In fact, attendance had been abysmal for years before the hiring, and during the two years thereafter it improved. Still, there were no guarantees that attendance numbers would not once again fall if the basketball team was not a high-quality product. Short-term planning might have focused on examining the attendance trends associated with the new coach for at least several years after he came to the University of Houston to see if his hiring would in fact increase the attendance numbers. After collecting some empirical data based on actual ticket sales and revenue for a one- or two-year period after the coach's hiring, the university could have made a more accurate short-term plan for capital expenditure during a deficit.

The University of Houston example highlights how most business decisions entail an element of both short- and long-term planning. Another example of how short-term planning can blend into long-term planning is the futures market. The futures market primarily involves commodities such as metals, meats and other foods, and money. Most commodities sales are conducted in the spot market, where an item is bought and sold for cash and the exchange is completed immediately. There are also transactions in which delivery and payment are to occur at a future date. The Celtics could pay a significant amount of money for a player, but the player might be delivered at a future date due to other contractual obligations. This future obligation often happens with foreign hockey and basketball players who might be drafted and signed with a United States team but still have to complete their contract with their foreign team. If the player was playing in Europe, the payment amount could be affected by fluctuations in the value of the U.S. dollar against the European currency during the waiting period. If the Celtics do not take short-term preventive steps such as floating the contract amount on the futures market, the price of the contract might be higher when the Celtics finally pay for the player.

Floating means paying a certain amount to buy future dollars or other currencies on the currency markets. Individuals are betting that the currency values will increase and others are betting that the values will decrease. A similar type of gamble often occurs when people buy stock with the intent that the shares will either go up or down in value. This process is often called **hedging,** which entails purchasing future contracts in situations in which a price change could positively or negatively affect profits. A business could purchase a long hedge when it anticipates a price increase. With a short hedge, a business sells future contracts to guard against price declines (Brigham & Gapenski, 1994).

The **short** sale is also used in the stock sale context when someone buys short with the intent of borrowing the stock from a broker and waiting for the price to decline before they actually pay for the stock. The difference between the amount they borrowed the stock for and the final amount they sold it for when the stock price declined is the profit generated by this short sale. This concept is covered in greater detail in chapter 9.

To put this example into numerical terms, assume that the Celtics are willing to pay $1 million for a player currently playing in the U.K. The team negotiates a contract with a British team and agrees to pay £500,000, which at the date of signing is worth approximately $1 million U.S. The contract is not to be paid for six months, when the British team's season is over. The Celtics' financial advisor tells the team that the dollar is going to be weaker against the pound in six months. That means that in six months it might take $1.2 million to pay the £500,000. The Celtics might buy a futures contract for $1.050 million now to deliver £500,000 in six months. Thus, by entering into a futures contract

the team can save $150,000 if the currency market acts as their advisor has predicted. If the market goes the other way, the team loses. Thus, if in six months the value of the pound has dropped, it would have been possible for the Celtics to pay $950,000 to complete the transaction if they had not entered into the futures contract. While this process can be considered a gamble, more often than not financial advisors have a good record of reading market trends based on years of statistical analysis that helps identify trends and patterns.

When purchasing a futures contract, the purchaser does not have to put up the full amount. The purchaser needs to put up only an initial **margin,** which for certain Treasury bonds is only $3,000 for each $100,000 in contracts (Brigham & Grapenski, 1994). Although it might seem that this purchase price is very inexpensive, investors need to maintain a certain value in their margin account, called a maintenance margin. If the contract value declines, the futures owner is required to pay more money to cover the maintenance margin.

A futures contract can be satisfied by the actual delivery of the commodities. A farmer could sell a futures contract for 5,000 bushels of oats for a September delivery. A sport nutrition bar company might buy the contract in March so the company knows how much it will need to pay for ingredients and the farmer will know how much he will be paid for the future delivery of oats. Thus, a futures contract is a definite agreement on the part of a given party to buy something on a specific date and at a specific price. No matter how the price might change, the contract guarantees that the purchaser has locked in a price to protect against such price fluctuations. Futures can be used speculatively or for hedging. People buy speculative futures if it appears that a price might decline or rise, resulting in profits.

By carefully examining financial markets, a business can help increase its profitability and reduce the chances of losing money through inactivity. That is why it is so important to scrutinize short-term strategies concerning all facets of a business. Long-term strategies also help guide businesses, as discussed next.

Long-Term Planning

Long-term goals are often less clear since there are too many variables to allow one to make accurate projections; but even so, obtaining additional research on which to base decisions can result in more accurate projections. Long-term planning focuses on planning for the future with a greater emphasis on external variables, such as industry trends and technological advancements. The Smiths' long-term analysis might focus on developing new exercise techniques or programs that combine some of the hottest fitness trends.

The long-term plan serves as the backbone for developing the proper documentation needed to secure capital support. Potential lenders such as banks or venture capitalists look to the managerial foresight highlighted in the plan. However, no mat-ter how much information the plan contains, a lender will not invest a penny without getting a picture of the business' future profit potential. The profit potential is reflected in the pro forma budget.

As discussed earlier in this chapter, numerous decisions in the sport industry entail both short- and long-term planning. An excellent example involves the XFL (see sidebar).

The Short Story of the XFL

World Wrestling Federation Entertainment, Inc. (WWF) went public in 2000 and is listed on the New York Stock Exchange. The WWF launched its own football league, called the Extreme Football League (XFL), in 2000-2001. The launch was undertaken with a broadcast partner, NBC, with the intent of capitalizing on the young male audience that dominates in wrestling. The games were scheduled for prime-time Saturday nights and were a complete disaster. The shows had declining ratings each week, and ended with WWF taking a $37 million charge to earnings (Grover & Lowry, 2001). A charge to earnings is a fancy term for a loss. Instead of a steady loss from poor sales, a charge represents a one-time loss that the business does not expect to arise in the future. **Wall Street** did not take the news well, as some analysts were skeptical about how the WWF could expand in a saturated market after the XFL collapsed (Grover & Lowry, 2001). The concern was also reflected in a drop in the stock price from $21 per share to around $12 per share after the XFL folded. By November 2001, the company had laid off almost 10% of its employees due to lower-than-expected revenues that resulted in year-end losses ("WWF Fires COO," 2001). After a legal battle with the World Wildlife Fund (WWF), the World Wrestling Federation changes its name to World Wrestling Entertainment (WWE).

The XFL example highlights how a long-term plan such as increasing revenues by launching a new football league to possibly compete with exist-ing leagues can backfire. With a significant amount of hype and planning, the league had a decent first night because of the novelty of the event. Once advertisers started complaining about the low rat-ings and the general lack of interest in the new league, a short-term exit planning process had to be undertaken. As the XFL crumbled, the WWE had to engage in short-term planning to find other options for continued growth. The WWE started pursuing other projects such as expanding overseas broad-casts, music sales, cookbooks, and children's storybooks, as well as launching a two-hour maga-zine-style show (Grover & Lowry, 2001). Thus, when the long-term plans failed, the WWE was forced to pursue short-term plans to fill the financial void left after the XFL failed to generate the expected future revenue streams.

Short-term financial planning deals with spe-cific internal variables such as working capi-tal and the cash budget for the immediate future. Long-term planning looks out beyond the next two years and focuses more on external variables such as industry trends.

Developing a Pro Forma Budget

As highlighted in chapter 5, budgets represent the key to financial planning. Financial planning is accomplished through the development of budgets as a road map for a business' financial success. Budgets help establish a means to forecast future performance based on past results and expected external changes such as changes in the market or the economy. The budget also helps management establish goals and objectives for the business. Thus, a **budget** is first and foremost a financial plan for the future. The financial plan highlights what results are anticipated if certain financial actions are taken. For example, if you want to buy a car, you might examine your financial position and know that you can afford only $100 a month for a car. Based on this amount, you can plan your purchase based on a financial plan centered on how much of a down payment you could make and your $100 a month available for monthly payments. A financial plan is often a key component of a pro forma budget and a business plan. A pro forma budget is simply a future budget based on past financial results and expected future financial results. The pro forma budget con-tains a financial plan for the business, and the two are often combined to help complete the business plan. The business plan is the road map for the business; it contains financial analysis along with marketing, production, and other key components that help an executive or lender determine the potential for future success of the business.

Before considering the pro forma budget as part of the planning process, we should note that there is a significant difference between forecasting and budgeting. A forecast is an estimate of anticipated operations, such as how many hours given machinery will operate. The sales force could be asked what sales they would forecast for the coming quarter. In contrast, a budget is a target agreed on by management as an indicator of success; for example, management might agree that a successful year would entail selling 1 million tickets. On the basis of this distinction, it is often best to view profit planning and appropriate budgeting from a product or division perspective in which less profitable products or divisions can be isolated for more thorough analysis.

Typical extensive pro forma budgets might incorporate the following:

- A sales budget
- A promotion budget
- A budget for materials, labor, and overhead
- A cash budget
- A capital appreciation budget

All the previously listed documents or components are contingent on developing a focused strategic plan. All the numbers in the world are meaningless if there is no direction to the business. While this text is not a strategic planning text, it is important to note that the hallmark of any business is a concise corporate purpose. This overall mission for the business leads to the development of the corporate scope—a definition of the business' area of concentration. The business' area of concentration is further refined through developing the corporate objectives, strategies, and plans, which focus on how the business can achieve its corporate purpose. The financial plan is a key document produced after significant foresight has shaped the business' future direction.

The financial plan can be developed in five steps. The first step is to develop a system of projected financial statements, which can help one analyze how the operating plan will affect the projected profits. The next step requires analysts to determine the funds that will be needed to help fund the long-term plans. The third step entails forecasting what funds will be available over the long term and how much of the funding will be generated internally and externally. The fourth step requires a business to establish and maintain a system of controls governing how funds are allocated and used. The last step requires analysts to examine the results and develop procedures for adjusting the plan if the forecasts are not met (Brigham & Gapenski, 1994).

A pro forma budget reflects the focused strategic plan and overall mission of a business expressed in financial terms.

Incorporating the Pro Forma Budget in the Business Plan

The hallmark of a successful business involves a detailed business plan that accentuates the pro forma budget. This chapter has focused so far on developing a financial plan, or "road map". Once this plan is developed, it has to be communicated. While some individuals with a strong financial background can examine the pro formas and get a decent picture concerning a business, most people need a little more guidance. That guidance comes from a business plan that expands on the financial plan and communicates the business' vision using both words and pro formas. Thus, a business plan represents a blend of a financial plan and a business strategy analysis that examines both long- and short-term goals and objectives. Although there is no one correct way to write a business plan, the following framework provides the most critical elements for a business plan that you might write to submit to a bank or other investors. Within the business plan, the pro forma budget is the concise document used to show that the business plan makes financial sense and is viable and accurate. An example of the first page of a pro forma budget is shown on page 119.

The following components represent the sections in a typical business plan and were developed by Florida Atlantic University's Small Business Development Center. There are countless potential variations, however, and software to help with writing business plans is available. The Small Business Administration also offers sample forms for writing a business plan at **www.sba.gov**.

- *The plan summary* should be written after all other sections have been written. It describes
  - the purpose of your plan,
  - the product or service that you will sell and why it is unique,

Profit and Loss Summary ($000)	Year 1	Year 2	Year 3	Year 4	Year 5	Year 6	Year 7	Year 8	Year 9	Year 10
*** CONFIDENTIAL ***										
Net revenue: Sports core (schedule A)	0	0	6,167	8,543	10,334	11,183	11,252	11,265	11,265	11,265
Leasing (schedule B)	0	0	1,782	2,158	2,214	2,247	2,278	2,310	2,310	2,310
Total net revenue	**0**	**0**	**7,949**	**10,701**	**12,548**	**13,430**	**13,530**	**13,576**	**13,576**	**13,576**
Net margin	0	0	4,210	6,659	8,288	9,013	9,007	8,947	8,947	8,947
Net margin %	**0**	**0**	**53.0%**	**62.2%**	**66.1%**	**67.1%**	**66.6%**	**65.9%**	**65.9%**	**65.9%**
Period costs:										
General and administrative (worksheet 2)	486	709	1,183	1,227	1,245	1,245	1,245	1,245	1,245	1,245
Depreciation (worksheet 2)	51	586	1,139	1,157	1,174	1,192	1,068	937	816	684
Vacancy cost (worksheet 2)	0	0	99	46	42	44	45	47	47	47
Total period costs	**537**	**1,294**	**2,421**	**2,429**	**2,461**	**2,481**	**2,359**	**2,230**	**2,108**	**1,976**
Income from operations	(537)	(1,294)	1,788	4,230	5,827	6,532	6,648	6,717	6,838	6,970
Other income/(expense) (See schedule E.)	0	(1,446)	(218)	(834)	(720)	(553)	(371)	(178)	12	209
Charge-out to cap. org. expense (except depreciation)	486	709	0	0	0	0	0	0	0	0
Pretax income	(51)	(2,031)	1,571	3,395	5,106	5,979	6,278	6,539	6,851	7,179
Provision for taxes (N/A due to LLC status)	0	0	0	0	0	0	0	0	0	0
Net income	**(51)**	**(2,031)**	**1,571**	**3,395**	**5,106**	**5,979**	**6,278**	**6,539**	**6,851**	**7,179**
Ratios and valuation (assumes owning land vs. leasing)										
ROE	N/A	N/A	30.0%	46.7%	49.4%	42.9%	35.5%	30.2%	26.6%	23.9%
ROA	N/A	N/A	22.5%	36.8%	40.9%	37.0%	31.5%	27.4%	24.5%	22.3%
Net income/net revenue	N/A	N/A	19.8%	31.7%	40.7%	44.5%	46.4%	48.2%	50.5%	52.9%
Book value	449	3,668	5,238	7,276	10,339	13,927	17,694	21,617	25,727	30,035
Liabilities to net worth	2.28	5.09	0.33	0.27	0.21	0.16	0.13	0.10	0.09	0.07
Interest coverage	N/A	N/A	16.26	38.45	52.97	59.39	60.44	61.06	62.17	63.37
Debt service coverage	N/A	N/A	25.64	42.38	58.10	66.19	67.88	68.97	70.69	72.48

1. Information on this and accompanying pages is confidential. It is being provided to the reader with the understanding that it shall not be shared with others without express permission.

2. As of this date the numbers provided here are preliminary and still undergoing analysis and revision. They are best, current, conservative estimates. We are in the process of refining the financial model, testing the investment, revenue and expense projections as well as exploring various capitalization strategies.

3. Interest expense based on assumption that mortgage principle payments are level over life of notes with interest payments declining.

4. Pro forma assumes organization as an LLC. In future years the company may elect to change to a corporate structure.

The first page of a pro forma budget.

Adapted by permission from The Peak Experience, LLC. Some numbers have been changed from the original.

- second- or third-generation products or services to help maintain sales,
- the market potential,
- specific highlights in the marketing plan,
- the skills provided by the management team,
- the financial projections for the first several years,
- your funding needs, and
- an exit strategy if the business does not succeed.

- *The industry section* should highlight the economics in the industry, industry trends, and potential legal or regulatory concerns and should critically analyze the competitive forces you might face. This section requires objective information that can be verified. Most of the information in this section should be documented through secondary data from reliable sources. Sources of secondary data could include government reports, Better Business Bureau reports, reports from national or international trade organizations, research conducted by competitors, or even magazine or newspaper articles. Primary data, as discussed earlier, are data generated by the business itself—for example, results of a customer satisfaction survey of a competitor's customers to help determine if the customers would prefer a different option or service. Regardless of the data used to substantiate statements in the industry section, all such data should be copied and attached to the business plan as exhibits.

- *The company section* describes the history and background of the business. It can include the mission statement, objectives, goals (long-term and short-term), and strategies. This section should also list the current principal owner(s) or majority stockholder(s), all members of the board of directors (if applicable), and all key executives. Last, this section should include the business' address; form of organization (sole proprietorship, partnership, limited liability company, or corporation); and any pertinent local, regional, or federal license requirements (such as requirements for handling pool chemicals). Any special circumstances concerning the company should be specified, such as what stock purchase options exist if the company goes public or whether key employees have noncompete

contracts. Any data an investor would need to make an investment decision should be included. For example, if a company-owned patent is about to expire, which would mean that competitors could start manufacturing the previously protected item, the company could face significant hardships. Similarly, if the Smiths had leased a fitness facility and the lease was about to expire, meaning they could be without a facility, such a fact would need to be disclosed. The plan needs to highlight such hardships even if they hurt the prospects for raising capital. The failure to include critical data can lead to allegations of fraud or negligent or intentional misrepresentation.

- *The analysis of the product or service* is a thorough analysis of the product's or service's unique qualities, which will help distinguish the product or service from those offered by competitors. You want to critically analyze the risks associated with the product or service and the reasons purchasers might not buy your product or service. You will need to critically analyze any market surveys or other research that helps you draw your conclusions about your product or service or that of the competition. Last, this section should identify any ancillary products or services that also might be produced to develop a more significant product or service line. If you were developing an indoor rock-climbing facility, for example, you would examine that facility in relation to
  - any home-based climbing apparatus,
  - any club-based climbing apparatus,
  - options available at health clubs,
  - the uniqueness of the industry,
  - the demand for leisure sports or recreational activities in a given community,
  - the availability of other climbing facilities within a 20-mile radius of the proposed facility,
  - the availability of natural climbing areas nearby and how weather patterns will affect usage,
  - the availability of safety-related products, and
  - the availability of trained instructors to work with patrons.

- *The market section* focuses on the demographic characteristics of the proposed market. Who is the target market? What is its size? Can these people be reached? And do they have the funds necessary to purchase the product or service? You will need to critically examine the market to determine whether the potential customers or clients buy on a regular basis or seasonally, whether they best respond to sales or coupons, whether there are better locations from which to reach the intended market. Look through the yellow pages and identify the competition by name, address, and phone number. Visit the competition to see how big they are, what products or services they offer, whether or not they are busy, and when they are busy. After you analyze the potential market and the competition, you should establish one-year and five-year sales goals.

- *The marketing strategy section* of the business plan applies the product or service characteristics to the customer's demands. This section focuses on how to sell or distribute the product or service to potential buyers and requires applying the four P's of marketing—place, product, price, and promotion. Sample brochures, advertisements, announcements, product packaging, product or service guarantees, and related materials should be included. The price for the product or service should be clearly explained and compared with prices charged by competitors. This section should include all relevant information that was obtained through the marketing research process and used as a basis for the marketing decisions.

- *The operation section* describes how the product will be developed and produced or how the service will be delivered. Here you should discuss critical dates—when production will begin, who will produce products, where the inventory will come from, what shipping schedule will be followed, how products will be delivered to clients, and so on. Writing this section requires that you have analyzed the financial and managerial control mechanisms for tracking production, inventory, and shipping, as well as accounting procedures and the like. This section should conclude by specifying the steps that will be taken if the sales goals are not reached, such as inventory liquidation, and the revenue such procedures can realize.

- *The management and personnel section* lists all the key individuals necessary for the business to be successful, with brief biographies of past accomplishments and potential references. This section should highlight the key skills that will be required for the business to succeed and indicate how the key individuals fit within the necessary skill areas. In addition to discussing qualifications here, you will typically analyze the compensation package key individuals are receiving or will receive.

- *The financial projections section* addresses when investors can make their money back and what profit they can realize. Anyone who might be interested in investing in your business will probably view this as the most important section of the business plan. Although the product or service, marketing strategy, and personnel are critical areas, investors may be most interested in the return on their money. Projected cash flow needs to be calculated on a month-to-month basis for the first year until a positive cash flow can be realized and then maintained. The cash flow should also be calculated annually for five years. These projections should be augmented with pro forma income statements and balance sheets. From these pro forma statements the potential investor can start making calculations to determine critical points for business growth and expansion, such as the break-even point or return on investment.

- *The capital needs section* covers what funds will be needed to launch the business and when the funds will be needed. The plan should highlight what the funds will be used for to help establish potential collateral. Thus, if the funds will be used to purchase a building, a lending institution will probably be more willing to extend the loan knowing that the loan proceeds could be secured by the building. This section also needs to detail how the money will be repaid, over what time period, and what penalties might apply for late payments. Last, this section should cover any ownership potential that might be available. If you are willing to sell a 10% stake in the business to the right investor, you need to explain the potential deal in great detail. Detail is required especially if someone else can purchase a controlling interest or can assume liability for financial obligations.

- *A miscellaneous section* can be added that contains relevant pictures, price lists, facility diagrams, a listing of necessary equipment, or a discussion of any unusual risks (Pounds, 1997).

Many business plans are written every day. Most never receive any funds. Most business plans fail due to lack of research, preparation, and presentation. The following is a top-10 list of characteristics seen in successful business plans:

1. Clear and realistic financial projections are the most important element.

2. The plan contains detailed and documented objective market research.

3. The plan includes a detailed analysis of all competitors.

4. The plan demonstrates that the management team is more than capable of leading the company.

5. There is a "killer" summary that is only two to three pages long and includes critical projections such as income statements.

6. The plan provides proof of the writer's vision by clearly differentiating the product or service from that of competition.

7. The document follows a clear plan and, most important, is written in proper English that is clear, precise, and free of grammatical mistakes.

8. The most effective plans are short, rarely exceeding 40 pages. Documents longer than this can become too cumbersome to read.

9. The writer clearly explains the bottom line— why the money is needed and how investors will be repaid.

10. The writer has taken the time to make the plan her own. When people write business plans using their own words, instead of hiring an outside writer or using canned computer software, the reader has a better feel for their sincerity (Elkins, 1996).

The business plan is a document that gives readers a complete and detailed picture of a proposed business. Realistic financial projections may be the most important element of a business plan.

CONCLUSION

Vigilance is the key to effective financial planning. Managers need to take the time to effectively research all prior actions and potential future actions. Planning cannot focus just on the past. Planning requires a critical analysis of the future, and estab-

lished criteria for success help show whether the plan in fact was successful. By doing their homework, managers can learn a great deal about their business. The research required to prepare budgets and develop business plans can provide a significant education about a business. All the individuals in the planning process have valuable information about the business. This insight can be of great help. If chief financial officers meet with individual salespeople, they may uncover reasons why certain products do not sell as well in particular regions or locations and can use this knowledge to help allocate resources more effectively. Thus, the planning process is not designed just to keep employees busy, but is the only technique available to prepare a business for the future. The hurdles and opportunities identified in the planning process lead to finalizing the capital budgeting process covered in chapter 11.

ASSIGNMENT

Take all the information presented in the text to this point, as well as information on a particular city as specified at the end of this paragraph, and develop a two- to three-page business plan for the Smiths comprising the 11 sections described in the chapter. Since you are in the Smiths' shoes when writing the plan, you can develop any special opportunities such as unique programs to attract new members or assume the Smiths' willingness to sell 25% of the company to an equity partner. Your focus should be on the research and not on a pro forma budget, which could be created using fictional numbers. Each student should be assigned a different city and should conduct real research on that city, analyzing such issues as competition, local costs, marketing opportunities, and related matters.

RESEARCH PROJECTS

1. Track stocks in a given industry group, and critically analyze the market segment to determine why the stocks are increasing or decreasing in price.

2. Conduct research using the school business library, the Internet, or both to find the following items:

   a. Which sport or recreational activity (such as walking or fishing) had the greatest number of participants last year?

   b. Which professional team among teams in the four major professional leagues had the highest attendance last year?

c. Which professional team among those in the four major professional leagues had the highest revenue from broadcasting last year?

CLASS DISCUSSION TOPICS

1. Discuss a rough budget for an individual's finances.

2. Discuss a short-term plan for a perennially losing team and identify specific steps that could be taken to increase income or generate victories.

3. Discuss a long-term plan for a perennially losing team and identify specific steps that could be taken to increase income or generate victories.

PART III
Capital Structuring

Obtaining Funding

CHAPTER OBJECTIVES

After studying this chapter, you should be able to do the following:

- Describe where money comes from.
- Compare various short-term borrowing strategies.
- Understand how to utilize personal funds and private financing as a source of capital.
- Understand how government-backed borrowing can spur economic growth.
- Understand how to utilize existing resources to leverage a business' financial position.
- Distinguish between leasing and other financial vehicles.

There is no one correct method to fund a sport business. Some individuals acquire a sport business through inheritance and do not need any funds to become owners. This has happened to many professional team owners as in the case of the Rooney family, who have owned the Pittsburgh Steelers for several generations. Other owners have tapped numerous sources such as their credit cards, relatives, and bank **loans** to keep a business alive. Each business is different and requires its own unique blend of financing. The various funding techniques combine to form the **capital** structure of a business.

The total number of options and techniques that can be used to obtain funds is all but limitless. Some individuals have made their fortunes through luck while others have relied upon hard work. Arthur Rooney, the famed founder of the Pittsburgh Steelers, bought the franchise for $2,500 in 1933. It is rumored that he obtained the money for the franchise by winning $250,000 at the horse track in 1932 ("Arthur J. Rooney," 2002). John Moores, the San Diego Padres' owner, invested a small amount in the late 1970s in BMC Software, Inc. Through hard work, designing innovative products, and a strong marketing push, he made a fortune ("Company," 2002). With these funds, he purchased the Padres. An individual could win the lottery and use these funds to start a business. Former athletes have taken the money they obtained from professional sport and used those funds to help launch or buy a business.

Examples include Dave Bing, who started the Bing Group, considered one of the largest black-owned businesses ("Bing Group Capsule," 2002), and Isiah Thomas, who purchased the entire Continental Basketball Association in 1999 for $9 to $10 million, which included a $5 million down payment and four future payments. Two years later the league was bankrupt, and Thomas' holding company owed at least $5 million to various lenders ("Left for Dead," 2001).

Although this chapter and the subsequent chapters on stocks and bonds (chapters 9 and 10) highlight for-profit businesses, we make some reference to funds utilized by government and tax-exempt businesses. This will be the case primarily in chapter 10; but, as with for-profit businesses, both government and nonprofit organizations can utilize countless other techniques to raise funds. Someone paying money from her own wallet, to cover initial costs, can help finance a Special Olympics event. Organizations can put expenses on credit cards; individuals can provide collateral to back a loan; a facility can be used as collateral for obtaining a loan. One of the major differences between government and nonprofit organizations is the opportunity to receive gifts and the potential tax consequences associated with such funding techniques. Tax issues associated with gifts are covered in chapter 14. One unique funding technique that was utilized to help support the 1976 Montreal Olympics is discussed in the following sidebar.

Fund-Raising Through Unique Financial Vehicles

Not all funds needed to fund sport events are derived from television rights payments, ticket sales, sponsorship contracts, or similar income-generating techniques. Obscure revenue-generating techniques can raise significant funds or can be significant failures. Olympic stamps and coins are a good example of both extremes and were both used by Canada in its effort to help finance the 1976 Olympic Games.

The Olympic Coin Program

The lineage of Olympic coinage is formidable. Anaxilas, a ruler of Sicily, ordered the first recorded minting of a coin struck especially to commemorate a sporting event in about 480 B.C. The silver tetradrachm coin honored his victory in a historic chariot race and appropriately depicted the winner bearing a laurel wreath. Since the 1950s, several Olympic host countries have issued a variety of commemorative coins to defray costs of the Games. However, Canada's coin program was considered one of the most successful (*Charlton Standard Catalogue*, 1990).

Basically, the program was aimed at selling collections of 28 specially minted silver $1, $5, and $10 coins. Canada was also the first country hosting the Olympics to issue a gold coin in the denomination of $100.

The margin between the cost of production and the face value of coins is known as seigniorage. According to the Canadian legislation authorizing the coins, it was the right of the seignior, or issuing authority, to retain that difference as profit. Profits from sales of the Olympic coins were initially expected to reach between $125 and $500 million. The coins were very successful, but they were issued at the height of an internationally depressed economy. However, through 1977, sales of the coins had reached

$386 million (of which $278.7 million represented the face value of all coins delivered), which by law had to be held in reserve by the Canadian government. The expenditures over and above the face value of the coins totaled only $8 million. Thus, the program netted a profit of close to $100 million.

The Olympic Stamp Program

The Olympic Stamp Program was yet another unique fund-raising effort designed to help finance the 1976 Olympic Games. Canada Post's fund-raising focused on four areas: Olympic action stamps, commemorative stamps, stamp sculptures, and stamp souvenirs. In 1974 Canada brought out its first set of semi-postal issues—postage stamps that carried a surcharge. The purpose of the surcharge was to give the public a convenient opportunity to support the Olympic Games on a voluntary basis. Germany, France, and Japan all have used semipostal stamps when hosting the Games. Additional sets were issued by Canada in 1975 and 1976 (Gandley & Stanley, 1978).

The Olympic action stamps bore two different prices, separated by a plus sign (+). The first price on each stamp indicated the postal value of the stamp, the other the amount of the surcharge; the two amounts combined gave the sale price of the stamp. Thus, a stamp with a 15 + 5 marking included $0.15 of postage and a $0.05 contribution to the Olympic effort. The post office collected $0.20 for each one of these stamps sold. A similar approach was utilized by the U.S. postal service in the 1990s to raise funds for breast cancer research.

To support the Olympic Stamp Program, Canada Post developed a promotional program under the umbrella theme Help It Happen. Advertisements were published in all major Canadian newspapers and magazines and in specialized publications the world over; commercials were aired on television and radio networks. Display stands, posters, and decals were used in post offices to attract the customer's attention. In spite of all the promotion, the stamps did not generate the target figure of $10 million. Purchasers either were opposed to the idea or were hesitant to try anything new.

The sidebar on the Olympic revenue-generating program highlights that any given effort to raise funds can be very unique and imaginative. However, most fund-raising for sport businesses follows established patterns that have been utilized for years by countless businesses. This chapter highlights the basic approaches to raising funds without necessarily having to incur significant costs or selling owners' equity. The chapter starts with an examination of basic funding sources for starting a business, such as personal bank loans, credit cards, or government assistance. The chapter then covers open market and short-term borrowing options. Next, the chapter examines several long-term borrowing options. The chapter concludes with an analysis of funding options for minority-owned businesses, including advice on how to obtain funding.

Where the Money Comes From

Most consumers have faced a financial crisis in which they needed money but found that sources of funds were lacking. Some people can approach their parents and ask for a loan. Money sometimes comes from an inheritance or in the form of a raise. Sometimes increased monetary streams can be expected—such as an annual cost-of-living salary increase to keep a salary at pace with inflation. At other times money might not come in when it is expected. You might anticipate receiving an Internal Revenue Service refund by a certain date and have to change your plans significantly if there is a delay. But what happens when you need a substantial amount of money and your likelihood of receiving a major gift is astronomically small? You have to analyze alternative approaches for raising the needed capital.

Not all capital needs arise from emergencies. Numerous capital structuring changes occur because of anticipated growth—growth that can occur only through the exploration of various capital financing options. This chapter deals with the various capital options available to those seeking to raise needed capital. We give special attention to individual borrowing, SBA loans, commercial lending, and venture capital. Subsequent chapters will cover issuing various types of stocks, issuing bonds, and obtaining capital assistance from the government. There is no one correct method of raising funds, and this chapter presents the diverse techniques available.

The Smiths are faced with the question of how to raise necessary start-up capital. They do not have a large amount of cash available to support their dreams. What if they want to purchase some expensive exercise equipment for their proposed facility? They do some initial research and discover that there are four primary means to obtain the equipment: renting, paying cash, obtaining a loan, and leasing (Haynie, 1998).

If the Smiths rent the machines there will be no up-front cash expenditures, except for a possible down payment or a security deposit. The Smiths will face lower upkeep and repair costs using this strategy and could return the equipment if they were not satisfied with the quality. However, renting equipment is normally not a good long-term option, as the final cost of renting equipment for several years could be double what it would have been with a conventional bank loan or with leasing (Haynie, 1998). Note that both rental and lease payments are 100% tax deductible as a business expense.

If the Smiths purchase the equipment with cash, they can avoid **finance charges** and depreciate the equipment. However, even if they had significant cash reserves and they did invest in a machine, they could no longer use those funds to pay for additional growth that might generate a greater return in the future.

A bank loan could be an effective technique for purchasing the equipment. A bank would require background material such as a credit check, tax returns, financial statements, and collateral. On the basis of the need to possibly sell the equipment upon loan default, a bank might provide a loan that covered only a certain percentage of the equipment's actual purchase price. If a new piece of equipment were to be purchased for $10,000 but would be worth only $8,000 by year's end, the bank might limit its exposure by lending only $6,500 toward the purchase.

If the Smiths lease the equipment, they can receive flexible terms and 100% financing. Initial expenses could include 2% to 5% of the purchase price as a down payment plus any applicable taxes and installation, delivery, and related "soft" costs. The key benefit of leasing involves the potential to expense 100% of the payments every month with pretax dollars (Haynie, 1998). Assume that the Smiths finance $36,000 in equipment for $843 per month. If they made $5,000 a month profit, $1,500 of this amount would go to

taxes if their tax rate was 30%. But if the Smiths reduced the $5,000 profit by $843, their potential taxes would decline from $1,500 to $1,247 (30% × $4,157). The $253 tax savings when subtracted from the $843 monthly lease obligation results in an actual payment of $590 for the leased equipment. When the $590 cost is multiplied over the actual term of the lease (60 months), the total cost is $35,400, which is less than the purchase price if they had purchased the equipment for $36,000 (Haynie, 1998). The **lease option** might be attractive, as there might not be an initial **capital outlay** to encumber the cash balances. In addition, the Smiths would face less risk if the product broke or became obsolete, and they could obtain a service agreement to keep the machine in working condition.

The same concerns that people face in deciding how to finance items such as a new business or equipment can apply to any decision requiring capital outlays. For example, if an investor wanted to build a golf course, he would need a significant amount of up-front capital to purchase the land and develop the course. It might be several years before the course would be suitable for use, and this would mean several years without any income. Most investors would shy away from a deal that was uncertain and that would not produce revenue for several years. A 1994 National Golf Foundation report concluded that financing for the average golf course loan requires 40% to 50% equity. This means that to build a $5 million course, developers would need to raise approximately $2 to $2.5 million from other sources such as their own money, limited partnerships, corporate investments, syndications, pension funds, or possibly **real estate investment trusts** (REITs) in order to obtain a bank loan (Turley, 1998). Such large equity requirements are based on the competitiveness of the golf course industry, a course's potential resale value, uncertain projected cash flow, uncontrollable factors such as weather conditions, and other variables. Nonetheless, there are experienced golf course lenders who search for opportunities. These lenders can utilize flexibility to design loans that could include

1. capitalizing working capital requirements and income shortfalls,
2. requiring sufficient cash reserves to cover any possible contingency, or
3. offering their own equity participation to help decrease the required borrower's equity,

which will help lower the debt interest rate (Turley, 1998).

Another option for a golf course would be to finance the course through the public coffers. Municipal golf courses have been built for years utilizing standard voter-approved bonds or the newer revenue bonds that could be paid back from the course's revenue. Other means to finance a municipal course could include general budget allocations (as a line item in a budget), the selling of bonds, and establishing a public development corporation, with the city having a contractor design and construct the course on a turnkey basis (Turley, 1998). Utilizing a turnkey basis, the contractor performs all the building construction and design functions for a set price and then turns the building over to the owner when all the work is completed ("Construction Glossary," 2002).

The same options that are possible for building a golf course can be applied to building a professional sport stadium or arena. Because of the hundreds of millions of dollars required to build a stadium or arena, the financing tools utilized by the Smiths or a golf course developer would typically not generate all the necessary funds. For a privately financed facility, the typical financing tools include loans, bonds, cash contribution, partnerships, equity offerings, and related investment pools. If the project was a public facility, the following financing techniques could be used:

- Loans
- General obligation bonds
- Project revenue bonds
- Tax revenue bonds
- Certificates of participation
- Tax incremental financing
- Tax exemptions
- Tax rebates (Miller, W.S., 1998)

Loans are simple borrowing agreements in which the borrower agrees to repay the borrowed amount at a set time at a set interest rate. General obligation bonds are bonds issued by a municipality that agrees to utilize any and all tax revenue it obtains to repay the bond. Project revenue bonds are more specific, with revenue generated from the project being dedicated to repay the bond. Tax revenue bonds are backed by general tax revenue collected by the municipality, such as property taxes. With certificates of participation, purchasers buy a share of the lease revenues, rather than the bond being secured by these revenues ("Certificate of Participation," 2002). These revenues are then usually used to construct a facility. Tax incremental financing, discussed in greater detail in chapter 14, represents a municipality's decision to forgo taxes from a landowner, such as a stadium owner, to encourage that landowner to build a facility in a given neighborhood. The municipality hopes that bringing the facility into the neighborhood will increase other property values and thus increase the general tax base for the entire municipality. A tax exemption refers to a waiver of tax obligations as an incentive to attract a business or build a new facility. The Texas Motor Speedway received such an exemption, and it was so significant that the school district subsequently sued to recover some of its lost tax revenue (Gibeaut, 1999). A tax rebate is similar to a refund: the municipality returns some or all the money a business has paid in whichever tax category is being rebated. Thus, a team could receive a rebate of their property taxes but still need to pay sales and utility taxes.

Thus there are numerous techniques available for funding business growth, whether a new gym needs to be built or a team is interested in renovating a stadium. The options are as countless as the number of individuals who have money to invest. Each deal can be structured to meet the needs of the parties involved. As an example of one combination, a deal might include financing from family, friends, corporate partners, and a venture capitalist. Obviously it would be impossible to describe every means of financing a business in this text; instead we will focus on several major sources for funds, including yourself, relatives and friends, banks, nonbank lenders, public stock offering, bonds, and venture capitalists. Before we discuss each capital acquisition method, it will be helpful to identify the three primary categories of sources of capital.

1. *Equity investors,* who purchase a portion of the business, in the form of stock, for example, with the hope of future returns through capital gains or dividend payments. Since equity owners assume significant risk that a business might not succeed, they typically require a higher rate of return to offset the higher risk. This reward is evidenced through either increased stock value or dividend payments to the stock (equity) owner.

2. *Long-term debt obligations,* such as bonds. A bondholder is interested in receiving an appropriate

rate of return on the investment with the lowest possible risk. Bondholders do not benefit the way equity investors do if the corporation becomes very successful. However, the risk of losing the investment is greatly reduced because the bonds are secured by collateral.

3. *Short-term loans.* Suppliers of merchandise or raw goods are often the source of loans of this type as they sell goods on the basis that the buyer will pay within 30 days, for example.

Personal Resources

Sometimes people accumulate money from a current job with the intention of someday starting their own business. Often these sums are wholly inadequate for that purpose. Industry professionals highlight the need to set aside at least two years' worth of living expenses in preparation for starting your own business. This is necessary because most new full-time businesses take at least a year, and sometimes many more years, to earn enough profit to pay the business owner a salary (Pounds, 1997). Proper financial planning can help eliminate numerous hurdles that might arise during a business' formative years. However, the planning process needs to begin long before a business starts up, and sufficient capital reserves are required to sustain the business through cyclical and seasonal downturns.

If you do not have enough cash or investments that could be liquidated to start the business, you might consider a home loan. Home equity financing requires borrowers to utilize their house as collateral when obtaining a loan from a bank or other lending institution. The loan amount is based on the equity the borrower has in the home. Suppose you have a house that is worth $100,000 on the market today. You paid $60,000 for the house 10 years ago, with $10,000 down and a $50,000 mortgage. You paid off $20,000 on the mortgage and still owe $30,000 on the mortgage. Thus, if you were to sell the house for $100,000, you would receive free and clear of the mortgage $70,000 ($100,000 − $30,000 remaining on the mortgage). The $70,000 represents the equity you have in the house and is the maximum amount you could borrow from a lending institution.

Home equity loans are traditionally favored over other loans because they carry a lower interest rate. Furthermore, some banks are willing to lend more than 100% of a home's value, depending on what the loan proceeds will be used to purchase. New businesses are highly speculative, and only 20% of new businesses survive (Zikmund & d'Amico, 1996). Therefore, some banks require substantial equity before loaning to a new business; established businesses with significant financial history are more reliable, and owners of these businesses can obtain larger mortgages.

Although most financial advisors do not recommend borrowing on a credit card because of the high interest rates, credit cards can also generate funds from which to start a business. However, anyone using this method of borrowing must be careful to repay the debt as quickly as possible, or the interest charges will negate any potential benefits that could have accrued from not having to approach other lenders such as banks. Furthermore, the high rate of small business failures should serve as a warning that a business owner could be paying off debts for years after a business has failed. With a high interest rate, the repayment obligation could force an individual into bankruptcy (see chapter 17).

The key to utilizing credit cards is to maintain a good **credit rating.** Especially if using personal credit cards, borrowers have to be vigilant in ensuring that purchases and repayments do not hurt their credit rating. A credit rating can plunge if the credit card bills are not paid on time or if payment is always late.

How Credit Card Applicants Are Rated

When determining whom to issue a credit card to, companies often utilize complex computer programs that score an applicant. The scoring technique analyzes distinct credit patterns to determine the likelihood that a borrower will repay any debts. Scores range from 375 to 900, with higher scores indicating lower likelihood of default (Sichelman, 1998). The key factors that can lower a score are late payments, collections, bankruptcies, outstanding debts, a short or nonexistent credit history, credit inquiries, and applications for new credit (Sichelman, 1998). If you are concerned about your potential score, you should have a lender order a report because traditional personal credit reports do not contain a score.

Percentage of Points Given to Help Determine Your Credit Score

Category	Percent
Payment history	35
Amounts owed	30
Length of credit history	15
New or attempted credit accounts	10
Variety of credit types	10

Data from "Planning for Success," 2000.

Can the Government Help You Get a Bank Loan?

An individual's credit history might limit her ability to obtain bank financing. However, the government has developed several programs to help small businesses borrow funds, even if the owner does not have the best credit history. The federal government realized the need for helping small businesses in the 1950s. In 1953 it created the Small Business Administration (SBA) to "aid, counsel, and protect the interest of the nation's small business community" (SBA, 2002). The SBA accomplishes this by working with lending institutions to encourage and promote loans and other financing to small businesses. For example, the SBA started the Microloan Program in 1992 with the express purpose of helping individuals realize the American dream of owning their own business (Hodges, 1997). The microloans range from $100 to $25,000; the average loan is around $10,000. These loans need to be paid back in four years at 10.8% interest. The SBA created over 100 loan outlets throughout the United States through various nonprofit organizations. The only requirement is for the company requesting funds to prepare a business plan that can meet the loan criteria.

The SBA also offers various other programs to encourage investing in small businesses. The SBA's 7(a) Loan Guarantee and Certified Development Company programs provide a guarantee for approved lenders if the borrower defaults on the SBA-backed loan. The SBA will not repay the loan. Instead, the SBA requires the lender to go after the borrower's collateral and then will supplement any remaining shortfall that might have been guaranteed.

 Assume that the Smiths use a 7(a) loan to finance their fitness center. The Smiths enter into a loan with their home as the collateral and 80% of the loan unguaranteed. If they borrow $100,000 from an SBA-approved lending institution, the loan is guaranteed by the SBA for $20,000; but the lending institution first needs to pursue recovery from the Smiths. If the Smiths' home is sold for $80,000 to pay the debt, the lending institution is still owed $20,000 and would look to the SBA to cover the $20,000 balance.

The SBA loans money to individuals starting a business if they have

- excellent credit, including no collection letters in the past three years;
- no bankruptcies in the past 10 years;
- a business plan;
- some type of collateral, such as a home; and
- up to one-third of the required capital to put into the business (Pounds, 1997).

Once these criteria have been met, the SBA has several lending programs available including the 7(a) and Microloan programs, as well as 504 and Certified Development Company, Certified Preferred Lender, and Surety Bond programs. The 7(a) program is the one that is most commonly used. In Hartford, Connecticut, 555 SBA-backed loans were approved in 1999, totaling $124 million. Over 94% of those loans (533) were 7(a) loans, and 50% (279) of all loans were for amounts under $100,000 (SBA, 2002). The market for SBA-guaranteed loans has become so big that a secondary market has been created to sell these loans. Lenders are able to sell the guaranteed portions of the SBA-guaranteed loans to investors and increase their yield on the unguaranteed portions of the SBA loans.

Self-Funding

Funds for a business can also come from the business itself. An established business might utilize depreciation allowances and profits not paid out as dividends as a way of fueling further expansion. For example, if a golf cart is purchased for $10,000 and has a five-year life, it can be depreciated $2,000 a year. The $2,000 deduction reduces total tax obligations and represents funds that should be set aside to help purchase another golf cart in the future. Most businesses also retain a percentage of their profits, whether at regular or random intervals, for future needs. These retained earnings are for future use and are not intended to pay salaries or other current expenses.

Companies often have extra cash that might be sitting around for one day or several months. Liquid assets can be invested in a bank, in commercial paper, or in Treasury bills for a short period and then withdrawn for any fiscal needs. The interest earned from such investments can be used for future development.

Another example of a self-funding concept is raising prices. If the Boston Celtics want to hire two new star players, they can anticipate their payroll increasing several million dollars a year. Borrowing funds from a bank or other lending institution can be risky. The Pittsburgh Penguins filed for bankruptcy in 1998, and part of their debt was attributable to players' salaries. Other teams face a similar problem when they attempt to cover their payrolls. A standard industry technique for covering such expenses is to raise ticket prices. If the Celtics' ticket prices were raised 10%, the resulting increased income might be enough to fund both players. Although the funds for the new players' salaries come from customers and constitute external funds, they are generated from internal marketing efforts rather than from debt or equity sources.

The University of Houston provides another good example of internally generated capital. Student fees are utilized as a revenue source to help fund the athletic department. If the athletic department needs additional funds, it can petition the students to increase their contribution level. As with Celtics customers, who can avoid purchasing higher-priced tickets, students can reject the higher prices by voting against raising fees. However, if the fees are raised, the athletic department will have a stable source of additional funds to fuel future expansion. The athletic department can also hold fund-raising events such as charity auctions or hoop-a-thons and generate additional revenue without having to tap any debt resources.

The Smiths could also try to raise funds before the fitness center even opens. They could develop a membership drive to sign up prospective members who will be entitled to pay $500 for a two-year membership and $200 a year in subsequent years. If the Smiths sell 200 such memberships, they will have $100,000 to pay for construction costs. However, some states require clubs to keep preopening revenue in escrow until the club is opened (Caro, 2000). Even if they cannot touch these initial funds, the Smiths would have 200 membership contracts that could be used as collateral for a loan. Such collateral is often called contractually obligated revenue or contractually obligated income. Large stadiums and arenas use naming rights and luxury box contracts as collateral to secure loans.

Although it is very difficult for business owners to finance capital growth by themselves, it can be done. Through savings, use of credit cards, government assistance, or internally generated funds, a business owner can find means to grow. More often than not, though, the business owner will need help from relatives or external investors.

Relatives and Friends

Some people are fortunate enough to have wealthy family members or friends who are willing to invest in a business. But most people do not have a Daddy Warbucks in their circle, and in this case they must go elsewhere for funding. However, if you are able to obtain money from a parent or another relative, there are specific steps you should take to maximize the benefits to yourself and the other parties. Many people borrow money from friends or relatives on a regular basis. Most of these arrangements are never documented. Most people would not think that their own flesh and blood or best friend could fail to pay a debt. But courtrooms are filled with individuals who have broken such promises.

If the Smiths' parents loaned them money and the venture failed, could the parents claim a bad investment? Under existing IRS regulations, the parents would be able to claim a tax deduction for the lost funds only if they first sued to collect (Marullo, 1998, March). If they sued and were unable to collect, they could claim a nonbusiness bad-debt deduction. The lost amount would be deducted from the parents' **long-** and **short-term capital gains.** If the loan loss exceeded the total capital gains, the parents could deduct $3,000 of the nonbusiness bad debt and carry over any remaining amounts to possibly deduct in $3,000 increments in future years (Marullo, 1998, March).

To avoid any improprieties, you should take the following steps whenever you borrow money from family members or friends who might have to write off a bad debt in the future:

1. Document the loan with a formal agreement.
2. Develop a formal repayment schedule.
3. Pledge security or collateralize the loan.
4. Keep accurate records of all repayments.
5. Make sure you have proof that the business was solvent when the loan was made.
6. Provide the lender with a detailed business plan specifying how the loan will be repaid (Marullo, 1998, March).

A relative or friend could also play the part of an "angel" who comes to the rescue. An angel is a major investor who can give a small amount or several million (Ambrosini, 2002). One of the most well-known angel investors in the sport industry is Paul Allen, a founder of Microsoft and owner of the Portland Trailblazers and Seattle Seahawks. Allen operates an angel investment firm that has invested in sport-related entities such as electronic ticketing businesses and Charter Communications, a major cable operator ("Paul Allen," 2002). Unlike venture capitalists, who want the business to go public and who invest only in larger projects, angel investors often come into a project before venture capital investors do or when they anticipate being part of a smaller but still profitable business. No matter who provides the capital, there are always risks associated with accepting money from others. Some concerns are

- whether the lender requires an ownership interest,
- whether the lender will demand a say in management decisions,
- whether there is an exit strategy once the business is sound enough to repay the angel and regain control, and
- whether interest payments will be tax deductible as a business expense.

Friends or acquaintances can also be a good source for funds. People often think they need to find someone with a fancy car or big house to approach for funds. However, research shows that the average millionaire does not live in such a grand style. In *The Millionaire Next Door,* Albert Hoffman concluded that of the 3.5 million millionaires in the United States in 1996, most owned less expensive cars such as Fords, ran mundane businesses, and lived well below their means (Stehle, 1997). Hoffman suggests that rather than trying to meet potential investors at the polo grounds or the opera house, individuals go to industry trade shows to meet people who might be willing to invest (Stehle, 1997).

Loyal customers also represent a potential funding source. The Mad River Glen Cooperative is one of the nation's smallest (and oldest) ski resorts, but it is financially sound. Loyal skiers are willing to pay $1,750 a share for stock in the cooperative and $200 a year thereafter. These funds and the dedicated following of loyal skiers help make the single-lift facility successful. The resort's management has critically examined expenses and determined that the resort needs to be open only 90 days a year to make a profit. Since the top customers are also owners, the resort understands its investment options and maintains a lower run price than other resorts. The company also does not invest a significant amount in new equipment like chairlifts or snow-making machines that could cost $1,000 an hour to operate. Customer loyalty is so strong that when a dividend was paid in 1998 ($16.43 per share), many stockholders suggested that the resort just keep the money (Goo, 2000).

Although family or friends can be a source for capital infusion, many business owners do not want to risk souring a good relationship. What if the initial capital infusion was not enough? What if more funds are needed, but the business owner does not want the initial investor to lose any money? What if the lender needs the money back immediately? Such issues associated with exit strategies are very critical. Individuals who do not want to make enemies of family members or friends might try to find funding through external sources such as the open market.

> *Start-up capital or additional capital for a sport business could come from many sources, including personal resources, government programs such as SBA-backed loans, the business itself (in the case of an existing business), and relatives or friends.*

Open Markets and Other Short-Term Borrowing

There are several effective techniques for raising funds on either a short- or a long-term basis. Long-term equity or capital funding techniques are discussed later in this chapter. Short-term funding techniques include borrowing to purchase inventories, supplies, or other items or pay expenses in situations in which the repayment period is expected to be less than 90 days. For purchases that require longer funding commitments, midterm, start-up, or long-term funding strategies might be needed.

People often find short-term and long-term funds in the open market. The open market is a free enterprise environment where anyone who wants to borrow and anyone who wants to loan money can enter into a relationship—somewhat similar to the traditional bazaar in which sellers and customers come together and negotiate on the price of goods. A bank is part of the open market because anyone can enter a bank and, with collateral or a good credit history, borrow money. Likewise, a successful business can be approached by numerous lenders interested in lending it money.

The Boston Celtics might need to use long-term funding options such as issuing stocks or bonds to purchase a new scoreboard or renovate their arena. They might require short-term funds to pay expenses or salaries if the players are on strike. The Smiths might need to use short-term borrowing to meet current accounts payable but need long-term funding to purchase expensive equipment. Sport Manufacturing Company (SMC) might need short-term funds to buy inventories or pay unexpected expenses such as settlement of a lawsuit. The company also might need long-term funds to buy manufacturing equipment or lease a new facility. In other words, every business at times experiences a need for long- or short-term funds.

Short-term funds may be needed in order for a business to meet monthly, seasonal, or other temporary financial needs. It does not make sense for a business to obligate itself to several years of interest payments if the money will be available to repay the loan in several months. A major advantage of short-term borrowing is the relative ease of such transactions. Banks and other lending institutions are accustomed to providing short-term loans, whether the money is required for several hours or several months. Many companies maintain a **line of credit** with a lending institution that allows them to borrow short-term funds on a preapproved basis.

The Celtics are such a large and financially strong business that several banks might each provide them with millions of dollars in lines of credit. For the purpose of this discussion, assume that the Celtics have a $5 million line of credit. The credit line does not entail any financial obligations until the money is actually utilized—if the Celtics never use the line of credit, they pay no interest. But if they borrow $5 million for several weeks, they pay interest on the $5 million amount for that period of time and still have $5 million to borrow if needed.

Even though the Celtics will pay no interest on any unborrowed amounts, they will probably pay a fee to keep the line of credit open. The fee is typically a percentage of the credit line. Thus, for a $5 million credit line the bank might charge 0.5% annually, which would require the Celtics to pay $25,000 annually to keep the line of credit open.

Another major benefit of short-term borrowing is that this strategy can be used to postpone long-term financing. Sometimes economic conditions or interest rates do not justify issuing bonds or stock. Thus, a "bridge gap" lending option such as short-term borrowing can help with any financial obligations until conditions are more favorable for obtaining long-term funding. Regardless of the purpose, short-term borrowing is critical for all businesses.

Sport Manufacturing Company is a seasonal business. During certain months the production line is closed. During those months the company does not need as much money for inventory expenses and related production costs, but very little money is coming in from sales. However, in springtime the company is flush with cash from surging seasonal sales. The seasonal character of the business creates a boom and bust cycle in which the company either has plenty of cash or is scraping by. During the good months, the excess cash can be deposited in liquid investments. During the lean times, SMC needs to borrow to pay bills. The various techniques SMC can use to secure short-term funding are discussed next.

Accounts Payable

One of the primary techniques for obtaining short-term funding involves accounts payable. Accounts payable represent amounts owed to vendors and suppliers for services that have been rendered or products that have been delivered.

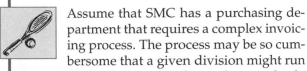

Assume that SMC has a purchasing department that requires a complex invoicing process. The process may be so cumbersome that a given division might run out of supplies before an order can be completely processed. However, the company might have an ongoing relationship with a supply company such that individual departments can purchase up to $100 a month without needing preapproval. All purchases that fall into this category can be calculated at the end of the month and then SMC can be billed for the total.

This example demonstrates that accounts payable can be more complex than a credit card arrangement. A credit card is another example of an account payable in that the purchaser uses the card to make purchases and is borrowing money from the card issuer until the balance is paid. If the balance is not paid in full at the end of the billing period, the card user is charged interest. Most businesses utilize a blend of short-term borrowing that includes accounts payable and other short-term borrowing options.

Assume that the Smiths need to hire a laundry service to clean gym towels. Instead of paying every week when the laundry is picked up and delivered, the Smiths may complete an account contract with the laundry service to pay the bill every month. At the end of the first month, the Smiths receive a bill for the prior month's service with specific repayment instructions. The laundry service might give a discount if the bill is paid within a week, offer no benefit if the account is paid in full within 30 days, and assess a penalty fee or an interest obligation on the owed amount if the required payment is not made within 30 days. The Smiths are engaging in a type of account payable called a trade credit that one business issues to another. In this example the trade credit is being offered pursuant to a cash discount option.

A major problem with accounts payable is the often slow turnaround time for repayment. If a business buys season tickets for a team's games but does not pay for them at the time of purchase, the team may have a problem with this receivable account if it never gets paid or is paid months later. Some suppliers may not mind slow repayment because they can obtain interest payments from the borrower. However other suppliers may count on

repayment to help pay other obligations. In this case the supplier may reduce the total amount owed in order to encourage fast repayment. The most common technique for encouraging fast repayment is the cash discount. A supplier might provide a business with a cash incentive for paying the obligation within 10 days. Cash discounts are often expressed in the formula 2/10/30. This refers to a 2% discount if the buyer pays in cash within 10 days or remits full payment within 30 days. If payment is not made within 30 days, the buyer has to pay interest or other penalties as defined by the purchase agreement. Although a 2% discount may not seem large, calculated out for the entire year it represents 36% per year (Bogen, 1966). To calculate the opportunity you lose in not paying early, take the 20 days each month that you do not receive a 2% discount. Then divide the 20 days into 365 days a year. The resulting 18.25 is then multiplied by the 2% discount that you could have obtained, for an annualized loss of 36.5%. This discount encourages purchasers to pay their bills quickly, which can also reduce collection fees for the supplier. The purchaser also receives a significant benefit in obtaining either a 10-day or a 30-day interest-free loan. That is why a cash discount is such a popular short-term funding technique. See chapter 12 for a discussion of cash discounts in the context of accounts receivable.

Bank Financing

As discussed in chapter 3, banks are among the cornerstones of the finance system. Banks provide numerous levels of financial assistance, whether through personal banking or comprehensive business banking services. Although accounts payable are a critical tool for commerce and most businesses utilize accounts payable on a daily basis, bank loans are the most economical and flexible means for short-term financing. Banks provide various services from savings accounts and business checking accounts to night deposit and automatic bill payment services. They often offer flexible short-term loans ranging from 30 or 60 days to several months. If a 30-day loan comes due, a bank has the flexibility to renew the debt. If the loan is for a longer time period, such as three to five years, it is referred to as a **term loan.** Banks prefer to issue short-term loans in order to get their money back as soon as possible (Spiro, 1996). Unlike short-term loans that come due at the end of the designated time period and are discharged with one payment, term loans often entail regular periodic payments and one **balloon payment.**

If the Celtics borrowed $5 million from a bank for five years, they might be required to pay $500,000 a year in principal and interest for four years with a large balloon payment approaching $4 million in the fifth year. If the loan was a conventional loan, the Celtics might have the $500,000 payment for 14 years to cover both the principal and interest.

No matter what services are utilized, a bank is more willing to negotiate and customize accounts with businesses that already have an established account. Some banks require businesses with active loans to maintain an average deposit balance equal to 20% of the loaned amount. Such a deposit is often called a compensating balance. This protective balance may not seem significant, but it does represent a cost of borrowing.

Suppose the Smiths borrow $100,000 from a bank but have to maintain $20,000 in a savings account at the bank throughout the life of the loan. If the Smiths pay 10% on the loan, maintaining the $20,000 in the bank at a low interest rate or with no interest would in essence bring the cost of borrowing to 12.5%, which is calculated as follows:

$$\frac{I}{L - B} = \text{cost of borrowing}$$

I = interest paid on loan

L = amount borrowed

B = compensating balance that needs to be maintained

$$\frac{\$10,000}{\$100,000 - \$20,000} = 12.5\%$$

A loan contingent on maintaining a minimum balance at the bank is a type of secured loan. Many loans require the use of collateral. Anything of value can be utilized to secure the loan. Some businesses pledge physical property such as land, buildings, inventory, or equipment. Other businesses pledge intangible assets such as accounts receivable or the rights to an invention or patent. Since loans against accounts receivable or inventory are often riskier, some banks do not offer such loans, and businesses need to go to nonbank lenders for these.

Collateral Values

The following table shows collateral values that might be needed to secure credit from potential financial institutions. According to these industry standards, if you have accounts receivable of $100,000 and you allow the bank to monitor the receivables, you could possibly obtain an $80,000 loan secured by the receivables.

Value of Factored Assets in Obtaining Loans

Collateral	Percent loaned
Accounts receivable—monitored	80
Accounts receivable—unmonitored	70
Inventory—monitored	50
Inventory—unmonitored	40
Owned equipment—% of book value	50
New equipment—% purchase price	80
Used equipment—% purchase price	75
Real estate	65-90
U.S. government securities	90
Investment grade municipal bonds	80
Bonds or preferred stock	75
Stocks below AA grade	50
NYSE, AMEX, NASDAQ shares	65
Cash value of insurance policies	100
Cash	100

Data from "Planning for Success," 2000.

Many businesses utilize real estate or machinery as collateral for a loan. However, assets such as inventory, investment assets, or accounts receivable can be pledged if other assets are already being used for collateral. In some instances businesses do not want to encumber an asset because they want to be able to sell it. A company that has pledged a factory as security cannot sell the factory because the factory does not have a **clear title;** the title is "clouded." Potential buyers can determine whether a property has a clouded title, as most debt instruments with any security (especially real property) are recorded by a city or county clerk. If someone tried to buy the pledged factory, the title could not be passed as free and clear of any encumbrances. After the obligation was paid in full, however, the factory could be sold. This same process operates when individuals buy a house. The mortgage on the house is recorded with a government agency and is discovered when a title search is conducted. The buyer can clear the title by paying the mortgage and having the mortgage company release its claim to the property.

Using current inventories as collateral is a technique that maximizes current value while affording the option to raise additional funds. Asset-based borrowing entails a revolving line of credit secured by accounts receivable, inventories, or both (Hovey, 1998, November). Bally's Total Fitness expanded its business by acquiring debt, and the debt is being secured by accounts receivable (Caro, 2000). Since the chain has numerous members throughout the world, it is guaranteed a certain amount each month from dues. These dues are part of the accounts receivable and are also called contractually obligated revenue or contractually obligated income since they are required by the membership contracts. Bally's can utilize these prospective assets to secure debt obligations, similar to the way a stadium can use the contractually obligated revenue from naming rights contracts as collateral for a bond or other debt instruments.

If the borrower defaults on one of these secured loans, the lender can seize the assets as with any other collateral. On the basis of the potential difficulty a lender might have in collecting receivables or selling inventory, the lender might loan only up to 65% to 85% of the value in receivables and 55% of the value of the inventories (Hovey, 1998, November). Asset-based loans normally are provided at the prime rate plus 2% for a creditworthy business. Although these loans are not especially hard to obtain, they do require significant paperwork. A borrower typically needs to provide three years' profit-and-loss statements, current and past financial statements, inventory aging reports, personal financial and tax return statements for the past three years, and sales projections for the coming year (Hovey, 1998, November). After receiving a loan, the borrower has to comply with additional paperwork requirements such as providing monthly reports concerning accounts payable and receivable.

Some commonly utilized documents that provide security for an asset-backed loan are bills of lading, trust receipts, and warehouse receipts. A bill of lading pledges commodities or merchandise in transit as collateral for a loan. Goods covered by a trust receipt are held in trust for the lending institution, but could be housed in a separate area at the borrower's business. Once those goods are sold, the cash from the sales is first paid to the bank to satisfy the debt. A warehouse receipt performs the same function as a bill of lading, but applies when the inventory is stored in a bonded warehouse to protect the bank's collateral. Title to the assets rests with the lender until a release document is provided to the warehouse. The warehouse can then release the specified assets. While secured loans provide significant protection for the lender, collateral may not be required if a business has a strong credit rating or a good relationship with the lending bank.

Banks have significant flexibility, within federal guidelines, to offer various customized services. Twenty years ago, banks were typically smaller than they are today and often had strong personal relationships with customers. Banks could provide a broader range of services for business owners whom the bank employees knew and had done business with in the past. However, having a "personal banker" is more unusual today. Recent mergers have consolidated numerous smaller banks into more impersonal businesses. But even with larger banks, it is still important for businesses to communicate with bank employees on a regular basis. Loan officers and their supervisors are important contacts. Knowing several bank employees in these positions provides protection if bank personnel move to different locations (Nelton, 1998, November). Developing personal relationships can help if you ever need to apply for a loan—it is to your advantage if you are more than just a name on an application, possibly a friend and someone the bankers would judge as highly credible.

Banks frequently expect the owner of a proposed new business to put some of his own money at risk. The underlying thinking is, why should the bank invest in the project if the owner is not willing to risk his own money? Equity capital represents a firm commitment by the owner to work for the business' best interest. The owner wants to succeed in order to avoid losing his own money, as well as the bank's money. A bank could require equity capital to approach approximately 40% of the amount needed to fund the new business (Horine, 1999). Even if no equity is required to obtain the bank loan, banks traditionally require audited financial statements to help calculate standard ratios, such as debt-equity and acid test ratios, and these figures can help determine the prospect for default. Banks might also require business plans, pro forma budgets, personnel profiles, sample products, and other information that can help them make a lending decision. Most banks require a borrower to complete a formal application, which could include a summary of the business, profiles of the top executives, financial statements, pro forma budgets, and a detailed repayment plan (Griffin, 1991).

The Five C's of Credit

Regardless of the requested loan amount, people should not quit their current job before obtaining a loan. A bank will check to see if you are currently employed in order to help establish your ability to repay or "service" the loan. The potential borrower's employment status is just one variable that banks and other lending institutions might investigate. Banks commonly refer to the **five C's** of credit when deciding whether or not to loan someone money. The five C's are character, capacity, collateral, capital, and condition.

1. *Character* refers to the applicant's credit history and the applicant's truthfulness. Did the applicant disclose all outstanding debt? Did the applicant list any prior bankruptcy? Does the applicant have favorable business or professional references? Does it appear that the applicant is willing to repay the loan? The answers to such questions help determine whether or not the lender can trust the applicant.

2. *Capacity* represents the lender's determination as to whether the potential business has the right management team and philosophy to become a profitable enterprise that will earn more than enough money to pay the loan.

3. *Collateral* refers to anything of value that can be pledged to guarantee final repayment of the loan. Collateral can include a home, property, equipment, collectibles, a legal judgment, or even a lottery payoff.

4. *Capital* represents the equity that the applicant will put into her own business. A lending institution will not be very interested in loaning money to help launch a new business if the business owner does not think the business will succeed. If the applicant feels that the business will be a success, then she must support her conviction by investing some of her own money. Banks typically require a 30% to 35% equity or cash investment in the business by the loan applicant (Pounds, 1997). Capital also refers to any excess cash that might be available to pay any unexpected expenses.

5. *Condition* represents the applicant's primary opportunity to sell the lender on the value of the business. The lender will want to know if the industry is growing, if there are competitors, whether the product has a long life cycle, whether a location or distribution channel is available to sell the product, and so on. By thoroughly researching the proposed business and presenting the lender with a comprehensive business plan that addresses these issues, the applicant greatly increases the chance of securing a loan (see chapter 7).

Once the loan papers have been approved, an agreement is signed between the parties. This document is called a promissory note. The note specifies the amount borrowed, the interest rate to be charged, any repayment terms, whether or not the loan is collateralized, and any and all other terms and conditions the parties have agreed upon. After the note is signed, the borrower receives the loan proceeds.

Whether the loan is backed by a personal guarantee, collateral, or a mortgage, banks offer numerous financial options that make short-term borrowing fairly simple. Lines of credit are more complicated but still represent an effective use of bank resources to cover immediate fiscal needs. A lending institution charges interest only on the amount actually borrowed from the credit line but can also charge a commitment fee that could range from 0.05% to 1%

(Battersby, 1999). The commitment fee can be waived if the borrower has compensating balances in other accounts. Three types of lines of credit are available:

1. A nonbinding line of credit is an open account for the business to borrow from. If the business experiences hardships and has financial trouble, however, the line of credit can be revoked.
2. A committed line of credit requires the potential borrower to pay a commitment fee to lock the line of credit into place, thus guaranteeing needed funds.
3. A revolving line of credit requires the borrower to undergo an annual review and renewal of the credit line (Battersby, 1999).

A **revolving credit** agreement is similar to a line of credit in allowing a company to borrow a specified sum, but there is a major distinction. A line of credit allows the borrower to access a certain amount of money if needed. However, the bank or the company can withdraw from the agreement at any time. A revolving credit agreement is a contract whereby the borrower agrees to pay an annual commitment fee, a small percentage of the unused amount, to compensate the bank for entering into the commitment (Brigham & Gapenski, 1994). If the

company uses only half of the available credit, it is charged the commitment fee for the unused amount and is charged the agreed-upon interest for the amount borrowed. Since the revolving credit agreement is a contract, both parties have to undertake formal contract cancellation steps to end it.

Commercial Paper

Businesses can raise short-term funds from other nonbank businesses by issuing commercial paper (CP). Commercial paper is a promissory note that might mature in one to nine months. Commercial paper is not seen too frequently in the sport industry; however, it is common among some large manufacturers and sales finance companies, such as General Motors Acceptance Corp (GMAC). Large corporations are also among the largest purchasers of CP, which they acquire with liquid funds to gain some interest. Similar to other short-term lending, if a large corporation needs money to pay bills, it can sell the CP it previously purchased. The business that issues the CP determines the interest rates charged based on what rates would draw the greatest investor interest. Specialized CP dealers quote CP prices on the open market. Rates and prices change as economic conditions change; and as companies need more money, they may offer better rates.

Commercial Paper

Commercial paper is one of the least understood financing techniques for major corporations. Smaller corporations cannot issue CP as effectively since CP is a short-term, unsecured instrument that is issued for a period of time from one month to 270 days. In 1990, less than $500 billion in CP was outstanding for larger corporations. By 2000, the amount of outstanding CP had increased to $1.4 trillion. In 2000, an Internet company was launched that was attempting to take 20% of this market online to sell CP directly to institutional investors. Companies that had signed contracts to offer their CP through this medium included Texaco, Exxon, Chevron, and numerous credit/acceptance units including IBM Credit, Ford Motor Credit, GM Acceptance, General Electric Capital, and Sears Roebuck Acceptance Corp. (Sherer, 2000).

Private Placement Through Nonbank Lenders

Various options are available for obtaining cash from other sources. **Private placement** refers to the process of obtaining funds from private parties such as investors, venture capital investors, or other companies interested in investing in a business. These investments can take the form of debt instruments, equity interest, or a blend of the two.

Nonbank lenders are the most frequent source other than banks for financing smaller businesses. Nonbank lenders do not include angel investors, family members, and friends, who can also serve as lenders. These lenders can be independent businesses or can work in conjunction with the government. Some companies that offer nonbank loans include AT&T Small Business Lending Corp., Heller First Capital Corp., Business Lenders, Money Store Investment Corp., and GE Capital Small Business

Finance Corp. These loans often have a higher interest rate based on risk factors, which might have been what dissuaded a bank from providing the loan in the first place. These loans also are often attached to special purchasing deals offered by suppliers (see discussion of supplier financing on p. 144). The list of potential lending sources is almost limitless. This section covers private companies, private investment group financing, factoring, installment sales, supplier financing, and leasing. These financing methods do not entail selling any equity position in the business. Thus, no ownership interest is given up to obtain the funds.

We discuss mergers and acquisitions in chapter 15, but every business owner has the option of selling a portion of the business or the entire business in order to acquire funds. Several **buyout** funds were established in 1999 for the sport industry and provide funds to businesses or purchase entire businesses. Chase Manhattan joined with International Management Group to form the IMG/Chase Sports Capital Fund. The fund had $170 million to help fund sport businesses and used some of those funds to purchase the Skip Barber Racing School in Connecticut (Tan, 2000). While selling an entire business entails obtaining funds for the sellers, the process should not be thought of as selling out. The owner may have sold the business, but the potential cash infusion from a financially stronger business might have been what was necessary to finance further expansion. There are many businesses that would have failed if they had not been purchased by a buyer who funded future growth.

Private Companies

Other nonbank lenders include private companies that are licensed by the U.S. SBA. These small business investment companies (SBICs) can provide either debt financing through issuing long-term loans or equity financing through acquiring an ownership interest in a company (Pryde, 1998). However, SBICs are barred by law from acquiring a controlling interest in a company. SBIC owners are required to contribute $5 million of their own money, which makes them highly selective in picking high-quality investments. The SBICs also prefer to invest close to home and typically invest around $500,000 in each company (Pryde, 1998). Many investments are in specialized companies that might include minority or socially or economically disadvantaged companies. To qualify for an SBIC loan or equity investment, a business's net worth must be less than $18 million and the business must have had after-

tax earnings of less than $6 million in the two previous years (Pryde, 1998).

Some private-placement investors, such as some venture capitalists, require significant control over managerial decisions. However some "hands-off" private-placement investors do not require any seats on the board of directors or managerial involvement. These individuals are typically content with a 25% return per year (Reynes, 1998, October). Hands-off private-placement deals are best suited for developed companies that are already publicly traded or that plan on pursuing a public offering in two to three years. There are local brokers, bankers, or regional brokerage firms in most cities that can help coordinate private-placement deals. These individuals typically get paid a percentage of the money they help raise (5%-15%). It is important to be careful when working with anyone trying to help you raise funds. Since deals are contingent on getting funding, numerous scams and incomplete deals can cost a company both money and lost time. If any broker or investment banker asks for money up front, there is no guarantee you will receive anything (Reynes, 1998, October). In contrast, individuals who receive a percentage after a deal has been completed are more likely to engage in more prudent conduct to guarantee payment for themselves and their firm.

Through private placement, an investor might purchase convertible debentures. A convertible debenture pays a certain predetermined interest rate to the investor. After a specified time period, convertible debentures can be converted into stock or maintained as a loan. The opportunity to convert the loan to stock is a choice made by the loan holder, the issuer, or both (Reynes, 1998, October). In one example involving a company that manufactured drug-screening kits, investors had the option to purchase convertible debentures in $5,000 blocks. The company's shares were selling for $0.38 each. After three years, the lenders could choose to get their money back and all interest owed, or could convert their debenture to stock at $0.75 a share. Converting to stocks would have been the best option for the lenders, as the stocks were then selling for $3 to $4 per share (Reynes, 1998, October). Debenture offerings are discussed further in chapter 10.

Private Investment Group Financing

Entrepreneurs can also turn to a private investment group (PIG) for nonbank funding. A PIG can pool money from a variety of sources including individuals, endowments, pension funds, private investors, and institutional investors (Hovey, 1997). Private investment groups traditionally invest in stable companies that have shown continued growth for several years. These investors typically prefer investing in manufacturing- or distribution-based companies rather than retail or service companies (Hovey, 1997). Private investment groups normally invest more than $1 million in a company and buy stocks and possibly secure loans to raise the necessary capital. However, such investments do not come without a hefty price. Private investment groups typically require a rate of return over 30% to 35% per year (Hovey, 1997). This rate of return may seem high, but venture capital or angel investors who invest in certain industries or products typically invest in riskier young firms and demand a higher **annual return**—*often over 50%* (Hovey, 1997).

A PIG deal might take 6 to 18 months to complete, and a $10 million deal might cost up to $340,000 to finalize. This figure is the sum of $100,000 to $200,000 for the mergers and acquisitions advisor, $30,000 to $100,000 for legal fees, and $25,000 to $40,000 for accounting fees (Hovey, 1997).

Factoring Accounts Receivable

Private parties can also provide short-term funds through factoring. Factoring entails selling assets. The assets that are sold are either inventories or accounts receivable and are purchased by a specialized financing company.

If the Smiths have $10,000 owed to them by members who have yet to pay their bills, the Smiths could possibly sell the accounts receivable for $7,500 and immediately utilize those funds.

There are several ways to accomplish factoring of receivables. One way is for a company to purchase the receivables, and another is for a company to purchase only the rights without transferal of actual administrative duties. The first technique is called factoring without recourse. A factor (the company that purchases the receivables) purchasing without recourse assumes complete responsibility in debt collection. Customers are instructed to send their payments to the factor. The factor receives a commission on the accounts that are paid and charges interest on the money loaned to the business until the accounts are paid.

Assume that the Smiths are owed $10,000 and that Acme Factoring purchases the accounts receivable without recourse. Acme might receive 10% of the $10,000, or $1,000, as commission and might loan the Smiths $7,000 on the remaining receivables at 5%. If Acme collects the entire $10,000, Acme profits from the $1,000 commission and from receiving 5% interest on the $7,000 loan. The remaining $3,000 might be returned to the Smiths according to the negotiated contract provisions.

In the second type of factoring—factoring with recourse—the original holder of the receivables is still responsible for obtaining repayment and collects all payments, but sends those payments to a finance company. This technique is also called accounts receivable financing. A finance company might advance money contingent on the borrower's agreeing to collect and actively manage the receivables. The factoring company might advance 70% to 95% of all receivables sold to it and then pay the remaining percentage when the last receivables are collected (Bogen, 1966). Again, the factoring company makes money by charging interest on the money advanced to the company selling the receivables. Regardless of the technique utilized, factoring accounts receivable is more expensive than bank borrowing, as the factor charges a higher interest rate based on the potential risk factors.

Installment Sales

Installment sales are common in the auto sales industry. An individual makes a down payment and makes monthly payments comprising principal and interest for a specified number of months or years. These contracts are typically for three or four years. The purchaser's failure to make timely payments gives the installment contract holder the right to repossess the car. Thus, the person holding the installment contract has title and true ownership. There are installment sales contracts in the sporting goods industry (for example, when someone buys an abdomen workout machine seen in an infomercial for three installments of $19.99 each). The purchaser has obtained the opportunity to receive the product contingent on future payments. Similar deals are made in almost all businesses, by which a party to a contract can make several payments. If the Celtics sold their broadcasting rights to a television station, the station might pay 33% when the contract is signed, 33% before the season starts, and 33% when the season ends.

Supplier Financing

Businesses can also obtain financial assistance from those who sell them necessary equipment or supplies. Such an arrangement can take a variety of forms, from loaning equipment to reducing purchase prices to extending credit or creating longer repayment terms (Hodges, 1997). Assistance from suppliers represents just one technique in **creative financing.** By casting a wide net, a business can find numerous potential co-entrepreneurs interested in possibly joining forces. Anaheim Pond is a good example of such a deal, as Aramark paid a significant amount for the rights to provide food and concession services for the facility. Aramark is hoping to write the building cost off as a tax expense and to generate significant long-term revenue from the exclusive contract.

The Smiths might enter into an agreement with a landlord interested in renting space. As an incentive to start the fitness center in a new shopping strip, the landlord might give the Smiths a construction allowance to build the facility to meet their specific needs.

Sport Manufacturing could also utilize supplier financing by entering into an agreement with a new company that manufactures pressing machines. The new company could provide the machines at a discount or offer more attractive financing options compared to other equipment providers and in return request using SMC as a referral for other potential buyers. The agreement could allow other prospective equipment buyers to visit SMC and see the machines in operation.

An established company might also offer financing options, but they might not be as favorable as a new company or a major competitor that is trying to gain market share. This example often can be seen in the consumer car sales area where various manufacturers offer lower interest loans to win a potential customer away from a different manufacturer.

Operating Versus Capital Leases

Leasing, whether from the selling company or from a leasing agent or corporation, can also provide the funds needed to obtain equipment or other assets. By leasing equipment, money can be saved to purchase other assets or equipment.

The Smiths might have to spend a significant amount to purchase new equipment. However, their initial expenditure would be much less if they leased the equipment instead. Fitness equipment leasing evolved in the mid-1990s; and in 1999, between 25% and 40% of all fitness equipment was being leased (Cohen, 1999). For a facility that leases equipment, the average leased amount is $40,000. This amount is based on the total equipment value, credit rating, financial conditions, and business experience. Fitness equipment does not depreciate as quickly as other assets, such as a car, and thus often serves as collateral for the lease. However, since the Smiths are still new to their profession, they might need to post a security deposit of 10% to 25% of the equipment's value (Cohen, 1999).

The Smiths could obtain either a capital or an operating lease. Under a capital lease, the Smiths would make their monthly lease payments and at the end of the lease term could pay a specified price, normally $1, and acquire the ownership rights for the equipment (Cohen, 1999). In contrast, an operating lease allows the lessee to return the equipment at the end of the lease or to buy it for a percentage of the original cost. Operating leases are often called service leases, as the contract normally requires both financing and maintenance. Operating leases are not fully amortized, which means that the lease payments are insufficient to recover the full cost of the equipment. A major advantage of the operating lease is a cancellation clause that gives the lessee (the Smiths) or the lessors (the equipment company) the opportunity to terminate the lease within a specified period. The cancellation clause could call for a 30-day written notice. Regardless of the time requirement, the benefit for the Smiths would be that they could, within 30 days, switch to a cheaper equipment supplier or one that provided more advanced equipment.

In contrast to the operating lease, the capital lease has one major advantage, the right to own the equipment when the lease ends. However, a capital lease does not have any maintenance provision, the lease is not cancelable, and the lease payments will equal the equipment's cost. A capital lease is often called a finance lease because of the nature of the lease arrangement.

The Smiths might find a nice piece of equipment sold by XYZ Manufacturing. They could negotiate price and delivery specifications with XYZ. The Smiths could then go to a finance company and apply for the finance company to buy the equipment and lease it back to them. The Smiths would have an amortized lease with an interest percentage built into it. If the equipment cost $10,000 and the interest rate was 10%, the Smiths would have paid $11,000 when all the lease payments had been rendered.

A similar type of lease arrangement is a sale-and-lease-back arrangement in which, for example, the Celtics sell their practice facility to another company. That company then turns around and leases the property back to the Celtics. The company has the collateral, as it now owns the facility; and the Celtics have immediate cash from the sale proceeds. The Celtics will be responsible for lease payments, and the company may become responsible for facility maintenance expenses.

There are several issues to examine when one is determining whether to purchase or lease new assets. Leasing new assets has the following advantages:

- Funds that would normally be used to purchase assets could be used for working capital and other needs.

- No external financing is required, or the amount of such funds would be minimal.

- The corporation's financial picture is strengthened as investments in fixed assets are reduced and debt service is not increased (however, additional debt obligation to pay for the lease would be required).

- No significant capital outlay is required, as most leases do not entail a significant down payment.

- Corporations can often avoid a large maturity payment such as is involved when a corporation retires a bond issue.

- Unlike the situation with stock sales, there is no increased dilution of the shareholder's equity through leasing.

- The entire lease payment is deducted from **taxable income,** which often produces a significant benefit over asset ownership. Other assets such as buildings and equipment can be depreciated if purchased, but the land is not deductible.

- Technological obsolescence due to the rapid increase in technology can be avoided when one is able to rapidly replace older leased equipment.

- Leasing equipment can eliminate numerous repair and upkeep expenses that could be covered by the lease agreement (Bogen, 1966).

Although there are significant advantages to leasing assets, such as lower up-front costs, tax deduction, and a positive effect on credit rating, there are also some distinct disadvantages:

- Gross lease costs are traditionally higher than financing costs if extended over the life of the asset.

- After the point at which an asset would have been paid for if purchased, the lessee is still making regular lease payments throughout the lease period rather than the life of the asset.

- Modifying the asset requires the lessor's permission, eliminating the lessee's ability to actually control the asset.

- A lessee loses the benefits associated with inflation, increased values, or increased salvage values, as the asset is turned over after the lease period ends and the lessor gains these benefits.

- A long lease obligation may force a company to keep using older equipment covered by the lease in order to avoid paying any penalties for breaching the lease (Bogen, 1966).

- Because leases entail no significant capital requirements, some companies may lease too much equipment and they may not realize that their fixed lease obligations are growing significantly and that the lease obligations would still be owed even if all their sales stopped.

- A lessor can always confiscate the equipment upon default, leaving the company without machinery.

Whichever leasing technique is used, there are specific tax and balance sheet impacts. The big tax benefit of a lease is the ability to deduct lease expenses as a business expense. If the Smiths buy the equipment instead, they will only be able to depreciate the equipment cost over five years as set forth by IRS regulations. The tax benefit is available only under specific circumstances if the lease meets the following conditions:

- The initial lease term cannot exceed 80% of the equipment's estimated useful life, which means that when the lease ends the equipment still should have at least 20% of its useful life remaining.

- The equipment's residual value at the end of the lease must equal at least 20% of its initial value.

- No party can be allowed to purchase the equipment at a predetermined price when the lease ends. This concern can be eliminated by allowing the lessee to purchase the equipment at the equipment's fair market value once the lease ends.

- The lessee cannot make any investments in or improvements to the equipment other than through the lease payments.

- There cannot be any contractual provision limiting the equipment's use until after the lease expires (Brigham & Gapenski, 1994).

An example of the depreciation versus business expense deduction highlights the value of a lease to the bottom line.

If the Smiths bought $2 million in equipment with a three-year-class life, they would receive a depreciation allowance of $660,000 the first year, $900,000 in the second year, $300,000 in the third year, and $140,000 in the fourth year. If the Smiths were taxed at 40% (federal and state taxes combined), the purchase would provide a total tax savings of $800,000. Assuming a discount rate of 6%, the present value of the tax savings would be $757,441. If the Smiths leased double the amount of equipment for one year for a $2 million lease payment, they would likewise have an $800,000 tax savings ($2,000,000 × 40%). However, since the lease option benefits are derived in the first year, there is a $42,559 savings compared with the present value from the purchase option (Brigham & Gapenski, 1994). The problem with this analysis is that the $2 million lease obligation appears very high when the purchase price is also $2 million. The example makes sense only because we are supposing that the Smiths would lease twice as much equipment as they would have purchased. If they were to lease the same amount of equipment, the tax savings as a function of present value would be significantly less. It is obviously important to make proper comparisons between items to be leased or purchased.

Leases also affect financial statements. Leases were called "off-balance-sheet financing" for many years because neither the leased asset nor the lease liability (payment requirements) appeared on a company's balance sheet. Since leased assets and obligations did not appear on the balance sheet, an investor might not know that all the equipment in a business was leased and that the business owed over a $1 million annually in lease obligations, for example. These facts would be critical for any investor. On the basis of this concern, the Financial Accounting Standards Board issued a ruling that leased assets need to be reported as fixed assets and the present value of future lease payments needs to be recorded as a liability (Brigham & Gapenski, 1994). Based on this ruling, an operating lease is recorded on the balance sheet. A capital lease is now recorded on the books as either an asset or an obligation. An asset is considered part of a capital lease if ownership of the asset is transferred to the lessee when the lease expires, if the lease contains a bargain purchase option, or if the lease term exceeds 75% of the asset's economic life (Spiro, 1996).

> *Businesses can borrow over the short term via arrangements related to accounts payable, as well as through various types of bank loans, private-placement investments, and other non-bank financing.*

Long-Term Borrowing

This chapter has covered various financing techniques that are often short-term solutions. Borrowing on a credit card is not a long-term option due to the high interest rates. Furthermore, factoring is a stop-gap solution and other funding options would need to be pursued in subsequent times of financial need. Other funding options, such as a bank's line of credit, can be both a short-term or long-term option. Installment contracts can be short-term for a car or long-term installment contracts can also be developed for equipment that might last longer than 10 years.

The most traditional forms of long-term funding are stocks and bonds (discussed in the next two chapters). Whereas these two options are normally available for larger businesses, smaller or new companies often do not have these options. Various long-term funding options, such as mortgages or long-term loans, exist for medium-sized businesses. Mezzanine financing is also available as a bridge loan for businesses that wish to expand but are not yet ready for a public offering. This section covers mezzanine financing and venture capital financing.

Mezzanine Financing

While raising short-term start-up capital is often very difficult, the scenario for existing companies is different. A company with a successful track record has fewer problems raising money because it should be able to show sustained income. These companies can utilize mezzanine financing, a type of financing available to established companies that show growth potential but that are not yet ready for a capital stock offering (Hovey, 1998, March). Companies can typically utilize mezzanine financing to raise between $1 million and $20 million through a combination of borrowing money from and selling stocks to the same investor (Hovey, 1998, March). Financing typically works through payment of interest on the borrowed amount for about five years. After that time period, the business can cash out the investor by going public or can **refinance** for a longer period. The investor has the benefit of earning a good rate of interest, typically prime plus 2 to 4 points, or, if the business has increased in value, can sell the stock for a capital gain (Hovey, 1998, March). There is no set amount that has to be raised; so the Smiths, after operating their business for several years, could possibly raise $2 million in unsecured, partially secured, or secured debt financing and perhaps $1 million in equity financing. Such deals typically take between three to five months to complete, and the total fee cost (attorneys, accountants, and investment bankers) can equal 5% of the deal (Hovey, 1998, March).

The rule of thumb for mezzanine lending is that a company can

[l]everage two to three times its cash flow in senior secured debt. It can raise total debt four to five times cash flow with a mezzanine deal. So if the company is doing $2 million in cash flow, it can probably raise $4 million to $6 million in senior debt and $4 million to $5 million more in mezzanine financing, for a total debt of $10 million or five times cash flow. (Hovey, 1998, March, p. 42)

Although mezzanine lending can help a company grow prior to a possible public offering, some businesses need a larger boost to expand more rapidly or to more expediently position themselves for a public offering. Whereas the previously discussed angel investor might stay with an investment for the long term, a venture capital investor normally remains with an investment until the business invested in goes bankrupt, gets purchased by someone else, or goes public.

Venture Capital

Venture capital represents an opportunity for individuals with marketable ideas or products to raise funds from private investors willing to take a risk in owning part of the company in exchange for their investment. Venture capital, commonly called VC, is similar to mezzanine financing in that it blends debt-based loans with the potential for equity interest if the borrower goes public. In 1996, capital investments of over $10.1 billion were made in U.S.-based companies (Reynes, 1997). The numbers were much greater for 1999 as numerous Internet businesses were launched through VC infusions.

 Venture capital investors might invest several million in the Smiths' proposed fitness facility, but at a price to the Smiths. The Smiths might have to give over a large percentage (possibly over 50% depending on the deal) of the company to the investor. Thus, they might no longer be the primary owners—and then would not be working for themselves. They might also have to give an investor a position on the board of directors and possibly give the investor some managerial control.

Venture Capital

Even with the decline of numerous Internet companies, VC firms poured a record amount of funds into start-up companies in 2000. Venture capitalists invested $22.68 billion into 1,557 companies in the first quarter of 2000. This was a staggering increase over the figure for the first quarter in 1999, when only $6.16 billion was invested in start-ups. The greatest portion of the invested funds, $14.04 billion (61.9%), went to expand currently existing businesses (McGee, 2000).

Venture capital investors are primarily interested in technology-based industries in which a winning company can pay off many times over, versus a mildly successful company that will show only marginal profits. Venture capitalists like to see gross margins of over 50%. A company making a 30%

profit a year represents too great a risk and does not attract the strong investor interest that could make an **initial public offering** (IPO) successful (Evanson, 1998, January). Venture capital investors have shied away from the sport industry in the past, but sport-related Internet companies are starting to garner VC interest. Not all Internet businesses are drawing VC interest, as venture capitalists are attracted to companies that have clear access to a channel of distribution, whether it is the company's own or someone else's (Evanson, 1998, January).

Regardless of the method used to obtain initial funding or short-term funding, any successful business will also require long-term financing. As just discussed, VC and mezzanine investors may pay a premium for the ability to transfer their investment from a debt instrument to an equity interest. The equity interest is developed through giving the investor a share of the business. Providing a share of the business is made easier with stock. It is preferable to give a VC investor 1 million shares of 2 million outstanding shares instead of a contract stating that she owns 50% of a business. That is, a contract indicating a 50% ownership in a business is often much harder to sell than stocks, especially stocks listed on an organized exchange.

Funding for Small or Minority-Owned Businesses

This section expands on prior analysis to look more closely at other capital options for smaller or minority-owned businesses and indicates where to go for help if you are having trouble finding funding.

Small Business Association Loans for the Inner City

An additional government source the Smiths could look to is the SBA, discussed earlier in the chapter. The SBA can offer assistance in obtaining various types of loans, including 7(a), 504, Microlenders, Small Business Lending Company, bank-regulated Certified Development Corporation, and SBIC-related loans or programs. In addition, the SBA can provide assistance to work in conjunction with other capital efforts. For example, Detroit obtained $100 million from the federal government to develop an empowerment zone ("Empowerment Zone Projects," n.d.). The empowerment zone is designed to foster revitalization of a community. Businesses moving to such a zone may receive wage credits, **tax-exempt bonds,** section 179 (depreciation) ex-

pensing, and assistance in obtaining SBA-backed loans. Property taxes also were to be frozen for those new businesses for five years. In conjunction with this effort, the Detroit Recreation Department put forth an empowerment zone initiative that received over $10 million in Title XX funding for such projects as Roving Recreation and Recreation Facilities Enhancement Project ("Empowerment Zone Projects," n.d.). Blending various government levels and agencies can help develop innovative capital acquisition programs and reduce operating costs. This is especially true in the context of minority-based programs.

> *Financing for smaller businesses in bad neighborhoods is often available from nonbank lenders including private SBA-licensed companies.*

A Helping Hand for Minority Business Owners

Although the capital sources just mentioned all present some strong opportunities for a new business or established business to obtain funds for growth, other companies might not have the same opportunities. Minorities and women have traditionally faced hardships in acquiring capital for their businesses. Some of these hardships were attributable to minimal or nonexistent credit histories for business owners who had never had credit cards in their own name or who represented too high a risk for traditional capital lenders. In order to prevent potential continued discrimination (whether disparate impact [unintentional] or disparate treatment [intentional]), numerous support opportunities have been established to help minorities and women obtain funding.

Although the Smiths are thinking about entering into an equal partnership, Cheryl could possibly become the primary owner/proprietor with a 51% stake in the fitness center. Under such an arrangement, the fitness center would probably be considered a female-owned business qualified for some special capital opportunities. As a female-owned business, the Smiths' business could also become eligible for specific government set-aside contracts.

Female-owned companies can utilize the Women's Prequalified Loan Program, guaranteed by the SBA, to borrow up to $250,000. Guarantees are for 80% of loans under $100,000 and 75% for loans over $100,000 (Broome, 1997). To qualify for the SBA-guaranteed loan, the business needs to be a female-owned business (at least 51% of the business needs to be owned, managed, or operated by women), have less than $5 million in sales, and employ fewer than 100 workers (Broome, 1997). If a loan under $100,000 is sought, the process just requires a one-page application. For loans over $100,000 the applicant needs to submit an expanded application, business plan, resumes of the primary officials, recent financial statements or tax returns, and a personal financial statement (Broome, 1997). Loans over $50,000 have an interest obligation at the prime rate. Loans under $50,000 can cost the prime rate plus up to 4% interest (Broome, 1997).

 The Smiths might also obtain additional partners who are minorities to help attract funding opportunities available only for minorities.

The following paragraphs describe some minority-oriented funding programs.

The National Minority Supplier Development Council (NMSDC) has 42 regional affiliates and works with 3,500 businesses to help minority-owned companies acquire goods and services. Such assistance is not meant to be charity. Rather the companies involved in NMSDC participate to help generate additional sales. Through the provision of flexible payment options or collateralized sales to minorities who otherwise might not obtain such preferential treatment, new sales and potential clients can be developed. The NMSDC has proceeded one step further to create the Business Consortium Fund, which helps minority business owners obtain financing for raw materials, employee salaries, and other contract-related expenses (Nelton, 1998, June). The Business Consortium Fund limits loans to $500,000 over a maximum of four years and requires the borrower to have a purchase order specifying where the funds will be spent.

While NMSDC aims to help minority-owned business owners, the definition of a minority has created a controversy. In 2000, NMSDC redefined the minority-owned business as a business with as little as 30% nonwhite ownership. But even if less than a third of a business needs to be minority owned in order for the business to qualify as a minority business for NMSDC, the rules also require qualified businesses to have 51% of their voting stock held by minorities (Wynter & Thomas, 2000). The change in the rule was designed to help give larger minority-controlled businesses that have a large number of nonminority investors the opportunity to compete more effectively with other businesses.

Apart from the Business Consortium Fund, minority-owned companies may obtain capital from specialized small business investment companies (SSBICs) licensed by the SBA. Local chambers of commerce, economic development committees, and various national associations also can help minorities and women find needed capital. Appendix C in this book lists several associations that can help in obtaining capital.

> *A number of programs have been established specifically to help minority- and female-owned businesses obtain funding.*

Basic Tools

No matter what capital source you attempt to tap, you will need several key tools. The primary tools you will need are either audited financial statements or pro forma statements (see chapter 7). You also will need a realistic road map for your business (i.e., a business plan) that will help investors determine what direction you will be taking to guarantee a strong likelihood of success. While having the proper documentation is important, you also need to have the right team of professionals helping you through the process. An accountant, attorney, and financial planner or investment banker might be critical for your capital acquisition success. These professionals may cost a significant amount, but are normally worth the investment. Some professionals are willing to forgo their customary fees and accept a percentage of the business or stock in the business in lieu of payment.

In addition to recruiting the right ensemble to help with your capital campaign, you need to develop a convincing sales pitch. However, selling investors on your project is significantly different from selling potential customers. Customers may be interested in product features, customer service, and warranties. In contrast, investors are interested in margin (profit), market size, competitive environment, return on investment, product development opportunities, and related financial issues (Evanson, 1997). The financial planning process (discussed in chapter 7) helps identify these issues.

Capital Acquisition Assistance

Capital acquisition might appear to be an unduly burdensome task. The task is much more difficult for new businesses than for established companies. The Smiths may have numerous doors closed in their faces while they search for funds. However, established businesses such as the Celtics treat capital acquisition as a routine management decision. Since the risks associated with issuing securities for established companies are much less than for new companies, underwriters charge the established companies a lower percentage in underwriting fees. An underwriter is a business, often an investment or financial services business, that helps prepare all the materials necessary to sell stocks or bonds to the investing public. Newer companies can reduce their costs by agreeing to pay an underwriter all out-of-pocket expenses and to grant the underwriter warrants on newly issued common stock (Spiro, 1996). The options available to help attract the top advisors in the capital acquisition game are limitless.

No matter what option is chosen, careful planning can reduce the potential costs and risks associated with acquiring funds. However, even the best plans can collapse in a heartbeat. In 2000, many Internet companies were in the process of securing funds through either VC or IPOs. Within a span of several months, a large number were unable to obtain any funds, and many others had to suspend their operation because they were not able to secure funding that a few months earlier had seemed certain to materialize.

Capital financing can be a complex process that is made possible by careful research, planning, and the assistance of industry professionals.

CONCLUSION

This chapter covers the basic elements of capital financing. Numerous options exist for finding necessary funds, but even people experienced in business can often face rejection. It is not uncommon for a businessperson to approach multiple lenders and be refused by all. This does not mean that the individual is a bad businessperson; it may mean that the economic environment is not right, the lending market is tight, or there is not enough collateral to secure the obligation, among a host of other things.

Persistency is the key to successfully securing capital. This chapter focuses more on short-term funding in situations in which quick decisions are necessary and businesses may not have the time necessary to pursue long-term funding options. It is always important to have in place the capital infrastructure, such as a line of credit, in case you might need money and do not have the time to try various options. The next two chapters discuss long-term funding options that often take months or years of planning to be successful.

ASSIGNMENTS

1. Go to a local bank and interview a loan officer to determine what loan officers look for when they consider a business loan. What can a business do to increase its chances of receiving a loan?

2. Interview a small sport business owner to determine how the owner funded the launch of the business and how he or she obtains any new capital requirements.

RESEARCH PROJECT

Search the archives on various Internet search engines for historical financial data on how some of the Internet sport businesses were funded. Examine such entities as MVP.com, fogdog.com, teamz.com, and possibly four or five other sport-related sites. Look to see if there is information on VC investment, angel investors, or multiple rounds of funding from banks, investment bankers, or public offerings. Additionally, if the company has subsequently closed or filed for bankruptcy, try to determine how they ran into financial trouble.

CLASS DISCUSSION TOPICS

1. If you have ever applied for a credit card, what were you required to show to obtain credit?

2. If you have ever borrowed money to buy a car, what was involved in that process?

3. If you ever borrowed money for college, what steps were involved in that process?

4. What would you want from a friend if you loaned the person $1,000 (for example, collateral, a contract)?

5. If a friend asked you for a $1,000 loan to start a business, what information would you want to obtain to help you make your decision?

9

Capital Stocks

CHAPTER OBJECTIVES

After studying this chapter, you should be able to do the following:

- Compare the different classes of stock available.
- Describe the rights of a stockholder.
- Understand how a company decides whether to go public.
- Describe how a smaller sport business can issue stock.
- Understand how stocks are issued.
- Understand the evolution of sport stocks.
- Compare the various publicly traded sport businesses.

Chapter 8 dealt with borrowing on the open market as a form of capital acquisition. Another major form of capital acquisition is to sell the business to a group of individuals who purchase stock in the company. Stocks, which represent ownership in the business, can be sold on the open market or through very private transactions. Whereas some businesses are owned by thousands of shareholders, others are owned by only one shareholder. Each business is different, and the number and types of shares sold are based on the capital needs of the company when it initially issues stock and when it experiences future financial needs that might warrant the issuance of additional shares.

Stock certificates represent an investor's ownership right in a business. A stockholder pays a designated amount to acquire an ownership interest in a company. Each share represents an ownership interest. That is why a stockholder is also referred to as a shareholder. If you owned 1,000 shares of a company's stock and 100,000 shares had been issued, you would own 1% of the company.

This chapter covers the types of stocks that can be purchased, the ways in which shareholders participate in a business, the process of issuing stock (often called "going public"), the reasons for increases in the value of shares, and the types of sport stocks that are available

Types of Stock

The two types of stock are **common stock** and **preferred stock.** These types of stock are explained in the sections that follow.

Common Stock

The type of stock that is most frequently issued and utilized is common stock, as the name implies.

 The Boston Celtics currently have 2.7 million units of partnership stocks outstanding. The individuals who own these shares would usually own the team. The Celtics are not the best example of a publicly traded sport business because they are owned by a partnership, which has issued a percentage of the team's profit for purchase by interested investors.

A more typical example might be a company such as Nike, which has issued millions of shares of both class A and class B common stock. Philip Knight, the original cofounder, owns 95.5% of the class A shares and 95,652,015 class B shares, which together represent approximately 36.1% of the outstanding shares.

Common stocks represent an equity ownership right in a company. Each share denotes a percentage ownership of the corporation. If Phil Knight, the CEO of Nike, owns over 95 million shares and Nike has in total 268 million shares outstanding, then he would own 35.7% (this number differs from the 36.1% previously mentioned due to the inclusion of the class A shares) of the business. As a partial owner, Knight is entitled to a proportional share of profits earned by Nike. If Nike had a $10 million profit and the board of directors decided to pay the entire amount to its common shareholders, then Knight would be entitled to a dividend of $3.57 million.

Knight has certain rights, risks, and obligations as an owner. His rights include the right to help set the direction of the corporation through voting his shares. He also faces risks, such as the ability to lose his investment and the prospect of any recovery if Nike ever goes bankrupt and there is no money left after the bondholders are repaid. Common stocks are low on the repayment list after secured creditors are repaid and holders of preferred shares are paid. Also, he has obligations to the business, which could include the prohibition of self-dealing or taking a business opportunity for himself.

Preferred Stock

Preferred stock earn its name from the dividend preference it carries in relation to common stock. While a corporation may not issue a dividend to common stock shareholders, it might be bound to provide dividends to the preferred stock shareholders. The dividend is cumulative in that if it is not paid to holders of preferred stock in a given year, the next year the corporation will owe two years' worth of dividends. The dividend to the preferred shareholders needs to be paid before common stockholders can receive their dividends. The requirement to pay a dividend, if one is issued, makes a preferred stock a blend between a bond with a required interest payment and a stock with its associated equity benefits. The requirement to pay a fixed dividend increases the issuing company's **financial leverage.** In the eyes of lenders, preferred stock represents equity and is shown in the equity section of the balance sheet.

Other benefits that are available for preferred stockholders can include

- the right to dividend payments before common stock shareholders receive dividend payments;
- preference as to assets in distribution;
- voting power for preferred stock, available under limited circumstances;

- strong redemption provisions;
- subscription privileges to future stock offerings; and
- the right to convert preferred stock to common stock (Bogen, 1966).

Some investors rely on dividend income as their primary return on an equity investment. For these investors, preferred shares would be the most prudent investment because preferred stock shareholders are entitled to a dividend payment before common stock shareholders receive any dividends.

Regarding preference upon distribution, some corporations specifically authorize preferred stockholders to receive the first of any return upon liquidation of a corporation's assets. If no such preference is provided for in the corporate bylaws, all classes of stock share equally in any distributions. Preferred stockholders often perceive their investment as riskier than bonds because the preferred shareholders' claims are subordinate to those of the bondholders in the event the company is liquidated. Furthermore, bondholders are more likely than preferred shareholders to continue receiving disbursements during hard times (Brigham & Gapenski, 1994).

The right to vote is given to preferred stockholders in limited situations such as when the board of directors fails to pay a required dividend over a specified number of quarters. Preferred stockholders can also vote on issues affecting their status when dividends are in **arrears.**

The conversion privilege attached to some preferred stocks can be a very attractive feature. Assume that a corporation issues a preferred stock that can be converted 2 to 1. Such a provision means that one preferred share could be exchanged at a given time for two common shares. Assume that the corporation's common stock is selling at $20, but the corporation decides to raise $5 million by selling 100,000 shares of preferred stock at $50 par value. At the $50 price, it would *not* be worthwhile to convert the preferred stock to common stock. However, if the common stock subsequently rises to $30 a share, it would be advantageous to convert the preferred stock to common stock (Bogen, 1966). It is advantageous to convert at $30 per share because the shareholder will receive two common shares valued at a combined $60, while his initial investment was only $50 per preferred share. This results in a $10 profit from the conversion. If the conversion had occurred when the common shares were valued at only $20 per share, the shareholder would have lost $10 in the conversion process. Thus, conversion typically occurs only when the conversion process will increase the investor's return. If preferred shares are not converted to common shares, they can continue to pay the required dividends or they might be called. Preferred shares could be issued with a **call provision.** The call provision might require that 2% of the shares be retired each year. A **sinking fund** could be established to help pay for buying back the preferred shares. Under a 2% buyback plan, the preferred shares would mature in a maximum of 50 years.

Preferred stock can also pose a risk if certain provisions are attached that might help sell the stock but can also be utilized as a weapon. In one case, a small meatpacking company sold preferred stock with a condition that no bonds could be issued without the approval of 75% of the preferred stockholders (Bogen, 1966). Although the restriction was onerous, management felt it would be a valuable tool to help sell the stock to skeptical buyers. Years later when the company needed funds for expansion, it discovered that a larger competitor had purchased over 25% of the preferred stock and could block the proposed sale of new bonds. This situation forced the smaller company to merge with the larger company on unfavorable terms.

The two types of stock, common stock and preferred stock, differ in the rights they confer on shareholders.

Shareholders' Rights

The basic rights and obligations of stockholders are set forth in the laws of the state in which the business is incorporated. Incorporation is the formal process of applying to be registered as a stock-issuing corporation, and each state has different laws. A disproportionately large number of businesses are incorporated in several states, including Delaware and Nevada, based on favorable tax or liability laws designed to attract corporations. Besides being spelled out in specific state laws, stockholders' rights can also be found in the corporation's bylaws, charter, or articles of incorporation.

Stockholders have the following legal rights:

- To receive evidence of ownership such as a stock certificate (see p. 154)
- To transfer the stock freely, within limited rules
- To exercise the right to vote in person or by proxy as set forth in the corporation's bylaws

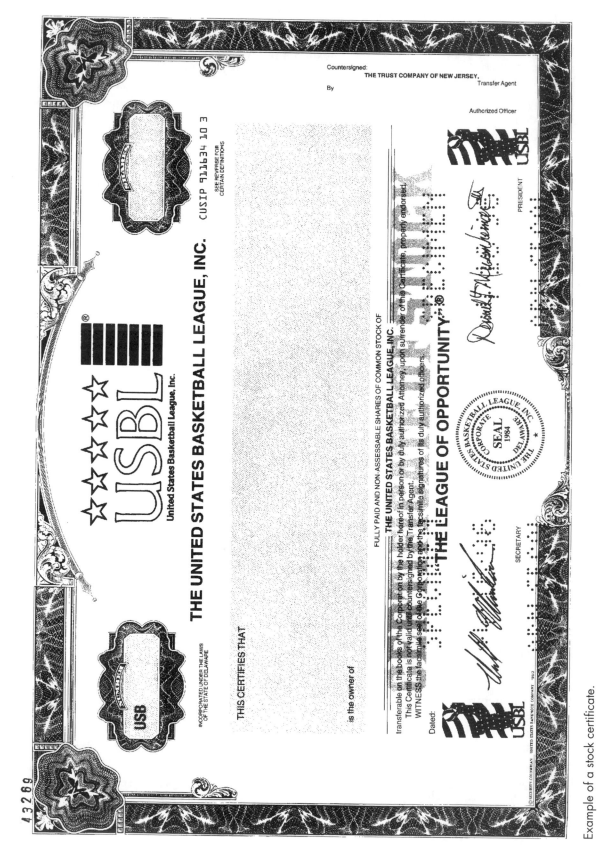

Example of a stock certificate.

- To receive dividends and other disbursements on a pro rata basis according to the number of shares held
- To receive disbursements on a pro rata basis when a partial or complete liquidation of corporate assets occurs
- To bring action on behalf of the corporation against board members who do not act in the corporation's best interest (commonly referred to as stockholders' derivative actions)
- To obtain information from the corporation to help safeguard the stockholder's investment (such as an annual report)
- To subscribe pro rata to new shares of company stocks when authorized by law (commonly referred to as stockholders' preemptive right) (Bogen, 1966)

As an owner of the business, a stockholder has the right to participate in profits earned by the company if the board of directors approves such a payment. The decision to issue a dividend is a very important decision for the board. If a dividend is declared, most investors see that decision as a sign that the business is doing well since the business is able to cover its internal fiscal needs and still has extra money available to pay the shareholders. In contrast, some investors and analysts may view paying a dividend as a sign that the business has no good investment prospects in which to reinvest its additional capital. The board of directors is responsible for making the final determination as to where the extra funds, if any, should be invested; and it is assumed that these decisions are made with the shareholders' interest in mind. The board of directors is elected by the shareholders to run the company on behalf of the shareholders. A successful board does more than just pay dividends to shareholders. A board is judged successful according to whether or not its decisions increase the stock's value.

The **preemptive right** is one of the stockholder's most important rights. Preemptive rights protect a stockholder's power of control and prevent dilution of the stock's value. Suppose Investor A owns all 1,000 shares of outstanding stock in a company and that the shares are valued at $100 each. The market value of the company would be $100,000. If the company sold an additional 1,000 shares at $40 each, the total market value for the company would be $140,000. When the total value is divided by the total shares, the stock value drops to $70 per share. To prevent such a loss to the prior investor and prevent a windfall to new investors, the preemptive right gives Investor A the right to buy the new stock before anyone else.

The right to exercise control over a business is one of the primary purposes of the preemptive right. If you own 10% of the business, you are entitled to purchase 10% of the newly issued shares. This gives you the right to exercise the same amount of control over the business that you did before even if new shares dilute the total number of outstanding shares. The right to control a corporation is one of the most basic stockholder rights, since if you have an investment in something you want to be able to protect that investment.

There are several ways stockholders can control a corporation's direction. These include the use of voting power, holding companies, and defensive tactics.

Voting Power

A major right for corporate owners is the right of certain stockholders to control the corporation through their voting power. Stockholders have the right to elect board members who then hire the company's management team. Smaller companies may have their major shareholders serving as owners, board members, and even managers. Larger businesses have board members who are elected for several-year terms only, to allow the opportunity to elect new board members. Board members are typically elected annually. Each shareholder is entitled to one vote for each share held. Control can be exercised by a large shareholder such as Mr. Jacobs, who controlled 99% of the Cleveland Indians' voting stock when they were publicly traded. Others can also exercise control: a block of family members who own significant shares in a business, a group of unrelated investors (from individuals to banks, corporations, foundations, and pension plans) that own a large voting block, a board member who might wield coercive control over fellow board members, or even bankers or financiers who can exercise considerable control. Regardless of who is in direct control, most larger businesses with traded stocks rely on the proxy process for voting on key matters such as electing new board members or changing the business' bylaws or articles of incorporation. A proxy is basically a power of attorney given by a registered stockholder who appoints someone else to vote on her behalf. Proxies are regularly mailed to all stockholders before the meeting of the board of directors.

The Securities and Exchange Commission (SEC) has very detailed laws to ensure equality and a democratic voting process for all shareholders of voting stocks. Thus, some regulations cover the process of hearing dissenting opinions or proposals and the requirement that management summarize these proposals in its proxy solicitation statement (Bogen, 1966). Although proxy fights typically do not occur on a regular basis, they can occur for a business in transition or one facing financial peril. A proxy fight can also occur when one company is trying to take over another company. A strong philosophical rift between key members of the management team can also lead to a proxy fight. Stockholders can be contacted by a marketing company that has been hired to try to sway their vote through letters, newspaper advertisements, or, in the case of large shareholders, personal phone calls.

> As an owner of a company through ownership of shares, a stockholder has a number of rights, which can include the right to vote on issues of importance to the direction of the company.

Holding Companies

Besides controlling the board of directors, parties can obtain control by investing in a company. A company that has 1 million outstanding shares can be effectively controlled by anyone who purchases 50.01% of the voting stock. Thus, a company can purchase 50.01% of another company and then effectively control the purchased company. A company does not even need to use its own money to acquire a controlling interest. In fact, some companies have been leveraged through another company, such as a holding company, that utilizes the financial resources of the company it is trying to control to help issue bonds or nonvoting preferred stock in order to help finance the purchase. Through this technique, a holding company can purchase controlling shares of several different businesses. The Boston Celtics, for example, could purchase a majority share of several television and radio stations to develop their own network without having to purchase each station in its entirety.

Defensive Tactics

Other businesses or individuals often purchase sport businesses. These transactions are often very amiable, as when private parties purchase the shares of a publicly traded company. This was the scenario when Larry Dolan purchased the publicly traded Cleveland Indians, buying the outstanding shares of the team from Jacobs and other shareholders for

$323 million (Kurdziel, 2000). But not all purchases or attempts to change a corporation are welcomed. An unwelcomed attempt to purchase the shares of a company is called a hostile takeover. Hostile takeovers can be vigorously defended against with significant funds being paid by each side or even several suitors trying to win a bidding war. Other times, a takeover might still be hostile, but if the acquired company does not have the resources to fight the takeover, they could be forced to accept the takeover without any recourse. However, most hostile takeovers are fought in court or financial markets if the company was not able to implement any defensive tactics. If a company cannot change its board or acquire other companies to make itself less attractive as a takeover option, it can utilize other techniques to appear less desirable for a hostile takeover. **Golden parachute** contracts requiring huge payments to executives if they are terminated can make a company less attractive. If a potential suitor discovers it might be necessary to pay an extra $20 million to former executives, a deal can quickly die. Stock purchase **warrants** can also be utilized as a defensive tool. Warrants that can be exercised at a price not much higher than the current market price can help discourage efforts by outsiders to acquire control. As an outside company attempts to buy shares on the open market, the price of the shares will continue to rise. However, management can buy shares at the fixed warrant price, which will allow them to purchase more shares. The mere fact that management has such an option can dissuade a potential hostile takeover. The potential for a takeover can also be affected if the corporation is in financial trouble and stockholder assistance is necessary in order for it to survive or a suitor is needed to save it from bankruptcy.

Although shareholders can benefit from profits as paid out through dividends, shareholders can also face losses that diminish the value of their investment. Stockholders cannot be punished or forced to pay more money if the business faces economic losses, but the share value can decline or the company can go out of business, rendering the stock valueless. Shareholders, much like any other business owner, have responsibilities for business losses. As discussed in chapter 4, shareholders are not personally liable for a corporation's debts, but they can be asked to contribute additional funds to keep the corporation from going bankrupt. Although no shareholder can be forced to purchase additional shares, they sometimes purchase additional shares to see if they can help the business through rough times.

Going Public

The first step for any corporation is the decision whether or not to go public. The decision is not simple; in fact it is very expensive and time-consuming. Chapter 4 outlined the advantages and disadvantages of the corporation as a legal entity. The primary benefits and disadvantages of going public are highlighted in table 9.1.

Besides the advantages and disadvantages of going public presented in table 9.1, specific advantages and disadvantages are associated with financing through the issuance of common stock. The primary advantages and disadvantages of financing through stock are presented in table 9.2.

The second step, after a corporation decides to go public, is to determine whether the stock will be publicly traded. Going public is the process of making a company's ownership available to new potential owners/investors. However, just because a company has issued stock and has gone public does not mean that the shares will be available to the general public. Whereas most large corporations are publicly owned and traded, small corporations are often owned by only a few shareholders, such as family members. Numerous stocks are privately held, or closely held, with only a few owners. Publicly held stocks are made available to an unlimited number of investors as long as shares are available for purchase. The company also has to decide whether it wants the shares listed on a major exchange or wants to have unlisted shares traded on the over-the-counter (OTC) market. Some companies might prefer to avoid some regulations imposed by larger listing exchanges and thus will opt for being an unlisted company. To be listed, a

Table 9.1 Advantages and Disadvantages of Going Public

Advantages	Disadvantages
Owners are allowed to diversify their investments instead of having all their assets locked into the company.	Increased operating costs are associated with all the quarterly and yearly reporting requirements.
A liquid asset is created (a privately held company would be harder to sell).	Company is required to disclose sensitive data that a competitor can use against the company.
Going public helps to raise new cash for growth.	Self-dealing and nepotism are not allowed.
A value for the company is established based on the combined value of outstanding shares.	There is a risk that the value of shares will drop if the market for the shares is slow and they are not traded enough, or if the company or its sector falls into disfavor.
	Loss of control of the business is possible if investors acquire enough stock.

Data from Brigham and Gapenski, 1994.

Table 9.2 Advantages and Disadvantages of Issuing Common Stock

Advantages	Disadvantages
There is no fixed cost associated with issuing stock, whereas a company that issues bonds or commercial paper (see chapter 10) will have to allocate a fixed amount in the budget for debt service.	Issuing bonds or commercial paper provides a predictable fixed cost for repayment in contrast to stocks, which represent a stake in the company's future profits.
Common stocks do not carry any fixed maturity date at which they will have to be paid.	The costs associated with issuing stocks and all ancillary activities can make issuing common stock more expensive than issuing preferred stocks or debt instruments.
Issuing common stock can help raise new capital without affecting the company's bond rating.	Some investors may see issuing new stock as a negative sign that the company has to sell more of itself in order to survive.
At times, such as when interest rates are low and the demand for bonds is also low, it is easier to sell common stock.	

Data from Brigham and Gapenski, 1994.

company has to pay a small fee and meet an exchange's minimum entrance requirements. The company also has to examine who the potential investors are. Institutional investors, such as pension funds or insurance companies, own about 55% of all common stocks and account for 80% of all stock transactions (Brigham & Gapenski, 1994).

Once a decision is made to sell shares to the general public, the shares will go through three possible phases. The first phase is the initial public offering (IPO). These shares are sold on the new-issue market. The first time shares are ever sold is called the **private offering.** The purpose of the IPO is to raise new capital for the business and to put

money into the owner's hands. Once shares have been sold during the IPO, the shares move into the second phase, the secondary market. The secondary market is the market in which stocks are bought and sold for all publicly traded businesses after the IPO. The first day Celtics stock was issued, the stock was part of the new market. Any subsequent transactions would occur in the secondary market, with one exception. If the Celtics decided to issue more shares, these shares would move into the third phase. The third phase is the primary market that exists for companies that have already had an IPO, but want to issue more shares to generate additional funds.

Initial Public Offerings

A record number of IPOs produced unprecedented results in 1999. In 1975, only 12 IPOs were issued; during the first day of trading, the average return was a net loss of 1.5%. By 1990, there were 111 IPOs, which produced a first day's return of 10.5%. In 1999, 485 IPOs were launched, with a net average return the first day of 69.5%. Eighteen of these IPOs had their shares increase over 1,000% during their first year. These dramatic increases do not always produce wonderful results for small investors. Typically 80% to 90% of the shares in an IPO are sold to institutional investors, so individual investors have not been able to reap these grand returns ("Doors to IPOs," 2000). In the fourth quarter of 2000, the total number of IPOs was 56 with a total value of $15.1 billion. By the fourth quarter of 2001, the economic downturn significantly affected the marketplace for IPOs, and the number was down to 26 with a total value of $10 billion ("Q4 IPO Scorecard," 2002).

New shares can be sold to five possible types of buyers:

1. Existing shareholders on a pro rata basis
2. Investment bankers, who will then sell the shares to the general public in an IPO
3. Several major purchasers in a private placement
4. Employees in an employee stock purchase plan
5. Buyers in a dividend reinvestment plan

Selling shares to existing shareholders is fairly simple and entails letting shareholders know when the shares will be available and at what price. Shareholders then have the opportunity to indicate whether they will subscribe. This is called preemption and is discussed earlier in this chapter.

Investment bankers operate as intermediaries to help facilitate the marketing and transfer of stock ownership. A large investor such as a mutual fund or a pension fund might contact an investment banker to secure a large position in an IPO. These large buyers often indicate in advance that they are interested in purchasing shares. Thus, the issuing

corporation knows in advance that a certain minimum number of shares will be purchased through the investment bankers.

A private-placement transaction occurs when one or more investors purchase most shares in a company. One advantage of such sales is the lower flotation costs associated with trying to find potential buyers, since one major potential shareholder is already identified. Flotation costs are the cost to sell shares to the general public. If a major purchaser is identified in advance, then less effort and cost needs to be expended because a majority of the shares are already sold. Another major advantage is the ability to circumvent the SEC requirements, since shares do not have to go through SEC registration. Although the prospects of gaining a large partner are great, private placements have the problem that since they do not comply with SEC requirements it is often hard to sell the shares except to another large investor or institutional investor. Private placements are discussed in greater detail later in this chapter.

Employees can obtain an equity interest in their place of employment by buying shares in the company. The process in which employees buy stock in a company is often referred to as an **employee stock ownership plan** (ESOP). In these plans, the company often uses its own profits to buy shares for the employees. Over time, enough shares are purchased that the employees eventually own the company. Since Congress feels that it is an important goal to allow employees the right to buy into their employer, the federal tax code provides specific benefits for companies engaged in ESOPs. Besides being able to deduct the interest on debt used to acquire the stock, a company can deduct some of the principal used to acquire the stock and can also deduct the dividend payments made to the employee stockholders. In addition to the tax benefits, an ESOP can help prevent takeovers by other firms because the employees can own a significant number of shares. Another benefit is that an ESOP can replace the employee retirement program. Thus, instead of pouring millions into a pension fund, the company can issue and then buy shares for its employees. The employees obtain a valuable asset that will hopefully increase over time, and the employer obtains a new avenue for selling additional shares. The final benefit associated with an ESOP is the potential for increased employee morale. Employees are more prone to work harder when they know that their productivity will benefit themselves fiscally. If employees work harder and generate increased income, the company benefits; and as owners, the employees will also eventually benefit.

Although ESOPs provide significant benefits, they can also have some disadvantages. The biggest disadvantage to an ESOP is the dynamic shift in power within a business as employees become owners. Assembly line workers who are used to being told what to do might now have a say in how the CEO acts. Labor negotiations can become very tricky as management has to try to produce a fair labor agreement with union workers; but the union workers might also be shareholders, and the more money paid in salary, the lower the profits for the company. The government (Department of Labor) can also cancel an ESOP if the ESOP was designed to fight a takeover and was not properly developed. Another concern arises in relation to retirees and pension holders whose entire **portfolio** might be composed of shares in the company. As long as the company is doing well, everyone will be happy. However, if the stock declines, the result can be devastating. A retiree could see his portfolio decline from $500,000 to $100,000 if the stock loses 80% of its value as a result of a negative industry analysis, for example.

A **dividend reinvestment plan** allows a shareholder to transfer all dividends back into the company to obtain more shares.

 Assume, for example, that the Celtics offered such an opportunity. Say the team paid a $0.50 dividend in a given quarter, and you had 20 shares and had the dividend reinvested to purchase additional shares. If the shares were selling for $10 each at that time, you would receive one additional share rather than a dividend check for $10.

Since the math usually does not involve round numbers like these, a shareholder normally obtains a percentage of a share. Thus, in a given quarter a shareholder might receive 0.756 of a share through dividend reinvestment and after the next dividend amount is reinvested might have built up to one complete share and start working on the next complete share.

Prospectus

Before making a stock offering, the issuer or underwriter has to develop a **prospectus** describing the company and all the potential risks and benefits associated with purchasing the stock. The prospectus often contains information on key employees and members of the board, information on how the funds will be used and the products that will be sold, audited financial statements, the sales forecast, pro forma budgets, the dividend policy, and related documentation. The audited financial statement, prepared by an independent accounting firm, describes the business and the management structure and explains what the managers are paid, who the principal shareholders are, what the underwriting agreement is, and who is involved in the stock sales syndicate. The SEC has to approve the prospectus before it can be sent to potential investors. However, the issuer or underwriter has the opportunity to distribute rough drafts of the prospectus prior to SEC approval to help generate investor interest. The preapproved document is called a red herring.

The **red herring,** along with company executives, is then shopped around in a marketing blitz by the underwriter through visits with potential major investors such as institutional investors. Significant oral information can be passed in this process, but no written material other than the prospectus can be given, and no sales can be made at these meetings. Once the SEC obtains all the necessary information, the SEC can approve the prospectus for general distribution.

Selling Shares

Stocks have value only if they are actually purchased. New issues need to be priced at a level that will interest potential investors. If the stock is priced too high, investors may see this as a sign that the stock "is out of their league." Other investors will see a high issue price as a sign of value. In contrast, people may perceive a low price either as an indication of an inferior company or as an attempt to garner ownership from smaller investors. Traditionally stock prices for new issues are based on the average price of similar stock issues (Spiro, 1996). Issuing new shares for existing stocks is simpler, as the current market value for the shares can be utilized as the benchmark price. If investors feel that the stock is correctly valued, they can purchase at the offering price or wait to see if investors bid the price up or down.

Current stockholders, institutional investors, investment bankers, potential investors, or even current employees can purchase stocks. Current stockholders might be the first choice for many corporations, as some laws require that current shareholders have the first right to buy stocks in order to maintain their pro rata interest in earnings, assets, and voting rights. The process of offering stocks first to existing shareholders is called a "privileged subscription." Shareholders often find this privilege a very important benefit, similar to receiving dividends.

Shareholders are given a right to subscribe to shares before they are offered to the general public. These shares are normally priced a little lower than the price at which the general public could purchase the same shares. The right might allow a shareholder to purchase one share of the new stock for every three shares of existing stock owned by the shareholder. However, shareholders do not need to purchase stocks through the right and can in fact sell their rights on the open market to others who would like to buy new shares at a lower price. No matter who exercises the right, the right becomes valueless after the subscription date expires.

 If the Boston Celtics offered current shareholders the right to buy one unit of new stock for every five units they currently own, such a right would normally vest (expire) after a set period such as three months. If the right is not exercised in that time period, the right is extinguished and any desired new shares would have to be purchased at their market price.

Although subscription rights can help ensure some purchases from dedicated investors, there are no guarantees for the issuer. Issuing stock can be like throwing a party—all the key individuals may be there, but perhaps no one will be there. To ensure that the stock is sold, an issuing company often utilizes the assistance of an investment banker to underwrite the stock offering. An underwriting is similar to an insurance policy. If sales are good and all the shares are bought, then the investment banker will not have to purchase any shares. However, if sales are mediocre, the investment banker may need to purchase a significant number of shares. The investment bankers charge either a commission or a set fee for their services. Investment bankers often attempt to sell stock concurrently with the issuing company to hedge the prospect of their having to buy a large number of shares.

Investment bankers also represent the primary vehicle for independent sales. The services offered by investment bankers or investment houses include the following:

- Giving advice on the security type to offer and the exact terms of the issue
- Giving assistance in underwriting a security issue
- Purchasing a security issue outright
- Helping a company to comply with state and federal requirements
- Distributing new securities to investors
- Helping to stabilize the price of a new issue by buying shares in the marketplace to support interest in the issue
- Providing additional advice after a security is issued (Bogen, 1966)

Private Placement

Private placement can occur in the borrowing market (the bond market in particular) as a loan is obtained from private parties. Similarly, private placement can occur with the issuing of stocks when stocks are sold by at least one institutional investor. Life insurance companies have been involved in numerous private placements because of their strong **purchasing power.** Companies that issue stocks are often interested in pursuing private-placement sale of their shares because this allows them to avoid some SEC rules and to drastically reduce the marketing costs. Since the SEC knows that companies would like to avoid stringent rules if possible, it has developed a two-part test for private offerings. The first is a consideration of the potential investor's sophistication. The investor must have enough knowledge to understand the risks and rewards inherent in the offering. The second component is a limitation of potential buyers to a maximum of 35 investors. Private-placement securities have other restrictions such as being restricted from resale to the public market for at least two years. Private placements are covered in greater detail in the next section.

> After a company decides to go public, it must decide whether to sell shares to the general public or on a private-placement basis.

Regulation D and Small Company Offering Registration (SCOR) Offerings

While professional teams or larger conglomerates can issue stock without significant difficulty, smaller companies often feel that a potential stock offering is unattainable. This misconception can deprive businesses of significant potential capital. Pursuant to federal securities laws, companies that wish to raise under $1 million in any given 12-month period are excused from certain burdensome requirements such as registering the security or submitting an audited financial statement. An audited financial statement can cost up to $100,000 (Evanson, 1998, January). This exemption is found in the Securities Exchange Act, Regulation D, Section 504; sales of such shares are commonly called Regulation D or 504 offerings. While federal laws govern these offerings, the issuing corporation still needs to comply with the incorporating state's laws. Colorado, Florida, and New York have some of the least restrictive laws for such offerings (Evanson, 1998, January). The keys to a 504 offering involve

1. contacting the security commission in the issuing state to determine what rules apply,

2. analyzing what financing structure can fit within the confines of the applicable laws, and

3. hiring competent professionals (accountant, lawyer, or financial consultant) for help through the process (Evanson, 1998, January).

If the Smiths were pursuing this route to finance their fitness center, they would have to complete a Form D with the SEC, which would qualify them for 504 status. Once they have completed the three steps just listed, the Smiths could contact the NASDAQ Bulletin Board to get their shares quoted and ultimately traded on the OTC Bulletin Board. The Smiths would probably feel that they were in the big time, as their company would now be publicly traded. All investors and potential investors have a more positive feeling when a national market exists for buying and selling shares. It should be noted, however, that bulletin-board stocks tend to be less liquid than stocks listed on an organized exchange because of less-frequent trading.

The key to issuing any Regulation D, SCOR, or private-placement offering is providing sufficient warning to potential investors concerning the potential risks inherent in the stocks. The disclosure information shown in figure 9.1 is adapted from a real offering.

The example in figure 9.1 was targeted to accredited investors. The SEC allows smaller offerings such as private-placement offerings to be conducted with no registration requirements at the federal level as long as the securities are sold only to accredited and nonaccredited investors. An offering can be made to an unlimited number of accredited investors. Accredited investors must fall into one of the following categories:

- Anyone with a net worth of at least $1 million
- Anyone with an annual income of at least $200,000 for the previous two years who reasonably expects to earn $200,000 in income during the current year
- Any corporation or partnership with over $5 million in total assets
- Insiders of the issuing company such as directors or officers
- Certain institutional investors such as pension plans or registered investment companies (Cheeseman, 1998)

Nonaccredited investors are persons who do not meet this definition. A private-placement or SCOR offering can have no more than 35 nonaccredited investors. Nonaccredited investors have to have a certain level of investing sophistication or be represented by an advisor such as a lawyer or accountant. A company cannot advertise to the general public in order to attract nonaccredited investors.

Although the SEC tries to reduce registration rules for smaller offerings, that does not mean there are no other possible regulations. Under SEC Rule 144, any security sold pursuant to a private-placement or SCOR offering must be held by the buyer for at least one year from the date when the securities were

Smith's Fitness Center

Summary of Offering

Smith's Fitness Center, Inc. ("the Company") is offering shares of Common Stock $0.001 par value ("Common Stock") pursuant to this offering on the following terms:
- The offering is intended to raise $2,000,000. This offering is not subject to receiving subscriptions for any minimum amount.
- The minimum investment is $50,000.
- The Company intends to accept subscriptions for shares of Common Stock in amounts in excess of $2,000,000 in this offering at its sole discretion. This offering is not subject to a maximum number of shares of Common Stock being sold.

Use of Proceeds

The proceeds from this offering will be used for the following purposes:
- Purchase existing fitness facilities or renovating warehouse space into new fitness facilities;
- Hire employees to work in sales and finance, and athletic trainers;
- Purchase/lease exercise equipment; and
- Ongoing working capital requirements.

Investors

The shares of Common Stock are being offered only to "accredited investors," as such term is defined in Regulation D promulgated under the Securities Act of 1933. Accredited investors are investors who either:
- had individual income in excess of $200,000 in each of 1998 and 1999 or joint income with their spouse in excess of $300,000 in each such year and have a reasonable expectation of reaching the same income level in 1999, or
- have an individual net worth (together with their spouse) in excess of $1,000,000.

These standards represent minimum requirements for investors and do not necessarily mean that these securities are a suitable investment for any investor meeting these requirements. See "Risk Factors and Other Important Considerations." Moreover, the Company reserves the right to reject subscriptions in whole or in part for any reason.

The Company has established a minimum purchase requirement of $50,000. The Company may, however, in its sole discretion, accept a subscription for less than the minimum requirement.

Restrictions on Transfer of Offered Securities

The Common Stock is not registered under the 1933 Act or the securities laws of any State ("State Acts") and the Common Stock may not be resold unless it is subsequently registered under the 1933 Act and any applicable State Acts, or an exemption from such registration is available. Holders of the Common Stock have no right to require such registration and the Company has no plans to register its securities. Shareholders may thus be required to retain their investment in the Common Stock for an indefinite period. Each certificate representing shares of Common Stock sold in this offering will bear a legend setting forth certain restrictions on transferability.

In addition, the securities laws of certain states may require that additional restrictions on transferability be imposed upon securities sold in such jurisdictions, and that additional restrictive legends be placed on the certificates representing the Common Stock.

Foreword

This Business Plan and Financing Memorandum ("the Business Plan") has been prepared by Smith's Fitness Center, Inc. ("SFC" or "the Company") to convey information about the Company and its plans.

The financial and sales projections contained herein are considered by SFC management to be reasonable. Management believes that the statements regarding the uniqueness and value of the Company's strategy are accurate as of the date of the Business Plan. The financial projections and statements contained herein constitute the baseline set of the Company's objectives for the near term, but should not be relied upon as a promise or representation of future performance.

This Business Plan is being made available to a limited number of accredited investors that are assumed to be familiar with the risks of investing in start-up enterprises, to be capable of evaluating these risks, and to be capable of protecting their own interests.

No person other than the officers of the Company has been authorized in connection with this Business Plan to give any information or to make any representation not contained herein. This document is not to be reproduced or distributed without the express written permission of AIM management.

For more information contact:

Bob Smith
President
SFC, Inc.
123 Anystreet
Anytown, CT USA
555-555-5555 phone
555-555-5555 fax

Figure 9.1 Disclosure information for Smith's Fitness Center (adapted from a template for a real offering).

purchased. These regulations are lifted after two years. However, between the first and second years there are additional restrictions on how many shares can be sold at any given time (Cheeseman, 1998). The following securities have no registration requirements and can be sold without significant regulation:

- Government-issued securities
- Short-term notes that mature in less than nine months
- Securities offered by nonprofit issuers such as youth sport organizations
- Insurance and annuity contracts issued by insurance companies
- Securities issued through a corporate reorganization in exchange for prior securities (Cheeseman, 1998)

In addition to 504 offerings, the Smiths could utilize a SCOR. These are available in every state except Alabama, Delaware, Hawaii, and Nebraska (Evanson, 1998, January). A SCOR offering might present a good opportunity for the Smiths to offer their stocks in several states if they are interested in raising less than $1 million annually. However, the Form U-7 requirements for a SCOR offering are so complex (even though only 50 questions are asked) that the Smiths would be better off filing a full-scale IPO and raising more than $1 million. Although the form is complex, it was designed for business owners to complete rather than an army of attorneys (Reynes, 1998, May). The Smiths could attempt to raise $200,000 to $400,000; but the cost associated with raising that sum, including personnel hours, would be between $30,000 and $120,000 (Reynes, 1998, May). Although this appears to be a large chunk of the money raised, it should be noted that a large **public offering** by a major corporation could cost between 15% and 25% of the amount raised. Besides the personnel hours needed to complete the SCOR forms, a filing fee is required that could range from as low as $200 to a high of $2,500 for registration in California (Reynes, 1998, May).

The SCOR filing process might be complex, but the SCOR marketing options have been simplified, so the Smiths could advertise for investors in the newspaper, by direct mail, or even over the Internet (Reynes, 1998, May). Furthermore, SCOR offerings are more attractive than venture capital infusion, as people with venture capital might want to have decision-making powers, impose certain rules, or both.

Exemptions in the Securities Exchange Act enable smaller businesses to raise capital through public stock offerings that are less complex than those for large businesses wishing to raise multimillion-dollar amounts.

Initial Public Offering

No matter what offering option is chosen, the business needs to hit the primary market with an IPO to launch its stock activities. The IPO can range from informal to very formal, depending on the stock offering. Before an IPO can be undertaken, the business needs to formalize its existence as a corporation. Corporation issues are covered in detail in chapter 11. However, we note here that the corporation's articles of incorporation specify how many shares can be issued. The corporate bylaws might specify how shares can be transferred and when shareholders can inspect the corporate records, as well as delineating similar rules affecting issuing and selling shares (Cheeseman, 1998).

For a full-scale common stock issue, a company first must file a registration statement with the SEC. The registration documents are very lengthy and require considerable time and expense to complete. The SEC can suspend or prohibit the offering if it finds any statements that are misleading or inaccurate. After filing for registration, the company and its underwriting syndicate of investment bankers distribute a preliminary prospectus. This prospectus could provide as follows:

A registration statement relating to these securities has been filed with the SEC but has not become effective. Information contained herein is subject to completion or amendment. These securities may not be sold nor may offers to buy be accepted prior to the time the registration statement becomes effective. This prospectus shall not constitute an offer to sell or the solicitation of an offer to buy, nor shall there be any sale of these securities in any state in which such offer, solicitation, or sale would be unlawful prior to registration or qualification under the securities laws of any such state. ("IPO Basics," 1999)

After the preliminary prospectus is issued, the company's top officials must go on a road show to promote the stock sale. During this time the SEC reviews the registration and might request additional information. If the SEC approves the registration, the company and its syndicate have to establish a price and the number of shares that will be sold. The final prospectus and any necessary amendments are distributed when the stocks are made available to the public. The IPO closes when the money is received and the stock certificates are delivered. This usually occurs around three days after trading has started. It takes approximately two to three and a half months from the start of the IPO process for the money to be received ("IPO Basics," 1999).

The decision to issue stocks is not something to be taken lightly. The costs are normally very steep. But also, it is not enough just to determine that a stock offering is the proper direction for a company. The company also has to determine what priority will be given to stock. This prioritization can be seen in preferred stock and the various rights given to different classes of shareholders.

Failed Offerings

Many companies go out of business each year. Even companies that have issued stock can face financial troubles and may have to go out of business. Publicly traded companies that flounder can find themselves being delisted by one of the exchanges. In 1998, Golden Bear Golf, a company primarily owned by Jack Nicklaus, faced some hard times, including suits by shareholders claiming that the company had underreported 1997 losses by $20 million (Mullen, 1998). Furthermore, the company's assets had decreased so that it no longer met the NASDAQ capital requirements (at least $4 million in assets), and it was delisted. **Delisting** meant that the shares would no longer be traded on NASDAQ and that shareholders would have to trade their shares on the less prestigious OTC Bulletin Board or the pink sheets (the least formal trading market for NASDAQ, which handles shares that are very infrequently traded, such as private-placement or Regulation D shares) ("Nicklaus Company's Stock," 1998). When the stock had been initially offered in 1996, the company was able to raise $37 million. Golden Bear sold its string of golf centers in 1998 and then shut down Paragon, the golf course construction subsidiary that had generated the questionable accounting practices. After the restructuring the company was taken private in 2000, when it was bought by Nicklaus and his family (Golden Bear, 2002).

Common or preferred stocks are sold when a company is interested in selling ownership or equity rights to others for needed funds. The primary benefit to such an approach is the elimination of a need to pay a set interest payment even during rough times. However, many companies do not want to dilute their ownership interest and prefer to finance growth through debt instruments. We have already discussed bank loans and various types of nonbank loans. An additional strategy for stronger companies such as the Celtics or Sport Manufacturing Company would be to issue bonds, which we discuss in the next chapter.

Increasing Stock Values

After selling shares, a corporation and all the employees are responsible for increasing the stock's value. One of the foremost benefits associated with purchasing stocks is the potential for increased equity value. If the business is doing well financially, the business increases in value. A business increases in value through a rise in the value of its shares. As noted previously, the success of any management team is based on the extent to which they can increase a stock's value and provide dividends to the company's owners. One can examine this success by looking at the company's PE ratio, the ratio of the stock price to the company earnings. A high ratio indicates that a company's stock is selling for much more than the per share earnings. If the earnings of such a company decrease, the value of the stock could plummet. The rapid rise in the stock market during 2000, propelled by Internet companies, provides such an example. Most prominent stocks in the largest traditional companies were trading at 20 times their earnings in 1999. Similarly, the top

NASDAQ shares in 1995 were trading at 20 times their earnings. However the demand for Internet stocks and the low earnings of Internet companies pushed the PE ratio of the NASDAQ 100 top firms to around 90 times earnings in March, 2000 (Browning, 2000). At the same time, the PE ratio for the Standard & Poor 500 was around 25 and for the Dow was around 20. The PE ratio of World Wrestling Entertainment, Inc. (WWE) in February 2002 was 19.07 (Yahoo! Finance—WWF, 2002). Price-earnings ratios can show significant fluctuation. Yahoo had a PE ratio of almost –1,000 at the start of 1999 and then had shot up to over 2,000 just one year later (Browning, 2000). By 2002, Yahoo's PE ratio had settled at 236.71 (Yahoo! Finance—YHOO, 2002).

 Shares can go up in price on the basis of a multitude of factors. One primary category of factors affecting stock prices is external factors. Examples of external factors that can affect the value of Boston Celtics stock, and that of other professional sport teams, include

- antitrust decisions affecting the league,
- labor disputes and unwillingness of players to cross the picket lines to play,
- environmental regulations affecting the arena,
- a change in workplace safety rules that apply to operating the team,
- new rules related to employment practices in the workplace such as the classification of food vendors as employees rather than independent contractors, and
- the folding of a rival league or the success of another league.

Stock prices can also be affected by internal strategic policy decisions. Examples of such decisions include

- whether to trade a star player or hire a new coach,
- whether to increase the number of preseason games,
- whether to borrow money for expansion or issue more stocks,
- whether to declare a dividend, and
- whether to consolidate television and radio broadcasting operations in-house.

Examples of Internal and External Factors' Influence on Publicly Traded Sport Organizations

Internal and external factors have played a part in the success and failure of several publicly traded sport organizations.

- The Cleveland Cavaliers went public in 1970 for $5 per share, but shares dropped to as low as $0.50 per share in 1982. The team went private in 1984 for $1.25 per share (Much, 1996).
- The New England Patriots went public in 1960 for $5 per share and went private in 1976 for $15 per share (Much, 1996).
- The Baltimore Orioles went on a roller-coaster ride in the 1970s, with their stock price ranging from $8 to $25.50. In 1979 the team went private, with liquidation value earning shareholders $49.60 per share over a three-year period (Much, 1996).
- The Milwaukee Bucks went public in 1968 for $5 per share and went private for $12 per share 11 years later (Much, 1996).

Teams that go public sell shares for an attractive price (normally under $25 per share) in odd lots to fans who wish to buy a few shares and frame the certificate as part of a sport memorabilia collection (Much, 1996).

The Cleveland Indians made a splash in the stock market, but were just as quickly taken off the market. The "tribe's" shares were doing well in the 1999 baseball season until the team lost in the division series. The day after the series ended, the stock declined 4.9% ("Go Figure," 1999). Several days later, a deal was announced in which an Ohio attorney (Larry Dolan) agreed to buy the team for $320 million, including assuming $35 million in debt (Walker, 1999). The planned purchase to take the Indians private only two years after they had gone public would mean a significant windfall for shareholders. At a price of over $22 per share if the purchase was approved, shareholders could have earned a 50% return on their investment in less than two years (Walker, 1999). The reward was worth the wait for investors who initially purchased shares for $15 each but then saw the stock drop to $10 per share for several months until the team's primary shareholder, Jacobs, announced his intent to sell.

There are publicly traded professional teams throughout the world. The country that has most recently had a team open itself to public ownership is Germany. Germany's 1995 and 1996 champion soccer team BV Borussia 09 Dortmund's owners voted to become a corporation and issue stock to the public. Publicly traded soccer teams already exist in England and Holland. In fact England has a "Kick-Index" that tracks 20 stocks of soccer teams in the United Kingdom. The index reached its highest point in 1997, but through 1999 it declined 35%. The only team that has shown financial strength is Manchester United, which was worth about a billion dollars before the 2000 market crash ("German Soccer," 1999).

While it is typically financially strong companies that are interested in launching an IPO, some businesses try to take advantage of a strong stock market to offer an IPO that might not be all that strong. For example, a San Diego A-league soccer team, the Flash, filed preliminary documents with the SEC in 1999 to go public. The announcement came even though the team was losing money (losses over $795,000 the first six months in 1999), had attendance of only around 3,000 per game, and had $67,196 in the bank (Palazzo, 1999). By 2002, the shares were trading for $0.17 each ("Stock Quote," 2002).

Sport entities besides professional teams also issued stock in the late 1990s to take advantage of the IPO craze. While numerous Internet-based companies were the primary beneficiaries of such IPOs, traditional businesses were also successful. WWE raised almost $200 million in a 1999 public offering fueled by WWE's success in such programs as "Raw is WAR" and "Smack Down" on national television ("Ready to Wrestle," 1999).

Some people purchase shares in publicly traded sport businesses to impress their friends. The Green Bay Packers shares are an excellent example of such a purchase, since the shares issued in 1997 have very little value on the open market (see next section). Other stocks have more value, but it might be harder to place a value on these shares other than the actual market value. However, ancillary benefits can be significant. For example, people who own shares in Tribune may have purchased them for their investment value but also in order to be eligible for the annual shareholders games at Wrigley Field for the Tribune-owned Chicago Cubs (Newberry, 2001).

After a company begins selling its stock, there are myriad factors, both external and internal to the company, that can cause the stock to increase or decrease in value.

Sport Stocks

Stock offerings in professional sport are not new. The Green Bay Packers sold their first 1,000 shares in 1923 for $5 each (Lascari, 1998). However, in 1935 the company went into receivership and was reorganized as a Wisconsin nonprofit stock corporation; it then issued another 3,000 shares at $5 each. In 1950 the Packers had another stock offering that raised $118,000. By 1997 there were 4,627 stockholders, who were given 1,000 shares for every share owned, which resulted in 4,627,000 shares outstanding. After amending their articles of incorporation the Packers were able to sell an additional 5,373,000 shares. A fourth sale was consummated in 1997, with each new share selling for $200 plus a handling fee of $15 (Lascari, 1998). There were significant restrictions that prohibited almost all transfers of the new stock except back to the Packers for $0.025 per share, to family members as gift, or as a bequest following death. Additional rules prohibit a stockholder from making any profit or even receiving a dividend. Furthermore, to comply with NFL rules, each stockholder had to represent that she had not been involved in any litigation alleging fraud, had not been convicted of a felony, and had not participated in sports gambling. Even with all these restrictions, the Packers sold 120,000 shares and raised over $24 million. Most purchasers bought the stock as a novelty to claim ownership in the Packers.

The Boston Celtics went public in 1986 when 40% of the team was sold for $17.50 per share. As of 1998, 5.3 million shares were outstanding and owned by over 50,000 shareholders (Lascari, 1998). Unlike the Packers shares, which are not approved by the SEC or covered by any federal or state laws, Celtics shares comply with all federal laws and were openly traded on the New York Stock Exchange (NYSE). The team's symbol on the NYSE was BOS. (Symbols for companies instead of company names are shown on ticker systems that display the most recent prices of shares.)

The Celtics have gone through several major changes over the years, including purchasing and selling radio and television stations. In 1998 the stock underwent additional changes forced by legislative requirements. In 1987 Congress passed the Revenue Act of 1987, which required that a limited partnership (a business structure similar to that of the Celtics when it was formed) be taxed at the partnership rate. On the basis of a grandfather clause, the Celtics' limited partnership would be taxed at the corporate rate beginning July 1, 1998. In June 1998, the Boston Celtics Limited Partnership reorganized into two separate entities:

1. Boston Celtics Limited Partnership II, which was formed to remain on the NYSE and be taxed as a corporation
2. Castle Creek Partners, LP, which was formed as a nonpublic entity with "pass-through" tax treatment (Much & Phillips, 1999)

Each stockholder had a choice of an interest in either entity.

As noted previously in this chapter and in chapter 1, several teams are attempting to cash in on the interest of sport fans to sell parts or all of their team to the general public. Some stocks have done very well while others have not. For example, the Cleveland Indians went public (a limited ownership right with very little voting rights) in 1998 with an initial price of $15 a share, which correlated to a team value of $232 million. However, within seven months the stock had fallen over 50% and was trading at $7.13 a share, which translated to a team value of approximately $113 million (Much & Phillips, 1999). Each of the 4 million shares of class A common shares was entitled to one vote. However, the 2,281,667 class B shares, all owned by the owner of the team, were each entitled to 10,000 votes (Lascari, 1998). Thus, Jacobs retained 99.98% control of the company and was entitled to elect the entire board of directors.

The Indians were unusually lucky with the timing of their stock offering. The year the Indians went public, they went to the World Series. The prospectus, which showed income through December 31, 1997, highlighted $140 million in revenue and $22.5 million in net income (see figure 9.2) (Much & Phillips, 1999). These numbers were very much inflated, as almost 90% of the income that year came from postseason and non-baseball activities. If interest income, gains from player transactions, league

	($000)
Reported net income	22,570
Interest income, net of interest expense	(2,371)
Gains on player transactions	(2,696)
League expansion proceeds	(9,286)
Playoff game revenue	(5,700)
Pretax income—adjusted to highlight only traditional revenue	**2,517**
Pro forma income taxes	(755)
Pro forma adjusted net income	**1,762**

Figure 9.2 Cleveland Indians 1997 adjusted income.

From Much and Phillips, 1999.

expansion proceeds, and postseason income are removed from the team's net income, the net income dropped to $1.76 million (Much & Phillips, 1999).

The $15 per share IPO, which implied a $232 million franchise value, priced the stock at 131.7 times the adjusted earnings from regular-season revenue (Much & Phillips, 1999). By pricing themselves so high, the Indians provided virtually no opportunity for price appreciation. Thus, when the 1998 revenue numbers were published for the quarter ending September 30, showing a 37% increase in third-quarter operating profit, the stock price barely budged (Much & Phillips, 1999). As previously mentioned, Larry Dolan purchased the team in 1999 for approximately $320 million.

Stocks in professional teams have had a mediocre reception from the investing public. "Pure-play" investments that include only a professional sport team have several major problems, such as seasonal revenue streams, potential labor strife, limited investment liquidity, reliance on other business owners to generate a product, and intense media and government scrutiny (Much & Phillips, 1999). A **pure play** refers to a corporation that participates in only one industry segment. For example, the Celtics are exclusively a sport team and are thus a pure play. In contrast, a blended company could encompass a team and other unrelated businesses; an example is the Florida Panthers team and their resort holdings.

While a pure-play stock offering for a team such as the Celtics might not be a sound investment option for stockholders other than the primary team owner, "blends" can produce more significant revenue streams through the addition of other revenue-producing units to a professional team. In the case of the NHL's Florida Panthers, additional units are combined with a pure play, producing a comprehensive business entity capable of utilizing additional revenue to offset potential losses associated with a professional team. In 1996, Florida Panthers Holdings, Inc. (parent company of the NHL's Florida Panthers—NYSE: PAW) sold 7.3 million shares of class A stock to the public, and team owner H. Wayne Huizenga retained 5.3 million shares (Much & Phillips, 1999). The shares sold for $10 each, which valued the team at $125 million. Shortly after issuing the stock, the company evolved from just the team to a diversified leisure and recreation company that included six resorts, an arena management company, two ice rinks, and one golf facility. This growth was funded through additional stock sales that increased outstanding shares from 12.6 million in 1996 to 35.1 million in 1998. Compared with the sport segment, the company's leisure and recreation side brought significant economic prosperity to the parent company. Table 9.3 presents the revenue, operating income, depreciation, and cash flow for the company's two divisions in 1997 and 1998.

As highlighted in table 9.3, the $235 million increase in revenue produced by the resorts helped offset the continued losses incurred by the sport side of the company. However, the marriage between the leisure and sport divisions would be short-lived, as management at the 1998 annual meeting announced the potential to spin off the sport division into a separate public company (Much & Phillips, 1999). A spin-off would indicate that in this particular attempt at blending, the company was not successful. In fact, in 2001, the team portion of the business was sold to concentrate the corporate efforts on the resort and property management side of the business. With the Panthers out of the corporate umbrella, former owner Huizenga concentrated his efforts on the resort side of the business and changed the **stock symbol** (ticker symbol) to RST, which is still traded on the NYSE ("Panthers' New Ownership," 2002).

The Panthers are not alone in their inability to fully develop a blended structure, as poor performance also has hounded Ascent Entertainment Group, Inc., which owns several businesses including the NHL's Colorado Avalanche and the NBA's Denver Nuggets. On the basis of double-digit losses for years, Ascent's parent company, Comsat Corp., divested its remaining interest in Ascent in 1996. Ascent suffered operating losses of $42.4 million in 1997 and was facing even larger losses in 1998

Table 9.3 Florida Panthers Holding, Inc. Financial Highlights

1997 ($000)

	Sports	Leisure	Total company
Revenue	$36,695	$17,567	$54,262
Operating income	(10,533)	4,053	(8,379)
Depreciation	4,239	1,459	5,698
Cash flow	(6,294)	5,512	(2,681)

1998 ($000)

	Sports	Leisure	Total company
Revenue	$43,586	$252,603	$296,189
Operating income	(17,503)	52,769	25,452
Depreciation	5,168	17,950	23,155
Cash flow	(12,335)	70,719	48,607

Data from Much and Phillips, 1999.

(Much & Phillips, 1999). In 1999 the Colorado Avalanche and Denver Nuggets were tentatively sold, along with their arena, for $400 million, with the buyer assuming some debt associated with the arena ("Two Denver Franchises," 1999). The sale has not gone unchallenged, as a potential suitor sued, saying that Ascent shareholders would make more money from a different offer to buy the team and that a potential conflict of interest had not been made public (Lewis, 1999). After several suits were filed, the teams were resold. The original buyers returned with a $450 million offer, which appeared to be enough to close the deal (Wal-Mart Heir," 2000). The team (as well as the Denver Avalanche and the Pepsi® Center) was eventually purchased for $450 million by Stanley Kroenke ("Owner," 2002).

In addition to pure-play and blended professional sport-related corporations, another variation has emerged recently—a vertically integrated combination whereby the sport team benefits other corporate units. The best examples of such combinations are Walt Disney (Mighty Ducks of Anaheim and the Anaheim Angels), Tribune (Chicago Cubs), and Fox Entertainment Group, Inc. (Los Angeles Dodgers and a minority interest in the New York Knicks, New York Rangers, Los Angeles Lakers, and Los Angeles Kings) (Much & Phillips, 1999). These vertically integrated combinations have proved to be much more effective than pure-play sport businesses because the broadcasting arms of each company can generate significant sport advertising income without having to pay significant broadcasting rights fees.

The history of sport stocks is reminiscent of a roller coaster. With strong interest in IPOs in the late 1990s, several more teams are considering public offerings. However, investor interest appears to be waning on new sport issues. If a team or other business does not have the ability or interest to pursue a larger public offering, it can still sell stock through a smaller stock offering such as a Regulation D or SCOR offering, discussed earlier in the chapter.

Beginning with the Green Bay Packers in the 1920s, many professional sport teams have sold stock, with greatly varying degrees of success.

CONCLUSION

The ability to reach more potential investors is a major advantage for a company issuing stock. Investors who might never express interest in a company might be willing to gamble and invest a small amount in order to be part of the ownership team. Large mutual funds could also purchase a large number of shares. No matter who owns the shares, a publicly traded company has greater access to capital than almost all non-publicly traded companies.

Teams such as the Boston Celtics, Cleveland Indians, Florida Panthers, and Green Bay Packers have all flirted with issuing stock to the public or are still publicly traded because of the potential for significant capital enhancement. Furthermore, large sport businesses such as Nike, Disney, and WWE cannot grow without the capital infusion afforded by issuing stocks.

Although shareholders have some obligations and significant rights, a publicly traded company has to comply with numerous regulations and reporting requirements, which can help make the decision to go public—regardless of how much money could be raised—unattractive. In fact, because of the often very quick decisions that need to be made in sport, public ownership may not be an attractive option. If the issuance of stock is not available as a capital acquisition tool, a company can entertain the idea of issuing bonds (see chapter 10) or other instruments to borrow funds.

ASSIGNMENTS

1. Track several publicly traded sport stocks over a period of two weeks to see how the stock fluctuates and what news or information causes the stock to change in value or causes the volume sold to change dramatically.

2. Contact several friends who own shares in publicly traded corporations and ask them why they purchased the stocks.

RESEARCH PROJECTS

1. Critically examine one of the publicly traded professional sport teams and review four or five recent analyst reports to determine what analysts are saying about the team. Decide whether you agree with what they are saying. Make sure you support your argument with specific facts.

2. Critically examine one of the publicly traded sport manufacturing companies and review four or five recent analyst reports to determine what they are saying about the company; determine whether or not you agree with what they are saying. Make sure you support your argument with specific facts.

CLASS DISCUSSION TOPICS

1. How many of you own stock?
2. Have you ever owned stock?
3. Have you ever thought about buying stock?
4. Would you ever buy any sport stocks?
5. What sport stocks would you possibly purchase, and why?

Bonds

CHAPTER OBJECTIVES

After studying this chapter, you should be able to do the following:

- Understand how issuing bonds creates a fixed-cost solution to raising funds.
- Describe the types of bonds that are available and how they are secured.
- Understand how a company has to repay bondholders.
- Understand the dynamics of government-issued bonds to finance sport facilities.
- Describe capital structuring through various examples.

10

In chapter 8, we considered short-term funding through bank loans and other capitalization techniques such as venture capital. Chapter 9 covers equity ownership through stocks as a means of raising capital. This chapter focuses on a tool utilized by both the private and the public sector—bonds. A **bond** is an obligation that needs to be repaid with interest, similar to a loan from a bank. The difference is that bonds are typically issued by larger corporations or government entities with a good repayment history and are sought after by investors because of either favorable interest rates or tax benefits. The high desirability of these bonds creates a market for their purchase and sale that is similar to the stock market. Thus, bonds have the financing characteristics of loans (covered in chapter 8), as well as a market in which they can be bought and sold, like stocks (covered in chapter 9).

This chapter first looks at the types of corporate bonds available, the costs associated with issuing such bonds, and various repayment methods. Next, we consider government bonds utilized to finance stadium and arena construction and related projects; this section highlights the various types of bonds issued by government entities and how they are issued. The last part of the chapter presents an example of a strategy in which various capital acquisition techniques are combined, and then examines concerns associated with raising too much or too little capital.

Corporate Bonds

Bonds issued by businesses are often referred to as **corporate bonds** because bonds can normally only be issued by the largest corporations. Similar to a mortgage loan, a mortgage bond is a bond backed by specified real estate. If the bond issuer defaults, the **bondholders** can foreclose on the property and sell the property to satisfy the claim.

A bond is similar to a long-term loan in that it is a contract under which a borrower agrees to make specified interest and principal payments on specified dates for a specified time period. Every bond has some restrictions attached. These restrictions (called bond covenants) are similar to typical contract terms that limit both parties. A company issuing bonds might attach restrictions that allow the company to pay a lesser amount if the investor tries to redeem the bond before its maturity date. Similarly, investors might demand restrictions on a company to protect their investment. These restrictions could include limiting the extent of acquisition activity and capital spending, requiring minimum levels of liquidity,

restricting a company's right to issue additional equity, and limiting the size of the debt-equity ratio.

In addition to the bonds already discussed, there are convertible bonds (discussed later in this chapter) and warrant bonds (not included in the scope of this book); income bonds that pay interest only when income is earned; indexed bonds whose interest rates increase if inflation rises (the index typically tracks a well-regarded index such as the **consumer price index**); and **zero coupon bonds** or original issue **discount bonds,** which carry no interest rate but are originally sold at a lower price than **par value** and appreciate in value over time (Brigham & Gapenski, 1994).

A type of bond that was popular in the 1970s and 1980s was the junk bond. In the late 1970s, Michael Milken of Drexel Burnham Lambert analyzed the often overlooked area of junk bonds and concluded that riskier bonds paid a higher return compared with other bonds. Thus, the two concluded that **junk bonds** were a strong investment even though they were associated with significant risk.

On the basis of his analysis, Milken convinced some institutional investors to buy risky bonds, and the market for junk bonds was born. These high-risk, high-yield bonds were often utilized in **leveraged buyouts** in which a company used debt instruments to help buy other companies. Ted Turner offered to buy CBS by offering CBS shareholders junk bonds for their shares. The shareholders balked at the offer, which then fizzled and disappeared. However, numerous savings and loans invested in other junk bonds, which helped usher in the savings and loan collapse. But savings and loans were not the only victims, as Drexel Burnham Lambert was also forced into bankruptcy in 1989 and Milken was jailed for his activities (Brigham & Gapenski, 1994). Milken faced a 98-count federal indictment alleging such acts as bribery, **insider trading,** and stock manipulation. These all stemmed from Milken's interest in pushing the often riskier junk bonds. He plea-bargained to six counts of minor security violations, including involvement with a client who failed to make Securities and Exchange Commission (SEC) disclosures. Even though the case was very weak, it appeared that the judge was trying to send the message that bond manipulation would be strictly scrutinized, and Milken was sentenced to 10 years in prison (Wanniski, 1991).

Bond Financing

Individuals often do not appreciate how important it is to choose the right funding vehicle for a busi-

Table 10.1 Advantages and Disadvantages of Bond Financing

Advantages	Disadvantages
Interest on bonds is tax deductible (vs. stock dividends, which are not deductible).	Interest is a fixed charge that needs to be paid regardless of whether income was or was not earned.
Bond financing can be reasonably inexpensive for an established company with a good credit rating.	The principal loaned amount must be paid in full when the bond matures.
There is a strong, established market for trading and issuing bonds.	Issuing bonds can harm a company's credit rating and make it more difficult for the company to borrow money in the future.
	If the bond is secured by collateral, a corporation might not be able to sell or otherwise dispose of the asset without bondholder approval.
	Bondholders have the upper hand whenever a company declares bankruptcy.

ness. If an owner makes a quick decision and the business has some poor years, the potential debt obligation could make an otherwise strong investment a fiscal disaster. Even with the potential downside associated with a financial obligation that can last over 30 years, bonds have significant positive attributes. The advantages and disadvantages of bond financing are listed in table 10.1.

Other factors that affect a business' decision to issue bonds include the general business environment and the prevailing interest in the specific business that is issuing bonds. If interest rates are generally low, then every business may have difficulty issuing bonds. But if a specific business is facing a potential hardship, it may be impossible for that business to issue bonds. For example, if a labor dispute has arisen with the players' association, the Celtics might face a difficult market in which to issue their bonds even though other businesses may not be having a problem in this regard. One way of avoiding such a problem is to provide some type of pledge to guarantee repayment (for example, by issuing a **secured bond**).

Secured Versus Unsecured Bonds

One disadvantage of secured bonds is related to a corporation's ability to control secured assets. If an asset is secured, by the terms of the security agreement the corporation does not have exclusive use of the asset and might need to obtain approval before using the asset for various activities. Unsecured bonds provide the greatest flexibility for the issuing corporation but minimal protection for the bond purchaser. A secured bondholder receives preferen-

tial treatment over subsequent bondholders, whether those subsequent bondholders are secured or unsecured. Various types of secured bonds can be issued. Collateral trust bonds are bonds secured by stock or other bonds. The collateral security is deposited with a trust company, which holds the assets for the bondholder's benefit (Bogen, 1966). An equipment trust obligation is a secured transaction whereby a corporation can acquire equipment under a collateral bill of sale. Title to the equipment does not pass to the corporation until the obligation has been paid, and a trustee retains title to the equipment until the obligation is **discharged.** In another type of arrangement, a second corporation, in addition to the original issuer, can guarantee a bond; and these guaranteed bonds can be very marketable if the backing corporation has an excellent credit rating because the bondholder has two guarantees for repayment—the original issuer and the guarantor. Guaranteed bonds are often issued in cases in which a large corporation is helping a small company expand and there is an existing or intended working relationship between the companies. For example, a professional sport team might guarantee the bond issued by a minor league affiliate. In another type of situation, similar to that with guarantees, a larger corporation can purchase a smaller corporation and assume the bond obligations incurred by the smaller corporation.

Debentures

A **debenture** is an unsecured bond, meaning that there are no assets to secure (guarantee repayment) the bond if the bond issuer defaults. Normally, because of the lack of protection for debenture bondholders, only companies with the best credit rating can issue such bonds. Although debenture bonds are generally unsecured, there are several techniques to extend protection to such bondholders. To provide investors with additional security that a debenture will be repaid, some companies issue **subordinate debentures.** These bonds provide some security as assets are pledged to back them. However, claims on these assets are subordinate to senior claims against the assets. For example, a mortgage bond issue could be secured by a business' equipment and any amount of the equipment value that is not securing the mortgage bond issue (senior claim) can be used to secure repayment of the subordinate debentures. Assume that a company backs a $10 million mortgage bond issue with property valued at $15 million. The company issues subordinate bonds in the amount of $10 million several years later, after the property has appreciated. However, when the company files for bankruptcy protection, the land is worth only $16 million. The mortgage bondholders will recover their $10 million. The subordinate bondholders are still in a better position than unsecured creditors, as there is still $6 million from the assets after the mortgage bond is satisfied. The $6 million will go to

the subordinate bondholders, who will probably be paid on a pro rata basis, $600 for each $1,000 bond they held.

In a covenant of equal coverage, the debenture bond is treated as equal to a secured mortgage if a mortgage is ever obtained in the future. Thus, both the mortgage and debenture bonds would be secured. Additionally, a debenture can be issued with a specific condition that no dividends will be paid to stockholders unless such moneys are derived from future earnings or unless the corporate assets exceed liabilities by a specified amount (Bogen, 1966).

Regardless of the asset used to secure a debt instrument, the security helps increase the instrument's liquidity, lowers the cost of capital to borrowers, and helps develop greater efficiency through the financial marketplace (Brigham & Gapenski, 1994). Thus, whether the Smiths pledge their home to secure a mortgage or the Celtics use contractually obligated revenue from their broadcasting contract, the security helps seal the deal and allows the flow of needed capital.

Whether a bond is secured or unsecured, bonds are covered by a contract called an indenture. The indenture is issued to a trust company that acts as a trustee for the bondholders. The indenture has to

An Unusual Way to Secure a Bond

In 1998 in an effort to acquire considerable cash in advance of his actual payday, Chicago White Sox slugger Frank Thomas, working with a New York City investment banking firm, was attempting to raise $20 million. The money would be raised through an offering of bonds in Thomas' name backed by his guaranteed annual salary of $7 million per year through 2006. The bonds would have probably paid a rate of approximately 9%. It was assumed that Thomas could earn more than 9% by reinvesting the $20 million somewhere else. Otherwise, there would be no benefit to him from borrowing the money ("Thomas Secures," 1998). However, shortly after an attempt was made to launch the bond, the idea was scrapped because there were too many inhibitive conditions in the player's contract, such as a moral clause, that could limit repayment. Furthermore, players can lose their entitlement to compensation if they are injured in a non-team-related event or if players go on strike; and in this case, Thomas would lose his entitlement to compensation if he decided to take the bond money and not play anymore (Kaplan, 1998, November). Since 1998, Thomas has often been injured and performed below par, which justifies the nervousness of potential investors back in 1998.

In February of 2001, William Andrews securitized the remaining $5 million that he was owed by the NFL's Atlanta Falcons. Andrews had last played in the NFL in 1996. But, as part of his playing contract, he was owed $200,000 per year over 25 years. Instead of waiting for these annual payments, Andrews decided to take the deferred compensation and sell it in the form of a bond to the sports insurance company of Hanleigh Co. Hanleigh paid $2 million to Andrews for the right to the future compensation stream. This marked the first sale of a bond securitized by an individual athlete's deferred compensation in the history of professional sports. While the $2 million is only 40% of the amount Andrews was to be paid over the next 25 years, the securitization gave the athlete immediate access to a large sum of money. He then had the ability to invest and grow that $2 million. The transaction was overseen by NDH Capital, a small Connecticut financing company (Kaplan, 2001).

follow specific SEC guidelines related to the trustees and their duties: trustees must have no conflict of interest and must have financial responsibility, make periodic reports to bondholders, provide appropriate default notice, protect bondholders after default, and fulfill related obligations (Bogen, 1966).

Most bonds are **bearer bonds,** with the bondholder retaining possession of the bond document. Bonds typically have **coupons** attached to them that the bondholder can redeem at the bondholder's bank on a semiannual basis to receive the specified interest payment. Such bonds are called coupon bonds. Coupon bonds are the easiest to transfer to other potential purchasers because the person in actual physical possession of the bond is entitled to redeem the coupon. In contrast, a registered bond is issued in the name of the bondholder. If such shares are transferred, the registered bondholder has to endorse the bonds to the new owner, and the new owner has to have his name added to the corporate books. Because of the registration requirement, such bonds are less marketable.

Some corporations have issued income bonds during reorganizations or in exchange for preferred stock. Income bonds pay interest only if the corporation earns income. If no income is earned, no interest is paid. Such a contingency requirement reduces the amount of fixed costs that would normally be allocated to pay the interest on a coupon or registered bond. Thus, if a company is facing rough financial times, they do not need to worry about paying interest to their bondholders. This frees up a significant amount of money to help the business staff in operation. However, when the company starts turning a profit, they are required to start paying interest to the bondholders. An indenture specifies the formula for calculating the required payments under an income bond. One rule typically applied to income bonds is that the interest is cumulative. This means that if interest is not paid in a given year because income is low, it has to be paid the next year, when there is more income, along with the interest for that next year.

Issue Size and Maturity

One of the primary concerns associated with bonds relates to determining the appropriate interest rate to attach to the bonds and determining how many bonds should be issued. When corporations are seeking millions of dollars, they do not resort to guesswork to determine the appropriate interest rate. Long- and short-term forecasting becomes a serious matter, as a difference of one-tenth of a percentage point can cost millions in interest or may make an offering so unattractive that no one purchases the issue.

There are several agencies that rate bonds, such as **Moody's Investor Service, Inc.** and Standard & Poor's. These entities examine the bond issuer and determine the potential for default based on various factors such as revenue stream to repay the bonds, current economic conditions, interest rates, and past repayment history. After analyzing all the relevant criteria, the rating agency establishes a rating for a bond. The highest rating is typically AAA or aaa depending on the agency. Bonds with such a rating have the lowest risk for default and do not have to pay as high an interest rate. Bonds that have a low rating are sometimes classified as junk bonds and have to pay a much higher interest rate to attract investors. Even if Moody's and Standard & Poor's give a bond a high rating, the potential for default always exists. Investors would not have considered Enron bonds high risk, but they turned out to be. Thus, the potential for default needs to be considered; the riskier the bond, the higher the interest rate needed to attract potential investors.

To help reduce the potential disasters associated with choosing an inappropriate interest rate, corporations appraise the supply and demand for money, which affect interest rates. Interest rates represent a true example of supply and demand in that if there is a glut of money on the market, whether as a result of government actions or strictly market forces, interest rates are lower than when there is a smaller money supply. However, if the money supply is tight, interest rates are higher as more corporations are fighting to obtain scarcer funds and the competition bids up the interest rates.

The demand for long-term funds arises from four major sources: mortgage borrowing, corporate bond financing, state and local government bond financing, and long-term U.S. Treasury borrowing (Bogen, 1966). The various entities that have money available and those that need funds are all affected by the Federal Reserve. As discussed in chapter 3, the Federal Reserve can control the supply and demand and affect interest rates through monetary policies. The Federal Reserve tends to relax the money supply during recessionary times and restrict the money during prosperous times. Such a strategy is designed to foster stable growth without significant fluctuation (Bogen, 1966).

The suppliers for long-term funds are very diverse; they include

- life insurance companies,
- saving and loans associations,
- mutual savings banks,

- commercial banks that might acquire bonds,
- insurance companies (fire, property, casualty),
- corporate pension funds,
- state and local government retirement funds (Bogen, 1966),
- union retirement plans, and
- mutual funds that purchase bonds.

A bond is similar to a long-term loan. In issuing bonds, a corporation is agreeing to make specific interest and principal payments for a specified period of time. Companies issue various types of bonds including debentures, junk bonds, and income bonds.

Costs of Issuing Bonds

Although bonds can raise substantial funds, they are very expensive to issue. The primary cost associated with issuing bonds is the required interest payments. Such payments are due on a semiannual basis for as long as the bond is outstanding. A $100 million 20-year bond issue with 10% interest would require semiannual payments of $5 million for 20 years.

Another cost associated with issuing bonds is the discount or **risk premium** at which they are sold. The discount for the $100 million bond issue might be $5 million, which means that the issuing or selling entity for the bonds would take $5 million (5%) as a fee to process and help sell the bonds. Every transaction is different, but the typical issuing fee for bonds is around 5%. This cost effectively increases the interest rate because the $10 million annual interest obligation is based on $100 million, but only $95 million was actually received. The company would still owe $100 million for the bonds, but it received only $95 million after paying the fee. This added cost has to be built into the bond's repayment schedule. Thus, the actual interest cost for such a bond would be 10.25%. The $5 million cost for the bond issue can be amortized over the bond's life by putting aside $250,000 a year for 20 years. Thus, the actual cost to the bond issuer is $10.25 million a year. Additional expenses could include legal fees for preparing the indenture, recording the mortgage(s), general legal advice, and marketing expenses.

The following case study is a good illustration of the importance of bond financing and the effect it can have on a company.

Sport Manufacturing Company (SMC) has 2 million shares of capital stock and has earnings of 20% on sales before taxes (see table 10.2).

While the company is interested in expanding sales, it realizes it needs to raise $6 million to double sales. Since stock is already outstanding, the company decides to sell $6 million in 5% bonds that would generate $300,000 in annual interest charges. The potential effect on stockholders would be as shown in table 10.3.

Table 10.2 Sport Manufacturing Company Financial Highlights ($000)

	Poor year	Normal year	Good year
Sales	$1,000	$2,000	$3,000
Expenses	800	1,600	2,400
Operating profit	**200**	**400**	**600**
Federal taxes	89	185	281
Profit after taxes	**111**	**215**	**319**
Earnings for stock	5.5%	10.7%	15.9%

Table 10.3 Sport Manufacturing Company Financial Highlights ($000)

	Poor year	Normal year	Good year
Sales	$2,000	$4,000	$6,000
Expenses	1,600	3,200	4,800
Operating profit	**400**	**800**	**1,200**
Interest on bonds	300	300	300
Profit after interest	**100**	**500**	**900**
Federal taxes	41	233	425
Profit after taxes	**59**	**267**	**475**
Earnings for stock	2.9%	13.3%	23.7%

As the example shows, by issuing $6 million in bonds to expand sales, the corporation is able to increase earnings 65% in a good year, from $319,000 to $475,000. However, the **fixed charge** of $300,000 can dramatically reduce earnings in a poor year, as the interest expense needs to be paid regardless of business conditions (Bogen, 1966). As the example highlights, bond financing exaggerates the effect of sales fluctuations through the new fixed business expense. If the $6 million had been raised with an additional stock offering, the stockholders' earnings would be lower in good years, but there would be no potential **deficit** in the poor year.

If SMC decided to issue $6 million in shares of common stock rather than $6 million in bonds, the impact would be significant. In a poor year the operating profit would increase to $400,000 a year, similar to what would happen with financing through bonds. However, with only 2 million shares outstanding, the earnings per share are 10% ($200,000 earnings divided by 2 million shares). Based on 8 million shares and $400,000 in earnings, the earnings per share decrease to 5%.

A corporation's cost of issuing bonds includes the major cost, which is the interest payments, and any discount or risk premium, issuing fees, legal fees, and other expenses.

Loan Repayment

Up to now we have looked at the types of bonds that can be issued. In this section we turn our attention to repayment and refunding mechanisms. Normally bond repayment occurs when the bond matures and the issuer repays all remaining obligations. Most bonds are redeemable when they mature. At that point the issuing company pays the bondholder the bond's cash value. Some bonds are redeemable at par, at the holder's option. The par value is the arbitrary initial value that the bond was issued for and which helps establish its value. These bonds are often sold at a lower interest rate: if the prevailing interest rate for bonds is 10%, the redeemable bonds might only pay 9.5%. The lower interest rate is justified in that the bondholder has the option of redeeming the bond before it matures and is then able to take the proceeds and invest in another bond. If the interest rate increases, then the investor may want to take the proceeds and purchase a bond with a higher rate. However, if the

interest rate declines, the investor still has a bond paying 9.5% interest.

Sometimes a company faces hardships that can force it to pay off the bondholders before maturity. If interest rates drop several percentage points, a company may not be able to afford the prior interest rate. Normally, changes in interest rates do not affect the maturity date and the issuer is stuck with the higher rate. However, if the bond was issued with a **call provision,** the issuer can exercise the call provision after a specified number of years. The call allows the issuer to pay the **face value** of the bond plus a fixed payment such as a year's worth of coupon payments. Once a bond is called and paid, the company can issue new bonds at the lower interest rate. Callable bonds have higher interest rates than noncallable bonds to compensate investors for the risk of the bonds being redeemed by the issuer before they mature.

Repayment can be accomplished through the following techniques:

- Sinking funds
- Serial bonds
- Bond redemption before maturity
- Convertible bonds

Sinking Funds

The most common technique for repaying a note is to use a sinking fund in which moneys are set aside either in preset amounts or on a variable basis. For example, a preset amount of $1 million a year could be deposited into a sinking fund account. The amount can grow to well over $20 million in 20 years, and the funds can be used to repay notes as they mature. In certain instances, the price of a bond may decline because the associated interest rates are unfavorable. In those instances, the sinking fund account can be used to buy bonds on the open market and retire them at an earlier date (Bogen, 1966). This practice can save significant interest obligations. Sinking funds can be created through various means. Annual payments of a fixed amount or a percentage of profit can also be utilized. Bonds issued for the purpose of acquiring fixed assets could also be retired through the establishment of a sinking fund using annual depreciation allowances for the asset. That means that the tax savings associated with depreciating an asset can be set aside to repay the bond. No matter what approach is used, the key is that a sinking fund is a way to actually set aside funds to repay the bonds in the future—a much better approach than trying to obtain funds at the last minute.

Serial Bonds

Serial bonds are a series of bonds issued with maturity dates at predetermined redemption dates. These types of bonds could include $1 million in bonds due in 20 years and a company can issue such bonds every year for a 10-year period so the bonds would have to be repaid in a series 20 to 30 years later. Serial bonds for a $50 million bond offering could include $5 million of bond obligations that mature in the 15th year with increased retirement obligations in subsequent years until the final bonds are retired in the 30th year. Serial bonds are often issued by states and municipalities, which have fairly reliable tax revenue. Since corporate revenue is more difficult to project in the long run, serial bonds are less popular as a way of meeting corporate funding needs. However, some corporations are willing to utilize serial bonds for **short-term debt** but utilize sinking funds for long-term obligations. Some corporations set equal serial maturities over several years and then provide a large balloon payment at the end. If a 10-year bond issue for $10 million was issued under this format, the corporation might have serial maturity of $400,000 a year for nine years and make a final balloon payment of $5.5 million in the 10th year (Bogen, 1966).

Bond Redemption Before Maturity

The sinking fund and serial maturation are just two techniques that companies can use to redeem bonds. Corporations can also issue newer bonds with more favorable interest rates and use the proceeds to buy older bonds on the open market. Numerous corporations issue bonds on a regular basis in an effort to take advantage of favorable interest rates and to avoid the potential impact if interest rates rise. Such bonds often have a call provision to allow the corporation to repurchase the bonds at a moderate premium if interest rates drastically change. Some bonds are **convertibles,** which means that they can be redeemed when the bondholder converts the bonds to stocks (see the next section). Other bonds are retired through retained earnings, the selling of assets, or issuing more equity. If all these techniques fail, the corporation can ask the bondholders for a voluntary extension of the bond's maturity date.

As just mentioned, a corporation may issue callable bonds that it can repurchase before the maturity date. If a bond is not callable, there are two other means of repurchasing. The company can purchase a bond on the open market or can purchase it from a bondholder who is willing to exchange it voluntarily. Note that even if a corporation issues callable bonds, the callable provision typically does not take effect on a 20-year bond until at least the 10th year. Until then, the bondholder is protected from an attempt by the corporation to call the bond any time interest rates decline or if the corporation attempts to issue new bonds with a lower interest rate. The protection against having a bond called can encourage larger investors such as life insurance companies to accept a lower yield, on the express condition that a bond will not be callable.

Convertible Bonds

Some corporations issue bonds that can be converted to common stock. These bonds are designed to redeem themselves and retire the debt through converting the debt to equity ownership. This approach increases equity ownership while reducing the total corporate debt. Reducing the corporate debt can dramatically increase the corporate credit rating, which can make it easier for the company to borrow additional funds or issue additional bonds. However, when a bond is converted to stock it does not bring any new funds into the business but merely redistributes debt obligations to owners' equity. Convertible bonds have some very strong benefits for both the issuing company and the potential bond buyer. Buyers often prefer convertible bonds because they can obtain interest payments on their investment, but can also choose to switch to the equity ownership option if the corporation starts to experience significant growth. Buyers also might prefer convertible bonds because they still retain the position of a secured creditor but also have an option to purchase stock. This might not be an important reason to purchase the bond, but if the stock price soars, it can suddenly become a key benefit. Corporations can benefit because when bonds are converted, the conversion usually occurs at a share price that is higher than it would have been if the shares had been purchased earlier. Thus, if the conversion occurs, the corporation can lower its debt obligation by exchanging that obligation for shares that are valued significantly less on the corporate books. This helps the corporation because it can sell its own shares at a higher rate compared with the bondholder who might buy stock on the open market that might not directly benefit the corporation. However, this benefit is also one of the primary reasons why some corporations do not want to issue convertible bonds. Some corporations do not want to dilute the stockholders' equity. Furthermore, since it is uncertain whether or when a bondholder might wish to convert bonds to stocks, convertible bonds add a degree of uncertainty to the corporation's capital structure.

Convertible securities are analyzed based on their conversion ratio. The conversion ratio (CR) represents the number of shares a bondholder will receive on conversion. Another important number is the conversion price (CP), which represents how much the company will receive when the bondholder purchases the shares. Assume that SMC issues a $1,000 bond that can be converted to 20 shares of common stock. The CR is 20, since 20 shares will be received. The CP is calculated with the following formula:

$$\frac{\text{par value of bond}}{\text{shares received}} = \text{conversion price}$$

$$\frac{\$1,000}{20} = \$50 \text{ CP per share}$$

The CP can conversely be used to calculate the CR, as follows (Brigham & Gapenski, 1994):

$$\frac{\text{par value of bond}}{\text{conversion price (CP)}} = \text{conversion ratio (CR)}$$

$$\frac{\$1,000}{\$50} = \$20 \text{ shares}$$

The issuing price for a convertible security is normally set at 10% to 30% above the prevailing market price for shares. Thus, the $50 CP would be appropriate if the shares were currently selling at the $35 to $45 price range. Most convertibles have fixed CPs and CRs for the bond's life. Some convertibles contain "step-up" clauses that allow the CP to increase over time. Thus, a bond could be issued with a $50 CP during the bond's first five years with the CP able to rise to $55 per share thereafter. The step-up is allowed if the conversion instrument contains specific language authorizing the increased cost for converting the bond to shares.

Almost all convertibles have specific clauses designed to protect the convertible holder from stock splits (discussed later in this chapter) and the sale of common stock below the CP. If the sales price decreases, then the CP must also be lowered. If the CP for a convertible was stated as $50 per share and the stock was selling for $35 per share, there would be no incentive to convert. If the stock price rose, there would be an incentive. Conversely, if the stock value drops significantly and the company has to issue new shares at $25 each, the company will renegoti-

ate the CP and reduce it to keep the bondholders happy. Similarly, if a stock split occurs and bondholders have the right to convert the bond to 40 shares at a CP of $20, they will receive 80 shares at $10 each if they exercise the conversion (Brigham & Gapenski, 1994).

Investors may not want to exercise a conversion, but a company can force a conversion if the bond issue had a call provision. Assume that SMC issues a $1,000 bond with a $50 CP, a 20-share CR, and a share price of $60 and that the bond has a call price of $1,050. If SMC wants to exercise the call provision, the bondholder will have to calculate under which scenario he would make the greatest income. If he accepts the call, he will receive $1,050. If he converts the bond, he will receive 20 shares valued at $60 each, or a total of $1,200 (Brigham & Gapenski, 1994). Most investors would rather take the $1,200 even if they did not favor equity ownership, since they could always sell the shares on the market.

> Companies that issue bonds use various methods to repay bondholders. Most commonly they set aside funds in a sinking fund that they will use when the bond matures.

Government-Issued Bonds

Bonds are documents representing a loan agreement and specifying the agreement's terms. Compared to the corporate bonds discussed in the previous sections, government-issued bonds for building sport facilities have several unique attributes. Special laws, elections, or referendums are often required in order for the bonds to be issued. Once the legal hurdles have been overcome, numerous additional steps need to be taken, from entering into a lease agreement with a professional team to acquiring funds for infrastructure repairs. The following example depicts this complex process.

In a general election, the citizens of Houston, Texas, voted to authorize a sports authority to issue bonds for the construction of a baseball and football stadium. The sports authority had been created after passage of a law by the Texas legislature providing for formation of the authority to raise taxes and issue bonds. The Harris County-Houston Sports Authority agreed to borrow $236.5 million to construct a new downtown baseball stadium (Williams, 1998). The money was to be borrowed in two ways: $34.7 million was to be raised through a zero-interest loan from business leaders with repayment due starting in 2009. The remaining $201.8 million was raised through **revenue bonds** with an interest rate of 5.61%, with debt service to start at $10.3 million in 1999 and increase to $22.8 million by 2028 (Williams, 1998). The revenue bonds are secured from revenue collected through special hotel and rental car taxes. Only $180 million of the offering was to go to stadium construction; the remaining $21.8 million was to be used to cover other finance-related costs such as issuing the bonds. The $21.8 million also went to purchase bond insurance, which helped increase the **bond rating** (Aaa from Moody's and AAA from Standard & Poor's). This in turn allowed the bonds to be issued at a lower interest rate (Williams, 1998). The bond underwriters included Salomon Smith Barney; Chase Securities of Texas, Inc.; Goldman, Sachs & Co.; Samuel A. Ramirez & Co.; Siebert Brandford Shank & Co., Inc.; Artemis Capital Group Inc.; Estrada Hinojosa & Co., Inc.; J.P. Morgan & Co.; and Paine Webber, Inc. Bond issues of this magnitude by government entities often have numerous companies helping to underwrite them, including some minority-owned firms and local firms that are involved for political reasons.

Types of Government-Issued Bonds

Numerous types of bonds can be issued in the sport industry. Earlier sections of this chapter cover several types of bonds that can help sport corporations. This section centers on bonds issued by various government entities. Bonds represent the most likely funding source for publicly financed projects such as stadiums and arenas.

Although bonds for stadiums and arenas are the type of bonds that are most typically studied, sport facilities are low on the list of total expenditures for bond proceeds. Other public projects garner a greater amount of bond dollars. The greatest amount of funding is directed to school projects. Other major projects funded by bonds include park and recreation departments, convention centers, and administrative offices. This section focuses on stadiums and arenas financed with bonds, as the same principles that relate to securing and repayment of bonds apply to all projects funded with government-issued bonds. The primary types of bonds considered here are general obligation bonds and revenue bonds. Other financing techniques, such as lease-backed financing (lease revenue bonds) and certificates of participation, can be used by the government entity, which then leases the facility to another government entity or sport authority (Greenberg & Gray, 1996).

General Obligation Bonds

General obligation bonds (GOBs) are among the instruments most commonly used to fund facilities. These bonds are often called **full faith and credit** obligations as the city, county, municipality, state, or other government unit pledges to repay the obligation with existing tax revenues or by levying new taxes (Greenberg & Gray, 1996). General obligation bonds and other bonds are rated by independent companies such as Moody's and Standard & Poor's based on the issuer's ability to repay the loan. General obligation bonds are often highly rated since currently existing and future tax revenue sources can be tapped for repayment. Bond ratings can be influenced by a multitude of factors, including

- the level of coverage (ability to repay the loan with existing revenue streams);
- the strength, breadth, and reliability of the tax base;
- the historical performance of the revenue stream;
- the risk associated with the project;
- the underlying economic strength of the stadium or arena or the community;
- political volatility; and
- whether or not the project is economically viable (Greenberg & Gray, 1996).

The strength of the tax base is one of the most important criteria for GOBs. A small city with a low tax base might suffer significantly if property values decrease or sales drop significantly. In contrast, a large city with hundreds of thousands of properties can experience downturns in the economy but still have a large enough tax base that the damage could be minimal.

Raters often look at the purpose of the project and the anticipated long-term benefits. Projects such as Camden Yards or Coors Field revolutionized the manner in which stadiums were viewed. These stadiums could be seen as catalysts for change that could revitalize an entire downtown community. If the downtown was revitalized, property values would increase. The increased property values would result in higher tax revenue, which would generate additional funds from which to repay bonds.

Revenue Bonds

A more specific type of bond is the revenue bond; here the tax revenue to support repayment may come from the project itself. For example, an entrance tax of $1.50 per ticket could be charged and all revenues from this tax would first be allocated to repaying the revenue bond. These bonds traditionally have a lower credit rating than other bonds because there are significant financial risks associated with limiting repayment requirements to a specific tax source. This concern arose during the 1998 NBA strike. If games were canceled and admission revenue was lost, some bond issuers might not have had any of their anticipated revenue sources to repay revenue bondholders whose bonds were secured by attendance taxes.

Sometimes a public entity targets a specific tax to finance a bond. Cleveland utilized a sin tax on alcohol and tobacco sales to help finance Jacobs Field and Gund Arena. San Antonio utilized a sales tax-based bond issue to help finance building the Alamodome. **Special tax bonds** are repayable from a specific pledged source and are not backed by the full faith and credit of the issuing entity. Thus, if the specific revenue source is inadequate, there may not be enough tax revenue to repay the bondholders. Tax and revenue anticipation notes can be issued to fund the project before revenue starts arriving. Similarly, a bond anticipation note or tax-exempt commercial paper can help bridge the gap during construction until revenue is generated to repay the interim note and start repaying special tax bonds (Greenberg & Gray, 1996).

Repayment Sources

Whichever type of bond is issued, repayment will always be the key concern for investors. There are other factors that can be very important to a potential investor, such as whether the bond is tax-exempt (see chapter 11 for tax-related factors), whether the government entity purchased bond repayment insurance, and whether contractually obligated revenue (COR) is sufficient to repay the bond. Even with these variables, investors will look toward a stable and adequate repayment source as an additional assurance that the bond will be paid. Significant funding sources include

- utility taxes,
- ticket surcharges,
- car rental taxes,
- real estate taxes,
- specific sales taxes,
- possessory interest taxes,
- tourist development taxes,
- restaurant sales taxes,
- excise or sin taxes,
- lottery and gaming revenue,
- nontax fees such as permits,
- general appropriations, and
- general sales and use taxes (Greenberg & Gray, 1996).

A utility tax, for example, is a cost added to an electric, water, or gas bill to help pay for the bond's debt service. In the 1990s, the San Francisco Giants were considering a move to San Jose, California. The proposed stadium was to be partially financed by a utility tax. Opponents to the stadium distributed light-switch covers to communicate the idea that every time people turned on the lights they would be paying for the proposed stadium. The stadium ballot measure was defeated by the strong activists against the tax.

A possessory interest tax is charged to whoever possesses control of the facility and is designed to tax the primary facility user. Tourist development taxes and car rental taxes are designed primarily to tax out-of-towners who visit the city. This is a popular technique because it is easy to tell a voting population that you are attempting to get out-of-towners to pay for the facility (Howard & Crompton, 1995).

Excise taxes are general taxes added to various products; sin taxes are more specifically geared to be added to the cost of alcohol and tobacco products. Sin taxes were utilized to help finance building the arena and stadium in Cleveland (see p. 182).

Nontax fees are special expenses passed on to particular parties; for example, the permit costs for other developers in the city could be raised. Such a tax can stimulate a backlash from citizens who do not want to pay a greater share of the funding for the facility than others are paying. General appropriations are among the most favored funding options. **Appropriations** are funds that are set aside for specific purposes. Through political dealings a municipality might convince the state legislature or federal government to give a "gift" appropriation from the budget to help pay the facility construction expenses or to fund bond repayments. The San Antonio Alamodome was built as a bus stop to help secure a federal appropriation for interstate transportation.

Although these revenue sources can often support significant repayment obligations, CORs can also provide a significant guarantee that a debt will be repaid. Contractually obligated revenues are any contract whereby a party agrees to pay a specific sum for a guaranteed number of years. Typical long-term contracts that form the basis of COR backing include

- premium seat contracts,
- luxury box contracts,
- concession and novelty rights contracts,
- naming rights contracts,
- pouring rights (beer and soft drink) contracts,
- personal seat licenses, and
- parking rights contracts (Greenberg & Gray, 1996).

Contractually obligated revenues have two primary functions. They can be used as a source of revenue to guarantee repayment of bonds or other loans. They also can be utilized as an independent funding source. If the bonds are all covered through other revenue streams, the team or facility may be able to sell the naming rights and use those funds to enhance its bottom line.

Several examples will suggest how stadium and arena builders can utilize a blend of bonds and CORs to finance a stadium. The Ballpark in Arlington was opened in 1994 at a cost of $190 million. A majority of the project (71%) was financed through a 30-year, 5% sales tax that was projected to raise $11 million yearly. The public sector also contributed 13% to the deal through a $1 per ticket surcharge. The Rangers contributed 16% to the project by selling $30 million in luxury suite contracts (Greenberg & Gray, 1996).

The Gateway project in Cleveland was financed through a tax-exempt county bond offering that raised 45% for the $152 million to build the Gund Arena. Liquor and cigarette taxes (sin taxes) covered another 42%, and private naming rights covered the remaining 13% (Greenberg & Gray, 1996). The bonds were sold to various investors, and the income stream used to repay the bonds came from state capital improvement funds and a countywide sin tax. The sin tax taxed alcohol at $3 per gallon of liquor and $0.16 per gallon of beer, and cigarettes were taxed at $0.045 per pack. These taxes were to be in place for 15 years (Greenberg & Gray, 1996).

The Ice Palace in Tampa may be one of the most complex projects in terms of the multitude of funding sources used to cover the $160 million needed to complete the facility in 1996. The Tampa Bay Lightning's parent company issued private-project revenue bonds to cover 30% of the costs. The Tampa Sports Authority issued tax-exempt bonds backed by a state sales tax rebate estimated at $2 million annually (19% of the costs) and a county tourist tax bond backed by non-ad valorem revenue, which would also generate $2 million annually. Another $750,000 per year (7%) was backed by city parking bonds. The sports authority also issued taxable bonds that included a requirement for a ticket surcharge of $0.50 per ticket, which was projected to generate $1.5 million annually (11%) and backed by a county loan or pledge. Additionally, the city issued a surcharge bond backed by a $0.25 surcharge per ticket, which was expected to generate $250,000 yearly (2%). Last, the city provided 2% of the construction costs through public land acquisition, which was accomplished through use of eminent domain (Greenberg & Gray, 1996).

Eminent domain is the process by which government units can take land from individual landowners. Land or property can be taken if the seized land will be used for the public good. Government units have to pay the fair market value for the land but utilize this process to build roads, new schools, or even new arenas or stadiums. In addition, eminent domain can be used to take more than just land. The city of Baltimore attempted to invoke eminent domain to take the Baltimore Colts, which prompted the team to pack all their belongings into trucks and move to Indianapolis in the middle of the night ("Eminent Domain," 2002).

Before any of the bonds discussed here are issued, the first step in the process is an examination of the potential municipal bond rating. Bond ratings for stadium projects are normally fairly high because of the backing of major cities that presumably will not go bankrupt. However, lenders have become somewhat more leery of these deals in recent years because of the possibility that the oversaturated television market might reduce future broadcast contracts. Lenders can also be concerned when teams and leagues face a multitude of challenges, from fickle fans to legal challenges of league policies. In the latest NBA lockout, for example, the NBA told its teams to refund suite and ticket money to ticket holders ("Securitizing Sports," 1998). Some facility bonds were secured with taxes or revenue linked with ticket sales. Actions of this type by the NBA and its teams could violate the terms associated with some bonds. This could lead to defaulting on loans or possible litigation.

Publicly financed stadiums and arenas are most often funded through government-issued bonds that are repaid with taxes or with revenues collected by the facility.

Bond Acquisition Process

The bond acquisition process is a complex process for sport facilities and can take several years. The first step often entails determining whether or not tax revenue can be raised from alternate sources. For example, the proposal for an arena in Denton County, Texas, included "calling" a half-cent sales tax to raise some of the required funds. The process starts with calling the election, which entails applying for the tax to appear on a future election ballot. Once an election is held and the half-cent tax is approved, the municipality needs to close the bond backed by the half-cent tax. With the prospect for the sales tax bonds, the municipality can then proceed with calling an election for the GOB. The GOB goes through the same process of being put on a future ballot. If the voters approve the GOB, the next step is closing the bond. The voting process alone can take 10 months to complete (*Overview*, 1995).

Even though some concerns exist with facility construction bonds, there are numerous major players in the sport facility bond market. Some of the largest holders of such bonds in 1997 are listed in table 10.4.

Table 10.4 Major Players in the Sport Facility Bond Market

Holder	Value in $ millions
Nuveen Perf Plus Municipal Fund	$44.7
Allstate Insurance Co.	31.9
Allstate Life Insurance Co.	30.2
Kemper Mutual Bond Fund	30.0
Vanguard Municipal Bond L-T	30.0
New York Life Insurance Co.	30.0
Franklin High Yield Tax-Free Income	21.1
Teachers Ins. & Annuity Assoc. of America	19.1
Nuveen Insured Municipal Bond Fund	19.1
Van Kampen Insured Tax Free	19.0

From "Top holders of stadium bonds," 1997.

Government Assistance: Industrial Development Bonds

So far, this chapter has focused on debt- and equity-based capital acquisition. The Celtics, the University of Houston, or SMC can utilize any one or several of the capital acquisition techniques we have considered. However, the Smiths may not have enough money to start the process to obtain needed capital. Many small businesses, including minority-owned businesses, need some additional help to acquire needed capital, while still relying on bonds.

While most bond offerings are too cost prohibitive for smaller companies to issue, there are other bond-based funding options that such businesses can secure with local government assistance. Government units in each state have the authority, through port authorities, economic development commissions, and similar divisions, to offer small-issue industrial development bonds (IDBs).

 Assume that the Smiths wish to build their fitness center in a run-down part of town that they think will turn around and become a prime location for young professionals. The Smiths can approach city hall with a request for assistance to help revive the area. Working with the city's economic development commission and planning committee, the Smiths present a deal to city hall that city hall approves. The city issues the IDB, which is really a corporate bond for the Smiths' business but appears to be a tax-free municipal bond issued by the city (Hovey, 1998, July). The proceeds from the bond are used to buy equipment or purchase the building.

Federal law allows a business owner to raise up to $10 million using IDBs. The IDBs, also called **industrial development bonds,** carry an interest rate ranging from half to three-quarters of the prime interest rate with a 30-year maturity. The one drawback to IDBs is the transaction costs. These costs can be between 2% and 5%, which can erase all interest savings and make smaller bonds uneconomical (Hovey, 1998, July). In 1996, over $2.7 billion was raised for businesses through use of this financing method, with these funds used to create new jobs (Hovey, 1998, July). The process requires a significant amount of paperwork and requires company owners to compete with other projects (such as public housing and urban renewal) that are trying to secure tax-free bonds. The key to obtaining these bonds is to show that you can generate jobs. A rule of thumb is that every $50,000 in bond funding should create one full-time-equivalent job (Hovey, 1998, July).

While these tax-free bonds have significant benefits, the Smiths would need to examine some rules and regulations to determine whether or not an IDB would be appropriate for their fitness center. If the IDB-generated funds paid for equipment, the money would go further than if it were used for construction. The reason is that many states require people using funds obtained from IDBs to pay union or prevailing wages. Union wages might need to be paid for construction, but wages are not relevant to equipment purchases. Another issue is that borrowers may need to contact a bank to secure a letter of credit guaranteeing repayment of the bond, and the letter of credit could cost around 1% of the borrowed amount (Hovey, 1998, July). Such added costs or restrictions might make IDBs impractical for some borrowers.

> A small sport business may be able to secure funding based on small-issue industrial development bonds.

Assume that the Smiths have been operating their fitness center for two years and decide to expand. Investors may be interested if the prospective earnings are high enough to meet their investment needs. However, many of the issues raised throughout this chapter come into play in determining exactly how the Smiths would pursue obtaining the funds. An attorney friend has suggested that they might want to incorporate to take advantage of liability reduction benefits. The Smiths decide not to issue bonds, but to have preferred stock issued to themselves, with a dividend requirement of $50,000 a year. Their business plan shows that future earnings before taxes should be $400,000 a year, but even in a poor year their COR will produce a minimum of $200,000 **pretax earnings.** Therefore, even in a poor year, and even if they received only $100,000 after-tax profit, they still could cover dividend obligations twice over.

The Smiths therefore decide to issue 20,000 shares of 5% preferred stock at $50 par value. Based on these figures, the yearly dividend will be $2.50 per share. The Smiths did not base their calculations on pie in the sky; they analyzed the worst possible earnings scenario and calculated how much they could withdraw from the business while still maintaining owner equity return. If the company has a strong year with $400,000 in earnings, reduced to $200,000 after taxes, they will have a $50,000 obligation for their preferred stocks and $150,000 for common stocks. The Smiths decide to sell common stock valued at 12.5 times expected earnings ($150,000) or $1,875,000 in potential value. If stocks at that time are selling for 10 times earnings on average, then the stock would be selling on the market for $1,500,000 in total.

The Smiths' next step is to determine a selling price for the stocks. On the basis of the $1,875,000 valuation for the common stocks, they choose to sell the stock for $10 per share. However, if they wanted to price the stock higher, at $50, for example, then they would not issue as many shares. To arrive at the requisite $1,875,000 value, they would issue only 37,500 shares at the $50 price. Using the $10 stock price, the initial capital structure for the business is as follows:

preferred stock ($50 par value), 20,000 shares = $1,000,000

common stock ($10 per share), 187,500 shares = $1,875,000

The fitness center's net assets would total $2,875,000 under these facts. The Smiths would have funded their business entirely through stocks.

Capitalization Problems and Issues

As highlighted throughout this chapter and chapters 8 and 9, a company needs to carefully examine its funding needs. Capital or debt structures are not random acts of choosing numbers. The consequences of issuing too many shares or bonds can have a significant negative impact. Likewise, the failure to issue enough shares or bonds can also be a disaster. This section covers the concerns associated with overcapitalization, undercapitalization, and recapitalization.

Overcapitalization

A critical concern that needs to be discussed before we move to part IV, Capital Budgeting, is overcapitalization. A company can raise too much money and not have the financial means to pay everything off. The most serious form of overcapitalization entails issuing too much bond-backed capital. Interest payments are due even if excess cash is lying around and not gaining any return. Too many cumulative preferred shares also can represent a significant cash flow problem, especially in periods of depression. Overcapitalization can also occur with stocks when too many shares are on the market, which reduces the earnings per share.

 If the Smiths issued 1 million shares and only earned $150,000 profit to use to pay common stockholders dividends, then the dividend would amount to only $0.15 per share. On the basis of the 12.5 times earnings figure used in the previous analysis, the Smiths' stock would now have a market value of only $1.87 per share (Bogen, 1966). Such a low stock price could scare away many investors who might think the stock was too speculative.

Undercapitalization

Besides having too many financial obligations, a company can issue too few shares or bonds in relation to the expected earnings. If a company becomes valuable and there are only a few shares available, the cost per share might be very high. Individual shares for various companies or partnerships have been worth several thousand dollars. Highly priced shares often scare away potential investors.

 Suppose that the Smiths issued only 10,000 shares of common stock and still had $150,000 in earnings with the entire amount to be used to pay dividends. Each stock would receive $15 per share in dividends. If the stock sold at 12.5 times earnings, the shares would sell for $187.50 (Bogen, 1966).

Another concern with undercapitalization relates to the fact that if most of the funds for growth come from internal sources such as retained earnings, the business may have a hard time raising funds externally. Similar to the situation for a consumer, a business needs to borrow through accounts payable and bank loans to develop a credit history. There are consumers who prefer to pay for everything with cash. Although you might think these people are being fiscally responsible, they in fact are hurting themselves by not developing a history of borrowing and paying debts in a timely manner. A business also needs to borrow enough from a variety of lenders to establish a credit history. Undercapitalization hampers the ability of a business to develop a strong credit history.

Companies need to be careful not to raise too much money, resulting in overcapitalization, as well as to borrow enough to develop a credit history.

Recapitalization

A key technique in capitalization is recapitalization, which can be performed through a **stock split.** If shares are trading at too high a price, the corporation's board of directors may decide to bring down the price by issuing a large number of shares in exchange for outstanding stock. Stock splits can be 2 for 1, or 3 for 1, or any other variation including fractions. Stocks can be split from common stock into either just common stock or common stock and preferred stock.

 Preferred stocks can also be recapitalized. For example, if SMC had to pay a 5% dividend on preferred stocks and had not paid the dividend in several years, the company might ask the shareholders to return the shares. The shareholders would receive in exchange additional shares that could include a higher interest rate to make up for the unpaid dividends.

Recapitalization can occur with bonds as well. However, the process for recapitalization of bonds is more elaborate. To recapitalize bonds, a corporation needs to go to the bondholders and ask them for approval before changing interest or principal payments. Any changes that do not affect principal or interest payments can be made by amending the indenture, if the indenture provides for changes. This might seem complex, but it is basically a change in the contractual terms and contract changes are not that difficult if all the parties agree to the changes. To help encourage bondholders to extend the principal repayment period, the corporation can offer to raise the interest rate, establish a sinking fund for retirement of the bonds or provide additional security as collateral (or both), or make the bond convertible (Bogen, 1966). If recapitalization does not appear feasible and the interest owed on the bonds is excessive, the corporation can ask bondholders to agree to postponing payments for a given period or have the bonds "stamped," indicating that interest will be paid only when earned (Bogen, 1966).

CONCLUSION

This chapter highlights various capital acquisition techniques. Sport businesses, whether for-profit or nonprofit, have to acquire funds in order to keep operating or to expand. Finding capital is often the most difficult task for new as well as established businesses. There is no one way to acquire capital, nor are there any guaranteed techniques. Issuing bonds is among the most difficult ways to raise funds.

It takes a significant amount of work to issue a bond, and typically only the largest companies do so. Most sport businesses utilize stock or bank financing rather than bonds. However, major privately financed construction projects, such as stadiums or arenas, can be financed through bonds secured by the facilities. Furthermore, stadiums and arenas built with public funds are almost always built using bonds guaranteed by a variety of taxes or revenue streams. Thus, bond financing is often the most visible form of capital acquisition in the sport industry.

ASSIGNMENT

In a library or on the Internet, find one of the bond-rating companies, such as Best or Standard & Poor's. Examine the company's criteria for ranking bonds and the requirements an entity has to meet in order to have the best rating. Examine several cities that have recently built stadiums or arenas to see how their bonds are rated.

RESEARCH PROJECTS

1. Take a look at one of the recently built stadium or arena projects and examine the entire process utilized to obtain approval for the bond issue. Determine any steps taken that possibly should not have been taken or what steps not taken should have been taken.

2. Research failed elections—the situation in which a city's population did not approve issuing a bond—and try to determine where the process went wrong. What suggestion(s) would you have given to help pass the bond?

CLASS DISCUSSION TOPICS

1. After reading about the various capital acquisition techniques, which one would you think would be the best for the Smiths, the University of Houston, SMC, or the Celtics, based on all that you have learned about the case studies to date?

2. Should the general population pay the debt service for bonds issued to pay for a stadium or arena that is used primarily by a privately owned professional team? What are the pros and cons? Debate the topic, citing all the pros and cons associated with the question. What innovative ideas could be used to help repay the bonds?

PART IV

Financial Management

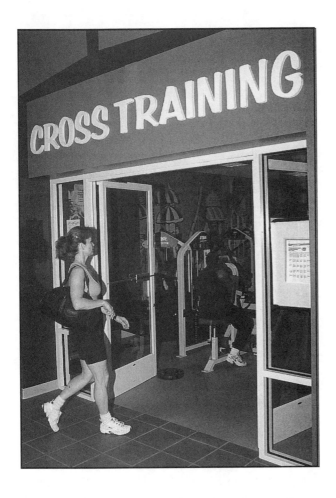

Capital Budgeting

CHAPTER OBJECTIVES

After studying this chapter, you should be able to do the following:

- Define capital budgeting.
- Distinguish between the different techniques of capital budgeting.
- Understand the process of calculating the cost of capital.
- Calculate and use the weighted average cost of capital and the capital asset pricing model formulas.
- Understand how to make capital decisions.
- Distinguish between present value and net present value calculations.
- Understand payback rules such as the internal rate of return.
- Describe cash flow and how it works.

Sport managers have many decisions to make with respect to financial management. One of the most important decisions involves the use of funds for long-term projects such as purchasing equipment or constructing a new facility. The process of making investments toward these types of fixed assets, both tangible and intangible, is known as capital budgeting. **Capital** is the long-term funding that is necessary for the acquisition of fixed assets (Brigham, Gapenski, & Ehrhardt, 1999). With respect to the sport industry, there has been a significant increase in the level of capital spending recently. In the 1990s, over $9 billion was spent on constructing new sport stadiums alone (Rogus, 1997). The construction boom has been fostered by several occurrences. On the financial side, team owners have believed that amenities such as luxury suites, club seats, concessions, and parking will result in new income streams.

New income streams are an important component of capital budgeting. A sport manager must decide if the positive future cash flow from a capital project will be large enough to offset the project's cost. This chapter focuses on the basics of capital budgeting. We will discuss the costs of capital, the methods of making capital budgeting decisions, and ways of projecting future cash flows from capital projects.

Our case studies provide several examples of the need to invest organizational funds into purchasing fixed assets. The Smiths must acquire fitness equipment, office furniture, and computers in order to start their business. The Boston Celtics often invest millions of dollars in signing high-priced free agents to long-term contracts. Colleges and universities invest in constructing and renovating facilities such as arenas, stadiums, administrative offices, and weight rooms. For example, Penn State University recently completed the construction of a $13.8 million facility for its football program. The Louis E. Lasch Building, opened in the summer of 1999, houses the football staff offices, meeting rooms, a 10,000-square-foot weight room, locker rooms, and athletic training facilities ("Penn State Sports Information," 1999). This is only one example of the many sport-related capital projects that are being undertaken at colleges and universities across the United States.

The goal of capital budgeting is to select those investment opportunities that are worth more than they cost. Also, businesses should initially invest in those projects that provide the greatest return for their investment. Given the long-term effects associated with any investment, we can see why capital budgeting is a primary focus for sport businesses or organizations.

A sport business can raise and spend capital funds in countless ways. An integral part of financial management is determining the best capital sources. Efficient capital spending leads to growth and success for a sport business. To grow, a business must invest some of its available capital in fixed assets such as land, equipment, or machinery. For example, the University of Houston (UH) cannot improve its recreational offerings without investing in new equipment and facilities. But while a for-profit business should invest in those projects that will result in the largest return on investment, this may not always be true for government or nonprofit organizations.

Before critically analyzing capital budgeting, we must focus on the meaning of capital spending. Capital spending is the net spending on fixed assets. Net spending is the total money a business uses to acquire **real assets,** less the sale of previously owned real assets (Brigham et al., 1999). It is important to note that sport businesses not only spend money on acquiring real assets; they may also sell some real assets. The sale of these real assets must be included when one calculates total capital spending.

 For example, if Sport Manufacturing Company (SMC) invests $10 million through purchasing fixed assets and also sells $4 million in fixed assets, its net spending on fixed assets is $6 million. Although the company budgeted $10 million to acquire new fixed assets, it produced income through the sale of existing assets that were part of the previous balance sheet.

It is also important to remember that capital budgeting and purchasing capital items are long-term endeavors. When we refer to items as long-term, this usually means a time frame greater than one year. Long-term assets such as equipment and facilities have a productive life that is longer than one year. With respect to capital, it is often not possible for a business to allocate the amount of money necessary for purchasing high-priced fixed assets in one single year. Therefore, the business must develop capital budgets that detail how the funds will be raised and allocated over an extended period of time. This is the primary reason for the separation of current, or short-term, items from capital items in financial statements.

The funding mix required for capital expenditures is referred to as the capital structure. In general, the traditional corporate capital structure includes debt (bonds and long-term loans), preferred stock, common stock, and retained earnings (Ross, Westerfield, & Jordan, 1995). These capital vehicles are discussed in part III, but are referred to again in this chapter within the context of analyzing their budgeting implications. All these capital sources have an accompanying cost. If a sport business wishes to borrow funds from a bank to construct a new facility, it must pay interest on the borrowed amount. The interest that is paid in addition to the principal being borrowed is referred to as the debt's cost. The next section deals with each form of capital and covers methods to measure the accompanying costs.

For nonprofit organizations such as UH, additional sources of funding are donations and gifts. Supporters of nonprofit organizations often make financial donations toward new capital projects. For example, a university alumnus may donate a significant amount of money toward constructing a new sport facility. Many nonprofit organizations rely on these donations for a portion, or all, of the funds necessary to complete capital projects. These donations are very important to nonprofit organizations because unlike corporations, they cannot raise capital through equity ownership.

Cost of Capital

Sport businesses can use four traditional forms of capital to fund growth: debt, common stock, preferred stock, and retained earnings. The four traditional forms of capital are known as capital components. They all have one common trait: the persons or institutions that provide the capital expect—or demand—a return on investment (Brigham et al., 1999). A bank or financial institution that loans money to a small business expects to be repaid the loan principal plus interest. A common stockholder or investor expects the firm to invest in capital spending projects that will increase the value of the company and ultimately result in increased stock value. This expected return on the investment means that there is a cost to the business in acquiring the capital funds. In the case of a bank loan, the cost of capital is the amount of interest that is owed to the creditor. This section develops methods to measure the cost of capital for debt and equity. Sport businesses need to understand and appreciate the fact that any capital acquisition technique has a cost, and that end cost will dictate how much capital can be raised.

We must make a quick point about retained earnings before moving forward. Retained earnings are funds that are kept by a business to be used for reinvestment in the company. This reinvestment often takes the form of capital spending. Management believes that the stockholders will benefit more from this reinvestment than from having the money returned through dividend payments. Because the retained earnings can be used by the business to purchase additional stock, the cost of retained earnings is considered to be the cost of common stock. Therefore, we will discuss the cost of retained earnings along with the cost of common stock.

It is important to mention that companies develop strategies concerning the manner in which their capital will be structured. For example, the Boston Celtics may have 40% of their capital in the form of debt, 40% in preferred stock, and 20% in common stock. These proportions, referred to as a target capital structure, may vary greatly across businesses and industries (Ross et al., 1995). Within some professional sport leagues, capital structure is somewhat controlled by the league. For example, the NFL has restrictions on the level of debt that each team can maintain. The NFL has the debt limit as a financial safeguard to ensure that none of its teams have excess debt that will lead to future financial difficulties. The debt limit was increased from $55 million to $100 million after the signing of a new league-wide television contract in 1998 (Kaplan, 1998, August-September). If a league member is at its debt limit, it must raise capital through other sources, perhaps by attracting new equity investors.

Most sport businesses finance their capital budgets through a combination of debt and equity. Each form of capital has an associated cost. Some businesses may decide to structure their capital budgets such that they rely on one single form of capital, but this is uncommon for large corporations. For government-owned and -operated institutions such as UH's athletic department, the sources of capital are primarily debt and money raised through gifts and donations. The University of Houston is operated by the state of Texas and has no individual private ownership rights. Its income comes from sources such as donations, ticket sales, sponsorships, student fees, and broadcast fees. These funds are used to cover the current expenses involved in operating a collegiate athletic program. The university usually raises money for capital projects from donations or the issuance of debt. The state is ultimately responsible for paying the bondholders if the university defaults. The Smiths, the Boston Celtics, and SMC can also raise capital by selling equity ownership rights or borrowing funds. For example, the Celtics have raised money in the past through the issuance of common stock to the public, but also could borrow from banks or could issue bonds. Other professional teams utilize similar capital funding techniques. For example, the city of Springfield, Massachusetts, recently passed a resolution to issue $2 million in city bonds to partially fund a new minor league baseball stadium (Goonan & McAuliffe, 1999).

Several factors can influence the decision on capital structuring. For example, a weak stock market may make the issuance of stock less attractive than it might be otherwise. As stock prices fall, a business needs to issue more shares in order to raise the capital funds that are necessary. Also, there is a cost associated with issuing new stock. Most businesses work with a financial institution to help with a public offering, and there is a cost for these services. The expenses related to issuing new stock are known as flotation costs (Ross et al., 1995). Immoo, Lochhead, Ritter, and Zhao (1996) found that a company that wants to raise $2 to $10 million in capital through a common stock offering will have flotation costs of approximately 13.28% of the total amount of capital being raised. Thus, if a business wants to raise $2 million in capital, it will actually need to raise approximately $2.26 million. The additional $260,000 will be needed to cover the flotation costs. Immoo et al. (1996) also found that the average flotation cost is significantly less when capital is raised through debt. In the $2 to $10 million debt range, the average flotation cost is 4.39%, one-third the level of common stock flotation costs. Whether debt or equity is used, many of the flotation costs, such as attorneys' fees, are fixed and are not greatly affected by the amount of capital being raised. Therefore, most businesses do not like to raise capital in relatively small quantities. Other businesses also elect to raise capital through one single source, debt or equity, each year in an effort to minimize flotation costs (Ross et al., 1995).

A professional sport team example will illustrate average cost of capital for debt. Assume that a professional baseball team goes public by issuing stock. Assume the team raises $200 million through its initial public offering. If the average flotation costs for such an offering are 8%, then $16 million will be paid to float the shares, and $3 to $4 million of that amount might represent attorneys' fees that need to be paid even if only $100 million is raised through the offering.

Selecting one capital source each year has short-term effects on a target capital structure. This strategy makes it difficult to maintain the target structure. A business' target capital structure may also be affected by outside economic forces such as the stock market or interest rates. Interest rates have an effect on the cost of issuing debt. Therefore, a business may want to select debt as its capital source (in order to maintain its capital target), but it may be more cost-effective to issue new stock. This is especially true when stock prices are relatively high.

Thus far, we have discussed the general principles of capital, the forms of capital, and the importance of capital cost. The next step is to develop a method for accurately measuring new capital costs. The most commonly used method to measure the cost of capital is the weighted average cost of capital (WACC). The WACC focuses on determining the average cost of each capital component and weights each based on its contribution to the total capital amount. In general, a sport business will maximize its value when it minimizes its WACC (Ross et al., 1995).

To calculate the WACC, we must separate capital into each of the three potential capital sources available for a business: debt, preferred stock, and common stock. As stated earlier, the cost of retaining earnings and the cost of issuing common stock are calculated similarly. In doing the calculation of the WACC as outlined in this chapter, retained earnings are implicitly included in the value of common stock. Whether new shares of stock are issued or whether retained earnings are used to finance a capital project, the cost of funds is identical (ignoring underwriting and flotation costs). The following sections deal with the cost of debt first, followed by the cost of equity and the cost of combining the capital mix in the WACC.

The traditional forms of capital that businesses, including sport businesses, use to finance their capital budgets are debt and equity.

Cost of Debt

Debt is important because many smaller businesses raise most of their capital through this capital component, usually in the form of bank loans (Brigham et al., 1999).

 For example, the Smiths have a relatively small business. They may borrow money from a bank or similar financial institution to fund new capital spending. The principal amount they borrow must be repaid over time with interest. The interest is the cost of borrowing the funds. If the Smiths borrow $100,000 at an interest rate of 8%, the cost of debt is, excluding taxes, also 8%. But, the cost of debt is misleading unless one extracts the potential tax implications. Taxes are covered in chapter 14, but it is important to note here that since the debt repayment of 8% is probably tax deductible, the Smiths will not pay 8% per year. The true cost will be $8,000 (8% × $100,000) minus what tax savings can be generated by reducing the Smiths' income by $8,000. Assuming a 40% combined federal and state tax rate for the business, the potential cost could drop from $8,000 to $4,800 ($8,000 – 40%).

Many large corporations also issue debt through bonds and debentures. A bond is a long-term promissory note issued by a business. For most bonds, the business agrees to pay back the amount borrowed at a specified future date (usually 10 to 30 years for long-term bonds) in addition to a coupon payment. The coupon payment for most corporate coupon bonds is made semiannually. The coupon payment is a percentage of the bond's value. For example, a business can sell 30-year bonds with a value of $1,000 and a semiannual coupon payment of 5%. Anyone who purchases a bond will receive semiannual payments of $50 for 30 years. Also at the end of the 30 years, the creditor will receive $1,000. In this example, the annual cost of debt for the life of the bond would average around 10%.

As discussed in the previous chapter, a debenture is a long-term bond. However, unlike regular bonds that are secured by corporate assets, a debenture is unsecured. The only protection a debenture holder has to guarantee repayment is the good name of the company that issues the debenture. If the corporation faces financial hardships, the debenture holders are similar to all other unsecured lenders in that they are often the last group to be repaid, if they are paid at all.

From these examples, it initially appears that measuring the rate of return required by debt holders is fairly straightforward. How much will debt holders demand in future payments in order to make the necessary funds available today? For a small business, ascertaining this may be as simple as determining the annual interest rate on a bank loan. However, it can be a bit more complex for a large corporation. Given that the WACC is used in the planning process for the issuance of future debt, a financial manager is making a prediction or estimation of the future cost of debt. It is not always easy to determine the coupon payment that must be

offered in order to attract future bond purchasers. If a business issues a new bond at a time when interest rates are on the rise, it will have a hard time selling the bonds without increasing the interest rate paid to purchasers. Therefore, determining the appropriate rate of return is not an exact science. Nevertheless, by using the correct information one can make a credible estimate.

What Is the Correct Information?

A financial manager can analyze historical data on past debt instruments to make a prediction about the future. For example, suppose that a business wants to issue new 30-year bonds to raise capital. Through past experience, the financial manager knows that similar bonds have been issued for each of the past five years. She also knows that the business' financial position has not changed over that time period and that those previous bonds were issued with a 10% coupon rate. Additionally, the financial manager should look at the current yield on a bond with the same maturity and credit rating, as determined by Moody's and Standard and Poor's, as well as the current debt costs for similar businesses. For example, suppose a team is investigating the issuance of debt to build a new stadium or arena. It would be beneficial for the team to gather information on the cost of debt incurred by other teams that have recently financed stadium construction.

Calculating the Cost of Debt

One other important debt feature is crucial to the cost-of-debt calculation. To encourage capital investment, the federal government and most state governments provide a tax deduction on the interest payments made to debt holders. For most corporations, the federal tax rate for interest deductions is 35% (Brigham et al., 1999). Most states also give tax allowances for interest deductions, usually at about a 5% rate (Brigham et al., 1999). In total, the average taxable rate for interest deductions is approximately 40%. This tax savings reduces the overall cost of debt for a sport business.

Assume we want to calculate the cost of debt for SMC. The cost of debt can be written as a mathematical formula:

$$D = R - (R \times T)$$

D = cost of debt

R = interest rate paid to debt holder

T = marginal tax rate on interest payments

The rate of return required by debt holders is the interest rate, or **R,** that is paid on the debt. The tax saving is the rate of return required by debt holders multiplied by the **marginal tax** rate on interest payments, which we will abbreviate as **T.** We can rewrite the cost of debt this way:

$$D = R \times (1 - T)$$

In our example, we will assume that SMC borrows $500,000 at an interest rate of 8% and has a marginal tax rate of 40%. Their actual cost of debt will be:

$$D = 8\% \times (1 - 0.4)$$
$$D = 4.8\%$$

Therefore, SMC's cost of debt is 4.8% annually. Multiplying 4.8% by $500,000 shows that the cost of debt in dollars is $24,000. The tax deduction associated with making interest payments will save SMC 3.2%, or $16,000, of the original $500,000 that was borrowed.

> A company's cost of debt can be calculated by subtracting the tax savings from the rate of return required by the debt holders.

Cost of Equity

Capital can also be acquired through selling ownership in the business, also known as the issuance of equity. Equity is separated into two different classifications: preferred stock and common stock.

Cost of Preferred Stock

Preferred stock has a few unique characteristics that are important when one is calculating its cost. First, dividend payments on preferred stock are not tax deductible (Ross et al., 1995). No tax savings such as we saw with debt are available for firms that issue preferred stock. Also, although firms have no legal requirement to pay yearly dividends on preferred stock, they usually make every attempt to do so. If a company misses a dividend payment, it has to pay the owed back dividend the next time a dividend payment is declared. The reason is that dividends must be paid on preferred stock before dividends are paid to common stockholders. Also, in some cases, preferred stockholders have the right to take control of a company if they do not receive dividend payments. To avoid defaulting on required payments, management pays dividends as regularly as possible to keep preferred stockholders happy. Also, the failure to make dividend payments to preferred stockholders is a signal that a firm may be in financial distress. This may eventually lead to difficulty

in issuing future capital in either the debt or the equity market (Ross et al., 1995).

As discussed in chapter 10, preferred stocks pay a fixed dividend to an investor, similar to a bond's coupon payment. Dividends can be postponed until future years; the firm's board of directors is responsible for making this decision (Ross et al., 1995). Also, as stated earlier, preferred stock dividends are not tax deductible, so we do not need to include a tax savings component in our cost calculation.

All preferred stock has a predetermined share value, called the par value, and a fixed dividend payment per share. For example, Nike preferred stock has a $1 par value and an annual fixed dividend payment of $0.10 (*Standard & Poor's*, 1999). The cost of preferred stock is the dividend payment, which we abbreviate as v, divided by the issuing price, **P.** In our calculations, we will also abbreviate the cost of preferred stock as **S.**

As stated earlier, there are flotation costs associated with issuing new stock. The flotation costs decrease the amount of cash the firm actually receives from the sale of new preferred stock. For example, if SMC issues new preferred stock for $100 per share and the flotation cost is 5%, SMC will receive only $95 per share. Therefore, we should include the flotation cost in the calculation of P and redefine P as the net issuing price. Given the information we have, the cost of preferred stock can be written as:

$$\text{cost of preferred stock} = \frac{\text{preferred stock dividend}}{\text{net issuing price}}$$

or

$$S = \frac{v}{P}$$

S = cost of preferred stock
v = preferred stock dividend
P = net issue price

Assume that the Boston Celtics want to issue $10 million of new preferred stock. The new preferred stock will have a $100 par value and pay an annual dividend of $8 per share, and the flotation cost will be 3%. The cost of preferred stock is then calculated as follows:

$$S = \frac{\$8}{\$100 - \$3} = \frac{\$8}{\$97} = 8.25\%$$

The cost of issuing new preferred stock for the Boston Celtics is 8.25%. As you can see, flotation costs have an effect on the cost of preferred stock. Without the flotation costs, the cost of preferred stock would be 8%. While the change of 0.25% may seem small, in this example in which $10 million of preferred stock is issued, the increased cost annually paid by the Celtics is $25,000.

Cost of Common Stock

The last capital component to be considered is common stock. With respect to common stock, a firm can raise capital through two methods. First, it can issue new common stock. To attract new common stock shareholders, the firm must sell the stock shares at an attractive price. Prospective stockholders will purchase the stock if they believe that the value of the stock will increase in the future. The annual percentage return (holding period return) associated with annual dividend payments and increases in stock price must exceed the returns on investments of equivalent risk. If it is not, people will invest their money in other opportunities.

A recent trend in the sport industry has been an increase in the number of initial public offerings of stock. As we saw in chapter 9, an initial public offering is the first offering of a stock to the general public. The shares that are made available can be primary offerings (new shares that are sold to raise additional capital) or secondary offerings, which occur when the company ownership sells a portion of their existing shares (Brealey & Myers, 1996). After being issued, the stock is bought and sold through a public market such as the New York Stock Exchange or the American Stock Exchange. Traditionally, sport teams were privately owned and operated. But we have recently seen organizations such as the Florida Panthers, Orlando Predators, and Boston Celtics go public.

A sport business can also raise capital through retaining earnings that would otherwise be used to pay common stockholder dividends. By not paying dividends, the firm is retaining funds for use in capital spending. The capital spending goal is to increase the business' value. If the business' value grows as a result of the capital spending, the common stock price should also increase. Most common stockholders will gladly forgo current dividend payments if the retained earnings will lead to an increase in the firm's stock price that is greater than the expected dividend payment.

Dividend policy is an important part of corporate finance. Financial managers continually struggle with the trade-off between dividend payments and retained earnings. They are looking for the appropriate levels of each that will keep the stockholders happy and also allow the firm to grow. It is impossible to make every investor happy, and there are never any guarantees. A business could pour $100 million into retained earnings and build a new physical plant. Investors might be ecstatic with the prospects of future increased value. However, a day after the plant opens a competitor can produce a better model and send the business' stock into a dramatic tailspin. Thus, retained earnings represent a potential risk, but all business decisions contain an element of risk.

Ultimately, the important aspect of common stock is that common stock shareholders require a return on their investment. This expected return on investment is vital for calculating the cost of common stock. In the simplest terms, the cost of common stock is the rate of return demanded by stockholders.

We must include several factors in calculating the cost of common stock. Similar to the situation with preferred stock, flotation costs are incurred when new common stock is issued. Also, issuing new common stock increases the overall supply of common shares available in the market. The increased supply of stock will cause the price of all shares to drop. This often forces the firm to sell the new stock at a lower price and reduce the amount of capital that is raised. All of these additional costs discourage some businesses from issuing new common stock. Most older and larger businesses do not regularly offer new common stock on the open market. Instead, they elect to raise capital through retained earnings that would otherwise be paid as dividends or by issuing bonds or commercial paper.

There is an **opportunity cost,** also known as **implicit cost,** to shareholders if a business retains earnings to raise capital. The shareholders are forgoing dividends when earnings are retained. Shareholders could have reinvested those dividend payments in stocks, bonds, and other opportunities that may have resulted in a positive return. Therefore, the retained earnings should result in an increase in a business' value that is greater than the amount a shareholder can expect to earn if the money is paid out as dividends. The difficult task for a financial manager is to calculate this amount in dollars and cents. Similar to the situation with issuing new stock, the amount shareholders could make by investing their dividend payments in the best alternative can also serve to help measure the cost of common stock. Thus, the cost of common stock involves many different factors such as dividend payments, flotation costs, the rate of return of other investment opportunities, and the risk involved in investing in common stock. The next sections present three different methods for measuring the cost of common stock.

Capital Asset Pricing Model   The first method of measuring the cost of common stock is the **capital asset pricing model** (CAPM). It is the most commonly used approach for measuring the cost of capital (Brigham et al., 1999). It begins by estimating the rate of return on a risk-free investment such as a U.S. Treasury bond. Within the mathematical formula for CAPM we will refer to the rate of return of a risk-free investment as **F**. In addition to risk-free investments, the shareholder can also purchase riskier investments such as corporate stocks and bonds. The CAPM also builds this into the calculation of the common stock cost. The most obvious investment decision would be for the shareholder to purchase more shares in the same business. Given this, we want to develop a measure of the expected return on the firm's stock. The return is, in part, based on the risk of the stock.

Risk is an important component of common stocks. Stocks with large price swings are considered more volatile than others and therefore have a higher risk level. Those stocks with a high level of risk must have the potential for a large increase in value. There are several accepted measures of a stock's level of risk. The CAPM incorporates the most commonly used measure, which is known as the beta coefficient. The beta coefficient is a measure of an individual stock's volatility. A stock with volatility similar to that of the overall stock market has a beta coefficient of 1.0. A stock that is one-half as volatile as the stock market has a beta of 0.5, and a stock that is twice as volatile has a beta of 2.0. The risk of a stock increases as the beta coefficient increases. Information on stocks' beta coefficients is readily available in publications such as *Value Line Investment Survey, Standard & Poor's,* and *Moody's.*

Another key component of CAPM is estimating the expected rate of return for the overall market. We want to develop the overall average return that can be expected from investing in the stock market. Using all of this information, we develop an equation that will measure the expected cost of common stock. The equation is:

$$C = F + \{(M - F) \times B\}$$

C = expected cost of common stock

M = expected rate of return for the overall market

F = expected rate of return from a risk-free investment

B = the company's beta coefficient

This equation attempts to measure the cost of common stock in two ways. First, it estimates the cost of a very safe investment through F, defined as the rate of return on a risk-free investment. In addition, the model builds in an additional measure of cost for the individual corporation being analyzed. This is done by first deducting the rate of return for a risk-free investment, F, from the overall stock market rate of return, M. This amount is then multiplied by the beta coefficient of the individual business' stock. The result is a measure of the additional cost, above that of a risk-free investment, for an individual business' common stock. This amount is then added to F, the cost of a risk-free investment. The sum is the total cost of common stock using the CAPM method. This method is popular because it incorporates several important variables (risk-free investment cost, overall market cost, and the individual stock's level of risk) into the computation of the cost of common stock.

Assume that SMC wants to raise capital by forgoing dividend payments to its stockholders. It will retain the earnings and use the funds to build a new distribution center. It must determine its cost of raising the capital through retained earnings. The company knows that under current economic conditions, a risk-free investment will return 6%; the firm's beta coefficient is 1.3, and the company estimates the expected rate of return for the overall stock market to be 10%. To summarize: F = 6%; M = 10%; and B = 1.3. The CAPM equation is as follows:

$$\begin{aligned} C &= F + \{(M - F) \times B\} \\ &= 6\% + [(10\% - 6\%)\ 1.3] \\ &= 11.2\% \end{aligned}$$

The estimated cost of common stock for SMC is 11.2%.

It is important to understand that the CAPM is not a perfect measure. While it arrives at an exact percentage, there is still some unpredictability in the various components used to help calculate CAPM and in the final CAPM figure. We are making an estimate of the overall stock market performance that may be inaccurate. It is very difficult to predict the future performance of the stock market. In addition, the beta coefficient is a measure of the individual stock's risk and can also change over time. Last, there may be some difficulty in selecting the appropriate risk-free investment. There are many different types of short- and long-term Treasury bonds, many of which have different rates of return. Any change in these variables greatly affects the final result when we are using the CAPM.

Bond-Yield-Plus-Risk-Premium Model The second method of estimating the cost of common stock is much simpler, but also much more subjective. Some financial analysts believe that the cost of common stock is closely related to the firm's cost of debt. The cost of common stock will be several percentage points higher than the firm's cost of debt because of the higher level of risk associated with stock. Intuitively this makes sense: firms with low-risk, low-interest-rate bonds should also have a low cost of common stock. Conversely, firms with high-risk and high-interest-rate debt should have a higher cost for issuing common stock. On the basis of this concept, the bond-yield-plus-risk-premium model was developed. It measures the cost of common stock as the yield from the firm's bonds plus some risk premium. The risk premium is usually in the 4% to 7% range and is selected by financial analysts (Brigham et al., 1999). One shortcoming of this model is that the risk premium is not an exact measure based on available financial data.

To return to the example of SMC, we may find that the company has outstanding bonds that were issued at 9%. We would add some risk premium to the 9% to arrive at the cost of common stock. If we say that the risk premium is 5%, we will estimate the overall cost of common stock as 14%. As with the CAPM, we cannot state that 14% will definitely be the cost of common stock for SMC. We are making an estimation of the cost.

Dividend Growth Model A third method for determining the cost of common stock is the dividend growth model. The price of common stock and its expected rate of return are, in part, related to the expected dividends that will be paid on the stock. Stockholders expect to earn some level of dividends. This is usually the amount paid in past years. But stockholders also expect that the annual dividend payments will increase in the future. Therefore, the cost of common stock is the sum of these two values (Griffin, 1991). We can represent the dividend growth model through the following equation:

$$C = \frac{E}{N} + G$$

C = required rate of return for stockholders (this serves as a measure of the cost of common stock)

E = annual dividend payment (for simplicity, we assume that these payments are fixed at the same level each year)

N = current price per share of the stock

G = annual growth rate of dividends.

The equation captures the notion that investors have some level of return that they expect to receive from purchasing a common stock. That return is the **dividend yield,** as measured by the annual dividend payment divided by the current stock price, plus the expected annual dividend growth rate. For a firm to invest capital in projects, capital that would otherwise go to common stock shareholders, it must assure stockholders that the capital investment will result in a higher return than C, the required rate of return for stockholders. Although this method seems fairly straightforward, there are some problems. It can be very difficult to accurately predict the annual growth rate of dividends, G. Security analysts spend countless hours analyzing company financial data to determine future performance and profitability. Despite such efforts, they are often wrong. This is especially true for companies with very abnormal past financial performances. Overall economic cycles and industry trends can also influence an individual business' future performance. This often occurs in some sport segments that rely on products with short life cycles. For example, beach volleyball was very popular in the late 1980s and early 1990s, but the sport saw some difficult times in the late 1990s as consumers shifted to other recreational activities. It is often difficult to predict these consumer trends.

The cost to the company of raising capital by issuing common stock can be calculated using three different methods: 1) the capital asset pricing model, 2) the bond-yield-plus-risk-premium model, and 3) the dividend growth model.

Calculation of the Weighted Average Cost of Capital

We now have measures for the three primary components of capital: debt, preferred stock, and common stock. The next step is to combine these measures and develop an overall cost of capital. As stated earlier, the most common method used is the WACC. The WACC uses the targeted levels, or proportions, of the three components along with the cost measures developed for each. Most firms have a targeted capital structure. The target is the proportion of debt to preferred stock to common stock that the business believes will be best for its future success. The proportions of target capital will be represented by weights that will be given to each capital type. When added up, the weights must equal 1. For example, if the debt portion has a weight of 0.1, this means that 10% of the business' targeted capital structure is funded through a debt instrument.

The reader can use any of the three previously discussed methods to calculate C, the cost of common stock. In the following example the CAPM is used. The equation that follows represents the WACC.

$$WACC = (W_D \times D) + (W_S \times S) + (W_C \times C)$$

WACC = weighted average cost of capital

W_D = target weight for debt

W_S = target weight for preferred stock

W_C = target weight for common stock

D = cost of debt

S = cost of preferred stock

C = cost of common stock

Also, remember that we have already highlighted methods to measure D, S, and C as highlighted by their formulas below.

$$D = R \times (1 - T)$$

$$S = \frac{v}{P}$$

$$C = F + \{(M - F) \times B\}$$

If we were to start from the beginning, we would first develop the costs of debt, preferred stock, and common stock and then weight each component, based on the target capital structure, to determine the WACC.

 Assume that SMC has a targeted capital structure in which 15% will be in the form of debt, 70% will be in preferred stock, and 15% will be common stock. In addition, through the use of the measures described earlier, SMC has found that its after-tax cost of debt (D) is 8.2%, its cost of preferred stock (S) is 9.7%, and its cost of common stock (C) is 12.3%. The company needs to raise $10 million in new capital to make major renovations of its administrative offices and production facility. Management wants to know what the average cost of the capital will be if the targeted capital structure is followed. The best way to show this is to solve the formula for WACC.

$$\begin{aligned} WACC &= (W_D \times D) + (W_S \times S) + (W_C \times C) \\ &= (0.15 \times 8.2\%) + (0.70 \times 9.7\%) + \\ &\quad (0.15 \times 12.3\%) \\ &= 9.87\% \end{aligned}$$

The WACC for SMC is 9.87%. In addition, for every $1 of new capital that is raised, 15% should be in the form of debt and have an after-tax cost of 8.2%. Seventy percent should be preferred stock and have a cost of 9.7%, and last, 15% should be raised through common stock and have a cost of 12.3%.

Note that the WACC is the cost of new capital only. We are attempting to develop cost measures as part of the capital budgeting process. This estimate should not be used to make statements about the cost of previously issued capital. Previous capital was raised under different economic and financial circumstances, and such circumstances can greatly influence the cost of capital. Last, note that the weights used are based on a targeted capital structure. If the firm actually raises capital in proportions that vary from the targets, this will greatly affect the WACC. Again, WACC is a method to estimate the cost of capital. Any changes in the variables used in the model will change the WACC.

The WACC is a commonly used method for determining the expected cost of raising new capital. As with any estimations of the future, it will not be accurate in every instance. As stated earlier, outside factors such as interest rates and tax rates play a role in determining WACC. Any changes in these factors would obviously affect the cost of capital. Additionally, a firm may change policies dealing with dividend payments, investment strategy, or capital structure. Any changes in these areas would greatly influence the WACC. For example, a change in investment assets may markedly affect the risk premium for the company. Ultimately, this may also affect the cost of common stock.

Last, our discussion of WACC and the cost of capital has primarily focused on publicly held businesses. Numerous businesses in the sport industry are small businesses or privately held companies (or both). Neither of these types of businesses have stocks that are openly bought and sold. This presents some unique problems when one is determining the cost of capital. The price of preferred and common stock is not easily obtainable because the stocks are not traded on the open market. Overall, the same principles of cost of capital determination apply for small businesses and privately held companies. It is, however, more difficult to obtain accurate and usable financial data. In addition, many small firms do not pay any dividends. Earnings are often retained and used to grow the company. This can make it very difficult to calculate accurate costs of preferred and common stock.

In addition, most small businesses do not have publicly traded bonds. The bond-yield-plus-risk-premium method for determining the cost of common stock relies on knowing a business' bond yield. This method is usually not appropriate when applied to small businesses.

We have now developed a method for measuring the cost of capital. The next step is to develop a method for making capital budgeting decisions. Sport managers are continually presented with a number of capital projects. They must decide which projects are worthy of being undertaken and which should be bypassed. The next section develops several different methods for making these capital budgeting decisions.

> *The method for calculating the overall cost of capital is the weighted average cost of capital.*

Trends in Stadium Financing

The past decade has seen an explosion in the construction of professional sport stadiums and arenas. As the 20th century came to a close, new facilities opened for teams such as the Seattle Mariners, Toronto Maple Leafs, Tennessee Titans, Washington Redskins, and Atlanta Hawks. In addition, new sport facilities were also under construction in cities such as Milwaukee, Detroit, Pittsburgh, and Philadelphia. There are several reasons for this trend in sport facility construction. Because of changes in facility design, a stadium such as FedEx Field in Washington, D.C., can produce substantially more revenue for the Redskins franchise than their previous home, Robert F. Kennedy Stadium. For example, FedEx Field has 208 luxury suites that bring in over $15 million annually, as well as 15,000 club seats that sell for $1,000 to $2,000 per year. The new income generated from the facility is critical to the financial success of the Redskins. As operating costs increase, due in part to rising player salaries, teams must find new income streams. Stadium revenues along with ticket sales, national broadcast rights fees, and team merchandise revenues are the main sources of income. However, unlike other revenue sources, most stadium income is not shared equally among all franchises. In the four major professional leagues, teams keep 100% of revenues from parking, concessions, advertising, and stadium naming rights. New facilities are often built to maximize these revenue sources.

Another important aspect of new professional sport facility construction is the source of funding. New facilities can cost between $250 and $500 million. It has been estimated that a new Yankee Stadium in New York could cost over $1 billion. In contrast, the Los Angeles Forum was built in 1967 for $15 million (Howard & Crompton, 1995). Given these high construction costs, the recent trend has been for new facilities to be jointly financed between the team ownership and the public sector. A popular financing method is for local and state governments to issue debt, through municipal bonds, that will be repaid at a later date. The public sector can use financing sources such as state lotteries, sales taxes, and ticket surcharges to raise the funds for debt repayment.

Cities and states have been involved in sport facility construction since the inception of professional sport. However, the end of the 20th century saw a new trend of franchise free agency. Team owners were willing to move to a city that would build a new stadium mostly financed by the public sector. Along with having a new stadium, team owners were allowed to keep a significant share of the stadium revenues. Many cities and states were willing to make such deals because of their strong interest in acquiring a professional franchise. The decade of the 1990s saw this occur several times. Art Modell moved his NFL

(continued)

(continued)

franchise to Baltimore when the city of Cleveland refused to build a new publicly financed football stadium. Baltimore was willing to build Modell a new stadium and also to allow the team to play rent free. Modell also received all revenues from concessions, parking, and in-stadium advertising. In addition, the city permitted Modell to keep up to $75 million from the sale of permanent seat licenses (PSLs). The money from the sale of PSLs was to be used to cover the costs associated with the team's relocation and the construction of a new practice facility in Maryland. In return, Modell agreed to sign a 30-year lease and cover all operational and maintenance costs associated with the new facility, estimated at $3 to $4 million annually (Stellino, 1995).

A similar deal was signed by Georgia Frontiere, the owner of the St. Louis Rams, when she moved the team from Los Angeles. The city of St. Louis spent $260 million to build a new domed stadium for the team. In addition, the city covered the Rams' operating losses from their last season in Los Angeles and paid off $30 million in debt that the team owed to Southern California. St. Louis also paid a $29 million league relocation fee and constructed a $15 million training center for the team. All of these benefits allowed the team to quickly remove itself from its financial difficulties and become profitable (Stellino, 1995). The new financial success of the team may have played a major role in its ability to acquire the necessary talent to win the 2000 Super Bowl. However, as the 20th century drew to a close, taxpayers in several cities began to rebel. Legislators in Minnesota and voters in North Carolina rejected stadium projects that would have used public subsidization to build a new baseball facility for the Minnesota Twins.

In most cases, team owners must contribute some funds for constructing the new facilities. In a few cases such as FedEx Field and Ericsson Stadium, the team ownership has contributed a majority of the funds and also retained facility ownership. Usually, the capital necessary for these projects is financed through debt. There have been several new trends in the issuance of private stadium debt. Historically, financial institutions viewed these projects and the accompanying revenue streams as fairly high risk. As a result, the team owner's cost of capital was relatively high. Owners were usually forced to use existing assets as collateral to secure the necessary loans. In some instances, it was difficult for team owners to find financial institutions that would provide the capital. However, as facilities such as Baltimore's Camden Yards, Denver's Coors Field, and the Palace of Auburn Hills have proved to be great sources of revenue, financial institutions have loosened the purse strings. Creditors have begun to issue debt based on the future revenue streams from the facilities. Some owners can now secure loans with the expectation of future revenue streams, as opposed to existing collateral.

Another recent trend has been the refinancing of facility debt. The late 1990s saw some of the lowest interest rates in decades. The interest rates for facility debt that was issued in the late 1980s and early 1990s were significantly higher. As a result, several sport organizations refinanced their preexisting facility debt and, in some instances, saved millions of dollars. For example, in 1999 the New Jersey Sports and Exposition Authority used a complex financial technique known as a "swaption" to refinance its debt. The authority saved $9.1 million that was used to help pay for renovation of the New York Giants' practice facility and the Continental Arena (Kaplan, 1999). The United States Tennis Association (USTA) used a similar technique to refinance a 1994 debt issuance that was used for renovations made to the National Tennis Center in Queens, New York. The USTA was able to save $3.25 million as the interest rate of its debt dropped from 6.4% to 5.94% (Kaplan, 1999). In a trend similar to that seen with American homeowners who refinanced their mortgages in the late 1990s, several sport organizations took advantage of low interest rates to save millions of dollars.

Capital Budgeting Decision Methods

Sport businesses have a variety of options with respect to spending funds. Capital spending on fixed assets such as equipment, facilities, and new technology is common. This section presents several methods for making decisions on how to allocate capital funds. Before examining decision making, we must consider the importance of time. Then we look at net present value, the payback rule, the discounted payback rule, and the **internal rate of return.** The first point of analysis needs to be the present value of an income stream as determined through the time value of money.

Importance of Time

An important element of capital budgeting is time. Capital spending and obtaining the returns from capital projects occur over many years. Therefore, the timing of the costs and revenues is critical. In chapter 6 we discussed the time value of money and the importance of determining the present value of a future stream of income. The following case study example can help explain the importance of understanding time, but is one you could skip if you feel you have a good grasp of the concept. For those wishing a quick review, please read the following example.

 The University of Houston (UH) is approached by a wealthy philanthropist who would like to make a large donation to the athletic department. The philanthropist offers two options for how the money will be paid:

1. The athletic department can receive a $100,000 check today.
2. The athletic department can receive a $110,000 check in one year.

The decision is based on which option is more valuable. If the present value of $110,000 in one year is greater than the present value of the $100,000 check received today, UH should select option 2. But how do we determine which option is more valuable? Obviously, $100,000 today is worth more than $100,000 a year from now, but is $100,000 today worth more than $110,000 a year from now? UH can invest the $100,000 today in an interest-bearing account and have more than $100,000 in one year. But can it make an additional $10,000 from the investment? Suppose that UH investigates the payoff from the best risk-free investment opportunity, probably a U.S. government security, and learns that the annual interest rate is 7.5%. Therefore, $100,000 invested in a U.S. government security will result in UH having $107,500 in one year. Under these circumstances, UH obviously should select option 2 and take the $110,000 in one year.

Another method for making this decision is to calculate the present value of option 2. Using this process, UH will determine the current dollar value of receiving $110,000 in one year. To make the decision, UH will need to know the expected rate of return. The rate of return is the reward demanded by investors for waiting one year to receive a payment. Assume that UH would expect no more than a 7.5% return from its best alternative risk-free investment. Therefore, we will use 7.5% as the rate of return. The rate of return is then used to develop a discount factor. Mathematically, the discount factor is expressed as:

$$\text{discount factor} = \frac{1}{1+r}$$

r = the expected return

The discount factor is then used to determine the present value of the $110,000 that will be received in one year. The future payout, in this case $110,000, is represented by FP. The following mathematical formula represents this concept.

$$PV = R \times FP$$

PV = present value

R = discount factor

FP = future payout

For our example:

$$PV = \frac{1}{1.075} \times FP$$
$$PV = \frac{1}{1.075} \times \$110,000$$
$$PV = \$102,325.58$$

Again, $102,325.58 represents the present value of receiving $110,000 in one year. Since this is greater than $100,000, UH would select option 2. However, if we went through the same process but assumed that UH's expected rate of return was 15%, this would cause the present value of option 2 to become $95,652.17. In this instance, the University would select option 1. The rate of return is very important in the determination of present value. In general, it represents the reward investors demand for accepting a payment made at a later date. This has obvious ramifications for capital spending, the investment of money today in an effort to receive future cash flows.

While the calculations in this example help establish which choice will be the most economical, they do not take into account other variables. For example, if UH does not build a park with the $100,000 this year, inflation and increased building costs might force the university to pay $117,000 next year. Furthermore, the future contains numerous variables that might make budgeting decisions that much more difficult. UH's athletic department might approve an additional $100,000 for a new field, but those funds might not be available if the athletic department waited a year to receive the $110,000 from the philanthropist.

Net Present Value

The calculation of present value leads us to the next important facet of capital budgeting. For all capital investments, a successful sport manager should calculate the present value of the expected future income related to the project. An investment is considered wise if the present value of this future income is greater than the necessary investment. The financial term associated with this process is **net present value** (NPV). The NPV is the difference between the present value of the future income and the required investment. It can be represented as follows:

$$NPV = PV - RI$$

NPV = net present value

PV = present value of future income

RI = required investment

The following case study example highlights how to apply NPV.

The University of Houston must decide if it wants to spend $1 million to construct 10 new luxury suites in the basketball arena. Each suite will last for 10 years. At the end of 10 years, we will assume that the suites will need to be replaced and will have no salvage value. For simplicity, it will also be assumed that each luxury suite can be rented for $30,000 per year and that no other income will be made from the suites. The construction project will take one year. Therefore, the first income from the suites will be made one year from today. If we think of one year from now as the end of year 1, income will flow into UH at the ends of years 1 through 10. Even though this example is not completely accurate, it depicts the concept of NPV in a simplified manner. The University of Houston must calculate the NPV of this investment opportunity prior to making the decision. So each year, starting next year, UH will have $300,000 in income for the next 10 years. Overall, the project will generate $3 million in income. However, the present value of the income stream must be calculated. Unlike the situation in the

previous example, in which one **payoff** was to be received one year into the future, here there is a stream of future payoffs. Thus, the present value of each future year's payoff must be calculated. The following mathematical formula is used to calculate cash flows in future years (Brigham et al., 1999):

$$PV = \left(\frac{1}{1+r} \times FP_1\right) + \left(\frac{1}{(1+r)^2} \times FP_2\right) +$$
$$\left(\frac{1}{(1+r)^3} \times FP_3\right) + \ldots\ldots + \left(\frac{1}{(1+r)^{10}} \times FP_{10}\right)$$

FP_1 = present value one year from now

FP_2 = present value two years from now and so on

These calculations will continue up to the end of year 10. In our example, the yearly income (FP) will always equal $300,000, and the rate of return will always equal 8%. We will assume that the rate of return for UH is 8%. We can rewrite the equation as:

$$PV = \left(\frac{1}{1.08} \times \$300,000\right) + \left(\frac{1}{1.08^2} \times \$300,000\right) +$$
$$\left(\frac{1}{1.08^3} \times \$300,000\right) + \ldots\ldots +$$
$$\left(\frac{1}{1.08^{10}} \times \$300,000\right)$$
$$= \$2,013,000$$

The present value of $2,013,000 can then be used to calculate the NPV of the capital expenditure. Note that these calculations can be done manually. However, if the rate of return and stream of income are constant throughout a project, an annuity table, such as table A.3 (pp. 314–315), can be used. The table will save a great deal of time and frustration! As stated previously, the initial investment is $1 million and the present value of the stream of income is $2,013,000. So, we can calculate the NPV as:

$$NPV = \$2,013,000 - \$1,000,000$$
$$= \$1,013,000$$

The NPV of the construction of five luxury boxes is positive and slightly over $1 million. The project definitely is worth more than it costs for the UH athletic department.

Net present value is an important capital budgeting component. Any project that has a negative NPV should not be undertaken. The reason is that the project's cost is higher than the projected income—financially, it is a losing proposition. However, not all projects that have a positive NPV must be undertaken. We will return to the selection of capital spending projects in a later section.

Next, it is important to note that there are other methods besides NPV for making a capital budgeting decision. All of these methods have strengths and weaknesses. The NPV method was presented first because it is the most often used and is regarded as the best. Although it is important to recognize and discuss these other methods, the NPV method is strongly recommended.

The Payback Rule

A second method of analyzing the value of a capital project is through the use of the payback rule. The payback rule analyzes how long it will take a business to receive its money back after investing in a capital project. The money is paid back through the stream of future income related to the project. The payback rule may be best explained through the following case study example.

Assume that UH has $1 million that it wants to invest in a capital project. The initial investment will result in a future cash flow into the university. The university has determined that it has two possible capital projects costing $1 million each. It must decide which one to select. These are the two choices:

Project A: A new outdoor aquatics facility. The facility will produce $250,000 in revenue in the first year and $300,000 per year for two subsequent years. In the fourth and final year, the cash flow will be $400,000. For simplicity, we will assume that there are no other costs or revenues. The total revenue for the next four years will total $1.25 million.

Project B: A new recreational gymnasium to be used for adult and youth sport leagues. This facility will produce $100,000 in the first year and $450,000 per year for the two subsequent years. However, it is estimated that because of a decrease in future demand, the cash flow for the fourth year will only be $100,000. The total revenue for the next four years will be $1.1 million.

The question is, which capital project should be selected? The university has decided to use the payback rule to make this decision. The university has decided that all of the initial $1 million investment must be paid back within three years. If this will not occur, capital funds will not be allocated for the project. Table 11.1 depicts the cash flows over time, the expected **payback periods,** and the NPV for each project.

Examining table 11.1, we see that it will take four years for Project A to repay the investment, whereas the investment for Project B will be repaid within three years. Given UH's payback rule of three years, Project B is the one to select. The cash flow from this project can repay the $1 million initial investment in three years. To reiterate, it will take four years to pay back the initial investment made in Project A.

The decision would change dramatically if we utilized the NPV method. To determine NPV, we assume that the opportunity cost of capital is 8%. We find that the NPV of Project A is $20,842, and the NPV for Project B is –$90,880. Using the NPV method, Project B would be rejected and UH would select Project A.

Table 11.1 Time Line of Cash Flows for Projects A and B

Project	P_0	P_1	P_2	P_3	P_4	Payback period	Net present value at 8%
A	–$1 million	$250,000	$300,000	$300,000	$400,000	4 years	$20,842
B	–$1 million	$100,000	$450,000	$450,000	$100,000	3 years	–$90,880

As you can see from the example, the selection of capital budgeting decision methods can have a major effect on capital budgeting. The reason for the difference is that the payback rule equally weights all cash flows. With use of the payback rule, the importance of time is ignored. This rule centers on which investment option will repay the initial outlay in the shortest amount of time. The NPV method discounts future cash flows based on the opportunity cost of capital. It also looks at the entire cash flow over the life of the project, in this case four years. Even if Project A had a cash flow of $1 billion in the fourth year, it would not be selected. The university's payback rule of three years means that only the cash flows in the first three years are important. The cash flow in the fourth year is meaningless in this example if we are using the payback rule. This is another obvious weakness of the payback rule; it ignores the cash flows after the arbitrarily selected payback date.

To account for the payback rule's failure to recognize the time value of money, the discounted payback rule has been developed.

Discounted Payback Rule

The discounted payback rule is the same as the payback rule but, based on the opportunity cost of capital, it discounts the future cash flows.

To return to our previous example, table 11.2 represents the cash flows when UH uses the discounted payback rule. The discounted payback rule applied to UH, and incorporating an 8% rate of return, produces the following results.

Using the discounted payback rule, the payback period remains at four years for Project A. Project B does not produce enough cash flow in four years to cover the initial investment. Therefore, using the discounted payback rule and a predetermined three-year maximum payback period, both projects are rejected. However, remember that using the NPV method would lead to the selection of Project A and that the original payback rule would result in selection of Project B. Again, the selection of capital budgeting decision methods has a major impact on the disbursement of long-term capital.

Table 11.2 Time Line of Discounted Cash Flows for Projects A and B

Project	P_0	P_1	P_2	P_3	P_4	Payback period	Net present value at 8%
A	–$1 million	$231,481	$257,210	$238,150	$294,009	4 years	$20,842
B	–$1 million	$92,593	$385,802	$357,225	$73,502	>4 years	–$90,880

Internal Rate of Return Method

The last method for making capital budgeting decisions is to use the internal rate of return (IRR). As with NPV and the discounted payback rule, IRR relies on the opportunity cost of capital and the time value of money. As stated earlier, the opportunity cost of capital is the return obtained by investing the capital in the next best alternative. For example, if you can place $100,000 in an interest-bearing investment that will result in your having $110,000 at the end of one year, the rate of return is 10%. Therefore, you would invest only in projects that can return more than $110,000. The IRR method emphasizes finding the rate of return for which NPV equals zero. Table 11.3 displays a situation in which a $1,000 capital investment results in a $750 cash flow in one year and a $500 cash flow in two years.

The goal of the IRR method is to find the rate of return for which NPV equals zero. The mathematical model for our example in table 11.3 is as follows:

$$NPV = P_0 + \frac{P_1}{1+r} + \frac{P_2}{1+r^2} = 0$$

P_0 = cash flow at time zero

P_1 = cash flow in first year

P_2 = cash flow in second year

r = rate of return

To complete the formula we need to solve for r, the rate of return. This can be quite difficult without the proper computer software. If you attempt to solve the formula manually, it will be a matter of trial and error. The trial-and-error process for manual calculation requires you to estimate for r and keep lowering or raising r until the equation equals zero. With a computer you can perform the analysis almost instantaneously. If we input the information from table 11.3, the equation can be rewritten as:

$$NPV = $1,000 + \frac{$750}{1+r} + \frac{$500}{1+r^2} = 0$$

We must now solve for r. Using trial and error, let's start with a 10% rate of return. If we solve the equation when r = 0.10, we find that the NPV equals $98.49. We now know that the IRR for which NPV

Table 11.3 Time Line of Cash Flows

Time 0 (P_0)	In one year (P_1)	In two years (P_2)
–$1,000	$750	$500

will equal zero is greater than 0.10. We continue this trial-and-error process until we find the rate of return at which NPV equals zero. In our example, NPV will equal zero when r equals 0.175. A wise sport manager would undertake this capital project if he believed that its opportunity cost of capital was less than 17.5%. In other words, the capital project would be undertaken if there were no other investment choices that had an expected rate of return greater than 17.5%.

> *Companies use various methods to decide how to allocate capital funds, including net present value, the payback rule, the discounted payback rule, and the internal rate of return.*

Risk and Capital Budgeting

Should the Smiths construct a new $1 million fitness center that will result in an increase of $100,000 in profit annually? Initially, one might answer yes, noting that an additional $100,000 in profit, a 10% return on investment, is fairly high. But what if the Smiths can also take that $1 million and purchase U.S. Treasury bonds that are guaranteed to provide a 9% return each year? Initially, the new fitness center still appears to be the best opportunity. But is the 10% return guaranteed? No. The 9% return from the U.S. Treasury bonds is definitely guaranteed. The expected return on the new fitness center is greater, but there is no guarantee that the return on investment will be 10%. It is an expected return.

This example illustrates the importance of risk and uncertainty. When one is calculating the return on investment for capital expenditures, risk is very important. Different capital projects have different levels of risk. In order to accept a higher level of risk for a project, one must expect the returns also to be higher. In every case, a wise sport manager faced with the choice of selecting one of two capital investment opportunities with equal returns will select the one with the lower risk.

There is some level of risk with all capital projects. Calculations of expected returns on investments and pro forma budgets are forecasts of future costs and revenues. Therefore, when discussing capital investment we will refer to expected payoffs and expected rates of return. Pro forma budgets are discussed in chapter 7.

Projecting Cash Flow

The discussion to this point has centered on capital budgeting from the cost side. The calculation of capital costs is an integral part of capital budgeting, but it is only half of the story. The other half deals with income and with developing methods to estimate future income that results from capital investment. The combination of expenses and income is known as the cash flow. The accurate projection of cash flows, both expenses and income, is a key to making wise capital budgeting decisions. Although no projection of future income is going to be totally accurate, it is imperative for a financial manager to make the best and most accurate attempt.

Chapter 5 dealt with the use of financial tools such as balance sheets and income statements to explain a business' current and past financial positions. Projecting cash flow also relies on financial tools, but the emphasis shifts to pro forma statements, discussed in chapter 7. Pro forma statements are very important to capital budgeting because an organization is investing capital today that will result in future cash flows.

The future cash flows that result from capital investment are dependent on many business factors. If UH plans to spend $100 million on a new 50,000-seat football stadium, the future cash flow resulting from this spending may be difficult to accurately estimate. The following is a list of factors that may affect future cash flow for such a project:

- Is there demand for 50,000 tickets to UH football games? An in-depth **market analysis** should be undertaken to determine spectator demand prior to construction.

- How important is ticket price to the spectators? Would an increase in the ticket price affect spectator demand?

- The University of Houston cannot assume that it will always put a winning team on the field. How will winning and losing affect spectator attendance?

- If the project succeeds and the 50,000 seats are filled on a regular basis, can the stadium be expanded in the future?

- If the capital is raised, in part, through booster donations, how will this affect fundraising efforts for other parts of the athletic program and the university? Will other projects or budgets be affected by the stadium project?

- How much additional cash will flow into the athletic department? If the new stadium is built, will it really have an effect on future cash flow as compared to the current cash flow from football games?

- In addition to football games, what other uses would the facility have, and what would the cash flow be from these uses?

- If luxury seating or boxes are included, is there a demand from corporate clients for these seats? What is the fair price for the luxury seating or boxes?

- How much will it cost to maintain and repair the stadium once it is built?

- What will be the cost for the capital required to construct the facility?

All of the factors listed are important when one is projecting the cash flow from a new university sport facility. It is necessary to ask questions dealing with market demand, sales projections, operating costs, and capital costs when attempting to project future cash flow. Again, remember that projecting future cash flow is not an exact science. A financial manager attempts to make the best possible estimation based on available data and research.

We will define a project's cash flows as the net cash inflows and investment expenditures associated with the project (Brigham et al., 1999). Again, projecting future cash flow is the most difficult facet of capital budgeting. For a sport organization, many different people and departments should be involved in making these projections.

 The University of Houston's stadium project can serve as an example of the departments that are involved in helping to project cash flow. The marketing department and ticket office need to make projections on ticket sales and ticket pricing. The university's construction planners and outside construction firms need to estimate construction costs. Perhaps the university's physical plant should be consulted to estimate maintenance costs. An event planner or promoter can help determine what revenues will be generated from other events being held in the stadium. The university's advancement or fundraising office can estimate the effect of stadium fund-raising on other university fund-raising endeavors.

As you can see, projecting cash flows for a capital project involves a large number of people and departments. Although this makes the process quite complex, it is essential to consult these people in order to make accurate estimations.

Several capital budgeting methods such as the payback rule, discounted payback rule, NPV, and IRR have already been presented. It is essential to remember that all of these sound financial techniques are worthless if poor cash flow projections are made. Poor decisions will result from any of these techniques if cash flow estimations are inaccurate.

An organization's financial staff must play a prominent role in projecting the cash flow. It is the job of the financial managers to take all of the information obtained from other departments and develop accurate projections. There are several common pitfalls that must be avoided. For a number of reasons such as career advancement, emotional ties, or possible benefits to their department, some individuals in other departments may be strong supporters of specific capital projects. This bias may affect the accuracy of the information they are providing to the financial staff. It is the responsibility of the financial staff to ensure that projections are as accurate as possible. Unfortunately, this is not always easy.

All businesses have a limited capital budget and many alternatives for capital spending. Each project must be evaluated on its own financial worth and also needs to be compared with other options. Those investment opportunities that fit within the capital budget and have the highest NPV are the most attractive. In the real world, the process of quantifying the NPV of investment choices is not this easy. Many confounding factors come into play. One capital spending project may affect another, and some may need to happen simultaneously to be successful. It is management's job to decipher all of this information.

Measuring Relevant Cash Flow

The first step in projecting cash flow is to measure the relevant cash flow for a capital project. All existing firms have a cash flow. The key to accurately measuring a single project's cash flow is to include only new cash flow. The new, or incremental, cash flow is the additional future cash flow, either internal or external to the business, that results only from the decision to undertake a project. Any cash flow that occurs regardless of the presence of a new project should not be included in the calculation of relevant cash flow. This is a very important concept that you need to remember throughout this discussion. With respect to measuring incremental cash flows, there are several common errors financial managers make.

The first common error relates to measuring sunk costs. **Sunk costs** are costs that have already occurred and do not change regardless of the decision to undertake a project.

For example, UH might pay $20,000 for a feasibility study on the construction of a new student recreation building. If as a result of this report UH decided not to construct the building, it would still have to pay for the feasibility study. The cost is incurred regardless of the outcome. According to our definition of incremental cash flow, the $20,000 is not important in making the capital spending decision. The money has already been spent, and it should not be included as a cost when UH is projecting cash flow for the capital project.

Another important aspect of projecting relevant cash flow, and the second common error, is opportunity cost. Opportunity cost refers to the most valuable alternative that is forgone if a particular capital project is undertaken.

Returning to the UH example, the recreation building must be built on a piece of land. The university has a parcel of land that can be used, but the land could also be used for new playing fields or a swimming pool. Initially, you might think that the cost of land is zero because UH already owns the land. This is not accurate. There is an opportunity cost associated with using that piece of land; the university is forgoing its next best alternative use of the land. The next best alternative may be to build a swimming pool. The university must estimate the value of the land and include this in its projection of project costs. This is especially true if the university will need to buy a new piece of land in the future to build the pool.

Failure to analyze the impact of any funding decision is a third common error. Most new capital spending projects have an effect on the overall organization.

If the university elects to build the new student recreation building, there may be side effects that will be felt by other parts of the university. Perhaps student fees will increase for activities that do not take place in the new recreation center. Visitors to the new facility will learn more about other activities at the university and might pay to attend them. This is an example of a positive side effect, also

known as a spillover effect. However, there can also be negative spillover effects. Students may decide to decrease their activities at other university venues or events in order to go to the new facility. This drop in attendance, and most likely income, at other locations is directly related to the new project. These types of spillover effects must be factored into projecting cash flows.

The failure to appreciate the impact of a capital decision on net working capital is another common error. New projects normally result in an increase in net working capital. Most projects need some cash on hand to pay for short-term expenses that arise.

For example, UH may need to purchase a scoreboard for the new facility using net working capital. Additional net working capital must be allotted for any new project. We could expect the increased investment in net working capital to be recouped by the university at the end of the project's life span. If the new facility has a life span of 30 years, at the end of that 30 years the scoreboard will no longer be needed. The scoreboard can possibly be sold for scrap value, and some of the initial investment in net working capital can be recouped. The increase in net working capital should almost be viewed as a loan that will be repaid at the end of the project's life span.

The last common error is including interest payments in the cash flow projections. We are interested only in the cash flows, both income and expense, that result directly from the project's assets. Interest payments and dividends are payments to creditors and shareholders. They are not expenses that result from the assets themselves. But perhaps more important, as already discussed, interest and dividend payments were included in calculating capital costs. If we also included them as cash outflows, we would be double-counting these payments. They have already been accounted for in the cost of capital so they do not need to be included as expenses (Brigham et al., 1999).

As you can see, some aspects of projecting cash flow are quite complex. The easiest way to explain the projection of cash flow for a capital project is probably through an example.

Let's assume that the Smiths are planning to expand their operations. As part of this expansion, they are investigating the possibility of constructing a new fitness facility. The following example will go through the process of projecting cash flows for a new fitness facility.

Projecting Cash Flow Example: New Fitness Facility

Pro forma financial statements must be developed to project cash flow for the Smiths' new fitness facility construction project. Pro formas are the easiest and most convenient method for projecting cash flow. To develop these pro forma statements we will need estimates of items such as fixed costs, variable costs, unit sales, and sales price per unit. Information must also be obtained on the change in net working capital and the total required investment. For our example, several numbers will be simplified. We will limit the life span of the facility to four years. A facility would probably last for over 20 years. Thus, while a four-year life span is somewhat unrealistic, it will make our example of projecting cash flow much easier to understand. The important thing is to understand the concepts of projecting cash flow.

Several assumptions will be made for the new facility. The new facility will be built on land valued at $250,000. The Smiths currently own the property and have already had an offer from another business to purchase the land for this amount. The construction cost of the building will be $400,000. The equipment that will be used, such as fitness machines, weights, and computers, will cost $100,000. The equipment can be fully depreciated over four years. For simplicity we will assume that the new facility can be constructed in one year and will open for business in the following year. Therefore, all of the land, building, and equipment costs will occur in the same **fiscal year** (2003), and income from the facility will occur from 2004 to 2007. This assumption is somewhat unrealistic, but it will make the example much easier to understand. Table 11.4 provides an overview of the investment costs for the project.

At the end of the building's four-year life span, the land will still have a value of $250,000 and the building will be worth $300,000. Therefore, straight-line depreciation will be used to depreciate the $200,000 loss in value over the four years. The value of the equipment will be equal to the cost of removing it from the site; therefore we will state that the overall value of the equipment in four years will be zero.

The Smiths believe that 1,000 memberships can be sold at an average price of $500 per year. The Smiths estimate that they will incur about $100 per person in variable costs such as staff salaries, benefits, and supplies such as towels. For a membership level of 1,000, fixed costs such as rent, electricity, and water will be approximately $70,000 per year. Again for simplicity, we will assume that there is no inflation and that the level of sales will remain at 1,000 memberships for each of the four years of operation.

Also, in order to open the new facility, the Smiths must initially increase their net working capital. The net working capital for the entire organization will be increased from its prior level of $65,000 to $75,000. The additional $10,000 in the first year must be included as a cash flow. However, the $10,000 will be retained at the end of the project, and that must also be included in the projections of total cash flow. The new facility will be subject to federal, state, and local taxes. The total cumulative tax rate will be 35%. Last, the WACC for the Smiths is 9.5%.

From all this information, we can construct our pro forma statement of cash flows as shown in table 11.5. As you can see, a pro forma cash flow statement can be quite complex. But it does capture the expected inflows and outflows of cash for the new facility during its four-year operational life span. There are several important aspects to discuss here. First, notice that depreciation is added back into the calculation of cash flow. Depreciation is an item that is included as part of a business' balance sheet in order to calculate its accounting value. However, it is not a flow of cash into or out of a firm. Therefore, although it is initially deducted in the cash flow statement, depreciation is ultimately added back into the cash flow. This is very important and is worth reemphasizing—the cash flow statement measures the inflows and outflows of cash for a firm, and depreciation is not a cash flow. The important result from the cash flow statement is that it provides a projection for the amount of cash that will accrue from operating the new facility. The cash flows range from $230,740 in 2004 to $250,740 in 2007. The difference in cash flows occurs because the Smiths must increase their net working capital in 2004 in order to start the operation. However, they will get this $10,000 back in 2007 when the facility closes.

The next step for the Smiths is to make the decision about under-

Table 11.4   Investment Outlays (2003—Year 1)

Fixed assets	Cost ($000)
Land	250
Building	400
Equipment	100
Total initial investment	**$750**

Table 11.5 Net Cash Flows

	2004 (Year 2)	2005 (Year 3)	2006 (Year 4)	2007 (Year 5)
Unit sales	1,000	1,000	1,000	1,000
Sales price	$500	$500	$500	$500
Net sales	**$500,000**	**$500,000**	**$500,000**	**$500,000**
Variable costs	$100,000	$100,000	$100,000	$100,000
Fixed costs	$70,000	$70,000	$70,000	$70,000
Depreciation (building)	$50,000	$50,000	$50,000	$50,000
Depreciation (equipment)	$25,000	$25,000	$25,000	$25,000
Earnings before taxes	**$255,000**	**$255,000**	**$255,000**	**$255,000**
Taxes (35%)	$89,250	$89,250	$89,250	$89,250
Projected net operating income	**$165,740**	**$165,740**	**$165,740**	**$165,740**
Add back noncash expenses*	$75,000	$75,000	$75,000	$75,000
Cash flow from operations	**$240,740**	**$240,740**	**$240,740**	**$240,740**
Investment in net working capital	($10,000)			$10,000
Total projected cash flow	**$230,740**	**$240,740**	**$240,740**	**$250,740**

* Depreciation is used for tax purposes. However, it is not a cash flow and therefore the $75,000 is added back into the cash flow statement.

taking this project. At this point, they have a projection on the cost of construction for the facility and the projected cash flows during the life of the operation. The importance of the time value of money must be mentioned. The Smiths are using capital today to construct a facility that will increase future cash flow. The future cash flow must be discounted to account for the time value of money.

 In the example of the Smiths' project, we will assume that there is no inflation. The time line in table 11.6 captures the cash flow analysis.

Based on the projected cash flows, it has been determined that the NPV of this project is $102,342.

Table 11.6 Time Line of Net Cash Flows (2003-2007)

Year	Net cash flow ($)
2003	–750,000
2004	230,000
2005	240,740
2006	240,740
2007	$250,740

Net present value: $102,364.
Internal rate of return: 10.7% versus 9.5% weighted average cost of capital.
Discounted payback period: 4.5 years from initial capital outlay at beginning of 2003 (Year 1).

Because the NPV is positive, it appears that this is a capital project that could be undertaken. However, the IRR is less than the cost of the WACC, 7.5% versus 9.5%. Therefore, a manager who uses IRR as a basis for capital budgeting decisions would reject this project. Finally, through use of the discounted payback method it was determined that it would take approximately 4.5 years to pay back the initial capital outlay of $750,000. As this example shows, there can be discrepancies across capital budgeting decision techniques.

All of these measures including IRR, NPV, WACC, and the discounted payback method can be used by a financial manager in making the capital budgeting decision for this project.

You should note that a project should not be undertaken solely because it has a positive NPV or an IRR that is higher than the WACC. Capital budgeting is one part of a sport organization's overall financial management strategy. The capital project must fit into the organization's long-term objectives. A sporting goods company may have an opportunity to invest in a capital project involving athlete representation that will result in a positive NPV. However, if this project does not fit into the overall organizational objective, it should not be undertaken.

Calculation of costs, along with estimates of future income resulting from capital investment, is used to project future cash flow, which is a key to making wise capital budgeting decisions.

CONCLUSION

Capital spending is an integral part of financial management. Ultimately, it ensures the long-term success of the organization. Sport businesses must develop capital budgets that will increase the stock value. The primary sources of capital for private or public sport businesses and organizations are debt and equity. Equity can take the form of preferred stock, common stock, and retained earnings. Government-owned and nonprofit sport organizations do not have ownership rights and therefore cannot raise capital through the sale of equity ownership interests. However, these organizations can raise money through donations and gifts. Many college athletic departments rely on donations as a major source of capital for spending in areas such as facility construction and equipment.

The cost of capital is a primary concern for all sport businesses. A capital project should be undertaken only if the projected revenue is greater than the projected cost. Otherwise, the funds can be more efficiently used in other ways; for example, they can be redistributed to shareholders or owners. There are several ways to calculate the costs of the various capital components. For example, the CAPM, bond-yield-plus-risk-premium model, and dividend growth model can all be used to calculate the cost of common stock. Once the cost of each capital component has been determined, the WACC method is most commonly used to calculate the overall cost of capital.

The cost of capital is only one piece of capital budgeting. Managers must also determine the additional revenue that will be generated from a capital project. Only new or marginal revenue should be considered when one is making this projection. Because of risk and uncertainty, it is best to establish a range of expected revenues. Best-case, worst-case, and most likely (also called middle-of-the-road) estimates of future revenues are recommended.

The next step is to use the cost and revenue estimates to project cash flow statements. These pro forma statements are critical to making a final capital budgeting decision. They allow a financial manager to organize and analyze a wealth of data related to a capital project.

A wise financial manager must analyze the validity of the projections that are included in calculating cash flows. If poor or inaccurate projections are used, the results are worthless. Accurate financial data are critical to the success of capital budgeting decisions. Businesses often develop several measures for projecting cash flows. For example, they might make several projections based on different economic conditions. Perhaps a business develops worst-case, best-case, and most likely projections. The worst-case projection would capture a situation in which sales are low, economic conditions are poor, and costs are larger than expected. Calculations of the WACC, NPV, and IRR would provide the financial manager with the absolutely worst result. This is valuable information to have when one is making a capital budgeting decision. Similarly, it is beneficial to know what the best-case scenario is. This projection provides a measure of the projected return when all variables are at their best. As you can probably guess, the most likely scenario would be the most realistic based on the available information. But although the most likely scenario is the most realistic, it is valuable to have projections for the range of other possible outcomes.

The final step is to make a decision on the capital project. The capital budgeting decision will affect the future direction of the sport organization. For example, constructing a new facility, signing a professional athlete to a long-term contract, or purchasing new technology has major effects on a sport business' future value. Three models used in capital budgeting are NPV, the discounted payback rule, and IRR. Each has inherent strengths and weaknesses. Financial managers should use the method or methods that they feel are most appropriate for their organization.

ASSIGNMENT

If you won $20 million in the lottery, would you rather receive one payment of $10 million or 25 payments of $500,000 a year for 20 years? Assume that the current interest rate is 10%.

RESEARCH PROJECTS

1. How would you project the cash flow for a planned golf course that you anticipate will cost $1 million a year in debt service, cost $1 million in operating expenses, and attract 4,000 rounds of golf per year?

2. Research the debt structure of any publicly traded sport company or corporation and analyze whether it is over- or undercapitalized.

CLASS DISCUSSION TOPICS

1. Why is a business' capital structure important?

2. What would happen if a business had too much in bonds or stocks as part of its capital structure?

3. Which funding option would be the most economical to issue if you were trying to raise $10 million?

4. What does flotation cost mean?

5. Why is the time value of money important?

6. Why is the payback rule important when we are analyzing financial issues?

7. What does the IRR mean?

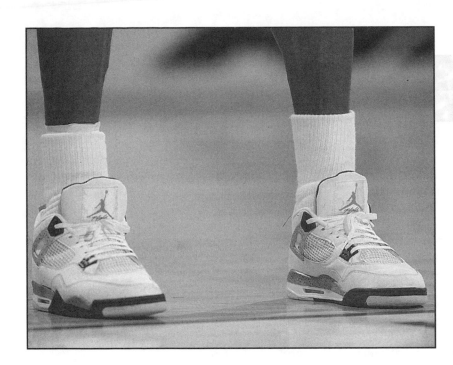

Short-Term Financial Management

CHAPTER OBJECTIVES

After studying this chapter, you should be able to do the following:

- Understand the definition of net working capital and see how net working capital is calculated.
- Discuss cash management by sport businesses, including how much cash to hold.
- Understand what is involved in the efficient collection and disbursement of cash.
- Describe how firms manage the granting of credit and how they set credit terms.
- Identify issues that arise as businesses engage in collections management, the conversion of accounts receivable to cash.

In chapters 7 and 11, we focused on long-range financing, particularly capital budgeting. In this chapter, our focus is the management of working capital, that is, the current assets and liabilities of a business. Working capital management can be viewed as short-term financial management because it centers on current assets and liabilities, which generate inflows or outflows of cash to or from a business within a year or less. For example, short-term financial management is occurring if Nike buys raw materials, pays for them in cash, and then uses the raw materials to produce and sell athletic shoes within one year for cash. By contrast, capital budgeting is not considered short-term financial management because it tends to focus on projects of several years' duration. For example, if Nike buys machinery to assemble athletic shoes, the machine may be used for several years until it either becomes obsolete or wears out. The analysis of the decision to buy the machinery relies on the tools of capital budgeting that were introduced in chapter 11.

In this chapter, we focus on several key areas of short-term financial management. These areas include cash management, credit management, and collections management. But first we briefly review current assets and liabilities.

Review of Current Assets and Liabilities

Figure 12.1 provides a breakdown of current assets and current liabilities for all manufacturing corporations in the United States in 2001. Current assets are cash and other assets that are expected to be converted to cash within one year. Current assets were $1,489.1 billion, while current liabilities were $1,219.8 billion. Net working capital (current assets minus current liabilities) equaled $269.3 billion.

As shown in figure 12.1, accounts receivable are an extremely important current asset based on the value of accounts receivable relative to other current assets. Accounts receivable consist of unpaid bills for goods and services that have been sold to customers.

 In the case of the Smiths, to operate the fitness center they would bill their patrons for membership dues. When the patrons are initially billed for membership dues, accounts receivable increase. As membership dues are paid, the **account balance** in accounts receivable declines and the balance in cash increases.

Inventories consist of raw materials, work in progress, and finished goods awaiting shipment to customers. Inventories are discussed in more detail in chapter 13. Cash consists of currency, funds in checking accounts, and funds in savings accounts. Marketable securities include commercial paper, short-term unsecured debt that is sold by other firms, U.S. Treasury bills, and state and local government-issued debt.

Other current assets include prepaid expenses, such as rent, utilities, and insurance, that have been purchased for use within one year. Prepaid expenses are items of value that have future usefulness in business operations. For example, all businesses purchase various types of insurance policies for protection against burglary, fire, personal injury, business interruption, and injury and death to employees (e.g., workers' compensation policies). Insurance premiums, the cost of insurance, are typically paid in advance. The unexpired portion of the already paid insurance policy is a current asset.

One of the key issues for financial managers in any business is choosing how much cash to hold. This choice involves various trade-offs. On the one hand, holding large amounts of cash reduces the likelihood that the business will run out of cash and have to raise more on short notice. On the other hand, there is a cost in the form of lost investment income as a result of holding cash balances rather than investing those proceeds in marketable securities that can earn a return.

From a balance sheet perspective, one business' assets are another business' liabilities. As an ex-

CURRENT ASSETS		CURRENT LIABILITIES	
	(in billions)		*(in billions)*
Cash	$187.9	Short-term debt	$195.5
Marketable securities	106.2	Accounts payable	333.9
Accounts receivable	463.3	Accrued income taxes	52.2
Inventories	470.9	Current payments due on long-term debt	85.3
Other current assets	260.8	Other current liabilities	552.9
Total	**1,489.1**	**Total**	**1,219.8**

Figure 12.1 Current assets and liabilities for all U.S. manufacturing corporations in 2001.

ample, assume that Nike buys laces for its Air Jordan athletic shoes from a wholesale shoelace supplier that bills Nike for the shoelaces after shipment. Until Nike pays the bill, the balance owed by Nike is part of the wholesale shoelace supplier's accounts receivable, a short-term asset. At the same time, the unpaid bill is a short-term liability for Nike. This is the reason that accounts payable are a major short-term liability for firms. Accounts payable are outstanding payments owed to other companies.

To finance investments in current assets, a company must rely on various short-term loans. Commercial banks are the largest source of short-term loans for most businesses (Brealey & Myers, 1996). Issuing commercial paper is another technique large corporations use to borrow needed funds. Although many short-term loans are unsecured, companies may offer inventories or receivables as security, or may sell inventories or accounts receivable to financial institutions at a discount. Short-term loans, including bank lending, commercial paper, secured loans, and inventories or receivables sold at a discount to financial institutions are discussed in chapter 8.

When businesses either issue long-term debt or take out a loan that is paid down over more than one year, all payments due within the next year or sooner are classified as current payments on long-term debt. Current payments on long-term debt are viewed as a current liability.

Another current liability is accrued income taxes. This category results from differences in the way revenues and expenses are reported for income tax purposes and the way they are accounted for in order to prepare an income statement. These differences in reporting income for tax purposes and for the objective of preparing financial statements are particularly prevalent in large publicly traded companies. For larger companies, it is not unusual to try to claim all available expenses that reduce tax liabilities while showing stockholders the largest amount of reported income possible under generally accepted accounting principles (GAAP; see chapter 5) (Fraser & Ormiston, 2001).[1] As a result of the differences in reporting of income for tax purposes, as opposed to GAAP, it is perfectly legal for companies to report net income on an income statement that differs from what is reported to the IRS.

Other current liabilities include accrued liabilities and unearned or deferred credits. Accrued liabilities result from the recording of expenses at the time they are incurred, but prior to the time they will actually be paid. Thus they are liabilities because there will be an eventual outflow of cash to satisfy particular obligations.

 As an example of an accrued liability, the Boston Celtics reported $1,226,316 in deferred compensation as a current liability as of June 30, 2001.[2] This consisted primarily of player salaries that would be paid within a one-year period.

Numerous companies record advance payments for services or products as a liability when the cash is received. When advance payments are recorded this way, they are recognized as unearned, or deferred, credits.

 The Boston Celtics reported as a current liability $6,498,726 in deferred game revenues as of June 30, 2001; these were either advance sales of single-game tickets or season tickets.[3]

Cash Management

In 1995, individuals and corporations in the United States held roughly $1.15 trillion in cash, consisting of $370 billion in currency and $780 billion in checking deposits in commercial banks (Brealey & Myers, 1996). Cash does not earn interest, yet individuals and corporations hold large amounts of it anyway. The reason for holding cash is the need for liquidity, that is, having an asset on hand for immediate transactions.

As a part of cash management, financial managers face decisions about how much liquidity their business should retain. If the business decides to keep excessive amounts of cash in the bank, then it loses interest that it could have earned through investing that cash in marketable securities. If the business keeps too little cash in the bank, it will be forced to make repeated sales of securities in order to pay its bills. These repeated sales of securities will also saddle the business with excessive brokerage and other costs associated with each transaction. Too little cash can also lead to frequent trips to banks to obtain loans or utilize lines of credit.

---

[1]See Fraser & Ormiston (2001, p. 65) for a more extensive discussion of differences between taxable and reported income.

[2]As reported on the balance sheet of Celtics Basketball Holdings, L.P., which is included in the Form 10-K filed with the Securities and Exchange Commission by the Boston Celtics Limited Partnership II on September 21, 2001.

[3]Celtics Basketball Holdings, L.P., balance sheet, Form 10-K.

In addition to dealing with trade-offs between holding cash and holding marketable securities, a second facet of cash management involves the efficient collection and disbursement of cash. This aspect of cash management requires an understanding of the relationship between businesses and their banks.

Liquidity

A simple way of looking at the trade-offs between holding cash and holding marketable securities was developed by Baumol (1952). In Baumol's framework, a firm has to choose between holding cash and holding U.S. Treasury bills. Baumol viewed cash as something that is steadily depleted to pay bills. When the business runs out of cash, it replenishes its cash supplies by selling Treasury bills that it holds. For each additional dollar of cash held, there is lost interest that could have been obtained through holding Treasury bills. If too little cash is held, a cost results from the brokerage expense associated with selling Treasury bills to replenish cash.

In the Baumol model, the cash management problem is shaped in terms of the optimum amount of Treasury bills sold each time the cash balance has to be replenished. The optimum amount of Treasury bills sold, **Q**, is equal to

$$Q = (2 \times a \times c/i)^{0.5}$$

Q = the optimum amount of Treasury bills sold

a = annual disbursements

c = cost per sale of Treasury bills

i = interest rate

Assume that the interest rate on Treasury bills is 5%, that the cost per sale is $30, and that the business pays out $1 million per year in cash. The optimum Q is then

$$Q = (2 \times 1,000,000 \times 30/.05)^{0.5}$$
$$= \$34,641$$

The firm will sell $34,641 of Treasury bills approximately 29 times per year ($1,000,000 / $34,461), or slightly more often than once every two weeks. The average cash balance held is equal to one-half of the amount of Treasury bills sold. In our example, the average cash balance is equal to

$$\$34,641 / 2 = \$17,321$$

We should note that in the Baumol formula the optimum amount of Treasury bills sold decreases as the interest rate rises. In other words, it pays to hold lower cash balances as interest rates increase. On the other hand, as the brokerage cost per sale of Treasury bills increases, the Baumol model implies that the business should hold higher cash balances to avoid the cost of selling Treasury bills, which would be greater than the interest earned.

 Assume that Sport Manufacturing Company (SMC) is finding that its outgoing cash is currently exceeding incoming cash by $500,000 per week. The company's financial managers need to determine the appropriate amount of cash for SMC to have on hand. If SMC begins the current week with $1 million in cash, its cash balance will drop to zero in exactly two weeks because $500,000 of the firm's initial cash will be consumed each week. Sport Manufacturing Company's average cash balance will then equal $1,000,000 / 2 = $500,000.

By contrast, if SMC started with $3 million in cash, cash would last exactly six weeks as a result of SMC's consuming $500,000 per week in cash. The average cash balance over the six-week period would be $3,000,000 / 2 = $1,500,000. What this illustrates is that if SMC sets the initial cash balance at a higher level, it will not have to replenish cash as frequently. As a result, SMC's brokerage expenses will be reduced. The trade-off is that by maintaining higher cash balances, SMC sacrifices interest income that could have been earned on marketable securities.

In order to use the Baumol model to determine the optimum cash balance, assume that the cost per sale of Treasury bills equals $1,000 and that the interest rate on Treasury bills equals 3%. Annual disbursements equal $500,000 × 52 weeks = $26,000,000. Based on the Baumol model,

$$Q = (2 \times \$26,000,000 \times \$1,000/0.03)^{0.5}$$
$$= \$1,316,561$$

Based on this calculation, Sport Manufacturing Company will liquidate Treasury bills approximately 20 times per year ($26,000,000 / $1,316,561).

Although the Baumol model demonstrates the analytical issues involved when we consider trade-offs between holding cash and marketable securities, it is simplistic relative to real-world business decisions. Unlike the situation described in the Baumol model, businesses do not deplete their cash reserves on a steady basis. Firms may find that over a one-month period there is a net inflow of cash as customers pay bills, whereas in the next month there is a net outflow of cash as suppliers are paid. There are more complicated models that allow for more unpredictable outflows and inflows (see Brealey & Myers, 1996).

Another limitation of the Baumol model is its assumption that the only option other than holding cash is to invest in Treasury bills. In the real world, it is possible to invest in other assets such as stocks. As discussed in detail in the section "Marketable Securities" in chapter 3, stocks are risky relative to Treasury bills.

In our discussion of cash management, we have ignored another possibility for cash replenishment, which is borrowing, rather than selling marketable securities. Numerous businesses draw on bank lines of credit when cash reserves are low. With borrowing, the analysis becomes more complicated since the interest rate paid to the bank is likely to be higher than the rate earned on marketable securities. If you were the financial manager of SMC, you would face a trade-off between the interest that would be sacrificed on sold-off marketable securities and the interest rate that would have to be paid on borrowings. If the interest charged on borrowed funds is substantially above the rate earned on marketable securities, selling off marketable securities as a means of raising cash would be preferable to borrowing additional amounts.

As a matter of practice, businesses that have idle cash will invest in marketable securities with maturities of one year or less, that is, money market instruments. Businesses may put their cash into **money market mutual funds,** which invest in short-term securities for a management fee. One of the benefits is the diversification provided by the fund manager's investment in many different short-term instruments. In addition, banks offer "sweep accounts" for corporate customers. The bank takes all available funds in a sweep account at the end of each business day and invests them for the corporate customer. Thus, the rate of return is higher than in other traditional bank accounts.

The reason that businesses invest idle cash balances in money market instruments is that for any given change in interest rates, the values of longer-maturity debt securities change more than those of shorter-maturity debt securities. Thus investors holding instruments with longer-term maturities face greater risk due to greater fluctuations in value associated with interest rate swings. This risk is known as interest rate risk. Given that the invested excess cash balances of the business may be needed at a moment's notice for large disbursements, busi-

nesses invest in money market instruments so that they are less subject to interest rate risk. As discussed in chapter 6, the expected returns on the instruments with shorter maturities are also lower because of the reduction in risk.

Collection and Disbursement of Cash

When businesses pay bills or receive payment for debts, they have the possibility of earning additional revenue or of losing the opportunity cost to earn additional revenue. Because of the time delays associated with writing, depositing, and cashing checks, some money can be lost. Checks that are written by the firm and not yet cleared represent payment **float.** Checks received by the firm and deposited, but not yet cleared, represent availability float. Net float represents the net effect of checks in the process of collection and is equal to the difference between payment float and availability float. The next example illustrates net float.

 Although we have discussed a business' liquidity, it is necessary to be more precise about how cash enters and exits the corporation and how the available cash balance is computed. Assume that SMC has $1 million on deposit in a bank checking account. Suppose also that SMC writes a $300,000 check to a supplier of graphite for its tennis rackets. Immediately, SMC will adjust its ledgers to show a cash balance of $700,000. The company's bank will not learn anything about this check until the supplier has received the check, the supplier has deposited the check at the supplier's bank, and that bank has presented the check to SMC's bank. While waiting for the check to clear, SMC's bank continues to show in its ledger that the company has $1 million in its account. Thus SMC gains the benefit of an extra $300,000 in the bank while the check is still clearing. This extra $300,000 is the payment float.

Although float sounds like something that SMC can take advantage of, it is really a two-way street. Assume that at the same time SMC writes the $300,000 check, SMC receives a $100,000 check from the purchasing department of Sports Authority, which keeps SMC's golf clubs in stock in its national chain of sporting goods stores. Sport Manufacturing Company deposits the $100,000 check, and both the company and bank ledger balances are increased by $100,000. Unfortunately for SMC, it does not have access to the $100,000 immediately; SMC's bank does not actually have the $100,000 until it has sent the check to and received the payment from Sports Authority's bank. While SMC's bank is waiting for the check, it makes SMC wait to have access to the $100,000 payment. Under current Federal Reserve regulations, this wait can be anywhere from one to five business days for most checks. While the bank waits for payment, the bank will show that SMC has an available balance of $1 million and an availability float equal to $100,000.

In effect, SMC gains from the payment float of $300,000, but loses as a result of the $100,000 availability float. The difference between payment float and availability float is the net float. In our example, the net float is $300,000 − $100,000 = $200,000. This can be important because if the net float exists for five days and the bank pays interest of 5% on the account, SMC will gain approximately $140 in interest during the five-day period. Although this may seem insignificant, if SMC is able to maintain an average of $200,000 per day in float because of the timing of all of its transactions, the interest earned per year would be $10,000.[4]

If you are a financial manager for SMC, your true concern is with the available balance, rather than the balance that is recorded on the bank ledger. If you know that there may be a one- or two-week delay before some of the checks written to suppliers are presented for payment, then you may be able to get by on a smaller cash balance. This is what is known as playing the float.

In effect, you can increase your available cash balance by increasing your net float. This means that checks received from customers should be cleared rapidly, while checks to suppliers are cleared more slowly. Although managing float may not seem like a significant activity for a business, for a large company it can be very significant. Assume that a company averages $100 million per day in sales. If it can increase collections by one day, it frees up $100 million, which is then available to the shareholders or for capital projects.

Although managing float is a legitimate business activity, there have been instances in which financial managers have gotten carried away. In 1985, the brokerage firm E.F. Hutton pleaded guilty to 2,000 separate counts of mail and wire fraud. E.F. Hutton admitted to creating nearly $1 billion of float by shuffling funds between its branches and through various accounts at different banks. These activities resulted in E.F. Hutton's incurring a $2 million fine and agreeing to repay various banks for losses that they incurred.[5]

There are several techniques for accelerating collections. One technique that many large companies use to speed up collections is concentration banking. This involves customers making payments at a local office as opposed to corporate headquarters. The local branch office then deposits the checks into a local bank branch. Surplus funds from the local bank account are then periodically transferred to a concentration account at one of the company's main banks. These transfers can be made electronically, which allows for next-day availability of the funds at corporate headquarters.

Concentration banking reduces float for two reasons. First, because the branch office is closer to the customer, mailing time is reduced. Second, since the customer's check is more likely to be drawn on a local bank, the time it takes for the check to clear is lessened.

Concentration banking can also be combined with a lockbox system. In a lockbox system, the company pays a local bank to handle the administrative chores, so that it is not necessary to establish a branch office to handle receipt of payments. A company with a national market will establish regions as collection points. Within each region, the company rents a locked post office box. All customers within a region are then required to send payments to the locked post office box in that region. The local bank, on behalf of the company, empties the box regularly and deposits the checks in the company's local bank account. Surplus funds are transferred periodically to one of the company's principal banks. The number of collection points, or regions, that are required depends on how quickly the mail is delivered.

 Assume that SMC decides to work with a West Coast bank in setting up a lockbox in Sacramento, California, for handling payments from customers in the western half of the United States. Suppose that the average number of daily payments to the lockbox is 500, the average size of payment is $1,000, the rate of interest per day that can be earned on funds invested in marketable securities is 0.02%, the savings in mailing time is 1.4 days, and the sav-

---

[4]This analysis does not include the additional interest earned because of compounding.

[5]This is discussed in Brealey & Myers, 1996.

ings in processing time is 0.5 days. The lockbox would result in SMC's increasing its collected balance by 500 items per day × $1,000 per item × (1.4 + 0.5) days saved = $950,000. The $950,000 invested at a return of 0.02% per day equals $950,000 × 0.0002 = $190 per day. Typically, the bank's charge for providing the lockbox service will be on a per check basis. Suppose the bank charges $0.30 per check. This results in a daily charge that equals $0.30 × 500 = $150 per day. Thus, SMC gains $190 − $150 = $40 per day, which does not include additional savings that result from SMC's not processing its own checks.

Slowing down disbursements is another technique for increasing net float. In extreme cases, businesses maintain disbursement accounts in several locations around the country. These businesses then use computer algorithms that look up each supplier's zip code so that a check is drawn on the most distant disbursement account.

Assume that SMC's corporate headquarters is located in Connecticut. If SMC pays its suppliers with checks drawn on a New York bank account, it may find that when the check is deposited by the supplier, it is only another one to two days before the check is presented to SMC's bank for payment. SMC can set up disbursement checking accounts in different parts of the United States (for example, arranging to write checks drawn on banks in such remote locations as Helena, Montana; Pierre, South Dakota; or Abilene, Texas). In these cases, it may be three to four days before each check is presented for payment. This allows SMC the opportunity to gain additional float days.

Historically, collection and disbursement activity involved movement of paper checks. There is currently a movement toward more electronic collection and disbursement. In the past, the main hindrance to paperless activities was that many smaller businesses and consumers were unable to operate electronically. This is changing as the IRS and state and local tax authorities are moving in the direction of electronic transmission of payroll and income tax payments. To the extent that businesses and individuals are increasingly using electronic funds transfers to pay bills, there is potential for faster collections and reduced availability float.

Companies that are electronically connected to their banks, suppliers, and customers have noticed various advantages. For example, in 1992, Campbell

Soup reported that it had costs of $7 per wire transfer while an automated clearinghouse transfer was only $0.08 (Moss, 1992). Record-keeping and basic transactions are easy to automate with electronic collections and disbursements. Campbell Soup was able to handle cash management, short-term borrowing and lending, and bank relationships with a total staff of seven, even though the company's domestic cash flow was $5 billion (Moss, 1992).

> *Cash management involves making decisions about liquidity, specifically about how much cash a business should have on hand. This in turn requires the business to examine and manage how it collects and disburses cash.*

Credit Management

The amount of accounts receivable held by the business is determined by the extent to which that business sells on credit, as opposed to cash. In addition, the terms of credit become important in determining the amount of accounts receivable appearing on the balance sheet. For example, if SMC offers its customers the terms of net 30 days, the customers have 30 days from the date of purchase to pay the amount owed. Under these circumstances, most of SMC's customers will pay near the end of the 30 days. If SMC wants to encourage its customers to pay earlier, SMC may offer terms of 1/10/30 (1%/10, net 30), which means that customers have 30 days to pay the balance owed and receive a 1% discount if payment occurs within 10 days of purchase. Another formula for credit terms is 2/10/30, which means that the discount is 2% if payment occurs within 10 days.

In the case of 1/10/30, the customer who pays SMC after 10 days in effect is receiving 20 days of credit at interest equal to the 1% forgone discount. Since there are roughly 18 such periods in the year (360 days a year / 20 days each period), the annual interest equals 18 × 1%, or 18%. If SMC changed the terms to 2/10/60, the cost of credit for 60 days minus the cost for 10 days (for paying early) would equal the cost for 50 days, which is 2% in lost discounts. This is equivalent to 360 / 50 = 7.2 such periods per year, or 7.2 × 2% = 14.4% interest per year.

To summarize thus far, the terms of a sale define what the cash customer pays for the merchandise.

In addition, the terms of sale set the interest rate charged for credit. If SMC increases the discount from 1/10/30 to 2/10/30, the price for the cash customer has been reduced, but there has been an increase in the interest rate charged to the credit buyer.

Generally speaking, competition causes companies within an industry to have similar credit terms. In the textile and jewelry industries, it is quite common for firms to offer such terms as 8/10/60 or 8/10/90 (8%/10, net 60 or 90) (Vaughn, 1997). At net 90, this is equivalent to a 36% annual interest rate, which suggests that the customer should borrow from a bank or other lender rather than buy on credit.

If a customer has a poor credit record, it may behoove SMC to insist that the buyer pay either COD (cash on delivery) or CBD (cash before delivery). There are various ways to assess the creditworthiness of a customer. One way is to have a credit agency perform a credit check. The most prominent of the credit agencies is Dun & Bradstreet. Credit agencies typically report the experience that other firms have had in collecting payments from the customer. Credit bureaus also provide this kind of information. Similar information is also available over the Internet through sites such as **www.BusinessCreditUSA.com,** which provides some basic credit information.

The business' own bank can do a credit check by contacting the customer's bank, which will provide information on the customer's average bank balance, access to bank credit, and reputation.

If the customer is a publicly traded firm, there are inexpensive ways of collecting information about how this customer is assessed in the financial markets. Although a precipitous drop in a company's stock price does not imply that the firm is going into bankruptcy, it indicates that the company's future prospects are no longer as bright as they were previously.

 For example, SMC may be supplying its tennis rackets and golf equipment to a publicly traded chain of sporting goods stores and can easily look up Moody's or Standard & Poor's rating. Moody's and Standard & Poor's rate the outstanding bonds of publicly traded companies in terms of the likelihood of default. Given the availability of stock price data on the Internet through such sites as Yahoo! Finance, SMC can look at recent behavior of the customer's stock price.

> *Companies manage credit by setting the terms of credit, that is, the length of the payment period and the size of any cash discounts.*

Collections Management

In addition to managing credit, it is important for businesses to manage collections. Collections management focuses on converting receivables to cash and refers to efforts made to obtain payment of past-due accounts. In addition, the credit manager needs to have records of the collections experience of the company in dealing with customers who currently have credit terms. This information is relevant for determining whether credit should continue to be extended in the future.

The Benefits of Electronic Funds Transfers

One of the most important developments in collections management over the past 20 years has been electronic funds transfers (EFTs). EFTs are now utilized by 80% to 90% of all health clubs in the United States. The EFT systems withdraw funds automatically from a customer's bank account. Because the withdrawals are done electronically and at set times, such as the fifth day of each month, the process streamlines the collection and accounting process (Ernest, 2002). This process can save a significant amount of time and lost cash due to payment delays. A third party, which can also provide additional support such as membership retention and marketing assistance, often administers the process. The Smiths could also utilize EFTs to establish an accurate flow of revenue upon which a bank loan or other borrowing could be secured. Another benefit of such a payment system is the time lag for terminating the service. If someone wants to cancel the service they have to give advance notice; otherwise they would have to make an additional payment, which represents additional cash the Smiths might not otherwise have received from that customer. Furthermore, if a customer breaches the contract, the Smiths could keep collecting the disputed amount until the matter is resolved without incurring a significant collection problem.

A business' general collections experience also needs to be monitored, since this will determine whether the firm's terms are appropriate. One reporting tool involves the average **days sales outstanding,** or days in receivables. Our example involving SMC can illustrate the use of this tool.

Assume that the terms on all SMC sales to customers are 1/10/30. Assume that 65% of the customers take the 1% discount and pay on day 10, while the remaining 35% pay on day 30. The average days sales outstanding equals 0.65×10 days + 0.35×30 days = 17 days.

Since payments to a business tend to arrive more sporadically than in our example, it is necessary to first calculate average daily sales. As noted in the Introduction to the Case Studies (p. 2), SMC's annual sales are $4 million. Therefore, its average daily sales = $4,000,000 / 365 days = $10,959 per day. The average daily sales outstanding is equal to the average daily sales divided by current accounts receivable. Once the average daily sales is calculated, then that figure is divided into the existing accounts receivable to obtain the average daily sales outstanding. Assume that accounts receivable equal $186,300; then average daily sales outstanding equals $186,300 / $10,959 = 17 days. This means that when making a purchase, the average SMC customer pays in 17 days.

If SMC uses daily or weekly data on sales and accounts receivable to compute average daily sales outstanding and finds that average daily sales outstanding stays at 17 days over a one-month period, then some customers are paying later. In addition, some accounts may be overdue. With sales outstanding staying at 17 days, a significant number of SMC customers are not paying their bills immediately or taking advantage of early payment discounts. Although some customers might pay early, it appears that more customers are waiting longer than the discount period. Keep in mind that for a company such as SMC that has seasonal sales patterns, the calculated average daily sales outstanding will fluctuate during the year. The reason is that for these businesses, receivables are low before the major selling season and high afterward. As a result, average daily sales outstanding on a particular date may need to be compared to past averages for the same date.

An aging report can provide more detailed information. An aging report tabulates receivables by the accounts' ages. Table 12.1 presents an example. Note that in table 12.1, a significant number of customers are past due (40% are accounts outstanding more than 30 days). Any company that displays a report like the one shown in table 12.1 has serious collections problems and should be reviewing its collections policies.

The usual procedure for collecting overdue accounts is to send an invoice to past-due accounts. If the invoice does not result in payment, then follow-up letters are sent to the customer concerning the delinquency of the account. In addition, several telephone calls can be made to the customer. There is a very fine line here that any company needs to appreciate. If a company is too aggressive, it could lose a customer who might be facing some temporary hard times. On the other hand, if the company does not push, it could face repeated abuses by customers who do not pay their debts as they come due. If all these efforts by the company are not fruitful, then the company may turn to a collections agency. Typically, collections agencies charge anywhere from 15% to 50% of the amount collected. An additional option is to retain an attorney in order to file suit against the customer. Yet another option is to write off the debt as a bad debt. However, to be able to deduct these losses from income for tax purposes, the company has to show that it made "reasonable" efforts to collect the debt.[6]

Table 12.1 Sample Aging Report

Age of account	Percent of total accounts receivable
0 to 30 days	60%
31 to 60 days	15%
61 to 90 days	15%
91 to 120 days	6%
Over 121 days	4%
Total	**100%**

---

[6]The rules governing the deduction of bad-debt losses are complicated. Whether a company has to go to court to obtain a judgment against the debtor depends on the particular situation. For example, if the company can show that a judgment from the court would be uncollectible, then going to court is unnecessary. Bankruptcy is generally considered evidence by the IRS that at least a portion of the debt can be viewed as bad debt. The deduction of bad-debt losses is summarized in IRS Publication 535, *Business Expenses* (2001).

For smaller businesses, it may be too expensive to employ someone in credit management and collections. Under these circumstances, the business may sell its accounts receivable directly to a financial institution, called a factor. The factor buys the receivables of the firm at a discount, which is typically 1% (Brealey & Myers, 1996). The company and the factor agree on credit terms for each customer. The customer sends payments to the factor, which bears the risk that the customer will not pay. Factors are discussed in chapter 8.

> *Collections management refers to the measures that businesses take to convert accounts receivable into cash and to obtain payment for past-due accounts.*

CONCLUSION

This chapter outlines the various types of current assets and liabilities, known as working capital on a company's balance sheet, including cash, marketable securities, accounts receivable, inventories, short-term loans, accounts payable, accrued income taxes, and current payments due on long-term debt. Net working capital refers to current assets minus current liabilities, as highlighted in chapter 5.

Financial managers face trade-offs between holding cash and holding interest-bearing securities. If interest rates are high, it is desirable to hold relatively less cash. Borrowing serves as an alternative to liquidating securities to replenish cash in the event of a deficiency. The cash that appears in company ledgers is not the same as the available balance in the company's bank account. The difference is net float. We discuss how companies can play the float so as to reduce their required cash holdings, as well as how companies can manage the float by speeding up collections and slowing down payments.

The chapter also deals with the intricacies of credit management, specifically establishing the length of the payment period and the size of any cash discounts. We discuss sources of information that can be used to assess a customer's creditworthiness, as well as collection measures and procedures. All these steps help create a plan of action to most effectively utilize a business' cash reserves for reinvestment or to pay expenses such as manufacturing and inventory costs, which are discussed in the next chapter.

ASSIGNMENTS

1. A sporting goods distributor has daily cash receipts of $60,000. A recent analysis of collections indicated that customer payments were in the mail an average of three days. Once the payments were received, it took two days to process and deposit them. It takes an additional three days to clear the banking system.

   a. What is the availability float in days?

   b. The distributor is able to earn 0.8% per day on deposits to its bank money market account. Is it advisable for the firm to pay the bank $5,000 to reduce the availability float by three days?

2. Sport Manufacturing Company's accounts receivable totaled $3,500,000 as of May 31, 2002. The following chart shows a breakdown of outstanding accounts on the basis of the month in which the initial credit sale was made. The firm extends 30-day credit terms to its customers.

Month of credit sale	Accounts receivable ($000)
May 2002	1,100
April 2002	900
March 2002	540
February 2002	760
March 2002 or earlier	200
	3,500

   a. Prepare an aging schedule for SMC's accounts receivable as of May 31, 2002.

   b. Use the aging schedule to evaluate SMC's credit and collection activities.

RESEARCH PROJECTS

1. Research some of the Internet-based innovations that are being introduced into the marketplace for collection and disbursement purposes and their relevance to sport business.

2. Review the financial statements of a publicly traded sport-related company to determine its net working capital.

CLASS DISCUSSION TOPICS

1. How does the appearance of lower-cost brokerage services over the Internet affect the cash balances that a firm must maintain?

2. How should a business monitor collections activity?

3. How has the advent of greater volumes of electronic funds transfers affected the accumulation of float by a business?

Inventory and Production Management

CHAPTER OBJECTIVES

After studying this chapter, you should be able to do the following:

- Distinguish between variable and fixed costs.
- Understand how to determine product costs and prices and how to reduce costs.
- Understand inventory management.
- Understand how to forecast inventory needs.
- Understand the costs associated with managing inventory.
- Calculate the optimum economic ordering quantity.
- Describe inventory turnover and inventory obsolescence.
- Calculate manufacturing costs, including labor costs.

This chapter focuses on inventory and production management, which are critical components of the manufacturing analysis process. All companies that manufacture products need to carefully examine how they use their inventory to insure they are not wasting any money. Similarly, companies need to examine how they produce products to maximize efficiency and minimize waste. Although we use SMC as an example throughout this chapter, the principles illustrated also apply to other sport-related businesses. The Smiths might have exercise equipment stored in inventory. They might also need to stock produce for the juice bar, and the produce would be subject to spoilage if not used soon enough. Similarly, the Celtics or the University of Houston have to purchase souvenir goods for the concession shops. This inventory would become obsolete if the team changed its logo. Thus, inventory management issues are critical for all sport businesses.

Although finance is not all about expenses, managing and controlling expenses is one of the primary financial disciplines. Controlling expenses is one of the most important elements in inventory and production management. If inventory is not utilized, money is wasted and expenses for storage costs increase. If a machine sits idle, the business loses money from the lack of production, and expenses increase for machine downtime. This chapter deals first with business costs and then with the entire inventory management process, including forecasting demand, purchasing optimum quantities, storing inventory, auditing inventory, and utilizing inventory. We then discuss production analysis with a primary focus on manufacturing costs, break-even analysis, variance analysis, and labor cost concerns.

Business Costs

As highlighted in chapter 7, a business has to plan for various expenses. Expenses can include office supplies, raw inventory, facility costs (from mortgages to electrical bills), corporate perks such as season tickets, and an endless number of other expenses. It is very difficult to categorize every dollar spent by a business because some expenses are often not recorded separately, but rather grouped into a generic category called general expenses. General expenses for a sport-related business can be highly diverse, as seen in the following example of the Boston Celtics.

 The Boston Celtics have significant expenses over and beyond player- and coaching-related expenses. The following are some of the possible operating expenses for the FleetCenter.

- Utilities, which can include lights, sewage, electricity, gas or propane, air conditioning, heating systems, and telephones
- Cleaning the facility after a game, which can include playing areas, seating areas, locker rooms, bathrooms, team offices, pressrooms, and concession areas
- Game day personnel, which can include ticket takers; ushers; security officers; and traffic control, police, fire, EMT, and related personnel (either directly hired or outsourced to an outside vendor)
- Insurance-related expenses, which could entail the following insurance policies: general liability, property damage, comprehensive, business interruption, air casualty, key person, and employee practices liability insurance, as well as other related policies
- Ordinary repair and maintenance costs for everything from computers and photocopiers to athletic trainers' equipment or the scoreboard
- Miscellaneous expenses, which can include the following:
  - Scoreboard operations
  - Maintenance costs for playing surfaces including repairing, repainting, and the like
  - Lighting systems
  - Floor crews
  - All office equipment and supplies
  - All employee benefits, whether health insurance or retirement accounts
  - Parking lot maintenance including lighting, repainting, and so on

These expenses can be diagrammed in the same way as the expenses faced by any sport business. An expense map is similar to a road map and identifies what areas of the business are incurring expenses and where possible cost savings can come from. A typical partial expense map could look like the following:

Expenses

Personnel	Maintenance
Player salaries	Storage
Coaches	Marketing
Scouts	Advertising
Administrative	Graphics
Legal	Travel
Accountant	Media
Insurance	Media food table
Facility	Media guides
Utilities	Modem lines

As discussed in chapter 7, if the Texas Rangers pay $250 million for Alex Rodriquez, how will such a salary affect ticket prices? Player salaries are a fixed expense; that is, at the start of the season the team knows what its total salary obligation will be except for possible bonuses and reductions in salaries if players are injured, cut, or traded. Knowing how much its payroll is, the team can determine all other expenses. Similarly, the team can determine the potential revenue from broadcast rights, luxury seating, and sponsorship income. On the basis of these potential income areas, the team can examine how much it might need to charge ticket holders to ensure that it can cover its costs. Thus expenses have a direct impact on prices of various items, from tickets to concessions.

We all know basic costs such as the cost of going to McDonald's® and spending $5 for a meal. When you do this, the cost to you is $5. If you earn $10 per hour, you can calculate your cost as 50% of your hourly wage. On the basis of an 8-hour day, you could calculate your $5 meal as 6.25% of your daily wage. In essence, cost analysis is similar for a sport business.

Types of Business Costs

There are several types of costs that any business might face. An example of a variable cost for a sport business might be salaries for the ushers, which could change from one game to the next according to the number of expected fans. An example of a fixed cost, on the other hand, is a team's lease payment to a city, which needs to be made no matter how many games are played. The following sections deal with the various types of costs that accrue in businesses.

Variable Costs

Variable costs vary with each unit produced as seen in the following SMC case study example.

If SMC acquired $2 million in steel in 1999, the company bought raw materials that would be classified as variable costs. The company might need to purchase more steel or might have too much. If SMC sees an increase in orders and needs to make 1,000 more golf clubs than it had previously planned to make, the variable costs would increase. However, even if SMC needs to purchase more steel, the variable cost per golf club could actually decrease because SMC might be able to buy the greater quantity of steel at a discount and the variable cost per club would then decline.

Semivariable Costs

Costs can also be classified as semivariable. These costs vary with the amount of activity, but they are not directly proportional to the amount of the activity. A good example of semivariable costs is maintenance costs. There is normally some uniformity with regard to the cost of regularly maintaining a piece of machinery. However, if SMC's club-making machine is running three hours more than usual each day, maintenance will probably have to be conducted more frequently. The costs of health care premiums paid by an employer could also be semivariable. The cost of a premium may be constant, but the total amount paid by the employer may vary with the number of employees covered by the plan.

Fixed Costs

Fixed costs are the last major cost category. Fixed costs stay the same no matter what changes occur in usage or sales. Property taxes and depreciation expenses are just two examples of fixed costs.

Other Ways of Classifying Costs

Through cost accounting, which is the method used to ferret out the true costs associated with any given activity, costs could be identified or classified according to additional levels other than variable, semivariable, and fixed costs. Some of these additional categories include material, manufacturing, labor, factory overhead, and general and administrative costs. Material costs are the costs of the material used to make a given product.

For SMC, the steel—identified earlier as a variable cost—also can be classified as a manufacturing cost. The company needs the steel to make its clubs.

Labor costs are the costs needed to transform the material into the finished product. Factory overhead is the cost associated with all the equipment and buildings used as the material is converted to a finished product. Factory overhead traditionally includes rent or mortgage, machine costs, depreciation, electricity, and so on. The last major category is general and administrative costs. These costs typically include salaries for employees in the sales or other nonmanufacturing departments, marketing expenses, research and development, and related expenses not associated with manufacturing.

Before we discuss costs further, it is important to note that many businesses use terms such as "overhead" or "indirect" costs. Overhead refers to all the additional costs (over and beyond all the combined manufacturing costs) associated with getting a product to market such as administrative, legal, marketing, and related costs. An indirect cost is a cost associated with—but not necessarily part of the process of—converting raw materials to the finished product. A good sport example of an indirect cost is scouts for a pro team. The scouts do not coach the athletes to become better or in any way enhance the value of a player; but without scouts, a team would not be able to put the best product on the field. Businesses should not use the terms *overhead* and *indirect* because they are misleading. They are misleading because all expenses, whether variable or fixed, add a cost component to the product. For example, we should not use the term *indirect labor* because either the labor is productive and needs to be accounted for or is unnecessary and needs to be eliminated. Nonetheless, because executives frequently use the terms *overhead* and *indirect expenses,* we briefly discuss them here.

Even though indirect expenses are not the most accurate measure for analyzing costs, direct and indirect labor costs are terms people use most frequently in referring to the manufacturing costs of a given product or service. Examples of **direct costs** are such items as raw materials for SMC's golf clubs and player salaries for the Celtics. **Indirect costs** could include employee salaries and benefits associated with office personnel, such as secretaries, who do not design, manufacture, or distribute the golf clubs. Traditionally, indirect costs are added directly to the cost of a manufactured item, even if these costs are wholly unrelated to the manufacturing process.

Hidden Costs

Some costs are "hidden" and thus hard to appreciate when one is making financial decisions. The building of a new facility involves numerous costs that are not obvious. These hidden costs can significantly affect such issues as building change orders or potential price increases based on the material used and any price increases that might pass through under the contract. For example, a new stadium is being built on a $100,000 budget. A construction company starts the building process and then a local homeowner sues everyone for diminishing the value of his property. The suit will cost money, but will not add any value to the facility or help pay for its construction. Thus, it was hidden in the initial budget, because it was not anticipated. Additionally, there could be hidden costs related to unexpected environmental issues. An environmental impact analysis as part of the due diligence process is a standard expense. Due diligence entails a thorough investigation of a proposed business deal to determine whether there are any potential legal or financial problems. The environmental impact analysis is designed to determine whether the land is contaminated or whether any environmental remediation might be required. Issues other than contamination or endangered species-related issues may also arise. These issues can undercut an entire project.

Local laws may require development of wetlands to replace areas converted by construction. It might be impossible to create or maintain wetlands if a stadium needs space for parking lots; thus a facility may not be able to comply with the law. Nevertheless, government entities still require compliance with the law. To address this conflict, some companies have developed wetland mitigation banks from which a business can buy its share of acreage and not have to retain wetlands at the construction site. For example, a stadium might be required to leave 2 acres as wetlands. Instead of losing all the possible parking spaces, the stadium can go to the mitigation bank and purchase 2 acres that might be located around a city park. The bank owners then assume the responsibility of keeping the wetlands in good shape and allowing wildlife to utilize the space. The cost of buying the space is offset by the high cost that would be involved in developing and maintaining the wetlands at the stadium site. Such a project was built outside Houston on 580 acres. The government granted credits for the acres, and the owners sold the credits to private companies that did not want to develop wetlands or wanted to avoid time delays associated with building a wetland project (Breyer, 1998).

Analyzing Costs

Regardless of how costs are classified, it is impossible to fully appreciate an item's cost without developing a cost summary sheet. The cost summary sheet breaks down all the costs incurred during manufacture of an item. One can also price services in this manner by calculating the labor cost for each activity that is part of the service.

The cost sheet shows the various categories of costs over and above the raw materials used to create the putter, such as taxes, depreciation, profits, and related expenses. Numerous pro forma budgets fail investor scrutiny because the pro forma fails to identify these cost categories. A cost sheet makes it more difficult to overlook any cost category.

 Table 13.1 could be a cost sheet for SMC's Super Putter. Using this cost sheet would help SMC determine optimum pricing strategies and allow management to identify where cost reductions can be made.

Table 13.1 Super Putter Cost Sheet

Description	Cost per packaged unit ($)
Part A	10.00
Part B	6.00
Part C	4.00
Part D	1.00
Primer	0.75
Paint	1.25
Packaging	2.00
Material costs	**$25.00**
Supplies and repairs	1.50
Utilities	1.00
Total	**$27.50**
Cost at step 1	14.00
Cost at step 2	5.00
Cost at step 3	1.50
Quality-related losses	4.00
Sales and distribution costs	5.00
Short-term interest	0.75
Total variable costs	**$57.75**
Manufacturing	7.25
Distribution	3.50
Research and development	2.50
Administrative	2.00
Long-term interest	1.25
Total manufacturing cost less depreciation	**$74.25**
Depreciation	10.00
Total cost	**$84.25**
Net profit	12.00
Target price after tax	**$96.25**
Provisions for taxes	7.75
Net target selling price	**$104.00**
Discount and terms	6.00
Total target price	**$110.00**

The cost sheet establishes several key variables that help SMC determine its profitability and related standards:

- SMC's profit is $12, which is built into the cost analysis.
- Profit as a percentage of sales price is 8% ($96.25 target price / $12 profit).
- Gross margin is net sales price ($104) minus the material costs ($25) = $79.
- Value added is the net sales price ($104) minus total purchases ($27.50) = $76.50.
- Cash flow is after-tax profits ($12) plus depreciation ($10) = $22.
- Contribution margin is the net sales price ($104) minus total variable cost ($57.75) = $46.25.

The value-added component is the key point for a specialized company such as SMC or the Celtics. Sport Manufacturing Company has unique skills as evidenced by its ability to manufacture a putter that is highly regarded by golf professionals. On the basis of this uniqueness, the company is able to charge more than other golf club manufacturers. The uniqueness adds value to the product, in the same way winning an NBA championship would add value to the Celtics. After winning the championship the Celtics would be able to charge a higher ticket price because people would be willing to pay more to see them.

Reducing Costs

Besides analyzing costs, it is important to examine techniques to reduce costs. Systematic cost reduction can be accomplished through various techniques, such as engineered standards and cost control reports. These techniques can help identify waste and appropriate remedial measures. For example, instead of having a secretary for each executive, a company could centralize the secretarial staff so that there are three secretaries for five executives—saving two salaries while still accommodating the executives' needs. Other cost reduction techniques are discussed elsewhere in this text, such as reissuing bonds at a lower interest rate (see "Loan Repayment," p. 177). Companies use capital cost reduction techniques to reduce the cost of issuing stocks or bonds. A company can issue more stock than it actually releases to the public in order to reduce future issuing expense. If and when the company needs to release the additional shares, the capital costs have already been covered, so most of the proceeds from sales of the additional shares go directly to the corporation. Although capital cost reduction produces significant benefits, cost reduction can also occur in other areas, such as inventory and the manufacturing process. First we discuss ways to reduce costs in the manufacturing process; then in the next section we consider inventory management, through which a company examines how much of the time inventory is just sitting in storage and wasting the company's money. Examining such costs gives a business an opportunity to identify where costs might be excessive and to reduce these costs.

The simplest means to meet a production and sales budget is to increase selling price. However, this strategy may lead to lost sales and lost goodwill. Reducing internal costs can also help make the budget. Cost reduction can result from various strategies, such as reducing labor costs or streamlining the manufacturing process. As an example, various cost reduction strategies can be undertaken to reduce utility expenses. Businesses can change the wattage of lightbulbs or reduce the amount of water used to flush a toilet. The electricity and water usage can be plotted, and the benefits associated with conservation efforts can also be tracked.

Numerous cost reduction strategies also apply to running machinery. Machinery can be very expensive to operate, and businesses that utilize machinery can identify ways to save in this area by doing the following:

- Analyzing costs based on machine centers (a group of similar machines working together) or groups versus product runs or other evaluation methods

- Examining preventive maintenance programs that can prolong machine life and reduce costly repairs

- Evaluating utility conservation programs to determine if machines are using energy as effectively as possible

- Ensuring that employees are not misusing the machines

- Analyzing true equipment requirements to reduce the need for certain equipment or reallocate floor space for more effective income generation

- Setting aside money (e.g., in a sinking fund) to help purchase new or refurbished equipment to replace outdated equipment (Feiner, 1977)

> Any sport business, such as a team, has to manage and control its expenses—whether they are variable expenses that change over time, semivariable expenses that change only to some extent over time, or fixed expenses.

Inventory Management

Most college, semiprofessional, and amateur sport facilities have similar costs. For example, each facility has maintenance, personnel, electricity, construction, and related costs. Similarly, each facility tries to minimize the operating costs while still providing the best services. No matter where expenses might arise, financial managers need to carefully track expenses to ensure that money is not being misspent. Inventory management is an effective tool for managing variable and semivariable costs. If excess inventory sits in a storage facility, the company not only loses the use of the money tied up in the inventory (and might even have to pay financing charges if the inventory was purchased with borrowed funds), but also has to pay inventory storage expenses. On the other hand, if there is not enough inventory available, customers may not receive items they have purchased; this can result in lower sales and the loss of consumer goodwill. To avoid these problems, managers utilize techniques such as order forecasting to help determine when they might have to purchase inventories or when certain expenses will arise.

Key Components of an Inventory Management System

The key components of any inventory management system are forecasting, purchasing, storing, auditing, and utilizing inventory. These five components are discussed in the sections that follow.

Forecasting Inventory

Here we briefly examine forecasting in general and then focus on one of the most critical forecasting areas, inventory forecasting. For example, we can develop a thorough forecast by analyzing what activities occur to generate a sale. Figure 13.1 shows a 35-point cost-of-sales questionnaire designed to help solicit the information we would need to develop a comprehensive forecast. The questionnaire identifies some of the dynamic issues associated with determining the potential costs associated with a manufactured item. Some individuals might feel that manufacturing cost reductions could be accomplished by just cutting costs. However, how can you reduce costs? The questionnaire poses questions that any manager needs to ask and answer to help identify variables that can affect pricing and which might represent a potential area for cost savings. Forecasting involves a little of both science and art to effectively set the stage for determining optimum sales, inventory, production levels, and manufacturing costs. Forecasts for some variables are simple, such as yearly property tax or insurance obligations, as in these cases the business knows what the expenses will be and when they must be paid. On the other hand, whereas the Smiths may be sure of certain expenses such as rent, they cannot know when a sound system will break or whether they will suffer any theft. Unpredictable variables will always come into play that can either positively or negatively affect projections. However, by developing a competently researched forecast, managers can either avoid or account for variability. Inventory forecasting helps establish what inventory purchases will need to be made throughout the year and the most effective techniques for reordering additional inventory.

Purchasing Inventory

Purchasing needed materials might appear to be a relatively easy process for most businesses. However, if you examine your own individual buying patterns, you may discover inefficiencies that cost you significantly. If you wait too long to buy gas on a highway, you may be stuck paying several more cents a gallon than you would otherwise. If you have a headache and buy aspirin at a convenience store, you will pay much more than if you had purchased it at a discount drugstore. Similarly, the failure of a business to effectively manage purchases and material costs can cost a company millions of dollars.

Some of the commonplace inefficiencies that a company might face are

- intermittent, ineffective, or short production runs (a production run is a manufactured amount that has been predetermined, such as when SMC has a production run of 1,000 clubs planned for February);

- double-handling of materials because some materials were not available when needed;

- inadequate development of proper tooling methods because the production runs are too short;

- failure to realize quantity discounts;

- failure to define economical order quantities; and

- downtime of machines that are waiting for parts but still incur all fixed operating costs (Feiner, 1977).

 The Smiths could be inefficient in their purchasing patterns for their fitness center. If the Smiths are charged $20 for each office supply delivery, they should forecast their potential needs for an extended period of time so they can order all the supplies possibly needed during that period; this will reduce delivery charges. Sound planning can help them consolidate orders.

Inventory Turnover Ratio The problems identified in the preceding section are just some of the concerns associated with poor management of the raw goods required to manufacture the final product. It is fairly easy to identify a machine that is not in use, and it is obvious when you have to pay an extra premium for a small order. However, it is often difficult or even impossible to notice when raw materials are just sitting in storage for extended periods and out of a manager's view. Inventory **turnover** is a method used to determine if in fact inventory is just sitting around. The inventory turnover ratio also helps identify whether management is adequately managing resources.

An inventory turnover ratio can be applied to both finished goods and raw goods. The calculation for finished-goods turnover is as follows:

$$\frac{\text{finished goods}}{\text{turnover ratio}} = \frac{\text{cost of goods sold}}{\text{average finished goods inventory}}$$

Assuming that the cost of goods sold is $385,000 and the average finished-goods inventory is $65,000, the turnover ratio will be $385,000 / $65,000 = 5.92.

35-Point Cost of Sales Questionnaire

Material Costs

1. What percentage of sales are direct materials?
2. How is the standard cost for materials established?
3. How often are these costs reviewed and by what procedure?
4. Are "free stock" items included as a direct or indirect cost?
5. How effectively and accurately are purchase parts invoiced and material (stores) requisitions processed?
6. Is a part-numbering system maintained?
7. Does cost accounting's purchase price agree with purchasing's current record and if not, what corrective action is required?

Direct Labor Costs

8. What percentage of sales is direct labor?
9. What percentage of total salary and wages is direct labor?
10. Which departments (cost centers) are being measured by performance reports, and are line managers making effective use of these reports?
11. Are standard labor hours based on historical actuals or industrial engineering standards?
12. How current are these standards?
13. How accurate are the standard dollar labor rates, and do they reflect shift differentials?
14. How is cost accounting notified of changes in the labor rate or in the standard hours?

Overhead Costs

15. What percentage of sales is overhead?
16. What percentage of overhead is classified as indirect labor, and is it all truly indirect?
17. What percentage of the overhead represents variable, semivariable, and fixed costs?
18. How is overhead applied, and is there more than one rate?
19. Is any of the overhead pool applied to materials, and is the rate sufficient to fully absorb actual expenses?
20. Do overhead expenses exist by department?

Variances

21. How are variances reported—by job, standard production runs, or on an exception basis?
22. Are material variances segregated from labor variances?
23. Are labor variances segregated by rate and efficiency factors?
24. Are material variances segregated by price and usage?
25. Are variance results oriented so that causes can be quickly identified and corrected?
26. How effective are variance reports? Who receives, reviews, and analyzes these reports?
27. Are sufficient data provided so all jobs can be adequately reviewed?
28. Who determines which jobs or production runs will be reviewed?
29. Is cost estimating plugged into your variance reporting?
30. Can any of these variances be honestly billed to the customer to reflect changes, etc.?

Inventory Related

31. Are book to physical adjustments recorded as discovered?
32. Are inventory cycles conducted, and how often?
33. How are production losses and shrinkages controlled, reported, and booked?

Other

34. Are gross profit margin analyses performed on a regular basis?
35. Are product line profit-and-loss statements prepared and shared with those who can make a definite contribution toward improving future results?

Figure 13.1 Points to consider when analyzing the cost of manufactured items. A manager needs to ask and answer these questions to help identify variables that can affect pricing and that might represent a potential area for cost savings.

Reprinted from R.R. Feiner, 1977, *Operational financial analysis: A practical handbook with forms* (Englewood Cliffs, NJ: Prentice Hall), 45–46. By permission of R.R. Feiner.

This number can also be expressed in working days: 42.7 days of unsold finished goods sitting in inventory. To calculate the number of working days, we divide the number of working days in the year (253) by the turnover ratio (5.92) (Feiner, 1977). The number of working days (253) is constant for any company that is closed on weekends and federal holidays. There is not one correct ratio for inventory turnover. However, the faster the inventory is turned over, the more money will be made. Some sport businesses are likely to have a high inventory turnover rate—for example, concession items are typically bought and sold very frequently. On the other hand, a yacht sales company might sell only a few boats each year, but their profit margin on each boat can sustain the business.

We can do the same calculation for raw materials using the following formula:

$$\frac{\text{raw materials}}{\text{turnover}} = \frac{\text{raw materials consumed/}}{\text{average raw materials inventory}}$$

Using the preceding formula, if a company spends $135,000 on raw materials and maintains an average inventory of $17,000 in raw goods, the company's turnover ratio would be the following:

$$\text{raw materials turnover} = \$135,000 / \$17,000 = 7.94$$

The 7.94 ratio translates to 31.9 days that raw materials are generally in inventory before they are consumed. The more quickly raw materials are consumed, the lower the inventory handling costs. This number is important, as it serves as a benchmark to help identify potential waste, and management has to vigilantly monitor whether this number increases or decreases. Knowing about any decrease is important because this will help the manager identify what is being done correctly in order to maintain the success. Any increases represent a trouble sign that raw materials are sitting around incurring unnecessary expenses.

Assume that SMC has incurred costs of $400,000 for the rackets it produces and $125,000 for the raw materials consumed. Also assume that the average finished-goods inventory is $50,000 and that the average raw-materials inventory is $15,000. Based on these numbers, the inventory turnover ratios would be as follows:

$$\text{finished goods} = \$400,000 / \$50,000 = \text{a turnover ratio of 8}$$

$$\text{raw materials} = \$125,000 / \$15,000 = \text{a turnover ratio of 8.33}$$

Thus, in our example, the number of working days required to turn over the inventory is 31.6 days for finished goods (253 / 8) and 30.4 days (253 / 8.33) for raw materials. The data obtained through this calculation can be compared with ratios from similar companies to determine whether SMC is storing and selling its inventory effectively. Comparison data can be obtained from banks and trade associations (Feiner, 1977).

Purchasing Concerns   Purchasing concerns arise when inventory is not ordered in a timely manner, ordered too quickly, or ordered in too small or too large an amount. Centralized purchasing is one technique for reducing these potential problems. Centralized purchasing moves the purchasing decision-making and execution function away from individual departments. Centralizing the purchasing function provides benefits such as the following:

- Managers can focus on their specialty rather than on administrative issues surrounding purchasing.
- Responsibility is given to a single person rather than numerous individual managers.
- Clerical effort and inventory control problems can be reduced.
- Problems of potential shortages can be identified early.
- Price negotiation can be improved because of the ability to buy bigger lots and redistribute the materials throughout an organization (Feiner, 1977).

Purchasing is only the second step in the inventory management process. Inventories are typically not purchased on an as-needed basis because the costs for ordering small amounts would be prohibitive. Thus a business places larger orders, and excess inventory needs to be stored for future use.

Storing Inventory

As you have already seen, inventory-related costs can be significant over and beyond the cost for the storage facility itself. Inventories can be classified as raw materials, work-in-process, and finished goods. At each level, the inventory needs to be stored, moved, modified, shipped, packaged, and sent through related processes; and all these steps cost money. Some of these expenses can be reduced through joint warehousing with other businesses or through the development of automated systems to more effectively move the right parts at the right time.

Raw materials can pose unique storage concerns when in liquid or bulk form. If SMC has purchased a large amount of steel for forging clubs, the metal might take up significant space or may need to be stored in special areas. Work-in-process is a term for refined raw materials that have not yet reached the finished-product stage. These materials need to be stored in a location from which they can easily be moved to the finishing area. In a typical manufacturing plant that produces millions of products each year, the amount of goods classified as work-in-process can be significant. This is especially true if the manufacturing process takes over a week and products are manufactured in a cycle in which new runs are started each or every-other week. If the product takes three weeks to manufacture and a new production run is launched every-other week, a significant amount of work-in-process is being stored at various stages of completion.

Inventory Storage Costs Inventory management is the process of lowering the total costs associated with all the inventories required to sustain efficient operations (Brigham & Gapenski, 1994). In other words, by effectively tracking inventory costs, a company can both reduce costs and keep operating efficiently. Costs can be broken down into four main areas: carrying costs, ordering costs, shipping and receiving costs, and costs associated with running out of inventory. The carrying, or storing, costs are the most expensive component of the inventory costs. These costs generally rise in direct proportion to the average amount of inventories carried. Thus the more inventory being stored, the greater the carrying costs, as the following example shows.

Assume that SMC sells S units of rackets each year and that the company has to place equal-sized orders N times a year for the raw materials needed to build the rackets. The ratio of S to N (S / N) will indicate how many units are purchased with each order. The average inventory level can be expressed with the following formula (Brigham & Gapenski, 1994):

$$A = \text{units per order} / 2$$
$$= (S / N) / 2$$

A = average inventory level

S = units of rackets sold in a year

N = number of orders or raw materials in a year

The number 2 is used to divide the total to obtain the "average" number of units to be ordered. If SMC sold 120,000 rackets and placed four orders a year for raw materials, the formula would be completed as follows:

$$A = (120,000 / 4) / 2$$
$$= 30,000 / 2$$
$$= 15,000 \text{ units}$$

Thus, SMC carries an average inventory of 15,000 units. The company orders 30,000 units at a time, so when a shipment is received, the inventory level should be close to 0 units; after the order is received, the inventory level will be slightly over 30,000 units. By knowing the average inventory level, we can calculate carrying costs.

If SMC pays $2 per unit, then the average inventory value is $2 × 15,000 units, or $30,000. Most businesses have a cost of capital based on having to borrow money to purchase inventory. If SMC has a cost of capital of 10%, then there will be $3,000 in inventory carrying costs for one year. This cost needs to be added to the storage costs, which include space, utilities, security, taxes, and so on. These annual costs come to $2,000 a year. In addition, the following annual costs also need to be added to the total carrying costs: $500 for insurance and $1,000 for inventory losses. SMC's total carrying costs for carrying the $30,000 average inventory are $3,000 + $2,000 + $500 + $1,000 = $6,500 (Brigham & Gapenski, 1994). We can calculate the $6,500 cost as a percentage (C) by dividing it by the $30,000 average inventory: $6,500 / $30,000 = 0.217, or 21.7%. The annual percentage cost can be used in subsequent forecasts to determine potential carrying costs.

$$TCC = (C)(P)(A)$$

TCC = total carrying costs

C = carrying costs divided by value of average inventory

P = product price

A = average inventory

If SMC increased its average inventory to $40,000, which would change A to 20,000, and the price (P) remained at $2, the carrying costs would be calculated as follows:

$$TCC = (0.217)(\$2)(20,000)$$
$$= \$8,680$$

The TCC of \$8,680 is a \$2,180 increase over the previous cost of \$6,500. This example highlights how the carrying costs increase when larger inventories are ordered. The increase would be reduced if the turnover rate was much greater. Thus, if 250,000 units were sold each year, the 100% increase in sales coupled with larger inventory purchases could reduce some of the carrying costs, which could result in increased profits and/or having funds to pay the capital costs earlier.

As noted at the start of this section, there are four types of costs associated with inventory. Carrying costs are the largest; but ordering costs, shipping and receiving costs, and the cost of running out of inventory are also important. These costs are often fixed and include such items as the cost of research on purchase options, interoffice memos, phone calls, taking delivery, and moving raw materials. The fixed costs associated with inventory ordering are represented by **F.** To calculate the total ordering cost we multiply F by N, with N representing the number of orders per year. The equation is often written as follows:

$$TOC = (F)(N)$$

TOC = total ordering costs

F = fixed cost of inventory ordering

N = number of orders per year, which is calculated as follows:

$$N = (S / 2A)$$

S = total units sold in a year

A = the average inventory

Thus TOC can also be written as (F)(S / 2A). This equation can be applied to our SMC example.

Based on SMC's previous number of 120,000 units sold and average inventory of 15,000 units, the formula would be calculated as follows if SMC incurred \$100 in expenses to place an order:

$$TOC = \$100 \times 120,000 / 30,000$$
$$= \$400$$

Thus, the total ordering cost is \$400 a year based on the four orders. Through knowing TOC and TCC, we can calculate the total inventory costs. In this case SMC's total inventory cost is \$400 + \$6,500 = \$6,900.

The numbers in the examples presented do not include certain other costs such as lost sales, loss of consumer goodwill, and the disruption of production schedules associated with not having enough inventory in storage (Brigham & Gapenski, 1994).

Inventory Valuation   Determining purchase costs, **replacement costs,** and the proper accounting technique to measure true revenue are critical components of the accounting process necessary to determine the effects of storing inventory over extended periods. This process is often called the cost-of-goods-sold method, which analyzes the replacement cost for sold inventory. Two basic techniques can be used to value inventory: LIFO and FIFO. LIFO, which stands for **last in, first out,** values inventory based on the current price of replacing an item. FIFO, which stands for **first in, first out,** reports valuation based on the price paid earlier for an item. Corporations prefer to use LIFO, as any increase in inventory prices results in less income and a corresponding lower tax obligation. Shareholders prefer FIFO, as the increased price generates additional revenue and possibly larger dividends.

Assume that the Celtics buy souvenir gold cups for their future championship celebrations. They pay \$30 per cup in 2002 and buy a supply that can last five years. However, by the year 2007 when the Celtics use the last of the gold cups, the cups are valued at \$500 each. The income statement for the mythical Celtics Souvenir Store, which sells nothing but the cups, might be as shown in table 13.2 for the LIFO and the FIFO methods:

Table 13.2   Celtics Souvenir Store Income Statement

LIFO	
Sales (100 units at \$1,000 each)	\$100,000
COGS (100 units at replacement value \$500)	50,000
Gross profit	**\$50,000**
Selling expense	20,000
Net profit before taxes	**\$30,000**
FIFO	
Sales (100 units at \$1,000 each)	\$100,000
COGS (100 units at replacement value \$30)	3,000
Gross profit	**\$97,000**
Selling expense	20,000
Net profit before taxes	**\$77,000**

COGS = cost of goods sold.

Another example should help highlight the difference between LIFO and FIFO. Assume that SMC has one item valued at $5, one valued at $6, and one valued at $7. Two items are sold for a combined $16 ($8 each). Under the FIFO method, the items that had cost $5 and $6 would be sold first. This would result in a $5 profit ($16 – $11) and leave $7 in the closing inventory T-account. In contrast, under the LIFO method, the two items sold would be the $6 and $7 items. Under this scenario SMC would generate only $3 profit ($16 – $13), and the closing inventory would be the $5 item.

Most accountants would want to recognize the loss associated with decreased inventory values in the current accounting period. Two valuation techniques can be utilized to do this: cost valuation and market valuation. The following example shows how the two values can be compared to help determine a decrease in inventory value. Assume that an item costs $5, the replacement cost is $3.50, the selling price is $6, the disposition cost is $2, and the normal profit is $1. The disposition cost is the cost to dispose of an item in inventory. Some items cannot just be thrown into the garbage. Items that are large or heavy, for example, may need to be hauled to a dump, and the cost of hauling them is their disposition cost. The replacement cost ($3.50) is lower than the net realizable value (NRV), which is $6 – $2 = $4. Since the replacement cost is lower than the NRV, the $3.50 amount is used. Since the initial cost was $5.00 and since the lower number (between cost and market) is $3.50, the loss that would be reported is $1.50 ($5 – $3.50). If the company buys another item at the $3.50 cost, the new item will generate a $0.50 profit. We calculate this profit by subtracting the replacement cost ($3.50) and the disposition cost ($2) from the $6 selling price. Thus, the higher-cost item would result in an initial loss, but the lower replacement cost will generate a profit in the long term.

The Celtics would earn a much higher rate of return if the FIFO method was used to calculate the store's pretax profit. However, the potential tax liability is also significantly higher. In the LIFO example, the income would be lower and taxes would be lower, but a more realistic estimate of the pretax profit is shown because any new cups would have to be purchased at the $500 price. Either technique is valid, and both conform to generally accepted accounting practices. A company has to decide which treatment of a given transaction is most appropriate for its needs. The FIFO method may be more appropriate if the Celtics want to show a higher rate of return for investors. Such financial maneuvering is not dishonest, since the Celtics' annual report will indicate that the FIFO method was used to calculate the inventory's value.

Lost Inventory One of the consequences of storing inventory is the possibility of losing inventory. Inventory can be lost for various reasons, from simple misplacement to theft, spoilage, or obsolescence. Inventory is an asset. As with any other asset, if care is not taken it can be lost. For example, if the Celtics did not properly track beer, they could lose beer as a consequence of concessionaires misreporting sales or even the cleaning crew taking beer. Employee honesty can be greatly enhanced when the employees know that inventory management practices are in place.

Besides losing money by paying to store inventory, inventory obsolescence can greatly increase inventory costs. A store that carried Shaquille O'Neal jerseys from the Orlando Magic definitely would find them a tough sell compared to Los Angeles Lakers jerseys. Although some consumers might be interested in buying an Orlando jersey as a collector's item, the costs associated with carrying the jersey for a possible sale once every six months might not justify keeping the jerseys. Factors that come into play when you are analyzing whether to carry an obsolete product include

- the potential activity or lack of activity in relation to the item,
- the amount of storage space required,
- the amount of physical activity required to move the item,
- the item's replacement cost if a replacement were ever required,
- whether replacement parts could ever be found and their potential cost, and
- how critical the item is for the overall business operation.

If these considerations indicate that the item is expendable, then the cost analysis should determine whether the company is wasting money by keeping it. Assume that the item would cost $100 a year to keep in inventory based on the cost per square foot for storage, utilities, human resources, and so on. If the replacement cost is $500 and there is a 50% chance the item could be used in the next 10 years, then disposing of the item would be a low-risk choice.

If inventory becomes obsolete (for example when a professional sport team such as the Houston Oilers becomes the Tennessee Titans), the inventory can be given away to charity or sold at a significant markdown. If your company is a subchapter S corporation, you can usually take a tax deduction for your cost of producing the goods. However, if you are a C corporation, you can deduct the cost of the inventory plus half the difference between the cost and the fair market value of the goods—which cannot exceed twice the cost of inventory (Marullo, 1997, December). S and C corporations are discussed in chapter 4.

Auditing Inventory

A key component to any inventory management system is taking a physical inventory. Whether one is counting production parts or supplies, physical inventory taking is a critical step in controlling inaccurate inventory purchasing behavior or determining a business' true value. Often people just count physical units, which is not the most effective way to take inventory. You may see this in supermarkets—for example, an inventory taker counts the number of potato chip bags on the shelf. In other settings, some people use a "line" system, drawing a line on a box and placing another order when items in the box dip below the line. Others use a two-bin system. They have two bins of parts, for example, and when one bin is emptied, they place an order, using the items in the second bin while waiting for the order to arrive.

As an alternative to just counting units, an inventory-taking protocol can help accurately determine the value of inventory units that might otherwise be difficult to track. An effective inventory-taking protocol could require the following steps:

- Analyzing the degree of obsolescence in the inventory
- Identifying fast- and slow-moving items
- Properly classifying the inventory based on need, value, or other variables
- Identifying the cause of lost or stolen inventory items
- Identifying techniques to help move slow inventory (Feiner, 1977)

Types of Inventory Tracking Systems   Numerous inventory management systems exist to help reduce carrying costs and optimize the production process.

Point of Sale

One key inventory management technique is the point-of-sale inventory management system. These systems are used at stores such as supermarkets, drugstores, and sporting goods stores. The system uses bar codes on packages. The bar code is scanned when an item enters a store and when it is sold. Computers track the item's movement, and sophisticated systems can identify when the items are selling, at what price they are sold, how often to reorder, and related information.

Just in Time

Just-in-time (JIT) inventory systems are often found in the manufacturing industry in cases in which numerous suppliers are required to provide multiple and flexible inventory options for a manufacturer. Japanese manufacturers developed the JIT system so that needed components could be delivered at the exact moment they would be needed to complete the production process. By utilizing such a strategy, businesses thought that they could avoid having a buffer or safety inventory and all the associated costs. The JIT system is a timing-based system. Everything has to be calculated to within minutes so that an entire assembly line is not shut down because of one missing screw. The JIT system was designed on the basis of highly predictable requirements, real-time communications between all parties, and coordinated suppliers (Spiro, 1996). Just-in-time systems can work and can save money, but if they are not perfectly coordinated, the process does not work. For example, the manufacturer must have strong faith that the supplier's deliveries will be at least 98% defect free. A shipment with too many defects would unduly hinder the entire process because the manufacturer would not have the benefit of possibly testing every component while in storage.

Another concern relating to JIT systems is the impact of sudden emergencies on the system. In the wake of the September 11 tragedies, according to a major study conducted by the trucking industry, 39% of companies surveyed experienced major disruptions in their supply chain as a result of the attacks ("Managers Rethinking," 2001). As a result of these disruptions, many companies started developing a new mind-set and looking toward just-in-case (JIC) systems. These systems are designed to maintain a safety stock so that the company can eliminate as much inefficiency as possible. Thus, JIT should not be taken as a directive to remove every item in inventory. Rather, a safety stock should be kept to guard against a major disaster or other concerns, while at the same time efforts are made to monitor and reduce inefficiencies.

Economic Order Quantity

One of the most important elements in the inventory auditing process is tracking how much to order. Determining the optimum order quantity is important for reducing storage and ordering costs.

Since the JIT system is not right for every manufacturer, other techniques need to be adopted to help reduce inventory costs while maintaining adequate reserves. One such technique is a mathematical model called the economic order quantity (EOQ) model. The EOQ model attempts to determine the optimum number of units to be ordered whenever an order is placed. Large inventories mean increased warehousing costs, interest expenses, insurance costs, and larger amounts of obsolete inventory. At the same time, the larger the order, the fewer orders need to be placed, which reduces ordering costs. By knowing the optimum numbers of components to order, a manager can reduce the number of orders that need to be placed and the number of extra units kept in inventory. The equation for the EOQ model is as follows:

$$EOQ = \sqrt{\frac{2(F)(U)}{C}}$$

F = cost for placing order

U = sales per year (in units)

C = carrying cost per year

In the model, F stands for the costs associated with placing an order, such as paperwork or personnel time to place an order or write a check, which are activities independent of the order size. U stands for the sales in units per year of the item that will be placed in inventory. C represents the costs per year associated with carrying the units in inventory and includes storage rental costs, insurance, handling charges, and so on. The model works only in cases in which the inventory and sales numbers behave in a predictable manner. The formula shown is based on the assumption that on average one-half of each shipment is carried in inventory. If the fixed cost per order (F) is $5, the number of units sold each year (U) is 5,000, and the carrying cost per unit per year (C) is $0.80, the formula would be completed as follows:

$$\sqrt{\frac{2 \times \$5 \times 5,000}{\$0.80}} = 250 \text{ units}$$

If the managers of this hypothetical company utilized good inventory management practices, they would place orders in lots of 250 units at a time (Spiro, 1996).

Some companies have a hard time identifying the exact cost of carrying an item and it is easier for them to calculate the EOQ based on industry norms. The formula for calculating EOQ based on industry norms or internally generated percentage of a product's selling price is:

$$EOQ = \sqrt{[2(F)(S)] / (C)(P)}$$

Under this version of the formula:

F = fixed cost of placing and receiving orders

S = units sold annually

C = annual carrying costs expressed as a percentage

P = purchase price of the inventory

 Assume that the Celtics order 26,000 shirts each year. The team calculates that the carrying costs are 25% of the inventory. The shirts are sold for $9 each, but the inventory cost is only $4.92 each. The fixed cost per order is $1,000. Plugging these numbers into the EOQ formula produces the following results (Brigham & Gapenski, 1994):

$$EOQ = \sqrt{[2(\$1,000)(26,000)] / (0.25)(\$4.92)}$$
$$= \sqrt{42,276,423}$$
$$= 6,500 \text{ units}$$

Dividing the 26,000 annual inventory by the EOQ of 6,500 units gives a total of four orders annually. Dividing 26,000 by 52 weeks gives a weekly usage rate of 500 shirts. Thus, after an order of 6,500 is received, 500 units will be subtracted from the inventory each week. Based on these numbers, the average inventory level will be 3,250 shirts at a cost of $4.92 each, which produces an inventory value of about $16,000. Economies of scale could be achieved if the Celtics sold 52,000 shirts, which would be a 100% increase in sales. Economies of scale represent the most beneficial purchasing or ordering quantity to receive a price reduction. Thus, through more efficient ordering or ordering larger quantities, a business can reduce the per unit cost significantly. Economies of scale can also be accomplished when companies join together to buy products when individually they might not be able to order a large enough quantity to obtain a break, but collectively they can place such an order. The EOQ would increase from 6,500 to 9,125—a 41% increase.

Although these ordering points provide an exact number to order, the world is not exact. The Celtics would not sell 500 shirts each week. Some weeks they might sell several thousand shirts and other weeks no shirts at all. This reality forces us to set an order point with flexibility. For example, a lag period needs to be built into the orders since it might take several weeks to receive an order. Thus, a several-week supply needs to exist before a reorder is placed. In addition, a safety stock should be maintained. A safety stock might be necessary to avoid delays in receiving orders or when sales suddenly increase. This concern is highlighted in the following Celtics example.

 Even though the preceding example showed an EOQ of 6,500 shirts, the Celtics might order 7,500 shirts to help maintain a 1,000-shirt safety stock. The Celtics also might order the shirts when there are still 1,000 shirts in inventory in order to maintain the EOQ and the necessary safety stock (Brigham & Gapenski, 1994). Note that any safety stock would increase the total carrying cost. If an additional 1,000 shirts were ordered, the additional carrying cost would be calculated as follows:

Additional carrying cost = (safety stock)(P)(C)

C = the annual carrying costs expressed as a percentage

P = the purchase price for the inventory

Using the definitions and numbers from above, the additional carrying costs for the Celtics would be:

$$\text{Additional carrying cost} = 1,000(\$4.92)(0.25)$$
$$= \$1,230$$

The 1,000 additional shirts will increase the Celtics' carrying costs from $4,000, as we will see, to $5,230 (Brigham & Gapenski, 1994).

The information we have can be plugged into the TOC and TCC formulas to calculate the total inventory costs (TIC). Remember, TOC = (F)(S / Q) and TCC = (C)(P)(Q / 2). Thus, the equations would be calculated as follows (Brigham & Gapenski, 1994):

$$\text{TIC} = \text{TOC} + \text{TCC}$$
$$= [(\$1,000)(26,000 / 6,500)] +$$
$$[(0.25)(\$4.92)(6,500 / 2)]$$
$$= \$4,000 + \$4,000$$
$$= \$8,000$$

This example shows that the total inventory costs, excluding the cost of the shirts, is $8,000.

Quantity Discounts

Another wrinkle can be added to the Celtics example. The EOQ is fine if no discounts are offered for larger orders. However, most suppliers are forced to provide larger purchasers with a discount to attract their business. Any discount can change the optimal ordering quantity since the discount can provide a tangible savings over and above any additional storage costs that might be incurred from having to store the extra inventory. The question then becomes, what would be the optimum ordering quantity if the supplier provided a discount for larger orders?

 Assume that the Celtics' supplier offered a 2% discount for orders equal to or greater than 10,000 shirts. Based on an order of 6,500 shirts in the previous example, the TIC was calculated at $8,000. We can rewrite the TIC equation using the 10,000-shirt order size and decreasing the price from $4.92 per shirt to $4.82 based on the 2% discount (Brigham & Gapenski, 1994).

$$\text{TIC} = [(\$1,000)(26,000 / 10,000)] +$$
$$[(0.25)(\$4.82)(10,000 / 2)]$$
$$= \$2,600 + \$6,025$$
$$= \$8,625$$

The carrying cost increases because the average inventory is larger, but the ordering cost declines since fewer orders are placed. Based on these numbers it would seem that adding 4,000 more shirts to the inventory increases inventory costs by only $625 per year. However, this analysis fails to take into consideration the savings of approximately 10 cents per shirt. The total yearly savings based on the 2% discount is $2,558. Thus, even after reducing the savings in shirt prices by the added inventory carrying cost ($625), the Celtics would generate a net savings of $1,933 each year by taking advantage of the larger-order discount (Brigham & Gapenski, 1994).

Inventory Conversion Period   Another calculation, one that is similar to the finished-goods or raw-materials turnover ratio, is the inventory conversion period (ICP) (Feiner, 1977). The ICP is the average length of time required to convert the raw materials to finished inventory and then sell the goods. We calculate the ICP by dividing inventory by the sales per day.

If we were to estimate that SMC had $5 million in inventory and $20 million in sales in the future, the calculation would be as follows:

$$ICP = inventory / sales\ per\ day$$
$$= \$5,000,000 / (\$20,000,000 / 360\ days)$$
$$= 90\ days$$

The equation indicates that it is 90 days from the time inventory is received until the rackets or clubs are manufactured and then sold.

The shorter the ICP, the more money the business will make if it makes a small profit on each item. For expensive items, the ICP may not be as relevant, since building one stadium might generate $20 million in profits for a builder but take three years to complete.

Amazon Floats

Amazon.com® uses a different inventory management system, which is referred to as a minimal inventory system utilizing a negative operating cycle. People also call the system a float as highlighted in chapter 12. The key to the system is that inventory is available through other suppliers so that the vendor does not really carry an inventory. The Internet bookseller Amazon carries only a small fraction of books in its inventory. Most book titles are not ordered until a customer places an order with Amazon. The result is that Amazon turns over the inventory 26 times a year compared with other booksellers such as Barnes & Noble, which has an inventory turnover of 10 (Mayer, 1998).

The negative operating cycles are what really separates Amazon from other booksellers and general retailers. Most companies need to buy a product, stock it, and move it to a different sales location before they can sell it. Amazon charges a customer's credit card account when the order is placed. The book distributor or publisher sends the book directly to the purchaser within days after it has been ordered. The credit card company pays Amazon within a day. Amazon then takes on average 46 days to pay its suppliers, the book distributors. Thus, instead of having to pay to finance sales (through borrowing money to purchase the books it sells—its inventory), Amazon makes even more money by having the customer's money for 45 days to reinvest and earn interest on (Mayer, 1998).

Regardless of the technique used to monitor inventory levels, a purchasing plan needs to be developed to optimize expenditures and carrying costs. This chapter provides several suggestions that will help with this decision. However, it is important to note that one of the best techniques to help optimize purchasing and inventory control is centralized purchasing. Imagine what would happen if a collegiate athletic department allowed each team to buy its own office supplies. Each team might have several hundred pens sitting in a drawer unused. In contrast, if the entire department bought several boxes of pens at a time, it could reduce total purchases. Centralized purchasing is designed to facilitate more effective purchasing, but it also allows a business to utilize inventories more effectively. The other benefits associated with centralized purchasing were addressed earlier in this chapter.

Utilizing Inventory

Businesses need to answer numerous questions in order to determine whether raw materials are being effectively utilized. The following are some of the key questions.

- How effective has management been in increasing the inventory turnover rate?
- How is purchasing controlled to make sure purchases are in economical quantities that do not unduly increase inventory carrying costs?
- Are any components of the manufacturing process sent to external sources for finishing, and can any such steps be completed internally?
- What is the relationship between direct and indirect labor costs?
- What steps are taken to reduce the need for overtime labor?
- Are the labor and materials costs clearly defined to allow accurate tracking?
- Are accurate records kept concerning equipment maintenance and repair costs?

- Who contracts for equipment rental or leasing, and how is that process supervised?
- What control mechanisms are in place to reduce pilferage and deterioration of supplies?

These are just some of the questions that are raised when a business starts putting the forecasting and inventory systems together with production and manufacturing. Before the manufacturing process could begin, SMC would need to develop a production budget.

Production Analysis

The production budget combines the desired inventory levels with forecast sales projections. The total production run that will be manufactured can be calculated by means of the following formula (Griffin, 1991):

total production = sales in units + desired ending inventory − projected beginning inventory

This formula can help a company determine if it needs to reduce the number of units produced if sales are low or if the inventory level is too high. This formula can be applied to calculate SMC's total production needs.

 Assume that SMC had forecast an ending inventory of 1,000 golf clubs in 2001. The beginning inventory is 500 clubs for 2001, which means that after the 2000 sales year was completed there were 500 clubs left in inventory. The company sold 10,000 clubs in 2001. The formula can be calculated as follows:

total production = 10,000 + 1,000 − 500
= 10,500 clubs

Thus, SMC would need to produce 10,500 clubs in order to serve all sales and to maintain an inventory of 1,000 clubs.

Another key component related to utilization is determining if a business is properly utilizing the workforce. Employers can calculate whether or not employees are performing their jobs efficiently. Time-motion studies undertaken by Frank Gilbreth (1868-1924) were conducted by industrialists to determine how long it would take for an assembly line worker to perform a given task (Bridges & Roquemore, 1996). Similarly, SMC could ascertain that an average golf club takes 4 hours to manufacture. Thus, in a 40-hour work week, an employee should manufacture 10 clubs. Employees who do not reach that goal are not utilizing their skills effectively. Management can track employee performance and engage in retraining or other steps to work with employees who are not effectively using their time.

The two steps outlined represent just two types of measurement techniques to help management identify costs associated with the production process. However, the manufacturing process entails unique components and costs that are necessary to transform the inventory, and utilizes the standards set forth in the production budget. Production management is the topic we turn to next.

> Managing inventory in a sport business involves forecasting, purchasing, storing, auditing, and utilizing inventory.

Production Management

This chapter has focused primarily on financing inventory and the costs associated with holding and liquidating inventory. However, most businesses do not maintain inventory in the same condition in which it was purchased unless they are in the wholesale business. Most companies utilize the inventory to develop some other marketable item. A professional team would have a useless inventory of players unless they actually competed. A golf club manufacturer must transform metal into a club in order to generate revenues. This transformation process costs money. Conversion costs entail direct materials, direct labor, and factory overhead. Direct materials are all the raw goods that will be used to make the product. For a golf club, the direct materials might include the metal as well as rubber for the grip. Direct labor entails the personnel time required to actually turn the metal and rubber into the club. The factory overhead involves the proportional costs of machinery and energy that are utilized to transform the metal and rubber into the club. Conversion costs do not include any nonmanufacturing costs such as administrative, advertising, and selling-related expenses.

The conversion costs associated with any manufacturing process are fairly simple to calculate. We can calculate direct material by dividing the cost of all the materials by the number of units that can be manufactured. If SMC paid $300,000 for metal and rubber and can produce 100,000 clubs with the materials, then the direct material cost is $3 per unit. Direct labor can be calculated in a similar manner.

If SMC employees can manufacture one club in 4 hours, the calculation to determine labor costs is very basic. The biggest mistake people make in determining labor costs is failing to include benefits in the calculation. If an SMC production line worker earned $10 per hour, the direct labor amount might not be $40 per club. If we assume that the employee's benefits amount to 40% of wages, the actual cost is not $40, but $56 per club.

The last component necessary for calculating conversion costs is factory overhead (FO). To determine factory overhead, a manufacturer calculates all the costs associated with the production process that do not include direct material or direct labor. Typical factory overhead costs could include lease expenses on equipment, interest payments owed for financed equipment, depreciation of factory equipment, utilities, insurance, maintenance, taxes, and any other expense that can be directly linked to the manufacturing process.

 Assume that SMC pays $20,000 annually for factory overhead costs. Furthermore, assume that the factory operates for 4,000 hours to produce a run of golf clubs. By dividing the $20,000 by the 4,000 hours we can determine that the factory overhead cost per hour is $5 per hour. Since it takes 4 hours to make a club, the FO is $20 per club assuming customized production of the clubs. By adding the direct materials, labor, and FO, we can calculate the manufacturing conversion costs for producing one golf club.

Direct material	$ 3
Direct labor	56
Factory overhead	20
Total	$79

The $79 conversion cost is critical because SMC needs this number to determine the lowest price it can charge a distributor for the clubs. Nonmanufacturing costs would need to be added to the $79 to determine the break-even point. If the total nonmanufacturing costs were $8 per unit, the club's break-even point would be $87.

Break-Even Analysis

The manufacturing process involves several key financial issues. One of the most important entails calculating an appropriate production run to maximize profits. In order to achieve the lowest production cost per unit, companies normally need to undertake large manufacturing runs. The setup cost

per unit is the measurement tool used to determine if the manufacturing process is economical. Break-even analysis can also be used to help calculate the number of additional items necessary to make a certain profit. Break-even analysis is discussed in chapter 5, but there the context is the financial statement rather than manufacturing. While the concepts are similar, break-even analysis associated with manufacturing focuses on specific manufactured items versus the business overall.

Instead of conversion costs, the following break-even analysis utilizes fixed costs. Fixed costs represent the costs that are incurred no matter how many units are manufactured. Variable costs change with the quantity being manufactured. The formula to calculate the break-even point is as follows:

$$\text{sale price} \times N = F + (\text{variable costs} \times N)$$

N = quantity

F = fixed costs

Quantity, often referred to as N as in this formula, denotes the units that need to be sold to break even. The break-even point is calculated in the next example.

 Assume that SMC has $100,000 in fixed costs for making tennis rackets. The variable cost per racket is $5. If these special-discount rackets sell for $10 each, we can calculate how many units need to be sold to break even. Applying the numbers, the equation is as follows:

$$\$10 \times N = \$100,000 + (\$5 \times N)$$
$$\$5N = \$100,000$$
$$N = 20,000$$

Thus, SMC needs to sell 20,000 of these rackets to break even. But what if SMC needs to make $40,000 from the rackets in order to undertake manufacturing them for an acceptable profit? The equation is as follows:

$$\$10 \times N = \$140,000 + (\$5 \times N)$$
$$\$5N = \$140,000$$
$$N = 28,000$$

The company would need to manufacture and sell 28,000 units to make the profit margin desired from this product line. Since the fixed costs are covered after 20,000 units have been manufactured, each unit over 20,000 has a $5 profit based on the $10 sales price minus the $5 variable costs.

Planning and pro forma budgets, discussed in chapter 7, also apply to manufacturing break-even analysis. We cannot perform a break-even analysis without referring to projected budgets for such items as sales and production runs. These data are critical for identifying how many units may be sold and how many units must be produced to meet the sales demand. A company can manufacture enough units to meet the break-even point; but if the units are not being sold, the company will not break even and will in fact be losing money as a consequence of having inventory sit on shelves.

All the factors addressed throughout this chapter help establish the numbers needed to create a realistic sales budget. The sales budget represents the number of units that the company anticipates should be sold in an upcoming time period. A sales budget is based on a multitude of factors or techniques. The unit costs, anticipated demand, the competition, consumer interest, and a host of additional variables help create the sales budget. In addition, salespeople can be asked what they anticipate future sales might be, and customers can be asked how much they might order in the future. A company can also estimate a specific percentage growth over the sales volume in the prior period. A sample sales budget was presented in the Introduction to the Case Studies (see p. 2).

Variance Analysis

It is relatively simple to calculate the break-even point or the optimum manufacturing run for making a specific profit, but these numbers are meaningless if the actual production runs are not monitored to ensure that the costs conform to the projections. Variance analysis is the process of establishing performance standards. Once the standards are established, a business needs to determine if it is reaching the standards. Are the actual fixed costs higher than projected? Why are they higher? For example, are energy prices higher than anticipated? Are variable costs above expectations? These costs could be higher because of an unanticipated increase in the price of iron if iron is one of the metals the business needs. If the costs are below expectations, the business will generate a greater profit than expected. If any cost is too high, the business must lower costs to meet the production budget. Cost reduction strategies might need to target a specific cost area or the entire production process. If costs are increasing across the board, a business may consider reducing some costs by taking drastic steps such as terminating employees or taking one day off from production each week.

Labor Costs

One of the greatest expenses associated with the manufacturing process is personnel cost. While most people do not consider people to be machines, they in fact are a part of the manufacturing process. Similar to a cutting machine that might help make a racket, a person can help make a sport product. In order to produce the product of a baseball game, you need to have players who can produce the game. Depending on the product's quality, the human machines that produce the games can either be very expensive or cheap. Thus, baseball players in the major league might get paid a significant amount for the product they produce, whereas players in the minor league might get paid very little for their product because even though both sets of players are producing the same product, they are producing at different quality levels. Whether for players or administrative personnel, expenses can be significant; and businesses need to carefully track labor costs. Salaries are among the primary components of labor costs, and these costs can be higher in the sport industry compared with other labor markets.

> To manage production effectively, a sport business must understand the cost of transforming inventory—whether raw materials for a manufacturing company or players for a team—into a marketable product.

Salaries for some positions may be straightforward (for example, minimum wage positions paying $5.15 an hour) (Fried & Miller, 1998). This is the current federal minimum wage rate, but some states have higher rates. New York's minimum wage mirrors the federal rate, but California's rate is $6.75 per hour and Connecticut's rate is $6.70 per hour. However, salaries in sport can be very complicated. Professional athletes have numerous clauses in their contracts that call for benefits several times over and beyond the base salaries. It is not only athletes who have complicated salaries, though. Table 13.3 shows the breakdown for the salary and benefits provided to Pat Richter, athletic director at the University of Wisconsin, for 1997-1998.

Table 13.3	Salary and Benefits Provided to Pat Richter
Base salary	$173,300
Radio show	3,000
Speaking	5,000
Radio/TV ads	7,000
Other	5,000
Total outside income	**$20,000**
Country club	6,400
Madison Club	1,100
Car payment	11,400
Total perks/benefits	**$18,900**
Total package	**$212,200**

From "UW Athletic Department," 1998.

Salary Packages

In 1998, football coach Barry Alvarez had a highly complex salary package totaling over $600,000 and including $210,000 for his TV show, $140,000 for a Reebok consulting contract, $71,000 from radio shows, $15,033 for two bowl game bonuses, and $864 in complimentary tickets. The coach also received $8,288 from camps and clinics ("UW Athletic Department," 1998). The income derived from the TV show, radio shows, and shoe endorsements was paid by external companies rather than the university, but still represents part of the overall employment package. The women's basketball coach also received a sizable package. Besides a base salary over $100,000 a year, Jane Albright-Dieterle received $43,500 from camps and clinics, $20,000 from Reebok, a $10,000 country club membership, and $5,200 from the Badger Store as part of her $186,700 total package ("UW Athletic Department," 1998).

The costs associated with labor can be immense. The biggest budget item for most businesses is salaries and benefits. Many businesses attempt to boost their bottom line by reducing salaries through terminations. Businesses are also reducing benefits and requiring employees to pay a greater share for health insurance to help decrease employee-related costs. Since labor is so expensive, businesses often need to determine if they are paying too much for their employees. This question can be answered through examination of the earnings per hour for a company (Feiner, 1977). A way to calculate earnings per hour is to divide total sales by the expected total number of hours worked. The earnings per hour ratio helps management determine how effectively a plant is running. The next example involves this ratio.

Assume that SMC forecasts sales to total $200,000 and that direct and indirect labor will entail 13,000 hours. By dividing the total sales by the expected total hours, we can develop the earnings per hour rate. In this example, the earnings per hour would be $200,000 / 13,000, which would be $15.38 per hour. If the labor costs are less than $15.38 per hour, SMC would be able to cover its labor costs. Note that this analysis does not include raw materials and other fixed costs that are over and above the labor costs.

Labor costs are such a significant component of the manufacturing process that the costs need to be compared to those for other companies in the same industry. Management can use such a benchmark as a negotiation tool if the competitors have a lower labor cost. If the competition pays more, a business can use its creativity to make up any difference. In the hot Internet market of the late 1990s, many compa-

nies were moving away from traditional salary-based motivation and toward stock options and other incentives that did not require a significant capital outlay. Although stock options can be a strong benefit, some observers felt that such deals helped lead executives to push for increasing their share value over true growth. This was seen in the WorldCom and Enron scandals. Through innovation, a company can reduce labor costs and increase its profitability.

Employers have often attempted to reduce employee-related costs. Employers need to reduce labor costs to maximize profit. That is one reason why employers fight so hard against unionization. Unionization might mean sharing power; but more important, when employees can negotiate as one, they normally can generate a higher per employee salary and larger group benefits. In order to combat rising employee-related expenses, employers are resorting to various tactics that they hope can lower costs. Several universities, most notably the University of Pennsylvania, Stanford University, and Tufts, have outsourced facility workers such as custodians (Nicklin, 1997). Outsourcing can allow the universities to concentrate more fully on their primary strengths (education and research), but it also can reduce benefit costs. A university employee who earns $30,000 per year and receives significant benefits, including tuition reimbursement, can cost the university well over $50,000. However, if the custodian is terminated and then signs with a janitorial service that has an exclusive contract with the university, the cost for the same worker could decrease to under $40,000. The $10,000 savings can be magnified by economies of scale, as the janitorial service can hire more people for less money and still make its profit. According to the principle of economies of scale, the larger the number of individuals involved, the greater the savings. Thus, although a $10,000 savings may not seem significant in itself, if the university requires the services of 100 janitors, the savings could be over $1 million. Outsourcing is just one technique organizations consider when attempting to reduce labor costs. Through lowering these costs, overall manufacturing costs can also be reduced. Thus, if inventory or manufacturing costs are too high, a business can consider reducing costs by controlling other expense areas such as labor costs.

CONCLUSION

Some of the material in this chapter, such as the information on manufacturing-related costs, does not apply to all businesses. However, all businesses need to manage their resources, and that is inventory management. Even an entity such as the University of Houston has inventory. It manages land, facilities, chemicals, equipment, and other assets. These assets need to be tracked, maintained, repurchased, and sold. Carrying and ordering costs need to be included in any budget.

Even businesses that do not traditionally manufacture products do manufacture value. The Celtics do not manufacture any products such as widgets. They manufacture basketball-related entertainment products. Thus, even the Celtics need to analyze manufacturing-related costs and to determine whether or not the players are working together cohesively. If the players are not working well together, the manufacturing process will not work as effectively, and the "machinery" for producing a winning season will need to be overhauled.

ASSIGNMENTS

1. Why is break-even analysis important?
2. If you had to explain the LIFO and FIFO process to the Smiths, what would you say and which system would you encourage them to use?
3. How frequently should SMC conduct an inventory audit and why?
4. Calculate the production cost and the break-even analysis for the 1930s baseball team highlighted in chapter 2.

RESEARCH PROJECT

Examine ticket pricing in professional sport and, selecting a specific team, track its ticket-pricing policies for the past five years. Examine the price and total attendance numbers to see if there is a correlation between increased pricing and lower attendance.

CLASS DISCUSSION TOPICS

1. What do you think is the most effective way to manage inventory?
2. What forecasting strategies would you utilize if you were managing a ski resort that had to deal with uncontrollable weather factors?
3. What strategies do you think might be useful in reducing employee pilfering?
4. What cost reduction strategies could be used by SMC or the University of Houston?
5. Should coaches receive large contractual perks and if so, what are some means to deal with Title IX or Equal Pay Act concerns?

PART V

Profits

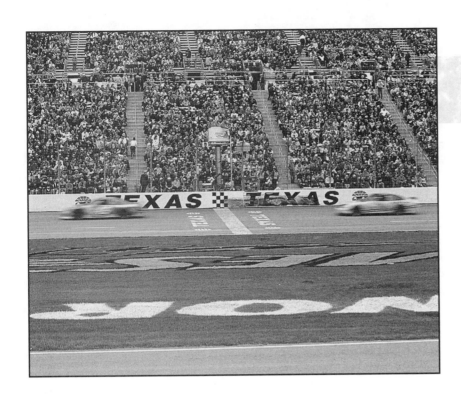

Taxation and Legal Issues

CHAPTER OBJECTIVES

After studying this chapter, you should be able to do the following:

- Understand some of the tax concerns affecting the sport industry.
- Understand the issues associated with minority ownership of a sport business.
- Describe the importance of tax planning in sport.
- Calculate the marginal tax rate.
- Understand how tax law is applied to athletes.
- Understand the basics of financial risk management.

Legal issues abound in the finance field. Securities and Exchange Commission regulations are voluminous. Legal issues can apply to the wording on the prospectus and to footnotes that need to be added to financial statements to provide details on transactions. Legal issues involve not only federal law but also numerous state laws. For example, blue-sky laws in almost all states regulate security dealers or the selling of securities in the state. In this chapter we start by focusing on the legal and tax ramifications of a sport business' structure and then expand on the discussion of corporations and partnerships from chapter 4. The chapter then deals with various tax-related concerns such as tax planning, taxes in sport, and taxes affecting teams and athletes. The topics of the final section are financial risk management and insurance as a financial parachute.

Benefits of Corporate Status

Chapter 4 highlighted some of the benefits afforded to corporations and partnerships. Corporations have several distinct advantages that can aid sport businesses, and professional sport teams have benefited from these opportunities for many years. Corporations and some partnerships can use losses to offset tax liabilities that occur in other business enterprises. Former San Francisco 49ers owner Edward DeBartolo transferred ownership in the team to his father's real estate company to create additional tax losses (Euchner, 1993). The New York Yankees reorganized in 1991, and the structural changes allowed limited partners to claim losses on their personal income taxes (Euchner, 1993).

Proper business and financial structuring can save millions of dollars. The **estates** of NFL team owners George Halas and Paul Brown were both assessed over $100 million in back taxes by the IRS. However, on the basis of shrewd business reorganization efforts, the estates in fact received an aggregate IRS refund of $2.5 million (Much, 1997, September 9). The tax benefit was established through the creation of minority ownership rights in the teams and the resultant lower value attributable to the minority interests. An example will clarify how this worked. Let's suppose that a company has 100 shares of stock. If numerous people own the shares, anyone interested in buying the company needs to buy a majority of the shares, but will not have complete control unless she buys all 100 shares. If someone owned 49 shares, that person's shares would represent 49% of the business. The reason for the lower value is that not as many people would be

interested in buying a minority interest since they would not be the primary owner and could never sell the entire business. As explained further on, by giving away shares to various relatives or colleagues, a team owner can dramatically reduce the values of all shares.

In the case involving the estate of the late Paul Brown, former owner of the Cincinnati Bengals, the IRS sought over $40 million in estate taxes. The controversy that brought the dispute before U.S. Tax Court Judge John O. Colvin entailed a 1983 stock option transaction that the government claimed was a scam. In that transaction, Brown had transferred 117 of his shares in the team to John Sawyer (another stockholder) for $30,000 per share. The sales contract allowed Brown to keep one share and still maintain complete control over the team. Another contract required Sawyer to sell, if Brown's sons exercised an option to buy, 329 of the now 330 shares Sawyer had for $25,000 each in 1993. The IRS unsuccessfully argued that the stock shares were sold significantly below the shares' true market value. The court ruled against the IRS based on the fact that even though the contract allowed the sons an option to buy back the team at a lower price, there was potential risk that the team would be worth less in 1993 than in 1983 (Much, 1997, September 9). If there had been no possibility of the value going down and the sons could have bought back the team at a lower price than what had been paid for the team, then the IRS would have prevailed.

Another key component in the Bengals deal involved the minority ownership interest. A minority owner traditionally does not have significant pull in any business; a minority share does, however, have the ability to drastically decrease the value of the team, as previously mentioned. Suppose you owned 99% of a house and your parents owned the remaining 1%. If the house was worth $100,000, no one would ever pay $100,000 for it because the individual would never be the complete owner. Someone might pay $70,000 for the house with the intent to buy the remaining 1% from your parents. There is no requirement that your parents in fact sell their percentage share of the house, so the buyer would be taking a risk. This risk element reduces the value of the majority share. The same concept applies to a professional sport team and other sport businesses. Although more people are willing to take a risk in buying a professional team, minority shares can still reduce the value of the majority shares. This reduced value can drastically decrease taxes that might be owed either on capital gains or on an inheritance, since the minority interests reduce all other values.

Although team values have significantly increased over the past decade, this does not necessarily increase value for some team's minority owners. Anyone interested in purchasing a business would attempt to pay a higher amount for the largest share and then pay a lower amount for smaller shares. A potential purchaser might be willing to pay more for a larger share after which they could assume managerial control and make life miserable for minority owners. In contrast, if a minority owner is a holdout, the majority shares can decrease in value. Assume that the developer of a stadium wants to buy 10 houses that are located on the land where the playing field will be. Nine homeowners are willing to sell, but the 10th owner refuses. The other nine owners will either receive reduced offers for their houses or a revocation of the offer, since the missing house reduces the value of the deal. The developer will not want to build the stadium if there will be a house on the 50-yard line. Thus, not owning all 10 houses reduces the value of all the houses. Similarly, not owning an entire team can reduce the team's value and save on taxes.

Although the Bengals deal held up in court, not every attempt to avoid estate taxes is successful. The Robbie family faced a $47 million tax bill after the death of former Miami Dolphins owner Joe Robbie. The family did not have the money and were forced to sell the team to Wayne Huizenga (Much, 1997, September 9). On the basis of these tax issues, the NFL has been considering changing the amount a general partner needs to own with the aim of helping families reduce estate tax concerns. In 2000, a general partner in an NFL team was required to own at least 30% of a team. The new rule would apply to someone who has been an owner of a team for at least 10 years and would allow him to remain a general partner while owning only 10% of the team as long as he maintained his decision-making power. The rule would allow an owner to transfer ownership to children in an effort to avoid the 55% estate tax ("NFL Looking," 2000).

As corporations or partnerships, sport teams take advantage of the tax benefits that these business structures are entitled to receive.

Taxes

No matter what organizational structure is chosen for a business, every manager needs to know some tax basics. The value of any financial asset or instrument is contingent on the cash flow produced by the investment. This cash flow is subject to taxation when disbursed and when received. If the tax rate on a given investment cash stream is too high, the investor will opt for a different investment that may have a lower return, but also lower taxes. For example, cautious investors often purchase tax-free bonds rather than stock or other types of investment vehicles. Although the interest rate is lower, tax-free bonds may be more practical than investments that pay a higher interest rate, as taxes on a taxable investment may cancel out any benefit derived from the higher interest rate.

An example will help show why this is so. If a municipality that is building a stadium issues a $1,000 tax-free bond that pays 5% interest each year, the investor will "take home" $50 each year. In contrast, if the investor buys a $1,000 face-value bond issued by the Celtics that pays 7%, her $70 per year interest will be subject to taxation. If her tax rate is 30%, then instead of taking home $70, she will take home only $49 after taxes. While in this example the difference is only a dollar, the purchaser of the tax-free bond also has the comfort of a secure investment, as most tax-free bonds are issued by government entities and have a low default rate. The difference could be much more significant when riskier bonds, such as junk bonds, are being purchased.

There are two formulas that can help an investor determine which of two investment options would return the most after taxes. Assume that Jane Doe wants to invest $10,000 in bonds. She is taxed at a rate of 31%. She is considering investing in a municipal tax-free bond (a "muni") with a 10% yield. Munis are attractive investment vehicles because they help communities grow and pay their holders interest that is tax free. Doe wants to determine the **tax-equivalent yield** for a taxable bond that would produce the same rate of return as the muni. The formula is as follows:

$$\text{tax-equivalent yield} = \text{yield on muni} / (1 - \text{marginal tax rate})$$
$$= 10\% / (1 - 0.31)$$
$$= 14.5\%$$

This formula determines the taxable bond yield, but what if we know the taxable bond yield and want to determine the equivalent muni yield? Another formula determines the desired minimum muni yield (Brigham & Gapenski, 1994):

$$\text{yield on muni} = (\text{taxable bond yield})(1 - \text{marginal tax rate})$$
$$= 14.5\%(1 - 0.31)$$
$$= 10.0\%$$

The formulas illustrate the types of calculations an investor or business needs to make in order to do tax planning. Making the wrong choice can cost an investor a significant amount of money. In contrast, through undertaking a simple analytical step, an investor can save a significant amount of money. The difference between the returns with the bonds would entice most investors to choose a taxable bond if the return is over 14.5% and tax-free bonds are paying less than 10% interest. Careful tax planning is not just an exercise in trying to keep Uncle Sam happy or to avoid an audit, but an exercise that gives people or businesses information about various investment options to help them maximize revenues.

Tax Planning

Almost everyone is familiar with taxes. We pay taxes at the gas pump in the form of gas taxes. We pay sales taxes at the cash register. We may pay a surcharge on the ticket to a game or other event. We also may pay **income tax** at the federal or state level or both. Thus, the average person is often all too familiar with taxes. However, corporations and businesses have unique tax concerns. We might not feel the impact of tax withholdings when our employers pay our taxes and we readjust the amount paid when we complete our tax forms. However, businesses often have to pay sales, employee, transportation, property, income, and possibly numerous additional taxes. If a business does not properly plan for all potential tax liabilities, it can lose significant revenue.

In 1958 the Federal Tax Code had 650 pages. By 1998 the Federal Tax Code had 2,862 pages ("Tax Numbers," 2000). The following case study example highlights how important tax planning is for a business.

Assume that the Smiths decided to retire after 20 years in the business. A potential purchaser offered to give them $1 million a year for 10 years. The Smiths thought this would help them retire. However, if they had not critically analyzed the sale's tax implications, their retirement plans could have been significantly affected if they had sold the business in 1999 versus 2000. Under previous law the Smiths would have paid a yearly income tax on the yearly payment. Thus, if they were in the 30% tax bracket they would have paid $300,000 a year in taxes and would have lived off the remaining $700,000. However, under a law signed by President Clinton in December, 1999, most installment purchase contracts for businesses would be taxable in a lump sum the first year. For the Smiths, this would have meant that they would have had to declare in the first year that they had sold the business for $10 million. Their tax bill at 30% would have been $3 million the first year even though they would have received only $1 million the first year. Under one system the Smiths could have retired in comfort, and under the other system they would have been in debt for over three years (Hube, 2000). On the basis of this potentially unforeseen hardship, the law was quickly overturned in 2000.

Taxing Visiting Athletes

To help finance the new sport facilities in Pittsburgh, the city's taxing authority (Department of Finance) decided to tax out-of-town athletes for games they played in Pittsburgh. The city estimated it would receive $1 million a year. The tax is based on a "duty day," which is calculated by determining what percentage of the athlete's income was earned in Pittsburgh during a given year. If an athlete played in Pittsburgh on only 5 of the 200 days on which he played or practiced his sport over the year, then the taxable income would be based on 5 days. For a player who earned $200,000 a year to play on 200 days, the tax would be only $50 a year. However, as of 2000 the city had obtained only a small portion of the expected $1 million ($26,000), and only 35 of the 47 teams playing in the city had registered to pay the tax ("Athlete's Tax Fails," 2000).

Businesses that fail to properly analyze tax implications can overstate anticipated income, which can lead to litigation from shareholders based on the inaccurate information. Numerous taxes can apply, including sales, property, and ad valorem taxes. While some taxes are direct pass-through taxes to the ultimate consumer, other taxes are borne by the company manufacturing the product. If a golf club manufacturing company is based in Europe, the host country may impose a value-added tax, which is a tax applied to the value added at every stage of the manufacturing process. When the raw aluminum is transformed into a shaft, a tax may be imposed. This type of tax may be imposed at all phases of the manufacturing process and is incorporated into the sales price. However, no separate sales tax is imposed on the clubs as they are sold. Furthermore, many European countries offer travelers a value-added tax refund as they leave the country. This tax example applies only to European companies.

The Cleveland Indians Before the Supreme Court

A case involving the Cleveland Indians wound up on the United States Supreme Court docket. Major League Baseball owners violated the players' free agency rights from 1986 through 1988. Pursuant to an agreement reached after a negative arbitration award, the owners agreed to pay $280 million to the players who had been harmed. A dispute arose over the percentage of the back pay that would be subject to Social Security taxes. The Indians were supposed to pay a total of $2.1 million to 22 players. The issue before the court was whether the team should have paid taxes at the 1994 rate when the arbitration award was finalized or at the lower 1986 rate when the disputed wages were earned. The team paid the higher rate and asked for a refund, and the trial court and appellate court each agreed that the lower rate should have been paid; but the IRS appealed the case to the highest court in the land (Greenberger, 2000). The Supreme Court ruled that the tax rate for 1994, when the payment was to be made, was the applicable tax year, not the year the money was initially earned ("Back Pay," 2001).

The two key concepts for analyzing taxing structures are marginal and average tax rates. The marginal tax rate is defined as the percentage tax liability imposed on the next dollar of income earned by the company or individual (Spiro, 1996). In contrast, the average tax rate is the total tax liability imposed on all taxable income. Suppose a tax structure called for a tax of 20% on all income under $100,000 and a 25% tax on income between $100,001 and $200,000. If the Smiths earned $140,000 in income, their taxes would be $30,000 ([0.20 × $100,000 = $20,000] + [0.25 × $40,000 = $10,000]). The marginal tax rate is 25% for all income over $140,000 (i.e., the next dollar of income earned). To calculate the average tax rate, we divide the $30,000 total tax burden by the $140,000 income, which produces an average tax rate of 21.4%. The average tax rate is important for historical purposes (for example, if we want to know how much of our income has been paid in taxes over the past five years). However, the more critical point of analysis for financial managers is the marginal tax rate, the rate on the next dollar earned. If a company knows that the next $100,000 earned will be taxed at a very high rate, it might decide not to earn that extra money because the resulting tax obligation would negate any added value from raising the next $100,000 in income. However, if additional income adds to the corporation's bottom line, then the corporation should attempt to earn that additional income even if a large percentage will go to taxes. The only exception is the situation in which a corporation earns just a few more dollars that send it into a higher tax bracket. In this case the additional income could in fact cost the business money because it has earned only a few more dollars but is now subject to a tax rate that might be 5% to 10% higher.

Taxing Sport

It is beyond the scope of this text to critically analyze all tax-related issues. However, in this section we overview some significant tax issues that affect the sport industry.

Various tax implications are associated with purchasing a professional sport team. For example, a major legal battle arose in connection with a 1997 tax court decision concerning whether or not stadium leases could be amortized when a professional team with a very good facility lease is purchased ("Portions of New Orleans," 1998). The case involved the New Orleans Saints, sold in 1985. When a team is sold, the primary assets are the players' contracts, franchise rights, and possibly a favorable lease. A business' goodwill is a Section 197 amortizable asset that can be amortized over 15 years. However, Section 197(e)(6) specifically excludes a sport franchise from such **amortization.** Thus, the team, or more specifically the expenditure directly attributable to the sport franchise rights, is not amortizable. However, if the team has switched some of the value away from the team franchise and allocated that sum to the lease, the lease value can be amortized over the time remaining on the lease. The cost of acquiring a leasehold is a capital expenditure recoverable through amortization. Such a benefit can be taken only if someone is willing to pay for the lease, which would occur only if the fair value exceeds the rent obligation established under the terms of the lease agreement. For example, if the team has been paying $100,000 a year to lease a facility and the fair market value for leasing the facility under a new lease would be $200,000, then the $100,000 value could be amortized over the remainder of the lease term.

The Saints were purchased for over $70 million. The team and the IRS took different approaches in establishing whether or not the lease was amortizable, but agreed that if it was, the value would be $16 million. The court concluded that the lease agreement, modified in 1975, was a premium lease and as such was amortizable. However, the court also held that if new lease terms are negotiated at the time the team is purchased, such new lease terms cannot be amortized ("Portions of New Orleans," 1998).

Besides potential tax implications associated with lease values, tax issues can arise as they relate to benefits generated through public tax dollars helping team owners. This concern can come up when a team negotiates a favorable contract that might be "too good." For example, Charlotte Hornets owner George Shinn was sued by a community activist for $4.1 million ("Shinn Faces Suit," 1998). The suit concerned the revenue Shinn had received from the Charlotte Coliseum based on parking and concession profits. Originally the lease between the Coliseum and Shinn had given the Coliseum 100% of parking and concession profits during Hornet games. This arrangement was changed in 1995 to give Shinn 50% of the profits, which over three seasons had totaled $4.1 million. The suit claimed that the lease agreement was unconstitutional as it conferred "privileges upon private parties without public benefit" ("Shinn Faces Suit," 1998). The activist was in essence claiming that in getting a change in the contract terms without public input, approval, or benefit, Shinn was receiving an unconstitutional benefit and that the benefits of the contractual change should revert back to Charlotte citizens. Thus, tax implications can benefit team owners or can raise the specter of the public coffers being raided by the wealthy and create a legal backlash.

Potential legal backlashes associated with favorable stadium financing deals were addressed by Congress in the 1986 Tax Act. Prior to passage of the act, municipalities were able to issue tax-exempt bonds for sport facilities. Tax-exempt bonds are more attractive for investors and might carry a better rate than taxable bonds. While the interest coupons are tax-exempt, any capital gains from the bonds are taxable. The benefit associated with tax-exempt bonds became problematic when the main tenant of the public building was a professional sport franchise. The government viewed such facilities, even if they were run by the local government, as private-purpose facilities and therefore not qualified for the tax-exempt status (Greenberg & Gray, 1996). One loophole was left in the legislation that allows bonds to retain their tax-exempt status. Under the private-activity test, a bond is not tax-exempt if 10% of the facility's use is controlled by a private business or if 10% of revenues to repay the bonds are derived from the private use. This loophole has been utilized by numerous stadium and arena projects with deals structured in such a way that if there is a primary facility user, that user will be charged less than 10% of the required principal and interest repayment amounts (Greenberg & Gray, 1996). Thus, many lease agreements limit the payment from the primary user to minimal amounts such as parking revenue, which normally would not come close to covering 10% of the annual debt service.

Additional attempts to prevent the raiding of public coffers or to deny a major advantage to a sport team could be seen in legislation proposed by Illinois Congressman William O. Lipinski entitled the Taxpayer's Right to View Act of 1992 (H.R. 4736, 1992). The bill, which eventually was not passed, was based on the premise that most sport facilities are funded by taxpayers and that it is unfair for taxpayers to pay for a facility but not be able to enjoy watching events broadcast from there if the events are aired on pay TV instead of "free" TV. The legislation also focused on nonprofit educational institutions that receive significant tax incentives and then try to broadcast events to taxpayers on a pay-per-view basis. The legislation called for taxpayers to have free access to events that are sponsored by nonprofit organizations and held in taxpayer-financed facilities. The bill also would have prohibited cable operators from charging or collecting a fee for pay-per-view broadcasts of an event held in a facility built, renovated, or maintained with taxpayers' financial support.

A sport business must analyze the tax implications of all its activities; one of the most important issues in relation to taxes is selecting or building a facility in which to play.

How Free Is "Free" TV?

Who pays for games to be aired on free TV? Pursuant to the $17.6 billion, eight-year contract to broadcast NFL games on ABC/ESPN, CBS, and Fox, CBS has asked its affiliates to ante up between $30 million and $50 million per year to help defray the costs. These costs would have to be passed on to advertisers, who would be obliged to increase prices to help cover their increased costs. ESPN has also asked affiliates for a 20% hike in cable fees that would probably be passed on to consumers (McGraw, 1998). Thus, it would be the consumer who would pay even more to watch games on either free TV or cable as a consequence of the increased price of consumer products advertised during the broadcast.

Although the Taxpayer's Right to View Act of 1992 was not successful, the IRS has been able to develop some equity by forcing nonprofit educational institutions such as schools involved in bowl games and some athletic departments to pay taxes if they are in fact engaged in a business enterprise. Two college football bowl games faced this issue in 1991 when the IRS ruled that Mobil Corp.'s contribution to the Cotton Bowl ($1.5 million) and John Hancock Mutual Life Insurance Co.'s $1 million payment to its bowl constituted unrelated business income (Lederman, 1991). The primary mission of the bowl games is educational, but the IRS concluded that the sponsorship payments were made in essence for advertisements whose benefit is not educational. Thus, since the advertisements were not "substantially related" to the primary mission of education, the revenue was taxable at about 34% (Lederman, 1991).

Nothing Is Free

So far we have considered just a few tax-related issues, but the IRS has developed so many complex rules that it is almost impossible to engage in any revenue-generating project without raising a potential tax-related concern.

If the University of Houston wanted to raise some money through a fund-raising campaign, most people would think that as a nonprofit organization it should not face significant tax hurdles. However, there is a complex set of tax requirements for treating gifts even to a nonprofit organization. Suppose that the University of Houston was trying to raise $100,000 for rebuilding a football field. The students decide to have a walk-a-thon and a raffle for a new car. They will also just ask people for donations and give donors gifts based on the size of the donation.

The IRS rules are fairly clear for the walk-a-thon; as there is no expected return to the donor, the donor can deduct the entire donation. Those who have lost money on the raffle can claim a donation for charitable purposes. The winner of the car will have to claim a gift on his tax return. However, the complexity arises with the last fund-raising option. As of 1998, the IRS requires individuals to reduce their donation amount by any premiums they receive if the premiums are valued at no more than 2% of the gift or $71, whichever is less (McAllister, 1998). Thus if a person gives $100 and receives a $10 gift, the total donation is only $90 (since $10 is greater than 2%, it cannot be disregarded). If a donor gives $4,000 and receives a plaque, the plaque can be disregarded if it is worth less than $71 (since $71 is less than 2%, which is $80 in this example) (McAllister, 1998). These rules are further complicated by additional rules that provide for disregarding low-cost logo premiums if the donation is over $35.50 and the total cost for the premium is under $7.10. The amounts applied to logo premiums are adjusted annually for inflation. Clarity becomes the key to helping donors understand their gift, and the IRS requires charitable organizations to give donors a breakdown of deductions that may be claimed whenever they contribute more than $75 and receive something of value (Blum, 1993). In 2002, the IRS ruled that the 2% rule was no longer being followed so premiums only need to be reported if they are valued at least at $71.

Charitable Planning

Various techniques can be utilized to raise funds for nonprofit organizations. The issue just discussed is only one tax-related concern associated with giving money. A more important concern relates to large donations and the various tax ramifications associated with such gifts. All nonprofits try to attract the large donations. While small gifts are nice, it is usually impossible to run larger programs without some large gifts. The manner in which these gifts are given significantly affects the ability of a donor to give the gift.

Assume that the University of Houston has an alumna who wishes to give $500,000 to the university. However, she does not want to just give the money over, because she bought the asset for $100,000 and would have to pay capital gains taxes on the $400,000 increase in value. The university could suggest using a charitable remainder trust to provide a benefit to the university and give the donor the option of reducing her tax liability. A charitable remainder trust (CRT) allows donors to give gifts at a future date but retain during their lifetime the interest income from the asset. The donor receives a current tax deduction, whereas if the gift was transferred after the individual's death, it would be the estate that would receive the deduction. The assets deposited in the trust can appreciate without the donor's having to pay tax on the income from the trust, and the donor does not have to pay capital gains taxes if the trust increases in value.

Using the $500,000 figure, assume that the donor currently receives a 3% return on the asset ($15,000 a year), that her tax bracket is 30%, and that the estate tax bracket is 55%. From the CRT the donor wishes to receive a 7% return, or $35,000 a year, over the course of her life. Table 14.1 shows the analysis for the options available to the donor if she deposits the asset in the CRT, keeps the asset, or sells the asset.

Table 14.1 shows that the lifetime net spendable income increases 181% when the CRT is compared with selling the asset and increases 256% when compared with keeping the asset (Fagan, 1999). If the donor kept the asset, she would have a lower income level but would be able to pass more money on to her heirs. If she sold the asset, she would receive the greatest upfront return, but her heirs would get the least amount with this option because of the high estate tax rate. If the donor's goal was to raise the highest amount of after-tax income over the life of the gift, then the CRT would be her best option. The example shows that proper tax planning can help educate donors about opportunities that can maximize their potential gifts.

Table 14.1

	Charitable remainder trust	Keep	Sell
Market value	$500,000	$500,000	$500,000
Capital gains	0	0	112,000
Charitable tax deduction	162,295	0	0
Income for donor	576,122	225,000	407,400
After-tax income	403,285	157,500	299,180
Value to heirs	0	225,000	174,600

Athletes and Taxes

While nonprofit organizations and their donors need to be concerned about tax implications of various gifts, professional sport teams can face the same challenges. For instance, in 1988 the Philadelphia Phillies gave Mike Schmidt a $2,150,000 contract that included a $100,000 charitable deduction made in Schmidt's name but with the tax deduction to go to the club ("1988 Baseball Salaries," 1988). Under this arrangement, Schmidt would have to include the $100,000 in his income even if he did not receive the money and if the club took the deduction pursuant to Federal Regulation 1.61-2(c). Teams regularly provide such bonuses to players as a means of increasing the player's take-home pay without increasing the player's salary. The additional amount usually is not counted against any salary cap constraints if it is an earnable bonus. Players appreciate the bonus because it can help their marketing and public relations effort, even if they have to pay taxes on the amount.

Numerous additional tax-related concerns can also arise for an athlete, such as how to categorize income. For example, a professional athlete's salary is subject to income tax withholdings, but signing bonuses are not considered remuneration for services and generally are not subject to the employer withholding taxes. However, the tax law clearly indicates that bonuses paid to baseball players that are predicated on continued employment are subject to withholding (Revenue Ruling, 1958). Numerous other revenue rulings issued by federal tax courts have also addressed bonuses and whether or not a player can give part of a bonus to a parent and claim the payment to the parent as a business expense. In one case a player gave $40,000 of his $70,000 bonus to his mother, but the tax court did not allow the expense deduction (*Allen v. Commissioner*, 1968). However, in another case, the tax court allowed the expense. In this case the player had paid his father a portion of the bonus, in part for his father's shrewd handling of the contract negotiation process and the years his father had spent coaching and training him (*Hundley v. Commissioner*, 1967).

Business expenses for a professional athlete can be highly diverse. The following are some of the expenditures that are classified as business expenses for athletes:

- Game tickets for individuals who train with the athlete to help improve the athlete's skills
- Expenses for operating a training camp or off-season conditioning
- Dues for a players' association
- Expenses for tax planning and investment advising
- Agent fees
- Fines imposed by a league or team for misconduct (*Ray Robinson v. Commissioner*, 1965)

Even though the case involving fines is over 35 years old, it is still the law of the land, and all the items listed are still considered valid expenses to reduce an athlete's tax obligations.

As the list suggests, careful planning by an athlete can reduce potential tax obligations. A professional athlete can run a summer camp and his own off-season training regime at the same facility using the same personnel. Through legal but creative accounting techniques, the expenses can be covered either under the athlete's personal business expenses or on the camp's tax return to help minimize tax obligations. It is important to recognize and appreciate that the failure to properly plan can destroy an athlete as easily as it can destroy a business. Former Dallas Cowboy great Tony Dorsett became so involved in ill-advised tax shelters that by 1985 the IRS had taken his paychecks and put liens on his homes to satisfy a $414,274 tax obligation (Rosenblatt, 1989).

The same tax issues associated with bonuses and business expenses also affect various other monetary matters, such as

- deferred income and nonqualified deferred income plans for player salaries,
- local and city taxes charged to players who earn money by playing in a given area or city such as Pittsburgh, and

- the creation of nonprofit charities by players that are designed to give family members jobs and to give the players a qualified tax deduction.

Taxing the Teams

Tax planning requires analyzing a company's or institution's long-term plans to determine the most appropriate path toward minimizing tax obligations. For example, a company expecting significant future profits may want to wait until the next tax year to purchase expensive equipment in order to maximize potential tax savings. The long-term plan can also help determine whether buying or leasing represents the greater tax benefit. In addition, long-term planning can help a business develop an appropriate strategy for categorizing income and expenses.

Depreciation of Assets

The way in which costs are categorized can help determine the total allowed tax benefits. Teams can incur current expenses and capital asset expenses, and can purchase nondepreciable assets. Current expenses can be written off the year they are incurred. Thus, if the Celtics spend $10,000 on office supplies, those expenses can be utilized to decrease income earned that year and ultimately reduce the tax burden.

Capital assets are expensive assets that have a longer life. Machinery is a good example of a capital asset; a machine used to form Sport Manufacturing Company's tennis rackets may be very expensive and may last over five years. The government allows companies to reduce their tax burden to help save money to repurchase another machine in the future. If a machine lasts about five years and costs $1 million, Sport Manufacturing Company can depreciate it by $200,000 a year for five years. If the machine is sold after five years to another business for $500,000, the new owners can keep depreciating the machine. These owners will be able to depreciate $100,000 a year for five years. Capital assets typically exclude salaries, which are normally classified as current expenses. This holds true for all industries except the sport industry. The salaries of athletes involved in professional sport are the only type of salaries that are depreciable (Euchner, 1993). The owner of a professional franchise can claim depreciation for five years after purchasing a franchise. In 1976, Congress passed the Tax Reform Act, which limited 50% of the franchise purchase price to players' salaries. Before that, a team buyer could claim 90% of the purchase price toward depreciable player salaries.

In 1986, Doubleday Co. sold the New York Mets to two major stockholders, Nelson Doubleday, Jr. and Fred Wilpon (Euchner, 1993). The new owners did not change the management structure, but technically there was a new ownership group. The transfer occurred exactly six years after Doubleday Co. had bought the team and at the time that the company had exhausted the player depreciation benefits. The new owners were then able to start the five-year depreciation clock over again.

Players are not the only assets that can be depreciated by a professional team. Other capital assets that can be depreciated include

- the franchise itself,
- lease contracts,
- concession contracts,
- broadcast contracts, and
- customer lists (Euchner, 1993).

All these contracts and marketing assets, as well as the goodwill inherent in the team, are assets that have value. The revenue stream available from luxury box lease contracts, concession contracts, and broadcast contracts can diminish over time; and although these are income-earning assets, they can be depreciated, as with all other major capital assets.

As previously indicated, the methods by which assets, expenses, and income are categorized in the planning process significantly affect all tax decisions. Income taxes can be markedly reduced on the basis of how income is classified. Active income is classified as **earned income.** Passive income is income derived from such transactions as renting that do not involve regular work activities.

Suppose the Smiths earn $100,000 a year but rent out a portion of their facility for a gymnastics tutor and as a result lose $20,000. The reason for the loss could be wear and tear or extra utility expenses. Even though this is a loss, it will not reduce the Smiths' tax obligation, as active and passive income are separate activities for the purposes of taxation. However, if the Smiths increased their business rental income by $20,000 and reduced their salaries by the same amount, they would reduce their taxable income by $20,000 (Goldhirsh, 1996).

This example suggests how income can be manipulated to reduce tax obligations. Although such moves are legal, they can raise concerns with IRS auditors. A business owner or manager should undertake such a strategy only after careful consultation with trained tax advisors.

Tax-related issues can be highly diverse and can cover every possible facet of a business. Even when money is paid to others, tax issues arise. An employee's withholding and Social Security taxes are just two of the many taxes an employer needs to consider. Pension plans also involve significant tax-related issues. Contributions to an approved pension plan are tax deductible for the employer. Thus, an expensive employee relations technique can be less costly when tax advantages are analyzed. We cannot consider every conceivable tax benefit or cost in this text. Instead the aim is to indicate the broad range of tax and legal constraints affecting sport businesses.

> *Nonprofit sport organizations such as collegiate athletic departments must consider the tax implications associated with fund-raising, and professional athletes and sport businesses must plan in order to minimize tax obligations.*

Financial Risk Management

Risk management is the process designed to identify problems and produce solutions for various risks that can range from tax concerns to litigation-based issues. One solution that any risk management plan must include involves insurance. Insurance protection can save a business a tremendous amount of money and represents an attempt to shift the risks associated with a financial loss.

There are people who prefer to run a business without insurance. Their thinking may be based on the calculation that if they do experience a loss, the cost of the loss will be lower than the premium payments that would have been required if they had purchased insurance. Others might base their gamble on the implementation of a significant risk management program that might reduce future claims. Although some managers are willing to take such risks or do not have the capital needed to purchase insurance, most are much more risk averse and prefer to have predictable outcomes that they can ensure through insurance or other risk reduction tools (Williams, Smith, & Young, 1995).

Risk management is designed to help reduce or eliminate potential hazards. A hazard is a condition that increases the likelihood of a loss. An example of a physical hazard is a defective gym floor; a moral hazard involves an effect on a person's behavior

(Williams et al., 1995). A moral hazard is present, for example, if there is a possibility that the owner or manager of a gym might not know whether a closet had been properly locked and thus not know whether a student could enter the closet, remove a trampoline, and get injured. Having an insurance policy to cover such an accident decreases the concern the person might have.

Insurance represents a finance technique termed risk transfer. The risk of a financial loss is transferred to another party. If a sport business does not have any insurance coverage, it is retaining the risk of any potential loss. Risk financing is a passive activity compared with risk management. Risk management is designed for **loss prevention.** Risk financing is designed to help settle a financial dispute after a loss has occurred. Risk financing establishes who will pay. Regardless, though, of whether the financial risk is transferred or retained, a business needs to allocate money for both risk financing and risk management.

For example, the Smiths might think that all they need to budget for is an insurance premium of $1,800 a year. However, they also need to calculate other expenses such as potential legal fees. Some of these, such as quarterly retainers for an attorney, may be easy to budget for; but the Smiths would not be able to easily budget for a new building in case a fire destroys the fitness center. Risk transfer would allow the Smiths to budget the insurance costs and then know that the insurance company would cover any significant losses in the future. The Smiths could also allocate $500 or more a month to pay for any future losses. Until these funds are used, they can be deposited into an interest-earning account. The Smiths would hope that they could save several thousand dollars and not have to pay any insurance premiums if they engage in self-insurance. If there are no losses for several years, the Smiths' reserves could be substantial; and if any loss did occur they might have enough in reserve to pay for it. If they faced a loss that the reserves could not cover, they would be forced to borrow funds.

In contrast, the Celtics might have a much more sophisticated self-insurance program. Because the Celtics have more money, and possibly more money to set aside, they could establish specific accounts to handle claims or could even own their own insurance company, which is referred to as a captive insurer (Williams et al., 1995). The Celtics could also join with other NBA teams to pool their resources and create an insurance fund to pay any loss incurred by any member of the group.

Lost Income

The risks that a sport business or organization can face could include various categories of decreased revenues:

- Lost rent if a subtenant does not pay its rent on time
- Interruption in business services through theft or vandalism of company property
- Interruption in the delivery of supplies (for example, when a power outage occurs)
- A reduced amount recovered from accounts receivable when debtors do not pay their accounts on time (Williams et al., 1995)

Other sources of lost income could include competition, environmental restrictions, legal changes, and numerous other internal and external variables. A risk management program can help identify all these potential ways in which income can be lost. Organizations can then develop proactive strategies to help reduce the potential impact of any given loss.

Legal Challenges

One risk management concern that any financial analysis must cover relates to potential future legal ramifications from any decision. For example, government entities can develop unique financing schemes to help build a facility. However, the fact that the government is involved does not guarantee that a legal challenge cannot invalidate provisions that might have made the deal financially beneficial. For example, a 1,500-acre cow pasture was converted into the 150,000-plus-seat Texas Motor Speedway. The developer and city entered into an agreement that the privately owned track would not have to pay any property taxes. A local school district sued the city to terminate what it called a "sweetheart deal" that deprived the school district of badly needed tax revenue.

The deal was founded on tax incremental financing (TIF). As noted in chapter 8, TIF is a financing vehicle whereby taxes for a facility such as a stadium are deferred. The municipality is gambling that with the new development, property around the stadium will increase in value, thus increasing the tax base. When the tax base increases, the municipality will receive higher taxes, which presumably will offset the tax savings given to encourage the stadium owners to build in a neighborhood with depressed property values. Tax incremental financing represents a potential win-win for all parties, as the stadium owner receives a tax break, local citizens see increases in property values, and the municipality earns more tax revenue. However, in the case of the Texas Motor Speedway, the school district claimed that the TIF led to unfair competition—that it allowed developers to receive undeserved government charity, which would eventually hurt homeowners. Homeowners would be forced to pay higher property taxes because of losses in the city's tax income resulting from the deal. The Texas Motor Speedway cost approximately $204.5 million. Tax money covered $9 million in road improvements, $20 million for land acquisition, and $100 million in waived property taxes (Gibeaut, 1999). The developer was required to make only $2.2 million in total lease payments and after 30 years could buy the facility from the city (Fort Worth) for $500,000. In comparison to tax abatements that allow reduced future taxes, the Speedway was built with a TIF that provided the upfront money. The TIF is supposed to generate increased tax revenue from other adjoining properties or businesses that are anticipated to grow because of the presence of the new facility.

Financial Risk Analysis

So far we have focused on business structure concerns affecting the bottom line, tax considerations, government regulations affecting sport financing, and risk financing. In addition, risk management can rely directly on financial ratios. For example, leverage ratios help measure the extent to which an organization is in debt. The more a business borrows, the higher the leverage ratio becomes. A highly leveraged business is more vulnerable to changes in business environments. A business facing significant leverage may be forced by a debt holder to buy insurance to help protect pledged assets. Two specific techniques that can help identify leverage-related financial risk are the long-term debt to net worth ratio and the times interest earned ratio discussed in chapter 5 (Williams et al., 1995).

Liquidity ratios measure the ability of a company to raise cash in the short run. If a company does not have the ability to raise cash for emergencies, it is not on strong footing to deal with fiscal risks. Several ratios that can be used to help evaluate a business' ability to cover short-term obligations are the net working capital to assets ratio, current ratio, and

the acid test ratio (Williams et al., 1995). These ratios are also covered in chapter 5.

Risk managers in sport also examine ratios to determine whether a team is in financial trouble. According to Fitch IBCA, an international rating agency, several measures can help determine the soundness of a professional sport team. Using collateral coverage, Fitch IBCA expects collateral to cover team debt at least two times (2 ×). The analysts also think that team debt to contractually obligated revenue should not exceed two times. Last, they recommended as a general guideline a minimum ratio of operating income to annual debt service of 1.5 times for investment-grade franchises in 1999 ("Changing Game," 1999).

Another financial measure for risks associated with a business is based on how stockholders view the business and whether they perceive the business as facing significant risks. Market valuation ratios such as the price-earnings (PE) ratio can provide a barometer of confidence. A high PE ratio is a strong sign that investors expect the organization's earnings to grow at a high rate. Another ratio is Tobin's q ratio, which analyzes the efficiency with which a business has invested its assets. Tobin's q is calculated by dividing the business' market value by the replacement value for the business' assets. A ratio above 1.0 implies that assets are worth more within the firm than if they were invested elsewhere. This number can be critical in risk management analysis when a buyer acquires a business and has to determine whether to liquidate the business' assets. If Tobin's q ratio is under 1.0, then an acquiring business might decide not to replace broken machinery because the added investment would not generate enough revenue to increase the business' value (Williams et al., 1995).

> *Financial risk management for a sport business includes identifying potential losses of income, understanding potential legal ramifications of any decision, and determining whether the business is in financial trouble.*

CONCLUSION

Legal issues are normally not the primary concern associated with financial management. However, every business decision has both financial and legal ramifications. If the financial statements do not comply with Securities and Exchange Commission reporting requirements, legal flags will wave. If a corporation engages in investments contrary to its bylaws, additional legal concerns can arise. The list of potential legal concerns goes on and on. The breadth of legal challenges facing a sport finance manager is equally significant. Chapter 15 deals with some of the legal issues associated with mergers. As seen in the business structure, taxation, and risk management sections in this chapter, a finance manager faces countless potential legal hurdles that are either self-imposed or imposed by external entities, such as bankruptcy-related issues (chapter 17). Although a business can proceed to bankruptcy on its own behalf, creditors can also force it into bankruptcy. One technique that many businesses use successfully to help identify potential legal problems is auditing. Auditing, covered in chapter 16, helps identify fiscal blunders and potential criminal misconduct.

ASSIGNMENTS

1. Based on material in chapter 4, what would be the best business structure for the Smiths, Sport Manufacturing Company, and the Bos-

ton Celtics? Would business structure affect taxes?
2. Is it worthwhile for the Celtics to buy liability insurance, and why or why not?
3. What is the benefit of liability insurance?

RESEARCH PROJECT

Research insurance policies and create a list of 10 different types of insurance policies or coverage that could be useful for a sport business.

CLASS DISCUSSION TOPICS

1. Should professional team owners be allowed to depreciate players' salaries? Take the pro or con side of this question.
2. Should the Mobil Cotton Bowl and The Ohio State University have been subject to taxes for unrelated business income even though funds from the advertising efforts were utilized for educational activities?

Spending Earnings

CHAPTER OBJECTIVES

After studying this chapter, you should be able to do the following:

- Describe different types of dividend policies and how they are used.
- Outline the dividend payment process.
- Describe how a business utilizes retained earnings.
- Understand how mergers and acquisitions are a way for a sport business to expand.
- Describe the legal concerns associated with mergers and acquisitions.
- Calculate the value of a consolidated business after a merger.

In earlier chapters, we focused on learning the fundamentals of sport finance and understanding the sources of revenues and expenses. If all goes well, a business will have the **ability to pay** all its costs from income. If income equals costs, the business will break even. However, the goal for a profit-driven business is not only to cover costs, but also to maximize profits. If a business generates positive earnings, it then has to decide how best to distribute the excess earnings. The earnings distribution process is a major decision for a sport business. It has significant short- and long-term ramifications.

The options a sport manager has with respect to distributing earnings differ depending on the business. Among our four case studies, the University of Houston athletic department is the government-owned entity. Therefore, the university does not have shareholders or a group of owners similar to the Smiths or the owners of Sport Manufacturing Company or the Boston Celtics. Given that this chapter centers on how earnings are distributed and used to increase the value of a firm, we focus primarily on for-profit corporations similar to the Smiths' fitness center, Sport Manufacturing Company, and the Boston Celtics.

Before discussing the earnings of for-profit organizations, we should note that nonprofit sport organizations, such as collegiate athletic departments, charitable foundations, and the YMCA/YWCA, might also have revenues that exceed costs. These organizations have several options for their earnings. They may elect to reinvest these funds back into the organization. For example, a college athletic department may elect to add new sports or improve sport facilities. Some major college athletic departments with excess funds have established scholarships for students who are not athletes. A YMCA may decide to increase the size of its staff or add new activities. In some cases, nonprofit sport organizations elect to save these excess funds to protect against future financial difficulty. While nonprofit organizations have a variety of options, what they cannot do is show an accounting profit for the fiscal year.

In general, sport businesses have three choices for using earnings:

1. Pay dividends to shareholders
2. Retain earnings for reinvestment in the business
3. Reinvest in other firms by purchasing a percentage or acquire other firms outright

Retained earnings are used primarily for long-term financial planning and capital budgeting. While retained earnings are discussed briefly in this chapter, the major focus is the payment of dividends and mergers with and acquisitions of other firms.

The key to making the right decision concerning earnings distributions is to select the option that will produce the greatest value to the ownership, or, in the case of a publicly held company, the shareholders. Although shareholders directly benefit from receiving a dividend payment, they may derive the greatest long-term value from forgoing dividend payments and allowing the earnings to be reinvested back into the firm. The reinvestment may be used to research and design a new product line, purchase new equipment, or hire additional human resources. Management may also attempt to increase the business' value by using the earnings to acquire another firm. It is management's responsibility to make these critical decisions. At all times, management must base the decision on selecting the option that is best for the shareholders or ownership. See the following case study example.

The Boston Celtics may decrease dividend payments to their shareholders and use the funds to construct a new practice facility. Although the reinvestment for capital improvements decreases the dividends received by shareholders, the Celtics' management believes that the end result will be an increase in the stock value.

Dividend Payments

A dividend is a payment made out of earnings, in the form of either cash or stock, to a business' owners or shareholders (Brigham, Gapenski, & Ehrhardt, 1999). Dividends are paid to reward stockholders for staying with the corporation. Some stocks steadily appreciate in value, and that capital appreciation is the reward stockholders need to justify their investment. Other corporations may have a steady stock price but reward stockholders by paying a regular dividend payment. Thus, while the Boston Celtics have not had a significant increase in their stock value over the years, they have paid steady dividends that sometimes amounted to about $0.50 per share. However, for the 2001 and 2002 fiscal years no dividends were paid to unit holders.

Paying dividends is one method for distributing profits. For many corporations, it is a major cash expenditure. Large companies such as IBM and Microsoft spend millions of dollars in making dividend payments to their shareholders. However, numerous companies also elect to make no dividend payments. A firm's board of directors determines the amounts of dividend payments and makes all other dividend decisions not otherwise specified in the corporate bylaws or on the stock certificates.

Initially, you would think that a firm would want to give as much money back to its shareholders as possible. But it also makes financial sense for the firm to take the money and invest it for the shareholders. Deciding which option to select can be quite difficult for financial managers and can be controversial. Shareholders and financial analysts can be quite critical if they believe management is pursuing a poor dividend policy. Such negative feelings can affect a stock's performance.

A business may also make distributions to its ownership. A distribution is similar to a dividend but it is paid out of sources other than current or accumulated retained earnings. For simplicity, we will refer to any payment by a firm to its shareholders as a dividend. Typically, dividends are most commonly paid by large corporations. Smaller corporations often need to reinvest the money in order to grow. For example, Speedway Motorsports is a growing company involved in the motor sport industry. It owns and operates several racetracks across the United States. In its 1998 annual report, the company stated that it would not pay dividends for the foreseeable future in order to reinvest money for company growth. In contrast, Nike paid a $0.12 **dividend per share** in 1999 (bloomberg.com, 1999).

Dividend policies can be somewhat confusing. There are many good reasons for a corporation to pay high dividends, but there are as many good reasons to pay relatively low dividends. This section covers the ways in which dividends are paid, the various types of dividends, and reasons for the payment of high and low dividends.

Dividend Payment Process

The process of paying dividends is well defined. The following case study example, adapted from an example in another industry (Ross, Westerfield, & Jordan, 1995) shows how the process works.

- On June 1, Sport Manufacturing Company passes a resolution to pay a dividend of a specified amount, let's say $2 per share. The date of the announcement, June 1, is referred to as the declaration date. Sport Manufacturing Company's board of directors also announces that the dividend will be paid on June 30 to all shareholders of record as of June 18.

- An important date in the process comes up four business days prior to June 18. June 14 is the ex-dividend date and is used to determine those shareholders who are eligible to receive dividends so that the dividend checks are distributed to the appropriate shareholders. Prior to June 14, the stock is traded "with dividend," meaning that shareholders are eligible for a dividend payment. After June 14, the stock trades as **ex-dividend,** meaning that the purchaser will not receive a dividend payment. This date is important in ensuring that there is no confusion as to who is to receive the dividend payment.

- June 18 is the record date, the date on which all shareholders of record are designated to receive their payment. The firm will prepare a list, based on the ex-dividend date, of those individuals who are believed to be shareholders. These persons are the **holders of record** and will receive dividend checks. Errors do sometimes occur and dividend checks get mailed to the wrong persons. However, the ex-dividend date helps minimize such errors.

- June 30 is the payment date. All dividend checks are mailed to the people who are believed to be the shareholders of record.

Cash Dividends

The most common type of dividend is a regular cash dividend. Some publicly traded companies typically pay cash dividends on a quarterly basis as a regular business practice. In addition to the regular cash dividend paid annually, semiannually, or quarterly, a business may also make special one-time payments. These special or additional dividend payments are called extra cash dividends or special dividends. For the most part, the extra payments differ from the regular dividends in name only. As the name implies, these dividends might not be repeated in the future. Last, a liquidating dividend is a payment made to shareholders as a result of some part of the business being liquidated, or sold off. All or part of the cash from the sale is distributed to the shareholders. Regardless of the name, a cash dividend payment reduces the firm's cash and retained earnings (Ross et al., 1995).

As discussed later, not all corporations pay dividends; and even if a dividend is paid one year, this does not mean that the board of directors will authorize a dividend the next year. However, any interruption in the payment cycle can have a chilling effect on analysts and shareholders, who may view the suspension of dividends as a sign of economic hardship.

Stock Dividends

Corporations have other alternatives to a cash dividend if they wish to distribute earnings back to their shareholders. A firm may elect to buy back stock or issue new stock to existing shareholders. The payment of a dividend in stock can have a dilutive effect on share price, which is not the case with cash dividends. There are also some differences between cash dividends and **stock dividends** related to tax policies. Dividend payments are taxed as income for shareholders, whereas the money earned from the sale of stock is taxed as capital gains. In recent U.S. history, the tax rates for income have been higher than the tax rate for capital gains, but the 1986 Tax Reform Act reduced the gap. However, the gap still exists, and it would appear that on the basis of taxation policy, many stockholders would prefer the repurchase of stock over dividend payments (Brealey & Myers, 1996). The decision to buy back shares is made by the corporation's board of directors, but the board considers the impact on the shareholders and market conditions. Typically a board with extra cash might buy back stocks when the value is depressed to help increase the stock value. When the company buys back stock, the number of shares outstanding decreases and the book value per share can increase.

Distribution of earnings is not the only reason for a company to repurchase stock. A business may also repurchase stock when it wants to change its capital structure. A business may borrow money, in other words go into debt, in order to repurchase stock from shareholders and lower equity. This action will have the final effect of changing the firm's capital structure (WACC). The WACC was discussed in chapter 11 as a tool to measure the effectiveness of a corporation's capital structure.

Determining the Appropriate Dividend Level

Another important aspect of dividend policy is arriving at the appropriate dividend level. According to Brealey and Myers (1996), there are three traditional views with respect to paying dividends. The groups of people who hold these views are the rightists, the leftists, and the middle-of-the-roaders.

The rightists believe that a business should pay the highest possible dividends. This group notes that the perceived business value increases as the level of dividend payments increases. Financial analysts believe that the perception of a business becomes more positive as higher dividends are paid, and this in turn increases the business' stock value. In addition, dividends are cash in hand whereas a capital gain is risky. There is always uncertainty surrounding the reinvestment of earnings; and the investments selected may not increase the business' value. This uncertainty and risk are eliminated if the excess cash is directly paid to the shareholders in the form of dividends.

Like all investors, financial analysts or researchers can fall anywhere on the spectrum, but some may be rightists because they feel there is no such thing in reality as an efficient and free capital market. That is, these researchers feel that it does not matter if high or low dividends are paid. In contrast, the leftists believe that the capital markets are imperfect and do not perform efficiently. Dividend policy therefore is quite important. This analysis is important for investors because boards of directors that follow the leftist ideology would be more inclined to pay dividends to insure that shareholders are happy. We should note that there are some investors who use their stock portfolio as a source of cash income. The quarterly dividend payments allow them to receive this cash. Without the dividends, these investors would need to periodically sell some of their stock and also incur the transaction costs associated with these sales. Also, these investors are more susceptible to the ups and downs of the stock market because they are selling pieces of their portfolio at different times.

Shareholders often demand that management make high dividend payments. The rightists have explained and justified this in several ways. The best justification may simply be that many shareholders do not trust management to spend the earnings properly. The shareholders may not believe that management has their best interests at heart and would prefer that the earnings be paid out through dividends. This gives shareholders the power to control the money, but it limits the business' investment decisions.

The leftists hold the opposite view of dividend policy. They strongly believe that dividend payments should be low. The focus of their argument is based on a single issue: taxes. As stated earlier, dividends are taxed as income, not capital gains. Therefore, the leftists believe that whenever income tax rates are higher than capital gains tax rates, the only option is to pay low dividends. The excess cash can be used in one of two ways.

First, the cash can be used for investment opportunities that will allow the business' value to grow. The company can engage in capital projects that will increase the business' value and ultimately its stock price. If a shareholder wants cash, he can sell his stock at the higher price and pay the capital gains tax, which is lower than the income tax. Second, the firm can use the excess cash to repurchase stock. The shareholders will receive cash for the shares they sell and will be taxed at the lower capital gains tax rate.

With respect to dividend policy, the third group is the middle-of-the-roaders. They believe that there is some middle ground between the two sides where the smart dividend policy lies. This group believes that the value of a company is not affected by dividend policy. They claim that if either raising or lowering dividend payments could increase the business' value, companies would already be using such strategies to affect their stock price. In fact, some businesses do use this strategy in an attempt to affect their share price. Most middle-of-the-road managers do not believe that stock prices could be manipulated simply through changes in the dividend policy. Each company arrives at some level of dividends that is appropriate for most of the shareholders. This middle-ground dividend payment satisfies the greatest number of shareholders and has no effect on business value. According to this view, smart managers would adjust the dividend policy if they believed the change would positively affect business value.

The dividend policy is an important issue for public companies. It is closely related to several other financial management decisions such as borrowing, capital structuring, and investment decisions. For example, if a business decides to use its excess cash to pay dividends, it must rely on more borrowing for investment opportunities. This will greatly affect its capital structure and long-term planning. Dividends can be very controversial. As we have discussed, there are several different views on their importance to the business and the appropriate dividend policy for a company to follow.

> *Paying dividends to shareholders, which is one of the ways a company can use its earnings, involves deciding how to pay the dividend, what type of dividend to pay, and how much the dividend should be.*

Reinvestment

As stated earlier, an alternative to distributing earnings to shareholders through dividends is to reinvest the funds back into the business. Reinvestment is a key component in financial management. A company must continually reinvest if it hopes to thrive and grow. One method of reinvesting funds is through retaining earnings. The business forgoes payment to stockholders and keeps the earnings for capital investment. The board of directors decides whether to cancel dividends and often sends out a press release when it files the quarterly report on the company's earnings. The suspension or canceling of a dividend is also reported in the corporation's annual report. As stated in chapter 11, the expected return from capital projects must be greater than the return stockholders receive from investing the dividend payments. If it is not, then the funds should be paid out as dividends.

The level of earnings that should be retained for capital investment is closely tied to a business' capital structure, capital budgeting decisions, and dividend policy. Obviously, businesses that prefer to pay relatively high dividends retain a smaller percentage of earnings. It is important to note that there are legal restrictions on the amount of dividends that can be paid. On a business' balance sheet, dividend payments cannot exceed retained earnings. This policy, known as the impairment of capital rule, was established to protect creditors. It prohibits a business that is in financial distress from liquidating its assets through dividend payments. In the absence of this legal stipulation, a business could distribute all its capital assets and creditors would have nothing to reclaim (Brigham et al., 1999).

The business' size also plays a role in the amount of funds that should be used for reinvestment. For smaller businesses, other capital sources such as debt or the issuance of new common stock may be relatively expensive. Thus, a smaller business would most likely elect to finance capital spending through retained earnings. Larger businesses can issue finance capital, such as stocks and bonds, at a much lower cost compared with small businesses. Therefore, they are more likely to pay higher dividends and retain a smaller percentage of earnings than smaller businesses.

As discussed in chapter 11, businesses also have a target capital structure. The capital structure target is the proportion of debt to equity that is believed to be best for increasing shareholder value. The level of reinvestment in the company is often a product of this capital structure. A business may lower retained earnings if it wants to repurchase stock. The result will be an alteration in the capital structure and level of reinvestment.

Last, managerial control may also affect the level of retained earnings. Some businesses with the need for additional capital are hesitant to issue new stock. In issuing new stock, management always faces the possibility of relinquishing control. To avoid this situation, management can take the alternative option of retaining a higher level of earnings. The earnings are then used to reinvest in the business.

Instead of paying dividends, a company may decide that the best way to increase long-term value to the ownership or shareholders is to reinvest earnings back into the company.

Mergers and Acquisitions

In a merger, one business blends its business with the acquired business. Thus, Company A can merge with Company B and the new entity could be called Company C. In contrast, in an acquisition the acquiring company still maintains control of the acquired company and serves in a dominant position over the acquired company. Thus, in an acquisition, Company A can acquire Company B and still be Company A. A merger can be part of an acquisition, such as the merger of accounting departments from two different companies. A merger is an investment, made under uncertainty, in which the acquiring business' goal is to increase its value or shareholders' wealth. As with other investment opportunities, a business should acquire another business only if it believes that a positive gain in net present value will occur. Unfortunately, given the level of uncertainty, it is very difficult to calculate the net present value of an acquisition candidate (Ross et al., 1996). Unlike the situation when a company decides to invest in long-term capital, it is difficult to place a value on the additional expenses and income associated with a merger.

Mergers and acquisitions are commonplace within the sport industry. Some sport businesses are continually looking to expand operations and improve earnings through acquiring other businesses as seen in the following case study example.

The Smiths may eventually turn their small fitness center into a highly successful operation. However, the growth potential for their single location is limited. If they wish to increase their business size, they may look to expanding into new locations. One method of expansion may be to acquire and operate other centers. After they acquired other centers, the Smiths would have the ability to increase income and grow their company.

The number of mergers in the sport industry has increased greatly over the past decade. Several sport and entertainment companies such as Disney, News Corp., and SFX Entertainment have acquired smaller companies to increase the scope of their operations. These acquisitions have been somewhat controversial and may have a large impact on the future financial landscape within the sport industry. Table 15.1 provides a list of sport holdings for some of the major corporate entities in the sport industry.

Aside from the major acquisitions, hundreds of smaller mergers and acquisitions occur each year within the sport industry. In 1995 alone, 9,030 mergers and acquisitions totaling over $500 billion were reported (Crow, Phillips, & Gillentine, 2000). The numbers have been skyrocketing since 1995. In the first three quarters of 1998, a total of 10,104 mergers were reported to the Department of Justice with a combined value of $1.3 trillion (Crow et al., 2000). Not all these were sport mergers, but they indicate a trend. Several sport mergers are discussed throughout this chapter.

It is important to realize that company acquisition for the sole sake of diversification is normally not a wise financial strategy. Companies normally should only merge if there is a belief that the new company will result in some additional value that is not possible if separate enterprises are maintained. If no additional value is earned through a merger or acquisition, it may not be in the best financial interest of either side. However, not all mergers are for financial growth. Some companies want to eliminate or reduce competition by purchasing a competitor and then shutting it down. Other companies may buy a competitor for leverage with unions so that the unions cannot use the other business as an example of concessions that they want. Still other businesses may merge to avoid a takeover by another company.

We need to remember also that many mergers are unwelcome. Although the purchase of a small corporation by a large corporation may make the owners of the small company wealthy, some owners do not want to sell. This can lead to the "hostile takeover." Hostile takeovers also can occur when one corporation is trying to buy another one and a third corporation arrives on the scene, offering more money. In December 2001, Monster.com offered to pay $355 million for HotJobs.com, and the companies worked on a merger for six months. However, at the last minute, Yahoo! upped the ante by $81 million, offering $436 million for HotJobs. Within three weeks, HotJobs agreed to Yahoo!'s hostile bid (Thornton, 2002). In fact, with the stock market down, hostile

Table 15.1 Selected Sport Holdings for Major Sport-Related Corporations

Corporation	Selected sport holdings
News Corp.	Los Angeles Dodgers, Dodger Stadium, New York Knicks (40%), New York Rangers (40%), Madison Square Garden (40%), Fox Broadcasting Co., Fox Sports Net, FX Network, British Sky Broadcasting (40%), and Fox Sports Online
Time Warner	Turner Sports, Atlanta Braves, Atlanta Hawks, Atlanta Thrashers, HBO Sports, Goodwill Games, *Sports Illustrated*, CNN/Sports Illustrated, Turner Field, and Philips Arena
Walt Disney	Anaheim Angels, Mighty Ducks of Anaheim, ESPN, ESPN2, ESPN Classic, ESPNews, ABC Sports, ESPN The Magazine, Walt Disney Wide World of Sports Complex, Lifetime, and ESPN.com
Comcast Corp.	Philadelphia Flyers, Philadelphia 76ers, Philadelphia Phantoms, First Union Center, First Union Spectrum, Comcast SportsNet, and The Golf Channel
SFX Entertainment/ Clear Channel	FAME, Hendricks Sports Management, Integrated Sports International, and The Marquee Group (which includes ProServ Marquee Football, Marquee Hockey, Marquee Baseball, Marquee Global Sports Ventures, Marquee UK, Tony Stephens Associates, Park Associates, and others)

Data from *Street & Smith's SportsBusiness Journal,* August 23-29, 1999, 24-31.

Schwinn Splits Up

One of the larger sport mergers in the past 10 years involved the bankruptcy and splitting of Schwinn/ GT Corp. Schwinn was one of the largest bicycle manufacturers in the world. Unfortunately the company faced hard financial times in 2000 and had to seek bankruptcy protection. Huffy Corp. placed an offer to the bankruptcy judge to pay $68.3 million for Schwinn. Another offer was received from Pacific Cycles, LLC and joined by Direct Focus, Inc. (Brennan, 2001). Pacific Cycles posted a $1.5 million deposit to challenge the "stalking-horse" sale agreement between Schwinn and Huffy. Pacific Cycles was required to surpass Huffy's offer by $5 million or lose its deposit. (A stalking-horse sale agreement, entered into when a company knows there may be other suitors, allows another suitor to top the existing offer and purchase the company. A company enters into this type of agreement when it knows that bidding will be spirited or thinks the sale price was too low and hopes that someone will come along and raise the offer. In other words, if Company A is being sought by several companies, it can enter into an agreement with Company X to sell the business to Company X. However, the agreement could provide that if another company, such as Company Z, comes along and offers more money, Company A can terminate its agreement with Company X and sell to Company Z.)

Schwinn, which had started operations in 1895, had 25% of the domestic bicycle market but had applied for bankruptcy in 1992 and again in 2001. Two divisions were going on sale, a bicycle division and a fitness division. The winner of the bicycle unit was Pacific Cycles, LLC. The fitness unit was purchased by Direct Focus, which also is the parent company for Bowlex and Nautilus. Direct Focus was interested in using its purchase of Schwinn's fitness unit to launch a major push in the indoor bike area to take advantage of the popularity of spinning (Janda, 2001).

bids were on the increase from $40 billion in 2000 to $94 billion in 2001. The surge was also prompted by changes in accounting practices. Recent rule changes do not require a company to reduce its earnings by the amortized value of the goodwill from the ac-

quired firm (Thornton, 2002). Goodwill is the difference between what an acquiring company pays for a business and what the acquired business' assets were valued at on its balance sheet. The potential goodwill for sport businesses such as professional teams is very high. The fact that an acquiring company can now capitalize goodwill rather than amortize it increases the balance sheet assets for the acquiring firm and makes it look stronger.

Not all hostile takeovers are successful, though, since companies can undertake various steps to protect themselves (see p. 156). Among these steps are issuing new shares to dilute the market, selling key assets, and approaching a "white knight" to make a counteroffer (Cheeseman, 1998). Other approaches include adopting "poison pills" that require the would-be buyer to possibly pay executives a large fee if it purchases the company or require the would-be buyer to pay more for the shares. In fact, poison pills have increased the value of the companies that have adopted them by 35.9% versus only a 31.9% premium for companies that did not have them (Thornton, 2002).

A successful sport manager must be highly attentive to the possibility of acquiring other companies or possibly becoming the target of an acquisition attempt. The discussion in the remainder of this section focuses on the types of mergers, justifications for mergers, the legal forms of acquisition that occur within sport, and other forms of acquisition.

Types of Mergers

Brealey and Myers (1996) separated mergers into three categories: horizontal, vertical, and conglomerate.

Horizontal Mergers

A horizontal merger takes place when two companies in the same line of business are joined. A recent sport example occurred when two concession service companies merged to form a new and larger business identity. In August 1998, Volume Services and Service America Corp. merged and started operations under the new name of Volume Service America Inc. ("For the Record," 1998, August 17-23). In such deals, management believes that the new, merged company will have a higher value than the two separate businesses. Other mergers have also occurred in this industry segment, with Aramark acquiring Volume Service America Inc. in 1999 and Ogden Corp.'s entertainment division for $236 million in 2000. SMG, another facility management company, which is partially owned by Aramark, merged with Leisure Management International in 2000 ("Aramark Acquires," 2000).

Vertical Mergers

In a vertical merger, a buyer expands operations forward toward the final consumer, or backward in the direction of the source of raw materials. Livingstone (1997) refers to these different levels in a market as upstream and downstream markets. A downstream market is one that is further along in the production process while an upstream market is closer to the original raw materials. In either situation, a business is expanding by acquiring other companies that are part of the production process. In 1998, Intrawest, the operator of several mountain resorts in North America, acquired Breeze Inc. and Max Snowboards Inc. Both companies rented ski and snowboard equipment. By acquiring these two businesses, Intrawest was able to extend its operations upstream because rental equipment is a necessity for many consumers who want to ski. Intrawest not only has control of the ski mountains and the corresponding income streams, but also rents the equipment needed to ski on its mountains ("For the Record," 1998, September 21-27).

Conglomerate Mergers

A conglomerate merger occurs when companies in unrelated lines of business come together. The merged companies can be involved in businesses that have no business link. SFX Entertainment Inc. has traditionally been in the entertainment industry through the ownership of amphitheaters and concert halls, as well as through participation in the music promotion business. With its recent acquisitions of the Marquee Group, Integrated Sports International, and FAME, SFX has expanded into sport marketing, sport event production, and athlete representation. It appeared with these deals that SFX was attempting to become the largest integrated sport and entertainment conglomerate in the world. However, in 2000, SFX was bought by an even larger entertainment company, Clear Channel. That purchase is discussed later in this chapter.

Companies can spend earnings in order to grow by purchasing a percentage of another firm or acquiring another firm.

Credible Justifications for Mergers

There must be credible justification for a merger to occur. As stated earlier, if no additional value is generated through a merger, then it is probably wisest to maintain the status quo and keep the companies independent. Perhaps the best justification for a merger, especially in the case of a horizontal merger, is economies of scale. A company achieves economies of scale by increasing its size. The adage "bigger is better" is a good way to sum up the idea of economies of scale. Two companies that duplicate activities may be more profitable if they merge operations. The acquisition of another fitness center by the Smiths may lead to achieving economies of scale. Corporate responsibilities such as accounting, staff development, and office management for the two facilities may be combined, and a substantial cost savings may result. While the consolidation of these operations should have little effect on revenues, it may lead to a decrease in expenses. Ultimately, this will increase earnings and the value of the merged company.

Another credible justification for a merger in the sport industry is the prospect that a company can save on costs not related to economies of scale. For example, Cablevision, the New York-based broad-casting company, has paid over $40 million annually for the local television broadcast rights of the New York Yankees. The 12-year, $486 million broadcasting deal between the Yankees and Cablevision ended in the year 2000. In the fall of 1998, Cablevision made a reported bid of $525 million to purchase 70% of the Yankees (King & Brockington, 1998). Part of the rationale for the acquisition was that it would allow Cablevision to save $40 million per year. Instead of annually paying local broadcast fees to the Yankees, Cablevision could purchase part ownership of the team and use the ownership rights to reduce or eliminate the broadcasting payments. Cablevision would have owned both the television outlet and the team. Ultimately, the two sides were unable to agree on some details within the acquisition such as team control, and the deal was abandoned.

A Fitness Merger

In December 2001, Bally Total Fitness merged with Crunch Fitness. The total purchase price was estimated at $90 million for the 19 Crunch Fitness clubs in five states. The merged company increased Bally's size to approximately 420 clubs throughout North America serving over 4 million members ("Bally," 2001).

A merger or acquisition is also a wise financial endeavor if the merged entity can generate revenues that are not possible if the firms remain separate. Two firms may have complementary resources or products that when combined will result in substantial revenues. As a consequence of the merger, there may be a very successful future for the combined company. For example, Action Sports Media Inc. is a sport marketing agency that works with colleges and universities on sponsorship and signage sales. In May, 1999, the firm filed a **letter of intent** to buy StadiaNet Sports. StadiaNet Sports installs and programs large-screen video displays and scoreboards primarily for college sport facilities ("For the Record," 1999). The acquisition allows Action Sports Media to be involved in not only the sales of signage and advertising for video displays, but also the installation and programming of the scoreboards. In theory, a college or university can work with Action Sports Media on the total process of installing and financing its video displays and scoreboards. This was not possible before Action Sports Media acquired StadiaNet Sports.

A corporate acquisition may also be a wise maneuver if a business believes that the targeted company is poorly managed. A business may view the other company as underperforming due to poor management and believe that it can transform the targeted company into a financially successful business. Through acquisition, the business believes it can improve its own value by instituting more effective management in the underperforming company.

Last, a merger can be the most effective way to invest surplus funds. As mentioned earlier, a successful business with a substantial amount of net income has several options. It can distribute the income to shareholders by increasing dividend payments or may repurchase its stock. A third option is for the business to invest its surplus cash by purchasing the stock of other companies. Often, businesses with surplus cash and a lack of good alternative investment choices redirect their capital toward purchasing other companies. The strategy may be very wise in that a business that fails to redirect its cash may itself become a target for takeover. Businesses with significant excess cash face the possibility of acquisition because other companies may believe that they can acquire the business and redirect the cash in a profitable manner.

Mergers and Antitrust Law

Within the legal system, mergers and acquisitions are regulated by antitrust law. There are three primary statutes that come into play. The first statute, passed in 1890, is the Sherman Antitrust Act. This act decrees that "every contract, combination . . . or conspiracy, in restraint of trade" is illegal (Sherman Antitrust Act, 1890, 15 U.S.C.A. Sec. 1). It was enacted in response to the monopolies that developed in the middle to late 1800s in industries such as steel, iron, and the railroads. The goal was to protect consumers from large corporations that controlled entire industries. However, the wording of the statute was quite vague and thus the law was difficult to enforce. The Federal Trade Commission Act of 1914 was a step toward tightening the restrictions on monopolies and collusive behavior. It prohibited unfair methods of competition, as well as unfair or deceptive acts or practices (Blair & Kaserman, 1985). The act also established an agency, the Federal Trade Commission, that was given the responsibility of enforcing the antitrust laws. The third and most enforceable of these statutes was the Clayton Act of 1914. Section 7 of the Clayton Act addressed mergers and acquisitions. It prohibited the acquisition of another firm's stock in cases in which the result would be to lessen competition and create a monopoly (Blair & Kaserman, 1985). However, the Clayton Act had one obvious loophole. It did not prohibit the acquisition of another firm's assets. The loophole was used extensively until 1950, when it was closed with the passage of the Cellar-Kefauver Act. Section 7 of the Clayton Act was amended to read:

[N]o corporation engaged in commerce shall acquire, directly or indirectly, the whole or any part of the stock or other share capital and no corporation subject to the jurisdiction of the Federal Trade Commission shall acquire the whole or any part of the assets of another corporation engaged also in commerce, where in any line of commerce in any section of the country, the effect of such acquisition may be substantially to lessen competition, or to tend to create a monopoly. (Blair & Kaserman, 1985, p. 226)

The improved Clayton Act not only forbade mergers that constrained trade or greatly lessened market competition, but also prohibited any merger that potentially restrained trade. Thus, the Clayton Act has been the primary statute used to stop mergers that could have created a monopoly within an industry.

Antitrust law is enforced by two federal government agencies: the Federal Trade Commission (FTC) and the U.S. Department of Justice. The Department of Justice has the power to file a civil suit to block any merger, and the FTC can initiate an official proceeding to analyze the effect of a merger on competition within an industry. Ultimately, either department can attempt to legally stop two firms from merging if it believes that the result will decrease competition and harm consumers. Since the passage of the Hart-Scott-Rodino Act of 1976, all firms are required by law to inform the government of any acquisitions of stock that exceed $15 million or involve greater than 15% of the targeted firm's stock, whichever is less (Brealey & Myers, 1996).

Very few mergers are contested by the Department of Justice or the FTC. Within the American sport industry, no major antitrust cases have arisen from a corporate merger. As the industry continues to develop and more mergers occur, it is likely that some acquisitions will be closely scrutinized by federal agencies such as the FTC.

Although there have not been any significant challenges to sport mergers, the government has become involved in several transactions. For example, when the NFL merged with the American Football League (AFL), Congress reviewed the proposed merger to assess its impact on broadcast football games. In response to the inquiry, the legislature passed the 1968 Sports Broadcasting Act, which allowed the merger to proceed so long as professional football did not air games on Saturdays during the college football season. Thus, even today, no NFL games are played on Saturday during the college football season. After the regular college football season ends, the NFL once again starts airing games on Saturdays. This legislation was developed to prevent professional football from overrunning college football.

As we see in the next section, there are three methods of legally acquiring another business. The first of these methods is the merger of two companies; the other two methods are purchasing voting stock and purchasing assets.

Various Forms of Acquisition

An acquisition can take many forms. Numerous issues play into how a company acquires another company. For example is the acquisition friendly or will it be strongly contested? The recent merger between Hewlett-Packard and Compaq was very contentious with millions being spent to convince individuals that the merger was right or wrong for

The NFL/AFL Merger

The NFL/AFL merger was not the first merger for the NFL. In 1949 the NFL merged with three teams from the rival All-American Football Conference, bringing Cleveland, San Francisco, and Baltimore into the NFL (Crow et al., 2000). The NFL/AFL merger was originally inked in 1966, but there were four years of political wrangling before Congress approved the deal and the merger was completed (Crow et al., 2000).

the shareholders. This section examines some acquisition concerns, such as whether it is better to purchase another business' stock or just their assets.

Merging Two Companies

A merger occurs when one company is completely absorbed by another. For example, in 1999, Easton Sports Inc., the aluminum baseball bat manufacturer, acquired Stix Baseball Inc., a wooden bat producer. The merged company would operate under the Easton Sports Inc. name and produce bats with both the Easton and Stix brand names (Byrd, 1999). The advantage for Easton was that the company would have a presence in the wooden and aluminum bat markets. This presence was important in view of debates in collegiate sport about abandoning aluminum bats. If the NCAA approved the new rules, Easton would lose a significant market. However, by acquiring a wood bat manufacturer, the company was anticipating being able to

fill a need for wood bats if the new rules were approved. There was no need to invest in new machinery or production sites. Easton simply purchased another company that already had those resources. The advantages of mergers are that they are legally quite simple and relatively inexpensive. There is no title transfer of property or assets. A disadvantage of a merger is that it must be approved by a stockholder vote within each company.

During a merger, the management team of the business being sold must cooperate and approve the deal. This is sometimes problematic because the merger may result in the termination of some top-level managers. These managers may make a concerted effort to block the merger. Because of this concern, some deals include clauses that guarantee management positions in the new company or provide for golden parachutes. A golden parachute is a large monetary payoff to a top-level manager in exchange for her support of a merger.

A Big Deal Falls Through

The best-laid plans can go awry in a minute. Similarly, major deals can fall apart very quickly. After finally obtaining an approved buyer for its Denver-based sport team, Ascent Entertainment Group was trying to finalize its purchase by Liberty Media Group, owned by AT&T. Liberty had agreed to purchase Ascent contingent on Ascent's unloading the Denver Nuggets, Colorado Avalanche, and Denver's Pepsi Center. The Sturm Group offer of $461 million for the assets was supposed to be completed by November 15, 1999; but outstanding issues with the city on lease arrangements pushed the deadline to December 1, and that deadline also was not met. On the basis that the sale had not been completed, Liberty terminated the acquisition agreement ("Ascent, Liberty," 1999).

What's in a Name?

Sport executives in a merger might overlook the merger's impact on naming rights. If Bank A has its name on a stadium under a 20-year contract, will that name change if Bank A is purchased by Bank B? The answer is yes. However, the potential costs of making such a changeover can be significant. Philadelphia's CoreStates Center was renamed First Union Center after CoreStates Financial Corp. was purchased by First Union in 1999. Likewise, the new Boston Garden was supposed to open as the Shawmut Center. However, Shawmut National Group was purchased by Fleet Financial Group, Inc., which renamed the facility the FleetCenter. Not all name changes go well after a merger. The name can be changed only if the contract provides for such a change. A dispute arose concerning Buffalo's Marine Midland Arena when Marine Midland was acquired by HSBC Holding PLC. The Buffalo Sabres initially did not want to change the facility's name since they argued that the contract with Marine Midland did not allow the name to be transferred ("Business Bulletin," 2000).

Purchasing Voting Stock

In another form of acquisition, a company purchases the voting stock in another company in exchange for cash, stock in the existing company, or both. This is achieved through a tender offer, or a public offer by one company to directly buy the stock of another. An advantage of this acquisition method is that shareholders' meetings do not have to take place and management can be bypassed. The buyer can go directly to the shareholders for their approval. If a majority of the shareholders agree to sell, the purchaser will have control of the company. In March 1999, Marquee Group stockholders approved a merger with SFX Entertainment. As part of the deal, Marquee common stockholders received 0.0815 shares of SFX class A common stock for every share of Marquee stock. Approximately 1.4 million shares of SFX stock were exchanged for the Marquee stock (Marquee Group, 1999).

Management sometimes fights the stock acquisition, and this can lead to conflict. The process has the potential to be much longer and more expensive if management attempts to block the acquisition. Shareholders may also hold out in an effort to increase the stock's acquisition price. If current shareholders can force up the sale price of the stock, they will receive more money when they ultimately sell the stock. As highlighted in chapter 9, several shareholder groups sued Ascent over the proposed sale of the Denver Nuggets based on the shareholders' opinion that the bid was too low and that higher bids had been rejected. The higher bids would have earned the shareholders a greater return. Any conflict typically raises the acquisition price for the purchasing firm. Note that many stock acquisitions ultimately become mergers. Management from both sides negotiates for a merger, usually protecting the self-interest of both.

Purchasing Assets

The last acquisition method to consider is the purchase of one business' assets by another company. This method requires voter approval by the acquired company and is the least common of the three forms. The benefit of purchasing assets is that the acquiring company can increase its inventory or capital assets without acquiring potential liability, debt, or other concerns from the seller. The legal process of acquiring assets such as real estate, production sites, and machinery can be very costly.

Merger Accounting

With respect to accounting issues, mergers and acquisitions can be highly complex. Using generally accepted accounting principles, mergers are handled as either a purchase of assets or a pooling of interests. The two methods have very little effect on the real value of the merged firm; however, there are some differences between the two that we discuss here. The results of a pooling of interests are shown in figure 15.1, a through c. With the pooling of interests method, the two companies are merged and their balance sheets are simply added together to form the balance sheet for the new company. The new company is jointly owned by all of the stockholders in the previously separate companies. The pooling of assets method is very simple, and the total assets are unchanged by the merger.

The purchase of assets method is somewhat more complex. This method requires applying the fair market value to the acquired company's assets. In addition, an asset category called goodwill is created for accounting purposes. Goodwill represents the difference between the acquisition price and the fair value of the acquired business' assets. Figure 15.2, a through c, provides an example of the purchase of assets method. The balance sheets used in figure 15.1, a and b, are again displayed. Assume that Company 1 is going to acquire Company 2 for $15 million in cash. The money is raised through borrowing from a financial institution. On its balance sheet, Company 2 has reported $6 million in fixed assets. However, at the time of acquisition Company 2 is appraised at $10 million. Since Company 2 also has $2 million in working capital, the balance sheet assets are $12 million. Therefore, Company 2 paid $3 million in excess of the estimated market value of Company 2's total net assets. The difference is represented on the combined balance sheet as goodwill. Figure 15.2c shows the new firm's balance sheet after acquisition.

a	ASSETS		LIABILITIES & SHAREHOLDERS' EQUITY		b	ASSETS		LIABILITIES & SHAREHOLDERS' EQUITY	
	(in millions)		*(in millions)*			*(in millions)*		*(in millions)*	
	Working capital	$ 3	Equity	$13		Working capital	$2	Equity	$8
	Fixed assets	10				Fixed assets	6		
	Total	**$13**	**Total**	**$13**		**Total**	**$8**	**Total**	**$8**

c	ASSETS		LIABILITIES & SHAREHOLDERS' EQUITY	
	(in millions)		*(in millions)*	
	Working capital	$ 5	Equity	$21
	Fixed assets	16		
	Total	**$21**	**Total**	**$21**

Figure 15.1 Company 1's balance sheet *(a)*, Company 2's balance sheet *(b)*, and their combined balance sheet *(c)*.

a	ASSETS		LIABILITIES & SHAREHOLDERS' EQUITY		b	ASSETS		LIABILITIES & SHAREHOLDERS' EQUITY	
	(in millions)		*(in millions)*			*(in millions)*		*(in millions)*	
	Working capital	$ 3	Equity	$13		Working capital	$2	Equity	$8
	Fixed assets	10				Fixed assets	6		
	Total	**$13**	**Total**	**$13**		**Total**	**$8**	**Total**	**$8**

c	ASSETS		LIABILITIES & SHAREHOLDERS' EQUITY	
	(in millions)		*(in millions)*	
	Working capital	$ 5	Equity	$15
	Fixed assets	20	Debt	13
	Goodwill	3		
	Total	**$28**	**Total**	**$28**

Figure 15.2 Company 1's balance sheet *(a)*, Company 2's balance sheet *(b)*, and their combined balance sheet *(c)*.

To recap, the total assets of the combined companies are $28 million, $7 million more than when the two company balance sheets were separate. Of that $7 million, $4 million is from the revaluation of Company 2's fixed assets and $3 million is from goodwill. The goodwill is the amount paid in excess of the fair market value of Company 2. A buyer may pay an additional amount such as this because there are a number of intangible assets that are not included on the balance sheet—assets such as employee talent and future growth opportunities. The additional $3 million pays for such assets.

Which of the two methods is best? As you can see, the major difference between them is goodwill. Goodwill has several important tax ramifications. Goodwill must be amortized over a period of years, not to exceed 40 years. The goodwill amortization expense is then deducted from reported income. However, unlike depreciation, goodwill is not tax deductible. Given the goodwill expense, the purchase of assets method usually results in lower reported income than the pooling of assets method. Also, since the fixed assets are revalued using the purchase of assets method, often the overall value of the merged company increases. The combined larger book value and lower reported income can have a negative effect on company performance measures such as return on equity (ROE) and return on assets (ROA). The resulting lower measures may paint a picture that is not as strong as when the pooling of assets method is used (Brealey & Myers, 1996).

Note that the choice of accounting methods used for acquisitions has no effect on tax-deductible expenses or cash flows. Therefore, the net present value of the merged firm is not affected by the selection of merger accounting methods. Also, no evidence exists to suggest that more value is created for the acquiring business under one method or the other (Ross et al., 1995). The differences are in the accounting methods only.

> A major purpose of a merger is to generate value above and beyond what would be possible if the two companies remained separate. Mergers involve issues such as antitrust law and can take a variety of forms.

Current Sport-Industry Examples

We have already discussed several merger and acquisition examples. However, two sport-specific examples illustrate concerns these types of transactions have raised in the sport industry and how these concerns were overcome.

Rupert Murdoch and News Corporation

An excellent example of a company acquiring another business in an attempt to increase its own value is News Corp., owned by Rupert Murdoch. News Corp. operates television networks such as the Fox Network, Fox Sports, and BSkyB. As part of

an overall business strategy, News Corp. acquired the Los Angeles Dodgers for $311 million in 1998 (Chass, 1998) One reason for the purchase was to provide broadcast content for the company's television networks. Therefore, although the Dodgers may not be a company that provides large profits, Murdoch is able to use them to help his other business ventures such as television and radio broadcasting.

Murdoch has used this strategy quite successfully in North America, Europe, and Australia, where he is involved in professional sports such as baseball, soccer, and rugby. In 1998, he also made a $1 billion bid for Manchester United, the English Premier League soccer club. Murdoch wanted to use the ownership right of the league's most popular team to improve his negotiating position with the English Premier League (Kaplan, 1998, September 14-20). The merger was blocked by antitrust regulators in Great Britain. News Corp. already owned BSkyB, the television outlet that has exclusive rights to broadcast all Premier League games. British regulators believed that cross ownership of a team and the exclusive television broadcaster could lead to anticompetitive behavior (Rofe, 1999). In addition, Murdoch was eyeing the possibility of starting a European "super league," which would also be broadcast on his network. Ultimately, because of antitrust concerns, the British government did not permit News Corp.'s purchase of Manchester United.

Murdoch has attempted to use acquisition in the past to compete in the sport broadcasting industry. In April 1999, he purchased one-half of Liberty Media's interests in regional cable networks. The price tag for the acquisition was $1.4 billion. The buyout gave Murdoch control over additional cable outlets along with the rights to several sport programs. News Corp. reportedly made the acquisition as part of an overall business strategy to build a network of regional cable outlets that would compete with ESPN for sport programming (Brockington & Rofe, 1999).

SFX Entertainment Incorporated

SFX Entertainment Inc. is another company that has greatly expanded its operations recently through the acquisition of existing companies. SFX had traditionally been involved in the entertainment industry through event and facility management. The company owns and operates amphitheaters and concert halls throughout North America, in addition to operating and promoting events such as rock concerts, Broadway shows, and specialized motor sport events (sfx.com, 1999). Within the past several years, SFX has acquired several companies that have resulted in the firm's expanding its operations into sport marketing and athlete representation.

Two of SFX's largest acquisitions have been Falk Associates Management Enterprises (FAME) and the Marquee Group. FAME was purchased in 1998 for $150 million from its owner David Falk. Through FAME, Falk had built one of the largest athlete representation companies in the world. Some of its clients, mostly in the NBA, have been Michael Jordan, Patrick Ewing, Stephon Marbury, and Dikembe Mutombo. As part of this merger and other similar acquisitions, SFX created the SFX Sports Group and appointed Falk as the chairman (Sandomir, 1999).

The Marquee Group is involved in several areas of the sport industry such as event management, television production, and talent representation. SFX Entertainment purchased the Marquee Group in 1998 for a reported $100 million. The deal was a stock acquisition in which Marquee Group stockholders received approximately $6 worth of SFX Entertainment stock for every Marquee share. The acquisition allowed SFX to strengthen its presence in sport marketing and athlete representation. The Marquee Group represents over 100 athletes, sport broadcasters, and entertainers. In addition, it has marketing relationships with more than 50 sport organizations and facilities. Its client list includes the Big 12 Conference, MLB, the International Hockey League, and the Professional Bowlers Tour. The Marquee Group also represents athletes such as Mark Chmura (football), Natasha Zvereva (tennis), John Daly (golf), and Orlando "El Duque" Hernandez (baseball) (Marquee Group, 1999).

Acquiring FAME and the Marquee Group was part of a long-term corporate strategy for SFX Entertainment. Its management wanted to be a major force in the sport and entertainment industries. Instead of starting its own sport marketing agency, SFX decided to acquire several preexisting firms. With these acquisitions, SFX also obtained the knowledge and experience of these companies' managers and staff. SFX now controlled many of the top facilities, events, and talent in the sport and entertainment industries. This would allow SFX to become involved in many new business ventures that might lead to financial success. Clear Channel Communications, Inc. of San Antonio, Texas, noticed the financial success. Clear Channel is the largest billboard and radio station owner in the United States. In an attempt to develop a comprehensive package including radio, television, billboard, facility, and concert promotion activities, Clear Channel paid

$3.3 billion to acquire SFX in 2000. Part of the purchase price included assuming $1.1 billion in debt ("Clear Channel," 2000).

> *Mergers and acquisitions involving sport are commonplace. Two recent examples are Rupert Murdoch's purchase of the Los Angeles Dodgers and Clear Channel's purchase of SFX Entertainment.*

CONCLUSION

Successful sport businesses must determine how to use their positive earnings. There are three primary ways in which companies use these funds: paying dividends to stockholders, acquiring other firms, and reinvesting in themselves. Paying dividends is often a popular choice with stockholders, but this may not be in the best long-term interests of the stockholders or the firm. There are three views on dividend payments. The rightists believe that the highest possible level of dividends should be paid to stockholders. The leftists feel that dividend payments should be relatively small. The middle-of-the-roaders feel that dividend payments should be at a level that satisfies the greatest number of stockholders. Paying dividends involves a somewhat complex process. The process has been established to ensure that the proper parties receive dividend payments in a fair and timely manner.

Another option for using earnings is to reinvest in the business. This reinvestment usually takes the form of spending on capital projects such as purchasing new equipment, investing in talent, or constructing new facilities. Sport is somewhat unique in that capital spending can take the form of hiring coaches and players. For example, the Minnesota Timberwolves signed Kevin Garnett to a six-year $126 million playing contract (Adamek, 1998). This is definitely a form of capital spending. In other industries, there are very few long-term employment contracts that make up such a large portion of a business' expenses. Reinvestment allows for growth and future financial success. It is an integral part of capital budgeting and long-term financial planning.

Last, earnings can be used to acquire other businesses. Acquisitions can entail horizontal mergers, vertical mergers, or conglomerates. For a merger to be successful, the value of the merged companies must be greater than the value of the two businesses if they were to remain as separate entities. Recently, there has been an increase in mergers and acquisitions in the sport industry. Entertainment companies such as Disney, Rupert Murdoch's News Corp., and

SFX Entertainment have acquired many other businesses in an attempt to expand their presence in the sport and entertainment industries. Using business earnings is an important aspect of financial management that plays a major role in determining long-term business success.

ASSIGNMENT

Examine the various case studies in this book and indicate how these businesses should spend any excess cash. Public entities may not have the luxury of making a profit, but they can still have revenue in excess of expenses that they can spend in various ways.

RESEARCH PROJECT

Examine two different mergers that have occurred in the sport, fitness, or recreation industry in the past 10 years and analyze whether or not the mergers were a success.

CLASS DISCUSSION TOPICS

1. Is consolidation in the sport industry good?
2. Do you think it would be worthwhile to create another football league similar to the United States Football League? Would another baseball league be a better investment?
3. If you could make 10% from a government bond or 10% from investing in a professional sport team, which one would you invest in and why?
4. Why should a business set a record date when issuing a dividend?
5. If you had this responsibility within a corporation, under what circumstances would you make a decision to reinvest versus issuing a dividend?
6. Which group (rightist, leftist, or middle-of-the-road) has the views that you feel make the most sense?

PART VI

Financial Troubleshooting

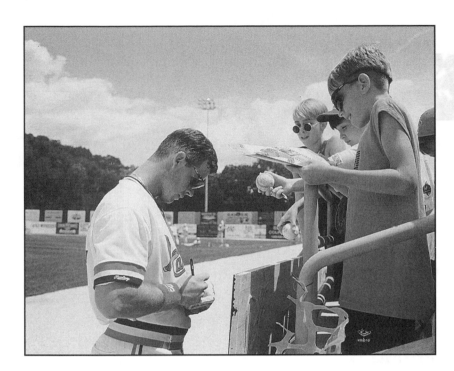

Auditing

CHAPTER OBJECTIVES

After studying this chapter, you should be able to do the following:

- Define the purposes of auditing.
- Understand the problems associated with poor auditing.
- Describe the types of audits.
- Understand the importance of selecting competent and unbiased auditors.
- Understand how the auditing process works.
- Understand how sport fraud can occur with sloppy financial analysis.

Auditing is one of the most important areas within the field of accounting. Although the focus of this textbook is on financial management, it is also beneficial for a sport manager to be knowledgeable in the basics of auditing. The importance of knowing how income or expenses can be excluded from financial statements was made abundantly clear in 2001 with the collapse of energy giant Enron amid allegations that numerous deals were not included in the balance sheets and income statements. Although such scandals are not common in sport businesses, they are possible. The goal of this chapter is to provide you with an introduction to auditing. If you wish to find out more about the field, you should consult a textbook devoted to the principles of auditing. This chapter deals primarily with the principles of auditing and their applicability to the sport industry.

The Purposes of Auditing

Auditing has two fundamental roles. First, auditing serves to ensure that all financial statements accurately portray a firm's financial position. Second, audits allow managers to analyze their operation's efficiency.

Ensuring Accuracy of Financial Information

The primary role of auditing is to ensure the accuracy of financial information. The purpose of auditing is to investigate and determine if the financial statements produced by the sport business have been prepared in accordance with financial reporting practices that are appropriate (Holmes & Burns,

1979). This may seem like a relatively simple matter, but it can be quite complex. In this text we discuss numerous financial measures that are predicated on accurate financial data. The ratios are only as good as the numbers used in the ratios. Auditing is not limited to simply analyzing financial statements, however. To ensure that the financial statements are accurate, an auditor must study the entire business. This often involves analyzing a business' internal processes to see whether they successfully control the flow of financial information. For example, an auditor must examine the processes involved in functional areas such as employee payroll, the purchase of goods and services, and inventory control to determine if the financial statements accurately represent the auditee. Thus, a benefit of auditing is to discourage and detect fraudulent activities (see Detecting Fraud on pp. 292–293). Additionally, an auditor must have knowledge of the industry being examined. It is important to note that all businesses and organizations, regardless of size, scope, and mission must undergo some type of periodic audit.

There is a need for honest and candid public disclosure of financial information by businesses and organizations, both public and private. It is just as important for publicly operated sport organizations, such as university athletic departments, to have accurate financial records as it is for private companies, such as professional sport franchises and sporting goods manufacturers. Auditing is designed to identify problems and to ensure investor confidence in a company's financial statements. However, if the independent auditors help manipulate the numbers, as is alleged to have occurred in the Enron scandal, the entire rationale for independent auditing is lost.

WorldCom

While it might be hard to replicate the complex schemes Enron used to cover its financial problems, WorldCom engaged in outright fraud that auditors should have checked. The WorldCom downfall was based on classifying debt as capital expenditures. This change resulted in a capitalization of expenses rather than having the expenses deducted as they were incurred and paid. This led to higher reported profits because approximately $3.8 billion worth of expenses were improperly classified ("WorldCom charged with fraud," 2002).

While it might be difficult for a sport business to engage in the same illegal activities that WorldCom did, SMC could face the same problem. If SMC's chief financial officer did not pay certain bills and wrote checks to himself, then the company could think they were paying their accounts payable when in fact their obligations were increasing every month. If SMC failed to properly audit its finances, such a scheme could go undetected for months until lawsuits are filed or accounts closed.

Legal but Not Necessarily Honest

Many companies "play games" with financial statements to present an interpretation of the data that shows the company in the best light. It is the role of the auditor to make sure these tricks are properly recorded and communicated to all interested parties. Some of the tricks that are legal, but not necessarily honest, include the following:

1. Companies might promote their earnings by publicizing a pro forma earnings that excludes many normal expense items such as interest and marketing expenses.
2. If the earnings are low or negative, a company might list instead EBITDA—earnings before interest, taxes, depreciation, and amortization.
3. Companies might not report the potential impact of stock-options grants on their earnings.
4. Especially in the late 1990s, some businesses reported large earnings acquired through selling their investments in start-ups. While these are real earnings, they are not the real earnings of the core business, but an offshoot, and there is no guarantee that any future similar earnings might ever be realized (Scherreik, 2000).

Auditing is designed to determine whether a business' financial statements are accurate and to identify problems, including possible fraud.

Analyzing Operational Efficiency

Audits may detect areas in which a sport business operates more efficiently, which could lead to an increase in profits (Arens & Loebbecke, 2000). For nonprofit organizations, this increased efficiency may allow the organization to do more with its available resources. For example, an athletic director at a small college is often given a fixed yearly budget. Efficient use of these funds will allow that athletic director to maximize the number of opportunities for the coaches and student-athletes. Therefore, it is as important for an athletic director to audit the organization to increase efficiency as it is for the manager of a multibillion-dollar private corporation.

Categories of Audits

Audits can be separated into two general categories: internal and independent. Internal audits are completed by staff members within a business. Most large businesses have a financial department that oversees internal audits. An internal auditor serves several different functions. Usually he is involved in preparing an organization's financial statements to ensure their accuracy. The auditor is also involved in the establishment of internal controls for the organization. An auditor may develop an internal control system to track the purchase, receipt, and distribution of inventory for a retail sales company such as Foot Locker or Athlete's Foot. As another example of establishing internal controls, an internal auditor may develop a system to track the use of office equipment such as computers, fax machines, and telephones. A phone tracking system might require a phone user to enter a special code to make a long distance call. The system can then track all calls to show if an employee is using the phone excessively or for personal purposes. Without a system that tracks the use and physical location of equipment, it may be quite easy for an employee to steal business property.

Independent audits, as the name implies, involve an external review of the finances by individuals who are not directly involved with the documents that are being reviewed. Thus, an independent audit can be performed by someone from another division in the company who has not been involved in generating the document that is being reviewed. Likewise, an independent audit can also be performed by external entities, such as public accounting firms, that can verify the truthfulness of the documents being reviewed. The latter is the type of audit most commonly seen in corporate finance. Independent audits are discussed in greater detail later in this chapter.

There is a third general category of audit that is outside the scope of this textbook. The IRS can request an audit of any business. Usually, the IRS audits a business to determine whether or not the correct amount of federal taxes has been paid. Businesses that fail to pay or that underpay taxes can face substantial monetary fines and penalties. In this chapter we will focus on independent audits because they are the most common type and are the type of audit that most directly affects sport finance managers.

> Two general categories of audits are internal audits, which are completed by personnel within the company, and independent audits, which are typically performed by auditors from outside the company.

Internal Controls

As stated earlier, auditing involves more than verifying a business' financial statements. An auditor must also examine a business' system of internal controls. Internal controls are the processes and mechanisms used in the management of a business (Meigs, Whittington, & Meigs, 1982). For example, all businesses have employees who are compensated for their labor. There are many steps in paying employees. A system must be developed to calculate the number of hours worked by each employee and the wage rate at which each will be compensated. In addition, deductions must be made for expenses such as income taxes, health benefits, and retirement plan payments. Last, paychecks must be processed and distributed to all employees. It is important that an efficient, consistent, and accurate system be developed for this process. An inferior system will mean a lack of internal control and increase the probability of financial errors. These errors could mean that an employee is not paid or is paid an inaccurate amount.

A strong internal control system is a means to avoid many financial errors. Therefore, those developing procedures for managing financial matters should stress internal control. A good example in the sport industry relates to parking lot attendants. At many large parking lots for stadiums and arenas, you will see two individuals helping process people through the gates. There may be two attendants because parking revenue is split between the team and the municipal entity that owns the facility. To guarantee accuracy, the team may employ a person to take the money, and the municipality may employ a person who has a counter to register how many cars have entered the parking lot. The number of cars clicked can be reconciled with the amount of money collected to make sure both sides have the right number. A system of strong internal controls also makes it easier for managers to prepare for financial audits because they will have the materials needed by the auditor.

Poor internal controls may also increase the likelihood of fraud. For example, if one person oversees the entire payroll system for a small sport organization, of say 20 employees, committing a fraud would be rather easy for that employee. A procedure must exist for ensuring the accuracy of this person's work; without oversight, a fraudulent act can easily occur. Perhaps the payroll officer overpays employees or places people on the payroll who are not actually working for the firm.

> An efficient internal control system should minimize the potential for financial errors and fraud.

Independent Audits

Independent auditors are auditors who are not associated with the business that is being audited. Although they are hired by the business, their responsibility is to provide assurance that the business' financial information is reliable and accurate. The issue of independence is very important. The audited business may not be pleased with the findings of an independent auditor, but the auditor has an ethical duty to honestly report her findings (Whittington & Pany, 1998). For public corporations, auditors must complete an auditor's report that summarizes their findings. As in the general field of accounting, auditors have standard procedures that they use to analyze and report their findings. There are also several professional associations that oversee the auditing field, some of which are listed in table 16.1.

The accuracy of an auditor's report is very important. Under U.S. common law and securities law, third parties such as investors, creditors, and government agencies can sue independent auditors. Monetary damages may have to be paid if it is determined that the independent auditor was guilty of a crime (Whittington & Pany, 1998). In March 2002, the accounting firm of Arthur Andersen was indicted in a federal court for its involvement with the Enron scandal. The U.S. Department of Justice claimed that Arthur Andersen obstructed justice by allegedly aiding Enron in the destruction of key financial documents. Deputy Attorney General Larry Thompson as quoted in *USA Today* stated that "Andersen personnel engaged in the wholesale destruction of tons of paperwork and attempted to purge huge volumes of electronic data or information. . . . At the time, Andersen knew full well that

Table 16.1 Professional Associations Related to Auditing

Abbreviation	Name
ASB	Auditing Standards Board
AICPA	American Institute of Certified Public Accountants
FAF	Financial Accounting Foundation
SSCPA	State Societies of Certified Public Accountants
AAA	American Accounting Association
FEI	Financial Executives Institute
NAA	National Association of Accountants
IIA	Institute of Internal Auditors

these documents were relevant to the inquiries into Enron's collapse" (Farrell, 2002). Although the ultimate result of the case was not known as this book was being prepared for publication, one outcome may be that Arthur Andersen will be forced to pay millions, or perhaps billions, of dollars in fines to the federal government. On a broader scale, the future of Arthur Andersen may be in doubt as a consequence of the possible loss of several key clients. The Enron scandal may also lead to much stricter auditing rules as the U.S. federal government attempts to protect corporate shareholders from misleading auditing practices (Farrell, 2002).

Types of Independent Audits

There are three distinct types of audits. The first, the audit of financial statements, is the most common, and this type of audit receives the bulk of attention in this chapter. The two other types of audits, operational audits and compliance audits, are usually referred to as audit activities (Arens & Loebbecke, 2000). While attestation and assurance are provided through these audits, as discussed later in the chapter, the central theme is to analyze a business' efficiency and regulatory compliance. What follows is a brief description of each of the three types of audits, which are also characterized in table 16.2.

1. *Financial statements audit.* This type of audit is done to determine if a business' financial statements meet generally accepted accounting principles. Most often, these financial statements include income statements, statements of cash flows, and the statement of financial position (i.e., balance sheets).

2. *Operational audit.* An operational audit reviews some part of a business' operating methods and procedures. The goal is to determine if the business is operating at its maximum efficiency and effectiveness. Usually, an operational audit assesses effi-

ciency and also yields recommendations for improved effectiveness. For example, a sporting goods manufacturer may undergo an operational audit to analyze the efficiency and effectiveness of its product distribution system. The result may be that the business uses the auditor's recommendations to develop new methods for transporting products from the production site to retailers.

3. *Compliance audit.* The goal of the compliance audit is to determine if the auditee is following the specific rules, regulations, and procedures set by some higher authority. Within collegiate athletics, the NCAA periodically visits member institutions to audit their operations. For example, the NCAA may analyze the system a college or university uses to ensure student-athlete eligibility. The NCAA has specific rules and regulations with respect to eligibility. Failure to follow these guidelines may lead to rules violations and probation. In an attempt to minimize these violations, the NCAA works with member institutions in developing effective mechanisms for following rules and regulations. In addition, the NCAA has instituted five-year self-studies and peer reviews for collegiate athletic programs as a method of instituting compliance audits.

Thus, the University of Houston would be required in the third or fourth year to start gathering data for its audit. The last year would be spent compiling the data and completing a report that would address both the positive and negative concerns raised by the self-study. If the university uncovered any potential academic or financial abuse, the audit would allow it to highlight such concerns. The process also will show that the university's own internal investigation system could uncover such problems and that the university could institute its own reforms or punishment.

Table 16.2 Types of Audits

Type of audit	Role of audit	Audit tasks
Financial statement audit	Ensure the accuracy of financial statements	Review documents, records, and other sources of financial evidence
Operational audit	Evaluate the efficiency and effectiveness of organizational acitvities	Interview employees; analyze processes and written reports
Compliance audit	Determine if specific rules, procedures, or regulations set by higher authorities are being met	Analyze written materials, stated regulations and standards, and methods for meeting these regulations and standards

Materiality and Meaningfulness

One of the most important concepts within auditing is materiality. Materiality has to do with the levels of misstatement that are allowable in financial information. Since no financial system is perfect, misstatements do occur. The auditor must determine the level of misstatement that will affect the fairness of the information. For example, a large sport marketing agency may have millions of dollars in revenues and expenses. For such an organization, a financial misstatement of $10,000 may be considered immaterial. With respect to the overall financial position of the business, such a small misstatement can be considered immaterial. However, a $10,000 misstatement for a small sport business such as an independent sporting goods store would probably be considered material. In each situation, the auditor must determine where to draw the line. In general, a misstatement can be considered material if knowledge of the misstatement affects a decision of a reasonable user of the statements (Arens & Loebbecke, 2000). A misstatement that is relatively small or one that does not affect the overall fairness of the financial statements is considered immaterial. If misstatements are relatively large or pervasively affect an organization's financial documents, an auditor may not be comfortable in issuing an unqualified auditor's report (see Receiving the Auditor's Report on pp. 290–292). In this case, the auditor may issue a qualified opinion or an adverse opinion about the documents. Obviously, an auditee wants to avoid this result. Such a finding may dramatically decrease the confidence that investors and creditors have in the company's financial statements.

The Role of Technology

The last 25 years have seen a revolution in auditing. Technology has drastically changed how businesses acquire, process, and manage financial information.

As a result, auditors have changed the manner in which they organize and analyze information. In the next sections we examine two technological advances that have greatly affected auditing.

Electronic Data Processing Systems

Electronic data processing (EDP) systems allow businesses to simplify operations such as accounts payable, payroll, and inventory control. This technology has increased efficiency and accuracy in the reporting of financial information. At the same time, businesses must take steps to make sure that information produced through use of an EDP system is accurate. First, they must ensure that the EDP systems themselves do not have errors. A poor EDP system can result in more misstatements than the old system of human recording and calculating. Second, as always, an EDP system is only as good as the data inputted. Errors in the inputting of data can be very costly. The increased efficiency gained through EDP may, in some cases, result in a loss of internal control. Too often, managers assume that financial information is accurate because it has been generated through an EDP system; this assumption can be costly. For example, a fitness center may use an EDP system to produce a monthly statement of the revenues generated through membership fees. This would appear to be a simple procedure, but problems may occur if the payment amounts are inaccurately entered by employees or are not entered in a timely fashion. If membership fees received on the last day of the month are not processed for several days, the monthly statement will not be accurate. An EDP system cannot recognize a discrepancy like this, yet it is still an obvious accounting error. As the saying goes, "garbage in, garbage out."

EDP can be a significant benefit, but if technological hurdles arise, the systems can also quickly become worthless. The recent Y2K scare was a great example of the possibility of errors due to technology. Many businesses invested substantial resources toward Y2K compliance in areas such as payroll and finance. As we all know, the investment was wise. January 1, 2000, came and went with very few problems attributable to computers and technology. However, without the precautions and safeguards, many businesses could have had substantial technological problems.

Today, more than ever before, businesses rely on computer technology and the Internet. When EDP was first developed, its cost made it attractive for only the largest businesses. Now it is cost-effective for even the smallest businesses. For a relatively low investment in software, any business can have an EDP system that is both powerful and user friendly. These systems have revolutionized the means by which businesses collect, process, and analyze financial information.

Because of the threat of computer viruses and bugs, all EDP systems must be backed up. Managers should be able to feel confident that if their primary EDP systems become inoperable, a backup system is in place. Auditors can help with this. First, through their work with the financial statements, auditors can help in analyzing a client's EDP and make recommendations for ensuring the safety and accuracy of financial information. In addition, businesses should undergo periodic operational audits in order to ensure the efficiency and effectiveness of their EDP.

The Internet and Electronic Mail

Another technological advance that has changed organizational finances and audits is the Internet and electronic mail. Organizations with multiple locations can now communicate much more efficiently. A sporting goods retailer with multiple stores could utilize technological advances to have the sales from each store automatically sent to a central location so management could track revenue. If sales are lower on one day as compared to other days, management could investigate what caused the decline to prevent its occurrence in the future. Transactions such as multiple electronic fund transfers from numerous bank accounts now occur without the use of paper and without human contact. While this increases efficiency, it also leads to new types of problems. Computer fraud is a new concern, and new internal controls have been developed to ensure the accuracy of transactions and processes.

Technology has also had a significant influence on how sport products are bought and sold. Organizations such as professional sport teams, collegiate athletic programs, and sporting goods manufactur-

ers sell their products over the Internet, place orders online, and market their products via Web sites. Electronic commerce has dramatically changed the sport industry and will continue to do so. Some analysts predict that ticket sales for sporting events over the Internet will be a $3 billion industry by 2003. With the increase in ticket sales via the Web, the threat of counterfeit tickets also arises. Sport managers must ensure that they have systems that can track these sales effectively. Auditors must be able to attest to the accuracy of these transactions and the financial statements that result from them.

In addition to the problems caused by viruses, computer-related crime is increasing at a rapid pace. Several major computer-related extortion cases occurred in 1999 when hackers broke into retail Web sites and stole credit card numbers, threatening to publish the numbers if they were not paid a specified amount. Customers will purchase with confidence only if a Web site protects financial transactions.

Technology has greatly changed the landscape of auditing and will continue to do so in the future. A successful sport manager must be prepared to use new technologies in making money, but also to effectively track these funds.

Benefits of Independent Audits

Companies derive several significant benefits from undergoing periodic independent audits. Additionally, there are societal benefits of independent audits. Poor decisions that businesses make based on inaccurate financial information can have a negative effect on a society at large. Resources may be mistakenly allotted to inefficient or unworthy projects, thereby decreasing overall economic productivity. Additionally, individual and institutional investors may make poor decisions in selecting investment options. In most instances, investors use corporate financial statements in their investment decision-making processes. While the positive effect of independent audits on individual businesses is obvious, the societal benefit of audits must not be overlooked. Accurate financial information about businesses is vital to maintaining an efficient economy. Holmes and Burns (1979) separated the benefits from accurate independent auditing into three categories based on who derives the benefit:

1. Benefits primarily for auditees:
   a. Independent audits provide credibility and reliability to financial statements.
   b. Audits serve to dissuade management and employees from committing acts of fraud.

c. Audited financial statements lessen the likelihood of government audits by ensuring that the basis for the preparation of tax returns and other financial documents is accurate.

d. Audited financial statements increase investor or creditor confidence and broaden the sources of outside financing.

e. Independent audits uncover errors in the auditee's financial records, which may lead to the recovery of lost revenue or may decrease costs.

f. Independent audits ensure that the business is consistently following stated policies and procedures.

2. Benefits primarily to other members of the business community:

a. Audited financial statements give vendors and other creditors a credible basis for making decisions about extending credit.

b. Audited statements are a credible basis on which potential and current investors can evaluate investment and management performance.

c. Audited statements provide insurance companies a credible and accurate basis for settling claims for insurance-covered losses.

d. Audited statements provide labor unions and the auditee an objective basis on which to settle disputes over wages and fringe benefits.

e. Audited statements provide the buyer and seller a basis for negotiating the terms for the sale or merger of business entities.

3. Benefits primarily to government entities and the legal community:

a. Government agencies gain additional assurance concerning the dependability and accuracy of tax returns and financial reports.

b. Independent audits of financial statements from public interest organizations such as banks and public utilities provide government agencies with an independent means to focus their special examination resources.

c. Audited financial statements provide the legal community an independent basis for settling bankruptcy actions.

> *An independent audit of a company's financial statements provides significant benefits to the company and to the business community, as well as to society at large.*

The Auditing Process

The next section of this chapter concerns the process of conducting an audit. The first step in the process is to select the appropriate auditor. After characterizing the selection process, we discuss how a business should prepare for an audit, the various types of audits that can be undertaken, and the auditor's report.

Selecting the Auditor

As stated earlier, an independent auditor plays a vital role in managing a sport business' finances. Despite any temptation to do so, the auditee should not influence the independent character of the audit. The auditor's report attests to the accuracy of financial statements. Creditors and stockholders have more confidence in organizations that have audits completed by credible auditing firms. Therefore, the selection of an auditor is very important. A business should seek out an auditor who has experience in the industry in question. Although audits can be expensive, with typical audits for medium-sized firms costing over $100,000, a specialized auditor in the sport industry is well worth the investment. The top accounting firms such as PricewaterhouseCoopers, KPMG Peat Marwick, Arthur Andersen, and other larger accounting firms have departments that specialize in the sport industry.

Each industry has its own unique characteristics that a specialized auditor can understand without needing to do as much research as other auditors would. For example, professional sport teams have several unique financial traits. Under federal tax laws, new team owners are permitted to depreciate the value of player contracts over five years. The players are treated as a capital investment similar to plants and equipment. Also, the pay structure for players can be complex because of signing bonuses, performance incentives, and deferred payments that are not seen in other industries. A professional team should seek out an auditor with experience in analyzing these types of financial documents. It would be easy for an inexperienced auditor to make an error that would call into question the accuracy of the team's financial statements.

Public companies have to meet certain requirements as they select their auditing firms. The New York Stock Exchange requires its member corporations to establish a committee to select their auditing firm (Holmes & Burns, 1979). This committee must consist of nonemployees of the corporation. Most firms elect to have their boards of directors choose their independent auditor. The goal of not having management select the auditing firm is to ensure objectivity from the audit. The possibility of fraud within the auditing process would be increased if management selected the auditing firm.

Preparing for the Auditor

After selecting the auditing firm, a business must prepare for the audit. An auditor needs specific types of information in order to do his job. The following are some of the organizational materials that should be collected in preparation for the auditor.

- *Internally prepared documents.* These include operating documents such as sales invoices, purchase orders, general ledgers, payroll records, receiving forms, and other standard accounting worksheets.
- *Externally prepared documents.* These include documents such as bank statements, loan documents, and vendor statements.
- *Nonfinancial records.* Auditors often need corporate information that is not financial. Documents in this category include articles of incorporation, minutes of organizational meetings, past internal or independent auditor's reports, organizational charts, and job descriptions.

Additionally, independent auditors may need to physically verify assets. For example, they may need to see direct evidence of assets such as inventory, equipment, computers, and office furniture. The auditor may literally walk through an office to verify that the organization has items such as chairs, desks, and computers that it claims as assets in financial statements.

An auditor may also wish to obtain oral testimony from management, employees, or customers to ensure that the organizational information is accurate. Arrangements should be made so that these people are available to the independent auditor. In general, there will be no problems with oral testimony unless there are misstatements—accidental or fraudulent.

The audit examines various business segments. We now focus on the areas of operation that are most important for a sport organization when it is undergoing an internal or independent audit.

> The independent auditing process involves considerable time and effort on the part of the company being audited, including selecting the auditor and gathering the organizational information the auditor will need.

Cash Auditing

For many sport businesses, cash is the most important current asset. For example, sporting goods stores and pro shops sell a high volume of their product inventory through cash transactions. Businesses or organizations that produce a sport event also have a high level of cash transactions. Items such as game tickets, team merchandise, and concessions are largely sold through cash transactions. Although customers are using credit cards at a higher rate than in the past, sport organizations such as college athletic departments, professional teams, and sport facilities must develop systems to control cash.

Unfortunately, cash is also the asset most susceptible to theft and fraud. It is easily transferable, liquid, and difficult to trace. Countless cases of fraud involving cash occur each year. In one example, a small business with two store locations had an employee who was responsible for both reconciling the organization's bank accounts and making the daily deposits. Each location would submit its daily cash amounts to the employee along with a completed bank deposit slip. The employee was then responsible for depositing the cash at the bank. This might appear to be an efficient and logical system. However, it also made cash fraud quite easy. The employee simply kept a portion of the daily cash receipts, completed a new deposit slip for the decreased amount, and deposited that amount. Since the employee did the bank **account reconciliation,** no one noticed that not all of the cash made it into the company bank account. On paper, everything seemed to be in order. In reality, the employee was keeping thousands of dollars in company revenue. The employee was eventually caught when another employee found an old deposit slip in the garbage. That employee notified the owner of the business, and the fraud was uncovered (Colbert & Bolton, 1998).

The role of the auditor is to ensure that cash assets are not overstated and that financial statements accurately represent the cash level. The usual method is to make sure that cash that should have been collected has been both collected and accurately recorded. For example, an audit of a sporting goods store involves matching the daily sales receipts from the cash registers with the cash deposit slips. All cash that is received through sales should be deposited into the business' bank account. Only the level of cash necessary for daily operations should be left in the cash register. Meigs et al. (1982) make the following suggestions for handling daily cash receipts:

- *No single employee should be responsible for handling cash transactions from beginning to end.* For example, the person who operates the cash register should not also oversee the daily cash deposits to the bank.

- *Cash handling should be separated from cash recording and deposit.* This can be accomplished by having one person open all letters and process all checks. Another person could be responsible for depositing the checks. Thus, each party can independently examine the cash or checks to be deposited to verify the amounts.

- *Cash receipts should be centralized.* For example, a sport facility may have several different locations where game tickets are sold. A system should be developed to track the cash activities at each location, and the cash should ultimately be collected in one location. A lack of cash centralization increases the number of people handling the cash and the likelihood for theft.

- *Cash receipts should be deposited on a daily basis.* Cash should not be left in the place of business for more than one day. The only exception may be a small amount of **petty cash** that is necessary for emergency or relatively small purchases.

- *When possible, make all payments by check.* Checks are easier to track and minimize the likelihood of theft.

Running Away With the Kids' Money

The former treasurer of the Southern Connecticut Youth Hockey League was accused of embezzling $21,462 from the league in a six-month period. She allegedly took checks for the league and deposited them in her own account. She left her position and was responsible for training the next treasurer. However, she allegedly delayed giving him the records, and when they were finally turned over there were many accounts that were delinquent and for which registration checks had been issued, but never deposited (Leo, 2000).

Another important responsibility for the auditor is to examine the auditee's management of cash balances to ensure operational efficiency. In some instances, a business may have too much cash on hand. An auditor may recommend that the organization reinvest the cash back into the business or invest in other opportunities. Conversely, the auditor may find that the organization has relatively low cash balances. It can be troublesome if the business does not have enough cash on hand to meet short-term debt obligations such as accounts payable to vendors or suppliers.

Inventory Auditing

Another large asset for most sport businesses is inventory. Chapter 13 covered inventory- and production-related issues. Apart from its conventional meaning, inventory can also be defined as products and materials that have a life of less than one year. For some sport businesses, inventories are not their greatest asset. For professional teams, whose primary assets are the players, inventory exists, but it is not as valuable as the players. Minor league players might be considered inventory, but they have little value until they make it to the highest professional ranks. The value of a minor league team stems from its goodwill. Recall that goodwill is any value over the team's book value that others might pay in order to purchase the team. If the team's assets are worth $1 million but someone is willing to pay $2 million to purchase it, then the team has $1 million in goodwill. The goodwill is value inherent in the minor league team, which might be based on the fact that there are only a limited number of minor league teams, that the team has a good relationship with a major league team, or that the facility the team plays in is brand new and has numerous amenities. Although it is very difficult to calculate goodwill, auditing items such as inventory and other assets can help establish a potential value range for goodwill. For example, through auditing the inventory a team might discover boxes of old uniforms, which might have limited value, but when used as a promotional item in an old-timers game, they can generate significant value based on the goodwill associated with the team's history. Inventory auditing will not determine a team's goodwill, but can be used in conjunction with other valuation techniques to develop a more accurate value.

Inventory auditing is the process of determining exactly what inventory exists and what is the inventory's value. Tracking entails the process of identifying where inventory might be located and the inventory's value. Inventory counting, on the other hand, refers to the process of identifying exactly how many units of a given item exist in inventory.

Internal control is a key to successfully managing inventory. A sport manager must develop a system that tracks all inventory from the time it is purchased to the time it is distributed to consumers or users. Inventory must be purchased, received, recorded, stored, and distributed. Management is responsible for developing internal systems to efficiently perform all of these operations (Whittington & Pany, 1998). At any point in this process an item might get lost, broken, stolen, or become obsolete, and only through auditing can a company truly know the status of most of their assets.

An accurate inventory count, whether of retail goods or materials used for production, leads to increased efficiency. Technology has been a key in improving systems of internal control. Computerized systems allow managers to track inventory quickly. This is especially helpful to businesses involved in the production of sport-related goods, for which inventory is a large component of total assets.

Two strategies in particular can be used to improve inventory control and also make the process of auditing, both internal and independent, much simpler. The first strategy is to have one centralized location where inventory is received and distributed (Holmes & Burns, 1979). For example, a concessionaire may be responsible for overseeing a dozen or more sales locations in a major sport facility. The concessionaire must ensure that each location has the products that will be prepared and sold. Inventory tracking is more accurate if all products are distributed from one central area. This allows management greater control over all products.

A second strategy is to develop a computer scanning system to track inventory (see chapter 13). Sporting goods stores are an example of a business that typically uses a computer scanning system. In most sporting goods stores, the products are bar coded. The computerized bar codes, usually placed on products by the manufacturer, are used to track material, determine its availability, and facilitate the sale. This type of integrated system allows management to determine exact inventory levels. When stock level is depleted, management has the information and can order more inventories from suppliers. Bar codes are another example of internal controls.

Computer tracking systems are also used by major manufacturing plants. Intermediate goods are maintained in some type of storage facility until they are to be used in the manufacturing process. Most often, computer systems are used to track when these intermediate goods are received, stored, and distributed to the production line.

With respect to auditing, technology and computerization have made it much easier to ensure that financial statements report inventory accurately. Computer programs can quickly produce reports on the types, amounts, and condition of inventory. Another important aspect of inventory auditing is the determination of fair value. An auditor must base the value of inventory on its quantity, quality, and condition. In addition to examining computer-generated inventory reports, the auditor may also physically locate inventory within the organization. Last, operational audits may lead to recommendations that will improve the efficiency of inventory control systems.

Plant, Property, and Equipment Auditing

Plant, property, and equipment are similar to inventory in that they are assets. The difference is that plant, property, and equipment are physical assets that have a productive life greater than one year. Examples of plant, property, and equipment for a collegiate athletic program are computers, facilities, and equipment such as goalposts, motor vehicles, and playing fields.

In the process of auditing, the auditor ascertains that all plant, property, and equipment that are listed as assets actually exist. This is usually not difficult for assets such as land, buildings, and heavy machinery. Often the difficult task is determining a fair value for these assets, especially with assets such as land that may fluctuate in value over time. Also, depreciation must be factored into the determination of fair value for plant, property, and equipment.

Similar to the situation with inventory, bar codes are often used to track equipment such as computers, copiers, and office furniture. Bar codes are usually placed on these items to clearly identify their owner. There are specialized bar-coded stickers that are nonremovable and that reduce the ability of a potential thief to hide the item's true ownership. An auditor may periodically visit various organizational locations to ensure that items such as computers are actually where they are supposed to be located.

Payroll Auditing

All sport businesses, regardless of size, scope, and mission, have one thing in common. They all have employees who are paid a wage in return for their labor. The ultimate result of a payroll system is that each employee receives a paycheck. The process of arriving at this final result can be complex. First, a system must be established to track the correct amount to be paid. For employees paid on an hourly basis, a system must be developed to accurately determine the number of hours worked. Employees may be required to fill out weekly time cards or use computerized time card machines. Payroll auditing is the process of tracking employee compensation to ensure accuracy. Payroll auditing can determine if employees are working too much overtime or whether personnel costs are in line with budgetary projections.

Computerized hand scanners are a new technology that has made auditing employee conduct simpler and that can improve the accuracy and reliability of the payroll process. The system requires making a handprint of all employees. A machine is then installed that identifies the handprint of each employee as she arrives for and departs from work. The computerized system can then calculate the total number of hours worked for each employee. Although such systems may be expensive to install, they can dramatically decrease the probability of payroll fraud. It is impossible for employees to fraudulently have other people clock in for them or fill out false time cards. The system also ensures that employees receive an accurate amount of pay. Other technology also exists to accomplish accurate track-

ing, such as swipe cards, retina detectors, and computerized punch systems that can track personnel activity.

In addition to determining the amount of gross pay, payroll preparation involves calculating income tax deductions, Social Security payments, and deductions for benefits such as retirement, union dues, and health insurance. An efficient and accurate system must be used for determining these payments. Failure to make payments for items such as federal or state income taxes will quickly lead to government audits.

When possible, all payroll duties and responsibilities should be separated. For example, the same person should not be responsible for the timekeeping system and the determination of employee wages. It would be very easy for this person to fraudulently overpay employees.

With respect to distributing paychecks, there needs to be a system to ensure that employees receive their own proper paychecks. One central location should be used to distribute all paychecks. Also, employees should be required to sign a document verifying that they have received their check. In large organizations, employees should be required to show proper identification. Additionally, unclaimed paychecks should not be left in the business' offices for an extended period of time. They are subject to possible theft if left in the office. The paychecks should be deposited in a special bank account for unclaimed wages. To reconcile the firm's accounts, efforts should be made to distribute the unclaimed checks to the persons to whom they were issued.

Last, at no time should employees be paid with cash. It is very difficult to track cash. An employee may claim that he did not receive his pay and request additional money. Also, there is little documentation associated with cash distributions. This makes it very difficult to accurately audit a payroll department. Checks are much easier to track because the employer receives the canceled checks and the withdrawals appear on the business' bank statement.

Areas of a business' operation that an audit normally encompasses include cash, inventory, plant, property, equipment, and payroll.

Receiving the Auditor's Report

For public corporations, the auditor is required to submit an independent auditor's report that is totally unbiased. Auditors usually provide a report when completing an audit for private corporations, nonprofit organizations, and government agencies. Of the several types of auditing reports, the standard unqualified auditor's report is the most common (see figure 16.1) (Arens & Loebbecke, 2000). The report is unqualified if no information was lacking and nothing that differs from the standard accounting practices set forth by the Auditing Standards Board was found. The standard unqualified auditor's report has seven parts:

1. *Report title.* Auditing standards require that a report have a title that includes the word "independent."

2. *Audit report address.* The report is usually addressed to the auditee, its board of directors, or stockholders.

3. *Introductory paragraph.* This paragraph explains management's role and responsibilities as they apply to the auditor (i.e., that management helped provide documentation or access to facilities). It also lists all the financial statements that were audited and the time periods of those statements.

4. *Scope paragraph.* This paragraph describes the nature of the audit and what the auditor did in the audit. It also outlines the business areas examined by the auditor.

5. *Opinion paragraph.* This last paragraph states the auditor's opinion. Within this section, the auditor attests to the accuracy of the financial information provided by the auditee.

6. *Name of the certified public accountant's firm.*

7. *Audit report date.*

Delong and Crimmins, PC
Certified Public Accountants
Box 324
Trunfio Park Central
Philadelphia, PA 18360
312-555-4433

Independent Auditor's Report

To the Stockholders
Diversified Sports Unlimited

We have audited the balance sheets of Diversified Sports Unlimited as of July 31, 2003 and 2002, and the related statements of retained earnings, income, and cash flows for the years then ended. These financial statements are the responsibility of Diversified Sports Unlimited's management. Our responsibility is to express an opinion on these financial statements based on our audits.

We conducted our audits in accordance with generally accepted auditing standards. Those standards require that we perform the audit to obtain assurance about whether the financial statements are free of material misstatement. An audit includes examining, on a test basis, evidence supporting the amounts and disclosures in the financial statements. An audit also includes assessing the accounting principles used and significant estimates made by management, as well as evaluating the overall financial statement presentation. We believe that our audits provide a reasonable basis for our opinion.

In our opinion, the financial statements referred to above present fairly, in all material respects, the financial position of Diversified Sports Unlimited as of July 31, 2003 and 2002, and the results of its operations and its cash flows for the years then ended in conformity with generally accepted accounting principles.

Delong and Crimmins, PC, CPAs

December 10, 2003

Figure 16.1 An example of a standard unqualified independent auditor's report for a sport organization. Can you identify each of the seven parts of an auditor's report?

Arens/Loebbecke, *Auditing: An integrated approach* 8/c © 1999. Adapted by permission of Pearson Education, Upper Saddle River, NJ.

The other possible audit opinions are as follows:

- Qualified opinion
- Adverse opinion
- Disclaimer of opinion

Although the use of qualified reports is common, these reports are being examined more carefully in the wake of the Enron scandal. A report is qualified because information was lacking or because other problems prevented the auditor from giving a more complete report. In a qualified opinion, the auditor will state that the company has departures from standard practices or perhaps that the company did not give them full access to necessary documents. Companies, auditors, and the government are all thinking about how to develop appropriate reports that contain as much additional information as possible to move the final report from qualified to unqualified status.

Detecting Fraud

Financial fraud can be a major problem for a sport business. Fraud can take many different forms. It can be as simple as theft of merchandise by a clerk in a sporting goods store or the filing of false time cards by employees in a sporting goods manufacturing plant. Inventory and payroll auditing are two of the types of auditing overviewed in this chapter that can help detect these types of fraud. Fraud can also involve complex schemes to embezzle millions of dollars from a sport business.

Later in the chapter, we look at the case of John Spano. Spano committed bank fraud in an attempt to acquire a professional hockey franchise. In part because of poor auditing of financial records submitted by Spano, several banks and the NHL were led to believe that Spano was a highly successful businessman. Ultimately, this was found to be incorrect. But Spano came very close to committing one of the largest frauds in sport history.

Fraud does not always mean theft. Managers may also prepare inaccurate financial statements in an effort to misrepresent the financial position of an organization. In 1997, management of Paragon Construction International, a subsidiary of Golden Bear Golf Inc., underrepresented its losses by more than $20 million. Management allegedly hid expenses and falsified records to conceal poor financial performance (Mullen, 1998). Shareholders and bondholders were injured when they made financial decisions about Golden Bear based on these fraudulent financial statements. The fraudulent acts were eventually uncovered, and Golden Bear refiled its financial statements. The new statements showed that the company had lost eight times the amount earlier reported. Stock in the company was eventually delisted from the NASDAQ stock exchange, and a class action lawsuit was filed on behalf of investors and creditors. In December of 1999, Golden Bear settled the lawsuit and paid investors $0.75 for each of the 2.7 million shares of outstanding stock. The money was paid by Golden Bear Golf, its insurance provider, and its auditor ("Golden Bear," 1999).

KnowledgeWare Inc.

Intentional misconduct can affect financial decisions. Employees can embezzle money, executives can engage in insider trading, and executives can manipulate financial reports. The Securities and Exchange Commission alleged that former football great Fran Tarkenton participated in a scheme to fraudulently inflate income for his company KnowledgeWare Inc. The income level was inflated in order to meet earning targets and included approximately $8 million in phony software sales. Tarkenton settled the case without admitting or denying wrongdoing and agreed to not violate any security laws in the future, paid a $100,000 fine, and paid the Securities and Exchange Commission over $50,000 from bonuses he received that were attributable to the company's success in 1994 (Schroeder & MacDonald, 1999).

Fraud can be a serious financial problem for a small sport business with limited resources. It is not easy for these businesses to recover from fraud. One incident of fraud could lead to bankruptcy, dissolution, or both. Additionally, small businesses are susceptible to fraud because employees usually have multiple duties and internal control is difficult. Often there are many employees who have access to assets such as cash, inventory, and office equipment. However, there are steps that can be taken to minimize the likelihood of fraud. Colbert and Bolton (1998) made the following recommendations for small businesses:

- *Segregation of duties.* Duties such as depositing cash and reconciling bank accounts should be given to different staff members. Also, different employees should complete duties such as preparing and signing checks. This will allow for a system of checks and balances so that no single person has total unfettered control.

- *Inventory of assets.* To prevent stolen assets such as plant, property, and equipment, a business should undergo periodic inventory checks. Each item listed in the financial statements as plant, property, and equipment should be physically located. In addition, the financial statements should be cross-checked to ensure that every listed asset is physically present.

- *Mandated vacations.* Each employee should use at least a portion of her allotted vacation time each year. It is also suggested that vacation days be taken as a block. This is an effective way to detect fraud. Some fraud cases, especially with cash, occur on a recurring or daily basis. It is much easier to detect the fraud if the employee is away from the business for an extended period of time.

- *Analytical procedures.* Simple analytical procedures such as tracking the daily deposits, weekly sales, and monthly sales totals may be enough to uncover some fraud.

- *Practical considerations.* For a small business, the first four recommendations may be difficult to implement. Employees may not want to take their vacation in a block, or there may not be enough employees to allow segregation of all duties. In addition to these recommendations, smaller companies can take some practical steps to minimize fraud. A small business owner may request that his bank send the business' bank statements to his home address instead of to the business. This allows the owner the opportunity to review deposit slips, bank statements, and canceled checks before other employees have access to them. Not only may the owner uncover fraud in this way, but the procedure may also deter employees from committing fraud.

> *Financial fraud may involve outright theft but also includes intentional misrepresentation on financial statements. Companies can take many steps relating to personnel in order to minimize the possibility of fraud.*

John Spano and the New York Islanders

One of the most infamous cases of fraud in the sport industry occurred in 1997. John Spano, a 33-year-old Dallas businessman, purchased the New York Islanders professional hockey team. He agreed to pay John Pickett, the previous team owner, $165 million. At the time, Spano claimed to have $55 million in available assets and a net worth of over $230 million. Spano stated that he had a $107 million trust fund, $52 million in Treasury bills, and $40 million in a money market account. He also claimed to have made millions of dollars in the South African stock market (Ranalli, 1997).

To finance the deal, Spano obtained an $80 million loan from Boston's Fleet Financial Group. Fleet is one of the largest lenders in the sport industry. Fleet has financed deals for teams such as the Baltimore Ravens, Washington Redskins, Phoenix Coyotes, and Los Angeles Lakers (Munroe, 1997). Unfortunately, Fleet was so enthusiastic about lending funds to Spano that it failed to correctly confirm Spano's net worth. As Fleet would later learn, Spano's actual net worth was less than $2 million.

Spano began by lying about his personal wealth and falsifying financial documents in order to obtain approval for a bank loan from the Fleet Financial Group. As part of the team purchase, on April 7, 1997, Spano was required to make a $24.4 million payment that was to cover the down payment for the team acquisition and interest prepayments on the bank loan. Spano did not make this payment, but did give the bank a wire-transfer number as proof that the funds were available. However, the wire-transfer number was a fake (Ranalli, 1997).

Shortly after the missed payment, the NHL, John Pickett, and the Fleet Financial Group started to question Spano's actual net worth. Federal investigators quickly uncovered Spano's scheme. Spano had begun by allegedly misrepresenting his financial wealth to Joseph Lynch, an executive for Detroit-based Comerica Bank. On the basis of financial statements supplied by Spano, Lynch attested to Spano's claimed net worth of over $230 million. However, Lynch did not obtain independent verification of the financial documents supplied by Spano. Spano then used the support from Comerica Bank to secure the $80 million loan from Fleet Financial Group ("Rumblings," 1997).

(continued)

(continued)

Spano's trouble began in earnest on April 7, 1997, when he was to make the $24.4 million payment to Fleet and Pickett. Obviously, he did not have the necessary funds. It was at that time that he provided the fake wire-transfer number to Fleet. In addition, Fleet Bank received a fax letter from Lynch verifying Spano's ability to make the $24.4 million payment. Federal investigators learned that the letter was a forgery. Spano had written the letter and reprogrammed his fax machine to make it appear that the letter had originated from Lynch's office. Investigators knew it was a forgery because it bore marks that were identical to those on a fax machine in one of Spano's companies ("Rumblings," 1997).

In July 1997, federal authorities pressed bank fraud charges against Spano. At the time, a Long Island newspaper reported that Spano was living in the Cayman Islands. However, Spano eventually surrendered to federal authorities and was charged with six counts of fraud in three different states, Texas, Massachusetts, and New York. If he had been convicted of all charges, Spano would have faced up to 60 years in prison ("Business Briefcase," 1997). After considerable negotiations between the federal government and defense attorneys, Spano agreed to a plea bargain. He pleaded guilty to six counts of fraud, two each in Texas, Massachusetts, and New York. In January 1998, Spano was sentenced to all six counts in New York and faced up to 63 months in prison. At the time, there were still several ongoing federal investigations related to alleged mail and wire fraud committed by Spano in New York and Massachusetts (Chase, 1998).

The fallout from Spano's attempt to financially misrepresent himself was considerable. On July 20, 1997, David Splaine resigned his position as senior vice president for Fleet Financial Group. Splaine was the loan officer who had approved the $80 million loan to Spano. Splaine had failed to accurately confirm Spano's real net worth (Vennochi, 1997). In addition, investigators for Comerica Bank learned that Joseph Lynch had been a guest of Spano at a four-star hotel on Long Island at a cost of over $2,000. The bank had clear policies stating that employees were not permitted to receive gifts, fees, or vacations from clients. In January 1998, Lynch resigned from his position with Comerica Bank ("Briefly," 1998).

As federal authorities further investigated Spano's business dealings, they uncovered several other acts of fraud. In one bizarre business deal, Spano formed a partnership with Lenco Holdings Limited, a South African company. The partnership was formed to sell kitchen pots and pans. Spano informed Lenco that he had secured an order for the cookware from the Nordstrom department store chain. Spano then allegedly sent a fraudulent Nordstrom invoice to Lenco, and Lenco in turn sent Spano the cookware to deliver it to Nordstrom. However, Spano failed to pay the $1.9 million due to Lenco for the cookware. The location of the now infamous cookware is still unknown (Bedell, 1997).

Spano also owed over $250,000 to a Dallas law firm that worked for him during his attempt to acquire the New York Islanders. In addition, Spano owed over $2.4 million to two different Dallas investment companies for loans they had made to him (Bedell, 1997).

The case of John Spano is unique in the sport industry in which there have been very few cases of financial fraud. However, as the professional sport industry becomes more profitable, the likelihood of financial fraud increases. The case of John Spano served as a wake-up call for all professional sport leagues. As a result, the NHL and other leagues have placed a greater emphasis on verifying the financial position of prospective owners. Similar steps are now taken by MLB after a scandal involving the first owner of the Colorado Rockies. The owner, Michael Monus, was also chairman of Phar-Mor Pharmacies and improperly used corporate assets to acquire sport teams. He funneled $10 million from Phar-Mor into a then fledgling and now defunct basketball league, World Basketball League (Schroeder & Schiller, 1992). Monus was convicted of a 109-count indictment including charges of mail, wire, and bank fraud.

CONCLUSION

Financial statement auditing is the objective examination of financial statements that are prepared by an organization. An auditor examines these statements to determine if they have been prepared according to generally accepted accounting standards. Financial audits are important because they ensure the accuracy of financial statements and deter management and employees from committing theft and fraud. Audits also lend credibility to financial statements, which can increase confidence on the part of other companies and investors. This makes it easier for businesses to work with investors and creditors. Last, accurate financial statements should lessen the possibility of government audits.

Two other types of audits are operational audits and compliance audits. Operational audits examine a business' policies and procedures to determine if they are appropriate and efficient. These audits can result in organizational changes that can affect a business' long-term efficiency and productivity. Compliance audits are undertaken to ensure that a business is adhering to rules and regulations established by an outside group such as a government agency. For example, any large employer in the United States must meet workplace regulations that have been developed by the Occupational Safety and Health Administration.

Technology has had a significant effect on auditing and financial operations in the sport industry over the past two decades. It allows businesses to quickly and efficiently process financial data and generate financial reports. Also, technology has been used to improve operational systems in areas such as payroll, inventory control, and accounting, which are critical to auditing. Last, technology has helped to minimize fraud and theft.

ASSIGNMENTS

1. What is the primary role of auditing? What function does auditing serve for a sport business?

2. What is financial fraud? Can you give examples of financial fraud?

3. Define internal control. Provide an example of an internal control system for a sport organization in each of the following areas:
   a. Personnel/payroll
   b. Inventory management
   c. Retail sales
   d. Accounts payable/accounts receivable
   e. Property, plant, equipment
   f. Preparation of financial statements

4. Explain the primary differences between internal and independent auditing.

5. Explain the three primary types of audits.

6. Identify the benefits of audits for the following four groups:
   a. Auditee
   b. Other members of the business community
   c. Government entities and legal community
   d. Investors

7. What is financial materiality with respect to auditing? How is financial materiality determined for a sport business?

8. In what ways has technology changed financial management, and specifically auditing?

9. What is contained within a standard unqualified auditor's report?

10. What steps should a sport business take to prepare for an independent audit?

11. Briefly describe the following types of audits:
    a. Cash audit
    b. Inventory audit
    c. Payroll audit
    d. Plant, property, and equipment audit

12. What are some measures that a sport business can take to minimize the likelihood of financial fraud?

RESEARCH PROJECT

Conduct an extensive literary and Internet search to examine a securities fraud case involving illegal stock manipulation. The case should be a case that the federal or a state government had to prosecute and can be in any industry.

CLASS DISCUSSION TOPICS

1. How would you go about auditing the Smiths, Sport Manufacturing Company, the University of Houston, or the Boston Celtics?

2. How can you balance the need for making sure accounts are accurate and the need to allow individuals to work without the fear that Big Brother is looking at their every move?

3. Why is accuracy so important?

4. Why should you choose an independent auditor versus an internal auditor?

5. Is it ethically correct to "permanently borrow" office supplies?

6. How would you approach someone if you thought that person had engaged in fraud?

Exit Strategy

CHAPTER OBJECTIVES

After studying this chapter, you should be able to do the following:

- Describe the techniques that can help spot financial trouble.
- Understand how to reorganize a troubled business.
- Compare the types of bankruptcies available.
- Describe the process of selling a business.
- Calculate the value of a sport business.

At various times during a business' life cycle, the going may get tough. Bills may go unpaid, debtors may not pay accounts receivable on time, shipments may be late or get canceled, distributors may stop extending credit, or a host of other problems can force a business owner to think about various options. Options that owners could consider are as diverse as the owners themselves. Some owners may just decide to transfer their business to a family member or a current business partner. Others may consider selling the company or just selling the assets. Still others may simply close shop or worse, be *forced* to close shop. No matter what strategy or technique the owner ultimately applies, each strategy or technique has particular legal and financial ramifications that the individual needs to consider to avoid increasing financial obligations or to reduce potential costs.

When management is stretched to the point of no return, there is often a tendency to try to resolve immediate difficulties rather than examining long-term financial problems. Such short-term thinking can result in lost concessions or bargaining power with creditors, or other long-term ramifications.

This chapter explains what to do at the point of no return. We start by examining red flags that might signal financial trouble. Next we discuss various options for dealing with financial problems, such as informal reorganization, informal liquidation, **bankruptcy-(chapters 7, 11, and 13),** involuntary bankruptcy, and removing business assets. The chapter ends with an analysis of what is required to sell a business and how to determine the value of a business that is being sold.

Red Flags

Before deciding to terminate operations, a business needs to know when it is in trouble. Most businesses cannot just decide to close their doors; there are usually existing financial obligations such as accounts payable, long-term labor contracts, long-term lease obligations, repayment to equity investors, and debts. The decision is not an easy one, nor is it made without significant managerial forethought. Most executives take pride in their managerial skills and would not want to be remembered as the person who lost a business.

Luckily, there are a significant number of indicators that can help signal financial trouble and provide adequate warning to an executive. For example, if orders start declining significantly, a business can examine the reasons and take corrective action to avoid losing market share. If a new competitor comes into the market with a more advanced and cheaper product, then the business needs to make adjustments to stay competitive. Key factors associated with business failures include economic weakness, industry downturns, poor location, too much debt, too little capital, and countless others. These concerns can lead to temporary cash flow problems that can often be worked out. However, sometimes the concerns indicate a permanent problem.

One sign of trouble is a lender's request for early repayment of a loan. A bank or other lender may call the loan under certain conditions; the primary reason is poor financial performance. If a sport business has been losing money steadily for several years, banks may feel uncomfortable with their loans and demand immediate repayment. The following are other conditions under which a bank might call a loan or not renew a line of credit:

- Loan covenants have been repeatedly violated.
- The bank is losing money on the relationship.
- New bank managers favor a different loan mix or institute new policies.
- The bank does not understand or is uncomfortable with the industry segment.
- The bank's credit exposure in the industry segment is too great.
- A loan guarantor's financial condition has deteriorated.
- The bank has lost faith in the business' management team (Broni, 1999).

If a bank or lending institution "pulls the plug," the business needs to establish a policy to deal with the lost cash. The first step is often to negotiate a short-term extension to try to resolve any problems or secure new funding. If the business is on strong financial ground, it might be easy to approach another bank. If a problem caused the bank to pull the funds, it might be worthwhile to ask the bank what the problem was. If the problem is one that can be fixed, such as untimely reporting, then the business owner can explain this to another potential lender and take measures to correct the problem.

If the business has assets, the assets could serve to help secure needed funds. Asset-based loans, as the name implies, can be obtained on the basis of the existing inventory or accounts receivable. If the business owns a valuable asset such as buildings or land, these could be pledged as collateral to secure more funds. However, if these options are not available, the business might need to approach a commercial finance company that specializes in "unbankable" loans. Since these loans are riskier, they entail a higher interest rate. The business also might have to report earnings frequently in order to keep the lender abreast of financial conditions. However, once the business can show sustained success and compliance with loan terms for one to two years, then usually the owner can apply again for conventional bank loans.

Losing a bank loan is just one sign that a business is in trouble. If the business cannot pull itself through the hard financial times, it may be necessary to resort to informal or formal attempts to satisfy debt holders. Debt holders can be satisfied through informal reorganization or liquidation, bankruptcy, removal of assets, or selling the business.

Bouncing Dividend Checks

A common concern of companies facing bankruptcy is the elimination of existing credit lines. Lenders are hesitant to increase the amount the company owes since there is no guarantee that they will get their money back. On the other hand, there is also the possibility that the additional funds will in fact save the business and allow for continued long-term profits for the creditor. Cutting off the credit line can cause significant hardships even if a company is not in bankruptcy. In 1999 a major publicity blunder occurred when the paying agent for the nation's largest bicycle manufacturer, Huffy Corp., announced that it would not honor the company's dividend checks. The company's lenders, including Bank One Corp. and BankAmerica Corp., cut off funding on the unsecured lines of credit after Huffy defaulted on its credit agreement. Unfortunately, however, Huffy had already sent out dividend payments of $900,000, or about $0.085 for each of the 10 million outstanding shares, and the checks bounced ("Huffy Checks," 1999). Thus, when banks start cutting off funding, a red flag should go off concerning the business' financial stability.

Among the warning signs of financial trouble for a business are declining orders, sharply increased competition, and a bank's request for early repayment of a loan.

Informal Reorganization

Informal reorganization allows a business to recover and reestablish itself after facing a temporary financial crisis. These voluntary plans in which all parties try to come to an agreement are often called "workouts." Workouts are successful only if the debtor is a good moral risk, if the debtor can show the ability to recover, and if the general business conditions are favorable for recovery (Brigham & Gapenski, 1994).

The informal reorganization process comprises extensions and composition. Extensions are extensions of the time allowed for repaying a debt. If a debt is owed and due in one year, an extension could be worked out for the borrower to repay the debt in two years instead. Composition is the process of asking to repay a lower amount. A debt holder would rather receive $900 from the company versus only $500 in bankruptcy proceedings from a $1,000 debt. Most often a workout involves a combination of these two methods.

 If SMC owed several lenders $10 million, it might be possible to develop a workout in which the company would pay 25% of the debt immediately and 20% a year for the next three years. Thus, in four years SMC would have repaid 85% of the original debt, and the debt would have been discharged.

Even though lenders would not receive the entire amount they were owed, most lenders would be happy to receive 85% of the original loaned amount versus possibly nothing, or a much smaller amount, if the borrower went bankrupt. Not all banks are willing to engage in workouts, but most understand the value of negotiating the best deal they can in order to receive the largest possible share of their initial loan. The lenders might demand interest payments during the payback period to help cover the extension and might also demand additional security such as personal pledges or asset-backed pledges.

A workout is an informal reorganization process that gives a business a chance to recover from a temporary financial crisis.

Informal Liquidation

Although informal reorganization is effective if the company can turn around, some companies cannot fix their problems. If the company's debt is larger than its net worth, the company will probably have to go through bankruptcy protection. However, if the company has more assets than debt, it is "worth more dead than alive." **Assignment** is the term used for the informal liquidation process. Lenders normally obtain a greater return through assignment than through bankruptcy. That is why lenders should focus on encouraging informal reorganization or liquidation rather than trying to force a company into bankruptcy.

Bankruptcy Protection

Bankruptcy is the primary technique used by business owners when they are facing mounting obligations and do not have the resources to finance continued operations. The U.S. bankruptcy laws were first passed in 1898. The laws were developed to prevent a creditor from racing to the courthouse against debtors. Prior to the bankruptcy laws, creditors would make a mad dash to the courthouse in an effort to be the first to file so that they could establish a higher repayment priority over subsequent filers. The bankruptcy laws were designed to give all creditors with equal standing (secured and unsecured creditors) the right to be put into a common pool with each creditor having the same rights. Thus, all secured creditors will be entitled to have their obligations repaid first with the sale of the secured assets. The unsecured creditors would then together receive proportional repayments of their loans based on what moneys remain after the secured creditors are paid.

Bankruptcy petitions peaked in 1988 at 1.44 million. That number declined 8.5% to 1.3 million petitions in 1999. Personal filings, which account for most bankruptcy petitions, declined 8.3%, while business filings declined 14.6% between 1998 and 1999 (Dreazen, 2000). There are 291 bankruptcy courts serving 90 judicial districts throughout the United States (Brigham & Gapenski, 1994). Although the newspapers do not typically report smaller bankruptcies, there have been several major sport-related bankruptcies affecting sport businesses in the past several years. The most highly publicized petitions include those of Starter Corp., Just For Feet, and the Pittsburgh Penguins.

Sammy Sosa's Charitable Foundation

Sammy Sosa may be hitting home runs, but his charity is not. The Sammy Sosa Charitable Foundation in the Dominican Republic was pushed to the brink of bankruptcy through mismanagement. Sosa's major contribution was an office building. The charity was established to benefit victims of hurricane George in 1998, but only $82,842 was allocated to relief supplies. An article in *Fortune* magazine highlighted various improprieties including failure of tenants to pay rent, the use of funds to buy Sosa's brother a sports car, and expenses of $2,000 a month for storing relief supplies in a Miami warehouse ("Sosa's Charity," 2000).

Two Recent Bankruptcies

In a perfect world, business would be able to thrive during both good and bad times. However, each year, numerous businesses go bankrupt. In recent years, several major sport businesses faced bankruptcy proceedings to protect creditors' investments in the businesses. Two of these bankruptcies involved Starter Corp. and Just For Feet.

In 1999 Starter Corp., which had been the premiere licensed apparel company for many years, faced a major creditor that felt uncomfortable with the company's debt and called the debt. The company was unable to secure additional funds and was forced to seek bankruptcy protection. The company's assets were liquidated, and the bank was able to obtain approximately 90% of its funds. However, Starter pursued litigation because the bank pulled its debt right before Starter's peak sales season. Starter had paid for inventory early in the year, and the debt would have been paid after the primary sales period in the fourth quarter (Sack & Nadim, 2002). The case was later settled without any admission to guilt or wrongdoing.

Just For Feet developed a unique bankruptcy plan to try to survive. The company faced bankruptcy protection after expanding too quickly through acquisitions and had excess inventory. In the second quarter of 1999, the company posted $25.9 million in losses compared with net income of $8 million the prior year. The financial hardships were forcing the shoe retailer to close 85 of its 362 stores. Just For Feet had $200 million of 11% senior subordinate notes due in 2009 and other unsecured creditors. A senior **subordinate debt** is a loan secured by a general claim on a company's assets and is repaid after all secured debts have been paid. These holders were to receive 100% of the common stocks in a newly reorganized company emerging from the shell of the former Just For Feet. The former shareholders would lose their shares and in exchange receive warrants allowing them to purchase up to 10% of the new company's shares ("Just For Feet," 1999). In 2000, Footstar purchased Just For Feet's major assets, including its name.

The Bankruptcy Reform Act of 1978 produced the bankruptcy system we currently utilize. The bankruptcy code contains nine chapters, but the chapters are not numbered consecutively. Chapters 1, 3, and 5 contain general provisions; chapter 9 applies to municipalities declaring bankruptcy; chapter 12 deals with family-owned farms; and chapter 15 establishes a system of trusts to administer bankruptcy proceedings. Three primary bankruptcy techniques are available to debtors to obtain court protection from creditors, depending on the existing circumstances; these are provided for in chapters 7, 11, and 13.

Chapter 7 Bankruptcy

Chapter 7 bankruptcies entail a procedure for the orderly liquidation of the debtor's assets to repay creditors based on a priority established by statute. Based on filing for chapter 7 protection, a trustee is appointed to gather and liquidate assets and then distribute the proceeds to creditors.

One of the many benefits associated with having a trustee to administer the bankruptcy estate is the power the trustee can wield. A trustee can invalidate a transaction made by the debtor if the trustee feels that the transaction was preferential or fraudulent. Thus, if the owner of a professional team pays her son-in-law $50,000 for some consulting work two weeks before the team declares bankruptcy, the trustee could invalidate the payment if the son-in-law in fact did not do anything.

Chapter 7 is designed to make sure that the debtor does not engage in fraud, provides for an equitable distribution of the debtor's assets among the creditors, and allows the debtor to clean the debts and start from scratch. Distribution of the assets is based on preference. Preference is allocated

from the most- to the least-secured creditors such that assets are distributed in the following order:

1. Proceeds of sold items pledged for a lien or mortgage to which secured creditors are entitled
2. Trustee-incurred costs associated with administering the bankrupt business
3. Expenses that were incurred after an involuntary case had been filed but before a trustee was appointed
4. Wages due to workers earned within three months prior to filing for bankruptcy
5. Claims related to unpaid contributions to employee benefits plans that should have been paid in the prior six months
6. Any unsecured claims for customer deposits
7. Any taxes due at the federal, state, or local level
8. Liabilities associated with unfunded pension plans
9. Payments to general or unsecured creditors
10. Preferred stock
11. Common stock (Brigham & Gapenski, 1994)

Chapter 11 Bankruptcy

Chapter 11 bankruptcy provides an outline for a formal business reorganization supervised by the court. When a business owner files a voluntary chapter 11 petition, he becomes a debtor in possession of the business, and the business becomes a property of the bankruptcy estate (Kupetz, 1998). The debtor is authorized to keep running the business and make all necessary business decisions until otherwise ordered by the bankruptcy court.

The reason the debtor is allowed to continue running the business is that chapter 11 bankruptcies are designed to rehabilitate the debtor, make sure all creditors are treated equally, and maximize the business' value to help pay as much of the debt as possible (Kupetz, 1998). A debtor can be issued debtor-in-possession financing for short-term liquidity purposes; these loans are given preference for repayment, as they are made with the knowledge that the borrower is in bankruptcy and with the hope that the funds may help him out of bankruptcy.

Specific protections are afforded a debtor in chapter 11 proceedings, including an automatic stay that prohibits the commencement or continuation of any legal action against the business (Cheeseman, 1998). Creditors can obtain relief from the stay, but courts traditionally attempt to assist the debtor as much as possible, including limiting the distractions caused by creditors pursuing litigation, through vigorously enforcing the stay.

While the debtor is authorized to sell assets and enter into transactions in the ordinary course of business that benefit the business, creditors can petition the court to appoint a trustee. A trustee can be appointed if the creditors can show that some improprieties are evident. Such improprieties can include debtor fraud, dishonesty, incompetence, or gross mismanagement (Kupetz, 1998).

The debtor has the obligation in chapter 11 proceedings to file a reorganization plan within 120 days after filing for bankruptcy protection. Such a plan gives a debtor the opportunity to try to turn the business around in four months. The debtor can stop making interest and principal payments until the plan is approved. Each creditor must be addressed in the plan, and the creditors have a final vote on whether they wish to accept the reorganization plan. Creditors have the right to vote against the plan, but this right is severely limited if the plan provides the creditors with at least as much as they might have obtained if the debtor had filed under chapter 7. Such a reorganization effort involves all creditors regardless of the amount each creditor is owed. This differs from the situation with a workout, which normally entails only the largest creditors. Workouts are more informal and, as discussed earlier, are generally voluntary actions taken by a creditor to reduce its losses or costs or to help create a future business opportunity with the same debtor at a different time.

Creditors can also be coerced into accepting an extension agreement, which does not reduce the obligation but delays repayment for a specified period of time. A standstill, or moratorium, agreement allows the debtor to delay repayment for a given time period without facing interest charges or penalties.

Chapter 13 Bankruptcy

Chapter 13 bankruptcy is designed only for consumers, so we will just touch on it. A debtor needs to voluntarily file a petition indicating that she is insolvent or unable to pay her debts as they come due. The trustee who administers the plan is paid 10% of the debts paid under the plan (Cheeseman, 1998).

 If the Smiths' fitness center is operated as a sole proprietorship, the business cannot file for bankruptcy under chapter 13; but the Smiths can file for chapter 13 personally if they still are earning money, have unsecured debts of less than $100,000, and have secured debts of less than $350,000. The Smiths would have to make a plan to repay the creditors and start making payments within 30 days after filing the plan.

The bankruptcy laws in chapters 7, 11, and 13 of the bankruptcy code protect debtors from creditors and provide for orderly procedures for repaying creditors.

Involuntary Bankruptcy

A business owner may think he can turn the business around, but creditors can force his hand if they think otherwise. An involuntary bankruptcy occurs when three or more unsecured creditors who hold bona fide debts of at least a combined $10,000 file a petition against the debtor. If there are fewer than 12 creditors in all, only one needs to file a petition for involuntary bankruptcy against the debtor. When a petition for involuntary bankruptcy is filed, a summons is issued to the debtor requiring the debtor to respond to the claims within 20 days. If the debtor does not respond in a timely manner, the court can enter an order for relief against the debtor. The order for relief might entail a creditor being allowed to seize some of the debtor's property. If the debtor responds, the court will grant relief only if the debtor does not pay his obligations as they become due. In most instances, the debtor is allowed to keep operating the business. However, if the creditors who petitioned for involuntary bankruptcy are concerned about the debtor's actions, under certain circumstances they can ask the court to appoint a trustee to take possession of the business (Kupetz, 1998).

Bankruptcy issues often arise in the health club industry as a result of mismanagement. However, bankruptcy actions can also take place in the professional sport arena. The American Basketball League, the first women's professional basketball league to show strong box office success, folded in its third year after competition arose from the Women's National Basketball Association. In 1998 the Pittsburgh Penguins filed for bankruptcy protection. The Penguins had filed for chapter 11 protection in 1975 when they owed $6.5 million. However, the 1998 Penguins owed over $35 million just to one former player, Mario Lemieux (Hoffman, 1998). To keep the team alive and in Pittsburgh, U.S. Bankruptcy Judge Bernard Markovitz approved Lemieux as the team's new owner ("Bankruptcy Judge," 1999).

Banks and other lenders are not the only option available when times become rough. When financial concerns arise, a business can sometimes look inside itself to find an answer. One such answer lies in liquidating assets such as stocks or other liquid assets. If no such assets exist, the business might have to sell other assets such as property.

Removing Business Assets

A business owner might decide to condense a business by removing assets. Selling assets can serve to reduce business costs or raise cash. Such transactions are often highlighted on annual reports as a footnote indicating a one-time write-off. Otherwise, these transactions would appear to boost the company's income when there is no possibility of ever generating these levels of funds again. Selling assets, or downsizing, occurs frequently. The Celtics used to own their own television and radio stations but sold them because these assets did not fit into the team's business plans. Owners can use several techniques to downsize a business and remove assets so that the new business will be smaller. The primary reason why a business would wish to downsize is reduced income. Instead of closing the business a business owner might wish to downsize and hope that at a later date they could once again grow. The first technique is taking out profits as dividends.

Dividends could be paid to the owner rather than reinvested into the business. Dividends can be paid at any time, but cannot be paid if such payments would make the company insolvent (Nicholas, 1990). When a business is paying dividends, it is essential to check government regulations, articles of incorporation, and bylaws to make sure all dividend restrictions are followed. Individual shareholders

can sue and recover damages for illegally paid dividends.

Other ways in which owners can remove assets from a business are to increase their own salaries, pay themselves bonuses, and fund benefits of various kinds. If a business owner wishes to increase her salary and the business is incorporated, the board of directors, shareholders, or both might have to approve the new salary. Owners of smaller businesses such as the Smiths may be able to take out as much as they want in salaries, especially if they do not have any debts. Business owners who have outstanding debt can still pay themselves a larger salary as long as the salary is reasonable. A salary could be considered unreasonable if it left the company insolvent or if the IRS viewed it as a way to give the business a tax deduction instead of paying nondeductible dividends (Nicholas, 1990). A salary is considered reasonable if it is justified based on such variables as extra work, more duties, or exceptional service. Business owners can also compensate themselves for independent projects in the same way an independent contractor is paid. Owners can pay themselves commissions on sales in order to remove additional dollars from the business. In bankruptcy proceedings it would be difficult for debtors to contest a commission payment if it was a payment for a legitimate service. If, on the other hand, the owner did not in fact do any work to earn the extra money, then a debtor could challenge such payments and demand that they be returned to the bankruptcy estate.

Money can also be removed through paying bonuses. The IRS might try to fight a bonus as a disguised dividend. However, the businesses can tie the bonus to the compensation package to protect its reasonableness. Similarly, a business owner can receive significant fringe benefits in the form of game tickets, company cars, and travel to business conferences. Owners who are considered employees could also receive employee benefits such as insurance, pensions, financial counseling, employee stock purchase plans, and any other benefit afforded to employees.

A business owner can loan himself money from the business. The risk of being rejected for the loan is eliminated, and leisurely repayment plans can be developed. The loan could also be interest free, and the owner might not have to pay taxes on the loaned amount. However, any time there exists self-dealing, the potential for abuse can arise and lead to disastrous results. The Rigas family, founders of cable television giant Adelphia, was under investigation in 2002 for off-balance-sheet loans to, among other things, help support the Buffalo Sabres to the tune of

$76.5 million. The Sabres were owned at the time of the loans by the Rigas family (Grover & Lowry, 2002). Issuing inappropriate loans can cause an incorporated business owner to lose her liability shield if a debtor pierces the corporate veil. Thus, even if you are loaning yourself money, you need to adequately document the transaction.

Finally, a business owner can sell or lease property to the business (Nicholas, 1990). If the Smiths owned a vacant lot, they could sell the lot to the fitness center for a price slightly above the market value and then build a new facility on the lot. Since the Smiths own the fitness center, they would be the primary beneficiaries of the sale. However, if the land was in their name and the fitness center was incorporated, then any debts owed by the fitness center could not be repaid with proceeds from selling the land, since the lot belongs to the Smiths as individuals and not to the fitness center.

Despite the many options for withdrawing assets from a business, most business owners would rather just sell the business in its entirety and obtain the funds immediately, rather than in a piecemeal fashion.

In the face of financial difficulties, businesses sometimes downsize by selling assets, paying the owner more in salary or bonuses, or loaning funds to the owner.

Selling a Business

Any business goes through ups and downs, but sometimes owners are not willing to accept the stress associated with such cyclical patterns. Business owners may decide to sell their business for a number of reasons, including the following:

- Wishing to retire
- Wanting to make a profit
- Wanting to change careers
- Wanting to get out while they can
- Finding the level of competition unacceptable

One trend that is helping to foster business sales is the fact that many baby boomers who own businesses are entering their 50s and 60s and want to retire, travel, or manage their pensions or investments.

The first step in selling any business is to gather together all relevant financial information. If an independent auditor has reviewed the company's financial condition, the audited statements are the best tool to use in selling a successful business. Having several years' worth of audited financial statements helps shorten the buyer's due diligence investigation time and can accelerate the process of acquiring financing to buy the business.

A key component of any purchase decision has to do with exactly what will be purchased. Footstar, Inc. purchased some assets of Just For Feet, Inc. for $66.8 million in 2000. Footstar purchased 79 Just For Feet superstores, 23 specialty stores, the Just For Feet name, and its Internet business ("Footstar," 2000).

Four options exist for selling a business: a taxable sale of company stock, a tax-free sale of company stock, a taxable sale of company assets, and a tax-free sale of company assets (Lee, 1999). Each option involves different concerns. For example, a cash purchase takes less time than a stock deal because there are fewer compliance issues. A sale can raise concerns for the buying company as well. For example, if a company issues more stock to buy another company, will the new shares give rise to preemptive rights to current shareholders? A sale can also raise concerns that typically would not be considered when making a typical asset purchase such as a car where the only issue might be determining if there exists a clear title.

 If SMC bought another golf club manufacturer, would it also acquire the employees? What if the employees had a pension plan? Who would be liable if the pension plan from the purchased business was underfunded? SMC would be dealing with employees who anticipated having a certain amount of money in their pension fund, and the money is not there. If this issue had not been resolved in the contract negotiations, SMC would be responsible for making up the deficit.

Asset Versus Equity Purchase

As already noted, one issue in selling a business is whether or not to sell stock, if the company is incorporated, or the company's assets. A person or another company interested in buying the business would prefer to buy assets rather than stock for various reasons. The primary reason has to do with reducing the purchasing company's liability, as stocks convey ownership and liability for all past obligations. Thus, if the business that had been purchased manufactured lawn dart games, and kids were being injured and suing the company, the new owners would be liable for all possible damages. On the other hand, if only the manufacturer's assets had been purchased, the company itself and all associated liabilities would have been dissolved.

There are also significant tax considerations for the seller and the purchaser of assets as opposed to stock. If you sell assets, the money you receive is taxed as ordinary income up to your basis (cost minus depreciation) in the asset. Any amount in excess of your basis is taxed as capital gains. Stock sales are taxed as long- or short-term capital gains. Ordinary income can be taxed up to 39.6% versus capital gains taxes for individuals, which are at most 20%. Thus, owners of a business would rather sell the stock; the difference between the buying and the selling price could be taxed at about half the rate that assets are (Marullo, 1998, August). On the basis of the unfavorable tax treatment a seller faces when selling assets, sellers can normally obtain a higher price for assets than for stock (Marullo, 1998, August).

Another significant benefit attached to selling assets involves the "step-down" basis for depreciable assets (Marullo, 1998, August) as illustrated in the following example.

 Assume that the Celtics purchased $100,000 worth of depreciable cameras for their television station. The cameras might have a depreciable life of five years, which means that the Celtics could depreciate $20,000 a year for five years. Assume that after five years the Celtics had depreciated the entire amount allowed, $100,000, but that the cameras still had a fair market value of $50,000. If the Celtics sold the cameras for $50,000, the purchaser would be entitled to the step-down, which means the purchaser could depreciate the cameras once again for five years. Thus, the new owner would be able to depreciate the $50,000 purchase price $10,000 a year over five years. If the new owner sold the cameras, the third owner would be able to depreciate the cameras from their purchase price. This process can continue for as long as the cameras still have value.

The step-down provision is particularly important in the professional sport industry in that players' contracts are considered depreciable assets. Buyers prefer to purchase assets if they can use the step-down basis to acquire added depreciation without assuming any liability. The step-down basis approach is covered in more detail in chapter 14 (see pp. 255–256).

If the Smiths wish to sell their now successful business, they face a major challenge—determining how much the business is worth. Owners put so much sweat equity into their business that they typically think it is worth much more than it actually is. Owners may have a misconception based on transactions associated with large publicly traded companies, which can sell for up to 20 times their earnings (Livingston, 1998). However, sales of smaller, closely held companies rarely reach such multiples of earnings. Larger corporations have a strong track record and can maintain consistent sales for extended periods, as well as significant goodwill associated with their product or service. An NFL franchise is valuable even with a losing record on the basis of the inherent value of an NFL team. The strong value of NFL teams is based on the strong broadcast agreement and shared revenue. In contrast, a small mom-and-pop gym has a less stable product, and customer loyalty might not transfer over in the same manner as with a large company. Some gym members might have been members just because they were friends of the owner. Fans of the Dallas Cowboys or any other NFL team would still be fans even if their franchise changed ownership several times over a decade.

Calculating Business Value

Several techniques can be used to calculate a business' value. The most common are asset-based valuation methods, the market-based approach, and income-based approaches. Next we briefly consider each of these.

The techniques presented here in no way represent a definite science. There is no one correct way to measure a business' value. Someone who loves golf might be willing to pay a premium to buy SMC just so she can own a golf club manufacturing business. This emotional element makes it almost impossible to create a foolproof valuation. Similarly, given the difficulty in valuing goodwill, there always has to be a subjective element to valuing a business.

Asset-Based Valuation Methods

In asset-based approaches to valuation, the business' value is determined based on the value of tangible and intangible assets net of liabilities. In essence, the net worth is computed based on factoring in assets that appear on the balance sheet, along with assets that might not appear on the balance sheet. Intangible assets, such as goodwill, might not appear on a balance sheet because of the difficulty in determining an accurate value, but nevertheless do add value to the business. Asset-based approaches (in particular the asset accumulation approach discussed next) are most relevant for valuing an established sport business or in cases in which the valuation is being done in response to the sale of an ownership stake that exceeds 50%.

There are two generally accepted asset-based approaches for valuing sport businesses: the asset accumulation approach and the excess earnings method.

Asset Accumulation Approach The asset accumulation approach is simply the identification and summation of the current economic values of all assets, tangible and intangible, that are controlled by the sport business as of the date of the valuation. Because the objective of the valuation is to determine the current net worth, or equity value, of the business, it is necessary to deduct all liabilities existing at the date of the valuation from the estimated value of the business' assets.

Excess Earnings Method In the excess earnings approach, the value of net tangible assets is estimated on the basis of the return that these assets can earn. As a separate process, intangible assets are valued based on the value of excess earnings that can be attributed to the intangible assets. The steps in the excess earnings approach can be summarized as follows:

1. Estimate the value of the tangible assets of the sport business net of liabilities.

2. Estimate the normal level of earnings for the sport business after a historical review of the business' financial results and subject to forecast of future results. To measure normalized earnings, the compensation of all equity owners, including salary, bonus, and profit sharing, is adjusted to reflect what the cost would be to hire a manager with nonownership status to perform the same tasks as owners.

3. Estimate the annual income that an owner would require to be interested in investing in the net tangible assets of the sport business.

4. Deduct the annual income computed in step 3 from the normal earnings estimated in step 2. This remainder can be viewed as the "excess earnings" that are attributable to the business' intangible assets.

5. This remainder is converted to an economic value by applying a **capitalization rate** that reflects the inherent riskiness in relation to the business' ability to generate the excess earnings over the long run. Capitalization refers to the conversion of a single value of economic income to a current economic value by dividing the measure of economic income by a capitalization rate that is expressed as a percentage. As an example, if the excess earnings generated by the intangible assets equal $400,000 per year and the appropriate capitalization rate is 20%, then the value of the excess earnings equals:

$$\frac{\$400,000}{0.20} = \$200,000,000$$

6. The value of the tangible assets and the value of the excess earnings are added together to produce the sport business' value.

Market-Based Approach

The market-based approach gives the value of the sport business based on some multiple of operating results, such as profits or revenues. The multiples are based on market transactions involving similar sport businesses. The inherent appeal of this approach is that the value of the business based on market-derived multiples reflects informed decisions negotiated between parties in transactions. When transactions are identified, notions of risk and return are incorporated into the multiples. Thus, the multiplier would vary within the same industry if one business has significant competition while the other business has no competition in a great location and should have a higher multiplier.

For many types of closely held businesses, market multiples are derived based on multiples of earnings and revenues that are obtained either from analysis of publicly traded companies similar to the business, or from data on actual transactions involving acquired or merging public and private companies. When market values of publicly traded companies are used to establish the value of a closely held business, it is necessary to apply a discount for lack of marketability to the value of the publicly traded companies. The lack-of-marketability discount results from a privately held company being less valuable than a comparable public company because it is not as quick and easy to convert a business ownership position to cash (i.e., a private company is less liquid). The appropriate lack-of-marketability discount should be between 40% and 63% based upon a recent survey of empirical studies (Pratt, Reilly, & Schweihs, 2000). For valuation analysis, there is limited information on transactions that involve sport businesses, and there are very few publicly traded sport businesses in existence.

Many people believe that simple rules of thumb concerning the market multiple should be applied. This would mean applying an arbitrary multiple to current annual revenues that is based on anecdotal information, rather than actual analysis of empirical data. Such rules do not adjust multiples to reflect differences in operating characteristics, and should not be used for any purpose other than as a reasonableness check on the values obtained from the use of other methodologies.

Income-Based Approaches

In income-based approaches, the value of the business is estimated based on the present value of all earnings and cash flow that the business provides to the owners during the time that it is owned. The appeal of this approach for valuing a sport business is that such a business is an operating entity that generates cash flow and earnings to the owners. The value resulting from the revenue- and profit-generating ability of the business is more relevant than the value that can be obtained from selling the business' assets because many sport businesses are not capital intensive.

One income-based approach, called the **discounted net cash flow** approach, is to estimate the present value of future economic income that is expected to result from the operations of the business. It is also common to use the net cash flow to equity formula, which requires the following steps:

1. Determine net income after taxes.
2. Add noncash charges (e.g., depreciation).
3. Subtract net capital expenditures necessary to support business operations.
4. Subtract changes in net working capital necessary to support business operations.
5. Add net changes in long-term debt necessary to support business operations.

Net cash flow is used because conceptually it represents all income that an investor can hypothetically take out of the business. Generally, annual net cash flows are projected over a 5- to 10-year period into the future. At the end of the projection period, a terminal value is estimated on the basis of the cash flows that are expected to be earned after the projection period.

The business' value is then computed as the sum of the present value of the annual net cash flows over the forecast period plus the present value of the terminal value (Shapiro, 1999). The present value of any single annual cash flow received in the future is computed by discounting the future cash flows. The concept of discounting recognizes that money received in the future is worth less than it would be today because money invested today can accrue

interest over time. Under the assumption that the investor can earn an interest rate of i, the present value of net cash flow (CF) received n years (CF$_n$) in the future is:

$$\frac{CF_n}{(1+i)^n}$$

For example, if the interest rate (i) is 10%, the present value of $1 million received five years from now is:

$$\frac{\$100,000,000}{1.10^5} = \$620,921$$

Additional Considerations When Selling a Business

In addition to determining the business' value, if you are selling a business you should keep the following guidelines in mind:

- Do not let employees know too early that you might be selling, as this can affect employee morale.
- Do not let competitors know too early about an impending sale, as they might try to steal customers or hinder the sales process.
- Do not accept a purchase agreement calling for the seller to receive cash and a note, as the note could be worthless if the new owner runs into financial hardships.
- Do not accept a significant bonus based on future financial success, as you will remain tied to the business and its potential success or failure.
- Do not get so involved in the sales process that the business suffers and becomes even more difficult to sell (Livingston, 1998).
- Do not specifically exclude certain assets from the final sale such as cash, past-due accounts receivable, deposits, refunds, and other valuable assets such as business records (Parish & Maloney, 1999). Although it might be hard to part with these valuable assets, their value should be reflected in the business' sale price.

Despite potential problems associated with special purchasing options, if a business has a strong financial future, the potential downside might be minimal and the seller might want to negotiate a contract attached to the company's future success. As with all contracts, the seller can negotiate a relatively risk-free deal by having the contract maximize success but minimize any losses. For example, the sales contract could specify that the seller is entitled to 10% of the company's profit for the first five years after the sale, but that if the company does not have any profits the seller will be entitled to a preferred collateral position on company assets. A preferred collateral position is a contractual agreement by which lenders can enhance their collateral positions. Thus, unsecured creditors can enter into agreements that provide them with a better position as long as such position does not harm any secured creditors or violate any bankruptcy estate.

Selling a Business to Employees

Employee stock ownership plans are plans in which employees are given the opportunity to buy the business. These plans normally funnel pension or retirement funds into company stock and at a certain point the employees can own a large percentage of the stock.

 Assume that the Smiths' employees decide they want to buy all the centers in the Smiths' fitness empire. The Smiths could negotiate an outright purchase of the centers or can undertake various strategies such as giving equity interest in lieu of some retirement benefits. The Smiths could also give the employees the opportunity to purchase the centers using the lease-to-own option in which the employees pay a lease amount for several years and then buy the centers at a set price.

External Sales Assistance

If you hire a business broker or investment banker, this individual can help focus your sales search by shopping the company only to those with interest in buying the company and the ability to do so. Many people would love to own a company but do not have the proper experience or the financial knowledge needed to complete the deal. External consultants can help provide an arm's-length, objective opinion about a purchaser. Professionals can prequalify potential candidates to make sure they have the necessary resources. If would-be buyers are not prequalified, another John Spano incident could occur (see chapter 16).

Business liquidators are experts in helping to establish a business' value and finding potential buyers for the entire business or just some key assets. They research businesses and find out what the best assets are and then come in, buy a business, sell all the valuables, and exit with a nice profit.

> *Sale of a business can take various forms, including sale of stock and sale of assets. In either case there are several techniques for calculating the business' value.*

CONCLUSION

People do not want to think that their business will ever go under. However, hard times do occur, and a business owner or manager needs to understand the signs of trouble. If the problem is caught soon enough, it may be possible to save the business. Losses can also result from events that an owner has no way to plan for. If the Celtics' star player died, ticket sales could plummet and ratings for game broadcasts could drop. Such a significant loss cannot be planned for. Nonetheless, a business does need to have some contingency plans.

By keeping meticulous records, managers can know how much their business is worth. They can be aware of impacts that economic changes or competition might have on the business. They can put themselves in a position to see the writing on the wall and determine the best time to sell a business. They can tell what is happening with the competition and how their business might be affected. They can plan for the future and stay one step ahead of the external factors.

ASSIGNMENTS

1. Which bankruptcy chapter should the Smiths, SMC, or the Boston Celtics use if they need to file for bankruptcy? Why?
2. Contact a local business broker to see if any sport-related businesses are for sale.

RESEARCH PROJECT

Research at least two sport businesses that have gone through bankruptcy and determine, if possible, why they were faced with bankruptcy.

CLASS DISCUSSION TOPICS

1. What is the best technique for determining a business' value?
2. If you were facing hard financial times, would you be willing to file for bankruptcy? What are the advantages and disadvantages you should consider?
3. Could the Smiths just shut their doors and not pay anything or sell anything?

Appendix A

Time Value of Money Tables

Table A.1   Future Value of $1 at the End of t Periods

Period	1%	2%	3%	4%	5%	6%	7%	8%	9%	10%	11%
1	1.0100	1.0200	1.0300	1.0400	1.0500	1.0600	1.0700	1.0800	1.0900	1.1000	1.1100
2	1.0201	1.0404	1.0609	1.0816	1.1025	1.1236	1.1449	1.1664	1.1881	1.2100	1.2321
3	1.0303	1.0612	1.0927	1.1249	1.1576	1.1910	1.2250	1.2597	1.2950	1.3310	1.3676
4	1.0406	1.0824	1.1255	1.1699	1.2155	1.2625	1.3108	1.3605	1.4116	1.4641	1.5181
5	1.0510	1.1041	1.1593	1.2167	1.2763	1.3382	1.4026	1.4693	1.5386	1.6105	1.6851
6	1.0615	1.1262	1.1941	1.2653	1.3401	1.4185	1.5007	1.5869	1.6771	1.7716	1.8704
7	1.0721	1.1487	1.2299	1.3159	1.4071	1.5036	1.6058	1.7138	1.8280	1.9487	2.0762
8	1.0829	1.1717	1.2668	1.3686	1.4775	1.5938	1.7182	1.8509	1.9926	2.1436	2.3045
9	1.0937	1.1951	1.3048	1.4233	1.5513	1.6895	1.8385	1.9990	2.1719	2.3579	2.5580
10	1.1046	1.2190	1.3439	1.4802	1.6289	1.7908	1.9672	2.1589	2.3674	2.5937	2.8394
11	1.1157	1.2434	1.3842	1.5395	1.7103	1.8983	2.1049	2.3316	2.5804	2.8531	3.1518
12	1.1268	1.2682	1.4258	1.6010	1.7959	2.0122	2.2522	2.5182	2.8127	3.1384	3.4985
13	1.1381	1.2936	1.4685	1.6651	1.8856	2.1329	2.4098	2.7196	3.0658	3.4523	3.8833
14	1.1495	1.3195	1.5126	1.7317	1.9799	2.2609	2.5785	2.9372	3.3417	3.7975	4.3104
15	1.1610	1.3459	1.5580	1.8009	2.0789	2.3966	2.7590	3.1722	3.6425	4.1772	4.7846
16	1.1726	1.3728	1.6047	1.8730	2.1829	2.5404	2.9522	3.4259	3.9703	4.5950	5.3109
17	1.1843	1.4002	1.6528	1.9479	2.2920	2.6928	3.1588	3.7000	4.3276	5.0545	5.8951
18	1.1961	1.4282	1.7024	2.0258	2.4066	2.8543	3.3799	3.9960	4.7171	5.5599	6.5436
19	1.2081	1.4568	1.7535	2.1068	2.5270	3.0256	3.6165	4.3157	5.1417	6.1159	7.2633
20	1.2202	1.4859	1.8061	2.1911	2.6533	3.2071	3.8697	4.6610	5.6044	6.7275	8.0623
21	1.2324	1.5157	1.8603	2.2788	2.7860	3.3996	4.1406	5.0338	6.1088	7.4002	8.9492
22	1.2447	1.5460	1.9161	2.3699	2.9253	3.6035	4.4304	5.4365	6.6586	8.1403	9.9336
23	1.2572	1.5769	1.9736	2.4647	3.0715	3.8197	4.7405	5.8715	7.2579	8.9543	11.0263
24	1.2697	1.6084	2.0328	2.5633	3.2251	4.0489	5.0724	6.3412	7.9111	9.8497	12.2392
25	1.2824	1.6406	2.0938	2.6658	3.3864	4.2919	5.4274	6.8485	8.6231	10.8347	13.5855
30	1.3478	1.8114	2.4273	3.2434	4.3219	5.7435	7.6123	10.0627	13.2677	17.4494	22.8923
40	1.4889	2.2080	3.2620	4.8010	7.0400	10.2857	14.9745	21.7245	31.4094	45.2593	65.0009
50	1.6446	2.6916	4.3839	7.1067	11.4674	18.4202	29.4570	46.9016	74.3575	117.3909	184.5648
60	1.8167	3.2810	5.8916	10.5196	18.6792	32.9877	57.9464	101.2571	176.0313	304.4816	524.0572

*Future value interest factor exceeds 99,999.

12%	14%	15%	16%	18%	20%	24%	28%	32%	36%
1.1200	1.1400	1.1500	1.1600	1.1800	1.2000	1.2400	1.2800	1.3200	1.3600
1.2544	1.2996	1.3225	1.3456	1.3924	1.4400	1.5376	1.6384	1.7424	1.8496
1.4049	1.4815	1.5209	1.5609	1.6430	1.7280	1.9066	2.0972	2.3000	2.5155
1.5735	1.6890	1.7490	1.8106	1.9388	2.0736	2.3642	2.6844	3.0360	3.4210
1.7623	1.9254	2.0114	2.1003	2.2878	2.4883	2.9316	3.4360	4.0075	4.6526
1.9738	2.1950	2.3131	2.4364	2.6996	2.9860	3.6352	4.3980	5.2899	6.3275
2.2107	2.5023	2.6600	2.8262	3.1855	3.5832	4.5077	5.6295	6.9826	8.6054
2.4760	2.8526	3.0590	3.2784	3.7589	4.2998	5.5895	7.2058	9.2170	11.7034
2.7731	3.2519	3.5179	3.8030	4.4355	5.1598	6.9310	9.2234	12.1665	15.9166
3.1058	3.7072	4.0456	4.4114	5.2338	6.1917	8.5944	11.8059	16.0598	21.6466
3.4785	4.2262	4.6524	5.1173	6.1759	7.4301	10.6571	15.1116	21.1989	29.4393
3.8960	4.8179	5.3503	5.9360	7.2876	8.9161	13.2148	19.3428	27.9825	40.0375
4.3635	5.4924	6.1528	6.8858	8.5994	10.6993	16.3863	24.7588	36.9370	54.4510
4.8871	6.2613	7.0757	7.9875	10.1472	12.8392	20.3191	31.6913	48.7568	74.0534
5.4736	7.1379	8.1371	9.2655	11.9737	15.4070	25.1956	40.5648	64.3590	100.7126
6.1304	8.1372	9.3576	10.7480	14.1290	18.4884	31.2426	51.9230	84.9538	136.9691
6.8660	9.2765	10.7613	12.4677	16.6722	22.1861	38.7408	66.4614	112.1390	186.2779
7.6900	10.5752	12.3755	14.4625	19.6733	26.6233	48.0386	85.0706	148.0235	253.3380
8.6128	12.0557	14.2318	16.7765	23.2144	31.9480	59.5679	108.8904	195.3911	344.5397
9.6463	13.7435	16.3665	19.4608	27.3930	38.3376	73.8641	139.3797	257.9162	468.5740
10.8038	15.6676	18.8215	22.5745	32.3238	46.0051	91.5915	178.4060	340.4494	637.2606
12.1003	17.8610	21.6447	26.1864	38.1421	55.2061	113.5735	228.3596	449.3932	866.6744
13.5523	20.3616	24.8915	30.3762	45.0076	66.2474	140.8312	292.3003	593.1990	1,178.6772
15.1786	23.2122	28.6252	35.2364	53.1090	79.4968	174.6306	374.1444	783.0227	1,603.0010
17.0001	26.4619	32.9190	40.8742	62.6686	95.3962	216.5420	478.9049	1,033.5900	2,180.0814
29.9599	50.9502	66.2118	85.8499	143.3706	237.3763	634.8199	1,645.5046	4,142.0748	10,143.0193
93.0510	188.8835	267.8635	378.7212	750.3783	1,469.7716	5,455.9126	19,426.6889	66,520.7670	*
289.0022	700.2330	1,083.6574	1,670.7038	3,927.3569	9,100.4382	46,890.4346	229,349.8616	*	*
897.5969	2,595.9187	4,383.9987	7,370.2014	20,555.1400	56,347.5144	*	*	*	*

Table A.2 Present Value of $1 Received at the End of t Periods

Period	1%	2%	3%	4%	5%	6%	7%	8%	9%	10%	11%
1	0.9901	0.9804	0.9709	0.9615	0.9524	0.9434	0.9346	0.9259	0.9174	0.9091	0.9009
2	0.9803	0.9612	0.9426	0.9246	0.9070	0.8900	0.8734	0.8573	0.8417	0.8264	0.8116
3	0.9706	0.9423	0.9151	0.8890	0.8638	0.8396	0.8163	0.7938	0.7722	0.7513	0.7312
4	0.9610	0.9238	0.8885	0.8548	0.8227	0.7921	0.7629	0.7350	0.7084	0.6830	0.6587
5	0.9515	0.9057	0.8626	0.8219	0.7835	0.7473	0.7130	0.6806	0.6499	0.6209	0.5935
6	0.9420	0.8880	0.8375	0.7903	0.7462	0.7050	0.6663	0.6302	0.5963	0.5645	0.5346
7	0.9327	0.8706	0.8131	0.7599	0.7107	0.6651	0.6227	0.5835	0.5470	0.5132	0.4817
8	0.9235	0.8535	0.7894	0.7307	0.6768	0.6274	0.5820	0.5403	0.5019	0.4665	0.4339
9	0.9143	0.8368	0.7664	0.7026	0.6446	0.5919	0.5439	0.5002	0.4604	0.4241	0.3909
10	0.9053	0.8203	0.7441	0.6756	0.6139	0.5584	0.5083	0.4632	0.4224	0.3855	0.3522
11	0.8963	0.8043	0.7224	0.6496	0.5847	0.5268	0.4751	0.4289	0.3875	0.3505	0.3173
12	0.8874	0.7885	0.7014	0.6246	0.5568	0.4970	0.4440	0.3971	0.3555	0.3186	0.2858
13	0.8787	0.7730	0.6810	0.6006	0.5303	0.4688	0.4150	0.3677	0.3262	0.2897	0.2575
14	0.8700	0.7579	0.6611	0.5775	0.5051	0.4423	0.3878	0.3405	0.2992	0.2633	0.2320
15	0.8613	0.7430	0.6419	0.5553	0.4810	0.4173	0.3624	0.3152	0.2745	0.2394	0.2090
16	0.8528	0.7284	0.6232	0.5339	0.4581	0.3936	0.3387	0.2919	0.2519	0.2176	0.1883
17	0.8444	0.7142	0.6050	0.5134	0.4363	0.3714	0.3166	0.2703	0.2311	0.1978	0.1696
18	0.8360	0.7002	0.5874	0.4936	0.4155	0.3503	0.2959	0.2502	0.2120	0.1799	0.1528
19	0.8277	0.6864	0.5703	0.4746	0.3957	0.3305	0.2765	0.2317	0.1945	0.1635	0.1377
20	0.8195	0.6730	0.5537	0.4564	0.3769	0.3118	0.2584	0.2145	0.1784	0.1486	0.1240
21	0.8114	0.6598	0.5375	0.4388	0.3589	0.2942	0.2415	0.1987	0.1637	0.1351	0.1117
22	0.8034	0.6468	0.5219	0.4220	0.3418	0.2775	0.2257	0.1839	0.1502	0.1228	0.1007
23	0.7954	0.6342	0.5067	0.4057	0.3256	0.2618	0.2109	0.1703	0.1378	0.1117	0.0907
24	0.7876	0.6217	0.4919	0.3901	0.3101	0.2470	0.1971	0.1577	0.1264	0.1015	0.0817
25	0.7798	0.6095	0.4776	0.3751	0.2953	0.2330	0.1842	0.1460	0.1160	0.0923	0.0736
30	0.7419	0.5521	0.4120	0.3083	0.2314	0.1741	0.1314	0.0994	0.0754	0.0573	0.0437
40	0.6717	0.4529	0.3066	0.2083	0.1420	0.0972	0.0668	0.0460	0.0318	0.0221	0.0154
50	0.6080	0.3715	0.2281	0.1407	0.0872	0.0543	0.0339	0.0213	0.0134	0.0085	0.0054
60	0.5504	0.3048	0.1697	0.0951	0.0535	0.0303	0.0173	0.0099	0.0057	0.0033	0.0019

Interest rate

* The present value factor is zero rounded to four decimal places.

12%	14%	15%	16%	18%	20%	24%	28%	32%	36%
0.8929	0.8772	0.8696	0.8621	0.8475	0.8333	0.8065	0.7813	0.7576	0.7353
0.7972	0.7695	0.7561	0.7432	0.7182	0.6944	0.6504	0.6104	0.5739	0.5407
0.7118	0.6750	0.6575	0.6407	0.6086	0.5787	0.5245	0.4768	0.4348	0.3975
0.6355	0.5921	0.5718	0.5523	0.5158	0.4823	0.4230	0.3725	0.3294	0.2923
0.5674	0.5194	0.4972	0.4761	0.4371	0.4019	0.3411	0.2910	0.2495	0.2149
0.5066	0.4556	0.4323	0.4104	0.3704	0.3349	0.2751	0.2274	0.1890	0.1580
0.4523	0.3996	0.3759	0.3538	0.3139	0.2791	0.2218	0.1776	0.1432	0.1162
0.4039	0.3506	0.3269	0.3050	0.2660	0.2326	0.1789	0.1388	0.1085	0.0854
0.3606	0.3075	0.2843	0.2630	0.2255	0.1938	0.1443	0.1084	0.0822	0.0628
0.3220	0.2697	0.2472	0.2267	0.1911	0.1615	0.1164	0.0847	0.0623	0.0462
0.2875	0.2366	0.2149	0.1954	0.1619	0.1346	0.0938	0.0662	0.0472	0.0340
0.2567	0.2076	0.1869	0.1685	0.1372	0.1122	0.0757	0.0517	0.0357	0.0250
0.2292	0.1821	0.1625	0.1452	0.1163	0.0935	0.0610	0.0404	0.0271	0.0184
0.2046	0.1597	0.1413	0.1252	0.0985	0.0779	0.0492	0.0316	0.0205	0.0135
0.1827	0.1401	0.1229	0.1079	0.0835	0.0649	0.0397	0.0247	0.0155	0.0099
0.1631	0.1229	0.1069	0.0930	0.0708	0.0541	0.0320	0.0193	0.0118	0.0073
0.1456	0.1078	0.0929	0.0802	0.0600	0.0451	0.0258	0.0150	0.0089	0.0054
0.1300	0.0946	0.0808	0.0691	0.0508	0.0376	0.0208	0.0118	0.0068	0.0039
0.1161	0.0829	0.0703	0.0596	0.0431	0.0313	0.0168	0.0092	0.0051	0.0029
0.1037	0.0728	0.0611	0.0514	0.0365	0.0261	0.0135	0.0072	0.0039	0.0021
0.0926	0.0638	0.0531	0.0443	0.0309	0.0217	0.0109	0.0056	0.0029	0.0016
0.0826	0.0560	0.0462	0.0382	0.0262	0.0181	0.0088	0.0044	0.0022	0.0012
0.0738	0.0491	0.0402	0.0329	0.0222	0.0151	0.0071	0.0034	0.0017	0.0008
0.0659	0.0431	0.0349	0.0284	0.0188	0.0126	0.0057	0.0027	0.0013	0.0006
0.0588	0.0378	0.0304	0.0245	0.0160	0.0105	0.0046	0.0021	0.0010	0.0005
0.0334	0.0196	0.0151	0.0116	0.0070	0.0042	0.0016	0.0006	0.0002	0.0001
0.0107	0.0053	0.0037	0.0026	0.0013	0.0007	0.0002	0.0001	*	*
0.0035	0.0014	0.0009	0.0006	0.0003	*	*	*	*	*
0.0011	0.0004	0.0002	0.0001	*	*	*	*	*	*

Table A.3 Present Value of $1 per Period for t Periods

Period	1%	2%	3%	4%	5%	6%	7%	8%	9%	10%	11%
1	0.9901	0.9804	0.9709	0.9615	0.9524	0.9434	0.9346	0.9259	0.9174	0.9091	0.9009
2	1.9704	1.9416	1.9135	1.8861	1.8594	1.8334	1.8080	1.7833	1.7591	1.7355	1.7125
3	2.9410	2.8839	2.8286	2.7751	2.7232	2.6730	2.6243	2.5771	2.5313	2.4869	2.4437
4	3.9020	3.8077	3.7171	3.6299	3.5460	3.4651	3.3872	3.3121	3.2397	3.1699	3.1024
5	4.8534	4.7135	4.5797	4.4518	4.3295	4.2124	4.1002	3.9927	3.8897	3.7908	3.6959
6	5.7955	5.6014	5.4172	5.2421	5.0757	4.9173	4.7665	4.6229	4.4859	4.3553	4.2305
7	6.7282	6.4720	6.2303	6.0021	5.7864	5.5824	5.3893	5.2064	5.0330	4.8684	4.7122
8	7.6517	7.3255	7.0197	6.7327	6.4632	6.2098	5.9713	5.7466	5.5348	5.3349	5.1461
9	8.5660	8.1622	7.7861	7.4353	7.1078	6.8017	6.5152	6.2469	5.9952	5.7590	5.5370
10	9.4713	8.9826	8.5302	8.1109	7.7217	7.3601	7.0236	6.7101	6.4177	6.1446	5.8892
11	10.3676	9.7868	9.2526	8.7605	8.3064	7.8869	7.4987	7.1390	6.8052	6.4951	6.2065
12	11.2551	10.5753	9.9540	9.3851	8.8633	8.3838	7.9427	7.5361	7.1607	6.8137	6.4924
13	12.1337	11.3484	10.6350	9.9856	9.3936	8.8527	8.3577	7.9038	7.4869	7.1034	6.7499
14	13.0037	12.1062	11.2961	10.5631	9.8986	9.2950	8.7455	8.2442	7.7862	7.3667	6.9819
15	13.8651	12.8493	11.9379	11.1184	10.3797	9.7122	9.1079	8.5595	8.0607	7.6061	7.1909
16	14.7179	13.5777	12.5611	11.6523	10.8378	10.1059	9.4466	8.8514	8.3126	7.8237	7.3792
17	15.5623	14.2919	13.1661	12.1657	11.2741	10.4773	9.7632	9.1216	8.5436	8.0216	7.5488
18	16.3983	14.9920	13.7535	12.6593	11.6896	10.8276	10.0591	9.3719	8.7556	8.2014	7.7016
19	17.2260	15.6785	14.3238	13.1339	12.0853	11.1581	10.3356	9.6036	8.9501	8.3649	7.8393
20	18.0456	16.3514	14.8775	13.5903	12.4622	11.4699	10.5940	9.8181	9.1285	8.5136	7.9633
21	18.8570	17.0112	15.4150	14.0292	12.8212	11.7641	10.8355	10.0168	9.2922	8.6487	8.0751
22	19.6604	17.6580	15.9369	14.4511	13.1630	12.0416	11.0612	10.2007	9.4424	8.7715	8.1757
23	20.4558	18.2922	16.4436	14.8568	13.4886	12.3034	11.2722	10.3711	9.5802	8.8832	8.2664
24	21.2434	18.9139	16.9355	15.2470	13.7986	12.5504	11.4693	10.5288	9.7066	8.9847	8.3481
25	22.0232	19.5235	17.4131	15.6221	14.0939	12.7834	11.6536	10.6748	9.8226	9.0770	8.4217
30	25.8077	22.3965	19.6004	17.2920	15.3725	13.7648	12.4090	11.2578	10.2737	9.4269	8.6938
40	32.8347	27.3555	23.1148	19.7928	17.1591	15.0463	13.3317	11.9246	10.7574	9.7791	8.9511
50	39.1961	31.4236	25.7298	21.4822	18.2559	15.7619	13.8007	12.2335	10.9617	9.9148	9.0417
60	44.9550	34.7609	27.6756	22.6235	18.9293	16.1614	14.0392	12.3766	11.0480	9.9672	9.0736

Interest rate

12%	14%	15%	16%	18%	20%	24%	28%	32%	36%
0.8929	0.8772	0.8696	0.8621	0.8475	0.8333	0.8065	0.7813	0.7576	0.7353
1.6901	1.6467	1.6257	1.6052	1.5656	1.5278	1.4568	1.3916	1.3315	1.2760
2.4018	2.3216	2.2832	2.2459	2.1743	2.1065	1.9813	1.8684	1.7663	1.6735
3.0373	2.9137	2.8550	2.7982	2.6901	2.5887	2.4043	2.2410	2.0957	1.9658
3.6048	3.4331	3.3522	3.2743	3.1272	2.9906	2.7454	2.5320	2.3452	2.1807
4.1114	3.8887	3.7845	3.6847	3.4976	3.3255	3.0205	2.7594	2.5342	2.3388
4.5638	4.2883	4.1604	4.0386	3.8115	3.6046	3.2423	2.9370	2.6775	2.4550
4.9676	4.6389	4.4873	4.3436	4.0776	3.8372	3.4212	3.0758	2.7860	2.5404
5.3282	4.9464	4.7716	4.6065	4.3030	4.0310	3.5655	3.1842	2.8681	2.6033
5.6502	5.2161	5.0188	4.8332	4.4941	4.1925	3.6819	3.2689	2.9304	2.6495
5.9377	5.4527	5.2337	5.0286	4.6560	4.3271	3.7757	3.3351	2.9776	2.6834
6.1944	5.6603	5.4206	5.1971	4.7932	4.4392	3.8514	3.3868	3.0133	2.7084
6.4235	5.8424	5.5831	5.3423	4.9095	4.5327	3.9124	3.4272	3.0404	2.7268
6.6282	6.0021	5.7245	5.4675	5.0081	4.6106	3.9616	3.4587	3.0609	2.7403
6.8109	6.1422	5.8474	5.5755	5.0916	4.6755	4.0013	3.4834	3.0764	2.7502
6.9740	6.2651	5.9542	5.6685	5.1624	4.7296	4.0333	3.5026	3.0882	2.7575
7.1196	6.3729	6.0472	5.7487	5.2223	4.7746	4.0591	3.5177	3.0971	2.7629
7.2497	6.4674	6.1280	5.8178	5.2732	4.8122	4.0799	3.5294	3.1039	2.7668
7.3658	6.5504	6.1982	5.8775	5.3162	4.8435	4.0967	3.5386	3.1090	2.7697
7.4694	6.6231	6.2593	5.9288	5.3527	4.8696	4.1103	3.5458	3.1129	2.7718
7.5620	6.6870	6.3125	5.9731	5.3837	4.8913	4.1212	3.5514	3.1158	2.7734
7.6446	6.7429	6.3587	6.0113	5.4099	4.9094	4.1300	3.5558	3.1180	2.7746
7.7184	6.7921	6.3988	6.0442	5.4321	4.9245	4.1371	3.5592	3.1197	2.7754
7.7843	6.8351	6.4338	6.0726	5.4509	4.9371	4.1428	3.5619	3.1210	2.7760
7.8431	6.8729	6.4641	6.0971	5.4669	4.9476	4.1474	3.5640	3.1220	2.7765
8.0552	7.0027	6.5660	6.1772	5.5168	4.9789	4.1601	3.5693	3.1242	2.7775
8.2438	7.1050	6.6418	6.2335	5.5482	4.9966	4.1659	3.5712	3.1250	2.7778
8.3045	7.1327	6.6605	6.2463	5.5541	4.9995	4.1666	3.5714	3.1250	2.7778
8.3240	7.1401	6.6651	6.2492	5.5553	4.9999	4.1667	3.5714	3.1250	2.7778

Appendix B
Formulas

The following balance sheet and income statement are interpreted through the financial analysis formulas and industry ratios in this appendix. These formulas and ratios are discussed in chapter 5.

Balance Sheet

ASSETS	($000)	LIABILITIES AND NET WORTH	($000)
Cash	100	Note payable	0
Accounts receivable	60	Accounts payable	150
Inventory	300	Taxes payable	40
Total current assets	**460**	Other accruals	30
		Total current liabilities	**220**
Plant and equipment	500		
Less depreciation	100	Mortgage payable	150
Net	400	Common stock	250
Total assets	**860**	Retained earnings	240
		Total liabilities and net worth	**860**

Income Statement

	($000)
Sales	500
Less: Material and labor	300
Manufacturing costs	30
Cost of goods sold	**330**
Gross profit	**170**
Depreciation	20
Selling expense	20
Profit before interest and taxes	**130**
Interest payments	10
Taxes	40
Profit after taxes	**80**
Dividends	40
Retained earnings	**40**

Additional facts include SMC's having 1 million outstanding shares currently selling for $10 a share. The stock was selling for $8 per share at the start of the year. SMC also has $10 million in outstanding bonds. The bonds are $1,000 face-value bonds redeemable in 20 years, paying 10% interest and currently selling for $1,100 each.

Profit

profit margin = profit after taxes / sales (i.e., $80,000 / $500,000 = 0.16, or 16%)

corporate earnings = sales − costs (i.e., $500,000 − $330,000 = $170,000)

earnings per share = earnings / total shares (i.e., $170,000 / 1,000,000 = $0.17)

PE ratio = price per share / earnings per share (i.e., $10.00 / $0.17 = 59 times earnings)

Liquidity

acid test ratio = liquid assets / current liabilities (i.e., $160,000 / $220,000 = 0.737)

current ratio = current assets / current liabilities (i.e., $460,000 / $220,000 = 2.09)

solvency ratio = net worth / total assets (i.e., $490,000 / $860,000 = 0.57)

working capital = current assets − current liabilities (i.e., $460,000 − $220,000 = $240,000)

Company Value

book value = total assets − total liabilities (i.e., $860,000 − $370,000 = $490,000)

book value per share = owners' equity / outstanding shares (i.e., $490,000 / 1,000,000 = $0.49)

owners' equity = common stock + retained earnings (i.e., $240,000 + $250,000 = $490,000)

dividend payout ratio = dividend per share / earnings per share (i.e., $0.04 / $0.17 = 0.235, or 23.5%)

net worth = common stock + retained earnings (i.e., $250,000 + $240,000 = $490,000)

turnover = sales / assets (i.e., $500,000 / $860,000 = 0.58)

Indebtedness

debt-equity ratio = total liabilities / shareholders' equity (i.e., $370,000 / $490,000 = 0.76)

interest coverage (IC) = (pretax income + interest expense) / interest expense (i.e., [$130,000 + $10,000] / $10,000 = 14 times)

Return on Investment

return on assets (ROA) = net income / total assets (i.e., $80,000 / $860,000 = 0.09, or 9%)

return on equity (ROE) = net income / owners' equity (i.e., $80,000 / $490,000 = 0.16, or 16%)

return on investment capital (ROIV) = net income / long-term debt + owners' equity (i.e., $80,000 / $640,000 [$150,000 + $490,000] = 0.125, or 12.5%)

bond yield = 10%

Investor Information

annual return (per share) = increase or decrease in value + any dividend (i.e., $2.00 + $0.04 = $2.04 per share). On a percentage basis, the annual return would be divided by the initial investment (i.e., $2.04 / $8.00 = 25.5%).

current yield = annual interest payment / current market value (i.e., $100*/ $1,100 = 9.09%). *Annual interest payment = bond face value $\times$ bond interest rate (i.e., $1,000 $\times$ 10%.)

dividend per share = dividends / outstanding shares (i.e., $40,000 / 1,000,000 = $0.04 a share)

holding period return (HPR) = (current income + capital gains) / purchase price (i.e., $0.04 + $2.00) / $8.00 = 0.255, or 25.5%)

simple rate of return (SRR) = investment's annual income / initial investment (i.e., $0.04 / $8.00 = 0.005, or 0.5%)

Appendix C
Suggested Resources

Stocks

North American Securities Administrators Association, Inc: 202-737-0900. U-7 registration forms and manuals can be obtained free of charge from the Web page at www.nasaa.org.

Small Business United of Texas (800-460-2448; www.score.org) offers for sale a Small Company Offering Registration (SCOR) kit for companies considering a SCOR offering. Local SCOR offices can be found throughout the United States.

The U.S. Securities and Exchange Commission: www.sec.gov

U.S. Securities and Exchange Commission EDGAR Database of filings by public companies: www.10kwizard.com or www.gsionline.com/info.htm

Yahoo! Finance: http://finance.yahoo.com

Minority Business Lenders or Suppliers

Business Consortium Fund: 212-243-7360

Certified Development Company (CDC): Call 800-972-2504 for the nearest CDC office.

National Association of Investment Companies: 202-289-4336; www.naicvc.com

National Association of Small Business Investment Companies: 202-628-5055; www.nasbic.org

National Association of Women Business Owners (NAWBO): 301-608-2590; www.nawbo.org

The National Minority Business Council, Inc.: 212-573-2385; www.nmbc.org

National Minority Supplier Development Council (NMSDC): 212-944-2430; www.nmsdc.org

Service Corps of Retired Executives (SCORE) Association: 800-634-0245; www.score.org

Women Incorporated: 800-930-3993; www.womeninc.org

Women's Growth Capital Fund of Washington, DC: www.womensgrowthcapital.com

Nonbank Lenders

AT&T Small Business Lending Corp.: 800-221-7252

Business Lenders: 800-646-7689; www.businesslenders.com

GE Capital Small Business Finance Corp.: 800-447-2025

Heller First Capital Corp.: 800-347-6430

The Money Store Investment Corp.: 800-722-3066

National Venture Capital Association: www.nvca.org

Mid-Atlantic Venture Funds: www.mavf.com

Venture Capital OnLine: www.vcapital.com

Commercial Finance Association: 225 W. 34th St., Ste. 1815, New York, NY 10122; 212-594-3490; www.cfa.com

Commercial Finance Group: www.cfgo.net

Factoring Lenders

There are several large factoring lenders including the businesses below. However, smaller businesses often have to go to smaller factoring lenders and a bank or loan broker might have some leads for smaller businesses.

CIT Group, Inc. of Livingston, NJ; www.cit.com

Finova Group, Inc. of Scottsdale, AZ; www.finova.com

GE Capital; www.gecapital.com

Quantum Corporate Funding, Ltd. of New York; www.quantumfunding.com

Vendor Financing

AT&T Capital Corp.: 201-397-3000

Canon Financial Services, Inc.: 800-220-0200; www.cfs.canon.com

GE Capital: 800-553-7287; www.ge.com

Hewlett-Packard: 415-960-5680; www.hp.com

IBM Credit Corp.: 800-678-6900; www.financing.ibm.com

IKON Capital: 912-471-2300; www.ikon.com

Oracle Credit Corp.: 415-506-7000; or www.oracle.com

Additional fund-raising information can be found at www.fundraiser.com.

Government Assistance

The Federal Reserve Board: www.federalreserve.gov

United States Small Business Administration: 800-827-5722; www.sbaonline.sba.gov

The National Association of Small Business Investment Companies (NASBIC): 666 11th St. NW, Ste. 750, Washington, DC 20001; 202-628-5055; www.nasbic.org

National Association of Investment Companies (NAIC): 1111 14th St. NW, Ste. 700, Washington, DC 20005; 202-289-4336; www.naicvc.com

Print Resources

Abrams, R.M. (1993). *The successful business plan: Secrets & strategies.* Grants Pass, OR: Oasis Press.

Athletic Business; www.athleticbusiness.com

Athletic Management; www.momentummedia.com

Barron's; www.barrons.com

Business Week; www.businessweek.com

Dun & Bradstreet

Fitness Management; www.fitnessmanagement.com

Forbes; www.forbes.com

Fulks, D.L. (2000). *Revenues and expenses of divisions I and II intercollegiate athletic programs: Financial trends and relationships-1999.* Indianapolis: National Collegiate Athletic Association.

Gabriel, C. (1998). *How to sell your business—and get what you want! A pragmatic guide with revealing tips from 57 sellers.* Westport, CT: Gwent Press.

Hagstrom, R.G. (1998). *The NASCAR way: The business that drives the sport.* New York: Wiley.

Helyar, J. (1994). *Lords of the realm: The real history of baseball.* New York: Ballantine.

Leeds, M., & von Allmen, P. (2002). *The economics of sports.* New York: Addison-Wesley.

Livingstone, J.L. (1997). *The portable MBA in finance and accounting,* 2nd ed., New York: Wiley.

Noll, R.G., & Zimbalist, A., eds. (1997). *Sports, jobs, and taxes: The economic impact of sports teams and stadiums.* Washington, DC: Brookings Institution Press.

Quirk, J., & Fort, R.D. (1992). *Pay dirt: The business of professional team sports.* Princeton, NJ: Princeton University Press.

Quirk, J., & Fort, R. (1999). *Hard ball: The abuse of power in pro team sports.* Princeton, NJ: Princeton University Press.

Staudohar, P.D. (1996). *Playing for dollars: Labor relations and the sports business.* Ithaca, NY: Cornell University Press.

Street & Smith's SportsBusiness Journal; www.sportsbusinessjournal.com

The NCAA News; www.ncaa.org

Sports Business Daily; www.sportsbusinessdaily.com

The Wall Street Journal; www.wsj.com

Zimbalist, A. (1999). *Unpaid professionals: Commerialism and conflict in big-time college sports.* Princeton, NJ: Princeton University Press.

Glossary

ability to pay—The ability to pay refers to a business' or customer's ability to make payment to a vendor. Thus, if you were trying to sell someone concession items, you would examine that individual's ability to purchase the items with either cash or credit.

acceleration clause—Such a clause is often included in a contract to force one party to pay the entire amount owed if another party misses a payment.

account—Accounts represent a record of a relationship between parties. A typical example is a line of credit with a bank or a simple checking account.

account balance—An account balance represents the current account status at the end of a given time period. Thus, at the end of each month a bank might send customers a checking account balance to help them identify how much money they have available for future purchases.

account reconciliation—If you have ever balanced your own checkbook, you have performed account reconciliation. Account reconciliation entails adjusting the difference between various accountings to ensure that all totals agree.

accounts payable—Accounts payable represent outstanding obligations that are owed to vendors, lenders, or anyone else from whom credit was received and goods were purchased on such credit.

accounts receivable (A/R)—Accounts receivable represent moneys that are owed to a business from customers who purchased merchandise or services on credit. Many customers do not have sufficient funds to make cash purchases and thus need credit in order to purchase necessary products or supplies. A/R are not bad, as they represent significant sales and can be used as collateral to borrow money. However, A/R can become a burden if they are not repaid in a timely manner.

accrual—Accrual is an accounting term that defines anticipated future expenses and revenues. For example, in some accounting systems (accrual accounting), expenditures and revenues are recorded when the act that results in them occurs, regardless of when the money is actually disbursed or received. In contrast, in the **cash basis budgeting** (or accounting) system, expenditures and revenues are recorded at the time they are actually disbursed or received.

accrued dividend—Sometimes a company decides to pay a dividend to shareholders but the company's board of directors does not make a formal declaration. Without a formal declaration, an accrued dividend does not represent a legal obligation, but still represents an obligation that should be paid to shareholders barring any unforeseen needs for such funds.

accrued interest—Similar to accrued dividends (dividends that have been earned but not yet paid), accrued interest is interest that is owed, but not yet paid.

acid test ratio (quick ratio)—The acid test is an analysis of the ability of a company to liquidate current assets (excluding harder-to-sell items such as inventory) to pay off current liabilities. Cash is added to marketable securities and accounts receivable, and these liquid assets are divided by current liabilities. If the resulting number is less than 1, then the company does not have enough liquid assets to pay current liabilities. If the ratio is greater than 1, then the company has more than enough liquid assets to pay off current liabilities. If a company has $100 in cash, no marketable securities, $200 in accounts receivable, and $400 in current liabilities, the acid test ratio is ($100 + $200) / $400 = 0.75. Since the ratio is lower than 1, the company cannot cover all its current liabilities.

activity—Activity refers to the number of transactions occurring in a given account during a given accounting time period.

actual value—Actual value refers to the **book value** of an asset. To determine book value, take an item's original purchase cost and subtract all accumulated depreciation. If you bought a computer with a five-year life for $5,000 and used straight-line depreciation, after one year the actual, or book, value would be $5,000 minus $1,000 (one year's worth of depreciation) = $4,000.

actuaries—Actuaries are expert mathematicians who analyze the risks and premiums for insurance coverage based on probability estimates. Probability estimates help determine the risk that a given event will occur and the potential loss that could be incurred from such an event.

adjustable basis—This term is typically used to describe a tax situation in which the value of an asset is increased through capital expenditures or reduced by depreciation. The adjustable basis for your house changes when you incur such capital expenditures as installing a new roof. Any increase in the house's value when you try to resell the house has to be adjusted by the cost of the new roof; this reduces your tax liability for any profits from the sale.

adjustable rate mortgage (ARM)—ARMs, also referred to as variable- or flexible-rate mortgages, are a type of mortgage for which the interest rate can change over the loan's lifetime. It is common for ARMs to be low cost for the first several years of the loan and for the interest rate to increase over time. In contrast, the interest rate for fixed rate mortgages remains stable throughout the loan's lifetime.

adjusted balance method (ABM)—ABM is one of several financing techniques (see also **average daily balance method** and **past-due balance method**) used to determine interest owed. As an example of how ABM is calculated, if you have a credit card that has an 18% annual interest rate, you will be paying 1.5% interest a month on your adjusted balance. If you used your credit card to buy sporting goods worth $400 in February and paid only $300 in March, you would owe 1.5% interest times the adjusted $100 balance ($400 – $300). If you made no more purchases in March, you would owe $101.50, representing the $100 balance and $1.50 in interest (Siegel, Shim, & Hartman, 1992).

adjusted gross income (AGI)—AGI is a tax term representing your total gross income minus allowed adjustments for such items as health care costs or mortgage interest.

ad valorem tax—An ad valorem tax is a levy that is imposed on business property (both real and possibly personal), based primarily on a percentage of the property's value.

after-tax cash flow (ATCF)—ATCF represents all income minus any taxes paid.

aggregate amount—An aggregate amount is the total, or gross, amount of a given item. For example, the aggregate income of the nation is the gross national product.

allowance—In finance terms, an allowance is a credit that a creditor allows a debtor to take for any of a number of reasons. For example, assume you bought 1,000 foam #1 fingers to sell and that 200 of them are defective. Instead of your owing $1,000 for the lot, the seller might give you a $200 allowance or reduction in the amount owed to compensate you for the defective products.

amortization—Amortization refers to repaying a loan in installments. As such payments are made, typically on a property mortgage, the debtor's equity in the property increases, as each installment comprises both interest and principal. Goodwill can also be amortized over several years instead of just the first year after a business has been purchased.

annual percentage rate (APR)—APR is the ratio of the finance charge to the average amount of credit in use during the lifetime of a loan (Siegel, Shim, & Hartman, 1992). Under the Truth in Lending Act, banks must disclose the APR (in percentage form) and the actual finance charge in dollars.

annual report—At the end of their fiscal years, companies produce an annual report to inform shareholders about the company's financial position. Annual reports are carefully scrutinized by more than just shareholders, as potential investors, creditors, lenders, and other interested parties rely upon the audited information to help make investment decisions.

annual return—The annual return is the return from a given investment over the course of a year. Assume you purchased a stock on January 1 for $1,000 and sold the stock on the following December 31 for $1,500. During the year, the stock paid a dividend of $50. Your total annual return is calculated as follows:

Increased value ($1,500 – $1,000) =	$500
Dividend income	+ 50
Total return	$550

The percentage annual return is calculated as follows:

$$\text{percentage annual return} = \text{total annual return} / \text{initial investment}$$
$$= \$550 / \$1,000$$
$$= 55\%$$

Thus, the annual return on this investment is $550, or 55%. However, not all investments are this successful. If the stock decreased to $800, the annual return would be calculated as follows:

$$\$1,000 \text{ decreased to } \$800 = -\$200 + \$50 \text{ dividend}$$
$$= -\$150 \text{ total revenue}$$

$$\text{percentage annual return} = \text{total return} / \text{initial investment}$$
$$= -\$150 / \$1,000$$
$$= -15\%$$

annuity—An annuity is typically a savings account or a retirement account with an insurance company or other investment placement company into which the investor can deposit a lump sum or scheduled deposits. When a particular event occurs, such as retirement, the investor receives regular repayments such as monthly distributions until the entire invested amount is repaid. Annuities have several significant benefits: the government does not tax the interest earned until the funds are distributed; compounding interest quickly increases the investment value; and unlike pensions and individual retirement accounts, annuities normally do not have any limitations on the amount an investor can contribute. One drawback, among several, is that investors normally cannot recover their funds until they reach the age of 59 1/2 without incurring significant penalties (Siegel, Shim, & Hartman, 1992).

appreciation—Appreciation is the increase in an item's value. If you bought 100 shares of a stock for $1,000 and sold them for $2,000, the investment would have appreciated $1,000.

appropriation—An appropriation is an amount of money set aside in a budget to cover a particular expense such as inventory or expected wages.

arrears—Being in arrears means being in default of an obligation. You are in arrears if you owe someone $10 to be paid on Friday but do not pay someone $10 to be paid on Friday but do not pay on Friday. Arrearage also refers to the situation in which cumulative preferred stock dividends have been declared, but not paid.

ask price—The ask price is the price that a seller would like to receive for the item they wish to sell.

assessed valuation—Government entities require landowners to pay property taxes based upon the assessed value of the property. The assessed value is not always the market value, but is often a percentage of the market value of the home and land.

asset—An asset is any resource or goods that might offer future benefits to a business and have value. Examples of assets are buildings, machinery, land, inventory, business goodwill, and related resources. "Hard assets" include such items as inventory and equipment that are tangible (can be touched). Intangible assets such as a company's goodwill, which has value but is hard to quantify, are called "soft assets."

assignment—Assignment refers to the transfer of property (real or personal) from one party to another. By assigning the property, the assignor gives the property to another (the assignee) with the assurance that there are no claims against the property and that the assignor has the right to transfer the property.

assumption—If you cannot pay your bills, someone can assume your debt and then become responsible for repaying the debt.

audit—An audit is an inspection by an independent external entity of all a company's accounting records and business operations. The primary purpose for audit of a company by a certified public accountant (CPA) is to validate all financial statements for accuracy so that the government, lenders, shareholders, and others can obtain an accurate view of the company.

average collection period—The average collection period is the average amount of time it takes a business to collect outstanding accounts receivable. The longer the average, the more money is lost due to the inability to use such outstanding funds for investment or other growth opportunities. Furthermore, if the average is long, that means there is a greater likelihood that some accounts receivables might be difficult to collect.

average daily balance method (ADBM)—ADBM is a method used by banks and credit card companies to calculate interest earned or owed. Using this method, a bank examines your average daily balance throughout the month and divides that amount by the number of days in the month. Assume that on the first day of the month you had $500 in the bank and on the 15th had only $100 in the bank. Also assume that your account earns 10% interest annually, or 0.83% a month. Your average daily balance is calculated as follows:

Number of days		Balance		Weighted balance
15	×	$500	=	$7,500
15	×	$100	=	$1,500
			Total	**$9,000**

The $9,000 weighted balance is divided by 30 days, equaling an average daily balance of $300, which if multiplied by the monthly interest rate produces an interest payment of $2.49.

backup withholding—Sometimes banks, investment companies, or other businesses cannot determine the Social Security number of someone to whom they are required to pay dividends, interest, or other payments. Instead of paying the full amount and possibly depriving the IRS of potential taxes, the entity withholds 20% of the payment and sends it to the IRS.

balance—For strict accounting purposes, one calculates balance by totaling all credits and subtracting all debt. However, in the context of **balance sheets**, balance refers to equality between all assets on the one hand and all liabilities plus owner's equity on the other hand, as shown in the equation assets = liabilities + owner's equity.

balance sheet—A balance sheet is a statement of financial condition prepared at the end of a set time period that lists a company's assets, liabilities, and owner's equity. The balance sheet is balanced when assets equal all liabilities plus the owner's equity. See the following balance sheet of Sport Manufacturing Company for the year ending October 31, 1999.

balloon payment—Some term loans (called balloon loans) require that only interest payments are made until the loan is due; then the entire principal and remaining interest are paid in a balloon payment.

bankruptcy—A business can face bankruptcy when its debt exceeds its assets' fair market value. If a company owes $1 million and its assets are worth only $500,000, the company can voluntarily pursue bankruptcy protection from creditors or can be forced by courts into bankruptcy to help protect any remaining value that the creditors might try to salvage. Three categories of bankruptcy are available: chapters 7, 11, and 13.

chapter 7 allows an individual's or business' property to be sold and the proceeds to be divided among creditors. Some specifically excluded items, such as a primary home and one auto, are not sold so that the debtor can still survive. Any debts that are not covered by the sale proceeds are discharged. Over 1 million chapter 7 bankruptcies were filed in 1997 (Cheeseman, 1998).

chapter 11 allows a company to reorganize and maintain control over its assets and operations while it attempts to resolve repayment schedules and amounts with debtors. Once the courts confirm a reorganization plan, all debts not included in the plan are discharged (Cheeseman, 1998).

Balance Sheet

ASSETS		LIABILITIES AND NET WORTH	
	($000)		**($000)**
Cash	100	Note payable	0
Accounts receivable	60	Accounts payable	150
Inventory	300	Taxes payable	40
		Other accruals	30
Total current assets	**460**	**Total current liabilities**	**220**
Plant and equipment	500		
Less depreciation	100	Mortgage payable	150
Net	400	Common stock	250
		Retained earnings	240
Total assets	**860**	**Total liabilities and net worth**	**860**

chapter 13, which is sometimes called the wage-earner plan, allows a debtor to repay debts over a three-year period. Debts are consolidated based on a court-coordinated and -approved schedule that allows for installment payments (Cheeseman, 1998).

bear and **bear market**—A bear is an individual who feels that the stock market will drop (typically more than 20%) and sells stocks, "goes **short,**" or buys a **put.** A bear market is a prolonged period during which stock prices continue to decline. Bear markets can be caused by poor economic conditions, political collapses, rising interest rates, or a host of other factors that foster pessimism among investors.

bearer bonds—Bearer bonds, or coupon bonds, do not require owners to register their names with the issuing company or government unit. The person who bears the bond can clip a coupon when it becomes due and cash it in.

Best's ratings—A.M. Best Co. performs an annual audit of insurance companies to help determine their financial stability, which is a valuable tool for those seeking to buy insurance from a solid company or those interested in investing in insurance company stocks. The highest rating is A+.

bid price—A bid price is the highest price a buyer is willing to pay for a security. The asking price is the price proposed by the seller of the security.

bill—There are several different types of bills, but in general, a bill is a written statement describing the terms and conditions of a particular sales transaction.

billing cycle—Companies traditionally bill their clients on a regular basis, typically monthly, bimonthly, quarterly, semiannually, or annually. These billing periods are referred to as billing cycles (they cycle through on a regular basis).

bill of sale—A bill of sale is formal documentation that represents the transfer of title to goods.

bills payable—Bills payable are bills or promissory notes that a company owes and represent a debt. See also **accounts payable.**

bills receivable—Bills receivable refers to notes, checks, drafts, or other contractually obligated instruments representing money or obligations owed to a person or entity. See also **accounts receivable.**

binder—A binder is a temporary payment representing a good faith deposit between contracting parties to go forward with a contract. The binder binds the parties to the agreement, but can be returned if the contract is not finalized. This distinguishes a binder from a deposit, which is normally not returned if the contract is not finalized.

blank endorsement—If you receive a check and sign the back, then you or anyone else who comes into possession of the check can cash it. To prevent others from cashing the check without your permission, you should sign the check and also write "For deposit only to the account of Jane Doe," or a similar phrase, on the check. The check no longer has a blank endorsement but now has a specified endorsement.

blind pool—Investors can join together as limited partners and each contribute a specific amount toward an investment. The combined money can then be invested by a general partner in investments such as stocks, bonds, or real estate. The pool is called a blind pool because the limited partners contribute without knowing exactly where the general partner might invest the money.

blind trust—In the traditional blind trust, one person or several individuals give their assets to a third party who will manage the funds in total independence. For example, President Bush owned part of the Texas Rangers before becoming the governor of Texas, and to avoid any potential conflict of interest, he transferred his ownership interest to a blind trust ("Bush Admits," 2000).

blue chip stocks—Blue chip stocks are stocks issued by the strongest companies—those that have a strong reputation for success, offer quality products or services, and are financially secure. Some blue chip companies are McDonald's, General Electric, IBM, Shell, AT&T, and Bank of America.

bond—A bond is a legal instrument through which a company or government entity promises to repay the bond purchaser both the principal and a specified interest rate; in return the bondholder receives a pledge of assets or can rely upon the **full faith and credit** of the issuer. Thus, if IBM wants to expand and issues $50 million in bonds, some investors may rely on IBM's past history of not defaulting on bonds and purchase the bond backed by their faith in the company. The full faith and credit of a company can back bonds not backed by assets. If the company collapses, there will be no collateral from which to repay the investment.

bond discount—Sometimes after a bond is issued the interest rate changes, making the bond less desirable than it was previously. A company's instability can also reduce the value of a bond. A bond is at a discount when the bond's **face value,** or **par value,** (what the bond is worth when it is issued) is greater than the **market value.** Market value represents what the bond would be worth if sold on a bond market. If the market value exceeds the face value, then the bond is being traded at a premium.

bondholder—A bondholder is anyone who holds legal title to a bond.

bond rating—Two companies, Moody's and Standard & Poor's, issue bond ratings that range from C or D to Aaa or AAA, respectively. An AAA- or Aaa-rated bond is the highest-quality bond, while ratings at the other extreme (C or D) indicate a lower chance that bondholders will be able to recover their investment. Blue chip companies or strong government entities (financially strong cities, municipalities, or states) typically have AAA or similar ratings.

bond valuation—Bond valuation is the complex mathematical process used to determine how much an investor should pay for a bond. The equation includes such criteria as present value, interest rate, investor-required rate of return, the bond's maturity date, and the degree of risk.

bond yield—The yield obtained from a bond represents its effective rate of return. One means to measure the yield is the current yield method, which is calculated by dividing the annual interest payment by the bond's current market value. Thus, if you have a bond with a 10% coupon rate and a $1,000 par value that is selling for $975, the **current yield** is (10% × $1,000) / $975 = 10.26%. This method shows that you are earning a little more than the stated interest rate, but it does not take into consideration the bond's maturity date, which can affect the attractiveness of the investment. Two other more complex formulas, **yield to call** and **yield to maturity,** can help provide a more detailed analysis if the bond is held for a set time period or held until it matures.

book value—Book value is calculated by subtracting total liabilities from total assets. See also **actual value.**

book value per share (BVPS)—BVPS represents the value of each share of stock based on its cost when the stock was originally issued. We can calculate BVPS by dividing total stockholders' equity by the number of outstanding shares. If a company's total shareholders' equity is $40 mil-

lion and there are 1 million outstanding shares, then the BVPS is $40.

break-even point—The break-even point is the level of revenue generation at which total revenue exactly matches total costs. The break-even analysis is used to help determine when profit could be made on a given product. Assume that you manufacture baseballs and that the variable costs (string, rubber, hourly wages, etc.) are $0.50 per ball. Assume also that fixed costs such as rent are $10,000 per month. If you manufactured and sold 5,000 balls per month, your total costs would be $2,500 (variable) + $10,000 (fixed) = $12,500. To break even, you would have to sell all 5,000 balls for an average price of $2.50 each. If you made 10,000 balls in a given month and kept the $2.50 per ball price, then you would have $15,000 in costs and $25,000 in sales that would generate a $10,000 profit.

break point—Sellers often indicate that if you buy 1 to 100 of an item, the price will be $1 each, for example. If you buy 101 to 500, the price will be reduced to $0.75 each. The break point for the discount is 101 units. A seller might have multiple break points at which the price continues to decline as the order quantity increases.

bridge loan—Sometimes a company needs a short-term loan while it is negotiating a long-term loan. A bridge loan is the solution, but it might cost more than traditional bank loans. A bridge loan might be needed by a buyer who wants to put a deposit down on some property prior to closing and securing a long-term mortgage.

budget—A budget is a road map or plan expressed in monetary terms that highlights all anticipated assets, debt, expenses, revenue, and net worth.

bull and **bull market**—A bull market is when there are prolonged market advances over a significant time period. A bull is an investor who has a favorable outlook on the economy and is willing to invest in stock, bonds, and other securities. See also **bear** and **bear market.**

business cycle—All businesses go through cyclical conditions in which they may have significant growth and then at a later time experience contraction. The entire economy can also go through cycles that include recovery and recession.

buying power—Buying power can be equated to liquid assets, which represent cash and marketable securities that could be quickly sold to make various purchases. If you do not have liquid assets, you do not have any buying power.

buy order—If you call your stockbroker and indicate that you want to purchase certain securities, you have just placed a buy order.

buyout—In a buyout, one investor, multiple investors, or a business can acquire a controlling interest in a company through buying a majority of that company's stock. Various professional sport teams have gone public and issued stock, and some of these teams were subsequently bought out by an individual investor or investment group and became privately owned teams.

call provision—Companies that issue bonds or preferred stock can pay an investor an amount over the face value of the security and redeem the security before it reaches maturity. A company might undertake this strategy if it wants to reduce amounts owed to bondholders or reduce the number of outstanding stock shares.

capital—Capital is wealth used to produce additional wealth.

capital asset pricing model (CAPM)—CAPM is a method of measuring the cost of common stock.

capital assets—The term *capital assets* commonly refers to fixed assets such as buildings, fields, stadiums, equipment, and other assets that can be depreciated.

capital gains and **capital losses**—Capital gains are the total gains in value of an investment excluding dividends. However, dividends can be included in the capital gains if the dividends are reinvested in additional shares of the same stock. Capital losses are all realized losses from an investment. There are both long-term and short-term capital gains and losses.

Long-term capital gains or losses are investments that have matured for over one year and result in capital gains or losses that must be reported to the IRS.

Short-term capital gains or losses apply to investments held for less than one year.

capitalization rate (cap rate)—The cap rate is used to determine the rate of return received from a real estate investment. To determine the cap rate, we divide the net operating income (NOI) from the investment's first year by the total investment cost. The higher the cap rate, the lower the perceived value of the investment. If you obtain $10,000 in NOI from a property and the property cost $200,000, then the cap rate is $10,000 / $200,000 = 5%. If banks are paying 8% interest, then the return on the real estate investment would be poor unless the real estate markedly increased in value.

capital markets—There are a number of capital markets in which long-term debt and securities are bought and sold. The most famous capital market is the New York Stock Exchange. Additional markets include the American Stock Exchange, the over-the-counter market (NASDAQ), and numerous regional and foreign exchanges.

capital outlay—A capital outlay is any expenditure for property or equipment for permanent use.

cash—There are many terms for cash, including legal tender and numerous slang terms. In the business world, cash includes money, coins, checks, bearer bonds, bank accounts, negotiable instruments, and related liquid assets.

cash basis budgeting—This budgeting process recognizes income and expenses when cash is actually received or paid and does not recognize accounts receivable or accounts payable.

cash discount—Manufacturers or wholesalers often offer discounts for those who purchase items with cash. A cash discount may be expressed by the formula 2/10/30. This formula means that the buyer has 30 days to pay the net amount. However, a buyer who pays the bill in 10 days will receive a 2% discount. Sellers can use multiple discounts in addition to cash discounts, such as seasonal or volume discounts, to obtain even greater savings.

cash flow—Cash flow refers to the difference between what a company brings in and what it pays out. Companies can keep track of cash payments and receipts with a cash flow statement.

cash system of accounting—The cash system of accounting calculates expenditures and income only when cash is actually paid or received. This system does not consider accounts receivable or accounts payable.

cats and dogs—A derogatory term referring to stocks that represent a poor investment choice because of their highly speculative nature.

certificate of deposit (CD)—CDs are a type of savings account that pay more than traditional passbook or other savings accounts. They earn higher interest because the depositor has to keep the money in the CD for a longer maturity period than for other types of accounts.

clear title—When real or personal property is sold, the buyer normally wants the property to have a clear title, which means that no liens or other claims exist against the property. If the property is subject to a court-ordered lien, it can still be resold, but with a clouded title.

collateral—Collateral is either real or personal property pledged as security for repaying a loan.

commercial paper (CP)—Larger, stable corporations issue commercial paper, or unsecured promissory notes from the corporation for amounts over $25,000. Commercial paper typically carries a higher interest rate than bank accounts or CDs and typically matures in 30, 60, or 90 days.

common stock—Common stocks are shares in either privately held or public companies and represent an equity interest in those companies. While common stock shareholders own an equity share in the company, if a company goes bankrupt, they are paid only after bondholders and preferred stock shareholders are paid. Stockholders have specific rights, including the right to elect the board of directors and the right of preemption that entitles them to buy any new stocks from the company before other investors can. Preemption helps the stockholder maintain a proportional share in the company.

compensating balance—Some banks allow a depositor to borrow money but demand that the borrower maintain a specified balance in the bank. Thus, the bank might loan you $10,000 but insist that you maintain a 10% compensating balance to help hedge against the possibility of your defaulting on the loan. The borrower normally does not earn interest on the compensating balance, which effectively increases the interest on the loan. For example, assume that the $10,000 loan has a required interest payment of 8%. Since the $1,000 compensating balance does not earn interest, the true interest rate for the loan is $800 / ($10,000 − $1,000), which equals 8.89%.

compounding—Compounding entails retaining an investment's return from subsequent years after the initial investment, which results in accruing more revenue than if the investment's return was withdrawn immediately upon receipt. Thus, compounding can significantly increase an investment's total return as highlighted in the **compound interest** example below.

compound interest—With many loans, interest is added to the principal loaned amount over the loan's life. If you borrowed $100 at 10% interest compounded annually, you would owe $110 after the first year, $121 for the second year ($110 × 110%), $133 for the third year ($121 × 110%), and so on throughout the life of the loan.

consumer credit—Consumer credit includes all nonbusiness debt (personal debt) excluding mortgages. Credit card debt represents part of the overall consumer credit.

Consumer Credit Protection Act (CCPA), also called the **Truth in Lending Act**—The CCPA requires a lender to clearly disclose the loan terms, interest rate, total payments, and total interest amount.

consumer finance companies—Sometimes a consumer has a poor credit history, and banks are unwilling to loan the individual any money. A consumer finance company can also loan the consumer money, through either a secured or an unsecured loan, for a short term and at a higher interest rate. The interest rate is higher because the loan is riskier.

consumer price index (CPI)—The Bureau of Labor Statistics publishes a monthly CPI number, which represents an average of the prices of various goods and services that consumers typically purchase in various urban areas. The CPI provides insight into the purchasing power of the U.S. dollar.

contingency fund—A contingency fund is a reserve account that an individual or entity has put money into to help pay unforeseen bills or cover emergency monetary needs.

conventional mortgage—Typically, mortgages are obtained after a buyer has provided a sizable down payment on real property and offers fixed monthly payments at a set interest rate over a 15- or 30-year term.

convertibles—Convertibles is the term used to describe bonds, debentures, or preferred stocks that can be converted to common stock or other securities. An investor might convert the bonds or preferred stock to obtain an ownership interest or to benefit from dividends or continued growth. Convertible preferred stock can be converted according to a preset conversion price formula at a specified date. Debentures can also be converted to stocks if they are convertible debentures.

corporate bond—A company can issue a debt security (bond) with semiannual interest payments that is traded on the major exchanges. These bonds typically have a $1,000 face value. Bonds are backed by either collateral or the full faith and credit of the corporation.

corporate earnings—Corporate earnings are calculated by subtracting costs from sales. If earnings increase, stock prices should increase; and if earnings decrease, stock prices should decrease. This happened in late 1998, when corporate earnings slid, causing the Dow Jones Industrial Average to drop almost 2,000 points.

cosign—Lending institutions may be reluctant to loan an individual or company money because of a poor credit history. However, if a cosigner agreed to repay the loan if it went into default, the lending institution would be much more likely to make the loan. The cosigner becomes liable for the entire loan if the borrower defaults.

coupon—When interest is due on a bond, the bondholder can clip the coupon from the bond and present it to a designated institution such as a bank to obtain payment.

creative financing—Sometimes a borrower cannot obtain a mortgage and may pursue creative financing to obtain money from a third party. Creative financing could entail a balloon payment, assumption of a prior mortgage on a property, or an adjustable rate mortgage.

credit—Credit refers to any purchase made on account, which would be paid at a later. In accounting terms, a credit represents an increase in funds and is usually listed on the right side in the T-account system. See also **debit.**

creditor—Anyone who is owed money is a creditor.

credit rating—Lenders use credit ratings to determine the risks associated with any given loan or extension of credit. Factors such as job history, housing, income, assets, and credit history help determine an individual's credit rating. Credit rating is a process that tracks an individual's or company's ability to repay borrowed money. Lenders use credit ratings to determine if any new moneys might be advanced.

current assets—Assets that are expected to be converted to cash in one year or less. Examples of current assets that appear on balance sheets are cash and short-term financial assets.

current ratio (CR)—Current ratio expresses a company's ability to cover current liabilities with current assets. To calculate CR, we divide current assets by current liabilities. If a company has $400 million in current assets and $100 million in current liabilities, the CR is 4 to 1, which means the current assets can cover current liabilities four times over.

current yield—The current yield is an investment's return in relation to its current value. For a bond, the annual interest payments are divided by the bond's current market value. If you had a $1,000 bond paying 10% interest, and the bond had a par value of $950, then your current yield would be $100 / $950 = 10.5%.

custodial account—A parent or guardian can establish a custodial account for a minor. The account belongs to the minor, but the minor is allowed to make transactions only with the custodian's approval.

days sales outstanding (DSO)—DSO is also referred to as the average collection period (ACP), which represents the length of time it is taking customers to repay debt owed to the company. A high DSO means that a company is not effectively collecting its accounts receivable or that credit is being extended to inappropriate customers.

debenture—Debentures are long-term bonds that are not secured by any collateral. As these bonds are backed by a company's good name and credit history, companies need good credit ratings to issue debentures.

debit—A debit represents any decrease in revenue or net worth and is documented by being listed on the left side of a T-account. See also **credit.**

debt—Debt is any money, goods, or services owed to someone else on the basis of a prior contractual agreement.

debt-equity ratio—The debt-equity ratio is one of the ratios obtained from analysis of financial statements and is used to determine how much protection creditors have. To calculate the ratio, divide total liabilities by total shareholders' equity. If a company has long-term debt of $200 million and shareholders' equity of $400 million, the debt-equity ratio is 0.5 to 1. If the debt-equity ratio is higher than 1, the company is not as good an investment as others, as the company is paying significant interest costs relative to its assets. If a company is highly leveraged, it is not as good a credit risk compared to companies with low debt-equity ratios.

debtor—A debtor is anyone who has a legal or moral obligation to pay a debt to a creditor.

debt securities—A debt security is any security such as a bond, note, or contract that proves the existence of a debt obligation. Stocks are not a debt security, but rather an **equity** security.

debt service—Debt service refers to the repayment of an obligation. The debt service on some new stadiums will be about $20 million per year for approximately 30 years.

deduction—The IRS allows specific deductions such as state and local taxes, employee expenses, and charitable contributions to reduce a taxpayer's **adjusted gross income (AGI).**

deep-discount bond—Bonds can fall out of favor with investors for various reasons (e.g., when the coupon rate is lower than current yield rates available from newer bonds); and when a bond declines over 25% below its face value, it is called a deep-discount bond.

deferred annuity—A deferred annuity is an **annuity** that begins paying out after a specified period of time. The payout could begin either on a specific date or on the date of a particular event, such as a person's retirement.

deferred profit-sharing plan—If a company has a good year, it can share a portion of the profit through an employee trust to give employees a percentage of their salary as a bonus. The primary benefit of such plans for the company is that they are deductible as a business expense if they meet IRS requirements.

deficit—A deficit represents any excess of expenses over income. In order to overcome the income-expense disparity, a company or individual needs to either reduce savings to cover losses or borrow money.

deflation—Deflation, which is the opposite of **inflation,** refers to conditions in which prices decline over a given period. The reduced prices are normally the result of fewer dollars in the economy.

delisting—If a company fails to follow specified stock exchange rules or regulations such as maintaining a minimum net worth, the company can be delisted from its exchange. Delisting can also occur when a company closes or merges with another company, in which case shareholders with stock in the company are issued different stocks.

demand deposit account—A checking account is an example of a demand deposit account. Funds can be withdrawn on demand through the writing or cashing of a check.

deposit insurance—Federal agencies such as the Federal Deposit Insurance Corporation can insure bank accounts to foster a sense of safety on the part of depositors.

depreciation—Every item deteriorates over time, and a business must replace items as they deteriorate. A business can better afford to purchase new equipment if it takes a charge against earnings (reduces earnings) to write off the costs of a depreciating asset based on a specified formula. The formula is derived from the depreciation base. Assume you buy a computer for $6,000 that has an estimated life of five years. After five years you could sell the computer for its salvage value of $1,000. The depreciation base is the initial cost minus the salvage value, or $5,000 in this case. The depreciation base is divided by the asset's life (five years) to produce a yearly depreciation of $1,000.

direct costs—Direct costs are directly associated with a given program. The direct costs for team promotion might include all costs associated with advertising, personnel, and related costs.

discharge—The completion of the debt process through repayment of a financial obligation is called discharging the debt. A discharge in bankruptcy is a final court order whereby the debtor is relieved of all further debt obligations.

disclaimer—Accountants or auditors who have not had enough time or information to make a conclusive decision about a company's financial statement can prepare a report with a disclaimer. The disclaimer can indicate that some uncertainties exist, for example a pending IRS audit or a lawsuit that can significantly jeopardize the company's financial position.

disclosure—All financial statements, including a company's annual report, must fully disclose all relevant facts such as contractual terms, debt issues, and equity adjustments. Under **Securities and Exchange Commission** regulations, a publicly traded company has to fully disclose to stockholders any disastrous event that could affect the company's financial condition, such as the death of a key executive or major research and development failures.

discount bond—A discount **bond** is sold in the marketplace below its **face value.**

discount broker—A discount broker is a stockbroker who does not give investment advice but performs trades for clients at a reduced price.

discounted net cash flow—This is a means to determine an investment's value by examining after-tax cash flows and return on an investment. By examining income streams and reducing them to represent the present value of money, an investor can critically examine how much should be paid for a given investment in order to generate a given rate of return.

discount factor, or **present value factor**—The discount factor is an arithmetic calculation that is used to help calculate the **present value** of a given investment.

discounting—Discounting is the formula used to determine the present value of a sum of money to be received in the future. Comprehensive tables allow individuals to easily determine the **present value** of given sums assuming various inflation rates.

discount rate—The discount rate is the interest rate or percent return that can be earned from an investment. The discount rate is used when determining the **present value** of an investment option.

discretionary funds—Discretionary funds are moneys set aside for incidental expenses. Typically an executive is given significant latitude in spending discretionary funds.

disposable income—Disposable income is the amount of money available to individuals after they have had taxes, contributions to benefits, union dues, and related deductions taken from their paycheck.

diversification—In order to reduce investment-related risks, investors often diversify their investments so that if one fails, the overall loss will not be as significant as it would with a single investment. Mutual funds are a classic example of diversification in that the funds traditionally purchase numerous stocks, which helps reduce investor risks.

dividend—A company's board of directors can set aside a portion of the company's net income to benefit the shareholders. Cash dividends can be given, but once received by the shareholder they are taxable. This double taxation (company pays taxes on income and then taxpayers get taxed on their dividends) is one of the key drawbacks to the corporation structure of business. **Stock dividends** consisting of additional shares of stock can also be allocated by the board of directors and are not taxed upon receipt by the shareholder. When additional stocks are given as a dividend, the stockholder pays taxes only when selling them.

dividend payout ratio—Dividend payments can be expressed as a percentage of net earnings: dividends per share are divided by earnings per share. Assume that a company has $1 million in earnings and that the board has approved a $50,000 dividend payout to the company's 25,000 outstanding shares. The **dividend per share** is $50,000 / 25,000 shares, or $2. The **earnings per share** are $1,000,000 / 25,000, or $40. The dividend payout ratio is $2 / $40, or 5%.

dividend per share (DPS)—If a $1 million dividend is declared and there are 1 million shares outstanding, the DPS is $1.

dividend reinvestment plan—Stockholders use a dividend reinvestment plan to plow their dividend payments back into purchasing more shares. This approach saves money, as the stockholder does not need to pay any stockbroker commissions.

dividend yield—This ratio helps determine what the percentage return is for a stock that pays a dividend. To calculate the dividend yield ratio, we divide the dividends per share by the stock's market price per share. A stock that is selling for $10 per share and receiving a $0.50 dividend per share has a 5% dividend yield ($0.50 / $10).

dollar-cost averaging—An investor can reduce the risks associated with stock volatility by investing a given amount of money in a stock on a regular basis no matter what the stock price is. Using this technique, an individual could put aside $100 a month to invest in a given company. Whether the price is $10 or $75 per share, the same $100 is always invested, and over the long haul the investor using this approach is normally very successful.

Dow Jones Industrial Average (Dow)—This average tracks the price of 30 blue chip stocks actively traded on the New York Stock Exchange to serve as a guide to how the stock market is performing. The price-weighted average takes the stocks' closing prices and adjusts the prices to reflect stock splits and dividends.

downside risk analysis—The downside risk analysis approach is a worst-case scenario process in which an investor examines the total potential loss from an investment to help determine whether to enter into an investment or whether to sell an investment.

dowry—A dowry is the total value of property, money, and other assets a prospective wife brings to a marriage.

draft—A draft is a note, such as a check, indicating the transfer of funds from one party to another. The person to whom the check is written is called the payee. The person writing the check is the drawer, and the institution being instructed to pay the payee is the drawee. See also **demand deposit**.

early-withdrawal penalty—Investors who have money deposited in certain investments such as individual retirement accounts or CDs may have to pay a penalty if they withdraw the investment before the investment's actual maturity date. Thus, you would have to pay a penalty if you had a six-month CD and cashed it in after only four months.

discount factor, or **present value factor**—The discount factor is an arithmetic calculation that is used to help calculate the present value of a given investment decision.

discount rate—The discount rate is the interest rate or percent return that can be earned from an investment. The discount rate is used when determining the present value of an investment option.

earned income—Earned income is any income obtained through performing labor. Earned income contrasts with passive income, which is income generated from sources, such as stocks or bonds, that do not require any labor.

earnest money—Earnest money is the sum of money given by a buyer to a seller for the purpose of holding a contract open to the buyer for a certain time period. Thus, if you wanted to buy a used car but wanted to check the car out for a day, you could put down an earnest-money deposit. If the car proved acceptable, you would complete the contractual process with the seller. The earnest-money deposit can serve as an earnest-money credit toward the purchase price.

earnings before interest and taxes (EBIT)—EBIT represent a company's earned income not taking into consideration any owed interest or taxes.

earnings per share (EPS)—Earnings per share helps highlight how much each share of stock is earning in dollar terms and represents one of the most important tools to measure a company's success. To calculate EPS, the company's net income is divided by the total number of outstanding shares. If the company's income is $1 million and there are 1 million outstanding shares, the EPS is $1.

earnings yield—Earnings yield is the opposite of the price-earnings ratio. This ratio measures the yield obtained from a stock. The higher the yield, the better. For example, if a company's earnings per share is $5 and the market price is $20, then the earnings yield is 25%.

economic indicators—The government, investors, and businesses analyze various economic indicators to help determine market conditions. Ex-

amples of leading economic indicators include the **gross national product,** the **consumer price index,** money supply indicators, and the **Dow Jones Industrial Average.**

economics—Economics blends art and science to help explain and chart the most effective and efficient use of scarce resources. Microeconomics analyzes individual markets such as baseball, football, or basketball. Macroeconomics analyzes the big picture, such as the national economy or global economy.

effective annual rate (EAR)—The EAR represents the real annual rate of return for an investment.

effective interest rate—The effective interest rate represents the real rate of interest paid on a loan. To calculate the effective interest rate, the nominal interest rate is divided by the loan amount.

employee stock ownership plan (ESOP)—An ESOP is a plan designed to give employees an ownership interest in the company through distributing company stocks to employees. ESOPs typically vest (allow for collection) when an employee leaves or retires. This allows the stocks to increase in value without the employees having to pay taxes until they are at a lower income level, thus reducing their final tax obligations.

Equal Credit Opportunity Act (ECOA)—The ECOA is a federal law that makes it illegal to discriminate against a loan applicant based on race, age, religion, or gender. The law requires all lenders to respond within 30 days to any applicant and to identify the specific reason an applicant was denied.

equity—Equity refers to an individual's net worth or a company's stock ownership value.

equity investment—An equity investment is an investment in a company through the purchase of company stock.

estate—All real and personal property owned by an individual at the time of the person's death belongs to that person's estate. If a person dies with a will, the will specifies how the estate should be distributed. The federal government charges an estate tax based on the estate's value; the first $600,000 (scheduled to increase to $1.2 million in 2007) is tax free.

even lot—Even lots are standard blocks of stocks. An even-lot block on the New York Stock Exchange contains 100 shares.

excise taxes—Numerous taxes exist for various consumed goods. These taxes are generally lumped under the designation excise taxes and are sometimes added to the purchase price of such items as gas, alcohol, and tobacco.

ex-dividend (XD)—Prior to the date on which a company records a stock dividend is a four-day freeze that allows the stock to trade, but without the right to obtain the dividend. The waiting period is based on the fact that stock transactions typically take five days to settle. Stocks subject to the XD provision normally trade at a reduced price that reflects the market price minus the expected dividend payment.

exempt income—Exempt income is income that is exempt from taxation, such as income from tax-exempt municipal bonds used to finance some stadiums or arenas.

expendable outlays—Expendable outlays are payments for items that are relatively low in cost and are frequently purchased, such as office supplies.

expenditure—An expenditure is any payment made to satisfy a financial obligation or to purchase assets.

expenses—Expenses are any payments, reduction in value (such as depreciation), or a new legal obligation (such as entering into a binding contract).

experience rating—Insurance companies use a statistical method to determine insurance premiums based on past claims and projections for future claims. Experience ratings allow an insurance company to properly determine the potential payout for a given policy, which helps set the premium price for the policy.

F—F, as used in financial calculations, represents a company's fixed operating costs or expected rate of return from a risk-free investment.

face value—The face value, or face amount, is the stated value for a bond or other security. Most bonds, for example, have a $1,000 face value, but can be sold for an amount higher or lower than the indicated value. In addition to a face value, a security has a face interest rate, which is the interest rate guaranteed for the security when the security was issued.

Fair Credit Billing Act (FCBA)—The FCBA is a federal law that is designed to correct problems in credit billing and complaints and that establishes time limits under which bills need to be sent and complaints filed. A similar law, the Fair Credit Reporting Act, establishes specific requirements concerning the use of and access to personal credit information.

Federal Deposit Insurance Corporation (FDIC)—The FDIC is a federal agency that insures bank accounts up to $100,000 per each depositor at the bank. All national banks and most commercial banks obtain FDIC insurance to reduce the risk for potential depositors. Prior to the savings and loan fallout in the 1980s, the federal government ran the Federal Savings and Loan Insurance Corporation, whose duties were assumed by the FDIC after the savings and loan disaster.

Federal Reserve System (Fed)—The Fed was established by Congress in 1913 and comprises 12 Federal Reserve district banks, branches, and all national and state banks (over 5,800). The system operates to manage the nation's money supply by raising or lowering the reserve amount that banks need to keep on hand, by changing the discount rate charged to commercial banks for borrowing money, and by purchasing and selling government securities (Siegel, Shim, & Hartman, 1992). The system operates similarly to a bank in that member banks can deposit funds in and borrow funds from the Fed in order to run more effectively.

finance charge—Nothing is free, and finance charges are a vehicle that assists in the transfer of money. The two types of finance charges are interest rates and points. Points can be charged when individuals apply for or are given a loan; each point charged represents 1% of the loan amount. Thus, if you were to refinance your home mortgage with a lower interest rate, the lending institution might charge you 1 or 2 points to process the loan, which for a $50,000 loan could be $500 or $1,000, just to obtain the loan.

financial assets—Financial assets are items of value that are intangible, but represent the ownership interest in a business or the investments that are funding the business. Financial assets include bonds, common stock, preferred stock, **money market certificates,** Treasury bills, and related instruments.

financial exigency—A financial exigency is an urgent financial situation, for example an athletic department losing a Title IX suit and having to add several new women's teams when it is already losing money.

financial leverage—Financial leverage represents the portion of a company's assets that are financed with debt rather than equity. It is normally beneficial to reinvest your own money (equity) rather than borrow funds; but if you can reinvest borrowed funds and obtain a rate of return greater than your interest and principal payments on the borrowed funds, then leveraging represents a potential strong option for growth.

financial leverage ratios—These are various ratios that help identify how a company is financed and whether it has undertaken too much debt to grow. These ratios include the acid test ratio, current ratio, debt ratio, and debt-equity ratio.

financial statements—Corporations report their financial condition in annual, semiannual, and quarterly reports that contain numerous financial statements such as balance sheets, income statements, and cash flow statements.

first in, first out (FIFO)—FIFO has different meanings in banking and inventory management. Using the FIFO method, a bank withdraws any debt from the earliest deposits in an account. Under this method, depositors lose interest, as earlier deposits are reduced by withdrawals, and this makes saving less beneficial. For example, if you deposited $1,000 in June and $1,000 in July but wrote a check for $500 in July, you would earn interest on only $500 in June ($1,000 – $500) but would earn interest on $1,000 for July. The same principle applies to inventory management application of FIFO.

fiscal year—A company's fiscal year is a one-year period used as a basis for analyzing the company's financial performance and creating new budgets for the coming year. Many companies have August 31 as the first date of the fiscal year and the following August 30 as the last day of the fiscal year.

five C's—Lenders often use five C's when reviewing a loan application. The five C's are (1) current economic *conditions*, (2) the **collateral** that will be used to secure the loan, (3) the **capital** available to the loan applicant (does the applicant have a positive net worth?), (4) the *capacity* of the applicant to earn enough to cover all expenses including the loan costs, and (5) the *character* of the loan applicant (is the loan applicant a reliable person or company?). After analyzing the five C's, a lender normally assigns a loan applicant a **credit rating** that will help determine the default risk for the applicant.

fixed assets—Fixed assets are permanent assets such as buildings or equipment required to run a business. Ice rinks, locker rooms, rental counters, spectator seating, and a Zamboni® are all examples of fixed assets.

fixed charge—Fixed charges are obligations that occur on a regular basis, such as taxes, rent, insurance, electrical bills, and related expenses.

fixed costs—Fixed costs are regular expenses that are incurred regardless of activity, inactivity, or level of activity. Rent is a fixed cost, as the same amount is owed regardless of potential business activity. Other examples are taxes, insurance premiums, and fixed-salaried personnel.

fixed income—Fixed income does not change over time; a fixed pension plan for former professional athletes, for example, might pay an athlete $2,000 a month for life.

fixed interest rate—A fixed interest rate does not change over time; in contrast, interest on a variable rate interest loan, such as on some credit cards that are tied to various federally adjusted interest rates, changes over time.

flat rate—Items that are purchased on a flat rate basis cost the same no matter what quantity is purchased. When the rate can change based on quantity purchased, the price is considered variable rate.

float—A float exists for money held by a bank or savings institution for checks that have not yet been cashed or deposits that have yet to be credited to a depositor's account.

Form 10-Q and **Form 10-K**—The Securities and Exchange Commission requires publicly traded companies to file specific quarterly (10-Q) and annual (10-K) reports featuring comprehensive financial statements.

formula budgeting—Formula budgeting involves establishing predetermined amounts that will be spent on various costs. Thus, if a team earns $1 per hot dog sold, the expenses and revenue can be calculated in the budget by estimating the total number of hot dogs that will be sold by both the purchase and potential sales price.

full faith and credit—See **bond.**

future value (FV)—Future value refers to the value that a given investment or security might have at a given time in the future. An investment's future value can be determined through various means, including the use of a future value table. FV_n is the future value at a specific (n) period. The opposite of future value is **present value.**

garnishment—An individual may lose in a legal proceeding or be required by law to make certain restitutions. Through garnishment, the person's wages, assets, or property can be attached, and any recovery can be used to pay the outstanding obligation. Attachment is the process where a court official or sheriff officially starts the collection process. For wage garnishment the sheriff could serve the employer with the court order requiring wage garnishment.

general mortgage bond—These bonds are collateralized by a blanket coverage over all company assets. However, these bonds are subordinate to (have lesser significance than) any bond collateralized by specific property. Thus, a general mortgage bond might cover all office equipment as collateral and be subordinate to another bond or obligation collateralized by photocopier machines.

general obligation bonds (GOBs)—GOBs are municipal bonds issued for such projects as stadiums or arenas, with the interest and principal payments backed by the **full faith and credit** of the municipality that issues the bonds. This means that the bonds are backed by all the taxes collected by the municipality even if such taxes are not used for the facility. Under such a bond, a stadium could be constructed from a bond backed by a ticket surcharge. If the host team moves and there are no other tenants, no ticket surcharges would be collected to pay back the bondholders. The bondholders could then proceed against property tax collections or any other taxes for repayment.

golden handcuff—In order to prevent key employees from leaving, a company can give key employees significant stock options and a pension plan that are designed to penalize them if they leave the company prior to a given date. Under such a plan, an employee might have 5,000 stock options available after two years, 10,000 after four years, and 25,000 after six years.

golden parachute—Golden parachutes are given to top-level executives, offering these individuals significant money, benefits, or both if the company is purchased and the executive is subsequently terminated. Such an agreement is often created to make a company less attractive for a hostile suitor to purchase.

goodwill—Goodwill represents the difference between a company's book value and its market value. The difference is based on the fact that the company has value that is not reflected on its books, or if goodwill is on the books, is an additional value based on various valuation techniques. The name Coca-Cola®, for example, represents a tremendous asset (a world-recognized name) that is hard to place a value on. However, some have placed the value on the goodwill of the name at over $2 billion since that is possibly how much it would cost to develop a similar brand name with world-wide recognition.

gross national product (GNP)—The GNP is a calculation of the total value of products manufactured and services provided in the United States in a given year.

gross national product deflator—The U.S. Department of Commerce publishes a quarterly weighted average of the gross national product to more accurately reflect the price changes for goods and services purchased by consumers, businesses, and the government.

gross profit margin—The gross profit margin is the income of a company before operating expenses, interest, and taxes are paid.

guaranteed dividend—Some stocks pay a regular dividend that is assured by a third party such as the government.

hedging—Investors understand that investments by their very nature comprise various risks. Thus, investors try to hedge potential losses by undertaking risk reduction strategies such as diversifying their holdings or purchasing insurance.

high-grade security—Stocks or bonds categorized as high grade have the best investment quality ratings, such as AAA. Independent companies establish the rating after reviewing a company's assets, liabilities, earnings, dividends, management, and related factors.

holder of record—The holder of record is the person whose name is recorded as the purchaser or owner of a given security. Proper recording of ownership is critical for determining who will receive dividends, as only the holder of record receives dividends.

holding period return (HPR)—This calculation determines the total return earned when an investment is held for a given period. HPR = (current income + capital gains) / purchase price. If you purchased a stock for $10 and sold it one year later for $12, and during the year received a $1 dividend, then the HPR would be ($1 + $12 − $10) / 10 = 3 / 10, or 30%.

illiquid—A company is illiquid when it does not have sufficient liquid assets such as stocks and marketable securities to cover short-term debt.

implicit costs—Also called **opportunity costs**, implicit costs represent the cost of the next best alternative forgone. If you build a stadium, you will receive a certain return. However, you also face certain lost income, because with the same money you could have built a convention center that might have had a greater impact on a given community.

incentive stock option (ISO)—An ISO is another option for transferring stocks to employees and is considered a benefit such as profit sharing. Compared with other stock-option plans, an ISO receives more favorable tax treatment.

income—Any money received during a given time period by either an individual or a company is considered income. Income can be derived from such sources as salaries, investment returns, asset sales, and many others.

income statement—An income statement tracks a company's revenue and expenses over any given time period. The following is a sample income statement for Sport Manufacturing Company.

Income Statement

	($000)
Sales	500
Less: Material and labor	300
Manufacturing costs	30
Cost of goods sold	**330**
Gross profit	**170**
Depreciation	20
Selling expense	20
Profit before interest and taxes	**130**
Interest payments	10
Taxes	40
Profit after taxes	**80**
Dividends	40
Retained earnings	**40**

income tax—Income tax is a levy imposed by the government on an individual's taxable income. The taxable income is calculated by deducting all allowable deductions (such as unreimbursed business expenses) from the gross income.

index of leading economic indicators—This index consists of several key economic indicators that help shed light on the economy's future direction. The index is published on a monthly basis by the U.S. Department of Commerce and analyzes such data as unemployment claims; stock prices; money supply; new building permits; changes in inventories; new orders for consumer and manufactured goods; vendor delivery delays; and the prices for oil, steel, and other essential materials.

indirect costs—Indirect costs are costs not associated with a specific activity. Administrative overhead and secretarial support are typical indirect costs, as these obligations arise even if a given activity does not appear to need such assistance.

industrial development bond (IDB)—Municipalities can issue tax-exempt bonds to fund the building of factories or facilities that are then leased to private industries. Such bonds are usually issued to help attract new businesses to a region.

inflation—Inflation represents an increase in the price level of products that could be due to increased demand. The increased demand for products can force prices to increase, which leads to a chain reaction of increasing wages and material costs.

initial public offering (IPO)—An IPO represents a company's first attempt at issuing and hopefully selling stocks to the public.

insider and **insider trading**—An insider is someone who has access to privileged information about a company that can affect the company's stock price. If the insider uses this information to make money on the stock or provides the information to anyone else to help that person make money, then everyone who has relied on such information has engaged in insider trading. Insider trading is a criminal offense if the trading is based on inside information. Insider trading is not always illegal if a company insider decides to purchase or sell company stocks and reports any such trades to the **Securities and Exchange Commission** within a specified time period.

interest (i)—Interest is the amount a lender charges for loaning money to a borrower. **Interest rates** are normally expressed in relation to an annual period. Interest can also mean an equity ownership position with a company. Thus, a professional sport team could own a 10% interest in a broadcast station, which means it owns 10% of the station.

interest coverage (IC)—IC represents a company's ability to repay a loan by making required interest payments. Interest coverage is calculated by adding pretax income and interest expense and then dividing that sum by the interest expense. Thus, if a company had $90 million in pretax income and $10 million in interest expense, the IC would be ($90 + $10) / $10 = 10 times.

interest rate—The interest rate represents the cost of borrowing money expressed in percentage terms over the course of a year. A bank might loan a business a certain sum at an interest rate of 10% a year.

interim financing—Businesses often need some money for a short period between deals or to help finance a quick deal; this borrowing is called interim financing.

internal rate of return (IRR)—This calculation is designed to provide an investor with the effective annual return from a given investment. The initial cash investment is analyzed in comparison with the present value of cash returns.

intrinsic value—Intrinsic value refers to the true value of any property or investment. The true value of a company can be determined through financial analysis, and this value may be different from the company's book value. Such a difference may be attributable to intangible assets such as a health club's goodwill associated with many years of quality client service.

inventory turnover ratio (ITR)—The ITR represents how frequently a business is able to process and sell inventory. The higher the ITR, the more frequently the business is buying inventory and selling finished goods. A high number is usually a good sign; however, if the business is a specialty manufacturer, such as handmade items, the ITR might be very low.

investment club—Single investors may not have the resources to make certain investments. However, people can create investment clubs in which multiple investors combine their money to acquire better investments through greater buying power.

jumbo certificate of deposit—A jumbo certificate of deposit is a CD with a minimum denomination of $100,000. Although jumbos carry a higher interest rate than CDs with lower values, they are not covered by the Federal Deposit Insurance Corporation.

junk bond—A high-yield bond with a low credit rating is called a junk bond. Smaller or new companies without a significant financial track record of sales or earnings often issue these bonds.

last in, first out (LIFO)—The LIFO method is used to calculate both bank interest payments and inventory values. This method does not penalize investors as much as the FIFO method, but still hurts investors compared with those who receive interest on the actual amount in a given bank account. When we use LIFO to analyze inventories, we calculate ending inventory levels by subtracting the cost of the most recently purchased inventory from the total inventory before we subtract earlier inventories. This formula takes into account the realities of repurchasing subsequent inventories at a higher price.

layering—In order to garner necessary protection, a baseball team can purchase a $100,000 property liability insurance policy from one broker, a similar policy for $50,000 from another insurer, and an umbrella policy for $1 million. This results in a layering of insurance policies and may be required if certain insurers are not willing to underwrite the entire protection amount required.

lease option—If the owners of a health club wish to rent a warehouse, they might not want to sign a long-term lease that could bind them for significant payments even if the venture was not successful. Instead, with a lease option, they can lease for a specific time period and then have the option of renewing the lease for additional specified periods. The benefit for the tenant is the ability to reduce long-term debt concerns if things go wrong. The landlord benefits in that such a lease option typically results in a higher rent, and the rent normally increases each time the option is exercised.

lender—A lender is any individual or entity that lends money to a borrower for a given interest rate for repayment within a specified time.

letter of credit (LC)—If you owned a sporting goods store, you could approach a bank for a letter of credit to help buy more inventory. An LC from the bank to the seller guarantees your credit for a given time period up to a certain amount. Thus, depending on its assessment of your financial strength, the bank could provide a $100,000 LC to be used to help buy inventory. The LC is like a loan from the bank that can be used at any time.

letter of intent—A letter of intent is a document among parties expressing intent to take or to refrain from taking certain actions. Two sporting goods stores could enter into a letter of intent to merge at a future date. Letters of intent are often a precursor to entering a formal contractual agreement, which often takes months; a letter of intent can provide very rough terms and can be completed in several hours.

leveraged buyout (LBO)—You can buy a professional sport franchise using borrowed funds in what is often called a leveraged buyout. The LBO is often completed using the assets of the purchased company as collateral to secure the borrowed funds, and the income or cash flow of the business is used to repay the loan.

leveraging—Leveraging is using borrowed money to make a greater return on investment than what could have been earned if no additional funds were available. Leverage is used only when the expected return on the investment will more than cover the expense of borrowing the funds.

liabilities—The term *liabilities* refers to any legal or financial obligation. Typical examples are long-term debt, retained earnings, shareholders' equity, and taxes owed. Liabilities are the opposite of **assets.**

life cycle costs—These are costs that are generated from the inception through termination of a product. If you owned a fitness equipment manufacturing company, your product life cycle costs would include all research, development, prototype, market research, test marketing, full sales, and product withdrawal or cancellation costs. Traditionally costs are greatest when a product is initially developed.

limited partner—Unlike traditional partners who are wholly liable for a partnership's losses, limited partners can be liable only for their own investment into a partnership. Limited partnerships are attractive in that the investor can maintain an ownership interest while reducing liability exposure. A general partner in a limited partnership invests capital, helps manage the business, and is personally liable for partnership debts.

line-item budget—A line-item budget lists every expense and revenue source on a separate line to help administrators identify every single source of revenue or expenses.

line of credit—A line of credit represents the maximum preapproved amount a company or individual can borrow without having to go to a different lending source.

liquid—Being liquid is a condition in which an individual or company has enough cash or liquid assets that can be sold quickly (CDs, Treasury bonds, high-quality corporate bonds, stocks, etc.) to meet current debt obligations. Inventories are traditionally not considered liquid because it can take time to sell inventory. Accounts receivable (A/R) are similar in that it can take time to collect them. Factoring, which entails selling inventories or A/R, is rapidly changing the nature of liquid assets, as inventories and A/R can now be sold in a relatively short amount of time.

liquidity—Liquidity can represent the number of stock shares available for investors to trade. Strong liquidity means there is a good supply of stocks available for purchase or trade.

loan—A loan is a transaction between a lender and a borrower in which the borrower contractually agrees to repay the principal amount and interest. By repaying the loan in a systematic manner, the borrower engages in loan **amortization.**

loan origination fee—In addition to principal, interest, and points, a lender can also impose additional fees on the borrower, including fees for credit checks, auditing of checks, appraisals, title searches, and related expenses required to protect the lender.

loan-to-value ratio (LTV)—The LTV is the ratio of the principal amount borrowed to the collateral's actual value or fair market value (amount borrowed divided by actual value). If you buy a house for $100,000 and take out a mortgage for $60,000, then the LTV is 60%.

loss prevention—Risk management techniques can be used to reduce the chances of being sued. One strategy for reducing financial risk involves purchasing liability, property, casualty, or other insurance policies.

low grade—Investments such as bonds that do not have strong industry ratings are considered low-grade investments and are riskier than high-grade investments.

lump sum distribution—Instead of borrowing money and making monthly payments to satisfy the loan, you could agree to make a lump sum payment at the loan's due date. A retirement pension or other obligation can also be repaid in a lump sum.

margin—If you do not have enough money to purchase stock with cash, you can purchase stock on credit with the remainder being advanced by the stockbroker. The stocks are kept by the broker as collateral. If you want to buy $10,000 worth of stock, you might need to put down an initial margin requirement of $6,000 while borrowing the remaining $4,000 from the broker. The stock purchaser in essence is borrowing money from the broker and has to pay the broker a given interest rate for using the money. If the price of the security declines and reduces the broker's equity, the broker can issue a margin call that requires the investor to put up more funds to protect the broker. The Federal Reserve Board sets limits on the amount of margins allowed.

margin (profit)—A profit margin (sometimes referred to as a net profit margin) represents profits after taxes divided by sales. This calculation shows whether a company made an acceptable percentage of profit based on total sales. A sport manufacturing company with millions in sales and minimal profits is possibly wasting money. In contrast, a company such as a sport services firm may have a lower income level but a higher profit margin. If Sport Manufacturing Company had an after-tax profit of $2 million based on $5 million in sales, then the profit margin would be 40% ($2 million / $5 million).

marginal cost—The marginal cost is the change in costs associated with the volume produced. If it costs $1 to produce each of 1,000 baseballs and $0.80 each to produce any additional balls, then the marginal cost of producing additional balls is $0.80.

marginal cost of capital (MCC)—When you are taking out a loan, MCC represents how much more you would have to pay to borrow an additional dollar. If the interest rate declines as the amount of a loan gets larger, the MCC will be lower for each additional dollar. If a bank offers a $1 million loan for 6% and a loan over $1 million for 5.75%, then the cost for borrowing each additional dollar over $1 million is .25% less.

marginal tax—The marginal tax is the tax paid on the last dollar earned. Thus, it can be unwise to earn more money after a certain point as the higher earning level results in a higher tax liability.

market—A market is any public location where products or services are bought and sold. There are a number of recognized financial markets, including the New York Stock Exchange, American Stock Exchange, and Chicago Livestock Exchange.

marketable title—A marketable title, one that is free of any problems including financial obligations (called encumbrances), is the most easily transferable property; it is marketable to anyone.

market analysis—A market analysis is any comprehensive analysis of current financial conditions concerning a given company, industry, or the economy.

market indexes, or **market averages**—Various market gauges exist to help investors appreciate market trends. The most famous index is the Dow Jones Industrial Average (Dow), compiled by *The Wall Street Journal* and composed of 30 blue chip stocks (high-quality stocks) that combined represent approximately 20% of the New York Stock Exchange's total value. In the early 1980s, the Dow was around 1,000, but by 1998 it had reached over 8,000. Other indexes include Barron's 50 Stock Average, Standard & Poor's 400 industrials, and Value Line Average.

market-to-book ratio (M/B)—The M/B ratio represents the difference between what a security is listed for on the books and its real market value.

market value—The market value is the true price in a competitive marketplace of a product, service, or investment vehicle. Supply and demand significantly affect the market value, which is why a ticket for the Super Bowl with a face value of $150 may be sold on the street for $2,000. The $2,000 price is the market value.

maturity—Maturity is the time when a loan, bond, or other obligation becomes due and payable. Maturity value is the amount owed once the maturity date is reached.

money—Any legal tender currency, whether in the form of coins, paper bills, or in some situations other valuable items, is considered money. During Napoleon's reign, soldiers were paid in salt, which was considered a form of money at that time.

money market certificate—Money market certificates are similar to certificates of deposit issued by banks, savings and loans, or credit unions; they usually mature in six months.

money market mutual fund—A money market mutual fund pools investors' money and purchases short-term debt securities such as government securities and commercial paper that will mature in less than one year.

Moody's Investor Service, Inc.—Moody's is one of the top investment rating services and is owned by Dun & Bradstreet. The other major investment rating business is Standard & Poor's.

mortgage loan—A mortgage is a long-term loan (typically 15 or 30 years) secured by real property. If the mortgage loan value is less than the property's market value, the property owner may be able to take out another loan called a second mortgage. Thus, if you bought a house for $100,000 but needed a mortgage loan for only $60,000, you might be able to take out a second mortgage loan for around $35,000 to raise money to start a business. A mortgage banker is the individual or company that originates the mortgage loan and can collect payments from the borrower.

multipayment loans—Such loans are often referred to as add-on loans, as the interest payments are added on to the principal. Under the actuarial method, interest is computed on unpaid principal at a fixed rate, with each initial payment being applied first to interest and the remainder to principal. The actuarial method is the simplest and most common method used for such consumer loans as mortgages, with the payment amounts often calculated through computer programs.

multiple of gross income rule—Lenders use a rule of thumb called the multiple of gross income rule to determine whether a borrower can afford a given loan. The formula multiplies the person's income by 2.5 to determine the maximum housing price the individual could afford. Thus, if you earned $50,000 per year, you should be approved for a mortgage loan (if there are no other credit problems, etc.) for a $125,000 home.

municipal bond insurance—Government-issued municipal bonds are traditionally very secure. However, to help attract investors and increase their security (and reduce the amount of interest that needs to be paid), municipalities can purchase insurance to guarantee repayment of the bond.

municipal bonds—Municipal bonds are issued by government entities and have significant benefits such as the security of a government entity to repay the loan and tax deductibility of income from the bond. However, the interest rates are typically lower than for corporate-issued bonds. Municipal bonds are nicknamed "munis."

mutual funds—Mutual funds provide an opportunity for investors to pool their money and buy a diverse collection of investment securities. These funds are very attractive to investors since they do not require a significant investment and the risk of loss is lower because the fund invests in numerous companies. Professional managers make the buy and sell decisions.

National Association of Security Dealers (NASD)—NASD is a self-regulatory organization for stockbrokers/dealers who sell **over-the-counter** stocks. The NASD has strong regulatory requirements including the requirement that dis-putes with brokers be heard in binding arbitration.

National Association of Security Dealers Automatic Quotations (NASDAQ)—NASDAQ is a subsidiary of the NASD and uses electronic networking to help facilitate buying and selling (trading) the **over-the-counter** market's 5,000 most active stocks.

negative amortization—Negative amortization occurs when someone fails to make outstanding loan payments in a high enough amount to cover the interest owed. The low payment then leads to an increase in the balance owed on the loan.

negative cash flow—Negative cash flow occurs when a business spends more than it makes in a given time period.

negotiable instrument—A negotiable instrument is any document that can easily be converted to cash. A bank draft (check written by a bank) represents a negotiable instrument, as any bank will accept and cash such an instrument.

net—Net represents the amount left after all expenses or deductions are subtracted.

net asset value (NAV)—NAV represents a mutual fund's total asset value less any debt, divided by the number of shares outstanding.

net current assets (NCA)—NCA (also called net working capital) refers to the total value of current assets minus current liabilities.

net earnings—Net earnings refers to an individual's take-home pay, which consists of the person's salary minus all tax, insurance, and related deductions.

net income—Net income is calculated by subtracting expenses from revenue.

net present value (NPV)—The NPV is the difference between the **present value** of the future income and the required investment.

net profit margin—The net profit margin is the net income of a company after interest and taxes are paid.

net working capital—Net working capital is the amount of money available to pay bills. It is calculated by subtracting current liabilities from current assets.

net worth—Net worth is the difference between a company's total assets and total liabilities. The resulting number is the owners' or shareholders' equity in the company.

New York Stock Exchange (NYSE)—The NYSE is the largest and most respected security exchange.

Often called the "big board," the NYSE requires new companies wishing to be listed to have, among other characteristics, over 3,000 shareholders and market value over $18 million. The NYSE is currently privately owned, but in 2000 it was exploring a possible public offering. The NYSE works as an auction floor where members who own seats can trade shares of listed companies on behalf of their clients. Current traders do not use actual seats, but the term has survived over the years. A seat can cost around $2 million and gives the owner the privilege of being able to buy and sell NYSE-listed stocks (Ceron, 2000).

no-load mutual fund—A no-load mutual fund is attractive for many investors in that no commission is charged for buying or selling shares.

nominal interest rate—The nominal interest rate is the stated interest rate on a loan or debt. If you had a $10,000 bond with a nominal interest rate of 5%, you would receive $500 in annual interest income.

note (promissory)—A note is a legally transferable debt instrument wherein the borrower agrees to pay a stated amount at a certain date and the obligation is good no matter who eventually owns the note. Thus, after you borrow money and sign a note to purchase a car, the note can be sold to several subsequent companies without affecting your obligation to repay.

not-sufficient-funds check (NSF)—If you buy something at a store and your check bounces, the store will receive an NSF notification from your bank.

novation—A novation is a new contract that can be entered into by various parties who take the place of a former party to a legal obligation. If you borrowed money from a bank to help buy a car but want to sell the car, you can have the car's new buyer sign a novation with the bank to assume your original obligation.

obligation—Any indebtedness, such as a student loan or a mortgage loan, that is owed to anyone else is an obligation.

odd lot—Stocks are traditionally sold in blocks such as 100 shares. An odd lot is any number of shares other than a standard block. An odd lot could consist of one share of stock or even a fraction of one share.

off board—Any purchase of a stock on the over-the-counter or any non-national stock exchange is considered an off-the-board trade.

offer price—The offer price is the initial price a seller asks for a given item or property. If a professional team owner mentions that she would sell a team for $200 million, then the $200 million price tag becomes the offer price.

open-end credit—A credit card is an example of open-end credit. The card holder is given a credit limit when the account is opened, but no debt is actually incurred until the card is used.

opportunity cost—Also called **implicit cost,** opportunity cost is the cost of the next best alternative forgone. If a city invests in a football stadium, then the city will have to forgo building a new convention center that would have been built but for the stadium. This is an additional cost associated with building the stadium, over and beyond the actual construction cost.

option—An option is a contractual right to buy or sell something at later date. If you wanted to buy a sport team for $1 million but needed to secure necessary financial backing, you could pay the team seller $1,000 for a one-month option. This option would give you the opportunity to try to raise necessary funds during that month. If you do not raise the funds, the team goes back on the market. If you do raise the funds, you can buy the team for $1 million. An option is not a deposit, which is why it does not reduce the purchase price.

overdraft—An overdraft occurs when you write a check without sufficient funds in your account, which can result in a not-sufficient-funds notice to the person cashing the check.

overextended—If you are approaching your credit limit, you might contact your credit card company to ask for an increase in the limit. If the card company increases your limit, even though you do not show the ability to afford the higher limit, the card company has overextended your credit.

over-the-counter (OTC) exchange—Unlike the New York Stock Exchange, which is a formal trading environment, the OTC is not one building or trading floor, but a means to trade unlisted securities. Dealers use electronics/telecommunication through the NASDAQ network to make trades. While the New York Stock Exchange requires companies to have significant capitalization, the OTC does not have the same requirements. There are some major companies, such as Microsoft, whose shares are traded over the counter.

owners' equity—Owners' equity is the value remaining after liabilities are subtracted from assets. Stock and accumulated earnings are added together, and then dividends are subtracted to calculate total owners' equity.

P—"P" has multiple meanings as a symbol, including the price of a stock on a per share basis, the price of a unit of output, and the probability that a given circumstance will occur.

paper profit—Paper profits or losses are unrealized increases or decreases in a security, which are not real profits or losses until the security is sold. This explains how people can lose millions one day and make millions the next without actually doing anything. Such gains and losses are only hypothetical, and real gains or losses occur only when the individual sells.

par value—So that shares can be valued and sold when they are issued, an arbitrary par value is assigned.

passed dividends—A company may have customary dividends, such as biannual dividends, but the board of directors may elect not to pay a dividend. A passed dividend is not a legal obligation owed to shareholders, but still needs to be paid to individuals who own cumulative preferred stocks.

past-due balance method—If you buy a product on credit and fail to make the necessary payment on time, you owe interest on the amount that is past due. If you pay during the specified time period, then there will be no past-due amount.

payback period—The payback period is the amount of time necessary to recover an initial investment. The payback period can be calculated by dividing the initial investment by the annual cash flow. If you invested $1,000 in a bond that would pay back $100 a year over 20 years, then the payback period would be $1,000 / $100, or 10 years.

payment in kind—Payment in kind can be compared to bartering, which involves trading valuable items or services rather than paying money.

payoff—Payoff occurs when a debt is completely satisfied.

penny stocks—Penny stocks is the term used to describe inexpensive, highly speculative stocks traded on the **over-the-counter** market.

pension fund—Pension funds incorporate deposits from employers, with or without employee contributions, into various investment vehicles to develop long-term growth capable of providing employees with money after they retire, quit, or get fired.

percent of monthly gross income rule—The percent of monthly gross income rule is a rule of thumb used by mortgage companies, stating that a person should not purchase a house if the monthly mortgage, insurance, and property taxes exceed 25% of the person's monthly gross income.

percent of sales method—The percent of sales method is a technique that ties variable costs to sales to help calculate expenditures.

performance stock—A performance stock is a stable, solid growth-oriented stock that has a better investment potential compared with other similar stocks.

perpetuity—A perpetuity is a single cash flow that lasts forever. If you win a lifetime lottery that pays you $1 million a year for life, that is a perpetuity.

personal property—Personal property includes items such as cars, clothes, and sporting goods that are not attached to the ground.

petty cash—Petty cash is a small amount of funds set aside to cover small purchases that do not meet the requirements for a formal purchase order. The purchase order is a formal document requesting the release of funds to cover an approved expenditure.

point(s)—Mortgage companies add to their loans a processing charge that is expressed in points. A point represents 1% of the face value of a loan. Thus, an $80,000 mortgage with 2 points would result in a mortgage-processing fee of $1,600.

portfolio—In order to increase an investor's diversity, the investor might create a portfolio that contains stocks, bonds, CDs, Treasury notes, stamps, Beanie Babies®, and any other item that could be considered an investment. Portfolios are created to protect the investor; any one investment vehicle might decline, but such a decline in a well-balanced portfolio would not hurt the investor as much as it would in a concentrated portfolio with few investments.

preemptive right—Allows a shareholder to purchase any future shares issued by the company in the same percentage of how many shares they currently own. This allows an investor to maintain the same percentage control of a business before shares are sold to the general public, which can dilute their ownership interest.

preferred stock—A preferred stock has some features similar to those of a stock and some similar to those of a bond. Preferred stocks represent ownership equity and can generate dividend income, but they also have a guaranteed dividend and a superior claim right over other stocks.

The superior claim rights allow preferred stock shareholders to sell assets or seize earnings if the company folds.

prepayment fee—Some mortgages or other loans have a provision imposing a prepayment fee or penalty if the note is completely paid before it matures.

present value (PV)—Present value is the current value of a future amount of money. If you win the lottery, you might be able to take several million now or 10 times that amount over a number of years. Such payouts are based on the fact that if you invested a certain sum now, it would be worth more in the future. Individuals can use a present value table to analyze the value of future income streams.

pretax earnings—Pretax earnings represent a company's net income prior to paying taxes.

price indexes—Various economic indicators (price indexes) help track inflation, the cost of living, and other economic measuring tools. Typical price indexes include the **consumer price index (CPI)**, which measures 400 typical consumer goods and services; and the producer price index (PPI), which tracks the costs of wholesale goods.

price-earnings (PE) ratio—The PE ratio is a comparison between a stock's market value and the strength of a company's earnings. The PE ratio can help determine a stock's market price. To calculate this, multiply the estimated earnings per share by the estimated PE ratio. Assume that a sporting goods company expects to have an after-tax profit of $500,000 and has 1 million outstanding shares. The estimated earnings per share is $0.50. If the estimated PE ratio was 8, then the estimated market price would be $0.50 × 8, or $4.00 per share.

primary market—The primary market is the market in which new securities are traded for the first time. The secondary market is the market in which securities are traded after they are initially sold.

prime interest rate—The prime rate is the interest rate that banks charge for loans to their most financially secure customers.

principal—Principal is the amount invested in any given security.

private offering—A private offering is a first-time offering of a given security by a company, traditionally made to current shareholders, executives, institutional buyers, or larger investment institutions before the security is offered to the general public.

private placement—Some securities are initially offered privately rather than in larger financial markets open to the public. A company may issue a bond that is placed solely with current shareholders or larger institutional investors such as pension funds or insurance companies.

profit—Profit is another term to describe revenue in excess of expenses. See also **margin (profit).**

program trading—Program trading involves computer-based decision making in which securities are bought and sold according to set parameters. Program trading creates a phenomenon called the triple witching hour, which occurs at 4:15 P.M. EST on the third Friday of March, June, September, and December when numerous securities expire all at once. The triple witching hour at times has produced significant market shifts. However, these shifts are normally corrected the following trading day.

prospectus—A prospectus from a company highlights key financial data about the company and the proposed security, but does not discuss when the security will be issued or the exact price.

proxy—A shareholder has a right to vote on company-related business issues. Shareholders who do not attend a shareholders' meeting can sign a proxy allowing a designated person to vote on their behalf.

public debt—A public debt is any debt incurred by a government institution. When a city builds a stadium or arena, it may issue bonds that represent public debt.

public offering—After filing the necessary registration with the **Securities and Exchange Commission,** a company is allowed to offer stock to the general public.

public syndicate—If two businesses wish to join together to buy a professional team, they might create a public syndicate to combine their money and make the purchase. The public syndicate allows the two companies to share costs and expenses on a predetermined basis.

purchasing power—After inflation has been adjusted for, a dollar has less purchasing power than it had at a prior time. Thus, employees are frequently given raises to maintain their purchasing power or standard of living. Purchasing power also refers to the credit available to someone who wishes to make a large purchase such as a car.

pure play—The stock of a company that has only one line of business (i.e., only the bowling industry) is a pure-play stock. An investor may want to play (invest in) one industry, and the company's exclusive position in that industry makes it a good investment prospect for that investor. Several mutual funds were started in the 1990s to invest in specific sport categories such as auto racing or companies that own or sponsor professional sport teams.

put—A put is an option to sell a commodity or shares of a security at a specified price during a specified time period. This risky investment alternative works as follows. You might pay $100 for an option to buy 100 shares of a given stock. Each put costs you $1 per share and represents an option to sell the 100 shares at $10 each, which is the stock's price when you purchase the put. If after three months (the time specified in the put) the stock decreases to $5 per share, you realize a $500 profit ($5 per share) minus the $100 spent on the put. If the stock increased to $15 per share, you would lose $500 plus the $100 for purchasing the put.

Q—The letter Q in a financial equation represents unit sales for a given product.

quoted price—The quoted price is the last price at which a security was bought and sold.

R—The uppercase letter R is used to represent the appropriate discount factor or interest rate in financial equations.

r—The lowercase letter r represents a correlation coefficient denoting the degree of correlation between given financial variables.

rally—A rally is a sharp upturn in stock prices and trading.

real assets—Real assets are tangible assets such as real estate, gold, and other items you can touch. Real property consists of land and any buildings or equipment on the land.

real estate investment trust (REIT)—A real estate investment trust provides short-term loans for some construction projects and long-term loans (mortgage REITs) for major projects such as stadiums and arenas.

realized profit or **loss**—After an investment is sold, the investor realizes a profit, a loss, or a **wash,** which means neither losing nor making any money.

realized yield—The realized yield measures the return available if a bond is sold prior to reaching its maturity. This measure is also called **yield to call** or **yield to maturity.** The calculation involves estimating the potential future value of a bond versus the current value to develop an estimated percentage rate of return on the investment.

receivables turnover ratio (RTR)—The RTR represents how quickly a company is obtaining repayments of accounts receivables. If a company takes too long to collect owed money, they would have a high RTR.

recession—A recession represents a downturn in the business cycle in which various economic indicators such as the gross national product, employment rate, consumer spending, and other indicators decline.

red herring—The initial information about a proposed new security is sometimes called a red herring.

refinance—Refinancing involves consolidating or reworking any and possibly all outstanding debts to make repayment easier or to avoid financial hardship such as bankruptcy.

registered security—Some securities such as registered bonds are registered in the owner's name and recorded by the issuing company and the registrar. The registrar is the trustee of a new security's records and is often a bank or similar institution that tracks the registration number of both old and new securities.

replacement cost—Replacement costs are the costs you would incur if you needed to replace property. Capital equipment in sport, such as a new Zamboni or a new air-conditioning system, can be very expensive. Thus, companies have to plan for replacement costs either by setting aside money over a long period of time or by ensuring the potential to issue new securities or borrow necessary funds.

return on assets (ROA)—ROA refers to the calculated investment return obtained from assets purchased by a company. Any new assets purchased should be able to generate increased return over and beyond what could have been earned if the money was invested in a CD or other liquid investment option. To calculate ROA, net income is divided by total assets.

return on equity (ROE)—Similar to ROA, ROE relates to whether or not an investment in an ownership position (equity) within a company produced a rate of return greater than what could have been earned if the money had been invested elsewhere. ROE is calculated by dividing net income by shareholders' equity.

revenue—Revenue is money coming into a business.

return on investment capital (ROIV)—ROIV shows whether or not an investment in a company produced a rate of return greater than what could have been earned if the money had been invested elsewhere. ROIV is calculated by dividing net income by the sum of long-term debt and shareholders' equity.

revenue bond—Revenue bonds are government-issued bonds whose interest and principal payments are repaid from specified revenue sources. A baseball stadium could be built using revenue bonds secured by hotel and rental car tax revenues.

reverse stock split—A company's board of directors can decide to reduce the number of shares outstanding. A reverse stock split reduces the number of shares every investor has, but does not reduce the equity percentage the owner has. Thus, the number of stock shares outstanding decreases, but the remaining shares increase in value. The opposite of a reverse stock split is a **stock split,** in which the total number of shares is increased and the share values are decreased.

revolving credit—Revolving credit accounts allow a purchaser to obtain a new line of credit as soon as old loans are paid.

risk-free return—A risk-free return is an investment that provides a low return because the investment's risk is so low. To obtain a greater return an investor needs to invest in a riskier investment. A T-Bill or CD is an example of an almost risk-free investment.

risk premium (RP)—RP refers to the fact that if a security is considered risky due to poor repayment history, the security has to pay a premium over other securities to garner investor interest. Thus, an RP could increase the interest on a bond from 4% to 6% on the basis of various risk factors.

roll-up—In a roll-up, an aggressive investment company buys numerous companies in similar industries. A well-funded company could start buying multiple health clubs in a region to gain market dominance.

round lot—A round lot, also called an even lot, is a block of 100 stock shares or a bond with a $1,000 face value.

rule of 69—The rule of 69 helps calculate how long it will take for an investment to double when a certain amount of money is being invested at a certain rate of return expressed as a percentage. The formula is 69 / r(%) + 0.35 periods. If you bought a security with a return of 25%, you would double your money in (69 / 25) + 0.35 = 2.76 + 0.35 = 3.11 years.

rule of 72—The rule of 72 determines how many years it takes to double an investment. The formula is: 72 / the fixed rate of return (r%). Thus, if you bought land with a fixed rate of return of 25%, it would take you 2.88 years to double your money (72 / 25 = 2.88).

S—The uppercase letter S can represent either a dollar sales volume or the total market value of a company's equity.

s—The lowercase letter s is used to represent the standard deviation.

scheduled payment—Scheduled payments are fixed payments owed on loans or bonds or pursuant to a contract or security.

schedule of estimated income—A schedule of estimated income lists expected revenue sources over a given time period. Such a schedule helps highlight what revenue can be expected so a budget can be developed.

secured bond—A secured bond is a bond secured by a specific item, or collateral, that can be sold if the bond is not repaid.

secured loan—Similar to a secured bond, a secured loan is guaranteed by specified collateral.

securities—Securities are any financial instruments that provide an ownership interest in the issuing company. Typical examples include stocks and bonds.

Securities and Exchange Commission (SEC)—The federal government established the SEC in the 1930s as an independent regulatory agency to regulate securities markets. To protect investors, the SEC requires full financial disclosure for all securities and regulates issues such as insider trading.

security exchanges—The Securities and Exchange Commission regulates several privately owned security exchanges, the most famous of these being the New York Stock Exchange, American Stock Exchange, and the over-the-counter exchange. Several regional exchanges also exist around the United States and in major foreign cities.

security interest, or **collateral interest**—A security interest gives a lender with a secured loan the right to go to court and take possession of the collateral if the borrower defaults on the loan.

seller's market—A seller's market is a market in which the seller has the advantage because numerous buyers are interested in purchasing the item being sold. This phenomenon is based on supply and demand when the supply is low and the demand is high. A seller's market exists for professional sport teams, as many people would like to buy a team but only a handful of teams are available in any given year.

sell order—When investors wish to sell a security, they can give their broker a sell order authorizing the sale. The sell order can be either oral or in writing.

senior debt—A senior debt is a superior obligation (loan) that a borrower has to repay before repaying any other obligations. If a company folds, senior debt would need to be paid before any shareholders could receive money, if any remains. A senior debt obligation can be secured by any, or all, corporate assets.

serial bond—A serial bond matures over regularly scheduled dates, in contrast to a bond that matures on only one given date.

Series E bonds—Series E bonds were issued by the U.S. government from 1941 through 1979, when they were replaced by Series EE and Series HH bonds. These bonds are purchased at 50% of the face amount, and the interest accumulates until the bonds reach their maturity date. These bonds can be redeemed before they mature, but the holder will have to pay a penalty.

shakeout—A shakeout occurs when security prices tumble with significant trading.

share—A share represents one unit of ownership interest in either a company or a financial vehicle (i.e., a mutual fund).

shareholder—An individual who owns a share in a company.

shareholders' report—Companies that issue stocks report to their owners on a regular basis. These reports highlight the company's current financial condition and other relevant facts. Shareholders' reports are often released annually and provide audited reviews of the company's financial statements by an independent accounting firm to substantiate the claims made by the company.

short—An investor can take a short position by borrowing a security from a broker and then selling the security on the open market. The idea is that the investor is hoping the stock price will decline, at which point the investor will buy the stock at a lower price and will have made a profit. For example, an investor can sell 100 short shares borrowed from the broker for $10 each. Ten days later the stock might have dropped to $5 per share, and at this point the investor buys the stock from the broker and makes a $500 profit. Buying short is very risky—if the stock price increases, you can lose a substantial amount of money because you have to buy the stock at its higher price.

short-term debt—Short-term debts are current liabilities that need to be repaid within one year, such as utility bills, payments for inventory, taxes owed, employee wages owed, and related liabilities.

signature loan—A signature loan is any personal loan secured only by the borrower's signature. No collateral is pledged.

simple interest—Simple interest is computed only on the original loan amount, whereas compound interest is applied to the original principal and all accumulated interest. The simple interest on a $1,000 loan at 10% interest would be $100.

simple rate of return (SRR)—The simple rate of return is a method used to calculate the return that can be obtained on a given investment. To calculate SRR, we divide the investment's annual income by the initial investment. If you invested $1,000 and receive an annual return of $75, the SRR is 75 / $1,000 = 7.5%.

simple yield—To calculate the simple yield of a bond, the bond's interest is divided by the face value. If you buy a $1,000 bond paying 5% interest for only $950, then the simple yield is (5% × 1,000) / 950 = 50 / 950, or 5.26%.

single-payment loans—Single-payment loans are paid in full on a given date, with the debtor repaying both the principal and required interest. There are two techniques for determining the appropriate annual percentage rate. Under the **simple interest** method, the amount repaid is computed by adding the original amount and interest, with the interest calculated by means of the following formula: interest = principal × interest rate × time period. Assume you borrow $1,000 for one year at a simple interest rate of 15%. The simple interest rate is 15%, and you would repay the lender $1,150 at the end of the year. The second method is the discount method; here the initial loan is discounted by the interest that will be owed. Using the same example, instead of receiving $1,000 and paying $1,150, you would borrow $1,000 at 15% but receive only $850, which represents the loan minus your prepayment of the interest you would owe. Unlike the 15% annual percentage rate (APR) under the simple interest method, the APR using the discount method would be 17.64%. The calculation is $150 (interest) / $850 (amount actually received). Thus, the discount method allows a lower payment upon maturity ($850 versus $1,150), but the simple interest method produces a lower APR.

sinking fund—A company can use a sinking fund to set aside money to invest in income-producing securities that are later cashed in to pay off a financial obligation. Without setting aside money in anticipation of repaying a loan, a company may be forced to issue additional securities to raise the necessary cash or may have to borrow the money.

skip-payment privilege—A lender might allow a borrower to skip a payment if the lender is notified in advance that the borrower will miss a payment.

solvency ratio—The solvency ratio is calculated by dividing net worth (assets minus liabilities) by total assets. A company with a high solvency ratio is financially very strong.

special tax bond—A special tax bond is a municipal bond paid for with revenue from excise taxes levied on such items as alcohol or tobacco sales. Such sin taxes have been used to fund stadium projects such as Jacobs Field in Cleveland.

speculative bond—A speculative bond is a low-rated bond that might be close to default. An investor might purchase such a bond at a deep discount with the hope that the company can turn around and pay off the bond.

stagflation—Stagflation represents an increase in prices that occurs when businesses are facing a slowdown.

statement of cash flows—A statement of cash flow is an accounting of where revenue is coming from and where it is being spent. These statements must be included in shareholders' annual reports.

stock dividend—If a company does not have enough cash to pay a dividend, the company can issue additional stock to shareholders. If a stock dividend is issued, the shares outstanding for the company are increased, and this reduces the per share value of all shares.

stock market, or **stock exchange**—A stock market or exchange is a marketplace where stock and other securities are traded.

stock split—A corporation's board of directors may authorize a stock split if the stock price is too high. Thus, for a share that sells for $200, after a 2-for-1 stock split the investor will have two shares, each worth $100. A stock split can take place for a variety of reasons and according to various formulas (e.g., 3 for 2; or 2.3 for 2).

stock symbol—Each company that issues stock on a given stock exchange is given a stock symbol (also called a ticker symbol) that is used to identify the stock.

stock types—Companies can issue various stocks such as common, preferred, and class A or class B stocks. The latter two types of stock give the stockholders different voting rights.

subchapter S corporation—Subchapter S corporations must follow strict rules; for example, they must have fewer than 35 shareholders. Their primary benefit is that the shareholders are taxed similarly to the way partners are taxed; this business structure avoids double taxation, or taxation of C corporations and then of their shareholders.

subordinate debenture—A subordinate debenture is an unsecured bond that would be paid only after senior bonds are paid.

subordinate debt—A subordinate debt is a loan secured by just a general claim on a company's assets that would be paid after a secured debt is paid.

sunk costs—Sunk costs represent past costs incurred that might affect a subsequent decision. If you bought a gym for $1 million 10 years ago, that cost is a sunk cost. The cost is irrelevant for many decisions, but it would be relevant if you wished to sell and would sell only for a specified rate of return higher than the initial purchase price.

T—The uppercase letter T represents a company's or individual's marginal tax rate on interest payments.

t—The lowercase letter t in a financial formula stands for the time frame for a given investment.

taxable income—Taxable income equals **adjusted gross income (AGI)** minus any allowed deductions or exemptions such as business expenses, capital losses, or charitable giving.

tax basis—The tax basis for an investment is the sum total of all expenses incurred for making a purchase, such as the security's cost, brokerage fee, registration fees, and any others.

tax credit—A tax credit can be created to reduce the total dollars owed to the government and can be associated with specific legislation; such legislation may call for a tax credit for starting a new business in a given neighborhood, for example.

tax-equivalent yield—A formula measures the yield of a tax-free municipal bond against other investments that might require tax payments. The formula is as follows: tax-equivalent yield = tax-exempt yield / (1 – tax rate). If a business has a 28% tax rate and a tax-exempt municipal bond pays 5% interest, the necessary return on a taxable investment would be 5% / (1 – 0.28) = 6.94%. Thus, to maximize your investment return, you should invest in the tax-exempt municipal bond unless you can find another investment that has a return greater than 6.94%.

tax-exempt bonds—Tax-exempt bonds allow investors the opportunity to receive interest income but not have to pay taxes on that income. Tax-exempt bonds were essential in the sport facility construction boom in the 1990s as investors were able to buy bonds backed by facility revenue but did not have to pay taxes on the interest income.

tax incremental financing (TIF)—TIF represents tax breaks given to a project with the hope that other businesses would move to the area and increase the property value. The increased property value and resulting greater tax base is supposed to help offset the tax break given to the company that received the TIF.

tax shield—A tax shield refers to any deduction that can ultimately reduce your tax burden. For example if you spend $3,000 a year on mortgage interest and pay tax at the 28% tax rate, you could have a tax shield of ($3,000 × 0.28) = $840.

term loan—A term loan calls for regular periodic payments, usually for three years or more.

time value of money—Money decreases in value over time, and time value of money represents this concept. As one dollar today is worth more than one dollar next year, investment decisions need to be made with a critical eye toward the future value of a dollar.

tombstone—A tombstone is a formal advertisement by a company or investment bank stating the financial terms of a pending security offering.

total asset turnover ratio—The total asset turnover ratio represents how quickly a company uses its assets to make money. A low ratio means that assets are not being turned over quickly enough to generate additional revenue.

trade—To trade is to exchange or sell a security on either a formal or an informal security exchange.

Those who buy and sell stocks for their own benefit are called traders.

Treasury bill (T-bill)—A T-bill is a short-term government obligation issued in a minimum denomination of $10,000 and scheduled to mature in three months, six months, or a year. T-bills are the safest investment vehicle, as they are 100% backed by the U.S. government.

Treasury bond—The federal government issues bonds in a minimum denomination of $1,000 that mature over 10 years and have semiannual payments of a fixed interest rate.

Treasury notes—Treasury notes are similar to T-bills and Treasury bonds, with similar security and interest rates.

treasury stocks—Treasury stocks are stocks that were once issued by a company and then subsequently repurchased by the company. Such repurchased stocks can be canceled or reissued, but while they are in the company's possession they pay no dividends and have no voting rights. Similar to treasury stocks, companies can also have treasury bonds, that is, bonds repurchased by the issuing company.

trust—A trust is a special account established to benefit a specified individual such as a minor.

turnover—Turnover is a means of determining how inventory is managed. A high turnover ratio means that a company is quickly replenishing inventory as old inventory is quickly sold. A low turnover ratio reflects that a company has inventory sitting around and is not maximizing its investment. To calculate turnover, sales are divided by assets. Turnover is also calculated for assets to determine how they are being managed.

usury—Usury refers to charging an excessive amount of interest on a loan. Loan sharks often represent a last resort for those who cannot obtain funds from any other source (i.e., their credit rating is bad or they have nothing to borrow against at a pawnshop). However, charging an excessively high interest rate is illegal.

value (V)—Value is the monetary worth of an item. Value can be expressed as what you could obtain on the market if you had to sell an item. Thus, baseball card price guides might list a card as worth $100, but if you can only find people willing to pay $20 for the card, then the card's value is only $20.

Value Line Investment Survey—Value Line is a publication and advisory service that ranks the quality of numerous companies and projects their possible successes or failures in the coming year.

variance—Variances represent the difference between the amount budgeted for a given expense and the actual expense incurred.

voluntary liquidation—As a consequence of severe financial concerns, shareholders may vote to liquidate a company by selling all company assets.

voting rights—Certain stocks carry with them a voting right that allows each shareholder to vote in person or by proxy on such issues as major expenditures, changing board members, or voluntary liquidation.

Wall Street—Wall Street is a street in New York City in the heart of the financial district where the New York Stock Exchange and the American Stock Exchange are located.

warrant—A warrant is an agreement that enables the holder to buy stock at a future date at an advantageous price.

warranty deed—A warranty deed guarantees that a given investment or property has clear title and is free from any encumbrances.

wash—A wash represents no gain or loss when a given investment is sold.

watered stock—A company can exchange capital stock for assets valued at less than the stock's par value. This transaction artificially inflates the value of the exchanged assets.

wholesale banking—Wholesale banking refers to significant volume of transactions with major corporations or financial institutions.

working capital—Working capital is the amount of money available to pay bills. To calculate working capital, current liabilities are subtracted from current assets. The term *working capital* is sometimes used to refer to only current assets.

year-end dividend—If a company is profitable or if the company's stock requires dividend payments, then the company can pay a dividend at the end of its fiscal year.

year to date (YTD)—The YTD notation on financial statements indicates financial activity from the start of the company's fiscal year to the date specified on the financial statement.

yield (rate of return)—The yield represents the income earned by a given investment.

yield to call (YTC)—YTC represents the yield obtained up to the point that a bond is called by the issuer.

yield to maturity (YTM)—YTM represents the annual yield that holders of a bond would receive if they held on to the bond until it matured. To calculate YTM we analyze the bond's face value, coupon rate, and market price taking into consideration the time remaining on the bond until it matures.

zero-based budgeting (ZBB)—The zero-based budget is founded on the concept that organizations and their programs need to justify their existence. The resulting budget would distribute money to the programs that produce the greatest benefits, and the components that produce lower benefits either would be eliminated from the budget or would receive fewer funds.

zero coupon bond—A zero coupon bond does not pay interest on a semiannual or annual basis; rather the semiannual interest payments are added to the principal, with the principal and interest being paid at maturity. These bonds are called zero coupon as the bondholder does not need to clip and redeem coupons in order to obtain the interest payments.

z score—The z score is a formula used to measure the probability that a company will go bankrupt, and analyzes a host of financial measures from retained earnings to total assets.

Bibliography

1988 baseball salaries. (1988, June). *Sport*, 24.

1997 stadium & arena managers' annual report. (1997). Tampa: Price Waterhouse Sports Group.

Adamek, S. (1988, July 1). Earth to union: Don't kill golden goose. *The Record* (Bergen County, NJ), p. 56.

Allen v. Commissioner, 50 T.C. 466 (1968).

Ambrosini, D. (2002, February 10). Bankrolled by an 'Angel.' *Connecticut Post*, p. F1.

Andelman, B. (1993). *Stadium for rent: Tampa Bay's quest for major league baseball.* Jefferson, NC: McFarland.

An introduction. (1992). Washington, DC: National Association of Security Dealers.

Appraisal. Available: http://homebuildingmanual.com/glossary.htm. Retrieved February 18, 2002.

Aramark acquires Ogden Entertainment. (2000, May-June). *Facility Manager*, 7.

Arens, A.A., & Loebbecke, J.K. (2000). *Auditing: An integrated approach* (8th ed.). Upper Saddle River, NJ: Prentice Hall.

Arthur J. Rooney. Available: www.profootballhof.com/players/enshrinees/arooney.cfm. Retrieved February 17, 2002.

Ascent, Liberty Media deal is scrapped on sale hitch. (1999, December 1). *The Wall Street Journal*, p. B3.

Athlete's tax fails to meet expectations in Pittsburgh. (2000). Available: www.sportslawnews.com/archive/articles/athletetax.htm.

Attorney general to check into Red Sox bidding process. (2001, December 23). *Connecticut Post*, p. D3.

Average salary tops $2 million. (2001, December 13). *Connecticut Post*, p. C5.

Baade, R.A. (1994, April 4). *Stadiums, professional sports, and economic development: Assessing the reality.* Heartland Policy Study No. 62. Chicago: The Heartland Institute.

Back pay subject to new tax. (2001, April 18). Available: www.acssonline.org / news / 200104018-backpaytax.asp. Retrieved February 18, 2002.

Baim, D. (1994). *The sports stadium as a municipal investment.* Westport, CT: Greenwood Press.

Baines, D. (1996, November 21). Canucks still on hook for liabilities incurred in buyout. *Vancouver Sun*, p. D2.

Bally Total Fitness and Crunch to merge. (2001, December). *Fitness Management*, 14.

Bankruptcy judge oks Lemieux's plan to save Penguins. (1999, June 25). *Houston Chronicle*, p. 15B.

Barron, D. (1996, June 28). Athletic programs lose money across the board. *Houston Chronicle*, p. 9B.

Battersby, M. (1999, July). Finance options. *Fitness Management*, 36–37.

Baumol, W. (1952, November). Transactions demand for cash: An inventory theoretic approach. *Quarterly Journal of Economics, 66*, 545–556.

Bedell, D. (1997, October 8). Dallas businessman pleads guilty to fraud in failed NHL deal. *Dallas Morning News*, p. 1.

Beltrame, J. (2000, January 24). Canada backs out of pledge to aid hockey teams. *The Wall Street Journal*, p. B10.

Bernstein, A. (1998, November 9-15). Sporting goods blues threatening to spread. *Street & Smith's SportsBusiness Journal*, 8.

The Bing Group capsule. Available: www.hoovers.com/uk / co / capsule / 3 / 0,2163,42033,00.html. Retrieved February 6, 2002.

Blair, R.D., & Kaserman, D.L. (1985). *Antitrust economics.* Homewood, IL: Irwin.

Bloomberg.com. (1999, August). Available: www.bloomberg.com.

Blum, D. (1993, September 22). Booster groups brace for law requiring charities to tell donors how much of a gift is tax-deductible. *Chronicle of Higher Education*, p. A36.

Bogen, J. (1966). *Corporation finance.* New York: Alexander Hamilton Institute.

Boudette, N. (2001, January 21). Muppet meltdown. *The Wall Street Journal*, p. 1.

Bowden, E., & Carlin, T. (1967). *Economics.* New York: Alexander Hamilton Institute.

Brealey, R.A., & Myers, S.C. (1996). *Principles of corporate finance* (5th ed.). New York: McGraw-Hill.

Brennan, T. (2001). Schwinn / GT bidding race begins. Available: www.thedeal.com / cgibin / gx.cg... / View&c=TDDArticle&cid=TDDLYIKOXPC&live=tru. Retrieved August 5, 2001.

Breyer, R. (1998, June 26). Wetlands "bankers" sell credits in land preserves to developers. *Austin American-Statesman*, p. C1.

Bridges, F., & Roquemore, L. (1996). *Management for athletic/sport administration: Theory and practice* (2nd ed.). Decatur, GA: ESM Books.

Briefly. (1998, January 8). *Detroit News*, p. F3.

Briefly. (2000, March 15). *Connecticut Post*, p. D4.

Brigham, E., & Gapenski, L. (1994). *Financial management: Theory and practice* (7th ed.). Fort Worth, TX: Dryden Press, Harcourt Brace College.

Brigham, E.F., Gapenski, L.C., & Ehrhardt, M.C. (1999). *Financial management: Theory and practice* (9th ed.). New York: Dryden Press.

Brockington, L., & Rofe, J. (1999, April 5-11). Murdoch grows his sports empire again. *Street & Smith's SportsBusiness Journal, 1*, 1, 47.

Broni, P. (1999, December). Take my loan . . . please. *Inc Magazine*, 163.

Broome, T., Jr. (1997, December). SBA gives women a foot in the door. *Nation's Business*, 44–45.

Brown family eludes IRS tackle. (1997, April 30). *Cincinnati Enquirer*, p. A5.

Browning, E.S. (2000, April 13). Industrials' skid mask strength in old economy. *The Wall Street Journal*, p. C1.

Budd, T. (1966). *Financial statements.* New York: Alexander Hamilton Institute.

Building information & history. (2001). Available: www.united-center.com / history / index.html. Retrieved December 26, 2001.

Burns, A. (1996, July 1). Athletics wake up and smell the deficit. *Daily Cougar*, p. 1.

Bush admits mistake. (2000, January 9). *Connecticut Post*, p. D11.

Business briefcase. (1997, December 17). *Boston Herald*, p. 41.

Business bulletin. (2000, February 10). *The Wall Street Journal*, p. A1.

Byrd, A. (1999, May 10-16). Easton adding wooden bats to lineup with Stix purchase. *Street & Smith's SportsBusiness Journal, 2*, 11.

Byrt, F. (2001, January 30). Converse's "Made in USA" ends its long run. *The Wall Street Journal*, p. B9A.

Calian, S., & Latour, A. (2000, May 15). Stockholm, once a David, is a high-tech Goliath. *The Wall Street Journal*, p. C1.

Canada eyes pro team subsidies. (1998, October 10). *Seattle Times*, p. C2.

Caro, R. (2000, January). A financial look at the next millennium. *Fitness Management*, 56.

CBA ceases operations. (2001, February 10). *Connecticut Post*, p. D3.

Ceron, G. (2000, March 13). Prices for a seat on the NYSE fall amid changes. *The Wall Street Journal*, p. B19.

Certificate of participation-COP. Available: http: / / investopedia.com/terms/c/cop.asp. Retrieved February 18, 2002.

Changing game of sports finance [pamphlet]. (1999, April 28). New York: Fitch IBCA.

The Charlton standard catalogue of Canadian coins, (44th ed.). (1990). Toronto: Charlton Press.

Chase, B. (1998, January 12). Hockey team buyer seen admitting $80 million fraud. *American Banker*, p. 1.

Chass, M. (1998, March 18). Turner's plan: Stop Murdoch. *New York Times*, p. C1.

Cheeseman, H. (1998). *Business law* (3rd ed.). Upper Saddle River, NJ: Prentice Hall.

Chi, V. (1992, September 30). Coping with the cash crunch. *San Jose Mercury News*, p. 1D.

Chiang, H., & Wilson, Y. (1998, December 24). Appeals court throws out stadium vote challenge. *San Francisco Chronicle*, p. A15.

Clear Channel plays new tune with purchase of SFX. (2000, May-June). *Facility Manager*, 25.

Cohen, A. (1999, July). Fit financing. *Athletic Business*, 11.

Coke signs new 4-year NFL deal. (1998, May 23). *Houston Chronicle*, p. 2C.

Colbert, J.L., & Bolton, D.L. (1998, November-December). Accounting: Recommendations for preventing and detecting fraud in a small business. *Forensic Examiner*, 29–31.

Company. (2002). Available: http://dmotorworks.com/company/bod.shtml. Retrieved February 17, 2002.

Construction glossary from Home Building Manual. (2002). Available: www.homebuildingmanual.com / glossary.htm. Retrieved February 18, 2002.

Copeland, T., Koller, T., & Murrin, J. (2000). *Valuation: Measuring and managing the value of companies* (3rd ed.). New York: Wiley.

Corporate debt may get more play to purchases of sports teams. (2000, March 2). *The Wall Street Journal*, p. A1.

Cravens, D., & Lamb, C., Jr. (1990). *Strategic marketing management cases and applications* (3rd ed.). Homewood, IL: Irwin.

Crow, B., Phillips, D., & Gillentine, M. (Winter, 2000). Corporate partnerships in sports. *International Sports Journal, 4*(1), 27.

Damadroran, A. (2001). The dark side of valuation: Valuing old tech, new tech, and new economy companies. Upper Saddle River, NJ: Prentice Hall.

Delaware InterCorp. (2000, June 27). Available: www.delawareintercorp.com/why.htm.

Detroit Empowerment Zone Transition Office. (n.d.). *Empowerment Zone Projects* [Brochure]. Detroit: City of Detroit.

Detroit Recreation Department Empowerment Zone Initiative. (n.d.). [Fact sheet]. Detroit: City of Detroit.

Doors to IPOs open slightly. (2000, March 31). *Connecticut Post*, p. C2.

Double play for New York. (2001, December 27). *Connecticut Post*, p. C6.

Dow Jones continues its losing streak. (2002, January 15). *Connecticut Post*, p. C3.

Dunphy, S.H. (1998, June 29). Understand the stock market—now. *Houston Chronicle*, pp. D1, D4.

Dreazen, Y. (2000, March 7). Bankruptcy bills may proceed despite new data. *The Wall Street Journal*, p. A4.

Elkins, L. (1996, June). Tips for preparing a business plan. *Nation's Business*, 58.

Emerson, J. (1985, December). *Public-commercial cooperative arrangements and the use of fees and charges in Texas municipal parks departments*. Austin, TX: Texas Parks and Wildlife Department.

Eminent domain. (2002). Available: www.sportslawnews.com/archive/jargon/LJEminent.html. Retrieved February 18, 2002.

Ernest, W. (2002, May). Seeing green. *Club Industry*, 41–42.

Euchner, C.C. (1993). *Playing the field: Why sports teams move and cities fight to keep them*. Baltimore: John Hopkins University Press.

Evanson, D.R. (1997, May). Capital pitches that succeed. *Nation's Business*, 40–41.

Evanson, D.R. (1998, January). Easier avenues to equity capital. *Nation's Business*, 44–46.

Evanson, D.R. (1998). Capital questions. *EntrepreneurMag.com*. [Online serial]. Available: www.entrepreneurmag.com / visa / visa_raise1.hts. Retrieved June 29, 1998.

Fagan, P. (1999, September). Charitable tax planning. *Jewish Action*, 89.

Farhi, P. (2001, December 30). It's a whole new ballgame. *Washington Post*, p. A01.

Farrell, G. (2002, March 15). Indictment could shred Andersen. *USA Today* [Online serial]. Available: www.usatoday.com/money/energy/enron/2002-03-15-indicted.htm.

Fatsis, S. (1998, May 8). Michael Jordan's agent scores big in takeover deal. *The Wall Street Journal*, p. B6.

Fatsis, S. (1998, May 14). In the NBA, shoe money is no longer a slam-dunk. *The Wall Street Journal*, p. B1.

FDIC. (2002). Available: www.fdic.gov/deposit/deposits /insure/index.html. Retrieved July 9, 2002.

Feiner, R. (1977). *Operational financial analysis: A practical handbook with forms*. Englewood Cliffs, NJ: Prentice Hall.

Fendrich, H. (2001, December 15). Sources: ABC/ESPN near NBA TV deal. Excite News. Available: http://news.excite.ca / news / ap / 011215 / 13 / bkn-nba-tv-contracts. Retrieved December 26, 2001.

Fiscally friendly football. (1996, July-August). *Sidelines* (College Football Association), 2.

Football strike? Who cares? (2001, March 26). *Business Week*, 34.

Footstar completes acquisition. (2000, March 8). *The Wall Street Journal*, p. A4.

For the record. (1998, August 17-23). *Street & Smith's SportsBusiness Journal*, 1, 36.

For the record. (1998, September 21-27). *Street & Smith's SportsBusiness Journal*, 1, 34.

For the record. (1999, May 10-16). *Street & Smith's SportsBusiness Journal*, 2, 38.

Fraser, L., & Ormiston, A. (2001). *Understanding financial statements* (6th ed.). Upper Saddle River, NJ: Prentice Hall.

Freeman, R.J., Shoulders, C.D., & Lynn, E.S. (1988). *Governmental and nonprofit accounting* (3rd ed.). Englewood Cliffs, NJ: Prentice Hall.

Fried, G., & Miller, L. (1998). *Employment law*. Greensboro, NC: Carolina Academic Press.

From $50 in 1922 to a half-billion today. (1999, December 26). *Connecticut Post*, p. D3.

From coins to credit cards. (1999, December 19). *Connecticut Post*, p. F4.

Frost, G. (2002). Longtime fans buy Boston Celtics for $360 million. *FindLaw*. [Online serial]. Avilable: http://news.findlaw.com/sports/s/20020927/nbabostoncelticsdc.html. Retrieved September 30, 2002.

Gandley, W., & Stanley, D. (1978). Canada/B.N.A. postage stamp catalouge (9th ed.). Ontario: Canadian Wholesale Supply.

Garrison, R. (1982). *Managerial accounting* (3rd ed.). Plano, TX: Business Publications.

German soccer team scores unusual goal: Approval to go public. (1999, November 29). *The Wall Street Journal*, p. B28.

Gibeaut, J. (1999, March). The money chase. *ABA Journal*, 58.

Gilpin, F. (1998, December 30). Officials cleared in arena probe. *Tampa Tribune*, p. 1.

Glier, R. (1997, July 20). With expectations unfulfilled, Atlantans still searching for legacy from games. *Houston Chronicle*, p. 18B.

Go figure. (1999, October 25). *Sports Illustrated*, 33.

Go figure. (2000, January 10). *Sports Illustrated*, 27.

Golden Bear Golf, Inc. Available: http: / / hoovers.com / print/printh.html. Retrieved February 18, 2002.

Golden Bear Golf Inc. announces settlement. (1999, December 23). Available: www.businesswire.com.

Goldhirsh, J. (1996, November). There's nothing passive about rental income. *Nation's Business*, 71.

Gomes, L. (2000, February 9). Nike forecasts disappointing sales as outlets for sneakers dwindle. *The Wall Street Journal*, p. B10.

Goo, S.K. (2000, January 26). Green Mountain: Loyalty helps VT ski co-op thrive. *The Wall Street Journal*, p. NE1.

Goonan, P., & McAuliffe, M. (1999, September 23). Springfield: City of homers? *Union News*, pp. A1, B4.

Gore hints at new Greenspan term. (1999, July 16). *Houston Chronicle*, p. 3C.

Greenberg, M., & Gray, J. (1996). *The stadium game*. Milwaukee: National Sports Law Institute of Marquette University Law School.

Greenberger, R. (2000, October 17). Supreme Court to decide tax case on back pay. *The Wall Street Journal*, p. B4.

Griffin, M.P. (1991). *Intermediate finance for nonfinancial managers*. Toronto, ON: Amacom.

Grover, R., & Lowry, T. (2001, September 3). Those smackdowns are taking their toll. *Business Week*, 40.

Grover, R., & Lowry, T. (2002, April 15). A cable clan on thin ice. *Business Week*, 48.

Haggerty, T., & Paton, G. (1984). *Financial management of sport-related organizations*. Champaign, IL: Stipes.

Harper, T. (1999, March 6). He shouts! He scares! *Toronto Star*, p. B1.

Haynie, W.H. (1998, July). Equipment financing. *Fitness Management*, 36–37.

Henderson, J. (1996, September 4). Voters say yes to sales tax. *Tampa Tribune*, p. 1.

Hiestand, M. (1992, October 1992). Illinois could eliminate funds for college teams. *USA Today*, p. 10C.

Hiestand, M. (1999, January 12). The B word—billion—no longer out of bounds. *USA Today*, p. 1A.

High-tech injection. (1999, October 27). *Connecticut Post*, p. C1.

Hoboken Arena. Available: www.sfo.com / ~csuppes / NHL / NewJerseyDevils / newindex.htm. Retrieved January 9, 2002.

Hodges, S. (1997, February). SBA microloans fuel big ideas. *Nation's Business*, 34–35.

Hoffman, D. (1998, November). Penguins file for bankruptcy. *Stadium & Arena Financing News*, 2(21), 1.

Holmes, A.W., & Burns, D.C. (1979). *Auditing: Standards and procedures* (9th ed.). Homewood, IL: Irwin.

Horine, L. (1999). *Administration of physical education and sport programs* (4th ed.). Boston: WCB/McGraw-Hill.

Hovey, J. (1997, September). A source of funds in search of work. *Nation's Business*, 37–38.

Hovey, J. (1998, March). A little-known pathway to growth. *Nation's Business*, 40–42.

Hovey, J. (1998, July). Cheap funding through bonds. *Nation's Business*, 50–51.

Hovey, J. (1998, November). Using inventory for collateral. *Nation's Business*, 42–43.

Howard, D.R., & Crompton, J.L. (1995). *Financing Sport*. Morgantown, WV: Fitness Information Technology.

H.R. 4736. (1992). Taxpayer's Right to View Act of 1992. 102d Congress, Energy and Commerce Committee.

Hube, K. (2000, January 26). Tax rule crimps small-business deals. *The Wall Street Journal*, p. C1.

Huffy checks bounce as lenders cut off credit lines funding. (1999, November 4). *The Wall Street Journal*, p. A6.

Hundley v. Commissioner, 48 T.C. 339 (1967).

Immoo, L., Lochhead, S., Ritter, R., & Zhao, Q. (1996). The costs of raising capital. *Journal of Financial Research, 19*, 59–74.

Inventory analyst—Easton Sports. (2000, March 3). Available: www.sportlink.com/employment/jobs/jobs2000-016.html

Investing's fast track? (1999, February 16). *Houston Chronicle*, p. C1.

Ip, G. (2000, March 10). NASDAQ pumps up to 5000. *The Wall Street Journal*, p. C1.

Ip, G. (2000, March 15). Archipelago to set up new stock market. *The Wall Street Journal*, p. C1.

IPO basics: A road map. (1999). FindLaw. Available: www.inc.com / articles / details / 0,6378,AGD2_ART15744_CNY56_SUB14,00.html

IRS. (n.d.). *Code of Federal Regulations*, 26 CFR 1.513-1. Washington, DC: Author.

Janda, J. (2001, December). Mad Dogg, Schwinn partnership ends. *Club Industry*, 24.

Just For Feet sets deal with creditors to seek bankruptcy. (1999, November 3). *The Wall Street Journal*, p. B10.

Kaplan, D. (2001, March 12-18). Securitization era opens for athletes. *Street & Smith's SportsBusiness Journal, 3*, 1, 43.

Kaplan, D. (1999, August 16-22). Lehman gives USTA fast-track refinance. *Street & Smith's SportsBusiness Journal, 2*, 16.

Kaplan, D. (1998, November 9-15). Slugger's bond plan striking out. *Street & Smith's SportsBusiness Journal, 1*, 3.

Kaplan, D. (1998, September 14-20). Soccer worth watching. *Street & Smith's SportsBusiness Journal, 1*, 1, 45.

Kaplan, D. (1998, August 31-September 6). NFL credit line may hit $800M. *Street & Smith's SportsBusiness Journal, 1*, 19.

Kapner, F. (2001, August 15). Juventus plans to play stock market game. *Financial Times*, 16.

King, B., & Brockington, L. (1998, December 14-20). Forces push both sides in Yanks' deal. *Street & Smith's SportsBusiness Journal, 1*, 1, 46.

Klise, E. (1972). *Money and banking* (5th ed.). Cincinnati: South-Western.

Kowall, S. (2001). The weekly tirade. Available: www.comedyzine.com / tirade154.shtml. Retrieved December 26, 2001.

Kraker, D. (1998). The economics of pro sports: The fans, the owners, and the rules. Institute for Local Self-Reliance. Available: www.ilsr.org / newrules / sportsbg.html

Kupetz, D.S. (1998, July). Resolving business financial crises. *California Lawyer*, 66–68.

Kurdziel, K. (2000, April 27). Dolan has one goal for the tribe: Win the World Series. *Sun News*, p. C1.

Lamiell, P. (1999, May 4). Dow index passes 11,000 in record time. *Houston Chronicle*, p. 1C.

Lascari, S. (1998, October-November). Sports facility issues, part two. Stock of sports franchises: A sound investment or scam? *For the Record* (Marquette University Law School), *9*(5), 3.

Lederman, D. (1991, December 11). IRS rules that 2 bowls must pay taxes on money they received from corporate sponsors. *Chronicle of Higher Education*, p. A33.

Lee, C. (1999, July). Managing the process. *ABA Journal*, 62.

Left for dead, CBA breathes new life. (2001). Available: http://lacrossetribune.com / rednews / 2001 / 07 / 30 / build / sports / 001lead.php. Retrieved February 6, 2002.

Leo, A. (2000, December 6). Fund looted from league, woman held. *Connecticut Post*, p. A2.

Lewis, A. (1999, June 8). Suits seek to halt Ascent sale prospective buyers wait as shareholders say $400 million bid by Lauries is too low. *Denver Rocky Mountain News*, p. 1B.

Lewis, J. (1936, February 29). Basehits, incorporated. *Liberty*, 48–49.

Lins, W., & Grillo, E. (1966). *Accounting principles*. New York: Alexander Hamilton Institute.

Lipin, S. (2000, February 28). Firms incorporated in Delaware are valued more by investors. *The Wall Street Journal*, p. C21.

Livingston, A. (1998, July). Avoiding pitfalls when selling a business. *Nation's Business*, 25–26.

Livingstone, J.L. (Ed.). (1997). *The portable MBA in finance and accounting* (2nd ed.). New York: Wiley.

Logo Athletic Inc. files for chapter 11. (2000, November 8). *Connecticut Post*, p. C4.

Managers rethinking "just-in-time" inventory management. (2001, December 28). [Trucking Technology Alert.] Available: www.ttnews.com / members / topNews/0008327.html. Retrieved February 18, 2002.

Markets consider merger. (2000, March 4). *Connecticut Post*, p. B1.

The Marquee Group. (1999). Available: www.marqueegroup.com

Marullo, G.G. (1997, February). Easier rules take effect for S corporations. *Nation's Business*, 63.

Marullo, G.G. (1997, December). Tax options for handling obsolete inventories. *Nation's Business*, 25.

Marullo, G.G. (1998, March). Rewards and risks in lending to your child. *Nation's Business*, 27–28.

Marullo, G.G. (1998, August). Selling your business: A preview of the process. *Nation's Business*, 25–26.

Mayer, C. (1998, July 26). Business model hikes Amazon's value. *Houston Chronicle*, p. 5D.

McAllister, P. (1998). Contributions & premiums. *Grantsmanship Center Magazine*, 9.

McCartney, S. (2000, December 27). Why a baseball superstar's megacontract can be less than it seems. *The Wall Street Journal*, p. B1.

McGee, S. (2000, May 3). Venture capitalists still love start-ups. *The Wall Street Journal*, p. C1.

McGraw, D. (1998, July 13). Big league troubles. *U.S. News and World Report*, 40–46.

Mclean, B. (2000, February). Chase's venture capital elite. *Fortune*, 47.

McMorris, F., Smith, R., & Schroeder, M. (2000, March 15). Insider case involves attempt at two brokers and Web ring. *The Wall Street Journal*, p. C1.

Meigs, W.B., Whittington, O.R., & Meigs, R.F. (1982). *Principles of auditing*. Homewood, IL: Irwin.

Mercer, J. (1996, October 11). In dollars and cents, colleges measure what they contribute to their communities. *Chronicle of Higher Education*, p. A47.

Miller, M. (1998, September 10). Murdoch soccer deal sets up bigger play. *Los Angeles Times*, p. D1.

Miller, W.S. (1998, August-September). Sport facility issues, part one. The boom in stadium construction & financing new facilities. *For the Record* (Marquette University Law School), *9*(4), 7.

Moffeit, M. (1999, March 28). Off to a fast start. *Houston Chronicle*, p. 8D.

Moss, J. (1992, September-October). Campbell Soup's cutting-edge cash management. *Financial Executive*, 8, 39–42.

Much, P. (1996, June 7). *Publicly traded sports team* [Marketing letter]. Chicago: Houlihan Lokey Howard & Zukin.

Much, P. (1997, September 9). *Estate planning for professional sports team owners* [Marketing letter]. Chicago: Houlihan Lokey Howard & Zukin.

Much, P. (1997, December 1). *Sports teams, IPOs, and some baseball nostalgia* [Marketing letter]. Chicago: Houlihan Lokey Howard & Zukin.

Much, P., & Friedman, A. (1996). *Inside the ownership of professional sports teams* [Team marketing report]. Chicago: Houlihan Lokey Howard & Zukin.

Much, P., & Phillips, J. (1999). *Sports teams and the stock market* [Marketing letter]. Chicago: Houlihan Lokey Howard & Zukin. 312-456-4700.

Mullen, L. (1998, November 30-December 6). Golden Bear Golf hit $14.3 million trap. *Street & Smith's SportsBusiness Journal*, 3.

Munroe, T. (1997, September 5). Fleet shuffles sports group lineup. *Boston Herald*, p. 26.

Naughton, J. (1996, November 22). Most intercollegiate-athletic programs lost money in 1995, NCAA report says. *Chronicle of Higher Education*, p. A46.

NCAA study shows athletic program costs rising at faster pace than revenues. (1998, October 9). *The NCAA News*, p. 1.

Nelton, S. (1998, June). Seeking funding? Get organized. *Nation's Business*, 40–42.

Nelton, S. (1998, November). Sizing up the megabanks. *Nation's Business*, 14–21.

Newberry, J. (2001, August). Free with purchase. *ABA Journal*, 78.

NFL looking at reducing minimum ownership stake for partners. (2000, June 1). *Sports Business Daily*, p. 8.

The NFL stadium financing landscape. (2001). Available: www.vikings.com/Stadium/Stadiumlandscape.htm. Retrieved December 26, 2001.

Nicholas, T. (1990). *Cash: How to get it into and out of your corporation*. Wilmington, DE: Enterprise.

Nicklaus company's stock doesn't make NASDAQ cut. (1998, August 14). *Houston Chronicle*, p. 3C.

Nicklin, J. (1997, November 21). Universities seek to cut costs by "outsourcing" more operations. *Chronicle of Higher Education*, p. A35.

Nike net rose 17%, revenue fell slightly in fiscal 3rd period. (2000, March 17). *The Wall Street Journal*, p. B17.

Noll, R., & Zimbalist, A. (1998). Are new stadiums worth the cost? Available: www.breadnotcircuses.org / brooking.html. Retrieved December 26, 2001.

Notebook. (2000, November 1). *Connecticut Post*, p. D3.

O'Brian, B., & Tam, P. (1999, October 4). Specialty funds seek piece of pie in growing market. *The Wall Street Journal*, p. R25.

Offering for investors to tackle. (1998, October 15). *Houston Chronicle*, p. 2C.

Overview of preliminary arena development process. (1995). Denton, TX: Denton County, TX.

Owner. (2002). Available: www.nba.com/nuggets/news/kroenke_bio.html. Retrieved June 23, 2002.

Owners unlikely to OK Redskins sale. (1999, April 7). *Houston Chronicle*, p. 7B.

Palazzo, A. (1999, October 4). Goal of minor league soccer team, the San Diego Flash, is to go public. *The Wall Street Journal*, p. B13E.

Panthers' new ownership group receives NHL approval. (2002). Available: www.flpanthers.com / pressbox / news/ownersapproval.shtml. Retrieved February 18, 2002.

Parrish, A., & Maloney, L. (1999, July). Documenting good intentions. *ABA Journal*, 63.

Paul Allen. (2002). Available: www.thestandard.com / people/profile/0,1923,1302,00.html. Retrieved February 6, 2002.

Penguins file for bankruptcy. (1998, November 2). *Stadium and Arena Financing News*, p. 1.

Penn State sports information. (1999). Available: www.psu.edu/sports/football

Pereira, J. (2001, January 23). Converse files for bankruptcy protection, plans to shutter North American plants. *The Wall Street Journal*, p. B8.

Pinches, G. (1984). *Essentials of financial management*. New York: Harper & Row.

Pitino resigns as Celtics coach, president. Available: http://dailynews.yahoo.com/h/nm/20010108/sp/nba_celtics_dc_2.html. Retrieved January 8, 2001.

Planning for success. (2000, November-December). *CampBusiness*, 8–11.

Portions of New Orleans Saints purchase price is allocable to Superdome lease. (1998, Spring/Summer). *Business of Sports*, 2–4. KPMG Peat Marwick, LLP, St. Petersburg, FL.

Pounds, M. (1997, October 27). Finding the money to start up a business and how to write a business plan. *Houston Chronicle*, pp. 1D–2D.

Pratt, S., Reilly, R., & Schweihs, R. (2000). *Valuing a business: The analysis and appraisal of closely held companies* (4th ed.). New York: McGraw-Hill.

Pritchard, C. (2001, December 21). Nike shares rise on earnings report. [CBS MarketWatch]. www.../yahoo&steid=yahoo&dist=yahoo&guid=%7B2C3848A2%2D0AA9%2D420A%2DA268%2D33. Retrieved January 8, 2002.

Profiles of success. (2001). Boston: International Health, Racquet & Sportsclub Association.

Pryde, J. (1998, February). A lending niche helps small firms. *Nation's Business*, 52–53.

Q4 IPO Scorecard. Available: http://hoovers.com/ipo/scorecard/0,1334,66,00.html. Retrieved February 18, 2002.

Ranalli, R. (1997, October 8). Islander buyer to plead guilty to fraud charges. *Boston Globe*, p. 35.

Ray Robinson v. Commissioner, 44 T.C. 20 (1965).

Ready to wrestle the bulls. (1999, August 4). *Houston Chronicle*, p. 1C.

Reports: Thomas agrees to sell CBA, owes $750,000. Available: www.canoe.ca/BasketballCBA/jun28_tho.html. Retrieved February 6, 2002.

Revenue Ruling 58-145, 1955-2 C.B., 25 (1958).

Revenue Ruling 88-76, 1988.

Reynes, R. (1997, November). Venturing out for rapid growth. *Nation's Business*, 54–55.

Reynes, R. (1998, May). Financing for do it yourselfers. *Nation's Business*, 38–40.

Reynes, R. (1998, October). Low-profile money sources. *Nation's Business,* 32–33.

Riggs, J., & Emerson, J. (1992). *Parks and recreation budget and staffing of Texas municipal, county and special district governments.* Austin, TX: Public Lands Division, Texas Parks and Wildlife Department.

Rodgers, R. (1966). *Banking.* New York: Alexander Hamilton Institute.

Rofe, J. (1999, August 23-39). The 800-pound gorilla keeps growing. *Street & Smith's SportsBusiness Journal, 2,* 24.

Rogus, D. (1997, June-July). America's sports stadiums: How much do they really cost you? *Your Money,* 70–79.

Rosenblatt, B. (1989, February 20). Have I got a deal for you, kid. . . . *Sportsinc,* 24.

Ross, S.A., Westerfield, R.W., & Jaffee, J. (1996). *Corporate finance* (4th ed.). New York: McGraw-Hill.

Ross, S.A., Westerfield, R.W., & Jordan, B.D. (1995). *Fundamentals of corporate finance* (3rd ed.). Chicago: Irwin.

Rumblings. (1997, August 25). *Crain's Detroit Business,* 34.

Ruxin, R. (1989). *An athlete's guide to agents.* New York: Penguin Books.

SBA. (2002). Available: http: / / sbaonline.sba.gov. Retrieved February 6, 2002.

Sack, A., & Nadim, A. (2002, January). Strategic choices in a turbulent environment: A case study of Starter Corporation. *Journal of Sport Management 16*(1), 36–53.

Salary scoreboard. (2001, December 13). *Connecticut Post,* p. C5.

Sandomir, R. (1999, December 14). SFX to consolidate acquired divisions. *New York Times,* p. D7.

Sapsford, J. (2000, March 14). Fed to make banks boost capital to cover venture-investing risk. *The Wall Street Journal,* p. A4.

Scherreik, S. (2000, December 16). What the earnings reports don't tell you. *Business Week,* 201.

Schreiner, J., & Damsell, K. (1998, November 11). Canucks blame record losses on dollar and taxes. *National Post,* p. CO1.

Schroeder, M., & MacDonald, E. (1999, September 29). SEC enforcement action targets 68, including former-NFL star. *The Wall Street Journal,* p. A4.

Schroeder, M., & Schiller, Z. (1992, August 24). A scandal waiting to happen. *Business Week,* 32.

Securities regulation in the United States. (1994). Gaithersburg, MD: National Association of Securities Dealers, Inc. (NASD).

Securitizing sports. (1998, November 16). *Stadium and Arena Financing News,* p. 8.

sfx.com. (1999). Available: www.sfx.com

Shapiro, S. (1999, Winter). Valuation of law practices. *Law Firm Governance 4*(2), 26–33.

Sheehan, R. (1996). *Keeping score: The economics of big time sports.* South Bend, IN: Diamond Communications.

Sherer, P. (2000, April 21). Upstart firm rolls out commercial paper on Web. *The Wall Street Journal,* p. C1.

Sherman Antitrust Act, 1890, 15 U.S.C.A. Sec. 1

Shinn faces suit over arena profits. (1998, October 24). *Herald Rock Hill,* p. 5B.

Sichelman, L. (1998, August 24). Trumping the credit bureau. *Houston Chronicle,* p. 1D.

Siegal, A. (2000). *Practical business statistics* (4th ed.). New York: McGraw-Hill.

Siegel, J., Shim, J., & Hartman, S. (1992). *Dictionary of personal finance.* New York: Macmillan.

Singer, T. (1998, May). Baseball's bargains and bandits. *Sport,* 35.

Smith, B. (2001, Fall). If you build it, will they come. *The Georgetown Public Policy Review, 7*(1), 45–60.

Soccer quotes. (2002). Available: www.soccerinvestor.com. Retrieved June 27, 2002.

SODA (Sportsplex Operators and Developers Association). (1993). *Sportspark Construction Costs.* Racine, WI: Author.

Sosa's charity mismanaged, on brink of bankruptcy. (2000, April 12). Available: www.sportslawnews.com / current/Sosacharity.htm

Sources: ABC/ESPN near NBA TV deal. (2001). Available: http://news.excite.ca/news/ap/011215/13/bkn-nba-tv-contracts. Retrieved December 26, 2001.

Speedway to report third-quarter loss; stock declines 38%. (1999, November 8). *The Wall Street Journal,* p. B13.

Spiro, H. (1996). *Finance for the nonfinancial manager.* New York: Wiley.

Sport management program standards and review protocol. (2000). Reston, VA: National Association for Sport and Physical Education and North American Society for Sport Management.

Sportsfund. (1996). Fields of opportunity [Promotional brochure]. Portland, ME: Author.

Sports in brief. (2001, January 8). *Seattle Union Record,* p. 1D.

Sportslaw jargon: Eminent domain. Available: http: / / sportslawnews.com/archieve/jargon/LJEminent.html. Retrieved February 18, 2002.

Sports stadiums as "wise investments": An evaluation. (1990, November 26). *The Heartland Institute, Executive Summary,* No. 32.

Standard & Poor's corporate description plus news. (1999). New York: McGraw-Hill.

Starter seeks Chapter 11. (1999, April 20). *Houston Chronicle,* p. 10B.

Stehle, V. (1997, November 27). Rich but not so different. *Chronicle of Philanthropy,* p. 11.

Stellino, V. (1995, November 6). Lease deal for Browns is 30 years. *Baltimore Sun,* p. 1A.

Steps for improving your firm's cash flow. (1998, November). *Nation's Business,* 12.

Stevenson, W. (1982). *Production/operations management.* Homewood, IL: Irwin.

Stock quote. Available: http://finance. yahoo.com/q?s= sds.pk. Retrieved June 12, 2002.

Tan, K. (2000, January 31). Interactive technology boosts sports business. *The Wall Street Journal,* p. B9A.

Tax numbers to know. (2000, January 30). *Connecticut Post,* p. F1.

Tejada, C. (2000, March 1). Clear Channel to acquire SFX for $2.99 billion. *The Wall Street Journal,* p. A4.

Texas Special Olympics, 1995 financial highlights. (1996). *Texas Special Olympics 1995 annual report.* Austin, TX: Texas Special Olympics.

Thomas secures his future. (1998, July 13). *Sports Illustrated, 89*(2), 32.

Thornton, E. (2002, January 12). It sure is getting hostile. *Business Week,* 28–30.

Top holders of stadium bonds. (1997, September 22). *Stadium and Arena Financing News,* p. 10.

Tough equations: Blame the profit drive on a marketing change in companies' costs. (2001, May 16). *The Wall Street Journal,* p. C1.

Trip to Super Bowl priceless (and pricey). (2001, January 16). *New Haven Register,* p. A4.

Truex, A. (1999, February 14). Going for broke. *Houston Chronicle,* p. 1B.

Turley, B. (1998, Fall). From tee to green: A primer on golf course development and financing. *Entertainment and Sports Lawyer, 16*(3), 3–5, 35.

Two Denver franchises sold. (1999, April 27). *Houston Chronicle,* p. 11B.

Undergraduate catalog, 1998-2000. (1998). West Haven, CT: University of New Haven.

Up, up and away. (1999, December 30). *Connecticut Post,* p. 1C.

U.S. standards. (2002) [NYSE]. Available: www.nyse / u.s.stsnadrads.html. Retrieved January 12, 2002.

UW athletic department personnel incomes. (1998, November 5). *Capital Times,* p. 3C.

Vaughn, D. (1997). *Financial planning for the entrepreneur.* Upper Saddle River, NJ: Prentice Hall.

Venator net surges, aided by cost-cutting and sales of stores. (2000, March 9). *The Wall Street Journal,* p. B14.

Vennochi, J. (1997, July 30). Does the puck stop here? *Boston Globe,* p. E1.

Verducci, T. (2000, December 18). Powerball. *Sports Illustrated,* 103–110.

Wahl, G. (2001, December 3). Billions for soccer. *Sports Illustrated,* 34.

Walker, S. (1999, November 5). Attorney set to buy Cleveland Indians in transaction totaling $320 million. *The Wall Street Journal,* p. B2.

Wal-Mart heir buying Denver teams, arena. (2000, April 25). *Connecticut Post,* p. D4.

Wanniski, J. (1991, October 9). Trial by press: James B. Stewart vs. Michael Milken. Available: www.polyeconomics.com/searchbase/10-09-91.html. Retrieved February 18, 2002.

Web billionaire to buy controlling interest in Dallas Mavericks. (2000, January 5). *The Wall Street Journal,* p. B16.

Where your tax dollar goes. (2000, January 30). *Connecticut Post,* p. F1.

White, K. (1966). *Production control.* New York: Alexander Hamilton Institute.

Whittington, O.R., & Pany, K. (1998). *Principles of auditing* (12th ed.). Boston: McGraw-Hill.

Williams, C.A., Jr., Smith, M., & Young, P. (1995). *Risk management and insurance* (7th ed.). New York: McGraw-Hill.

Williams, J. (1998, August 14). Stadium financing plan is completed. *Houston Chronicle,* p. 40A.

Winters, C. (2000, November). Budgeting 101. *Club Industry,* 90–91.

Wixon, R. (1966). *Budgetary control.* New York: Alexander Hamilton Institute.

Woolworth Corp. agrees to buy Sports Authority for $579.6 million. (1998, May 8). *The Wall Street Journal,* p. B9.

WorldCom charged with fraud. (2002, June 27). *Connecticut Post,* p. C1.

WWF fires COO, 39 employees to aid profits. (2001, November 10). *Connecticut Post,* p. B1.

www.delawareintercorp.com/why.htm. (2000, June 27).

Wynter, L., & Thomas, P. (2000, February 2). New definition of "minority business" splits blacks. *The Wall Street Journal,* p. B1.

XFL's hefty losses slam WWF profits. (2001, June 29). *Connecticut Post,* p. B14.

YankeeNets affiliate to buy hockey's New Jersey Devils. (2000, March 17). *The Wall Street Journal,* p. B6.

Yahoo! Finance—BOS. (2002). Available: http://?finance.yahoo.com/q?d=t&s-BOS+. Retrieved February 18, 2002.

Yahoo! Finance—WWF. (2002). Available: http://?finance.yahoo.com/q?d=t&s-WWF+. Retrieved February 18, 2002.

Yahoo! Finance—YHOO. (2002). Available: http://?finance.yahoo.com/q?d=t&s-YHOO+. Retrieved February 18, 2002.

Yip, P. (1999, March 30). Changes paved way to 10K. *Houston Chronicle,* p. 1C.

Zikmund, W., & d'Amico, M. (1996). *Basic marketing.* St. Paul: West.

Zimbalist, A. (1999, October 13). The NFL's new math. *The Wall Street Journal,* p. A30.

Index

Note: The italicized *f* and *t* following page numbers refer to figures and tables, respectively.

About the Authors

Gil Fried, JD, is an associate professor at the University of New Haven School of Business in Connecticut, where he teaches sport finance at the graduate and undergraduate levels. He holds both a master's degree with a concentration in sport management and a law degree from The Ohio State University.

Extensively published and well spoken on the subject of sport finance, Dr. Fried has worked closely with the International Association of Assembly Managers on a variety of projects. He also has served as general counsel for several sport facilities and associations, including the Sportsplex Operators and Developers Association and the Resort and Commercial Recreation Association. Additionally, Dr. Fried has served as an expert witness in several major sport valuation cases involving businesses or lost income due to professional athlete injury.

A member of the California State Bar, Dr. Fried is chief executive officer of Gil Fried & Association, LLC, a consulting firm specializing in sport law and finance-related issues. He makes his home in New Haven, Connecticut, with his wife, Susan, and their children. In his free time, he enjoys playing badminton (he is the head coach of the Yale Badminton Club) and volunteering in his community.

Steven J. Shapiro, PhD, is the chair of the Department of Economics and Finance and an associate professor of economics and finance at the University of New Haven. Dr. Shapiro received his BA in economics and mathematics from the University of Virginia and his MA and PhD in economics from Georgetown University. He serves on the board of governors of the Society of Litigation Economists and is the coeditor of *Litigation Economics Review*.

Dr. Shapiro has written and presented numerous papers on the valuation of employee stock options, the appraisal of closely held firms, the calculation of damages, and applications of financial event study methodologies to examine the effects of litigation on shareholders. In addition, he has provided expert testimony and served as a consultant in legal matters that required the measurement of damages resulting from wrongful death, personal injury, and wrongful employment termination; the computation of lost profits in commercial litigation; and the analysis of relevant markets in antitrust cases.

Dr. Shapiro's professional memberships include the American Economic Association, American Finance Association, American Statistical Association, National Association of Business Economists, National Association of Forensic Economists, and American Academy of Economics and Financial Experts. Dr. Shapiro resides in Orange, Connecticut, with his wife, Phyliss. He enjoys hiking, photography, and reading history and biographies.

Timothy D. DeSchriver, EdD, is an assistant professor in the Department of Sport Management at the University of Massachusetts, Amherst. He completed his undergraduate education at Villanova University, holds a master's degree in economics from Penn State University, and earned his doctorate in sport management from the University of Northern Colorado.

Widely published in several major sport management and economics journals such as the *Journal of Sports Management*, *Sport Marketing Quarterly*, and the *Eastern Economic Journal*, Dr. DeSchriver also serves on the editorial board of *Sport Marketing Quarterly*. He coauthored a chapter on sport finance and economics in *Introduction to Sport Management, Third Edition*. He served as a field economist for the U.S. Department of Labor and was also the interim associate athletic director at the University of Northern Colorado.

A member of the North American Society for Sport Management, Dr. DeSchriver serves as an executive council member for the organization's annual conference. As a member of the UMass Center for Spectator Sport Research, he has also helped to complete research contracts for sport organizations such as the National Steeplechase Association, the National Collegiate Athletic Association, and the Anschutz Entertainment Group. Dr. DeSchriver makes his home in Sunderland, Massachusetts, where he enjoys mountain biking and hiking in his free time.